IDENTITY, CAUSE, AND MIND

Identity, Cause, and Mind

Philosophical Essays

EXPANDED EDITION

SYDNEY SHOEMAKER

CLARENDON PRESS · OXFORD

OXFORD

UNIVERSITY PRESS

Great Clarendon Street, Oxford OX2 6DP

Oxford University Press is a department of the University of Oxford.
It furthers the University's objective of excellence in research, scholarship,
and education by publishing worldwide in

Oxford New York

Auckland Bangkok Buenos Aires Cape Town Chennai
Dar es Salaam Delhi Hong Kong Istanbul Karachi Kolkata
Kuala Lumpur Madrid Melbourne Mexico City Mumbai Nairobi
São Paulo Shanghai Taipei Tokyo Toronto

Oxford is a registered trade mark of Oxford University Press
in the UK and in certain other countries

Published in the United States
by Oxford University Press Inc., New York

This edition © Sydney Shoemaker 2003

The moral rights of the author have been asserted
Database right Oxford University Press (maker)

First edition published by Cambridge University Press 1984

British Library Cataloguing in Publication Data

Data available

Library of Congress Cataloging in Publication Data

Data available

ISBN 0–19–926469–4
ISBN 0–19–926470–8 (pbk.)

1 3 5 7 9 10 8 6 4 2

Typeset by Cambrian Typesetters, Frimley, Surrey
Printed in Great Britain
on acid-free paper by
Bookcraft (Bath) Ltd.

For my son Peter

Contents

Acknowledgments

The dates and places of the original publication of these essays are as given below. I am grateful to the editors and publishers for permission to reprint the essays here.

1. "Self-Reference and Self-Awareness," *The Journal of Philosophy*, 65, 19 (October 1968), 555–567. This was delivered as part of a symposium on "Self and Reference" at the meetings of the Eastern Division of the American Philosophical Association in Washington, D.C.; the other symposiast was Michael Woods.

2. "Persons and Their Pasts," *American Philosophical Quarterly*, 7, 4 (October 1970), 269–285. This is a revised version of a paper that was read at a conference on "The Concept of a Person" at the University of Michigan in November 1967.

3. "Time Without Change," *The Journal of Philosophy*, 66, 12 (June 1969), 363–381.

4. "On Projecting the Unprojectible," *The Philosophical Review*, 94, 2 (April 1975), 178–219. This was first presented, in an earlier version, at a meeting of the Moral Sciences Club at Cambridge University in the spring of 1972.

5. "Conceptual Connections and Other Minds" was originally part of a larger essay, "The Problem of Other Minds," which appeared in Joel Feinberg (ed.), *Reason and Responsibility*, 3rd edn. (Dickenson Publishing Co., Encino, California, and Belmont, California, 1975).

6. "Embodiment and Behavior," in Amelie Rorty (ed.), *The Identities of Persons* (The University of California Press, Berkeley and Los Angeles, 1976).

7. "Immorality and Dualism," in Stuart C. Brown (ed.), *Reason and Religion* (Cornell University Press, Ithaca, N.Y., 1977). This was originally presented at a conference sponsored by the Royal Institute of Philosophy and held at the University of Lancaster in 1975. The other symposiast was Hywel Lewis. Copyright © 1977 by the Royal Institute of Philosophy.

8. "Phenomenal Similarity," *Critica*, 7, 20 (October 1975), 3–34. This

was first presented at the Western Washington Philosophy Colloquium at Bellingham, Washington, in March 1974.

9. "Functionalism and Qualia," *Philosophical Studies*, 27 (1975), 291–315. Reprinted with minor revisions in Ned Block (ed.), *Readings in the Philosophy of Psychology* (Harvard University Press, Cambridge, Mass., 1980), vol. 1. Copyright © 1975 by D. Reidel Publishing Company, Dordrecht, Netherlands.

10. "Causality and Properties," in Peter van Inwagen (ed.), *Time and Cause* (D. Reidel Publishing Co., Dordrecht, Netherlands, 1980), pp. 109–135. Copyright © 1980 by D. Reidel Publishing Company, Dordrecht, Netherlands.

11. "Identity, Properties, and Causality," *Midwest Studies in Philosophy*, 4 (1979).

12. "Some Varieties of Functionalism," *Philosophical Topics*, 12, 1 (1981), 83–118.

13. "On An Argument for Dualism," in Carl Ginet and Sydney Shoemaker (eds.), *Knowledge and Mind, Philosophical Essays* (Oxford University Press, New York, 1983). Copyright © by Oxford University Press.

14. "Absent Qualia Are Impossible," *The Philosophical Review*, 90, 4 (October 1981), 581–599.

15. "The Inverted Spectrum," *The Journal of Philosophy*, 74, 7 (July 1981), 357–381.

16. "On What There Are," *Philosophical Topics*, 16, 1 (Spring, 1988), 201–223.

17. "Self and Substance," *Philosophical Perspectives*, 11, *Mind, Causation, and World* (1997), 283–304.

18. "Causal and Metaphysical Necessity," *Pacific Philosophical Quarterly*, 79 (1998), 59–77.

19. "Realization and Mental Causation," in Carl Gillett and Barry Loewer (eds.), *Physicalism and Its Discontents* (Cambridge University Press, Cambridge, 2001), 74–98.

Preface to Second Edition

This volume contains all of the essays originally published in the first edition of this work, together with four more recent essays. Some of these four were written too late for inclusion in my 1996 collection of essays,[1] while others had topics that made them unsuitable for inclusion in that collection. All develop my views on themes that figured in the original version of this work.

Three of the added essays relate, in one way or another, to the essays in the original collection ("Causality and Properties," "Identity, Properties and Causality," and "On Projecting the Projectible") that discuss the ways in which causal considerations enter into the individuation of properties. "Causal and Metaphysical Necessity" develops the idea that properties are individuated by their causal features in a way that makes causal laws metaphysically necessary. It discusses, as the earlier essays did not (except in a postscript), the role of "backward-looking" causal features of properties (having to do with how the instantiation of a property can be caused) in the individuation of properties. And it attempts to clarify the central argument for the claim about metaphysical necessity. "Realization and Mental Causation" gives an account of what it is for one property to be "realized" in another, e.g., what it is for mental properties to be realized in neurophysiological ones, that starts from the view that properties are individuated by their causal features. And "On What There Are" is concerned with the general question of what it is for putative things and properties to be "genuine." It considers among other things the question of whether we can dispose of what Quine called "*entia non gratia*" by invoking considerations having to do with the role of causation in the individuation of properties and in the persistence conditions of objects.

The fourth of the added papers, "Self and Substance," presents my current view on the topic of personal identity, a topic I have revisited a number of times over the last forty years or so. The view it develops is a version of the neo-Lockean view I presented in "Persons and Their

---

[1] *The First Person Perspective, and Other Essays* (Cambridge, 1996).

Pasts,"[2] included in the original collection, but attempts to do justice to intuitions (traditionally associated with Butler and Reid) that appear to conflict with that view.

I have not undertaken to revise any of the essays in the original collection. The one thing in them I now firmly disown is the flirtation in the "postscript" to "The Inverted Spectrum" with the "Frege–Schlick view," i.e., the view that qualitative similarity of experiences is well defined only for the intrasubjective case. (My current view about that is in an essay entitled "Intrasubjective/intersubjective" which appears in a different collection.[3]) Given that some of these essays were written over thirty years ago, I probably should find more in them to disagree with than I do. But, fleeting doubts aside, the views presented in these essays are, by and large, ones that I am still willing to stand by. (Nelson Goodman's "grue" figures in several of these essays, and the passage of time has made it necessary for me to change the date in its definition so as to keep it in the future.)

In addition to those thanked in the Introduction to the original edition of this work, I would like to thank the following for helpful comments on one or more of these essays: George Bealer, Gail Fine, Phil Gasper, Tamar Gendler, Eric Hiddleston, Christopher Hill, Harold Langsam, Barry Loewer, Jill Riatt, Mark Richard, Eleonore Stump, Zoltan Szabo, Peter Unger, Michael Watkins, and Steve Yablo.

---

[2] Also in my "Personal Identity: A Materialist's Account," in S. Shoemaker and R. Swinburne, *Personal Identity* (Oxford, 1984).

[3] It is in my *The First-Person Perspective, and Other Essays,* cited above.

Introduction
(to original edition)

The essays in this volume were written over a period of approximately fifteen years. The earliest of them were begun a few years after the publication of my book *Self-Knowledge and Self-Identity* (*SK&SI*), and many of the themes that figure in these essays were already present in that earlier work. By the time I began writing these essays, however, my thinking had changed in important ways from that represented in *SK&SI*. A brief account of some of the changes may help to orient the reader to the present work (which, however, assumes no familiarity with the earlier one).

In *SK&SI* I relied heavily, and I now think uncritically, on the notion of a criterion. The problem of personal identity was put by asking what the criteria of personal identity are; my view about this then was that bodily identity is the primary criterion, although I allowed that in exceptional cases this can be overridden by a memory criterion. The special character of each person's access to his own identity was put by saying that this first-person knowledge is "non-criterial," i.e., not grounded on criteria. The notion of a criterion also figured prominently in my discussions of knowledge of other minds and the relation of mental phenomena to bodily and behavioral facts. Following Wittgenstein, I held that "an 'inner process' stands in need of outer criteria." And I interpreted this as implying that mental concepts are given by specifying bodily criteria for their application, this yielding conceptually necessary truths to the effect that the existence of such and such behavior in thus and such circumstances implies the (probable) existence of certain mental states, or (what I did not distinguish from this) that given the behavior and circumstances, one would be justified in ascribing those mental states. This has sometimes been called the "criteriological view" of mental concepts. My view then was that only by adopting such a view can we avoid skepticism about other minds.

In the essays in the present volume I have largely avoided the term "criterion," partly to avoid any appearance of conflating questions which, however closely they may be related, ought to be kept distinct – e.g., the metaphysical question of what personal identity consists in, and the epistemological question of how it is known. But I have also abandoned or modified a number of the views, in particular those just mentioned, which I formerly used this term to express.

"Persons and Their Pasts" (Essay 2) marks my abandonment of the view that bodily identity is constitutive of personal identity, and my adoption of the view that what is constitutive of it is psychological continuity (with memory continuity playing a crucial role). It may strike some readers as puzzling that this occurred at about the same time that I came to regard my position in the philosophy of mind as a "materialist" one. But, as I hope the essays in this volume make clear, there is no inconsistency in holding on the one hand that as a matter of fact mental states are all realized physically, and even insisting (as I do in "Embodiment and Behavior," Essay 6) on the conceptual import-ance of embodiment *vis-à-vis* the existence of mental states, while maintaining on the other hand that the identity conditions of persons (and subjects of mental states generally) are most illuminatingly put in psychological terms, and do not require that a person have the *same* body at all times at which he exists.

"Persons and Their Pasts" also marks a change in my views about the special access each person has to his own identity. In "Self-Reference and Self-Awareness" (Essay 1) the claim that certain self-ascriptions are "non-criterial" was recast as the claim that they are "immune to error through misidentification." And while in that essay I held that such immunity is "preserved in memory," and thus that self-ascriptions of past actions and experiences have such immunity when grounded on memory, I qualified this in "Persons and Their Pasts." The qualification was required by the recognition of the logical possibility of what I there call "branching" (e.g., a person's splitting into two distinct persons), or, what comes to the same thing, the possibility of "quasi-remembering" that is not remembering.

The "criteriological" view I held in *SK&SI* is only one version of the view, what I have sometimes called the "conceptual connection view," that it belongs to the concepts of certain basic sorts of mental states that these states are connected in certain ways with bodily behavior; and while the former view is entirely absent from these essays, the latter remains in the form of "analytical" or "conceptual" function-alism – the view that mental states are definable in terms of their relations to sensory inputs, behavioral outputs, and other mental states, and (what distinguishes analytical functionalism from other varieties of functionalism) that such definitions reflect the nature of our mental concepts and the meanings of our mental terms. One line of argument in favor of the conceptual connection view is presented in

"Embodiment and Behavior." This is (roughly) to the effect that certain psychophysical connections are required (logically) by embodiment, and that embodiment, in turn, is the conceptually "paradigmatic" condition for the existence of subjects of mental states. Another line of argument in its support is what in "Some Varieties of Functionalism" (Essay 12) I called the "argument from science fiction," and is presented most explicitly in "Conceptual Connections and Other Minds" (Essay 5). It is to the effect that some version of the conceptual connection view is needed to explain our intuitions about the mentality of certain possible creatures – imaginary Martians and the like. This should not be confused with the argument in *SK&SI* that we must accept the criteriological view in order to avoid skepticism about other minds. That argument now seems to be doubly mistaken. Even if the avoidance of skepticism did require that we accept some version of the conceptual connection view, the criteriological view would not be the one to accept. And in any case, I no longer think that we must accept any version of the conceptual connection view in order to explain how we can be justified making the behaviorally based judgments we actually make about the mental states of other human beings. But a satisfactory account of mental concepts, and of the semantics of mental terms, must not only account for our judgments about actual situations; it must also account for our epistemological intuitions about what mental state ascriptions would be justified in a variety of possible situations. It is here that some version of the conceptual connection view seems to me to be required. (I should stress, however, that on the version of functionalism I favor the connections of mental states to other mental states are if anything more important than their connections to behavior; in the terminology of Essay 5, the "rationality condition" on mental states is more fundamental than the "perceptual" and "volitional" conditions.)

If the term "criterion" is conspicuous by its presence in *SK&SI* and its absence in the present work, just the reverse is true of the term "causality" and its cognates. Martin and Deutscher's "Remembering" persuaded me that the notion of memory is a causal concept, and this was one of the main factors that led me to the view of personal identity presented in "Persons and Their Pasts" and the causal account of the identity over time of "continuants" generally which is suggested in "Identity, Properties, and Causality" (Essay 11). At about the same time I became persuaded that the conceptual connections view is best put as the view that mental states are defined by their "causal roles"; influential here were writings of David Armstrong, Donald Davidson, David Lewis, and Hilary Putnam.

The notion of causality figures in yet another way in "Time Without Change" (Essay 3), where a connection begins to emerge between causality and "genuine" change – as opposed to what I have called "McTaggartian" change, or, following Geach, "mere-Cambridge" change. (I am at present uncertain whether the existence of this connection undermines the argument given in that essay for the claim that there can be time without change.) Eventually reflection on this connection led me to the causal account of properties presented in "Causality and Properties" (Essay 10). In "Identity, Properties, and Causality" I relate this to the causal account of identity through time, and in "Some Varieties of Functionalism" I relate it to the functionalist account of mind.

My interest in the notion of "genuineness" of changes and properties, and in the connection of this with causality, has been closely related to two other interests. One concerns the cluster of issues raised by Nelson Goodman's "grue." This is the subject of "On Projecting the Unprojectible" (Essay 4), which argues (among other things) that there is an incoherence involved in the supposition that someone might systematically "project," inductively, predicates that are "grue-like" relative to those we project.

The other interest concerns the cluster of issues having to do with "qualia," i.e., the (supposed) qualitative or phenomenal features of sensations and sensory states. Many of the issues are most vividly raised by reflection on the (apparent) conceivability of "qualia inversion," e.g., "spectrum inversion." I was first led to think about this topic by reflecting on Wittgenstein's discussions of private language and privacy of sensation. More recently my concern with it has focused on the task of showing that, contrary to the claims of Ned Block, Jerry Fodor, and others, allowing the existence of qualia (in whatever sense they can reasonably be supposed to exist), and allowing the possibility of "qualia inversion," is perfectly compatible with accepting a functionalist account of mind. This compatibility claim is defended in "Functionalism and Qualia" (Essay 9) and "Absent Qualia are Impossible" (Essay 14). "The Inverted Spectrum" (Essay 15) is concerned with the epistemological and metaphysical issues posed by the possibility of spectrum inversion. My interest in qualia comes together with my interest in "genuine" vs. "grue-like" properties in "Phenomenal Similarity" (Essay 8).

A final theme to be mentioned is dualism. The question whether mind–body dualism is coherent was only obliquely addressed in *SK&SI*, but the implicit answer was negative. In the present volume the answer becomes "yes and no – it depends on what version of dualism you have in mind." This question is connected, via the question of whether disembodied existence of minds is possible, with the issue of the nature of the connection between mental states and behavior, and is discussed together with this in "Embodiment and Behavior," "Immortality and Dualism" (Essay 7), and "On an Argument for Dualism" (Essay 13).

The essays appear here in pretty much the order in which they were written, although in a few cases I have departed slightly from this order to produce a more natural grouping. Reading the essays over now, I find some things I would now put differently, and some I am doubtful about; but by and large I stand by what they say. My revisions of the text are limited to minor stylistic changes and a few deletions aimed at reducing repetitiousness. Some footnotes have been deleted, others have been amplified or modified, and a few have been added. I have added "postscripts" to two of the essays which reflect my most recent thinking about their topics.

A major impetus to the development of many of the ideas presented here was the invitation to deliver the John Locke lectures at Oxford University in 1972. The essays that are most directly descended from those lectures are "Conceptual Connections and Other Minds," "Embodiment and Behavior" and "Phenomenal Similarity," but there are traces of them in a number of the others. A number of the essays were written during a sabbatic leave in 1973–74, during which I was a fellow at the Center for Advanced Study in the Behavioral Sciences in Stanford, California, and a subsequent sabbatic leave in 1980–81, during which I held a fellowship from the National Endowment for the Humanities. For these opportunities and leaves I am grateful to Oxford University, the Center, the National Endowment, and Cornell University. The earliest essays in the volume were written while I was on the faculty of Rockefeller University, the rest while I have been on the faculty of Cornell University. I am grateful to my colleagues at Rockefeller, Cornell, and the Center, and to philosophers at many universities at which I have read papers, for helpful advice, comments, and criticism. I would especially like to thank the following people, each of whom has provided helpful comments on one or more of these essays: John G. Bennett, Jonathan Bennett, Ned Block, Richard Boyd, John V. Canfield, Hector-Neri Castañeda, Oswaldo Chateaubriand, Robert Cummins, Harry Frankfurt, Carl Ginet, Jaegwon Kim, Norman Kretzmann, Keith Lehrer, Robert Nozick, David Reeve, David Sanford, Michael Slote, Robert Stalnaker, Nicholas Sturgeon, Peter van Inwagen, and Margaret Wilson.

Self-reference and self-awareness

If we consider the logical powers of first-person statements and the role played by the first-person pronoun in communication, nothing seems clearer than that in all first-person statements, including "avowals," the word 'I' functions as a singular term or singular referring expression. Statements expressed by the sentence "I feel pain" have it in common with those expressed by sentences like "He feels pain" and "Jones feels pain" that they contradict the proposition "Nobody feels pain" and entail the proposition "Someone feels pain." In these and other ways "I feel pain" behaves logically as a value of the propositional function "X feels pain." Moreover, in all first-person statements, including "psychological" or "experience" statements, the word 'I' serves the function of identifying for the audience the subject to which the predicate of the statement must apply if the statement is to be true (what it indicates, of course, is that the subject is the speaker, the maker of the statement). And this is precisely the function of a referring expression.

Yet philosophers have often found the referring role of 'I' perplexing, and some have been led to hold that in at least some of its uses it is not a referring expression at all. Thus Wittgenstein reportedly held at one time that "I have toothache" and "He has toothache" are not values of a common propositional function, that in "I have toothache" the word 'I' does not "denote a possessor," and that "Just as no (physical) eye is involved in seeing, so no Ego is involved in thinking or in having toothache." He is also reported to have viewed with approval Lichtenberg's saying that instead of "I think" we ought to say "It thinks" (with 'it' used as it is in "It is snowing").[1] At apparently the opposite extreme from this, yet stemming from much the same sources, is the view that 'I' refers to a "transcendental ego," an entity that is in principle inaccessible to sense experience. In this essay I shall try to diagnose the source of, and to dispel, some of the mysteriousness which surrounds the use of the

[1] See G. E. Moore, "Wittgenstein's Lectures in 1930–33," *Philosophical Papers* (London, 1959), pp. 306–310.

word 'I' and which underlies the perennial attractiveness of such unacceptable views about the self and self-reference.

I

In the *Blue Book* Wittgenstein distinguished "two different uses of the word 'I' (or 'my')," which he calls "the use as object" and "the use as subject." As examples of the first of these he gives such sentences as "My arm is broken" and "I have grown six inches." As examples of the second he gives "I see so and so," "I try to lift my arm," "I think it will rain," and "I have toothache." He goes on to say:

One can point to the differences between these two categories by saying: The cases of the first category involved the recognition of a particular person, and there is in these cases the possibility of an error, or as I should rather put it: the possibility of an error has been provided for. . . On the other hand, there is no question of recognizing a person when I say I have tooth-ache. To ask "are you sure it is *you* who have pains?" would be nonsensical.[2]

It is important to see that the distinction Wittgenstein is drawing here is not the controversial distinction between "corrigible" and "incorrigible" first-person statements. It is easy to overlook this, for Wittgenstein's examples of "the use as subject" are mostly statements that many philosophers have held to be incorrigible. But Wittgenstein's point is not that these statements are totally immune to error, though he may have believed this to be true of some of them, but is rather that they are immune to a certain sort of error: they are immune to error due to a misrecognition of a person, or, as I shall put it, they are immune to error through misidentification relative to the first-person pronouns. It is the use of 'I' in such statements, i.e., its use "as subject," that philosophers have found puzzling.

If I say "I am bleeding," it can happen that what I say is false even though I am giving expression to the knowledge that a certain person is bleeding; it may be that I do see a bleeding arm or leg, but that because my body is tangled up with that of someone else (e.g., we are wrestling) or because I am seeing my identical twin or double in a mirror, I am mistaken in thinking the person who is bleeding to be myself. Such statements are subject to error through misidentification relative to the first-person pronouns, where to say that a statement "*a* is φ" is subject to error through misidentification relative to the term '*a*' means that the following is possible: the speaker knows some

<hr>

[2] *The Blue and Brown Books* (Oxford, 1958), pp. 66–67.

particular thing to be φ, but makes the mistake of asserting "*a* is φ" because, and only because, he mistakenly thinks that the thing he knows to be φ is what '*a*' refers to. The statement "I feel pain" is not subject to error through misidentification relative to 'I': it cannot happen that I am mistaken in saying "I feel pain" because, although I do know of someone that feels pain, I am mistaken in thinking that person to be myself. But this is also true of first-person statements that are clearly not incorrigible; I can be mistaken in saying "I see a canary," since I can be mistaken in thinking that what I see is a canary or (in the case of hallucination) that there is anything at all that I see, but it cannot happen that I am mistaken in saying this because I have misidentified as myself the person I know to see a canary. And whereas the statement "My arm is moving" is subject to error through misidentification, the statement "I am waving my arm" is not.

First-person statements that are immune to error through mis-identification in the sense just defined, those in which 'I' is used "as subject," could be said to have "absolute immunity" to error through misidentification. A statement like "I am facing a table" does not have this sort of immunity, for we can imagine circumstances in which someone might make this statement on the basis of having misidenti-fied someone else (e.g., the person he sees in a mirror) as himself. But there will be no possibility of such a misidentification if one makes this statement on the basis of seeing a table in front of one in the ordinary way (without aid of mirrors, etc.); let us say that when made in this way the statement has "circumstantial immunity" to error through misidentification relative to 'I.' It would appear that, when a self-ascription is circumstantially immune to error through misidentifi-cation, this is always because the speaker knows or believes it to be true as a consequence of some other self-ascription, which the speaker knows or is entitled to believe, that is absolutely immune to error through misidentification; e.g., in the circumstances just imagined the proposition "I am facing a table" would be known or believed as a consequence of the proposition "I see a table in the center of my field of vision."[3]

---

[3] A qualification is needed here. Someone who lacks the concept of seeing and the concept of a field of vision and who, therefore, is in one sense incapable of believing that he sees a table in the center of his field of vision, might nevertheless make (and be entitled to make) the statement "I am facing a table" in the circumstances imagined, i.e., when it is in fact true of him that he sees a table in the center of his field of vision. For our present purposes we can perhaps stretch the notion of being entitled to believe that p to cover the case of someone who lacks the concepts needed to express 'p' but who would be entitled to believe that p if only he had these concepts.

If I say "I feel pain" or "I see a canary," I may be identifying for someone else the person of whom I am saying that he feels pain or sees a canary. But there is also a sense in which my reference does not involve an identification. My use of the word 'I' as the subject of my statement is not due to my having identified as myself something of which I know, or believe, or wish to say, that the predicate of my statement applies to it.

But to say that self-reference in these cases does not involve identification does not adequately capture what is peculiar to it, for these first-person statements are not alone in involving reference without identification. Consider two cases in which I might say "This is red." Suppose that I am selling neckties, that a customer wants a red necktie, and that I believe I have put a particular red silk necktie on a shelf of the showcase that is visible to the customer but not to me. Putting my hand on a necktie on that shelf, and feeling it to be silk, I might say "This one is red." Here it could be said that I have identified, correctly or incorrectly, the object I refer to in saying "this" as the object I "have in mind," i.e., as the object of which I wish to say that it is red. We can contrast this with a case in which I simply point to a necktie that I see and say "This is red." In the latter case there is, in the present sense, no identification and hence no possibility of misidentification. In the first case I intend to refer to a certain red necktie I believe to be on the shelf, but there is also a sense in which I intend to refer, and do refer, to the necktie actually on the shelf, and there is a possibility of a disparity between my intended reference and my actual reference. But there can be no such disparity in the second case. In this case my intention is simply to refer to one (a specific one) of the objects I see, and in such a case the speaker's intention determines what the reference of his demonstrative pronoun is and that reference cannot be other than what he intends it to be.

But now let us compare this sort of reference without identification with that which occurs in first-person statements. The rules governing the use of a demonstrative like 'this' do not by themselves determine what its reference is on any given occasion of its use; this is determined, as we have noted, by the speaker's intentions. When a man says "This is red," there are generally any number of things to which he could be referring without misusing the word 'this,' and there is of course no requirement that different tokens of 'this' in a man's discourse should all refer to the same thing. This permits the reference of 'this' on a particular occasion to be fixed by the speaker's intention to say of a particular thing that it is red, i.e., fixed in such a way that it can refer to nothing other than that thing and, consequently, in such a way that his statement "This is red" does not involve an identification. But we cannot explain in this way the reference without identification that occurs in first-person statements. One can choose whether or not to use the word 'I,' but the rules governing the use of this word determine once and for all what its reference is to be on any given occasion of its use, namely, that its reference is to the speaker, and leave no latitude to the speaker's intentions in the determination of its reference.[4]

There are other important differences between 'I' and demonstratives like 'this.' Although there are cases in which the reference of a demonstrative cannot be other than what the speaker intends it to be, there is in even these cases the logical possibility of failure of reference; it may happen, e.g., in cases of hallucination, that there simply is no object to which a speaker can truly be said to be referring in saying "This is red." But there is, as Descartes's "*cogito* argument" brings out, no such possibility of failure of reference in the use of the word 'I.' Again, if I retain in my memory an item of knowledge which at the time of its acquisition I could have expressed by saying "This is red" and if I wish at a later time to express that knowledge, it will not do for me simply to utter the past-tense version of the sentence that originally expressed it. In the expression of my memory knowledge the word 'this' will typically give way to a description of some kind, e.g., 'the thing that was in front of me,' or 'the thing I was looking at.' I may of course say at a later time "This *was* red," pointing to something then in front of me, but this statement will involve an identification and will be subject to error through misidentification. But the appropriate way of expressing the retained (memory) knowledge that at the time of its acquisition was expressed by the sentence "I see a canary" is to utter the past-tense version of that sentence, namely, "I saw a canary." This, if said on the basis of memory, does not involve an identification and is not subject to error through misidentification.[5]

I think that many philosophers have assumed that where self-reference does not involve identification it must involve the sort of demonstrative reference that occurs when one says "This is red" of something one sees. If one makes this assumption, but then notices

---

[4] I now think that it is a mistake to think that the immunity to error through misidentification of first-person statements has to do with the peculiarities of the first-person pronoun; see footnote 5 of Essay 2.

[5] See Hector-Neri Castañeda's paper "'He': A Study in the Logic of Self-Consciousness," *Ratio*, 8 (1966), p. 145, for a closely related point. In Essay 2 I discuss further, and to some extent qualify, the claim that first-person memory statements are immune to error through identification.

that 'I' is no more a demonstrative pronoun than it is a name or "disguised description," one will quite naturally conclude that in its use "as subject" the word 'I' is not a referring expression at all, or, as Wittgenstein put it, that it does not "denote a possessor."

II

Philosophers who have reflected on the "use as subject" of the first-person pronouns have often been inclined to say such things as that one cannot be an object to oneself, that one's self is not one of the things one can find or encounter in the world. The most commonly drawn conclusion, of course, is that one's self, what one "calls 'I,'" cannot be any of the *physical* or *material* things one finds in the world. But as is well known to readers of Hume and Kant, among others, it is also widely denied that any *immaterial* object of experience could be the subject of thought and experience. These views lead naturally to the conclusion that 'I' does not refer, that there is no self, or that the self is somehow not "in the world."

In the *Blue Book* (p. 74) Wittgenstein observed that in "I feel pains" we "can't substitute for 'I' a description of a body." And Thomas Nagel has recently pointed out, in effect, that there is no description at all which is free of token-reflexive expressions and which can be substituted for 'I'; no matter how detailed a token-reflexive-free description of a person is, and whether or not it is couched in physicalistic terms, it cannot possibly entail that *I* am that person.[6] Inspired by these considerations, someone might argue as follows: "Nothing that I find in the world can be myself (or my Self), for there is nothing that I could observe or establish concerning any object I find in the world from which I could conclude that it is myself." This would clearly be a very bad argument, for even if its premise were true it would not establish that I cannot find what is in fact myself in the world; it would only establish that if I found what is myself in the world I could not *know* that it was myself that I had found. But it does not even establish that, for its premise is false. It is true that there is no token-reflexive-free description of any person from which it would follow that that person is myself, but there is no reason why, in

[6] See Nagel's "Physicalism," *The Philosophical Review*, 74 (1965), pp. 353–355.
After the above was written it came to my attention that Castañeda has argued, very persuasively, that there is no description, not even one containing indexicals (other, presumably, than the first-person pronouns themselves), that can be substituted for 'I.' See his "'He'" and his "Indicators and Quasi-Indicators," *American Philosophical Quarterly*, 4 (1967), pp. 87 and 95.

establishing whether someone is myself, I should be limited to facts about him that can be described without the use of token-reflexive expressions.

In our world there seldom occurs anything that it would be natural to describe as "finding oneself in the world" or "being an object to oneself." It is relatively seldom that we observe ourselves in the ways in which we observe others. But we can easily imagine a world full of reflecting surfaces, in which most seeing involves the intervention of one or more mirrors between what sees and what is seen. And one can perhaps imagine a world in which light rays follow curved paths, or a non-Euclidean world in which light rays following "straight" paths sometimes return to their point of origin. In such worlds one could be, visually at least, an object to oneself in just the way in which others are objects to one. It is clear that there would be no guarantee, in such a world, that, when observing oneself, one would know that it was oneself one was observing. But it is also clear that there would be no reason in principle why one should not find this out. Presumably one could find it out in much the way in which, in our world, one finds that it is oneself one is seeing in a mirror.

But while there can occur something that is describable as "finding oneself in the world" or "being an object to oneself," it is not and could not be on the basis of this that one makes the first-person statements in which 'I' is used "as subject." It is clear, to begin with, that not every self-ascription could be grounded on an identification of a presented object as oneself. Identifying something as oneself would have to involve either (a) finding something to be true of it that one independently knows to be true of oneself, i.e., something that identifies it as oneself, or (b) finding that it stands to oneself in some relationship (e.g., *being in the same place as*) in which only oneself could stand to one. In either case it would involve possessing self-knowledge – the knowledge that one has a certain identifying feature, or the knowledge that one stands in a certain relationship to the presented object – which would not itself be grounded on the identification in question. This self-knowledge might in some cases be grounded on some *other* identification, but the supposition that *every* item of self-knowledge rests on an identification leads to a vicious infinite regress. But in any case, and this is perhaps the most important point, the identification of a presented object as oneself would have to go together with the possibility of misidentification, and it is precisely the absence of this possibility that characterizes the use of 'I' that concerns us. I think that this is one of the main sources of the mistaken opinion that one cannot be an object to oneself, which in turn is a source of the view that 'I' does not refer. One feels that if one ever encounters the referent of 'I' in experience, this ought to occur on those occasions on which one's right to say 'I' is most secure, and that nothing that is not an object to one on those occasions can be its referent at all.

I have just said that identification necessarily goes together with the possibility of misidentification. It is clear enough why this is so in the case of the identification as oneself of a flesh-and-blood person who is observed by means of ordinary sense perception, but it may be questioned whether an identification of a self as oneself would be subject to error if selves were conceived as introspectable immaterial substances. And even if my "self" is a flesh-and-blood person, why shouldn't it be accessible to me (itself) in a way in which it is not accessible to others, so that in knowing that what is presented to me is presented in this special way – from the inside, as it were – I would know that it can be nothing other than myself?

Now there is a perfectly good sense in which my self is accessible to me in a way in which it is not to others. There are predicates which I apply to others, and which others apply to me, on the basis of observations of behavior, but which I do not ascribe to myself on this basis, and these predicates are precisely those the self-ascription of which is immune to error through misidentification. I see nothing wrong with describing the self-ascription of such predicates as manifestations of self-knowledge or self-awareness. But it is plainly not the occurrence of self-awareness in *this* sense that has been denied by those philosophers who have denied that one is an object to oneself; e.g., it is not what Hume denied when he said: "I can never catch *myself* at any time without a perception, and never can observe anything but the perception."[7] What those philosophers have wanted to deny, and rightly so, is that this self-awareness is to be explained in a certain way. They have wanted to deny that there is an experiencing or perceiving of one's self that explains one's awareness that one is, for example, in pain in a way analogous to that in which one's sense perception of John explains one's knowledge that John has a beard. An essential part of the explanation of my perceptual awareness that John has a beard is the fact that the observed properties of the man I perceive, together with other things I know, are sufficient to identify him for me as John. If the awareness that I am in pain had an explanation analogous to this, it would have to be that I "perceive," by "inner sense," something whose "observed properties" identify it

[7] *A Treatise of Human Nature*, ed. by L. A. Selby-Bigge (Oxford, 1888), p. 252.

to me as myself. And if the supposition that the perception is by "inner sense" is supposed to preclude the possibility of misidentification, presumably this must be because it guarantees that the perceived self would have a property, namely, the property of being an object of *my* inner sense, which no self other than myself could (logically) have and by which I could infallibly identify it as myself. But of course, in order to identify a self as myself by its possession of *this* property, I would have to know that *I* observe it by inner sense, and *this* self-knowledge, being the ground of my identification of the self as myself, could not itself be grounded on that identification. Yet if it were possible in this one case for my self-knowledge not to be grounded on an identification of a self as myself, there seems to be no reason at all why this should not be possible in other cases, e.g., in the case of my knowledge that I feel pain or my knowledge that I see a canary. Thus the supposition that there is observation by inner sense of oneself – where this is something that is supposed to explain, and therefore cannot be simply equated with, the ability to self-ascribe those predicates whose self-ascription is immune to error through misidentification – is at best a superfluous hypothesis: it explains nothing that cannot be just as easily, and more economically, explained without it.

Yet despite these considerations, it can seem puzzling that self-awareness, of the sort we are concerned with, does not involve being presented to oneself as an object. I cannot see the redness of a thing without seeing the thing that is red, and it would seem that it should be equally impossible to be aware of a state of oneself without being aware of that which has that state, i.e., oneself. It may seem to follow from the view I have been advancing that one is aware of the predicates of self-ascriptions, or aware of the instantiation of these predicates, without being aware of their subject, i.e., that in which they are instantiated. Thus we have Hume's view, that one observes "perceptions" but not anything that has them, and the view that one sometimes finds in discussions of Descartes's *Cogito*, that one seems, mysteriously, to be aware of thoughts, or of thinking, but not of that which thinks. If this strikes one as impossible, and if one is nevertheless persuaded that what is called "self-awareness" does not involve being aware of oneself as an object, it may seem that the only possible conclusion is that, when used in first-person statements, the expressions 'feel pain,' 'am angry,' 'see a tree,' etc., are pseudo-predicates, like 'is raining,' and that, in its use as subject, the word 'I' is a pseudo-subject, like the 'it' in "It is raining."

I think that the main source of trouble here is a tendency to think of awareness as a kind of perception, i.e., to think of it on the model of sense perception. I have been denying that self-awareness involves any sort of perception of oneself, but this should not be taken to mean that in making a judgment like "I feel pain" one is aware of anything less than the fact that one does, oneself, feel pain; in being aware that one feels pain one is, tautologically, aware, not simply that the attribute *feel(s) pain* is instantiated, but that it is instantiated *in oneself*. What makes the matter seem puzzling, I think is that one starts off by trying to construe self-awareness on the model of the observational know-ledge that a perceived thing has a certain sensory property, and fails to abandon this model, or to abandon it completely and consistently, when one becomes persuaded that self-awareness does not involve any sort of perception of one's self, i.e., does not involve what I have called "being presented to oneself as an object." One tries to construe one's knowledge of the instantiation of the attribute ascribed in a self-ascription on the model of a case in which one sees or otherwise observes the instantiation of a sensory attribute, like redness, while at the same time denying that one perceives that in which the attribute is instantiated. And this, of course, leads to incoherence. The way out of this incoherence is to abandon completely, not just in part, the perceptual model of self-knowledge.

What perhaps makes it difficult to abandon the perceptual model is the fact that it can seem to be implied by the very vocabulary we use to express certain psychological predicates. Thus, for example, we speak of a person as *feeling* a pain in his back or an itch on his nose, and there is an almost irresistible temptation to construe the cases thus described as cases of someone perceiving a particular of a certain sort – a private, mental, object. But even if we do so construe them, this does not really support the perceptual model. The attribute self-ascribed in the statement "I feel a pain" is that of feeling or having a pain, not that of being a pain or of being painful. And whether or not we construe 'feel' as a perceptual verb and allow that I can be said to feel something to be a pain, I can hardly be described as feeling anything to have the attribute of feeling a pain or as feeling this attribute to be instantiated. Our language may suggest that pains are perceived, but it does not suggest – and it seems to me clearly not to be true – that one perceives the feeling or the "having" of one's pains.

III

If one finds it puzzling that there can be the sort of self-reference that occurs in the use "as subject" of the first-person pronouns, i.e., that there can be self-ascriptions that are absolutely immune to error through misidentification and are not based on self-observation, one should reflect on the fact that if this were not possible there would be much else, and much that we take for granted, that would also not be possible. The question of how it is possible that there should be such self-reference is equivalent to the question of how it is possible that there should be predicates, or attributes, the self-ascription of which is immune to error through misidentification. And this question seems to me to be at the root of the larger question of how it is possible that there should be psychological attributes, or, what is almost though not quite the same thing, the question of how it is possible that there should be what Strawson has called "P-predicates." It has often been held to be one of the defining features of the realm of the mental, or the psychological, that each person knows of his own mental or psychological states in a way in which no other person could know of them. We can put what is true in this by saying that there is an important and central class of psychological predicates, let us call them "P*-predicates," each of which can be known to be instantiated in such a way that knowing it to be instantiated in that way is equivalent to knowing it to be instantiated in oneself.[8] There are

---

[8] A more explicit formulation is this: φ is a P*-predicate if and only if there is a way w of knowing φ to be instantiated such that, necessarily, S knows φ to be instantiated in way w if and only if S knows that he himself is φ. It is a consequence of this that, although self-ascriptions of P*-predicates need not be incorrigible and although it is not necessarily the case that if a P*-predicate applies to a person that person knows that it applies to him, it is necessarily the case that if a person knows that a P*-predicate applies to him he knows that it applies to him in the "special way" appropriate to that predicate (which does not preclude that he should *also* be in a position to know that it applies to him in other ways, i.e., ways in which others might know that it applies to him). Thus if one construes 'feeling pain' as the "special way" in which a person knows that he is in pain and holds that it is possible for a person to be in pain and know that he is in pain (e.g., on the basis of his behavior) without feeling pain, one should hold that the predicate of 'is (am) in pain' is not a P*-predicate and that its self-ascription is not immune to error through misidentification. But I can see no reason for holding this view.

My "P*" notation was suggested by H. N. Castañeda's use of the term "he*" to mark the special and interesting use of third-person pronouns in sentences of the form "S knows (believes, says, etc.) that he is φ," where 'he' has the force of "he himself." See Castañeda's "'He.'"

[(1983) The above definition of "P*-predicate" will not do as it stands. Unless we restrict in some way what counts as a "way of knowing," any predicate that one can know to apply to oneself will count as a P*-predicate according to the definition, which obviously is not what is intended. What is wanted is that there should be a way of knowing that satisfies the stated condition *and* does not resolve into (1) a way of knowing the predicate to be instantiated that does not satisfy the condition plus (2) an identification of that in which it is instantiated as oneself.]

psychological predicates that are not P*-predicates – e.g., "is highly intelligent." But I think that those which are not P*-predicates are classified as psychological predicates only because they are related in certain ways to those which are; e.g., they are predicable only of things of which some P*-predicates are also predicable, and many of them ascribe dispositions that manifest themselves in the having of P*-predicates.[9] If this is right, the question of how it is possible that there should be psychological predicates turns essentially on the question of how it is possible that there should be P*-predicates, and this is the same as the question of how it is possible that there should be predicates the self-ascription of which is absolutely immune to error through misidentification.

There is another question that seems to me to turn essentially on this question, namely, the question of how it is possible that there should be a first-person pronoun at all; i.e., how it is possible that people should be able to employ a referring expression whose meaning is given by the rule that it refers to the person who uses it. There is, I think, an important sense in which the "use as subject" of the first-person pronouns is more fundamental than their "use as object."

It is possible to imagine a people who speak a primitive language containing a first-person pronoun but no P*-predicates – let us suppose that the only predicates in this language, and thus the only predicates self-ascribed by its speakers, are what Strawson calls "M-predicates," i.e., predicates that do not "imply the possession of consciousness on the part of that to which they are ascribed" (p. 105). As I have already noted, it is possible for there to be self-ascriptions involving self-identification only if there are some self-ascriptions that do not involve self-identification. Now there are M-predicates, e.g., "is facing a table," which can in some circumstances be self-ascribed without identification. But in order to describe the circumstances in which such self-ascriptions could occur and in order to formulate the grounds of such self-ascriptions, it would be necessary to employ predicates, P*-predicates, that could not be expressed in our imaginary language. A speaker of this language would have to learn to self-ascribe such M-predicates as 'is facing a table' under just those circumstances in which he would be entitled to self-ascribe certain P*-predicates, e.g., 'sees a table in the center of one's field of vision,' if only he had these P*-predicates in his vocabulary. And if he can be taught to self-ascribe an M-predicate in this way, thus showing that he

---

[9] Strawson makes closely related points about what he refers to as "some important classes of P-predicates"; see his *Individuals* (London, 1959), pp. 107–110.

can discriminate between cases in which a certain P*-predicate applies to him and cases in which it does not, there would seem to be no reason in principle why he could not be taught to self-ascribe the P*-predicate itself. I think we can say that anyone who can self-ascribe any predicate whatever thereby shows that he is potentially capable of self-ascribing some P*-predicates, and that if he is presently incapable of doing so this is due simply to a correctable lack of his vocabulary or his stock of concepts. Something similar can be said of other sorts of reference. It is a condition of someone's being able to make a demonstrative reference, of the sort that does not involve identification, that he should in some way perceive the object referred to. Anyone who can correctly employ referring expressions of the form 'this so and so' thereby shows that he is potentially capable of self-ascribing P*-predicates of the form 'perceives a so and so.'

There is another way of indicating the priority I am claiming for the use "as subject" of 'I' over its use "as object." The clearest cases of the use "as object" are those in which the predicate self-ascribed is an M-predicate. Now where 'φ' is an M-predicate, to say that I am φ is to say that my body is φ. And if asked what it means to call a body "my body" I could say something like this: "My body is the body from whose eyes I see, the body whose mouth emits sounds when I speak, the body whose arm goes up when I raise my arm, the body that has something pressing against it when I feel pressure, and so on." All the uses of 'I' that occur in this explanation of the meaning of the phrase 'my body,' which in turn can be used to explicate the use "as object" of the first-person pronouns in the self-ascription of M-predicates, are themselves uses "as subject." To put this in another way, M-predicates are mine in virtue of being connected in a certain way with P*-predicates that are mine.

There is, I think, a tendency to find the use "as subject" of 'I' mysterious and to think that it is perhaps not reference at all, because it cannot be assimilated to other sorts of reference, e.g., to the use "as object" of 'I' or to demonstrative reference, the latter being taken as paradigms of unproblematic reference. This tendency ought not to survive the realization that these other sorts of reference are possible only because this sort of self-reference, that involving the use "as subject" of 'I,' is possible. There is an important sense in which each person's system of reference has that person himself as its anchoring point, and it is important for an understanding of the notion of reference, and also for an understanding of the notion of the mental, that we understand why and how this is so.

2

Persons and their pasts

Persons have, in memory, a special access to facts about their own past histories and their own identities, a kind of access they do not have to the histories and identities of other persons and other things. John Locke thought this special access important enough to warrant a special mention in his definition of "person," viz., "a thinking, intelligent Being, that has reason and reflection, *and can consider it self as it self, the same thinking thing, in different times and places. . .*"[1] In this essay I shall attempt to explain the nature and status of this special access and to defend Locke's view of its conceptual importance. I shall also attempt to correct what now seem to me to be errors and oversights in my own previous writings on this topic.

I

As a first approximation, the claim that persons have in memory a special access to their own past histories can be expressed in two related claims, both of which will be considerably qualified in the course of this essay. The first is that it is a necessary condition of its being true that a person remembers a given past event that he, that same person, should have observed or experienced the event, or known of it in some other direct way, at the time of its occurrence. I shall refer to this as the "previous awareness condition" for remembering.[2]

---

[1] Locke, *Essay Concerning Human Understanding*, ed. by Peter H. Nidditch (Oxford, 1975), p. 335 (bk. II, ch. 27, sect. IX). Italics added.

[2] In their paper "Remembering" (*The Philosophical Review*, 75 (1966)) C. B. Martin and Max Deutscher express what I call the previous awareness condition by saying that "a person can be said to remember something happening or, in general, remember something directly, only if he has observed or experienced it." Their notion of direct remembering seems to be much the same as Norman Malcolm's notion of "personal memory" (see his "Three Forms of Memory" in *Knowledge and Certainty* (Englewood Cliffs, N.J., 1963), pp. 203–221). To remember that Caesar invaded Britain I need not have had any experience of the invasion, but no one who lacked such

The second claim is that an important class of first-person memory claims are in a certain respect immune to what I shall call "error through misidentification." Consider a case in which I say, on the basis of my memory of a past incident, "I shouted that Johnson should be impeached," and compare this with a case in which I say, again on the basis of my memory of a past incident, "John shouted that Johnson should be impeached." In the latter case it could turn out that I do remember someone who looked and sounded just like John shouting that Johnson should be impeached, but that the man who shouted this was nevertheless not John – it may be that I misidentified the person as John at the time I observed the incident, and that I have preserved this misidentification in memory, or it may be that I subsequently misidentified him as John on the basis of what I (correctly) remembered about him. Here my statement would be false, but its falsity would not be due to a mistake or fault of my memory; my memory could be as accurate and complete as any memory could be without precluding this sort of error. But this sort of misidentification is not possible in the former case. My memory report could of course be mistaken, for one can misremember such incidents, but it could not be the case that I have a full and accurate memory of the past incident but am mistaken in thinking that the person I remember shouting was myself. I shall speak of such memory judgments as being immune to error through misidentification with respect to the first-person pronouns, or other "self-referring" expressions, contained in them.[3]

I do not contend that all memory claims are immune to error through misidentification with respect to the first-person pronouns

experience could directly or personally remember that Caesar invaded Britain. In this essay I am primarily concerned with memories that are of events, i.e., of something happening, and do not explicitly consider what Malcolm calls "factual memory," i.e., memories *that* such and such was (or is, or will be) the case, but what I say can be extended to cover all cases of direct or personal memory. Martin and Deutscher hold, and I agree, that remembering something happening is always direct remembering.

There are apparent counterexamples to the previous witnessing condition as I have formulated it. I can be said to remember Kennedy's assassination, which is presumably an event, yet I did not witness or observe it, and the knowledge I had of it at the time was indirect. But while I can be said to remember the assassination, I could hardly be said to remember Kennedy being shot (what I do remember is hearing about it, and the impact this made on me and those around me). Perhaps I can be said to remember the assassination because we sometimes mean by "the assassination" not only the events in Dallas but their immediate effects throughout the nation and world. In any case, when I speak of memories of events in this essay I mean what Martin and Deutscher speak of as memories of something happening.

[3] Although self-reference is typically done with first-person pronouns, it can be done with names, and even with definite descriptions – as when de Gaulle says "De Gaulle intends . . .," and the chairman of a meeting says "The Chair recognizes . . ."

contained in them. If I say "I blushed when Jones made that remark" because I remember seeing in a mirror someone, whom I took (or now take) to be myself, blushing, it could turn out that my statement is false, not because my memory is in any way incomplete or inaccurate, but because the person I saw in the mirror was my identical twin or double.[4] In general, if at some past time I could have known of someone that he was φ, and could at the same time have been mistaken in taking that person to be myself, then the subsequent memory claims I make about the past occasion will be subject to error through misidentification with respect to the first-person pronouns. But if, as is frequently the case, I could not have been mistaken in this way in the past in asserting what I then knew by saying "I *am* φ," then my subsequent memory claim "I *was* φ" will be immune to error through misidentification relative to 'I'; that is, it is impossible in such cases that I should accurately remember someone being φ but mistakenly take that person to be myself. We might express this by saying that where the present-tense version of a judgment is immune to error through misidentification relative to the first-person pronouns contained in it, this immunity is *preserved* in memory.[5] Thus if I claim on the strength of memory that I saw John yesterday, and have a full and accurate memory of the incident, it cannot be the case that I remember

In such cases these expressions are "self-referring," not merely because their reference is in fact to the speaker, but also because the speaker intends in using them to refer to himself.

[4] There is a subtle distinction between this sort of case and cases like the following, which I would not count as a case of error through misidentification. Suppose that Jones says "You are a fool," and I mistakenly think that he is speaking to me. Subsequently I say "I remember Jones calling me a fool," and my statement is false through no fault of my memory. While this is a case of knowing *that* Jones called someone (someone or other) a fool and mistakenly thinking that he was calling me a fool, it is not a case of knowing *of* some particular person that Jones called him a fool but mistakenly identifying that person as oneself. Whereas in the other case we can say, not merely that I know that someone or other blushed, and mistakenly think that it was I, but that I know *of* some particular person (namely the man I saw in the mirror) that he blushed and have mistakenly identified him as myself.

[5] I have discussed the immunity to error through misidentification of first-person present-tense statements in Essay 1. There I made the mistake of associating this feature with the peculiarities of the first-person pronouns. But in fact present-tense statements having the appropriate sorts of predicates are immune to error through misidentification with respect to any expressions that are "self-referring" in the sense of footnote 3, including names and definite descriptions. If someone says "De Gaulle intends to remove France from NATO," and is using "de Gaulle" to refer to himself, his statement is in the relevant sense immune to error through misidentification, regardless of whether he is right in thinking that his name is "de Gaulle" and that he is the President of France.

someone seeing John but have misidentified that person as myself; my
memory claim "I saw John" is subject to error through misidentification with respect to the term "John" (for it could have been John's
twin or double that I saw), but not with respect to 'I.'

II

In his early paper, "Personal Identity," H. P. Grice held that the
proposition "One can only remember one's own past experiences" is
analytic, but pointed out that this would be analytic in only a trivial
way "if 'memory' were to be defined in terms of 'having knowledge of
one's own past experiences.' " He says that "even if we were to define
'memory' in this sort of way, we should still be left with a question
about the proposition, 'one can only have knowledge of one's own
past experiences,' which seems to me a necessary proposition."[6] Now
I doubt very much if Grice, or any other philosopher, would now want
to hold that it is necessarily true, or that it is true at all, that one's own
past experiences are the only past experiences of which one can have
knowledge. But one does not have to hold this to hold, with Grice, that
it is not just a trivial analytic truth that one's own experiences are the
only ones that one can remember, i.e., that it is not the case that the
necessity of this truth derives merely from the fact that we refuse to
call someone's having knowledge of a past experience a case of his
remembering it unless the past experience belonged to the rememberer
himself.

Grice's remarks are explicitly about memory of past experiences,
but they raise an important question about all sorts of "event
memory." Supposing it to be a necessary truth that the previous
witnessing condition must be satisfied in any genuine case of
remembering, is this necessarily true because we would refuse to *count*
knowing about a past event as remembering it if the previous
awareness condition were not satisfied, or is it necessary for some
deeper reason? I think that many philosophers would hold that if this
is a necessary truth at all, it is so only in the former way, i.e., in such a
way as to make its necessity trivial and uninteresting. Thus G. C.
Nerlich, in a footnote to his paper "On Evidence for Identity," says
that it is true only of *our* world, not of all possible worlds, that only by
being identical with a witness to past events can one have the sort of
knowledge of them one has in memory.[7] On this view it is logically

---

[6] H. P. Grice, "Personal Identity," *Mind* 50 (1941), 330–350, p. 344.
[7] G. C. Nerlich, "On Evidence for Identity," *Australasian Journal of Philosophy*, 37
(1959), 201–214, p. 208.

possible that we should have knowledge of past events which we did not ourselves witness, of experiences we did not ourselves have, and of actions we did not ourselves perform, that is in all important respects like the knowledge we have of past events, experiences, and actions in remembering them. If one takes this view it will seem a matter of small importance, if indeed it is true, that the having of such knowledge could not be called "remembering."

It is of course not absolutely clear just what it means to speak of knowledge as being "in all important respects like" memory knowledge, if this is not intended to imply that the knowledge *is* memory knowledge. Presumably, knowledge of past events that is "just like" memory knowledge must not be inferred from present data (diaries, photographs, rock strata, etc.) on the basis of empirical laws and generalizations. But while this is necessary, it is not sufficient. When a person remembers a past event there is a correspondence between his present cognitive state and some past cognitive and sensory state of his that existed at the time of the remembered event and consisted in his experiencing the event or otherwise being aware of its occurrence.[8] I shall say that remembering a past event involves there being a correspondence between the rememberer's present cognitive state and a past cognitive and sensory state that was "of" the event.[9] In actual memory this past cognitive and sensory state is always a past state of the rememberer himself. What we need to consider is whether there

[8] I am not here endorsing the view, which I in fact reject, that remembering consists in the having of an image, or some other sort of mental "representation," in which the memory content is in some way encoded. It is sufficient for the existence at *t* of the "cognitive state" of remembering such and such that it be true of the person at *t* that he remembers such and such; I am not here committing myself to any account of what, if anything, someone's remembering such and such "consists in."

[9] I should make it clear that I am not saying that what we remember is always, or even normally, a past cognitive and sensory state. I am not propounding the view, which is sometimes held but which is clearly false, that "strictly speaking" one can remember only one's own past experiences. I am saying only that if a person remembers an event that occurred at time *t* then at *t* there must have been a corresponding cognitive and sensory state – which the person may or may not remember – that was of that event. It would not be easy to specify just what sort of correspondence is required here, and I shall not attempt to do so. But I take it as obvious that the claim to remember firing a gun requires, for its truth, a different sort of past cognitive and sensory state than the claim to remember hearing someone else fire a gun, and that the latter, in turn, requires a different sort of past cognitive and sensory state than the claim to remember seeing someone fire a gun. Sometimes one remembers a past event but no longer remembers just how one knew of it at the time of its occurrence; in such a case one's memory, because of vagueness and incompleteness, corresponds to a wider range of possible cognitive and sensory states than (say) a memory of seeing the event or a memory of being told about it.

could be a kind of knowledge of past events such that someone's having this sort of knowledge of an event does involve there being a correspondence between his present cognitive state and a past cognitive and sensory state that was of the event, but such that this correspondence, although otherwise just like that which exists in memory, does not necessarily involve that past state's having been a state of the very same person who subsequently has the knowledge. Let us speak of such knowledge, supposing for the moment that it is possible, as "quasi-memory knowledge," and let us say that a person who has this sort of knowledge of a past event "quasi-remembers" that past event. Quasi-remembering, as I shall use the term, includes remembering as a special case. One way of characterizing the difference between quasi-remembering and remembering is by saying that the former is subject to a weaker previous awareness condition than the latter. Whereas someone's claim to remember a past event implies that he himself was aware of the event at the time of its occurrence, the claim to quasi-remember a past event implies only that someone or other was aware of it. Except when I indicate otherwise, I shall use the expression "previous awareness condition" to refer to the stronger of these conditions.

Our faculty of memory constitutes our most direct access to the past, and this means, given the previous awareness condition, that our most direct access to the past is in the first instance an access to *our own* past histories. One of the main questions I shall be considering in this essay is whether it is conceivable that our most direct access to the past should be a faculty of quasi-remembering which is not a faculty of remembering. Is it conceivable that we should have, as a matter of course, knowledge that is related to past experiences and actions other than our own in just the way in which, as things are, our memory knowledge is related to our own past experiences and actions? In our world all quasi-remembering is remembering; what we must consider is whether the world could be such that most quasi-remembering is not remembering.

Before going on to consider this question I should mention two reasons why I think it important. The first is its obvious bearing on the question of the relationship between the concepts of memory and personal identity. If there can be quasi-remembering that is not remembering, and if remembering can be defined as quasi-remembering that is of events the quasi-rememberer was aware of at the time of their occurrence (thus making it a trivial analytic truth that one can remember an event only if one was previously aware of it), then it would seem that any attempt to define or analyze the notion of personal identity in terms of the notion of remembering will be viciously circular. I shall have more to say about this in section v. But this question also has an important bearing on the question of how a person's memory claims concerning his own past are grounded. In previous writings I have claimed, and made a great deal of the claim, that our memory knowledge of our own past histories, unlike our knowledge of the past histories of other things, is not grounded on criteria of identity.[10] Strawson makes a similar claim in *The Bounds of Sense*, saying that "When a man (a subject of experience) ascribes a current or directly remembered state of consciousness to himself, no use whatever of any criteria of personal identity is required to justify his use of the pronoun 'I' to refer to the subject of that experience." He remarks that "it is because Kant recognized this truth that his treatment of the subject is so greatly superior to Hume's."[11] Now it can easily seem that this claim follows immediately from the fact that remembering necessarily involves the satisfaction of the previous awareness condition. If one remembers a past experience then it has to have been one's own, and from this it may seem to follow that it makes no sense to inquire concerning a remembered experience whether it was one's own and then to try to answer this question on the basis of empirical criteria of identity. But suppose that it were only a trivial analytic truth that remembering involves the satisfaction of the previous awareness condition, and suppose that it were possible to quasi-remember experiences other than one's own. If this were so one might remember a past experience but not know whether one was remembering it or only quasi-remembering it. Here, it seems, it would be perfectly appropriate to employ a criterion of identity to determine whether the quasi-remembered experience was one's own, i.e., whether one remembered it as opposed to merely quasi-remembering it. Thus the question of whether the knowledge of our own identities provided us by memory is essentially non-critical turns on the question of whether it is possible to quasi-remember past actions and experiences without remembering them.

III

There is an important respect in which my characterization of quasi-remembering leaves that notion inadequately specified. Until now I

[10] See my book *Self-Knowledge and Self-Identity* (Ithaca, N.Y. 1963), especially ch. 4, and my paper "Personal Identity and Memory," *The Journal of Philosophy*, 56 (1959), 868–882.

[11] P. F. Strawson, *The Bounds of Sense* (London, 1966), p. 165.

have been ignoring the fact that a claim to remember a past event implies, not merely that the rememberer experienced such an event, but that his present memory is in some way *due to*, that it came about *because of*, a cognitive and sensory state the rememberer had at the time he experienced the event. I am going to assume, although this is controversial, that it is part of the previous awareness condition for memory that a veridical memory must not only correspond to, but must also stand in an appropriate *causal* relationship to, a past cognitive and sensory state of the rememberer.[12] It may seem that if quasi-memory is to be as much like memory as possible, we should build a similar requirement into the previous awareness condition for quasi-memory, i.e., that we should require that a veridical quasi-memory must not only correspond to, but must also stand in an appropriate causal relationship to, a past cognitive and sensory state of someone or other. On the other hand, it is not immediately obvious that building such a requirement into the previous awareness condition for quasi-memory would not make it equivalent to the previous awareness condition for memory, and thus destroy the intended difference between memory and quasi-memory. But there is no need for us to choose between a previous awareness condition that includes the causal requirement and one that does not, for it is possible and useful to consider both. In the present section I shall assume that the previous awareness condition for quasi-memory does not include the causal requirement, and that it includes nothing more than the requirement that a quasi-memory must, to be a veridical quasi-memory of a given event, correspond in content to a past cognitive and sensory state that was of that event. In the sections that follow I shall consider the consequences of strengthening this condition to include the causal requirement.

The first thing we must consider is what becomes of the immunity of first-person memory claims to error through misidentification if we imagine the faculty of memory replaced by a faculty of quasi-memory.

---

[12] I owe to Norman Malcolm the point that to be memory knowledge one's knowledge must be in some way due to, must exist because of, a past cognitive and sensory state of oneself – see his "Three Forms of Memory." Malcolm holds that "due to" does not here express a causal relationship, but I have been persuaded otherwise by Martin's and Deutscher's "Remembering." See also my paper "On Knowing Who One Is" (*Common Factor*, 4 (1966)), and David Wiggins's *Identity and Spatio-Temporal Continuity* (Oxford, 1967), especially pp. 50ff. The view that there is a causal element in the concept of memory is attacked by Roger Squires in his recent paper "Memory Unchained" (*The Philosophical Review*, 78 (1969), 178–196); I make a very limited reply to this in section v of this essay.

As things are now, there is a difference between, on the one hand, remembering an action of someone else's – this might consist, for example, in having a memory of seeing someone do the action – and, on the other hand, remembering *doing* an action, which can be equated with remembering *oneself* doing the action. In the case of quasi-remembering the distinction corresponding to this is that between, on the one hand, the sort of quasi-memory of a past action whose corresponding past cognitive and sensory state belonged to someone who was watching someone else do the action, and, on the other hand, the sort of quasi-memory of a past action whose corresponding past cognitive and sensory state belonged to the very person who did the action. Let us call these, respectively, quasi-memories of an action "from the outside" and quasi-memories of an action "from the inside." Now whereas I can remember an action from the inside only if it was my action, a world in which there is quasi-remembering that is not remembering will be one in which it is not true that any action one quasi-remembers from the inside is thereby an action he himself did. So – assuming that ours may be such a world – if I quasi-remember an action from the inside, and say on this basis that I did the action, my statement will be subject to error through misidentification; it may be that my quasi-memory of the action is as accurate and complete as it could be, but that I am mistaken in thinking that I am the person who did it. There is another way in which a first-person quasi-memory claim could be mistaken through misidentification. If there can be quasi-remembering that is not remembering, it will be possible for a person to quasi-remember an action of his own from the outside. That is, one might quasi-remember an action of one's own as it appeared to someone else who observed it; one might, as it were, quasi-remember it through the eyes of another person. But of course, if I were to quasi-remember someone who looks like me doing a certain action, and were to say on that basis that I did the action, I might be mistaken through no fault of my quasi-memory; it might be that the person who did the action was my identical twin or someone disguised to look like me.

What I have just said about the quasi-remembering of past actions also applies to the quasi-remembering of past experiences and of other mental phenomena. If I remember a past pain from the inside – i.e., remember the pain itself, or remember having the pain, as opposed to remembering seeing someone manifest pain behavior – then the pain must have been mine. But the fact that I *quasi*-remember a pain from the inside will be no guarantee that the pain was mine. Any quasi-memory claim to have been in pain on some past occasion, or to have had a certain thought, or to have made a certain decision, will be subject to error through misidentification.

What is shown by the foregoing is that the immunity of first-person memory claims to error through misidentification exists only because remembering requires the satisfaction of the previous awareness condition, and that this feature disappears once we imagine this requirement dropped. Quasi-memory, unlike memory, does not preserve immunity to error through misidentification relative to the first-person pronouns. To consider the further consequences of replacing memory with quasi-memory, I must first say something more about memory.

To refer to an event of a certain sort as one that one remembers does not always uniquely identify it, since one may remember more than one event of a given sort, but it does go some way toward identifying it. In referring to an event in this way one to a certain extent locates it in space and time, even if the description of the event contains no place-names, no names of objects by reference to which places can be identified, and no dates or other temporal indicators. For in saying that one remembers the event one locates it within a spatiotemporal region which is defined by one's own personal history. The spatiotemporal region which is "rememberable" by a given person can be charted by specifying the intervals of past time during which the person was conscious and by specifying the person's spatial location, and indicating what portions of his environment he was in a position to witness, at each moment during these intervals. If someone reports that he remembers an event of a certain kind, we know that unless his memory is mistaken an event of that kind occurred within the spatiotemporal region rememberable by him, and in principle we can chart this region by tracing his history back to its beginning.

Ordinarily, of course, we have far more knowledge than this of the spatiotemporal location of a remembered event, for usually a memory report will fix this position by means of dates, place-names, and other spatial and temporal indicators. But it must be noted that memory claims are subject to error through misidentification with respect to spatial indicators. If a man says "I remember an explosion occurring right in front of that building," it is possible for this to be false even if the memory it expresses is accurate and detailed; the remembered explosion may have occurred, not in front of the building indicated, but in front of another building exactly like it. This remains true no matter how elaborate and detailed we imagine the memory claim to be. For any set of objects that has actually existed in the world, even if this be as extensive as the set of buildings, streets, parks, bridges, etc., that presently make up New York City, it is logically possible that there should somewhere exist, or that there should somewhere and at some time have existed, a numerically different but exactly similar set of objects arranged in exactly the same way. So memory claims are, in principle, subject to error through misidentification even with respect to such place names as "New York City." Here I am appealing to what Strawson has referred to as the possibility of "massive reduplication."[13]

When a memory report attempts to fix the location of a remembered event by reference to some landmark, we are ordinarily justified in not regarding it as a real possibility that the claim involves error through misidentification owing to the reduplication of that landmark. Certainly we are so justified if the landmark is New York City. But it is important to see why this is so. It is not that we have established that nowhere and at no time has there existed another city exactly like New York; as a self-consistent, unrestricted, negative existential claim, this is something that it would be impossible in principle for us to establish.[14] What we can and do know is that New York is not reduplicated within any spatiotemporal region of which anyone with

---

[13] P. F. Strawson, *Individuals* (London, 1959), p. 20.

[14] It will perhaps be objected that the dictum that unrestricted negative existential claims are unverifiable in principle is brought into question by the possibility that we might discover – what some cosmologists hold there is good reason for believing – that space and past time are finite. If we discovered this, why shouldn't we be able, at least in principle, to establish that at no place does there exist, and at no time in the past has there existed, a duplicate of New York?

One way of countering this objection would be to introduce the possibility, which has been argued by Anthony Quinton in his paper "Spaces and Times" (*Philosophy* 57 (1962), 130–141), of there being a multiplicity of different and spatially unrelated spaces. Establishing that there is no duplicate of New York in our space would not establish that there is no space in which there is such a duplicate, and if it is possible for there to be multiplicity of spaces there would seem to be no way in which the latter could be established.

But we needn't have recourse to such recondite possibilities in order to counter this objection, if it is viewed as an objection to my claim that it is the fact that remembering involves the satisfaction of the previous awareness condition that makes it possible for us to rule out the possibility that memory claims are false through misidentification owing to the reduplication of landmarks. For to discover that space or past time is finite, and that massive reduplication does not occur, one would have to have a vast amount of empirical information about the world, including information about the histories of particular things. But, as I think the remainder of my discussion should make clear, one could not be provided with such information by memory (or by quasi-memory) unless one were *already* entitled in a large number of cases to refer to particular places and things in one's memory reports without having to regard it as possible that one's references were mistaken owing to massive reduplication. So this entitlement would have to precede the discovery that space and past time are finite, and could not depend on it.

whom we converse can have had experience. Whether or not New York is reduplicated in some remote galaxy or at some remote time in the past, we know that the man who claims to remember doing or experiencing something in a New York-like city cannot have been in any such duplicate. And from this we can conclude that if he does remember doing or experiencing something in a New York-like city, then it was indeed in New York, and not in any duplicate of it, that the remembered action or event occurred. But we can conclude this only because remembering involves the satisfaction of the previous awareness condition.

Even when a landmark referred to in someone's memory claim is reduplicated within the spatiotemporal region rememberable by that person, we can often be confident that the claim does not involve error through misidentification. Suppose that someone locates a remembered event, say an explosion, by saying that it occurred in front of his house, and we know that there are many houses, some of which he has seen, that are exactly like his. If he reported that he had simply found himself in front of his house, with no recollection of how he had gotten there, and that after seeing the explosion he had passed out and awakened later in a hospital, we would think it quite possible that he had misidentified the place at which the remembered explosion occurred. But suppose instead that he reports that he remembers walking home from work, seeing the explosion in front of his house, and then going inside and being greeted by his family. Here a misidentification of the place of the explosion would require the reduplication, not merely of his house, but also of his family, his place of work, and the route he follows in walking home from work. We could know that no such reduplication exists within the spatiotemporal region of which he has had experience, and could conclude that his report did not involve an error through misidentification. But again, what would enable us to conclude this is the fact that remembering involves the satisfaction of the previous awareness condition.

Presumably, what justifies any of us in using such expressions as "New York" and "my house" in his own memory reports are considerations of the same kind as those that justify others in ruling out the possibility that claims containing such expressions involve error through misidentification. What justifies one is the knowledge that certain sorts of reduplication do not in fact occur within the spatiotemporal regions of which any of us have had experience. Normally no such justification is needed for the use of 'I' in memory reports; this is what is involved in saying that memory claims are normally immune to error through misidentification relative to the first-person pronouns. But what makes such a justification possible in the case of "New York" is the same as what makes it unnecessary in the case of 'I,' namely the fact that remembering involves the satisfaction of the previous awareness condition. So it is because of this fact that remembering can provide us, not merely with the information that an event of a certain sort has occurred somewhere or other in the vicinity of persons and things satisfying certain general descriptions, but with the information that such an event occurred in a certain specified place, in a certain specifiable spatial relationship to events presently observed, and in the vicinity of certain specified persons or things. But this is also to say that it is this fact about remembering that makes it possible for us to know that an object or person to which one remembers something happening is, or is not, identical with an object or person presently observed. And it will emerge later that it is also this fact about remembering that makes it possible to know that different memories are, or are not, of events in the history of a single object or person.

But now let us consider the consequences of replacing the faculty of memory by a faculty of quasi-memory. Quasi-remembering does not necessarily involve the satisfaction of the previous awareness condition, and first-person quasi-memory claims are, as we have seen, subject to error through misidentification. It is a consequence of this that even if we are given that someone's faculty of quasi-memory is highly reliable, in the sense that when he seems to quasi-remember an event of a certain sort he almost always does quasi-remember such an event, nevertheless his quasi-memory will provide neither him nor us with any positive information concerning the spatial location of the events he quasi-remembers, or with any information concerning the identity, or concerning the history, of any object or person to which he quasi-remembers something happening. The fact that he quasi-remembers an event of a certain sort will not provide us with the information that such an event has occurred within the spatiotemporal region of which he has had experience. But in consequence of this, if he attempts to locate the quasi-remembered event by reference to some object or place known to us, e.g., New York or Mt. Everest, it is impossible for us to rule out on empirical grounds the possibility that his claim involves error through misidentification owing to the reduplication of that object or place. To rule this out we would have to have adequate grounds for asserting, not merely that there is no duplicate of New York (say) in the spatiotemporal region of which he has had experience, but that at no place and time has there been a duplicate of New York. And this we could not have.[15] But this means that in expressing his quasi-memories he could not be justified in using such expressions as "New York" and "Mt. Everest," or such expressions as 'I,' "this," and "here," to refer to the places, persons, and things in or to which he quasi-remembers certain things happening. The most he could be entitled to assert on the basis of his quasi-memories would be a set of general propositions of the form "An event of type φ at some time occurred in the history of an object of type A while it stood in relations $R_1, R_2, R_3 \ldots$ to objects of types $B, C, D \ldots$" And given only a set of propositions of this sort, no matter how extensive, one could not even begin to reconstruct any part of the history of the world; one could not even have grounds for asserting that an object mentioned in one proposition in the set was one and the same as an object mentioned in another proposition of the set.

So far I have been ignoring the fact that the events and actions we remember generally have temporal duration, and the fact that we sometimes remember connected sequences of events and actions lasting considerable lengths of time. What will correspond to this if remembering is replaced with quasi-remembering? If someone says "I remember doing X and then doing Y," it would make no sense to say to him, "Granted that your memory is accurate, and that such a sequence of actions did occur, are you sure that it was one and the same person who did both X and Y?" But now suppose that someone says "I quasi-remember doing X and then doing Y," and that the world is such that there is quasi-remembering that is not remembering. Here it is compatible with the accuracy of the man's quasi-memory that he should be mistaken in thinking that he himself did X and Y. And as I shall now try to show, it must also be compatible with the accuracy of this man's quasi-memories that he should be mistaken in thinking even that one and the same person did both X and Y.

Suppose that at time t_1 a person, call him A, does action Y and has while doing it a quasi-memory from the inside of the immediately previous occurrence of the doing of action X. A's having this quasi-memory of the doing of X is of course compatible with X's having been done by someone other than himself. At t_1 A's cognitive state includes this quasi-memory from the inside of the doing of X together with knowledge from the inside of the doing of Y; we might say that it

[15] The point made in the preceding footnote can now be expressed by saying that even if we, who have the faculty of memory, could establish that at no place and time has there been a duplicate of New York, this could not be established by someone whose faculty of knowing the past was a faculty of quasi-memory.

includes knowledge from the inside of the action sequence X-followed-by-Y. But now suppose that at a later time t_2 someone, call him B, has a quasi-memory corresponding to the cognitive state of A at t_1. It would seem that B's quasi-memory will be a quasi-memory from the inside of the action sequence X-followed-by-Y. This quasi-memory will be veridical in the sense that it corresponds to a past cognitive state that was itself a state of knowledge, yet its being veridical in this way is compatible with X and Y having been done by different persons. If A were mistakenly to assert at t_1 that X and Y were done by the same person, his mistake would not be due to a faulty quasi-memory. And if B's cognitive state at t_2 corresponds to A's cognitive state at t_1, then if B were mistaken at t_2 in thinking that X and Y were done by the same person, this mistake would not be due to a faulty quasi-memory.

If, as I have been arguing, someone's quasi-remembering from the inside the *action* sequence X-followed-by-Y provides no guarantee that X and Y were done by the same person, then by the same reasoning someone's quasi-remembering the *event* sequence X-followed-by-Y provides no guarantee that X and Y were witnessed by the same person, and therefore no guarantee that they occurred in spatial proximity to one another. But any temporally extended event can be thought of as a succession of temporally and spatially contiguous events; e.g., a stone's rolling down a hill can be thought of as consisting in its rolling half of the way down followed by its rolling the other half of the way. Suppose, then, that someone has a quasi-memory of the following event sequence: stone rolling from top of hill to middle followed by stone rolling from middle of hill to bottom. If we knew this to be a memory, and not just a quasi-memory, we would know that if it is veridical then one and the same person observed both of these events, one immediately after the other, and this together with the contents of the memory could guarantee that one and the same hill and one and the same stone were involved in both, and that a single stone had indeed rolled all the way down a hill. But the veridicality of this quasi-memory *qua* quasi-memory would be compatible with these events having been observed by different persons, and with their involving different stones and different hills; it would be compatible with no stone's having rolled all of the way down any hill. And since any temporally extended event can be thought of as a succession of temporally and spatially contiguous events, it follows that someone's quasi-remembering what is ostensibly a temporally extended event of a certain kind is always compatible with there actually being no such event that he quasi-remembers, for it is compatible with his quasi-

memory being, as it were, compounded out of quasi-memories of a
number of different events that were causally unrelated and spatiotemporally remote from one another. The knowledge of the past provided
by such a faculty of quasi-memory would be minimal indeed.[16]

IV

But now we must consider the consequences of strengthening the
previous awareness condition for quasi-remembering to include the
requirement that a veridical quasi-memory must not only correspond
to, but must also stand in an appropriate causal relationship to, a past
cognitive and sensory state of someone or other. Clearly, much of
what I have said about quasi-remembering ceases to hold once its
previous awareness condition is strengthened in this way. If, as is
commonly supposed, causal chains must be spatiotemporally continuous, then if quasi-memory claims implied the satisfaction of this
strengthened previous awareness condition they would, when true,
provide some information concerning the location of the quasi-
remembered events and actions. We would know at a minimum that
the spatiotemporal relationship between the quasi-remembered event
and the making of the quasi-memory claim is such that it is possible
for them to be linked by a spatiotemporally continuous causal chain,
and if we could trace the causal ancestry of the quasi-memory we could
determine precisely when and where the quasi-remembered event

[16] It may be objected that I have overlooked one way in which a quasi-rememberer
might begin to reconstruct his own past history, and the histories of other things, from
the information provided him by his quasi-memories. The quasi-rememberer's
difficulties would be solved if he had a way of sorting out those of his quasi-memories
that are of his own past, i.e., are memories, from those that are not. But it may seem
that the quasi-rememberer could easily tell which of his quasi-memories of the very
recent past are of his own past, namely by noting which of them have contents very
similar to the contents of his *present* experiences; e.g., if he quasi-remembers from the
inside the very recent seeing of a scene that resembles very closely the scene he
presently sees, it may seem that he can justifiably conclude that the quasi-remembered
seeing was his own. And it may seem that by starting in this way he could trace back
his own history by finding among his quasi-memories a subset of situations that form
a spatiotemporally continuous series of situations, that series terminating in the
situation he presently perceives.
  This objection assumes that the quasi-rememberer can know the degree of
recentness of the situations of which he has quasi-memories, but I shall not here
question this assumption. What I shall question is the assumption that if the quasi-
rememberer knows that a quasi-remembered scene occurred only a moment or so ago,
and that it closely resembles the scene he presently sees, he is entitled to believe that it
is numerically the same scene as the one he presently sees and that in all probability it

occurred. Thus if we construe the previous awareness condition of quasi-memory as including this causal requirement, it seems that a faculty of quasi-remembering could enable us to identify past events and to reidentify persons and things, and it seems at first glance (though not, I think, on closer examination) that it would enable us to do this without giving us a special access to our own past histories.

It must be stressed that this strengthened previous awareness condition is an improvement on the weaker one *only* on the assumption that causal chains (or at any rate the causal chains that link cognitive and sensory states with subsequent quasi-memories) must be spatiotemporally continuous, or at least must satisfy a condition similar to spatiotemporal continuity. If the sort of causality operating here allowed for action at a spatial or temporal distance, and if there were no limit on the size of the spatial or temporal gaps that could exist in a causal chain linking a cognitive and sensory state with a subsequent quasi-memory, then the claim that a quasi-memory originated in a corresponding cognitive and sensory state would be as unfalsifiable, and as uninformative, as the claim that it corresponds to a past cognitive and sensory state of someone or other.

To consider the consequences of strengthening the previous awareness condition for quasi-memory in the way just suggested I shall have to introduce a few technical expressions. First, I shall use the expressions "quasi$_c$-remember" and "quasi$_c$-memory" when speaking of the sort of quasi-remembering whose previous awareness condition includes the causal requirement. Second, I shall use the term "M-type causal chain" to refer to the sort of causal chain that must link a quasi$_c$-memory with a corresponding past cognitive and sensory state if they are to be "of" the same event, or if the former is to be "of" the latter. Since quasi$_c$-remembering is to be as much like remember-

---

was he who saw it. For of course it could be the case that there is somewhere else a duplicate of the scene he sees, and that his quasi-memory is of that duplicate. It will perhaps be objected that while this is logically possible (given the possibility of quasi-remembering that is not remembering), it is highly improbable. But while it may be intrinsically improbable that a highly complicated situation should be reduplicated within some limited spatiotemporal area, it does not seem intrinsically improbable that such a situation should be reduplicated somewhere or other in the universe – unless the universe is finite, which is something the quasi-rememberer could have no reason for believing (see footnotes 14 and 15). Moreover, one could not be in a position to know how rare or frequent such reduplication is in fact, and therefore how likely or unlikely it is that a given situation is reduplicated, unless one already had a way of reidentifying places and things. So the quasi-rememberer could not be in a position to know this, for he could have a way of reidentifying places and things only if he were already in a position to rule out reduplication as improbable.

ing as is compatible with the failure of the strong previous awareness condition, M-type causal chains should resemble as much as possible the causal chains that are responsible for actual remembering, i.e., should resemble them as much as is compatible with their sometimes linking mental states belonging to different persons. At any given time a person can be said to have a total mental state which includes his memories or quasi$_c$memories and whatever other mental states the person has at that time. Let us say that two total mental states, existing at different times, are directly M-connected if the later of them contains a quasi$_c$-memory which is linked by an M-type causal chain to a corresponding cognitive and sensory state contained in the earlier. And let us say, by way of giving a recursive definition, that two total mental states are M-connected if either (1) they are directly M-connected, or (2) there is some third total mental state to which each of them is M-connected.[17]

Now there are two cases we must consider. Either the world will be such, or it will not, that a total mental state existing at a particular time can be M-connected with at most one total mental state existing at each other moment in time. Or, what comes to the same thing, either the world will be such, or it will not, that no two total mental states existing at the same time can be M-connected. Let us begin by considering the case in which the former of these alternatives holds. This is the case that will exist if there is no "branching" of M-type causal chains, i.e., if it never happens that an M-type causal chain branches into two such chains which then produce quasi$_c$-memories belonging to different and simultaneously existing total mental states, and if it never happens that different M-type causal chains coalesce

---

[17] It is worth mentioning that if quasi$_c$-remembering is to be as much like remembering as possible then not just any causal chain linking a past cognitive and sensory state with a subsequent quasi$_c$-memory can be allowed to count as an M-type causal chain. For as Martin and Deutscher ("Remembering") point out, there are various sorts of cases in which a man's knowledge of a past event is causally due to his previous experience of it but in which the causal connection is obviously not of the right kind to permit us to say that he remembers the event. E.g., I have completely forgotten the event, but know of it now because you told me about it, and you came to know about it through my telling you about it prior to my forgetting it. It is easier to decide in particular cases whether the causal connection is "of the right kind" than it is to give a general account of what it is for the causal connection to be of the right kind, i.e., what it is for there to be an M-type causal chain. I shall not attempt to do the latter here. The notion of an M-type causal chain would of course be completely useless if it were impossible to determine in any particular case whether the causal connection is "of the right kind" without already having determined that the case is one of remembering – but I shall argue in section v that this is not impossible.

and produce in a single total mental state quasi$_c$-memories whose corresponding past cognitive and sensory states belonged to different and simultaneously existing total mental states. This is presumably the situation that exists in the actual world. And I think that in any world in which this situation exists M-connected total mental states will be, to use a term of Bertrand Russell's, "copersonal," i.e., states of one and the same person, and quasi$_c$-remembering will reduce to remembering. There seems to me to be at least this much truth in the claim that memory is constitutive of personal identity.[18] (But more about this in section v.)

Now let us consider the case in which M-type causal chains do sometimes branch, and in which, as a result, it can happen that two or more simultaneously existing total mental states are M-connected. Here we cannot claim that if two total mental states are M-connected they are thereby copersonal without committing ourselves to the unattractive conclusion that a person can be in two different places, and can have two different total mental states, at one and the same time. But it is still open to us to say that if a total mental state existing at time t_1 and a total mental state existing at time t_2 are M-connected then they are copersonal *unless* the M-type causal chain connecting them branched at some time during the interval t_1–t_2. If we can say this, as I think we can, then even in a world in which there is branching of M-type causal chains the fact that a person quasi$_c$-remembers a past event or action would create a presumption that he, that same person, experienced the event or did the action, and therefore a presumption that the quasi$_c$-memory was actually a memory. This presumption would stand as long as there was no evidence that the M-type causal

---

[18] In his paper "Bodily Continuity and Personal Identity: A Reply" (*Analysis*, 21 (1960), 42–48), B. A. O. Williams says that "identity is a one–one relation, and . . . no principle can be a criterion of identity for things of type T if it relies on what is logically a one–many or many–many relation between things of type T," and remarks that the relation "being disposed to make sincere memory claims which exactly fit the life of" is a many–one relation and "hence cannot possibly be adequate in logic to constitute a criterion of identity" (pp. 44–45). Now it may seem that my version of the view that memory is a criterion of personal identity is open to the same objection, for if M-type causal chains can branch and coalesce then the relation "has a quasi-memory which is linked by an M-type causal chain with a cognitive and sensory state of" is not logically a one–one relation. But while this relationship is not logically one–one, the relationship "has a quasi-memory which is linked by a *non-branching* M-type causal chain with a cognitive and sensory state of" is logically one–one, and it is the holding of the latter relationship that I would hold to be a criterion, in the sense of being a sufficient condition, for personal identity.

chain linking the past action or experience with the subsequent quasi$_c$-memory had branched during the interval between them.

Worlds of the sort we are now considering, i.e., worlds in which M-type causal chains sometimes branch, could be of several kinds. Consider first a world in which people occasionally undergo fission or fusion; i.e., people sometimes split, like amoebas, both offshoots having quasi$_c$-memories of the actions done prior to the fission by the person who underwent it, and two people sometimes coalesce into a single person who then has quasi$_c$-memories of both of their past histories. Here we cannot say that a person did whatever actions he quasi$_c$-remembers from the inside without running afoul of Leibniz' Law and the principle of the transitivity of identity. But we can say something close to this. Suppose that someone, call him Jones, splits into two persons, one of whom is me and the other is someone I shall call Jones II. Both Jones II and I have quasi$_c$-memories from the inside of Jones's past actions, and no one else does. If anyone now alive is identical with Jones it is either myself or Jones II, and any objection to saying that I am Jones is equally an objection to saying that Jones II is Jones. I think that we can say here that I am identical with Jones if anyone now alive is identical with him. Or suppose that two people, call them Brown and Smith, coalesce, resulting in me. I have quasi$_c$-memories from the inside of Brown's actions and also of Smith's actions. There are serious objections to identifying me with either Brown or Smith, but it seems clear here that if anyone now alive is identical with either Brown or Smith, I am. So in such a world the following principle holds: if at time t a person A quasi$_c$-remembers a past action X from the inside then A is identical with the person who did X if anyone alive at t is identical with him.[19]

[19] A. N. Prior has defended the view that in cases of fission *both* offshoots can be identified with the original person, although not with each other. This of course involves modifying the usual account of the logical features of identity. See his "'Opposite Number'" (*Review of Metaphysics*, II (1957), 196–201) and his "Time, Existence and Identity" (*Proceedings of the Aristotelian Society* (1965–66) 183–192). Roderick Chisholm takes a very different view. Considering the supposition that "you knew that your body, like that of an amoeba, would one day undergo fission and that you would go off, so to speak, in two different directions," he says "it seems to me, first, that there is no possibility whatever that *you* would be *both* the person on the right and the person on the left. It seems to me, secondly, that there *is* a possibility that you would be one or the other of those two persons" ("The Loose and Popular and the Strict and Philosophical Senses of Identity," in Norman S. Care and Robert H. Grimm (eds.), *Perception and Personal Identity* (Cleveland, 1969), p. 106). It is not clear to me whether Chisholm would hold that one (but not both) of the offshoots might be me if the memories of each stood in the same causal relationships to my actions and experiences as the memories of the other, and if each resembled me, in personality, appearance, etc., as much as the other. If so, I would disagree.

But I think that we can imagine a world in which this principle would not hold. In the case in which two persons coalesce the M-type causal chains involved might be represented by a river having two "forks" of equal width. Suppose that instead of this we have an M-type causal chain, or a connected set of such causal chains, that could be represented by a river having several small tributaries. For example, suppose, very fancifully, that memories were stored, by some sort of chemical coding, in the blood rather than in the brain cells, and that as a result of being given a blood transfusion one sometimes acquired quasi$_c$-memories "from the inside" of a few of the actions of the blood donor. Here the blood transfusion would be a "tributary" into what apart from its tributaries would be the sort of M-type causal chain that occurs in the history of a single person. Now I do not think that we would deny that A, existing at time t_2, was the same person as B, who existed at an earlier time t_1, merely because A quasi$_c$-remembers from the inside, as the result of a blood transfusion, an action at t_1 that was not done by B. Nor would we deny that another person C, the blood donor, is the person who did that past action merely because there is someone other than himself, namely A, who quasi$_c$-remembers it from the inside. So here it would not be true that if at time t a person quasi$_c$-remembers a past action from the inside then he is identical with the person who did it if anyone existing at t is identical with the person who did it.

Yet even in such a world it seems essential that in any total mental state the memories, i.e., the quasi$_c$-memories produced by the past history of the person whose total mental state it is, should outnumber the quasi$_c$-memories produced by any given tributary. If the quasi$_c$-memories produced by a given tributary outnumbered the memories then surely the tributary would not be a tributary at all, but would instead be the main stream. But this implies that if a person quasi$_c$-remembers an action from the inside then, in the absence of evidence to the contrary, he is entitled to regard it as more likely that the action was done by him than that it was done by any other given person. And this, taken together with my earlier point that if someone quasi$_c$-remembers an action from the inside there is a presumption that he is the person who did it, gives us a sense in which quasi$_c$-memory can be said to provide the quasi$_c$-rememberer with "special access" to his own past history. This is of course a much weaker sense of "special access" than that explained in section I – but in this sense it will be true in *any* possible world, and not merely in ours, that people have a special access to their own past histories.

V

In the preceding sections it was assumed that remembering, as opposed to (mere) quasi$_c$-remembering, necessarily involves the satisfaction of the strong previous awareness condition; that is, it was assumed that in any genuine case of event memory the memory must correspond to a past cognitive and sensory state of the rememberer himself. And this is commonly supposed in discussions of memory and personal identity. But it is not really clear that this assumption is correct. For consider again the hypothetical case in which a man's body "splits" like an amoeba into two physiologically identical bodies, and in which both offshoots produce memory claims corresponding to the past life of the original person. Or, to take a case that lies closer to the realm of real possibility, consider the hypothetical case in which a human brain is split, its two hemispheres are transplanted into the newly vacated skulls of different bodies, and both transplant recipients survive, regain consciousness, and begin to make memory claims that correspond to the past history of the brain "donor."[20] In neither case can we identify both of the physiological offshoots of a person with the original person, unless we are willing to take the drastic step of giving up Leibniz' Law and the transitivity of identity. But is it clear that it would be wrong to say that each of the offshoots remembers the actions, experiences, etc., of the original person? There is, to be sure, an awkwardness about saying that each offshoot remembers *doing* an action done by the original person, for this seems to imply that an action done by one and only one person was done by each of the two nonidentical offshoots. But perhaps we can say that each of the offshoots does remember the action "from the inside." In our world, where such bizarre cases do not occur, the only actions anyone remembers from the inside are those that he himself performed, so it is not surprising that the only idiomatic way of reporting that one remembers an action from the inside is by saying that one remembers doing the action. But this need not prevent us from describing my hypothetical cases by saying that both offshoots do remember the actions of the original person, and it does not seem to me unnatural to describe them in this way. If this is a correct way of describing them, then perhaps my second sort of quasi-remembering,

[20] See Wiggins, *Identity and Spatio-Temporal Continuity*, p. 53, where such a case is discussed.

i.e., quasi$_c$-remembering, turns out to be just remembering, and the previous awareness condition for remembering turns out to be the causal requirement discussed in the preceding section rather than the stronger condition I have been assuming it to be.

If the suggestion just made about the conditions for remembering is correct, the logical connection between remembering and personal identity is looser than I have been supposing it to be. Yet adopting this suggestion does not prevent one from defending the claim that remembering is constitutive of and criterial for personal identity; on the contrary, this makes it possible to defend the letter of this claim, and not just its spirit, against the very common objection that any attempt to analyze personal identity in terms of memory will turn out to be circular.

Bishop Butler objected against Locke's account of personal identity that "one should really think it self-evident, that consciousness of personal identity presupposes, and therefore cannot constitute, personal identity, any more than knowledge, in any other case, can constitute truth, which it presupposes."[21] More recently several writers have argued that while "S remembers doing A" entails "S did A" (and so entails "S is identical with the person who did A"), this is only because "S remembers doing A" is elliptical for "S remembers himself doing A."[22] To offer as a partial analysis of the notion of personal identity, and as a criterion of personal identity, the formula "If S remembers (himself) doing action A, S is the same as the person who did A" would be like offering as a partial definition of the word "red," and as a criterion of redness, the formula "If S knows that X is red, then X is red." In both cases the concept allegedly being defined is illicitly employed in the formulation of the defining condition. Likewise, it has been argued that while someone's remembering a past event is a sufficient condition of his being identical with a witness to the event, we cannot use the former as a criterion for the latter, since in order to establish that a person really does remember a given past event we have to establish that he, that very person, was a witness to the event. And if this is so, the formula "If S remembers E, S is identical

[21] Joseph Butler, "Of Personal Identity," First Dissertation to the *Analogy of Religion*. Reprinted in J. Perry (ed.), *Personal Identity* (Berkeley and Los Angeles, 1975).

[22] See A. J. Ayer, *The Problem of Knowledge* (Harmondsworth, Middlesex, 1956), p. 196, and B. A. O. Williams, "Personal Identity and Individuation," *Problems of the Self* (Cambridge, 1973), pp. 3–4.

with someone who witnessed *E*" will be circular if offered as a partial analysis of the concept of personal identity.[23]

Such objections assume that remembering involves the satisfaction of the strong previous awareness condition, and they can be avoided on the assumption that the previous awareness condition is weaker than this, e.g., is that given for quasi$_c$-remembering in section IV. Or, better, they can be avoided if we explicitly use "remember" in a "weak" sense ("remember$_w$") rather than in a "strong" sense ("remember$_s$"), the strength of the sense depending on the strength of the associated previous awareness condition. Although there are perhaps other possibilities, let us take "remember$_w$" to be synonymous with "quasi$_c$-remember." Clearly, to establish that *S* remembers$_w$ event *E* (or remembers$_w$ action *A* from the inside) it is not necessary to establish that *S* himself witnessed *E* (or did *A*), for it will be enough if *S* is the offshoot of someone who witnessed *E* (did *A*). And while we cannot claim that statements about what events or actions a man remembers$_w$ logically entail statements about his identity and past history, this does not prevent the truth of the former from being criterial evidence for, and from being partially constitutive of, the truth of the latter. For we can still assert as a logical truth that if *S* remembers$_w$ event *E* (or remembers$_w$ action *A* from the inside), *and if* there has been no branching of M-type causal chains during the relevant stretch of *S*'s history, then *S* is one of the witnesses of *E* (is the person who did *A*). Here we avoid the circularity that Butler and others have thought to be involved in any attempt to give an account of personal identity, and of the criteria of personal identity, in terms of memory.

In the actual world, people remember$_s$ whatever they remember$_w$, and this makes it difficult to settle the question of whether it is the weak or the strong sense of "remember" that is employed in ordinary discourse. It is possible that this question has no answer; since branching of M-type causal chains does not in fact occur, and is seldom envisaged, people have had no practical motive for distinguishing between the strong and the weak senses of "remember."

---

[23] See Williams, "Personal Identity and Individuation," pp. 4–5, and my "Personal Identity and Memory," pp. 869–870 and 877. In the latter, and in *Self-Knowledge and Self-Identity*, I attempted to reduce the force of this objection by arguing that it is a "conceptual truth" that memory claims are generally true, and that we can therefore be entitled to say that a person remembers a past event without already having established, or having inductive evidence, that some other criterion of personal identity (one not involving memory) is satisfied. This way of handling the objection no longer seems to me satisfactory.

But I do not think that this question is especially important. We can defend the spirit of the claim that memory is a criterion of personal identity without settling this question, although in order to defend the letter of that claim we must maintain that in its ordinary use "remember" means "remember$_w$."

At this point I should say something about why it is important to insist on the claim that there is a causal element in the notion of memory. For this claim has recently come under attack.[24] It has been argued that the notion of memory should be analyzed in terms of the *retention*, rather than the causation, of knowledge, and that the notion of retention is not itself a causal notion. Now I have no objection to saying that remembering$_s$ consists in the retention of knowledge. But I believe that unless we understand the notion of retention, as well as that of memory, as involving a causal component, we cannot account for the role played by the notion of memory, or even the concept of similarity, in judgments of personal identity.

Here it will be useful to consider a hypothetical case I have discussed at some length elsewhere.[25] Let us suppose that the brain from the body of one man, Brown, is transplanted into the body of another man, Robinson, and that the resulting creature – I call him "Brownson" – survives and upon regaining consciousness begins making memory claims corresponding to the past history of Brown rather than that of Robinson. We can also suppose that Brownson manifests personality traits strikingly like those previously manifested by Brown and quite unlike those manifested by Robinson. Although Brownson has Robinson's (former) body, I doubt if anyone would want to say that Brownson is Robinson, and I think that most people would want to say that Brownson is (is the same person as) Brown.

But what can we offer as evidence that Brownson is Brown? Clearly the mere correspondence of Brownson's ostensible memories to Brown's past history, and the similarity of Brownson's personality to Brown's, is far from being sufficient evidence. And it is equally clear that the notion of the *retention* of knowledge and traits is of no use here. To be sure, once we take ourselves to have established that Brownson is Brown we can say that Brownson retains knowledge, and also personality traits, acquired by Brownson in the past. But the latter assertion presupposes the identity of Brownson and Brown, and cannot without circularity be offered as evidence for it. Indeed, the circularity is the same as what would be involved in offering as

---

[24] See Squires's "Memory Unchained."
[25] *Self-Knowledge and Self-Identity*, pp. 23–25 and 245–247.

evidence of this identity the fact that Brownson remembers$_s$ Brown's past experiences and actions.

We do not, however, beg the question about identity if we take Brownson's possession of what used to be Brown's brain, together with the empirical facts about the role played by the brain in memory, as establishing that Brown's ostensible memories are directly M-connected with Brown's past actions and experiences, i.e., are causally related to them in essentially the same ways as people's memories are generally connected with their own past experiences and actions. This in turn establishes that Brownson quasi$_c$-remembers, and so re-members$_w$, Brown's past experiences and actions. And from this in turn, and from the fact that we have good reason to suppose that no other person's memories are M-connected with Brown's past history in this way, i.e., that there has been no "branching" of M-type causal chains, we can conclude that Brownson is Brown.[26]

We can reason in this way only if we can assert that there is a causal connection between Brownson's past history and Brownson's os-tensible memories. And this, it seems to me, we are clearly entitled to do. Given that Brownson has Brown's former brain, there is every reason to think that had Brown's history been different in certain ways, there would (*ceteris paribus*) be corresponding differences in what Brownson ostensibly remembers. I can see no reason for doubting that such counterfactuals assert causal connections. Similar remarks can be made about the similarity between Brownson's and Brown's personality traits. Given that Brownson has Brown's former brain, we have reason to think that had Brown developed a different set of personality traits, Brownson would (*ceteris paribus*) have those personality traits rather than the ones he has. And while we cannot naturally speak of Brown's having a certain trait at one time as causing Brownson to have the same trait at a subsequent time, we can speak of the former as being an important part of a causally sufficient condition for the latter. It is only where we suppose that the traits of things at different times are causally related in this way that we are entitled to

---

[26] In *Self-Knowledge and Self-Identity* I held that saying that Brownson is Brown would involve making a "decision" about the relative weights to be assigned to different criteria of personal identity, and that in the absence of such a decision there is no right answer to the question whether Brownson is Brown. I have come to believe that there is a right answer to this question, namely that Brownson is Brown, and that my former view overlooked the importance of the causal component in the notion of memory (see my treatment of this example in "On Knowing Who One Is").

take the similarity of something at one time and something at another time as evidence of identity.

VI

We are now in a position to reassess the view, mentioned in section II, that the knowledge of our own pasts and our own identities provided us by memory is essentially "noncriterial." If I remember$_s$ an action or experience from the inside, and know that I do, it makes no sense for me to inquire whether that action or experience was my own. But it seems logically possible that one should remember$_w$ an action or experience from the inside (i.e., quasi$_c$-remember it) without remembering$_s$ it. So if one remembers$_w$ an action or experience from the inside it can make sense to inquire whether it was one's own (whether one remembers$_s$ it), and it would seem offhand that there is no reason why one should not attempt to answer this question on the basis of criteria of personal identity.

But while an action I remember$_w$ from the inside can fail to be mine, there is only one way in which this can happen, namely through there having been branching in the M-type causal chain linking it with my present memory. So in asking whether the action was mine, the only question I can significantly be asking is whether there was such branching. If I go on to verify that there was no branching, I thereby establish that a sufficient criterion of personal identity is satisfied. If instead I conclude on inductive grounds that there was no branching, relying on my general knowledge that M-type causal chains seldom or never branch (or that it is physiologically impossible for them to do so), I thereby conclude that a sufficient criterion of personal identity is satisfied. But an important part of what the satisfaction of this criterion consists in, namely my remembering$_w$ the past action from the inside, is not something I establish, and not something I necessarily presuppose in inquiring concerning my relation to the remembered$_w$ action. In cases where one remembers$_w$ a past action from the inside, and knows of it only on that basis, one cannot significantly inquire concerning it whether one does remember$_w$ it – for as I tried to bring out in my discussion of quasi-remembering, there is no way of knowing the past that stands to remembering$_w$ as remembering$_w$ stands to remembering$_s$, i.e., is such that one can know of a past event in this way and regard it as an open question whether in so knowing of it one is remembering$_w$ it. So in such cases the satisfaction of this part of the memory criterion for personal identity is a precondition of one's being able to raise the question of identity, and cannot be something one establishes in attempting to answer that question.

That one remembers$_w$ a past action is not (and could not be) one of the things one remembers$_w$ about it, and neither is the fact that there is no branching in the M-type causal chain linking it with one's memory of it. And normally there is no set of remembered$_w$ features of an action one remembers$_w$ from the inside, or of the person who did the action, by which one identifies the action as one's own and the agent as oneself. If one has not identified a remembered person as oneself on the basis of his remembered$_w$ features, then of course it cannot be the case that one has *mis*-identified him on this basis. This is not to say that there is no basis on which one might misidentify a remembered$_w$ person as oneself. If there can, logically, be remembering$_w$ that is not remembering$_s$, then where one remembers$_w$ an action from the inside one's judgment that one did the action will not be logically immune to error through misidentification in the sense defined in section II – though given the contingent fact that all remembering$_w$ is remembering$_s$, such judgments can be said to have a *de facto* immunity to error through misidentification. But the sort of error through misidentification to which a statement like "I saw a canary" is liable, if based on a memory$_w$ from the inside, is utterly different from that to which a statement like "John saw a canary" is liable when based on a memory$_w$ of the incident reported. If the making of the latter statement involves an error through misidentification, this will be because either (1) the speaker misidentified someone as John at the time the reported incident occurred, and retained this misidentification in memory, or (2) at some subsequent time, perhaps at the time of speaking, the speaker misidentified a remembered$_w$ person as John on the basis of his remembered$_w$ features. But if I remember$_w$ from the inside someone seeing a canary, and am mistaken in thinking that person to have been myself, it is absurd to suppose that this mistake originated at the time at which the remembered$_w$ seeing occurred. Nor, as I have said, will this be a misidentification based on the remembered$_w$ features of the person who saw the canary. What could be the basis for a misidentification in this case is the mistaken belief that there is no branching in the M-type causal chain linking one's memory with the past incident. But a misidentification on this basis, while logically possible, would be radically unlike the misidentifications that actually occur in the making of third-person reports.

VII

Because I have taken seriously the possibility of worlds in which M-type causal chains sometimes branch, and thus the possibility of quasi$_c$-remembering (remembering$_w$) that is not remembering$_s$, I have had to qualify and weaken my initial claims about the "special access" people have to their own past histories. But if our concern is with the elucidation of our present concept of personal identity, and with personal identity as something that has a special sort of importance for us, then it is not clear that the possibility of such worlds, and the qualifications this requires, should be taken as seriously as I have taken them. For there is reason to think (1) that some of our concepts, perhaps including the concept of a person, would necessarily undergo significant modification in their application to such worlds, and (2) that in such worlds personal identity would not *matter* to people in quite the way it does in the actual world.

There are important connections between the concept of personal identity and the concepts of various "backward looking" and "forward looking" mental states. Thus the appropriate objects of remorse, and of a central sort of pride, are past actions done by the very person who is remorseful or proud, and the appropriate objects of fear and dread, and of delighted anticipation, are events which the subject of these emotions envisages as happening to himself. And intentions have as their "intentional objects" actions to be done by the very person who has the intention. It is difficult to see how the notion of a person could be applied, *with these conceptual connections remaining intact*, to a world in which M-type causal chains frequently branch, e.g., one in which persons frequently undergo fission. If I remember$_w$ from the inside a cruel or deceitful action, am I to be relieved of all tendency to feel remorse if I discover that because of fission someone else remembers$_w$ it too? May I not feel proud of an action I remember$_w$ from the inside even though I know that I am only one of several offshoots of the person who did it, and so cannot claim to be identical with him? Am I not to be afraid of horrible things I expect to happen to my future offshoots, and not to view with pleasant anticipation the delights that are in prospect for them? And is it to be impossible, or logically inappropriate, for me knowingly to form intentions, and make decisions and plans, which because of the prospect of imminent fission will have to be carried out by my offshoots rather than by me? To the extent that I can imagine such a world, I find it incredible to suppose that these questions must be answered in the affirmative. The prospect of immanent fission might not be appealing, but it seems highly implausible to suppose that the only rational attitude toward it would be that appropriate to the prospect of immanent death (for fission, unlike death, would be something "lived through"). It seems equally implausible to suppose that a person's concern for the well-being of his offshoots should be construed as altruism; surely this concern would, or at any rate could, be just like the self-interested concern each of us has for his own future well-being. Yet a negative answer to my rhetorical questions would suggest that either the concept of a person or such concepts as those of pride, remorse, fear, etc., would undergo significant modification in being applied to such a world.[27]

A person's past history is the most important source of his knowledge of the world, but it is also an important source of his knowledge, and his conception, of himself; a person's "self-image," his conception of his own character, values, and potentialities, is determined in a considerable degree by the way in which he views his own past actions. And a person's future history is the primary focus of his desires, hopes, and fears.[28] If these remarks do not express truths about the concept of personal identity, they at least express truths about the *importance* of this concept in our conceptual scheme, or in our "form of life." It seems plausible to suppose that in a world in which fission was common personal identity would not have this sort of importance. Roughly speaking, the portion of past history that would matter to a person in this special way would be that which it is possible for him to remember$_w$, and not merely that which it is possible for him to remember$_s$. And the focus of people's "self-interested" attitudes and emotions would be the future histories of their offshoots, and of their offshoots' offshoots, and so on, as well as their own future histories. In the actual world it is true both that (1) remembering$_w$ is always remembering$_s$ (and thus that there is special access in the strong sense characterized in section 1), and that (2) the primary focus of a person's "self-interested" attitudes and emotions is his own past and future history. It is surely no accident that (1) and (2) go together.

[27] On this and related questions, see my exchange with Chisholm in *Perception and Personal Identity*, pp. 107–127.

[28] This is not to deny the possibility or occurrence of unselfish attitudes and emotions. Even the most unselfish man, who is willing to suffer that others may prosper, does not and cannot regard the pleasures and pains that are in prospect for him in the same light as he regards those that are in prospect for others. He may submit to torture, but he would hardly be human if he could regularly view his own future sufferings with the same detachment (which is not indifference) as he views the future suffering of others.

3

Time without change

It is a widely held view that the passage of time necessarily involves change in such a way that there cannot be an interval of time in which no changes whatever occur. Aristotle spoke of time as "a kind of affection of motion," and said that, although time cannot be simply equated with motion or with change, "neither does time exist without change."[1] Hume claimed that "'tis impossible to conceive . . . a time when there was no succession or change in any real existence."[2] And McTaggart presented as something "universally admitted" the contention that "there could be no time if nothing changed" (from which, he claimed, it follows that everything is always changing, at least in its relational qualities).[3] Similar claims can be found in the works of contemporary writers.[4]

The claim that time involves change must of course be distinguished from the truism that change involves time. And, as it will be understood in this essay, it must also be distinguished from a truism that Aristotle expressed by saying "if the 'now' were not different but one and the same, there would not have been time," i.e., the truism that if at time t' some time has elapsed since time t, then t' is a different time than t.[5] I do not think that this truism is what Aristotle had in mind in asserting that time involves change, but it, and certain related truisms, have seemed to some philosophers, e.g., to McTaggart, to imply that there are changes that occur with a logically necessary inevitability and relentlessness. Thus the date and time of day is constantly changing, it is constantly becoming later and later,

[1] *Physics*, bk. IV, ch. 11, 218b.
[2] *A Treatise of Human Nature*, ed. by L. A. Selby-Bigge (Oxford, 1888), p. 40.
[3] J. M. E. McTaggart, *The Nature of Existence* (Cambridge, 1927), vol. II, p. 11.
[4] See, for example, Bruce Aune's "Fatalism and Professor Taylor," *The Philosophical Review*, 71 (1962), 512–519, p. 518, and, for a somewhat more qualified statement of the view, Jonathan Bennett's *Kant's Analytic* (Cambridge, 1966), p. 175. Bennett makes the acute point that, because of multidimensionality of space and the unidimensionality of time, empty space is measurable in ways in which empty time necessarily is not.
[5] Aristotle, *Physics*, bk. IV, ch. 11, 218b.

whatever exists is constantly becoming older and older (whether or not it "shows its age"), and not a moment goes by without something that had been future becoming present and something that had been present becoming past. Such changes, if indeed they are changes, are bound to occur no matter how much things remain the same; whatever else happens or fails to happen in the next twenty-four hours, the death of Queen Anne (to use Broad's example) is bound to recede another day into the past.

I do not wish to become embroiled, in this essay, in the controversy as to whether these "McTaggartian" changes deserve to be regarded as genuine changes. My own view is that they do not. But my concern in this essay is with ordinary becoming, not "pure becoming"; my concern is with changes with respect to such properties as color, size, shape, weight, etc., i.e., properties with respect to which something *can* remain *un*changed for any length of time. And though McTaggart may be an exception, I think that philosophers who have claimed that time involves change have generally meant, not of course that everything must always be changing with respect to every such non-McTaggartian property, but that during every interval of time, no matter how short, something or other must change with respect to some such property or other.

This view, unlike the truism that time involves McTaggartian change, has important cosmological consequences. It implies, for example, that the universe cannot have had a temporal beginning unless time itself had a beginning and that the universe cannot come to an end unless time itself can come to an end. The claim that time involves McTaggartian change is compatible with the universe having had a beginning preceded by an infinite span of empty time, for throughout such a span the beginning of the universe, and the various events in its history, would have been "moving" from the remote future toward the present, and this itself would be McTaggartian change. But the kinds of change I am here concerned with are changes of things or substances, not of events, and such a change can occur only while the subject of change exists; the occurrence of such changes involves the existence of a universe of things, and if time involves change then there can be no time during which the universe does not exist.

There is another sort of change, or ostensible change, which must be ruled out of consideration if the claim that time involves change is to assert more than a triviality. Consider Nelson Goodman's term 'grue,' and suppose that this is given the following definition (which, though not Goodman's definition, is common in the literature): "*x* is grue at t if and only if t is earlier than A.D. 2000 and x is green at t or t is A.D. 2000 or later and x is blue at t." Anything that is green up to A.D. 2000 and remains green for some time after A.D. 2000 necessarily changes at A.D. 2000 from being grue to being nongrue. Clearly, for any interval during which something remains unchanged with respect to any property whatever, we can invent a "grue"-like predicate which that thing either comes to exemplify or ceases to exemplify during that interval. And if we take there to be a genuine property corresponding to every grue-like predicate and count the acquisition or loss of such properties as genuine change, it follows that whenever anything remains unchanged in any respect it changes in some other respect. Now it is notoriously difficult to justify or explicate the intuition that there is a distinction between greenness and grueness which justifies regarding the former but not the latter as a genuine property, and it is correspondingly difficult to justify or explicate the intuition that something does not undergo a genuine change when at the advent of the year A.D. 2000 it ceases to be grue by continuing to be green. But I shall assume in this essay that these intuitions are well founded and shall exclude from consideration "changes" that, intuitively, consist in the acquisition or loss of "positional," i.e., grue-like, qualities. If we do not do this, the view that time involves change becomes trivially and uninterestingly true, and the considerations usually advanced in its favor become irrelevant to it.

Aristotle's statement of his grounds for thinking that time involves change is unclear but suggestive. He says that "when the state of our own minds does not change at all, or we have not noticed its changing, we do not realize that time has elapsed, any more than those who are fabled to sleep among the heroes in Sardinia do when they are awakened; for they connect the earlier 'now' with the later and make them one, cutting out the interval because of their failure to notice it" (*ibid.*). It is not clear to me why Aristotle focuses here on change of "the state of our own minds," although later on I shall venture a suggestion about this. But if we leave this aside, the argument seems to be that time involves change because the awareness, or realization, that an interval of time has elapsed necessarily involves the awareness of changes occurring during the interval. It is not a serious objection to this that sometimes, e.g., when we have been asleep, we are prepared to allow that a good deal of time has elapsed since a given event occurred even though we were not ourselves aware of any changes during the interval, for in such cases it is plausible to hold that our belief that an interval of a certain duration has elapsed is founded on the inductively grounded belief that changes did occur that we could have been aware of had we been awake and suitably situated.

What Aristotle says here seems to be supported by the obvious and often mentioned fact that it is by observing certain sorts of changes, e.g., the movements of clock hands, pendulums, and the sun and stars, that we measure time. Even if what we are measuring is the length of time during which a given object remained *un*changed, it seems necessary that something, namely whatever we are using as our clock, should have changed during that interval. This is perhaps what Aristotle meant when he said that time is directly the measure of motion and only indirectly the measure of rest. At any rate, the fact that we measure time by observing changes lends plausibility to the view that there cannot be an interval of time in which no changes occur. The contrary view can seem to lead to total skepticism about the possibility of measuring time. If it is possible for there to be changeless intervals, then it may seem compatible with my total experience that any number of such intervals, each of them lasting billions of years, should have elapsed since I ate my last meal, despite the fact that the hour hand of my watch has made only one revolution and the fact that my lunch is still being digested. For if such intervals can occur there is apparently no way in which we can be assured of their nonoccurrence; as Aristotle put it, "the non-realization of the existence of time happens to us when we do not distinguish any change" (*ibid.*). And if this is so, we can never know how much time has elapsed since the occurrence of any given past event. But, it may be held, if the supposition that changeless intervals are possible leads to this sort of skepticism, this itself is proof that the supposition is false.

Of course, it is not only by measurement, i.e., by the use of clocks and the like, that we are aware of the existence and extent of intervals of time. We are all possessed of a "sense of time," an ability to judge fairly accurately the length of intervals of time, at least of short intervals, without using any observed change as a standard; one can tell whether the second hand of a clock is slowing down without comparing its movements with those of another clock, and if one hears three sounds in succession one can often tell without the aid of a clock or metronome how the length of the interval between the first and second compares with that of the interval between the second and third. But, although the exercise of this ability to judge the length of temporal intervals need not involve *observing* any change, it is plausible to suppose that as long as one is aware of the passage of time some change must be occurring, namely, at a minimum, a change in one's own cognitive state. Suppose that throughout an interval of five minutes I observe just one object, call it o, which remains completely unchanged throughout the interval, and that at each point during the interval I know how long I have observed o to remain unchanged. Then the content of my knowledge will be different at different moments during the interval. For example, at one time I will know that I have been observing o for two minutes, and a minute later I will know that I have been observing o for three minutes. And this means that there will be a constant change in my cognitive state as the interval progresses.[6] Possibly it was considerations of this sort that led Aristotle to stress change "in the state of our own minds" in his discussion of the relationship between time and change – although it does not seem to be true to say, as he does, that one must *notice* a change in the state of one's own mind in order to be aware of the passage of time.

These considerations suggest that it is logically impossible for someone to know that nothing, including the state of his own mind, is changing, i.e., for someone to be aware of the existence of a changeless

---

[6] Suppose, however, that what I am aware of, at each moment during the interval (after the first minute of it), is only that o has remained unchanged – has remained in a certain state which I will call "*S*" – during the immediately preceding minute. (I have, let us suppose, an incredibly short memory span, and after the first minute of the interval my memory does not extend back to the beginning of it.) Would this continuous awareness of lack of change in o involve a continuous change in my own state of mind? One might argue that it does, on the grounds that at each instant I know something I did not previously know, namely that at *that* instant o is, and has been continuously for one minute, in state *S*. On the other hand, one could argue that my cognitive state at any instant during the interval (after the first minute) consists in a certain predicate's being true of me, namely the predicate "knows that o has remained in state *S* for the last minute," and that since the very *same* predicate is true of me throughout there is no change. I shall not here try to resolve the tricky issue of which of these ways of viewing the matter is correct. I shall only remark that the former, according to which awareness, even of changelessness, involves change on the part of the subject of awareness, seems to me essentially the same as C. D. Broad's view that as long as one is conscious there is a "steady movement of the quality of presentedness" along the series of one's experiences; see his *An Examination of McTaggart's Philosophy* (Cambridge, 1938), vol. II, pt. I, p. 308. My present inclination is to regard this kind of "change" as a species of McTaggartian pseudochange. The issues raised by this example are similar to those raised by a very interesting argument of Norman Kretzmann's, to the effect that God must always be changing if he always knows what time it is, and that there is therefore an incompatibility between the claim that God is omniscient and the claim that he is immutable. See Kretzmann's "Omniscience and Immutability," *The Journal of Philosophy*, 63 (1966), 409–421.

interval during that interval itself. But it does not of course follow from this that it is impossible for someone to be aware of the existence of such an interval before or after its occurrence. To take an analogous case, it is logically impossible that anyone should know, at any given time, that the then current state of the universe is such as to make impossible the existence in it of life and consciousness, yet most of us believe that we have very good reasons for thinking that the universe has been in the very remote past, and will again be in the very remote future, in just such a state. In what follows I shall try to show that it is conceivable that people should have very good reasons for thinking that there are changeless intervals, that they should have well-grounded beliefs about when in the past such intervals have occurred and when in the future they will occur again, and that they should be able to say how long such intervals have lasted or will last. Of course, the fact that people might have good reasons for thinking that something happens does not prove that it is logically possible for that thing to happen; people have had good reasons for thinking that the circle has been squared. But I think that the sorts of grounds there could conceivably be for believing in the existence of changeless intervals are such that no sound argument against the possibility of such intervals can be built on a consideration of how time is measured and of how we are aware of the passage of time.

To the best of my knowledge, it follows from well-established principles of physics that our universe is a perpetually changing one. But what is in question here is not whether it is physically possible for there to be time without change but whether this is logically or conceptually possible. Accordingly, I shall allow myself in what follows to consider "possible worlds" in which the physical laws differ drastically from those which obtain in the actual world. It may be objected that scientific progress brings conceptual change and that within modern physical theory it is not possible to make any sharp distinction between those propositions about time which express logical, or conceptual, claims and those which purport to express synthetic truths of physics. But I think that it is fair to say that those philosophers who have claimed that time involves change have not generally rested their case on recent developments in physics, e.g., relativity theory, and have thought that this claim holds for our ordinary, prescientific, concept of time as well as for the more sophisticated conceptions provided by the physicists. And in dealing with such a view it seems to me legitimate to consider possible worlds in which quite different physical theories would be called for. If someone wishes to maintain that the occupants of such a world would necessarily have a different concept of time than that which the physicists tell us is applicable to our world, I have no objection to make – as long as it is granted that their concept would have enough in common with our notion of time to make it legitimate to regard it as a concept of *time*. I should concede that in allowing myself to speak of worlds that are logically but not physically possible I am making the somewhat controversial assumption that there is a tenable distinction between logically contingent and logically necessary truths. But this assumption is one that I share with the philosophers against whom I am arguing, those who say that time involves change – for I think that this claim is philosophically interesting only if we understand the 'involves' in it as meaning "necessarily involves."

Consider, then, the following world. To the best of the knowledge of the inhabitants of this world all of its matter is contained in three relatively small regions, which I shall call A, B, and C. These regions are separated by natural boundaries, but it is possible, usually, for the inhabitants of this world to pass back and forth from one region to another, and it is possible for much of what occurs in any of the regions to be seen by observers situated in the other regions. Periodically there is observed to occur in this world a phenomenon which I shall call a "local freeze." During a local freeze all processes occurring in one of the three regions come to a complete halt; there is no motion, no growth, no decay, and so on. At least this is how it appears to observers in the other regions. During a local freeze it is impossible for people from other regions to pass into the region where the freeze exists, but when inhabitants of other regions enter it immediately following the end of a freeze they find that everything is as it would have been if the period of the freeze had not occurred. Eggs laid just prior to the beginning of a freeze lasting a year are found to be perfectly fresh; a glass of beer drawn just prior to the beginning of the freeze still has its head of foam, and so forth. And this remains so even when they make the finest measurements, and the most sophisticated tests, available to them; even radioactive decay, if such exists in this world, is found to be completely arrested during the period of a local freeze. Those people who were in the region during the freeze will initially be completely unaware that the period of the freeze has elapsed, unless at the beginning of the freeze they happened to be observing one of the other regions. A man who was stopped in the middle of a sentence by the onset of the freeze will resume the sentence at the end of it, and neither he nor his hearers will be aware that there has been any interruption. However, things will seem out of the ordinary to any inhabitant of a frozen region who at the beginning of the freeze was looking into one of the other regions. To such a person it will appear as if all sorts of major changes have occurred instantaneously in the other region: people and objects will appear to have moved in a discontinuous manner or to have vanished into thin air or to have materialized out of thin air; saplings will appear to have grown instantaneously into mature trees; and so on. Although people might initially refuse to believe that events that seem to them to have only just occurred in fact occurred a year before and that they have been unconscious for a full year, it would seem that they would eventually come to believe this after hearing the reports of observers from other regions and, more important, after they themselves have observed local freezes in other regions.

The possibility of what I have described so far is compatible with the claim that there can be no time without change. That claim is that *something or other* must change during any interval of time and not that everything must change during every interval, and all that I have so far described is a case in which a fairly large percentage of the things in my imaginary world remain unchanged (or apparently unchanged) throughout an interval of time. But now the following seems possible. We can imagine, first, that the inhabitants of this world discover, by the use of clocks located in unfrozen regions, that local freezes always last the same amount of time – let us suppose that the length of freezes is always exactly one year. We can also imagine that they keep records of local freezes and find that they occur at regular intervals – let us suppose that it is found that in region A local freezes have occurred every third year, that in region B local freezes have occurred every fourth year, and that in region C local freezes have occurred every fifth year. Having noticed this they could easily calculate that, given these frequencies, there should be simultaneous local freezes in regions A and B every twelfth year, in regions A and C every fifteenth year, in regions B and C every twentieth year, and in all three regions every sixtieth year. Since these three regions exhaust their universe, to say that there will be simultaneous local freezes in all three regions every sixtieth year is to say that every sixtieth year there will be a *total* freeze lasting one year. Let us suppose that the predicted simultaneous two-region freezes are observed to occur as scheduled (the observers being, in each case, the inhabitants of whichever region remains unfrozen), that no freeze is observed to begin by anyone at the time at which local freezes are scheduled to begin simultaneously in all three regions, and that the subsequent pattern of freezes is found to be in accord with the original generalization about the frequency of freezes. If all of this happened, I submit, the inhabitants of this world would have grounds for believing that there are intervals during which no changes occur anywhere.[7]

The objections that might be made to this (and they are many) can be divided into two sorts. Objections of the first sort maintain, on various grounds, that the inhabitants of my imaginary world could not really have good reasons for believing that no changes whatever occur in a region during an ostensible local freeze in that region. For example, it might be held that, even if the hypothesis that no changes occur in such regions has survived a large number of refinements of their instruments and techniques of measurement, they could never be entitled to believe that further refinements of their instruments and techniques would not show that very slight changes occur during such intervals. Or it might be held that visual observation of an ostensibly frozen region would itself involve the occurrence of changes in that region, namely the transmission of light rays or photons. Objections of the second sort do not question the possibility of there being good reasons for believing in the occurrence of local freezes, but do question the legitimacy of extrapolating from these to the periodic occurrence of total freezes. Later on two objections of this sort will be considered in detail.

I shall not in this essay consider, except in a very general way, objections of the first sort. For though I am inclined to think that all such objections can be met, I think that such objections have limited force even if correct.[8] Even if the inhabitants of this world could not have good grounds for thinking there are intervals in which no changes at all occur, it seems clear that they could have good grounds for thinking there are intervals in which no changes occur that are

---

[7] It is obvious that during a local freeze objects in the frozen region will undergo changes of a kind; they will undergo changes in their relational properties in virtue of the changes that are still going on in the unfrozen regions. But during a total freeze there are no unfrozen regions, and so no changes occur even with respect to relational properties.

[8] Of the two objections of this sort I have mentioned, I think that the first can be met by supposing that the scientific investigations of these people support a "quantum" theory of change which rules out the possibility of changes so slight that they are undetectable by certain instruments. The second could be met by supposing that visual observation in this world does not involve the occurrence of processes in the vicinity of the thing perceived, does not involve the transmission at finite velocities of waves or particles. Alternatively, we can avoid the objection by supposing that while a local freeze exists in a region it is as if the region were divided from the rest of the world by an opaque (and impenetrable) curtain, and that what serves as evidence that no change occurs in regions thus insulated is the fact that when such a region again becomes observable everything appears to be just as it was immediately before the region became insulated.

detectable by available techniques and instruments. And this goes against the view, suggested by Aristotle's remarks, that when we have the well-grounded belief that two events are separated by an interval of time this belief is always grounded, ultimately, on evidence that changes occurred between these events, i.e., is grounded either on observations of such changes or on inductive evidence that such changes occurred. Moreover, if one thinks that the possibility of time without change can be ruled out on verificationist grounds and if it is only objections of the first sort that enable one to maintain that it is impossible to verify the existence of changeless intervals, then one seems to be committed to a view which is much stronger, and intuitively less plausible, than the view that *something or other* must change during every interval of time; one seems committed to the view that *everything* must change during every interval of time. Now there is of course a sense in which a change in any given thing involves a change in the relational properties of everything else. But it now appears that the verificationist must rest his case on the (alleged) impossibility of verifying that anything has remained wholly un-changed even with respect to its *non*relational properties and that he ought to conclude that it is logically impossible for anything to remain unchanged with respect to its nonrelational properties. But this seems no more plausible than the argument from the fact (if it is one) that it is impossible to verify that two things are exactly equal in length to the conclusion that any two things necessarily differ in length.

   I turn now to objections of the second sort, and to the first objection that I shall consider in any detail. I have imagined that the inhabitants of my imaginary world come to accept the generalization that local freezes occur in region A every three years, in region B every four years, and in region C every five years, from which it follows that there is a total freeze every sixty years. But why should they accept this generalization? What they observe is equally compatible with the generalization that freezes occur with these frequencies *with the exception* that all three regions skip a freeze every fifty-nine years; or in other words (to put this in a way that makes it sound less ad hoc): one-year local freezes occur in A in cycles in which nineteen freezes occur at the rate of one every third year, with four "freezeless" years between the last freeze of one cycle and the first freeze of the next; they occur in B in cycles in which fourteen freezes occur at the rate of one every fourth year, with six years between cycles; and they occur in C in cycles in which eleven freezes occur at the rate of one every fifth year, with eight years between cycles. This generalization does not imply that there are ever freezes in all three regions at the same time, and it may be held that for just this reason it should be preferred to the generalization that does imply this.

Now it seems to be generally agreed that if two hypotheses are compatible with the same observed data, we should prefer the simpler of the hypotheses in the absence of a good reason for preferring the other. And the first generalization stated above seems clearly simpler than the second. One reason for preferring the second is the belief that total freezes, i.e., changeless intervals, are impossible. And the most common basis for this belief is the conviction that the existence of changeless intervals is unverifiable. But, on the assumption that the simpler hypothesis is a possible one, the existence of total freezes is verifiable by standard inductive procedures; so one cannot claim that the existence of changeless intervals is unverifiable without begging the question against the possibility of the simpler hypothesis. Of course, the existence of total freezes is not "directly" verifiable, if direct verification of the occurrence of something involves knowing of its occurrence while it is actually occurring. But there are all sorts of things whose occurrence is not directly verifiable in this sense and yet is perfectly possible and knowable; it would be impossible to verify directly, in this sense, that the rotation of the earth would continue if everyone in the universe were sound asleep, yet it is clearly possible that everyone in the universe should at some time be sound asleep, and we all have excellent reasons for believing that if this ever happens the rotation of the earth will continue. I conclude that considerations of verification give no reason for preferring the second hypothesis to the first, and that the first, being simpler, should be preferred unless some other reason for preferring the second can be found.

If one does not find this wholly convincing, this is probably because the generalization that implies the existence of total freezes does not strike one as significantly simpler than its competitor, and because one views the latter not really as a "hypothesis" at all, but rather as a straightforward description of what would actually be observed over a long period of time by the inhabitants of my imaginary world. But I think that this way of viewing the matter becomes less plausible if we introduce some modifications into the example.

So far I have supposed that local freezes are always of the same length, and that whenever local freezes in different regions coincide they do so completely, i.e., begin and end at the same times. Let us now suppose instead that freezes vary in length and that sometimes freezes in two different regions overlap, so that the inhabitants of each region can observe part of the freeze in the other region, namely the part that does not coincide with a freeze in their own region. Let us further suppose that the length of local freezes is found to be correlated with other features of the world. For example, we can suppose that immediately prior to the beginning of a local freeze there is a period of "sluggishness" during which the inhabitants of the region find that it takes more than the usual amount of effort for them to move the limbs of their bodies, and we can suppose that the length of this period of sluggishness is found to be correlated with the length of the freeze. Finally, let us replace the supposition that observed freezes always last one year with the supposition that they always last longer than six months.

It now becomes possible to decide empirically between the two hypotheses stated earlier. First, it is compatible with the first and simpler hypothesis, but not with the second, that during the sixtieth year after the beginning of a cycle some periods of freeze should be observed. For now we are allowing local freezes to overlap and to last for less than a full year, and this allows freezes to be observed even in a year in which there are freezes in all three regions. Perhaps the second hypothesis could be modified in such a way as to allow there to be local freezes during the sixtieth year, as long as there is no interval during which all three regions are simultaneously frozen. This would of course involve asserting that there are exceptions to the rule that freezes always last longer than six months. Moreover, it obviously could turn out that on occasions on which the local freezes in the sixtieth year could not have lasted longer than, say, four months without there having been a period of total freeze, the periods of sluggishness preceding them were observed to be of a length that had been found in other cases to be correlated with freezes lasting, say, seven months. We can of course modify the second hypothesis still further, so that it will assert that there are exceptions to the rule that the length of the freeze is always proportional to the length of the adjacent period of sluggishness, and that these exceptions occur every fifty-nine or sixty years. But this does seem to me to make the hypothesis patently ad hoc. By positing these sorts of exceptions to observed regularities one can of course make the second hypothesis compatible with the observed facts, but it seems to me that this is no more intellectually respectable than the use of the same procedure to protect from empirical falsification the quasi-Berkelian hypothesis that objects disappear when no one is looking at them, or, to take a case closer to home, the hypothesis that it is impossible for there to be an interval of time during which everyone in the world is sound asleep.

This brings me to the last objection that I shall consider. Suppose for the moment that it is correct to describe my imaginary world as one in which there are intervals during which no changes, and hence no events or processes, occur. A question arises as to how, in such a world, processes could get started again after the end of such an interval, i.e., how a total freeze could come to an end. What could *cause* the first changes that occur after there has been a total freeze? In the case of local freezes we might initially suppose that the end of a freeze, i.e., the changes that mark its termination, are caused by immediately preceding events (changes) in regions adjoining the region in which the freeze existed. But we cannot suppose that local freezes are terminated in this way if we want to defend the legitimacy of extrapolating from the frequency of their occurrence to the periodic occurrence of total freezes. For such an extrapolation to be legitimate, we must think of a total freeze as consisting in the simultaneous occurrence of a number of local freezes, the beginnings and endings of which are caused in the same way as are those of the local freezes from which the extrapolation is made. And if a freeze is total, there is no "unfrozen" region adjoining any frozen region, and hence there is no possibility that the end of the freeze in any such region is caused by an immediately preceding event in an adjoining region. If there were evidence that the changes that terminate local freezes are always caused by immediately preceding events in adjoining regions, this would be a reason for rejecting the extrapolation to the existence of total freezes of fixed and finite durations. Nor does it seem open to a defender of the possibility of total freezes to hold that the changes that terminate freezes are uncaused events. For if that were so, it would apparently have to be sheer coincidence that observed freezes always last exactly one year (or, in the modified version of the example, that their length is proportional to that of the temporally adjoining intervals of sluggishness) – and it is illegitimate to extrapolate from an observed uniformity that one admits to be coincidental. So we are faced with the question: by what, if not by an immediately preceding event in an adjoining unfrozen region, could the end of any freeze be caused? And a special case of this is the question of how the end of a total freeze could be caused.

If we make the simplifying assumption that time is discrete, i.e., that for any instant there is a next instant and an immediately preceding instant, it is clear that the cause of the change that ends a total freeze cannot be, and cannot be part of, the state of the world in the immediately preceding instant. For the immediately preceding instant will have occurred during the freeze (will have been the last instant of the freeze), and since no change occurs during a total freeze the state of the world at that instant will be the same as its state at any other

instant during the freeze, including the first one. If the state of the
world at that instant were causally sufficient to produce a generically
different world-state in the immediately following instant, then the
freeze would not have occurred at all, for then the change that ends the
freeze would have begun immediately after the first instant of the
freeze – and a freeze "lasting" only an instant would be no freeze at all.

If time is dense or continuous, of course, we cannot in any case
speak of a change as being caused by the state of the world at the
immediately preceding instant, for in that case there is no immediately
preceding instant. But I think that it is rather commonly supposed that
if an event E occurs at time t and is caused, then, for any interval i, no
matter how short, that begins at some time prior to t and includes all
the instants between that time and t, the sequence of world states that
exist during i contains a sufficient cause of E. If this is so, however, the
first change that occurs after a total freeze could not have a cause. For
let i be an interval with a duration of one second. If the freeze lasted
more than one second, then the sequence of states that occurred
during i was part of the freeze, and consequently the very same
sequence of states occurred during the first second of the freeze. If the
occurrence of that sequence of states had been sufficient to initiate the
change that ended the freeze, the freeze could not have lasted more
than one second. But since we can let i be as small an interval as we
like, we can show that if the change that ends the freeze was caused,
then the duration of the freeze was shorter than any assignable length,
and this is to say that no freeze occurred at all.

It would seem that the only alternative to the view that the
termination of a total freeze cannot be caused is the view that there can
be a kind of causality that might be called "action at a temporal
distance" and that the mere passage of time itself can have causal
efficacy. To hold this is to deny the principle, stated above, that if an
event is caused then any temporal interval immediately preceding it,
no matter how short, contains a sufficient cause of its occurrence. I
shall refer to this principle as "P." To suppose P false is to suppose that
an event might be caused directly, and not via a mediating causal
chain, by an event that occurred a year earlier, or that an event might
be caused by such and such's having been the case for a period of one
year, where this does not mean that it was caused by the final stage of a
process lasting one year. Now I think that we are in fact unwilling to
accept the existence of this sort of causality in our dealings with the
actual world. If we found that a flash is always followed, after an
interval of ten minutes, by a bang, we would never be willing to say
that the flashes were the immediate causes of the bangs; we would look

for some kind of spatiotemporally continuous causal chain connecting flashes and bangs, and would not be content until we had found one. And if we found that things always explode after having been red for an hour, we would never suppose that what causes the explosion is simply a thing's having been red for an hour; we would assume that there must be some process occurring in something that is red, e.g., the burning of a fuse or the uncoiling of a spring or the building up of an electric charge, and that the explosion occurs as the culmination of this process.

In the *Treatise* (though not in the *Inquiry*) Hume made it part of his definition of "cause" that causes are "contiguous" with their effects. And I think that there is some temptation to think that principle P, which could be thought of as expressing (among other things) the requirement that causes and their effects be temporally contiguous, is an analytic or conceptual truth. Establishing that this is so would not show directly that it is not logically possible for there to be changeless intervals, but it would undermine my strategy for arguing that this is logically possible. For, as we have seen, this would make it illegitimate for the inhabitants of my imaginary world to argue for the existence of total freezes on the basis of the observed frequency of local freezes.

But is P analytically or conceptually true? Here it is useful to distinguish two ostensible sorts of "action at a temporal distance," both of which are ruled out by P. The first might be called "delayed-action causality," and would be possible if the following were possible: X's happening at t is causally sufficient for Y's happening at a subsequent time t', and is compatible with t and t' being separated by an interval during which nothing happens that is sufficient for the occurrence of Y at t'. If in my earlier example we deny that the flash can be the "direct" cause of the bang, we are denying that this sort of causality is operating. I think that it is commonly believed that this sort of causality is logically impossible, and I am inclined to believe this myself. But in order to save the intelligibility of my freeze example we do not need to assume the possibility of this extreme sort of causality at a temporal distance. All that we need to assume is the possibility of the following: X's happening at t is a necessary but not sufficient part of an actually obtaining sufficient condition for Y's happening at t', and t and t' are separated by an interval during which nothing happens that is sufficient for Y's happening at t'. To posit this sort of causality is not necessarily to deny the principle that causes must be temporally contiguous with their effects. If we take something's exploding at t to be the result of its having been red for the preceding hour, there is a sense in which the cause (the thing's having been red for an hour) is temporally contiguous with the effect (the explosion); yet here the thing's having been red at *t*-minus-one-half-hour is taken to be a necessary though insufficient part of a sufficient condition of its exploding at *t*, and it is assumed that nothing that happens during the intervening half hour is sufficient to bring about the explosion. Likewise, if *S* is the state the world is in at every instant during a given total freeze and if *E* is the event (the change) that terminates the freeze, we can suppose that *E* is caused by the world's having been in state *S* for one year without violating the principle that causes are temporally contiguous with their effects, although not without violating principle P. Now we are, as I have already said, quite unwilling to believe that this sort of causality ever occurs in our world. But I am unable to see any conceptual reason why it could not be reasonable for the inhabitants of a world very different from ours to believe that such causality does occur in their world, and so to reject any principle, such as P, which excludes the possibility of such causality. And if this is possible, then in such a world there could, I think, be strong reasons for believing in the existence of changeless intervals.[9]

But here an important reservation must be made. Early in this essay I ruled out of consideration what I called "McTaggartian changes," and in doing so I was implicitly refusing to count certain predicates, e.g., "present" and "ten-years old," as designating genuine properties – these (which I will call "McTaggartian predicates") are predicates something comes to exemplify or ceases to exemplify simply in virtue of the passage of time. In ruling such predicates, and also grue-like predicates, out of consideration, I relied on what seem to be widely shared intuitions as to what are and what are not "genuine" changes and properties. But these intuitions become somewhat cloudy if we try to apply them to a world in which there is action (or causal efficacy) at a temporal distance. Supposing "*F*" to be a non-McTaggartian predicate, let us define the predicate "*F'*" as follows: "*x* is F' at *t*" = $_{\text{df}}$

---

[9] It may be objected that allowing for this sort of causality would complicate the scientific theories of these people so much that it would always be simpler for them to avoid the need of allowing for it by adopting a hypothesis according to which total freezes never occur. But this supposes that they *can* avoid the need for allowing it by adopting such a hypothesis. It seems entirely possible to me that they might find that in order to subsume even *local* freezes under causal laws they have to accept the existence of this sort of causality (e.g., they never succeed in explaining the termination of local freezes in terms of immediately preceding events in adjacent unfrozen regions), and that they might find other phenomena in their world that they are unable to explain except on the assumption that such causality exists.

"at *t* *x* is *F* and has been *F* for exactly six months." It follows from this definition that if something is F' at *t* it ceases to be F' immediately thereafter, simply in virtue of the "passage" of *t* into the past. "F'" seems clearly to be a McTaggartian predicate, like "ten-years old," and one is inclined to say that something does not undergo genuine change in coming or ceasing to be F'. But now suppose that the basic causal laws governing the world are such that the following is true: something's having been *F* for a period of one year is a causally sufficient condition of its becoming *G* at the end of that year (where "*G*" is another non-McTaggartian predicate), and it is not the case that something's having been *F* for any interval of less than a year is a causally sufficient condition of its becoming *G* at the end of that interval. Given this, the causal implications of something's being F' at *t* are different from those of its being *F* at *t*; from the fact that something is F' at *t*, but not from the fact that it is *F* at *t*, we can infer that if it continues to be *F* for another six months it will then become *G*. And if we introduce another predicate "F''," defining it like "F'" except that "exactly six months" is replaced by "more than six months," we see that "F'" and "F''" are incompatible predicates having different causal implications. Now we are accustomed to regarding the causal properties of things, their "powers," as intrinsic to them, and it is thus plausible to say that, when predicates differ as "F'" and "F''" do in their causal implications, then something does undergo genuine change in ceasing to exemplify one and coming to exemplify the other. But if we say this, then we will have to allow that, in remaining *F* for a year and not undergoing change with respect to any other non-McTaggartian property, a thing nevertheless undergoes genuine change. And this of course goes counter to the intuition that McTaggartian change is not genuine change. It remains true, I think, that the inhabitants of my imaginary world could have good reasons for thinking that there are intervals during which no non-McTaggartian changes occur – but given the sorts of causal laws they would have to accept in order for it to be reasonable for them to believe this, it is not so clear whether they would be justified, as I think we are in our world, in dismissing McTaggartian changes as not being genuine changes. The determination of whether this is so must wait on a closer examination of the considerations that underlie our intuitions as to the genuineness, or otherwise, of ostensible changes and properties.[10]

[10] The need for this reservation was impressed on me by Ruth Barcan Marcus, who observed in a discussion of this essay that, if the "mere" passage of time can itself have causal efficacy, it is not clear that it can be dismissed as not being genuine change.

Supposing that it is possible for there to be time without change, how are we to answer the skeptical argument mentioned at the beginning of this essay – the argument that we can never be justified in believing that a given amount of time has elapsed since the occurrence of a certain event, since there is no way in which we can know that the interval between that event and the present does not contain one or more changeless intervals, perhaps lasting billions of years? I think the answer to this is that the logical possibility of such intervals, and the fact that such intervals would necessarily be unnoticed while they were occurring, do not prevent us from knowing that such intervals do not in fact occur. Given the nature of our experience of the world, the simplest theories and hypotheses that do justice to the observed facts are ones according to which changeless intervals do not occur. We do not indeed have a set of hypotheses that explain all observed phenomena, but none of the unexplained phenomena are such that there is any reason to think that positing changeless intervals would help to explain them. If our experience of the world were different in describable ways, e.g., if it were like that of the inhabitants of my imaginary world, then, so I have argued, it would be reasonable to believe in the existence of changeless intervals. But even then there would be no basis for skepticism about the measurement of time. The simplest set of hypotheses that did justice to the observed facts would then be one according to which changeless intervals occur only at specified intervals, or under certain specified conditions, where their existence and extent could be known (although not while they were occurring). If anything leads to skepticism it is not the claim that changeless intervals can occur but the claim that they might occur in such a way that their existence could never be detected. But it is not clear to me that even this is a *logical* impossibility, or at any rate that we must assert that it is in order to avoid skepticism. The claim that changeless intervals *do* occur in such a way that their existence cannot in any way be detected could not – and this is a logical "could not" – constitute part of the theory that provides the simplest and most coherent explanation of the observed facts, and this seems to me a sufficient reason to reject it. It is "senseless" in the sense that it could never be sensible to believe it; but it seems to me unnecessary to maintain, in order to avoid skepticism, that it is also senseless in the sense of being meaningless or self-contradictory. This is, in any case, irrelevant to what I have been arguing in this essay, for what I have suggested is that there are conceivable circumstances in which the existence of changeless intervals *could* be detected.

4

On projecting the unprojectible

I

This essay deals with one of the issues raised by Nelson Goodman's predicate "grue" and other similarly defined predicates. Goodman defines "grue" as applying "to all things examined before t just in case they are green but to other things just in case they are blue," where t is some particular time in the future – say, 12:01 a.m., E.S.T., 1 January 2010.[1] I take this to mean that something is grue at a given time if and only if either (1) it is green at that time and is (has been or will be) first examined before t, or (2) it is blue at that time and is not (has not been and will not be) examined before t. Goodman defines another predicate, "bleen," which is defined as applying to all things examined before t just in case they are blue and to other things just in case they are green. And he points out that while we can define "grue" and "bleen" in terms of "green" and "blue," we can also define "green" and "blue" in terms of "grue" and "bleen"; for example, we can say that something is green just in case it is grue and examined before t or bleen and not so examined. When predicates are related as "green" and "grue" are, or as "blue" and "bleen" are, I will say that they are " 'grue'-like" relative to each other.[2]

Following Goodman's precedent I shall assume that the statement "All emeralds are green" is not analytic, or true by definition, but that we do believe on inductive grounds that it is true as a matter of fact.

[1] Nelson Goodman, *Fact, Fiction and Forecast*, 2nd edn (New York, 1965), p. 74.
[2] There are various ways in which " 'grue'-like" could be defined. We could say that two terms are "grue"-like relative to each other *at a given time* if and only if they are so defined that (1) in the case of objects examined at that time or earlier they are coextensive, and (2) in the case of some objects not examined at that time or earlier, one of the terms applies only if the other does not. This definition permits two terms to be "grue"-like relative to each other at one time and not at a later time; e.g., after the time t mentioned in Goodman's definition of "grue," the terms "grue" and "green" will no longer be "grue"-like relative to each other in this sense. If this is thought undesirable, we can define a second sense of " 'grue'-like" such that terms are "grue"-like relative to each other in the second sense if there is any time at which they would be "grue"-like relative to each other in the first sense.

Since we believe that there are emeralds that will not be examined before *t*, we do not believe that all emeralds are grue – for the latter generalization implies that emeralds not examined prior to *t* are blue. Yet while it is true that all *examined* emeralds have been green, it is equally true that all *examined* emeralds have been grue. Every positive instance of the generalization "All emeralds are green" has likewise been a positive instance of the generalization "All emeralds are grue," and nothing so far examined has been a negative instance of either generalization. How, then, do we take ourselves to be entitled to believe the former generalization, and to reject the latter, on the basis of examined cases? This, in a nutshell, is Goodman's "New Riddle of Induction." The puzzle is easily generalized; since for virtually any predicate we can introduce a predicate that is "grue"-like relative to it,[3] it is apparent that for virtually any inductive inference that seems intuitively acceptable we can, by introducing an appropriate "grue"-like predicate, construct an inductive inference which has the same form as the original one but which draws an incompatible conclusion on the basis of the same examined cases.

It has been said of Hume that in the passages in which he is taken as posing the "problem of induction" what is presented is really, in the first instance, not a difficulty or a problem but a *demonstration* – a demonstration of (in the words of one commentator) "the impossibility of deducing any universal proposition from any evidence which can be provided by experience – unless of course that universal proposition is a mere epitome of some aspect of that experience."[4] In a similar vein it might be said that what Goodman presents here is, in the first instance, a demonstration rather than a difficulty or problem; the demonstration is that there can be no purely formal logic of induction, and no purely syntactical criterion of empirical confirmation. But Hume's "demonstration" left various problems or seeming problems in its wake, and the same is true of Goodman's. Following Goodman, let us say that a hypothesis is "projectible" if, or to the extent that, it tends to be confirmed by the discovery of positive instances. Goodman sees the problem posed by "grue" as that of devising a satisfactory definition of the predicate "projectible," where this will consist (if I understand him rightly) in finding a set of principles which yield a classification of hypotheses as projectible or not, and an assignment to hypotheses of degrees of projectibility,

---

[3] An apparent exception, pointed out by an anonymous referee of this essay, is the predicate "examined before *t*."

[4] A. G. N. Flew, *Hume's Philosophy of Belief* (London, 1961), pp. 71–72.

which accord with our inductive practice – that is, our actual judgments about the acceptability, or otherwise, of particular inductive inferences. His solution to this problem is his theory of "entrenchment," which says, to oversimplify it grossly, that hypotheses are projectible to the extent that the predicates in them are "entrenched," where predicates are entrenched to the extent that they, or other predicates having the same extensions, have been projected in the past – that is, have been involved in actual predictions and inductive extrapolations.[5] Thus "All emeralds are green" is much more projectible than "All emeralds are grue," and this is attributed to the fact that the predicate "green" is much better entrenched than the predicate "grue."

Goodman's theory of entrenchment is unlikely to afford relief to anyone who is troubled by skeptical doubts about induction. Nor do I think that it was intended to afford such relief; skepticism is not one of Goodman's concerns. But it is natural to feel that in addition to raising the problem (or setting the task) of defining the predicate "projectible," Goodman's predicates also raise questions that bear on the issue of whether we can show (without begging any questions) that skepticism about induction is irrational or incoherent. One question can be put simply by asking what justifies us in projecting the predicate "green" rather than the predicate "grue." More generally, what justifies us in projecting the predicates that are actually entrenched rather than non-entrenched predicates that are "grue"-like relative to them? And it is natural to approach such questions by considering the hypothetical case of someone who actually does project the predicate "grue," or other predicates that are "grue"-like relative to predicates we project, and asking whether we can show, without simply assuming that our policies of projection are reasonable, that the projective policy of the hypothetical person is unreasonable or in some way logically incoherent. If it is not already apparent that Goodman's theory does not provide us with a satisfactory way of answering this question in the affirmative, this is perhaps shown by the following consideration. If there actually were such "grue" projectors, and if they were numerous enough, and if they persisted long enough in adhering to their projective policies, then given Goodman's criteria for projectibility the degree of projectibility of their predicates (or hypotheses) might eventually approach that of

[5] To be slightly more accurate, what I have characterized in this sentence is not entrenchment *simpliciter* but what Goodman calls "earned entrenchment." There is also what he calls "inherited entrenchment." See *Fact, Fiction and Forecast*, ch. 4.

our own, or even exceed it – yet it seems evident that even if this happened their projective policy would be unreasonable.

II

If someone systematically projects the predicates "grue" and "bleen," his predictions about objects examined for the first time after t will conflict with those of someone who systematically projects the predicates "green" and "blue" – or at any rate this will be true if, as I will suppose until further notice, the two people otherwise project the same predicates. We would like to be able to find some basis on which we could say in advance, prior to time t, that one of these sets of predictions is reasonable and the other not, and we would expect, of course, that the reasonable ones would be those involving the projection of "green." But even if one can find no such basis one is inclined to say that come time t the projections of "green" will be shown to have been by and large correct while those of "grue" which conflict with them will be shown to have been by and large incorrect. And it seems to be just a matter of logic that if the appropriate observations are made after t then one or the other of these sets of projections will be shown to have been incorrect, even if we cannot justify in advance a claim about which set that will be.

But far from being true as a matter of logic, this last claim does not appear to be true at all. To see this, consider the case of Mr. A and Mr. B. Mr. A, a sensible fellow like ourselves, projects the predicate "green"; he predicts, among other things, that emeralds examined for the first time after t will be green. But Mr. B systematically projects the predicate "grue," and predicts, among other things, that emeralds examined for the first time after t will be grue. Mr. A, like us, regards Mr. B's practice as perverse, and casts about for an argument to show that Mr. B's projections are unreasonable. Like many philosophers he can find no such argument. Mr. A remains convinced, however, that his own predictions will be confirmed by future experience, and he settles down for a long wait. Finally time t arrives and Mr. A leads Mr. B into an emerald mine. Together they extract a previously un-examined emerald, and bring it up into the light. Mr. A is pleased, although not of course surprised, by what he sees. "There you are," he says, "it is as green as any emerald could be. It looks just like the emeralds we examined in the past." Noticing, somewhat to his bewilderment, that Mr. B looks unperturbed, he says, "Still not convinced? Surely you agree that the lighting conditions here are perfectly normal. And look, I happen to have brought with me a portable spectroscope. There you are: the light coming off it is of wave length Z, which you will agree is just the sort of light that has come off green things in the past. And just to clinch matters, I have brought with me from the archives the Standard Green Emerald. Look, the emerald we've just uncovered is indistinguishable from it – if I switch them around you can't even tell which is which."

Mr. B takes all of this in his stride. "Yes," he says, "I agree that the lighting conditions here are normal. I also agree that the new emerald looks just the way the green emeralds looked in the past, and that it is indistinguishable from what you call the 'Standard Green Emerald' – and I don't deny that the latter is green. And I agree that the light coming from these emeralds is just the sort of light that came from the green emeralds in the past. Nevertheless, this emerald looks just the way I predicted it would, and I take it as confirming my predictions. You seem to have overlooked the fact that my policy has been to project the predicate 'grue' systematically – that is, to project it wherever you project 'green.' One thing that was true of all grue emeralds examined before *t* was that they reflected light of wave length Z, so of course I expected this one to reflect light of wave length Z. Another generalization that held prior to *t* was that if something *x* examined at one time was grue, and something *y* examined at a later time looked just the way *x* looked at the first time, then given that lighting conditions were normal at both times *y* was grue at the later time. And conversely, if something was grue it resembled previously examined grue things. My policy of projection involves expecting generalizations involving grueness which hold up to a certain time to continue to hold after that time. So of course I am not surprised to find that this emerald looks the way grue emeralds looked in the past. As for the fact that this emerald matches, and is in fact indistinguishable from, what you call the 'Standard Green Emerald,' let me remind you that you yourself are committed to saying that the latter is *now* grue – for you say it is green, and admit that it was first examined before *t*, and from this it follows that it is grue. I also say that it is grue (and, since it was examined before *t*, green). But it was true in the past that things indistinguishable from grue things were themselves grue, and since I am a consistent 'grue' projector you can hardly expect me to be surprised at finding that this emerald, which I predicted would be grue, is indistinguishable from an emerald which we both agree to be grue."

Mr. B continues: "It has rather amused me over these years that you have so confidently expected me to find my predictions defeated by my observations after *t*. I, of course, realized that you would not be surprised and disappointed by the appearance of emeralds examined for the first time after *t*; or rather, I realized that you would be surprised and disappointed only if I too were surprised and disappointed. And if you had been more acute, you would have realized the same thing about me and my expectations. You systematically project the predicate 'green,' and I systematically project the predicate 'grue.' This means, among other things, that on the basis of the regularities observed to hold before *t* you expected things indistinguishable from green things, and things that look the way previous green things looked, to be themselves green, and expected green things to look similar to other and previously examined green things, while I expected things indistinguishable from grue things, and things that looked exactly the way previous grue things looked, to be themselves grue, and expected grue things to look similar to other and previously examined grue things. Since prior to *t* something was grue just in case it was green, it was inevitable that we would have the same expectations about the appearance of objects examined for the first time after *t*, given our respective policies of projection."

None of this will convince A, and none of it should convince us, that there is not something perverse or worse about Mr. B's having, or claiming to have, a policy of systematically projecting the predicates "grue" and "bleen" and refusing to project "green" and "blue." But we have yet to see why this is perverse. And something of importance does seem to emerge about Goodman's puzzle. It has commonly been supposed, I think, that the task of showing that "green" is projectible and "grue" not is equivalent to the task of showing that it is reasonable to believe of a policy of systematically projecting "green" that it will lead to expectations about future experience that in general will not be disappointed, and that it is unreasonable to believe this of a policy of systematically projecting "grue." But Mr. B's argument seems to show that this is a mistake. The expectations of a systematic "grue" and "bleen" projector will be disappointed only in case the expectations of a systematic "green" and "blue" projector will also be disappointed – assuming, again, that there is no other difference between their policies of projection. It is, we will suppose, conceivable that the emerald uncovered by Mr. A and Mr. B after *t* should have looked the way blue (and bleen) things looked before *t*. In that case the expectations of *both* Mr. A and Mr. B would have been defeated. But as I described the case, the only expectation that was defeated was Mr. A's unfounded expectation that Mr. B would be surprised.

III

At this point, however, a doubt should arise as to whether the predicate "grue" which Mr. B projects can really be Goodman's predicate "grue" – that is, the predicate defined as being true of green things examined before *t* and blue things not so examined. We can of course suppose that Mr. B *says* that it is. But why should anyone believe him? And how could *he* believe this? Given that it seems to be predicted by both his projective policy and Mr. A's that after *t*, as well as before, he will apply his predicate "grue" to just the things Mr. A calls green, surely the most plausible hypothesis for Mr. A to adopt is that Mr. B means by "grue" what Mr. A means by "green" – no matter what he *says* he means. Indeed, it seems that this is what Mr. B should think as well.

It would seem that a projector of Goodman's "grue" ought to have different expectations from the rest of us about the appearance of emeralds and the like after *t*, and that this should show itself in what he says and does after *t*, when making the observations he takes as verifying or falsifying his expectations. If we find our predictions about emeralds first examined after *t* to be confirmed, he ought to agree that his have been defeated. And what goes with this, he ought to agree with us after *t* (as well as before) in his application of the terms "green," "blue," "grue," and "bleen" to examined objects – or, rather, he should agree with us as much as we agree with one another. Let us call this the "agreement-after-*t* condition," and let us call the situation in which it is satisfied the "agreement-after-*t* situation."[6] It would seem that if it is to be plausible to say of someone who projects a predicate spelled and pronounced "grue" that his "grue" is Goodman's "grue" – that is, is definable *à la* Goodman in terms of our "green" and "blue" and time *t* – the case must be such that the agreement-after-*t* condition is satisfied. What we saw in the preceding section is that in the case of Mr. A and Mr. B, as I have described it so far, the condition clearly is not satisfied.

When I speak of the agreement-after-*t* condition being satisfied (or not satisfied) in a given case, this will be elliptical for saying that it is satisfied (or not) *on the assumption* (the "analytical hypothesis") that the words "grue" and "bleen" (or other such words) are definable *à la* Goodman in terms of words (like "green" and "blue") which we

---

[6] Prof. Mary Hesse lays down a similar requirement in "Ramifications of 'Grue,'" *The British Journal of the Philosophy of Science*, 20 (1969), 13–24. See esp. pp. 14–15.

project. Thus when I say that the condition is not satisfied in my story of Mr. A and Mr. B, this does not mean that it is true *simpliciter* that Mr. A and Mr. B disagree after *t* about the color of newly observed emeralds – for if, as I have suggested, it would be reasonable to conclude in this case that Mr. B's "grue" means the same as Mr. A's "green," then it would be reasonable to conclude that they do not disagree (or that their "disagreement" is "merely verbal"). What is true is that *if* Mr. B's "grue" is definable *à la* Goodman in terms of Mr. A's (and our) "green" and "blue," *then* he and Mr. A cannot agree after *t* about the colors of emeralds newly observed for the first time. What I am maintaining, among other things, is that the truth of this conditional is grounds for regarding its antecedent as false.

IV

But there is, as may already have been noticed, an incoherence in my story of Mr. A and Mr. B. I have supposed that the only difference between the projective policies of the two men is that Mr. B projects "grue" and "bleen" where Mr. A projects "green" and "blue." But this will not do. We can suppose that the relational predicate "is exactly similar in color to" has been true of all pairs of emeralds examined prior to *t*. If Mr. B projects *this* predicate, as we can suppose Mr. A to do, he will have to predict that emeralds first examined after *t* will be exactly similar in color to emeralds first examined before *t*. But he *also* predicts that these emeralds will be grue, and so blue. So he will have to predict that some blue things first examined after *t* will be exactly similar in color to some green things first examined before *t*. And this seems inconsistent. Surely Mr. B must agree that green and blue are colors, while grue and bleen are not, and that something exactly similar *in color* to something green must be green.

We can get around this difficulty by introducing, following J. S. Ullian, a term "schmolor" which is so defined that grue and bleen are schmolors while green and blue are not, and by supposing that Mr. B projects the relational predicate "is exactly similar in schmolor to" instead of the relational predicate "is exactly similar in color to," these predicates being "grue"-like relative to each other.[7] This notion will be such that something green and something blue can be exactly similar in schmolor if one of them was examined before *t* and the other was first examined after *t*. And if we are going to have Mr. B project

    [7] J. S. Ullian, "More on 'Grue' and Grue," *The Philosophical Review*, 70 (1961), 386–389.

the predicate "*is* exactly similar in schmolor to," it seems that we had better also have him project the predicate "*looks* exactly similar in schmolor to," and also such predicates as "looks more similar in schmolor to *x* than to *y*."

Now it seems, at first blush, that by increasing the "gruification" of Mr. B's projective vocabulary in this way we not only eliminate the incoherence in that policy just pointed out, but also bring it about that the case satisfies the agreement-after-*t* condition, and that we thereby eliminate the grounds for doubting whether Mr. B's "grue" can really be Goodman's "grue."[8] For now it may seem that if after *t* Mr. A finds a newly discovered emerald to be green, and so not grue, Mr. B will agree with him. If the emerald looks similar in color to previously examined green (and hence grue) things, it will (being itself first examined after *t*) look exactly similar in schmolor to previously examined blue (and hence bleen) things. So, it seems, Mr. B should declare such an emerald bleen and, since it is first examined after *t*, green, thus agreeing with Mr. A.

But this overlooks a number of things. First, and least important, it overlooks the fact that in the original story Mr. B had various reasons for regarding the newly examined emerald as grue, and not all of these had to do with the way it looked. For example, there was the evidence of the spectroscope and the fact that in the past things giving off light of wave length Z had been grue. But the important point is that there is simply no warrant for the claim that Mr. B will find the new emerald similar in schmolor to previously examined bleen (blue) things; on the contrary, there is every reason to think he will find it similar in schmolor to previously examined grue (green) things. After all, on the basis of the generalizations he knows to have held prior to *t* he is committed to the generalization "Things indistinguishable by sight from grue things look exactly similar in schmolor" and to the generalization "Under normal viewing conditions, things indistinguishable by sight from grue things are grue." Since it was part of our story that the emerald first examined after *t* was visually indistinguishable, by both Mr. A and Mr. B, from an emerald (the "Standard Green Emerald") which both agree to be grue, Mr. B's commitment to the latter generalization certainly commits him to saying that the new emerald is itself grue. And given the former generalization, he is committed to saying that the new emerald looks exactly similar in schmolor to previously examined grue things; which

---

[8] One projective vocabulary is "gruified" relative to another to the extent that it contains predicates that are "grue"-like relative to predicates contained in the other.

of course indicates (given his projective policy) that it is grue. Hence this change in Mr. B's projective policy, this expansion of the gruification of his vocabulary, does not bring about the agreement-after-*t* situation. And so the doubt raised about the original case arises about this one as well, the only difference being that it now concerns a slightly larger set of terms; it now seems that Mr. A, at any rate, would be entitled to suspect that Mr. B's "grue" and "bleen" are just new words for "green" and "blue," and that his "schmolor" is just a new word for "color" (also that in Mr. B's idiolect "green," "blue," and "color" mean what "grue," "bleen," and "schmolor" mean in Mr. A's).

Of course, we can resort to further gruification in our attempt to bring about the agreement-after-*t* situation – that is, to describe a case in which it would be reasonable to say that the agreement-after-*t* condition is satisfied. Presumably we can introduce a predicate that is related to "is visually indistinguishable from" in the way the predicate "is similar with respect to schmolor to" is supposed to be related to the predicate "is similar with respect to color to." Let this predicate be "is ingrustinguishable from." If things *x* and *y* were both examined before *t*, or both examined for the first time after *t*, or if neither is grue or bleen, they will count as ingrustinguishable just in case they are visually indistinguishable. But where *x* and *y* are grue or bleen things, and one of them was first examined before *t* while the other was first examined after *t*, then they will count as ingrustinguishable if and only if (*a*) they look exactly similar with respect to schmolor (that is, appear to be of exactly the same shade of grue or bleen; that is, one looks green and the other looks a corresponding shade of blue), and (*b*) they look exactly alike with respect to all of those visually detectable properties, such as size and shape, which Mr. A and Mr. B agree in projecting. It may be thought that by supposing Mr. B to project the predicate "is ingrustinguishable from" rather than the predicate "is visually indistinguishable from" we can bring about the agreement-after-*t* situation.

But this is not so. We would of course get the agreement-after-*t* situation if after *t*, as well as before, Mr. A and Mr. B agreed in their judgments about what examined objects are visually indistinguishable and what examined objects are ingrustinguishable. But now we must take note of the fact that there are behavioral criteria for indistinguishability. Mr. B will not agree with Mr. A after time *t* about what objects are visually indistinguishable unless he also agrees with him about what behavioral phenomena establish that a person is, or is not, able to distinguish certain objects by sight. And he will do the latter only if he accepts various generalizations linking these behavioral phenomena with visual indistinguishability. Now, he and Mr. A agree that these generalizations held prior to time t. But they must also agree that prior to t there held another set of generalizations that are exactly like these except that a generalization in the second set has the word "ingrustinguishable" where its counterpart in the first set has the words "visually indistinguishable." For prior to t examined objects were ingrustinguishable just in case they were visually indistinguishable, so positive instances of generalizations in the first set were also positive instances of their counterparts in the second set. It would appear that if Mr. B's policy is to project the predicate "ingrustinguishable," he should project the generalizations in the second set rather than the generalizations in the first set. But if he does this, he will in effect appropriate as criteria for ingrustinguishability what Mr. A regards as criteria for visual indistinguishability; that is, whatever facts Mr. A takes as showing that objects x and y are visually indistinguishable to person S, Mr. B will take as showing that x and y are ingrustinguishable to S. And this will have the consequence that after t he will say that objects are ingrustinguishable when Mr. A says they are visually indistinguishable, even in cases in which one of the objects is an emerald first examined before t and the other an emerald first examined after t. And then he will disagree with Mr. A about which objects are grue and which are green, and will take objects which Mr. A takes as confirming his "green" projections as confirming his own "grue" projections, even in cases in which the "grue" and "green" projections are supposed to be incompatible. So again we have failed to achieve the agreement-after-t situation, and again the doubt arises as to whether Mr. B's terms can really mean what they are supposed to mean. Nor does it seem plausible, given the way the discussion has gone, to suppose that further gruification of Mr. B's projective vocabulary is going to help matters.

It should be fairly clear what the source of this difficulty is. On the one hand, projection is a matter of accepting generalizations on the basis of observing what we take to be positive instances of them (and observing no negative instances). On the other hand, what properties we take observed items to have, and so what generalizations we take them to be positive instances of, is determined in part by what generalizations we already accept. For the generalizations we already accept determine what we count as evidence concerning what properties observed things have. Let us call generalizations that play this role "evidential generalizations." (It may be that virtually any generalization could function, in some context, as an evidential generalization.) If in our thought experiments we tamper with inductive policies by supposing people to project predicates that are "grue"-like relative to those we project, we have got to expect this to affect their judgments about observed objects as well as their judgments about objects not yet observed; for it will affect what evidential generalizations are accepted and hence what is taken to be evidence for the instantiation of various properties. And this interferes with the satisfaction of the agreement-after-t condition.

Sometimes Goodman's definition of "grue" has been read differently from the way I read it; it has been read as meaning that for any time t, a thing x is grue at t if and only if either t is earlier than T, and x is green at t, or t is T or later, and x is blue at t, where T is the time mentioned in Goodman's definition. Since the prevalence of this reading is due to an influential paper by Barker and Achinstein, let us call this the Barker–Achinstein definition.[9] If we understand "grue" in accordance with this definition, the argument of the last few sections will have to go somewhat differently. The main difference is that it will not be possible for Mr. B to claim, in justification of his claim that an emerald newly observed after t is grue, that it is indistinguishable from an object (the "Standard Green Emerald") which Mr. A agrees to be grue; for using the Barker–Achinstein definition, Mr. A will say that since the time is after t, the Standard Green Emerald is no longer grue (the fact that it was observed prior to t is not, on this definition, sufficient to make it grue at all times at which it is green). But it will still be possible for Mr. B to claim that the new emerald looks just the way grue emeralds looked in the past. More generally, he will still have a case for saying the new object is grue which exactly parallels Mr. A's case for saying it is green – and this remains so even if we increase the gruification of his vocabulary. Thus the satisfaction of the agreement-after-t condition seems as elusive when we use this definition as it is when we use the other.

V

It may be thought that it is only if a predicate is not an "observation predicate" that whether it is applied to observed items will depend to a significant extent on what generalizations the speaker accepts. Color predicates are usually thought to be paradigms of observation predicates; and I think that it is no accident that the standard examples

    [9] See S. F. Barker and P. Achinstein, "On the New Riddle of Induction," *The Philosophical Review*, 69 (1960), 511–522.

used in discussing Goodman's projection problem have been color predicates and predicates that are "grue"-like relative to color predicates. And it is certainly true that in applying a predicate like "green" to observed items we do not ordinarily invoke generalizations of the form "If something is Φ it is green." But it is too often overlooked that in applying these predicates in the way we do we are committed to generalizations of this sort. If I think that I can tell whether something is green from the way it looks, I think that I am a reliable visual color detector, where this involves my having, in Quine's terminology, a "quality space," or an "innate subjective spacing of qualities," which accords with objective color similarities in the world.[10] And to say this is to say, among other things, that there are lawlike connections between things being similar in color and their looking alike to me, and between things being different in color and their looking different to me, one consequence of these lawlike connections being that under normal viewing conditions things visually indistinguishable by me from (central cases of) green things are themselves green.[11] It was primarily this, of course, that led to the nonsatisfaction of the agreement-after-t condition in the original story of Mr. A and Mr. B. Let us use the term "Looks-Green propositions" to refer to the generalizations containing the words "green" and "blue" that I am committed to in regarding myself as a reliable visual color detector, and the term "Looks-Grue propositions" to refer to the generalizations we get if we substitute "grue" for "green" and "bleen" for "blue" in the "Looks-Green propositions." If Mr. B subscribes to the generalizations we get if we make these substitutions in all of the generalizations which Mr. A accepts, he will of course subscribe to the "Looks-Grue propositions"; and then, it seems, he will apply "grue" after t to just the things to which Mr. A applies "green," thus violating the agreement-after-t condition – on the assumption, of course, that his "grue" is Goodman's "grue." It is just

[10] See W. V. O. Quine, "Natural Kinds," in *Ontological Relativity and Other Essays* (New York, 1969), pp. 121 ff.

[11] Without the qualifying phrase "central cases of," this generalization would imply the falsehood that everything is green. For between any shade of green and any shade of any color whatever we can (in principle) find a series of shades of color such that adjacent shades in that series are indistinguishable by me under normal viewing conditions. (I was led to see this by a remark of Mr. Vanda McMurtry.) But no such absurd consequence follows from the claim that things indistinguishable by me from central cases of green things are themselves green – though we must of course insist, in order to avoid this consequence, that something can be green without being a central case of a green thing. By a central case of a green thing I mean something that is green and not near the borderline area between green and some other color.

this that led to the doubt as to whether his "grue" can be Goodman's "grue." We have seen that increasing the gruification of Mr. B's projective vocabulary does not remove this doubt.

This doubt seems to be reinforced by the following consideration. There is an obvious connection between a person's being capable of being a reliable visual color detector and his being capable of learning color words ostensively. And it would seem to be a necessary condition of the latter, as well as of the former, that at least some of the Looks-Green propositions should be true of the person, and true of him in a lawlike way. For ostensive definition (or ostensive teaching) to "take," for it to bestow meaning on a predicate or establish understanding of a predicate in a person, it must be the case that the ostensive procedure establishes some sort of lawlike connection involving the person's use of the predicate or his tendency to use it, and, more specifically, some sort of lawlike connection between his thinking that the predicate applies to something and its actually applying. A satisfactory specification of what sort of connection must be established would require a full theory of meaning. But it seems plain that in the case of a predicate which is introduced as the name of a sensible quality, the connection must be one between something's looking (feeling, sounding, and so forth) a certain way to the person and his being disposed to apply the predicate to the thing. And in the case of the predicate "green," it would seem that the establishment of such a connection will amount to a person's having learned the correct meaning of the predicate only if the Looks-Green propositions are true, and true in a lawlike way, of that person.

But if something like this is right, Mr. B seems to be impaled on the horns of a dilemma. For suppose that Mr. A puts to him the question whether it was "grue" or "green" that he, Mr. B, learned ostensively. If he answers that he learned "grue" ostensively, this seems to clinch the case for saying that his "grue" cannot be Goodman's "grue," and is instead just another word for "green." For if someone learns a word ostensively, and applies it, on the basis of looking, to just the things to which we apply the word "green," that is surely the best evidence there could be that he means by it what we mean by "green." On the other hand, if Mr. B says that he learned "green" ostensively, his position seems incoherent. For he is then committed to the Looks-Green propositions being true of him, and true in a lawlike way, and this is incompatible with his professed policy of systematically projecting the predicate "grue."

VI

So far my concern has been with whether we can describe a case in which someone (Mr. B) *systematically* projects Goodman's "grue." It is not luminously clear what it means to speak of someone projecting a term "systematically." This must not be taken to mean that the person projects every undefeated hypothesis that contains that term; for I want to be able to say that we project the term "green" systematically, and I do not want this to mean that in addition to projecting "All emeralds are green" we also project "All emerires are green" (where "emerire" is defined as being true of emeralds examined before *t* and sapphires not so examined). For the purposes of this discussion, I shall take the expression "projects *T* systematically" (where *T* is a term) as short for "projects *T* systematically relative to our projective policy," where the latter expression is defined as follows. A speaker *S* projects a term *T* systematically relative to our projective policy if and only if *T* belongs to a set of terms *K* which can be put in one–one correspondence with the terms in our projective vocabulary (the set of terms we sometimes project) in such a way that (1) every term in *K* is true of the same examined cases as the corresponding term in our projective vocabulary, and (2) for every hypothesis that we project, *S* projects (given the same examined cases as evidence) the hypothesis that results if we replace in that hypothesis the terms in our projective vocabulary with their counterparts in *K*. This of course makes it trivially true that we project "green" systematically relative to our projective policy; for "green" belongs to our projective vocabulary, and if we make *K* our projective vocabulary, it is trivially true that it can be mapped onto our projective vocabulary in a way that satisfies conditions (1) and (2) – the mapping would be one in which each term is mapped onto itself. And in the cases I have considered so far, Mr. B projects his term "grue" systematically relative to our projective policy.

Now it may be suggested that if we make Mr. B's projection of "grue" selective rather than systematic, we avoid the difficulties I have been raising about the satisfaction of the agreement-after-*t* condition. For example, we might suppose that the only generalizations containing "grue" that Mr. B projects are "All emeralds are grue" and generalizations that are entailed by it (for example, "All emeralds of above average size are grue"). This would leave him free to project the Looks-Green propositions, and such evidential generalizations as "Things that reflect light of wave length Z are green," and thus enable him to agree with Mr. A in his application of "green" and "blue" (and so also "grue" and "bleen") to things first examined after t.

But this suggestion is fraught with difficulties. To begin with, if Mr. B follows this policy he will project the generalization (G1) "Things visually indistinguishable from green things are themselves green." But now suppose (as could easily be the case) that all emeralds so far examined have been exactly similar in color, luster, degree of transparency, and so forth, and hence that all emeralds of exactly the same size and shape have been visually indistinguishable from each other. On the basis of this Mr. B should project the generalization (G2) "All emeralds of exactly the same size and shape are visually indistinguishable from each other." But since emeralds examined before t were green, it follows from G1 and G2, together with the empirical facts, that any emerald first examined after t that is of the same shape and size as an emerald examined before t will be green. So Mr. B will be committed to believing that *either* some emeralds first examined after t will be green (and so not grue) *or* no emerald first examined after t will be of the same shape and size as some emerald first examined before t. He cannot believe the first disjunct of this disjunction without giving up the generalization "All emeralds are grue," which he is supposed to be projecting. And it is *prima facie* unreasonable for him to believe the second disjunct of it – certainly he would be ill-advised to take bets on its truth, since it would seem that after t it will be within the power of any competent gem cutter to falsify it.

We might of course try to avoid this difficulty by having Mr. B project instead of G2 a generalization G2′ which is the result of replacing "visually indistinguishable" in G2 with "ingrustinguishable." But as we saw earlier, and will see again now, increased "gruification" merely postpones the difficulty and does not solve it. Although I have been treating visual indistinguishability as a dyadic relationship, it is really triadic (at least): things are visually indistinguishable *to* (or *by*) someone. And as I remarked earlier, there are behavioral criteria for saying that things are, or are not, visually indistinguishable to someone. Consider, then, a behavioral predicate "$B(x, y, z)$" whose satisfaction by a person x and objects y and z we would take as showing that y and z were visually indistinguishable to x. And suppose that the positive instances of G2 and G2′ observed prior to t were all positive instances of the generalization "$(x)(y)(z)$ (if x is a person, and y and z are emeralds, and y and z are of exactly the same size and shape, then $B(x, y, z)$)." If we project this generalization, and also project the generalization "$(x)(y)(z)$ (if $B(x, y, z)$ then

y and z are visually indistinguishable to x)," and also project G1, we will be committed to the conclusion that all emeralds of the same shape and size as already examined emeralds are green. And I can see no satisfactory way in which Mr. B could reconcile this conclusion with his projection of "All emeralds are grue." It does not seem likely that we can help matters by supposing Mr. B to project, in some cases, a predicate "grue"-like relative to "$B(x, y, z)$."

But even if this difficulty can somehow be handled, another difficulty arises. The only thing to be gained by having Mr. B project "grue" selectively rather than systematically is to permit him to project the same "evidential generalizations" as Mr. A, thereby bringing about the agreement-after-t situation. These evidential generalizations will include, of course, the Looks-Green propositions – for example, such propositions as "Things visually indistinguishable from (centrally) green things are themselves green." An inevitable consequence of this strategy is to make Mr. B's "green" and "blue" ascriptions epistemologically prior to his "grue" and "bleen" ascriptions, in the sense that he will defend the latter by reference to the former (and to information about the date) and not vice versa. So if we must pursue this strategy in order to make sense of the notion of someone's projecting "grue," there is an epistemological asymmetry between "grue" and "green." Now many philosophers have maintained that there is such an asymmetry, and have argued from this that a policy of projecting "grue" would be unreasonable. For example, Professor Judith Thompson maintains that "in order to be supposed to know now that all so far examined beryls are grue, a man must be supposed to know that they are all green and examined before T and to have deduced from this that they are grue," whereas, obviously, it is not true that in order to know that all examined "beryls" are green a man must know that they are all grue and examined before t and have deduced from this that they are green.[12] (Thompson talks of "beryls" rather than emeralds, because she takes "All emeralds are green" to be analytic.) And she shows – by an argument too complex to be summarized here – that it follows from this asymmetry, and from a highly plausible principle about reasons, that we have reason to prefer the green hypothesis (about emeralds, or, as she has it, about beryls) to the grue hypothesis. Other philosophers have argued to the same conclusion in other ways; but what is common to many such arguments is the claim that there is such an epistemological asym-

[12] Judith Jarvis Thomson, "Grue," *The Journal of Philosophy*, 63 (1966), p. 304.

metry between "grue" and "green."[13] Those who have sought to keep
Goodman's puzzle alive (or to defend the view that the only possible
solution to it is along the lines of Goodman's theory of entrenchment)
have generally sought to show that no such asymmetry can be made
out. But there is no hope of showing this if the only way of avoiding
the difficulties raised in earlier sections is by supposing Mr. B to
project "grue" selectively rather than systematically; for if those
difficulties can be avoided in cases involving selective projection of
"grue," this is only because these are cases in which the asymmetry
exists.

Thus Mr. B seems to be impaled (again) on the horns of a dilemma.
If he claims to be projecting Goodman's "grue" systematically, he
must face the objection that all of the evidence points to the conclusion
that his term "grue" is not Goodman's "grue" at all, but merely
another name for the color green. It does not seem that he can avoid
this objection by increased gruification. If to avoid this objection he
adopts the policy of projecting his "grue" selectively, then, in addition
to other difficulties, he must face the objection that he is admitting that
there is an epistemological asymmetry between "grue" and "green"
and thereby making his position vulnerable to objections like
Thompson's.

VII

But now we must consider what may seem to be a way out for Mr. B.
In arguing that the agreement-after-t condition is not satisfied in the
various versions of our story that I have considered, I have assumed
that Mr. A and Mr. B are alike, after t as well as before, in their
discriminatory abilities and their visual "quality spaces." It seems,
however, that by abandoning this assumption we can get a version of
our story that satisfies the agreement-after-t condition, and does so
without introducing any epistemological asymmetries between
"grue" and "green."

Let us suppose, then, that when after time t Mr. A and Mr. B
uncover a hitherto unexamined emerald, Mr. B agrees with Mr. A that
it is green and admits that he was mistaken in predicting that it would
be grue. When asked how he knows that it is green, he says that this

[13] See, e.g., Michael Slote, *Reason and Scepticism* (London, 1970), ch. 5, and Simon
Blackburn, *Reason and Prediction* (Cambridge, 1973), ch. 4. The claim that there is an
epistemological asymmetry between "green" and "grue," of the sort claimed by
Thomson, is clearly involved in Blackburn's argument, and I think that it is involved
in Slote's as well.

follows from the fact that it is bleen and the fact that it was first examined after t. And when asked how he knows that it is bleen, he says that it looks similar in color to, and in some cases indistinguishable from, previously examined bleen things; for example, he finds it quite indistinguishable from the Standard Sapphire, which he and Mr. A agree to be bleen. On the other hand, he says, it is clearly not grue, for it looks very different from the Standard Emerald, which he and Mr. A agree to be grue. Mr. A finds this very surprising. He finds the newly examined emerald easily distinguishable from the Standard Sapphire – they look as different to him as grass and sky – but finds it visually quite indistinguishable from the Standard Emerald. But Mr. A and Mr. B are able to persuade each other, by giving each other discrimination tests of various sorts, that each is able to discriminate very easily between objects which the other finds indistinguishable. This happens, however, only in cases in which the two objects compared are blue or green things of which one had been first examined before t while the other had not been examined until after t. More generally, they find that in judging about similarities and dissimilarities in the way things look to them, where the size and shape of the objects are held constant and only their color is varied, they make the same judgments if the compared objects are both examined before t or both first examined after t, but make different judgments in the case of blue or green objects if one of the compared objects was first examined before t and the other was first examined after t; in the latter case Mr. A finds objects that are both green or both blue more similar than objects that are both grue or both bleen, while Mr. B finds objects that are both grue or both bleen more similar than objects that are both green or both blue. The upshot of this is that after t, as well as before, Mr. B applies the terms "green," "blue," "grue," and "bleen" to just the examined things to which Mr. A would apply them. Thus we seem to have the agreement-after-t situation.

But while the satisfaction of the agreement-after-t condition is (*ceteris paribus*) a necessary condition of its being reasonable to say that Mr. A and Mr. B mean the same by these various words (among other things, that Mr. B's "grue" is definable *à la* Goodman in terms of Mr. A's "green" and "blue"), it is not a sufficient condition of this. For whether this is reasonable depends not only on what objects they apply these words to but also on what *explains* (or what we can reasonably take to explain) their applying these words to those objects. And the explanation of this, whatever it is, will not be independent of the explanation of the remarkable difference we have supposed there to be between the discriminatory abilities, and the visual "quality spaces," of Mr. A and Mr. B. Since we are already up to our necks in science fiction, I shall now give a sketch of a theory that would explain all this.

We will suppose first that there are two hitherto undiscovered sorts of radiation – call them alpha radiation and beta radiation – and that prior to being first observed every object emits alpha radiation when green and beta radiation when blue. These are sorts of radiation an object emits in addition to the light it emits or reflects. Second, we will suppose that human eyes emit another sort of radiation – call it gamma radiation – and that the first irradiation of an object by gamma radiation leaves a permanent effect on it; the effect is that henceforth the object emits alpha radiation when blue and beta radiation when green. Human eyes, or the eyes of whatever creatures count as observers, are the only source of gamma radiation. But it is only up until time t that the first observation of an object has this effect on it. At that time, human eyes cease to emit gamma radiation. So if an object remains unobserved until t, then throughout its history it emits alpha radiation when green and beta radiation when blue, even if it does get observed after t. Finally, we will suppose that one of our two men – let it be Mr. B – has sensory receptors that are sensitive to alpha and beta radiation, but not to green and blue light as such. Since green things that were examined before t and blue things not examined before t both emit beta radiation, such things "look alike to" Mr. B, and that is why he applies the term "grue" to both. Likewise, since blue things that were examined before t and green things not examined before t both emit alpha radiation, such things look alike to Mr. B, and that is why he applies the term "bleen" to both. But if one green thing was examined before t and the other was not so examined, then the first emits beta radiation and the other emits alpha radiation; this is why Mr. B says that such things look different, and is able to distinguish some things that are indistinguishable by sight to Mr. A. Likewise, if one blue thing was examined before t and the other was not so examined, then the first emits alpha radiation and the other emits beta radiation; this is why Mr. B says that such things look different and is able to distinguish them by sight.

No doubt this explanation sounds bizarre. But then the imagined phenomena were bizarre. And I think that what seems bizarre about this theory would have to be a feature of any theory that explained these phenomena; any such theory would have to involve the supposition that prior to t, but not afterward, the first observation of an object makes a permanent change in it, and that the permanent state thus induced influences the way the object acts on the sensory receptors of one of our two men, either Mr. A or Mr. B, but not on the way it acts on the sensory receptors of the other. If it is impossible that this supposition should be true, it is likewise impossible that the imagined phenomena should occur – except by an incredible, and inexplicable, coincidence.

But suppose now that the imagined phenomena were to occur, and that this explanation of them, or something like it, were accepted. Could it then be claimed that Mr. A and Mr. B mean the same by the terms "green," "blue," "grue," and "bleen" (despite the fact that Mr. A defines his "grue" and "bleen" *à la* Goodman in terms of his "green" and "blue" and time *t*, while Mr. B defines his "green" and "blue" *à la* Goodman in terms of his "grue" and "bleen" and time *t*)? It should be noted that this claim would not have been at all plausible prior to time *t*. For prior to *t* Mr. A and Mr. B would *both* have predicted, on the basis of the uniformities they had observed, that after *t*, as well as before, Mr. B would call "grue" and "bleen," respectively, those things Mr. A calls "green" and "blue," respectively. Moreover, the coherence of our story requires that Mr. B learned "grue" and "bleen" ostensively, or at any rate that he did not learn "green" and "blue" ostensively. Given what we are supposing about the "quality spaces" of the two men, if Mr. B had learned "green" ostensively before *t* by reference to things Mr. A calls "green," then after *t* he would have applied it to newly examined things which Mr. A calls "blue," contrary to what we have supposed. Plainly, the reasonable hypothesis for both men to have adopted prior to *t* would have been that Mr. B means by "grue" and "bleen," respectively, what Mr. A means by "green" and "blue," respectively, and that Mr. A means by "grue" and "bleen," respectively, what Mr. B means by "green" and "blue," respectively. This hypothesis, of course, would have to be abandoned after *t*, given what we have imagined. But it would *remain* unreasonable after *t* for them to accept the hypothesis that each means by these terms what the other means by them. And this hypothesis would be *totally* out of the question if the theory sketched above were accepted. According to that theory, the physical properties of objects that are causally responsible for Mr. B's ascriptions of the predicates "grue" and "bleen," and hence, indirectly, for his ascriptions of "green" and "blue," have to do with the emission or reflection of alpha or beta radiation, and not at all with the emission or reflection of light. It seems to me that the only reasonable description of the case, given this, is that the properties he uses these terms to ascribe are different from, and logically and nomologically independent of, those Mr. A ascribes by means of his predicates "green," "blue," "grue," and "bleen." So if Mr. B says that something is grue, and Mr. A says of the same thing that it is green and examined before *t*, or that it is blue and not examined before *t*, they are saying utterly different things about it, and are not agreeing about anything. Also, when prior to *t* Mr. A predicted that emeralds first examined after *t* would be green, and Mr. B predicted that such emeralds would be grue, they were not making incompatible predictions. To be sure, it is part of the description of the case that Mr. A's predictions turned out to be true while Mr. B's turned out to be false. But that is no reason for saying that the predictions were incompatible, as they would have to be if Mr. A and Mr. B meant the same by all of these terms.[14]

A further reason for saying that Mr. A and Mr. B would not mean the same by their various terms (given the truth of the imagined theory), is that Mr. B's terms would not even be coextensive with the similarly spelled and pronounced terms in Mr. A's vocabulary. For compare Mr. B's "grue" and "bleen" with Mr. A's "grue" and "bleen" (the latter being Goodman's "grue" and "bleen"). Whereas the first observation of something green before *t* changes it from being an alpha emitter to being a beta emitter, and hence from being bleen to grue in Mr. B's sense, it does not change it from being bleen to grue in Mr. A's (and Goodman's) sense – for if the thing was green before it

---

[14] Apparently Goodman intends the word "conflict" to be understood in such a way that these predictions do conflict; for in "On Kahane's Confusions," *The Journal of Philosophy*, 69 (1972), he says that "Two hypotheses conflict only if neither follows from the other and they ascribe to something different predicates such that only one actually applies. 'All emeralds are green' conflicts with 'all emeralds are nongreen' if there are any emeralds, conflicts with 'all emeralds are grue' if there are any emeralds not examined before *t*, and incidentally even conflicts with 'all emeralds are hard' if there is an emerald that is either green or hard but not both" (p. 84). Given the remark about "all emeralds are hard," it appears that the "only if" in the first sentence should read "if and only if." This is, to say the least, an unusual way of using "conflict." Goodman says in this article that "when two supported, unviolated, unexhausted hypotheses conflict and are equally well entrenched, the conflict awaits resolution through one or the other of them either being discredited by new evidence or acquiring superior entrenchment or being overridden by some other hypothesis" (p. 83), and that until this happens "the hypotheses are not projectible, or unprojectible." But one wonders why, in such a case, *both* hypotheses could not be projectible. It is not at all to be expected that hypotheses that "conflict" in this sense should be known to conflict; and when there is no reason to suppose they conflict, it can surely be reasonable to project both (as it is now reasonable to project both "All emeralds are green" and "All emeralds are hard," even if, unbeknownst to us, these do "conflict" in Goodman's sense).

was first examined, it was (in Mr. A's sense) grue at that time, even though it was then an alpha radiation emitter.[15]

I have not shown, of course, that the theory I have sketched is the only one that would explain the imagined phenomena. But I think that any other explanation of them would have the same consequences. And the fact that the imagined phenomena could be so explained is sufficient to show that the possibility of the phenomena does not establish the possibility that someone might systematically project predicates that are "grue"-like relative to those we project.[16]

VIII

In the preceding section I used the words "grue" and "bleen" in the senses explained in section I – that is, in the senses I think Goodman intended. Let us see now how the argument would go if, instead, we understand "grue" and "bleen" in terms of the Barker–Achinstein definitions.[17]

We are to suppose, again, that the agreement-after-*t* condition is satisfied. This means, given the Barker–Achinstein definition, that

---

[15] This was pointed out to me by Oswaldo Chateaubriand. It does not, of course, conflict with the claim (or stipulation) that Mr. A and Mr. B apply their terms to the same examined objects, both before and after *t*, and that the case satisfies the agreement-after-*t* condition. If we were to try to modify the case so as to make Mr. B's "grue" coextensive with Mr. A's "grue," I think we would have to posit a bizarre sort of backwards causality. We would have to suppose that the first observation of an object determines not merely which sort of radiation (alpha or beta) it will emit in the future when green (and which when blue) but also which sort it emitted in the past when green (and which when blue). Even if we do suppose this, my main reason for denying that Mr. A and Mr. B mean the same by their terms would still apply. But it is at least questionable whether this supposition is coherent.

It is worth noting, in this connection, that from the point of view of a "green" and "blue" projector (like ourselves) one can have it in one's power at a given time (prior to *t*) to bring it about that at an *earlier* time something was, or was not, grue; confronted with an as yet unexamined emerald (which like all emeralds is green) I can either examine it now, and so bring about that it has always been grue, or place it in a vault with a time lock which guarantees that it will not be examined before *t*, thereby bringing it about that it has always been bleen. And of course a "grue" projector, supposing there could be such a person, would be committed to holding that it can be within his power to bring it about either that something has always been green or that something has always been blue.

[16] Points similar to those made in this section were made by Kenneth Small in "Professor Goodman's Puzzle," *The Philosophical Review*, 70 (1961), 544–552 – although he adopts the Barker–Achinstein interpretation of Goodman's definitions.

[17] See footnote 9, and the final paragraph of section IV.

after *t* Mr. B applies his term "grue" to just the things Mr. A calls "blue," applies his term "bleen" to just the things Mr. A calls "green," and regards his predictions (made before *t*) about the colors (or schmolors) after *t* of emeralds, sapphires, and so forth as having been defeated. If asked why he thinks that emeralds are now bleen, he says that they look the way he remembers bleen things (for example, sapphires) looking in the past. Likewise, he takes sapphires to be grue because, he says, they look the way grue things (for example, emeralds) looked in the past. Indeed, according to him there occurred at *t* a marked change in the appearance of all those things that had been grue (green) or bleen (blue) before *t*; the grue things came to look the way the bleen things had previously looked, and the bleen things came to look the way the grue things had previously looked. For Mr. B the claim that there was such a change is not simply the (nearly) empty claim that there are predicates that were true of (or appeared to be true of) these objects before *t* and were no longer true of (or no longer appeared to be true of) them after *t*. For at *t* Mr. B spontaneously (without knowing the time) began applying "grue" to blue things rather than green things, and "bleen" to green things rather than blue things, and his behavior showed that he expected from green things what he had previously expected (in terms of flavor, say) from similarly shaped and sized blue things, and vice versa, and was surprised when these expectations were not fulfilled.

As before, we must ask what could explain these imagined phenomena, and whether any of the explanations is compatible with the view that Mr. A and Mr. B mean the same by the relevant terms.

One possible explanation is similar to the explanation offered in the preceding section of phenomena imagined there. We can suppose that prior to *t* green things emitted alpha radiation and blue things emitted beta radiation, and that for some reason (or none) a change occurred at *t* which resulted in its henceforth being the case that blue things emitted alpha radiation while green things emitted beta radiation. And, as before, we can suppose that Mr. B's eyes are sensitive to alpha and beta radiation, but not to green and blue light. If this were the explanation it would be quite out of the question to translate Mr. B's "grue" as being definable *à la* Goodman in terms of Mr. A's "green" and "blue," and to count Mr. A and Mr. B as agreeing when each applies his word "grue" to a thing or as disagreeing when Mr. A predicts that emeralds will be green (in *his* sense of "green") after *t* and Mr. B predicts that emeralds will be grue (in *his* sense of "grue") after *t*.

But there is another way in which we might try to explain the phenomena imagined in this case, and one such that there is, so far as I can see, no analogous way of explaining the phenomena imagined in section VII. This time we will suppose that Mr. B's eyes are sensitive to green and blue light. But we will also suppose that his physiological makeup (or, if you like, his unconscious psychological makeup) includes an internal timing device which is set to produce a change at t, this being either (1) a change in the way blue and green things look to him, or (2) a change in the way he remembers blue and green things looking prior to t. The upshot of this is that after t grue (blue) things look to him the way he remembers grue (green) things looking to him prior to t, and bleen (green) things look to him the way he remembers bleen (blue) things looking to him prior to t.

There may be some temptation to say that such a person (that is, a person who is the way Mr. B is here imagined as being) would perceive grueness in just the way we perceive greenness, and that he would be able to learn "grue" ostensively. After all, if we introduced such a person to the word "grue" before t by pointing out samples of grueness (these all being samples of greenness), it is to be expected (given our supposition about his internal makeup) that after t, as well as before, he would apply "grue" to grue things – that is, that after t he would apply it to blue things. But if this is true, it must also be true that if such a person were introduced to the word "green" ostensively he would learn to use it, not as the word for the color green, but as the word for the schmolor grue (for after t he would apply it to blue things). But in the latter case there is (given the imagined explanation) a far more plausible account available; what we should say, surely, is that the person learns the word "green" as the word for the color green, but that he is so constituted that beginning at time t he will (either because of a change in his color experience or because of systematic misremembering) regularly mistake green things for blue things and blue things for green things, and will continue to do so until he allows himself to be corrected by the judgments of others (or by spectroscopic evidence and the like). And this seems to me what we should say of the case of the man, having the same internal makeup, who learns "grue" ostensively; such a man will have learned "grue" as a word for the color green, despite the fact that after t he will tend (unless corrected) to apply it to blue things.

IX

I have been concerned in this essay with the question of whether there could be a Mr. B who systematically projects predicates that are "grue"-like relative to predicates we project (and so "grue"-like relative to those projected by a hypothetical Mr. A whose projective policy is the same as ours). The first difficulty I raised about this, in sections II–V, was that on certain natural assumptions it seems impossible for the agreement-after-t condition to be satisfied in a putative case of systematic "grue" projection, and that this makes it unreasonable to count such putative cases as genuine cases. One assumption that seemed to block the satisfaction of the agreement-after-t condition was that Mr. B's visual "quality space" was the same as that of Mr. A – that is, the same as ours. In sections VII and VIII I considered the consequences of dropping this assumption, and argued that while this enables us to describe cases in which the agreement-after-t condition is satisfied, it does so in such a way as to make it unreasonable on other grounds to say that the "grue" projected in these cases is Goodman's "grue" (or, more generally, to say that predicates projected in those cases are "grue"-like relative to predicates we project).

I have thus moved, in the course of the essay, from arguing against the possibility of the agreement-after-t condition being satisfied to arguing that even if we stipulate that this condition is satisfied (in a hypothetical case), and make such adjustments in our description of the case as are required to make this stipulation coherent, it remains unreasonable to take Mr. B (or anyone) to be projecting predicates that are "grue"-like relative to those we project. The latter argument involved the point that if we consider possible explanations of the satisfaction of the agreement-after-t condition in such cases, we see that these are incompatible with the claim that these cases are what they purport to be (that is, cases in which "grue"-like predicates are systematically projected). In this section I shall pursue this line of argument further, and shall apply it to the suggestion, already discussed in section IV, that we can bring about the agreement-after-t situation by increasing the gruification of Mr. B's vocabulary. The argument against this suggestion in section IV was inconclusive. My discussion there did strongly suggest that if we increase the gruification of Mr. B's vocabulary by stages, each successive stage of gruification will leave us as far from the agreement-after-t situation as we were before. But I could consider only a few stages of gruification before the discussion threatened to become unmanageable. And I lack the means of showing that a massive dose of gruification, introduced all at once rather than by stages, could not bring about the agreement-after-t situation. So it is worth considering the consequences of simply stipulating that the agreement-after-t condition is satisfied and then introducing, as we need it, whatever gruification seems to be required in order to preserve the coherence of this stipulation and of the claim that Mr. B projects "grue" (and other such predicates) systematically.

Earlier I pointed out that what generalizations we accept affects what properties we ascribe to observed items. It might seem to follow from this that if someone systematically projected predicates that are "grue"-like relative to predicates we project, he would necessarily differ from us in some of the evidential generalizations he accepts and hence in some of his judgments about items first observed after *t*, and that the number of such disagreements will increase as we increase the "gruification" of his projective vocabulary relative to ours. If this were so, it would follow immediately that the agreement-after-*t* condition cannot be satisfied. But this line of thought is mistaken. It assumes that if two people differ about the projectibility of a generalization, they necessarily differ about the acceptability, and the truth, of the generalization. And this is not so. Suppose, for example, that Mr. B projects the generalization "All emerires are grue," where "emerire" is defined as applying to things examined before *t* just in case they are emeralds and to other things just in case they are sapphires. This is not a generalization that Mr. A projects; for Mr. A holds that this generalization is not supported by the fact that all so far examined emerires have been grue – that is, that all examined emeralds have been green. Nevertheless, it is a generalization he *accepts*; for it is equivalent to a conjunction of two generalizations he accepts – namely, "All emeralds examined before *t* are green" and "All sapphires not examined before *t* are blue."[18] Hence, even if Mr. B's projective vocabulary were entirely gruified relative to Mr. A's, it still might be the case that a number of the generalizations Mr. A projects translate into generalizations Mr. B accepts, and that a number of the generalizations Mr. B projects translate into generalizations Mr. A accepts. And for all I have shown so far, the agreement about these generalizations might be enough to bring about the agreement-after-*t* situation.

But now let us try to suppose that the agreement-after-*t* situation is brought about in this way. To avoid certain complications, I shall shift my attention from the predicate "grue" to the predicate "emeruby," which is defined, *à la* Goodman, as applying to emeralds examined before *t* and to rubies not so examined. We will suppose that Mr. B has

[18] On such generalizations, see Donald Davidson, "Emeroses by Other Names," *The Journal of Philosophy*, 63, (1966), 778–780; and Goodman, "Comments" and "Two Replies," *The Journal of Philosophy*, 63 (1966), 328–331, and 64 (1967), 286–287.

terms that he pronounces and spells "emerald," "ruby," and "emeruby," that he regards these as interdefinable *à la* Goodman, that he projects "emeruby" rather than "emerald" and "ruby," and that he applies these terms, after *t* as well as before, to the same examined objects to which Mr. A applies the identically spelled and pronounced predicates in his vocabulary. What we must consider is whether we can make the case such that it would be reasonable for Mr. A, or for Mr. B, to claim that Mr. B's "emerald," "ruby," and "emeruby" mean what Mr. A's "emerald," "ruby," and "emeruby" mean.

Presumably our two men have grounds for applying their various predicates to particular examined objects. Let us suppose that the term "emerald-like" stands for a cluster of properties that Mr. A takes as showing something to be an emerald, and that the term "ruby-like" stands for a cluster of properties that Mr. A takes as showing something to be a ruby. Mr. A of course projects these terms, and accepts the generalizations "If something is emerald-like, it is an emerald" and "If something is ruby-like, it is a ruby" (where these are to be understood as synthetic propositions). If Mr. B projects these terms along with the term "emeruby," the agreement-after-*t* condition will be violated on the supposition that he means by "emeruby" and the rest what Mr. A means by them; for then he will accept the generalization "If something is emerald-like, it is an emeruby," and so will either disagree with Mr. A about the application of the predicate "emerald-like" to objects first examined after *t*, or, if he does not, will end up applying his term "emeruby" (and so also his term "ruby") to what Mr. A claims are *emeralds* first examined after *t*. So let us suppose instead that Mr. B projects a predicate that is "grue-like" relative to the predicate "emerald-like"; specifically, he projects a predicate, "emeruby-like," which is defined as applying to emerald-like things examined before *t* and to ruby-like things not so examined. Mr. B will therefore project the generalization "If something is emeruby-like, it is an emeruby." This generalization translates into something Mr. A accepts – namely, "If something is emerald-like, and examined before *t*, it is an emerald, and if something is ruby-like and not examined before *t*, it is a ruby." And it will lead Mr. B to apply the terms "emeruby" and "ruby" to those objects first examined after *t* which Mr. A takes to be rubies (and so emerubies). Thus the agreement-after-*t* condition appears to be satisfied.

But now let us view this case through the eyes of Mr. A. It seems clear that at first – that is, prior to *t* – Mr. A could have had no good reason to think that Mr. B's term "emeruby" was definable *à la* Goodman in terms of his own terms "emerald" and "ruby," and would have been entitled to think that it was just another name for emeralds. But now he finds, after *t*, that while Mr. B still applies "emeruby" to emeralds first examined before *t*, he refuses to apply it to emeralds first examined after *t*, and applies it to rubies first examined after *t*. It may seem that he now has good grounds for saying that Mr. B's "emeruby" is his own "emeruby" – that is, is definable *à la* Goodman in terms of his own "emerald" and "ruby." But I think that this is not so. For if Mr. A reflects on the matter he must see that he is committed to holding that *if* Mr. B's terms do mean what he himself means by words with the same spellings and pronunciations, *then* Mr. B has totally unacceptable reasons, irrelevant reasons in fact, for applying them as he does to objects first examined after *t*. For consider again, by way of analogy, the generalization "All emerires are grue." As already noted, this is equivalent to something Mr. A accepts – namely, the conjunction of the generalizations "All emeralds examined before *t* are green" and "All sapphires not examined before *t* are blue." But if someone accepted this generalization on the grounds that so far examined emerires have been grue, and predicted on this basis that emerires first examined after *t* will be grue, then we and Mr. A would have to object that he was making this prediction on irrelevant grounds; for he would be predicting that sapphires first examined after *t* will be blue on the grounds that emeralds examined before *t* were green. That the conclusion happens to be true does not make the grounds less irrelevant. Now from Mr. A's point of view, Mr. B would be involved in the same sort of irrelevance if he takes something first examined after *t* to be an emeruby on the grounds that it is emeruby-like and that prior to *t* things that were emeruby-like were emerubies. For this would amount, given the definitions, to inferring that after *t* things that are ruby-like are rubies on the grounds that prior to *t* things that were emerald-like were emeralds; and while Mr. A regards the conclusion of this inference as true, he is committed to regarding these grounds for it as totally irrelevant. Now if someone applies a term on the basis of irrelevant grounds, it is not to be expected that he will apply it to things it correctly applies to. And if it does nevertheless get applied to things it correctly applies to, this will be a coincidence; in such a case the application of the term to examined objects is not explained in the ordinary way by the speaker's meaning by the term what he does. So from Mr. A's point of view the fact that Mr. B applies the terms "emeruby" and "ruby" to the things to which he applies them is not explained by, and so does not provide evidence for, the hypothesis that Mr. B means by these terms what Mr. A means by them.

Since this argument is important, I should perhaps expand on it briefly. I assume that translation involves what Gilbert Harman has called "inference to the best explanation."[19] Now let us grant, although this would have to be qualified in all sorts of ways, that normally the best explanation of someone's applying a term to an object involves the supposition that his meaning of the term is such that it correctly applies to the object. So under normal circumstances, if two people apply the same word, or the same sound, to the same objects, this is good evidence that they mean the same by that word (or sound). But the term "normal circumstances" must be construed here to rule out not only such things as perceptual illusion but also such things as extreme irrationality or illogicality; for it is only if these are absent that a person can be expected to apply his terms to things which (given what he means by them) they correctly apply to. Irrelevance is a species of illogicality. So from Mr. A's point of view, if Mr. B means by his terms what Mr. A means by them then the apparent evidence of this is not evidence of it, since it follows from this supposition that the conditions are not "normal." I am not here begging the question against the possibility of projecting "grue"-like terms. I have not said that Mr. B is guilty of irrelevancy, or even (categorically) that he is if he means by "ruby" and the rest what Mr. A means by them; what I have said is that in having the projective policy he has (a policy we share) Mr. A is committed to saying that *if* Mr. B means by these terms what he, Mr. A, means by them, *then* his grounds for applying them as he does after *t* are irrelevant.

The situation remains the same if we shift to the point of view of Mr. B. Given his projective policies, he will be committed to the claim that if he and Mr. A mean the same by their terms, then Mr. A's grounds for thinking that objects first examined after *t* are rubies are totally irrelevant grounds. So he too has no reason to think that this is so. Nor is there any third point of view from which it would be reasonable to believe this. If, *per impossibile*, we suspend judgment as to what projective policy to employ, we will be in no position to infer anything about what Mr. A and Mr. B mean by their predicates from their applications of them. And if we have a projective policy, it must either be that of Mr. A or that of Mr. B, or else must involve the projection of some third set of predicates. It should not be necessary for me to argue that it will get us nowhere to suppose the latter.

[19] See Gilbert Harman, "The Inference to the Best Explanation," *The Philosophical Review*, 74 (1965), 88–95.

X

Now let us leave Mr. A and Mr. B and consider what this shows about ourselves. We can be said to have a projective policy that involves projecting a particular set of predicates, which I shall speak of as constituting our projective vocabulary. This policy is considerably more complicated than I have so far indicated. For one thing, we do not regard all undefeated hypotheses formulated in this vocabulary as equally projectible, and we regard the projectibility of some such hypotheses as depending on that of others in at least roughly the ways described in Goodman's theory of entrenchment.[20] But now suppose that we are presented with another set of predicates, a set of definitions of them, and a one–one mapping of them onto the predicates of our own projective vocabulary which is such that some or all of them are "grue"-like relative to their counterparts in our vocabulary. And suppose we are asked to contemplate a projective policy which is just like the one we actually have except that it involves projecting the predicates in this new vocabulary instead of their counterparts in our present vocabulary; so that if our present policy requires us, given the observed facts, to assign a certain degree of confirmation to a given hypothesis, the other policy would require us, given the same observed facts, to assign that degree of confirmation to the hypothesis obtained from the first hypothesis by replacing each term in it with its counterpart in the other vocabulary. Now what I hope to have shown is that nothing that could happen would be good evidence that someone *else* had adopted and was following such an alternative policy. But if this is so, is it intelligible for *us* to contemplate adopting such a policy in place of the one we now have? It seems to me that it is not. For one thing, it seems no more possible that I should know that I had adopted such a policy than that I should know that someone else had adopted it. Suppose that I do start projecting the *words* in the vocabulary associated with that policy; what could entitle me to think

[20] Here I have in mind Goodman's discussion of the way in which the projectibility of a hypothesis is affected by the degree of confirmation of "overhypotheses" of it – where, e.g., if *B* is a bagful of marbles in Utah, "All bagfuls of marbles in Utah are uniform in color" is a positive overhypothesis of "All marbles in *B* are red." See *Fact, Fiction and Forecast*, pp. 106ff. However, serious difficulties with Goodman's account have been brought out by Paul Teller, in "Goodman's Theory of Projection," *The British Journal for the Philosophy of Science*, 20 (1969), 219–238; and Andrzej Zabludowski, "Concerning a Fiction about How Facts are Forecast," *The Journal of Philosophy*, 71 (1974), 97–112.

that I was applying them in accordance with the definitions that render them "grue"-like relative to predicates I now project? To be entitled to think this I would have to be entitled to think that my new policy involves applying them, after *t* as well as before, to the things to which someone projecting my present vocabulary would apply them if he applied them, with justification, on the basis of those definitions. But I think that my argument about Mr. B's term "emeruby" shows that I could not be entitled to think this. If I started doing the sort of thing Mr. B was described as doing, then what applies to Mr. B would apply to me; and I have already argued that Mr. B could have no reason for thinking that the terms in his projective vocabulary are definable *à la* Goodman as "grue"-like counterparts of the predicates in our actual projective vocabulary. But if, as I think, I could have no reason for thinking that I had adopted such a policy, it surely makes no sense for me to contemplate adopting such a policy. And if it makes no sense for me to contemplate adopting such a policy, it also makes no sense to ask for reasons why I should continue to pursue my present policy *rather than* adopting such an alternative policy.

XI

Suppose there is a man, Omar, who has an instrument he calls an "alpha-meter." This instrument, he says, indicates, by emitting a clicking noise, the presence of a property he calls "alpha." For Omar the reference of the term "alpha" is "fixed" (in Kripke's sense) by the description "the property whose presence causes this instrument to emit a clicking noise."[21] Omar projects hypotheses containing "alpha," and to date the predictions implied by these hypotheses have been much more often confirmed than disconfirmed. He has found, among other things, that apples are invariably alpha, while pears are invariably non-alpha, and that alpha things always weigh more than four ounces and less than ten pounds; or so it has been in examined cases. But now suppose that Omar, having read *Fact, Fiction and Forecast*, expresses to us the worry that perhaps some predicate "grue"-like relative to "alpha" is projectible, and "alpha" itself is unprojectible. It is clear, I think, that we can assure him that this is a groundless worry. Omar could, of course, be mistaken in thinking that there is any (one) property that causes his "alpha-meter" to emit its clicking sound. If that were true, the definite description which supposedly fixes the reference of "alpha" would not be uniquely satisfied, and no reference for that term would have been fixed – and so the corresponding predicate would lack an extension ("alpha," I will suppose, is like "red" in that it functions both as an abstract singular term and as a predicate). And in that case sentences containing "alpha" would lack truth value, and so would sentences containing "predicates" defined in terms of "alpha"; and then the question of whether it is "alpha" or some term "grue"-like relative to it that is projectible would be simply misplaced. But if a reference for "alpha" has been fixed, then there can be no question of "alpha" 's being an unprojectible predicate. For in that case there are lawlike truths expressible in sentences containing "alpha" – for example, "Alpha things cause this instrument to emit a clicking noise." And projectibility is supposed to be what distinguishes generalizations that are "lawlike" from those that are not.[22] Omar could, of course, have evidence (or what he regards as evidence) that his alpha-meter really does detect the presence of a property, and that "alpha" really does have a (fairly) definite extension; for example, its readings might correlate with other phenomena in just the ways they would if they were caused by a property which interacted causally in certain ways with those other phenomena. Indeed, one could claim that the success (to date) of his predictions about the alpha-meter readings of apples and pears is evidence of this. To the extent that his belief that there is

[22] See *Fact, Fiction and Forecast*, pp. 72ff., where the notion of projectibility is linked with the notion of lawlikeness.

It might be questioned whether the connection between projectibility and lawlikeness is as close as my argument about Omar's "alpha" requires it to be. Consider the case of George, who has good eyesight, has a good grasp of the color vocabulary, always knows the date and time of day, is always honest and co-operative, and is familiar with Goodman's definition of "grue." It will be true of George that (1) if he calls something he sees "grue," it is grue, and (2) that if something is grue, then if George sees it he will assent to its being grue (here we must read "grue" in accordance with the Barker–Achinstein definition). Of these two generalizations, (1) has a nonprojectible predicate ("grue") as a consequent, and (2) has one as antecedent. Neither (1) nor (2) seems to be confirmed by positive instances, as lawlike generalizations are supposed to be. And it is at least problematic whether they can be said to "sustain counterfactuals" in the way lawlike generalizations are supposed to. Nevertheless, there is some inclination to say that (1) and (2) express lawlike truths. At any rate, it seems misleading to characterize them as "accidental" generalizations. For we can be entitled to believe these generalizations in such a way as to make it reasonable for us to rely on them in making inferences and predictions. Now it might be suggested that in order for Omar's "alpha" to have a definite extension it is sufficient that the generalization "Alpha things cause . . . etc." have the status of (1)

such a property rests on such evidence, it commits him to believing
that there are lawlike generalizations linking this property with other
features of the world (and, incidentally, commits him to holding that
these other features, or the corresponding predicates, are projectible).
So both in thinking that that "alpha" has an extension, and in
thinking that he has good reasons for thinking this, Omar is
committed to thinking that "alpha" is projectible.

As I may have indicated already by my remarks in section v, I think
that the case with the predicates "green" and "blue" is much the same
as the case with Omar's predicate "alpha." The belief that these terms
have extensions is inseparable (for a rational person) from the belief
that we ourselves are "visual color detectors," and thus inseparable
from the belief that there are true lawlike generalizations containing
color words (for example, the "Looks-Green propositions" of section
v), and thus inseparable from the belief that these words are
inductively projectible (at least to some appreciable degree). It is also
inseparable from the belief that all sorts of other predicates are
projectible. For if we were called upon to defend the claim that our
color words do have relatively determinate extensions (and, what I
think this essentially involves, that there are properties of objects that
cause our experiences of color and account for the fact that ostensive
teaching of color words leads people to apply them to the same
objects), we would invoke all sorts of generalizations involving other

and (2), and that it is not necessary that it be lawlike in what I shall call the "strong
sense" – i.e., that it be projectible. And if this were so, Omar's belief that he had
successfully fixed a reference for "alpha" would not commit him to the belief that
"alpha" is projectible. (Generalizations like (1) and (2) were brought to my attention
by Michael Slote.)

It is obvious, however, that our reliance on (1) and (2) is based ultimately on our
reliance on generalizations to the effect that (3) George is regularly right about
whether observed things are green or blue, that (4) he is regularly right about the date
and time of day, that (5) he regularly sees simple logical consequences of relatively
simple definitions (e.g., from "It is still before t" and "I see X to be green" he will
deduce "X is grue"), and so on. And these generalizations are lawlike in the strong
sense, and do not contain unprojectible predicates as antecedents or consequents.
Thus it seems appropriate to say that the lawlike truths asserted by (3)-(5) are "basic,"
while those asserted by (1)-(2) are "derivative." (In introducing George to Goodman's
"grue," we might say, we harness basic lawlike connections in order to bring about
the derivative ones asserted by (1) and (2).) It is in regarding a generalization as
asserting a basic lawlike truth that one seems committed to regarding its antecedent
and consequent predicates as projectible. And to return to Omar, it would seem that in
taking the reference of "alpha" as being fixed in the way I have supposed, he is
committed to its being a basic lawlike truth that alpha things cause certain readings on
his alpha-meter.

predicates – and in claiming to know (or have reason to believe) that these generalizations are true, we would be committed to holding that they, and the predicates in them, are projectible. This is not to say, of course, that we must regard a predicate as projectible in order to be justified in regarding it as having an extension. For we can justifiably believe of Goodman's "grue" both that it has a definite extension and that it is unprojectible. But what makes this possible is precisely the fact that "grue" is definable in terms of predicates which, given the way we learned them and the way we use them, we cannot regard as having extensions except on the assumption that they are projectible.

This perhaps throws some light on the connection between projectibility and entrenchment. For any speaker there will be a vast set of predicates which, given the way they entered his vocabulary and the way he uses them, he can reasonably regard as having definite meanings and extensions only on the assumption that they are, to some appreciable degree, projectible. This set will include not only predicates that are ostensively learned but also predicates that are linked to ostensively learned predicates in "evidential generaliz-ations" which serve as the person's basis for applying them. His vocabulary may also include predicates that are "grue"-like relative to those in this set. But he can reasonably regard the latter as having definite meanings and extensions only if he regards the former as having definite meanings and extensions, and so only if he regards the former as projectible. Moreover, terms in the first set will have entered his vocabulary before their "grue"-like counterparts, and if he is at all reasonable it will be terms in the first set that he will have been projecting. So it is these that will be entrenched, at least in his "idiolect." And he will continue to project these terms, not because they are entrenched, but because it will continue to be the case that in regarding them as having meanings and extensions the man is committed to regarding them as projectible. Where it can be reasonable to take entrenchment as evidence of projectibility is where the term in question belongs to the vocabulary of another person and is not, as yet, part of one's own vocabulary. But this will not be a matter of first understanding the term and then using its entrenchment (in the inductive practice of other persons) as evidence of its projectibility. Rather, the fact that a term is entrenched will be an important indication as to how it is to be understood – that is, how it is to be translated into one's own idiolect; it is evidence that if it is translatable at all it must be translated by a term that one regards as projectible.

Goodman has said, in summary of his theory of entrenchment, that "the roots of inductive validity are to be found in our use of language" and that "the line between valid and invalid predictions (or inductions or projections) is drawn upon the basis of how the world is and has been described and anticipated in words."[23] I can give these words a sense I can agree with, but I am not at all sure that this sense is that intended by Goodman. For him, apparently, whatever it is that endows particular words with the extensions they have (and about this he says virtually nothing) is independent of what makes certain words, and not others, projectible (namely, their being employed in actual projections). For me, the crucial point is that the fact that words are used, meant, and understood in such a way as to have particular extensions is part of "how the world is" (if you like, a fact about the natural history of human beings), and consists in lawlike, or causal, truths which cannot be stated in a way that is noncommittal as to what terms are projectible and what terms not.

[23] *Fact, Fiction and Forecast*, p. 119.

5
Conceptual connections and other minds

I wish to consider a view which is often labelled "behaviorist," but which seems to me not open to the objections that are fatal to logical behaviorism properly so-called. This is the view that some of the connections between mental states and behavior are "logical" or "essential" or "conceptual" rather than "contingent." I shall call this the "conceptual connection view."

One source of this view has been the conviction that it is our only defense against complete skepticism concerning other minds; those who think this argue that the analogical position is mistaken, and conclude from this that if all connections between mental states and behavior were contingent there would be no way at all in which such connections could be known, and so no way at all in which the mental states of others could be known. But it is, quite independently of this, quite plausible to maintain that there is *some* sort of logical, or conceptual, connection between (for example) fearing something and avoiding it, or between desiring something and pursuing it. It is easy to imagine a world in which fear has no tendency to give rise to perspiration and trembling, in which embarrassment has no tendency to give rise to blushing, and so on; that these mental states have, or tend to have, *these* behavioral manifestations seems clearly to be a contingent, empirical fact. But can we imagine a world in which fear has no tendency to give rise to avoidance of the thing feared, or in which desire has no tendency to give rise to pursuit of the thing desired? Offhand it would seem not. People might at some future time use the *word* "desire" to name a state which is unconnected with pursuit of the things they say they "desire"; but if they did, they could hardly mean by the word "desire" what we mean by it.

At this point we had better make some distinctions. If a proposition says that under certain conditions a certain mental state (or set of mental states) gives rise to, or tends to give rise to, certain behavior, let us call it a Mental-to-Behavior generalization, and let us say that it asserts a Mental-to-Behavior connection. If a proposition says that under certain conditions a certain sort of behavior is accompanied by, or tends to be accompanied by, certain mental states, let us call it a

Behavior-to-Mental connection. What I claimed in the preceding paragraph is that it is plausible to hold that some Mental-to-Behavior generalizations are conceptually (or logically) true. But what some advocates of the conceptual connection view have apparently held is that some Behavior-to-Mental generalizations are conceptually (logically) true. And that is a different matter.

If we are liberal enough about what counts as a description of behavior, it is easy to find Behavior-to-Mental generalizations that are logically true. Clearly enough, it is logically true that shouting in anger is typically (in fact always) accompanied by anger. But, what is equally clear, this logical truth is of no help whatever in explaining our knowledge that someone is angry, since we have to know that someone is angry in order to know that his behavior counts as "shouting in anger." To describe someone's behavior as "shouting in anger" is to give a "mentalistically loaded" description of it. And if we limit ourselves, in formulating Behavior-to-Mental generalizations, to descriptions that are not mentalistically loaded, and are instead expressed in purely physical terms, then it is quite implausible to suppose that any such generalizations are logically or conceptually true. The bodily movements, sound emissions, etc., that make up human behavior could all occur in the "behavior" of an automated clothing store mannequin, and any combination or sequence of these that could occur in the behavior of an actual person could (in principle) occur in the behavior of such a mechanical puppet without its thereby coming to "have a mind."

It is worth noting that it is Behavior-to-Mental generalizations which the analogical position holds to be justified by the argument by analogy. It is a shared assumption of this version of the analogical position and of the version of the conceptual connection view which I have just criticized that it is Behavior-to-Mental generalizations that play the crucial role in the justification of inferences from behavior to mental states; where the two positions differ is in what they say about the logical status of these generalizations (whether they are logically true or contingently true) and about how we know them (whether we know them a priori or empirically). But this shared assumption of the two positions seems to me to be mistaken. There is perhaps a sense in which any behaviorally based mental state ascription commits one to a Behavior-to-Mental generalization; if in certain circumstances I take the occurrence of certain behavior as entitling me to ascribe a certain mental state, I would seem to be committed to the general claim that whenever *exactly* similar behavior exists in *exactly* similar circumstances, the mental state in question is likely to exist. But such generalizations are useless as licenses for inference; in fact behavior and circumstances are never exactly duplicated, and in any case it would be impossible to establish that they were exactly duplicated. Indeed, it seems clear that one knows such generalizations by knowing that particular inferences are warranted, and not vice versa. And if we consider cases in which we do invoke generalizations relating mental states and behavior in justification of our other minds beliefs, I think it turns out that the generalizations are for the most part Mental-to-Behavior generalizations rather than Behavior-to-Mental generalizations. In talking of the connections between mental states and behavior we characteristically say that a certain mental state *manifests* itself in, or is *expressed* by, or *gives rise to* certain behavior; or that someone's having certain mental states *makes* him behave in certain ways, or *leads* him to behave in certain ways. The locutions we use highlight the causal or quasi-causal character of the connections; and of course it is typically mental states that cause or produce behavior, and not vice versa. And when we arrive at a mental state ascription by explicit reasoning, the reasoning usually constitutes what has been aptly called an "inference to the best explanation."[1] We begin (in effect) by asking "Why is he doing that?" or "Why would someone behave in that way?" and then proceed by evaluating the possible answers for adequacy, simplicity, consistency with what we know about the person and his circumstances, and so forth, finally settling upon one of them as the most plausible explanation of the behavior in question. What we have to know about mental states and behavior in order to conduct such reasoning is what sorts of mental states will produce, or give rise to, what sorts of behavior – in other words, what we need to know are Mental-to-Behavior connections. Thus it appears to be Mental-to-Behavior generalizations and connections, rather than Behavior-to-Mental generalizations and connections, that are of primary importance *vis-à-vis* our knowledge of other minds.

But now we should take notice of the fact that our reasoning concerning other minds involves generalizations and connections that do not have to do with behavior at all. These include generalizations asserting connections between mental states and their physical causes, e.g., "If someone's hand is burnt, he feels pain" (for short, these are Physical-to-Mental generalizations, and assert Physical-to-Mental connections); and generalizations asserting connections between

---

[1] For this notion, see Gilbert Harman, "The Inference to the Best Explanation," *The Philosophical Review*, 74 (1965), 88–95.

different mental states, e.g., "People want to avoid things they believe to be painful" (for short, these are Mental-Mental generalizations, and assert Mental-Mental connections). If we make explicit everything that is taken for granted in reasoning concerning other minds, a typical case of such reasoning will be found to involve generalizations of both of these sorts as well as Mental-to-Behavior generalizations. To take a very simple example, we see John, teeth clenched and red in the face, walk up to Tom and strike him, and we conclude that John is angry at Tom. Although such a judgment would be unlikely to involve explicit inference, anyone who judged in this way could be said to be taking for granted a number of generalizations, and these are precisely the generalizations that would be required to justify an "inference to the best explanation" from John's behavior to the conclusion that he is angry at Tom. Among these generalizations, which usually go unmentioned and unformulated because of their obviousness, is a Physical-to-Mental generalization to the effect that if someone's eyes are open and directed toward an object in good light, then normally he will, if conscious, have veridical sense-impressions of the object, and so will perceive it. Also among these generalizations is a Mental-Mental generalization to the effect that if someone has sense impressions of a man of a certain appearance, he will (normally) believe that there is a man of that appearance before him. We take for granted generalizations like these in believing that John knew that Tom was before him and knew that he was striking Tom. Further, in taking the striking as evidence of anger we take for granted some Mental-to-Behavior generalization to the effect that if X is angry at Y, and believes that Y is before him, then in the absence of interfering factors (including scruples and self-control) he is likely to behave violently towards what he believes to be Y. We also take for granted a Mental-to-Behavior generalization to the effect that (normally) if someone tries to strike someone, his arm makes a striking movement. And we take for granted some Mental-to-Behavior generalization to the effect that anger tends to manifest itself in teeth clenching and reddening of the face.

While sometimes such generalizations are presupposed by reasoning from behavior to other minds, at other times they figure in the conclusions of such reasoning; for that certain such generalizations are true of a set of creatures can be part of what we conclude from their behavior. Suppose, what is perhaps no longer a merely fanciful possibility, we were to come into contact with intelligent creatures "from outer space" whose evolutionary development had been completely independent of ours. If the behavior and facial expressions of such creatures sometimes resembled what we call smiling, frowning, grimacing, blushing, teeth clenching, sweating, etc., this resemblance might be as superficial, psychologically speaking, as that between the tail wagging of dogs and the tail waving of cats. What looks like smiling in them might be a manifestation of hostility, or of some emotion that is completely alien to us. Such creatures might differ from us in their sensory apparatus (e.g., they might be equipped with something like sonar, or something like radar) and in their method of reproduction (perhaps theirs would not involve sexual differentiation), and they might, accordingly, differ radically from us with respect to the sorts of sensations, feelings, and emotions they are capable of having. And their bodies might be quite different from ours; they might be equipped with pincers instead of hands, wheels instead of legs, and so on. But despite all this, it is surely possible that we should recognize such creatures as intelligent and sentient beings, and come to know a great deal about their mental states. For we could observe them engaging in complex patterns of behavior – behavior we perceive as "intelligent" and "purposive" – which we find to be inexplicable except on the assumption that they have certain motivational states (goals, needs, wants, desires, likes, dislikes, etc.), that they have modes of sense perception that provide them with information concerning their environment that is relevant to the satisfaction of their wants and needs, that they are sufficiently intelligent and rational to draw a significant number of the deductive and inductive consequences of their beliefs and thus to anticipate the consequences of their actions, and, finally, that they have a significant degree of voluntary control over their bodily movements. Especially compelling, as a reason for attributing "minds" to such creatures, would be the fact that their output of sounds or gestures is interpretable as a sequence of sentences in a language, many of these sentences constituting true descriptions of their surroundings and many of them having a content relevant to purposes seemingly manifested in their nonverbal behavior. This, it is plausible to say, is something that could *only* be explained by the creatures having minds.

Let us speak of any subject of mental states as having a "psychology" consisting of all of the Physical-to-Mental, Mental-Mental, and Mental-to-Behavior generalizations that are true of it. Given the ways other subjects of mental states might differ from us in their sensory apparatus, in what sensory and emotional states they are capable of having, and in the nature of their bodies and the nature and extent of their control over their bodies, it does not seem to be a necessary condition of our having behaviorally grounded knowledge of the mental states of other creatures that their psychologies should be the same as ours. (This is, incidentally, a further reason for rejecting the analogical position and its assumption that one's knowledge of other minds rests on an inductive extrapolation of generalizations one has found to hold in one's own case.) But it does seem to be a necessary condition of our having such knowledge (a) that some of the Physical-to-Mental generalizations true of the creatures describe connections that constitute (amount to, or add up to) their having the power to perceive facts about their physical situation and surroundings (call this the *Perceptual* condition); (b) that some of the Mental-Mental generalizations describe connections that constitute their having a significant degree of intelligence and rationality (call this the *Rationality* condition); and (c) that some of the Mental-to-Behavior generalizations describe connections that constitute their having a significant degree of voluntary control over their bodily movements (call this the *Volitional* condition). Where these conditions are satisfied, let us refer to the generalizations in virtue of which they are satisfied as, respectively, the Perceptual generalizations, the Rationality generalizations, and the Volitional generalizations. The conjunction of these three conditions I shall call the Informed Agency condition (since informed, intelligent action requires the satisfaction of this condition). What I am claiming is that this condition must be satisfied by the psychology of a set of creatures if it is to be possible for us to have behaviorally grounded knowledge of their mental states. It is precisely when behavior can be seen as manifesting a psychology satisfying this condition that it can be seen as "intelligent" and "purposive," and as calling for an explanation in terms of mental states. When the behavior of creatures is never of this sort (as is true of trees, except in fairy stories), it is at best idle to suppose that mental states play any role in its production; such behavior is most appropriately explained in nonmentalistic terms.

What accounts for the presumption that creatures having mental states are creatures whose psychologies satisfy the Informed Agency condition? Three possible answers come to mind. (1) It might be held that for each of us this presumption is an inductive extrapolation from the fact that his own psychology satisfies this condition (this can be thought of as a version of the analogical position). (2) It might be held that explanations of behavior in terms of psychologies that satisfy this condition are always simpler than competing explanations in terms of psychologies that do not satisfy it. (3) It might be held that our mental concepts impose constraints on the ways mental states can meaningfully or consistently be supposed to be related to one another and to bodily states, and that this delimits the class of possible psychologies in such a way that only those that satisfy the Informed Agency condition are capable of explaining behavior (this can be thought of as a version of the conceptual connection view). Let us consider these in turn.

It should be noted that the Perceptual part of the Informed Agency condition seems to involve the Volitional part in a rather fundamental way; for having the ability to perceive facts about one's surroundings seems to involve having some degree of voluntary control over one's bodily movements (those of one's hands, etc., in the case of tactual perception, and those of one's head and eyes in the case of visual perception). Now in order to discover anything about one's bodily states (and their relation to one's mental states) one must satisfy the Perceptual condition (and hence also the Volitional condition), while in order to discover anything at all one must satisfy the Rationality condition. Hence, the only sort of psychology anyone could discover himself to have is one satisfying the Informed Agency condition (or at least the Perceptual and Rationality conditions). So if other sorts of psychologies are logically possible, one's own case constitutes a biased sample (with respect to the property of satisfying the Informed Agency condition), and an inductive extrapolation from it (involving this property) would be illegitimate. And if other sorts of psychologies are not possible, the extrapolation from one's own case is superfluous. Hence (again) the analogical position seems to be of no help.

Turning now to the second answer, let us pretend that we could write out all of the sentences you would accept as expressing true propositions about how human mental states are connected with one another and with physical states of affairs. Let us say that you accept the "hypothesis" (call it H-1) that the psychology expressed by this set of sentences (or a psychology similar to it) is true of the human-appearing creatures you see around you. Now there is a simple recipe for constructing countless other "hypotheses," incompatible with H-1, which are (assuming them to be internally consistent and conceptually coherent) just as simple as H-1 and equivalent to it in their power to predict and explain behavior. (That is, all of these hypotheses predict the same behavior on the part of a creature as H-1, given the same information about its past behavior and physical stimuli.) To get such a hypothesis, start with the set of sentences associated with H-1, and systematically intersubstitute in these sentences two mental terms that differ in meaning, leaving the sentences otherwise unchanged. For example, replace "like" with "dislike" wherever it occurs, and vice versa. Or systematically interchange "believe" and "disbelieve." The set of sentences resulting from such a systematic intersubstitution will express an alternative psychology; and corresponding to each such psychology will be a hypothesis to the effect that the psychology is true of the human-appearing creatures around you. Clearly there are countless different psychologies and hypotheses we could construct in this way. And most of these will violate some part of the Informed Agency condition. For example, the psychology we get by interchanging "believe" and "disbelieve" will violate the Perceptual condition, since the corresponding hypothesis will imply that people are systematically mistaken about (and so lack the ability to perceive facts about) their physical surroundings. Yet since this hypothesis attributes to disbelief precisely the behavioral effects (as well as the causes) which hypothesis H-1 attributes to belief, it will predict the same behavior as H-1. And for the same reason, all of the alternative hypotheses constructable in this way have the same predictive power as H-1; so far as their observable consequences are concerned, the differences between these hypotheses "cancel out." Moreover, there is no obvious sense in which H-1 is "simpler" than any of the other hypotheses. Yet the other hypotheses will be full of such bizarre generalizations as "People dread, and if possible avoid, the things they like, and they seek out, and look forward to with delight, the things they dislike." Anyone would reject as absurd the suggestion that it is perhaps one of these hypotheses, rather than H-1, that is true of his friends and neighbors. But this rejection cannot be justified on the grounds that H-1 is superior to the other hypotheses in simplicity and explanatory power.

It may be suggested that what is decisive here is our adherence to the principle "Like causes have like effects." You know (to a considerable extent) what the causes and effects of mental states are in your own case, and you get a simpler account of the world (other things being equal) if you suppose that they are the same in other people; *given* that H-1 is true of you, the simplest hypothesis is that it is true of other similarly behaving creatures as well (even though H-1 is not itself simpler than other hypotheses that could equally well predict the behavior of these creatures). This suggestion has some force. But it is doubtful that it adequately explains the confidence with which we reject the hypotheses that result from systematic intersubstitution in H-1. Let us divide the generalizations in the H-1 psychology into two groups, A and B; group A will consist of the Perceptual, Rationality, and Volitional generalizations, and group B will consist of all the rest (including such generalizations as "Angry people tend to scowl," "Happy people tend to smile," "Fearful people tend to tremble," and

"Embarrassed people tend to blush"). One way of producing an alternative psychology would be to leave the group A generalizations unchanged while systematically intersubstituting certain mental terms in the group B generalizations. Another way would be to leave the group B generalizations unchanged while systematically intersubstituting certain mental terms in the group A generalizations. Psychologies produced in the first way do not violate the Informed Agency condition, while those produced in the second way do violate it. Clearly the behavior of actual human beings is not satisfactorily explained or predicted by psychologies of either of these sorts. But whereas we can imagine fairly easily that a psychology of the first sort might be true of the Martians (e.g., that the same Perceptual, Rationality, and Volitional generalizations are true of them as of us, but that they smile when angry, scowl when happy, blush only when at ease, and so on), it seems quite out of the question that a psychology of the second sort should be true of them (e.g., that while smiles, scowls, blushes, etc. have the same causes and effects in them as in us, believing has in them the causes, and the effects on voluntary behavior, that disbelieving has in us, and vice versa). That matters strike us this way cannot, I think, be explained by our adherence to the principle "Like causes have like effects"; for given that H-1 is true of us, that principle is violated as much by the hypothesis that a psychology of the first sort is true of the Martians as by the hypothesis that a psychology of the second sort is true of them.

This brings us to the third and last explanation of the presumption that other subjects of mental states have psychologies that satisfy the Informed Agency condition, namely that this is a consequence of constraints imposed by the very concepts of mental states (or, if you like, by the very meaning of mental terms). While I have characterized this as a version of the conceptual connection view, it is very different from behaviorism, at least as behaviorism is usually conceived; for it does not imply that mental concepts are "reducible" to physical concepts. Rather, we have here a version of what recently has been called the "causal" or "functional" theory of mental states and processes. Such a theory says, roughly, that what defines a mental state as being the mental state it is (e.g., what makes it a particular belief, or a particular desire) is some fact about the causal or functional role it plays in a complex system of states which include physical states (including behavior) as well as other mental states.[2] This explains why

[2] See David Armstrong, *A Materialist Theory of Mind* (London, 1968), and David Lewis, "An Argument for the Identity Theory," *The Journal of Philosophy*, 63 (1966), 17–25.

we get outrageous results if we intersubstitute (for example) the terms "believe" and "disbelieve" and the terms "belief" and disbelief" in the psychology H-1, leaving it otherwise unchanged. For this assigns to belief the causal or functional role which H-1 assigns to disbelief, and vice versa; and this will be incoherent if belief and disbelief are *defined* by roles assigned them in H-1. On the version of this theory suggested here, it is not all of the causal facts about mental states, but only (or primarily) those that are relevant to the satisfaction of the Informed Agency condition, that make them the mental states they are.

6

Embodiment and behavior

A prominent question in recent philosophy of mind is whether some of the connections between mental states and behavior are (in some interesting sense) "logical," "necessary," "internal," or "conceptual," as opposed to being "purely contingent." Another prominent question, a much older one, is whether subjects of mental states, in particular persons, can exist in "disembodied form," that is, whether it is possible (logically possible) for there to be something (or someone) that has mental states without having (or being) a body and so without having any physical states whatever.[1] While both of these questions concern the relationships that hold between the realm of the mental and the realm of the physical, they are on the face of it very different questions, and they are often discussed as if their answers were independent of one another.

But suppose that it could be made out that it is a necessary truth that *if* a person is embodied (has a body) *then* certain of his mental states

---

[1] It is important to distinguish the question of whether there could be disembodied subjects of mental states from the question of whether actually existing people are such that it is possible that they should exist in disembodied form, e.g., whether it is possible that I should exist in disembodied form. A negative answer to the first question implies a negative answer to the second, but the converse does not hold. It is arguable that if it is so much as logically possible that I should at some time exist without having a body, then even now, when I do have a body, I cannot be identical with that body and cannot be the subject of its physical states (or of any other physical states). On this view, dualism is true of whatever creatures are capable (logically capable) of existing in disembodied form – the idea behind this being, roughly, that whatever has physical states is *essentially* something having physical states (and, what follows from this, that whatever can fail to have physical states essentially lacks physical states). But even if this is so, and even if I and other human beings have physical states and so are essentially embodied, it does not follow that it is impossible that there should be subjects of mental states which are capable of existing in disembodied form. Note that a materialist, while he must deny that he and other actually existing human beings are capable of disembodied existence (or, at least, must do so if the essentialist view just stated is correct), can consistently allow that it is logically possible that there should be disembodied subjects of mental states. (For further development of this point, see Essay 13.)

will (*ceteris paribus*) manifest themselves in certain ways in the behavior of whatever body is his. By itself this would not conflict with the view that all psychophysical connections (lawlike connections between mental and physical states) are basically contingent. A Cartesian dualist, who thinks that disembodied existence of persons or minds is at least a logical possibility, need not dispute the claim that this conditional proposition is necessarily (logically, conceptually) true; but he would claim that if it is necessarily true, it is so merely because it spells out part of what it means to say that a person is embodied in a particular body, and that this leaves it a purely contingent fact that the causal connections between minds and bodies are such that the minds count as being embodied in the bodies.[2] (Analogously, we could introduce a notion of "automotive embodiment" which is so defined that an engine counts as being automotively embodied in a particular automobile body just in case it is so related to it that certain movements in the engine result in locomotion of the automobile body, thus making it a logical truth that if an automotively embodied engine is operating in a certain way the associated automobile body will move in a certain way. We would hardly take this as showing that there is (in any interesting sense) a conceptual or logical connection between the operation of an internal combustion engine and automotive locomotion.) But if we conjoin the claim that this conditional proposition is necessarily true with the radically anti-Cartesian claim that disembodiment is logically impossible (that being a subject of mental states necessarily involves being embodied), we get the conclusion that it is a necessary truth that certain mental states lead (*ceteris paribus*) to certain sorts of behavior; and this certainly does conflict with the view that all psychophysical connections are basically contingent.

So far I have been simply supposing that it could be made out that some conditional proposition linking embodiment with the existence of certain psychophysical connections is necessarily true. I have not given any reason to suppose that any such proposition has this status, and have not produced any proposition that is a plausible candidate for having it. I have hinted, however, that some such proposition may be necessarily true in virtue of what it means to say that a particular

---

[2] I do not mean to suggest that it is only Cartesian dualists who will take this line; it can equally well be taken by a materialist who happens to believe that disembodied existence is a logically possible, although in fact nonexistent, phenomenon. See footnote 1.

body is the body of a particular person.³ If this is so, we should not expect the consequent of that proposition to assert the existence of *all* of the psychophysical connections that we believe to hold in the case of normal human beings, for it seems plain that many of these connections could fail to hold, in the case of someone or in the case of everyone, without this affecting anyone's embodiment. If embodiment consists in the holding of certain psychophysical connections, these must be a proper subset of all the psychophysical connections we believe to hold in normal cases. What subset might this be?

In what follows I shall assume an account of action, or at least of central cases of action, according to which the connection between wants and beliefs, on the one hand, and the overt behavior to which they give rise, on the other, is always mediated by a mental event which can be characterized as an attempt or effort on the part of the person to do a certain thing, as the person's trying to do a certain thing, or, in philosophical jargon, as a "volition" to do a certain thing. I realize that this account is controversial, but I have not the space to defend it here.⁴ I shall also assume an account of perception according to which veridical perception, as well as sensory illusion and hallucination, always involves the occurrence of mental states or events that can be characterized as sense-impressions or sense-experiences, and which a person is sometimes reporting when he says how things look, feel, sound, and so forth, to him.⁵

³ For an explicit statement of this view, see Jerome Shaffer, "Persons and Their Bodies," *The Philosophical Review,* 75 (1966), especially p. 72. Shaffer defends in this paper a view he calls Cartesian, although he does not commit himself to the possibility of disembodied existence. See also C. J. Ducasse, "Mind, Matter and Bodies," in J. R. Smythies (ed.), *Brain and Mind* (London, 1965), p. 96.

⁴ Such an account is defended in Brian O'Shaughnessy, "Trying (as the Mental 'Pineal Gland')," *The Journal of Philosophy* 70 (1973), 365–386, and by David Armstrong in "Acting and Trying," *Philosophical Papers* (1973), reprinted in Armstrong's *The Nature of Mind* (Ithaca, N.Y., 1980).

⁵ The most common objection to this view about perception – that under normal circumstances it cannot appropriately be said of someone who sees something red (for example) that it looks to him as if he were seeing something red, or that he is having a visual impression or visual experience of something red – seems to me to have been decisively answered by H. P. Grice in his paper "The Causal Theory of Perception," *Proceedings of the Aristotelian Society,* supp. vol. 35 (1961). And I think that Grice's analysis can be used to answer a parallel and equally common objection to the view that all cases of intentional action involve a mental episode of trying, or what I am calling a volition. It is true that in ordinary circumstances it would be inappropriate to say of someone who raised his arm that he tried to raise it, because saying this carries the implication that in the circumstances raising his arm was, or might have been

Many connections between mental states and behavior are not mediated by volitions. Fear sometimes gives rise to perspiration and trembling, but not because the fearful person *tries* to perspire or to tremble. Likewise, embarrassment sometimes leads to blushing, but not by leading someone to try to blush. In cases like these there is, I think, very little plausibility in the view that the mental states and their associated bodily manifestations are logically or conceptually connected; it is not difficult to imagine that a change in human physiology might result in its no longer being the case that fear leads to perspiration or trembling, and it is quite implausible to suppose that it is only in an altered sense of the word "fear" that it would apply to people after such a change. And in such cases it is likewise implausible to say that the holding of the psychophysical connections is partially constitutive of the relationship of embodiment – for example, it is surely implausible to hold that part of what it *means* to say that a body is my body is that fear on my part tends to produce perspiration and trembling in that body, that embarrassment on my part tends to produce blushing in that body, and so on.[6] This suggests that any connections between mental states and behavior that are "conceptual," and any that are constitutive of embodiment, are ones involving volitions.

The connection between fear and "avoidance behavior," unlike that between fear and perspiration, is one that many philosophers have found it plausible to regard as a conceptual or logical connection. But this connection seems to resolve into more elementary connections; roughly speaking, my fear of the snake before me leads to a desire to be elsewhere, which leads to an attempt to run (a "volition"), which leads to the bodily movements constitutive of running. Some of the links in this chain, for example the connection between the fear of snakes and

---

supposed to be, difficult or impossible for the person to do. But this implication is, in Grice's terminology, "cancellable"; having said that someone tried to raise his arm one can go on to say without inconsistency that he experienced no difficulty in raising his arm and that no one had supposed that he would have difficulty. And this is because the implication is carried, not by the meaning of what is said (that the person tried to raise his arm) but by the saying of it; the speaker's calling attention to the fact that someone tried to raise his arm indicates that the case is an atypical case of arm raising, not because it is unusual for such trying to occur but because it is unusual for it to be worth commenting on.

[6] After writing this I found that on this point I am apparently in disagreement with Ducasse, who writes that one of the "decisive marks" of one's own body (as contrasted with such "accidental marks of it" as that one never sees its eyes) is that it is "the only body in which one's being ashamed causes blushing automatically" (Ducasse, "Mind, Matter and Bodies," p. 96).

the desire to be elsewhere, are connections between different mental states rather than between mental states and behavior (they are "psycho-psycho" rather than psychophysical), and can hardly be expected to be constitutive of the psychophysical relationship of embodiment. The one link that is itself psychophysical is that between the volition and the movements constitutive of the action one is trying to perform – in this case, the movements constitutive of running. The existence of this sort of causal connection does seem to me a central aspect of embodiment, and I will say that a person is "volitionally embodied" in a certain body to the extent that volitions of the person produce in that body movements that conform to them or fulfill them, that is, movements that the person is trying to produce or which are constitutive of actions he is trying to perform. (Henceforth I shall abbreviate this by saying that the volitions produce movements "appropriate to them.")

In somewhat the way in which volitions mediate the connection between desires, and so forth, and behavior, sense experiences mediate the connections between a person's bodily circumstances and his beliefs. This points to another central aspect of embodiment; I will say that a person is "sensorily embodied" in a certain body to the extent that the interactions of that body with its surroundings produce in the person sense-experiences corresponding to, and constituting veridical perceptions of, aspects of those surroundings. And I suggest that volitional embodiment and sensory embodiment are together the primary criteria of, or constitutive factors in, embodiment *simpliciter*.[7]

Most people would be prepared to allow that it is at least logically possible for someone to have mental states while being not only completely paralyzed but also blind, deaf, and otherwise cut off from

---

[7] Talk of "criteria" of embodiment will strike some readers as odd. For when do we have occasion to employ such criteria? Ordinarily a question of the form "Which body is S's body?" would ask for the identification of a corpse, and it would not seem that such an identification requires the use or possession of criteria of embodiment. But recent work on the problem of personal identity strongly indicates that the identity conditions for persons are different from those for bodies, in such a way as to make it possible for a person to have different bodies at different times; that persons cannot, therefore, be identical with their bodies; and that at any given time in a person's life it is a contingent fact that he has the body he has instead of some other one. This indicates that there is a relationship of "being embodied in" or "having as one's body" which persons have to bodies; and an account is needed of what this relationship consists in which explains, when combined with an account of personal identity, how we know that in fact people retain the same bodies throughout their lives and how we would detect a change of body if it occurred.

sensory contact with the world. And such a person would certainly
have a body. This may seem to conflict with what I have claimed about
volitional and sensory embodiment; but I shall try to show, by means
of a "Gedankenexperiment," that it does not.

Let us suppose that at some time in the future, when biological
science and technology are much more highly developed than now, a
new disease strikes mankind; those afflicted by the disease can be kept
alive for indefinitely long periods of time by intravenous feeding and
the like, but they are completely paralyzed, and are totally blind, deaf,
and otherwise cut off from ordinary sensory stimuli. I shall assume
that it is possible that we should discover correlations between mental
states and brain states that would enable us to "read off" a good deal
of information about someone's mental states from the states of his
brain, and that there could be devised a brain state recording device – a
"cerebroscope" – which would inform us of the relevant brain states.
We will suppose that while it is impossible to communicate with
victims of this disease, except perhaps by direct brain stimulation,
cerebroscopes reveal that they have intervals of consciousness.
Although the brain itself remains healthy in these cases, the deterior-
ation of the rest of the body is irreversible. It seems at first that the only
solution is to transplant the healthy brains into other bodies, and for
this purpose duplicates of bodies are grown (by an accelerated
process) from cells taken from them prior to the onset of the disease.
But alas, in this possible world, unlike others that have been imagined,
brain transplantation proves to be impossible. Finally, however, a
solution, or at least what some regard as a solution, is found. Highly
sensitive cerebroscopes are developed which are capable of recording
the brain states of afflicted persons and transmitting information
about them to receivers planted in the skulls of duplicate bodies, and
the receivers in turn are connected with the nervous and muscular
systems of the duplicate bodies. And transmitters placed in the skulls
of the duplicate bodies are fed information from their nervous systems
and sense organs, and transmit this information to receivers planted in
the brains of the afflicted persons, which in turn provide sensory
input into those brains. The effect of this is that the afflicted person
has just the sense-impressions he would have if his brain were in the
duplicate body and connected up with it in the ordinary way, and he
has voluntary control over the movements of that body – so if his
duplicate body's eyes are open and directed toward a tree, he has
sense-impressions as of a tree, and if he tries to raise his arm, then, in
the absence of "countervailing factors," the arm of his duplicate body
goes up.

Let us grant that there is a criterion of embodiment – I will call it the "biological criterion" – which assigns a body to a person if his brain is inside the skull of that body and stands to it in certain biological relationships that do not exclude paralysis, blindness, deafness, and so forth, that is, do not guarantee any degree of volitional or sensory embodiment. In the actual world, I will assume, anyone who is embodied in a body according to the volitional and sensory criteria is also embodied in it according to the biological criterion – although because of the existence of paralytics, the converse does not hold. The world I have imagined is one in which it is possible for a person to be, at one and the same time, embodied in one body according to the biological criterion and in a different body according to the volitional and sensory criteria. If this happened, which body should we say is *really* the person's body? Perhaps this question can be bypassed. If cases of this sort actually occurred, people would probably distinguish different senses of expressions like "my body"; much as we now speak of natural parents and adopted parents, they might speak of a person's "biological body" and his "volitional-sensory body." But I think that it is clear that most of the work now done by the notion of a person's body would be done by the notion of a person's volitional-sensory body rather than by the notion of a person's biological body; for example, when a person uses expressions like "my arm," "my leg," and so forth, he would mostly be taken to be referring to parts of his volitional-sensory body, and when someone locates something by its relation to himself – for example, when he says "It is right in front of me" – he would usually be taken to be locating it in relation to his volitional-sensory body. This gives support to the claim that the volitional and sensory criteria are primary, and that biological embodiment derives its status as a criterion from the fact that in normal circumstances it is a causally necessary condition of volitional and sensory embodiment.

It should also be noted that it makes sense to speak of a biological criterion of embodiment only on the assumption that we have already identified some kind of bodily organ, for example the brain, as the primary physiological seat of consciousness and mental functioning, or as what we might call the physiological core of a person; only so can we identify a person by reference to an organ of this sort and ask how a larger biological entity must be related to that organ in order to be the body of the person so identified. But of course a biological criterion for answering this question does not tell us what it is that makes an organ of that sort the physiological core of a person – and so it falls far short of giving us a full account of embodiment. It seems obvious that what

does single out the brain as the physiological core of a person is mainly
its role in bringing about or controlling on the physiological level the
behavior that on the psychological (or mentalistic) level we take to be
brought about or controlled by mental states of persons; and this is a
role it can play only in cases in which there is a significant degree of
sensory and volitional embodiment. This points up again the primacy
of the volitional and sensory criteria of embodiment.

Let us say that normal, healthy human beings are "paradigmatically
embodied" in their bodies in virtue of the significant extent to which
they are volitionally and sensorily embodied in them. While I can thus
indicate the intended extension of the notion of paradigmatic
embodiment, I cannot define it to my satisfaction; for I am unable to
specify, in general terms, the "significant extent" of volitional and
sensory embodiment which it involves. But one obvious requirement
for paradigmatic embodiment is that the extent of sensory embodiment (and also the rationality and learning capacity of the person) be
sufficient to enable the person to determine the extent of his volitional
embodiment. Let us say that a person is volitionally embodied relative
to volition-type V and body B if his having a volition of type V results,
ceteris paribus, in movements appropriate to V occurring in B. Then
this requirement for paradigmatic embodiment can be put by saying
that the extent of sensory embodiment (and of rationality and learning
capacity) must be such that the person will not as a rule be mistaken in
thinking that he is volitionally embodied relative to a particular
volition-type. And whatever definition we give of paradigmatic
embodiment, it ought to be such as to make it a definitional tautology
that if a person is paradigmatically embodied in a body, then (a) for
some volition-types he is volitionally embodied relative to those
volition-types and that body, and (b) if he believes that he is
volitionally embodied relative to a volition-type and that body, then as
a rule he *is* volitionally embodied relative to them. And given the
centrality of volitional and sensory embodiment as criteria of
embodiment *simpliciter*, it seems reasonable to characterize paradigmatic embodiment as normal embodiment (where "normal"
implies a conceptually central and paradigmatic status rather than
statistical predominance), and to say that it is a conceptual truth that if
a person is embodied then his volitions, or at least those volitions that
are of types relative to which he believes himself to be volitionally
embodied, normally issue in movements of his body which are
appropriate to them.

The conceptual truth we have uncovered (supposing we have
uncovered one) is of the form "If someone has a body, such and such

of his mental states manifest themselves in such and such ways in the behavior of that body." As I noted at the beginning of this essay, the claim that some propositions of this form are necessarily or conceptually true is perfectly compatible with Cartesian dualism and with the view that all connections between mental states and behavior are at bottom purely contingent. We must consider whether this conceptual claim can be supplemented in such a way as to warrant a philosophically interesting version of the claim that there are conceptual connections between mental states and behavior. What obviously has to be considered is whether disembodied existence of persons is possible, or, what is the same thing, whether persons are necessarily embodied. But before I do this I want to look again at the notion of volitional embodiment.

My most recent definition of "volitionally embodied" makes it a necessary truth that if a person is volitionally embodied relative to his body and the volition to raise his right arm, then, *ceteris paribus*, his trying to raise his right arm results in the right arm of his body going up. But we could introduce a notion of X-embodiment (or, if you like, X-misembodiment) which is so defined as to make it a necessary truth that if a person is X-embodied relative to a certain body and the volition to raise his right arm, then, *ceteris paribus*, his trying to raise his right arm results in the *left leg* of that body moving in a certain way – and this certainly would not establish any interesting conceptual connection between trying to raise one's arm and some leg's moving. So what is it, if anything, that gives conceptual importance to the necessary truths generated by the notion of volitional embodiment but not to those generated by the notion of X-embodiment (and by other notions of volitional misembodiment we might devise)? It is a partial answer to this, but I think only a partial answer, that volitional embodiment is, while X-embodiment most definitely is not, partially constitutive of embodiment *simpliciter*.

One fact worth noting is that the notion of X-embodiment could not play any significant role in the explanation of observed behavior. To be sure, it might be true of a paralytic that he is X-embodied relative to his body and the volition to raise his arm, and if we knew this we might explain his leg movements by reference to his attempts to move his arm. But it would be essential to the intelligibility of such an explanation that we suppose that the man is ignorant of the effects of his volitions, that is, does not know or believe that he is X-embodied relative to those volitions. For if he knew that what formerly constituted trying to move his arm now results (as a matter of course) in leg movements rather than arm movements, it could no longer constitute trying to move his arm; it would have come to constitute trying to move his leg. And it seems clear that the hypothesis that someone having certain mental states is *systematically mis*embodied (e.g., X-embodied) in a certain body relative to certain sorts of volitions could not, except in very special circumstances, constitute the best explanation of any substantial stretch of behavior of that body. Since volitional misembodiment would have to involve mistaken beliefs about the effects of one's volitions, it would have to be accompanied by sensory misembodiment in order to persist for any period of time – otherwise (assuming a minimal degree of rationality) the mistaken beliefs would be corrected on the basis of the person's sense-experiences. And certainly the hypothesis that someone is volitionally *and* sensorily misembodied in a certain body would provide no ready explanation of the fact that the movements of that body are such as to keep it nourished and out of danger, to say nothing of the fact that some of its movements and interactions with its environment are of the complex and intricate sorts which in a paradigmatically animated body would constitute threading a needle, repairing a radio, or painting a portrait. So if the behavior of a body is anything like normal human behavior, the misembodiment hypothesis would not provide much competition to the hypothesis that the body is paradigmatically animated, that is, is the body of someone who is volitionally and sensorily embodied in it to a significant degree. On the other hand, if the movements of a body are not such as to call for an explanation in terms of its being paradigmatically animated – that is, do not seem to constitute "appropriate" responses to its circumstances, and do not appear to show intelligence and purpose – then there will normally be no reason to invoke mental states in their explanation at all; such "behavior" will be most economically explained in nonmentalistic terms. To be sure, if an outlandish hypothesis is suitably supplemented with other outlandish hypotheses, it can be made to explain virtually anything. If we suppose that the connections between mental states and states of a body are mediated by the machinations of a Cartesian evil genius or a malicious remote-controlling physiologist, we can suppose any series of mental states to lead to any series of bodily states, and vice versa. But presumably we have more than ample grounds for rejecting such outlandish hypotheses, despite the logical possibility (if it be such) of their being true. So unless we have evidence for believing in the existence of certain volitions which is independent of the occurrence of the behavior to which they give rise, the existence of these volitions cannot enter into a plausible explanation of that behavior except on the supposition that the person having the volitions is paradigmatically embodied in the body exhibiting the behavior.

What this last argument shows, if correct, is that volitional embodiment, and more generally paradigmatic embodiment, has a kind of epistemological necessity; it is a necessary condition of our knowing about the mental states (especially volitional states) of other persons in the way we normally do that they be volitionally embodied to a significant degree (indeed, that they be paradigmatically embodied), and we could not know them in any other way if we could not sometimes know them in this way. But of course, to show that something must be true of persons and their volitions if they are to be known is not the same as showing that something must be true of them if they are to exist; the epistemological necessity of volitional embodiment does not establish its ontological necessity.

There is, however, another difference between the notion of volitional embodiment and such notions as that of X-embodiment. The notion of volitional embodiment and that of X-embodiment are of course alike in involving the notion of a volition. In the case of X-embodiment this "involvement" goes in only one direction; the notion of a volition does not in any natural or interesting sense involve the notion of X-embodiment. There is a fairly clear sense, however, in which the notion of a volition involves, as well as being involved by, the notion of volitional embodiment. A volition is always a volition to perform some bodily action. And the notion of bodily action involves the notion of volitional embodiment; for in order for the movements of a body to constitute the performance of a certain action by a certain person, it must be the case that the person is volitionally embodied relative to that body and the volition to perform that action. For example, my arm's going up constitutes my raising my arm only if I am volitionally embodied relative to my body and the volition to raise my arm, that is, am such that my trying to raise my arm results, *ceteris paribus*, in my arm's going up. Thus it can be said that the connection between the having of volitions and volitional embodiment is an internal one, the notion of each of these involving the notion of the other. This being so, the necessary truth linking volitions and behavior which is generated by the definition of volitional embodiment can be said to be explicative of the notion of a volition as well as of the notion of volitional embodiment. And this constitutes a difference between this necessary truth and that generated by the notion of X-(mis)embodiment, and also between it and the necessary truth generated by the notion of automotive embodiment mentioned at the beginning of this essay. For there is no such internal connection between the having of volitions and X-embodiment, or between the existence of a certain sort of engine and automotive embodiment.

But if this is all there is to the "conceptual connection" between mental states and behavior, it is not what it has been cracked up to be. The existence of this "internal connection" between volitions and volitional embodiment does not entail that volitional embodiment, or anything approaching volitional embodiment, is required for the *existence* of volitions; and so it does not entail that it is a conceptual truth that volitions typically or normally occur in people who are volitionally embodied relative to them and so typically or normally give rise to bodily movements that are appropriate to them. To see whether the latter is so we shall have to consider what sort of degree of embodiment, if any, is required for the existence of a person (or, more generally, subject of mental states). It is to the latter question that I now turn.

We know, of course, that it is not necessary for a person to be *paradigmatically* embodied in order to exist and be a subject of mental states. Paralysis actually occurs, and complete paralysis coupled with blindness, deafness, and the like, seems to be at least possible. And both states seem compatible with the possession of mental states and incompatible with paradigmatic embodiment.

It is natural to feel that the case of complete paralysis coupled with blindness, and so forth, is not significantly different, with respect to its possibility and its compatibility with the possession of mental states, from the hypothetical case of a "brain in a vat," that is, a detached brain kept alive *in vitro*. If information about the brain states of the blind, deaf paralytic could justify ascribing mental states to him, it would seem that the same information about the states of a detached brain could justify us in regarding it as the brain of a still existing and still conscious person having those mental states. And such a person would be, in one sense, without a body.

I shall not dispute the claim that a brain in a vat can be a subject of mental states – or, better, that such a brain can be the brain of (and all that physically remains of) a still existing person having mental states. But I am concerned to draw the teeth of this claim, insofar as it is thought to show that there is no essential connection between the having of mental states and embodiment (and the potential for behavior it involves). The view I wish to defend is that what I have called "paradigmatic embodiment" is paradigmatic not only of the *embodiment* of persons but of their very *existence*. While we can give sense to the idea of a person existing without being paradigmatically embodied, this is essentially the idea of a person having a damaged, defective, or truncated body. In general we can know what it is for something to be a damaged or defective so-and-so only by knowing what it is for something to be an undamaged and nondefective so-and-so. It is also true, I think, that in order to be able to characterize something as damaged or defective we must have *some* notion of what it would be for the damage to be repaired or the defect remedied; in still other terms, we must have a notion of what it would be for the thing to be restored or brought to a condition in which each of its parts, if it has parts, performs its proper function. And so it seems to me to be with persons. The body of a person can be thought of as having among its parts various mechanisms each of which has the function of contributing in a determinate way to the person's paradigmatic embodiment. These include sense organs, limbs, muscles, nerves, and so on – and of course the brain, which can be said to function as the "control mechanism" for the entire organism. If enough of these perform their functions satisfactorily, the person is paradigmatically embodied. If something has some of these parts, including the brain, but lacks others whose proper functioning is required for paradigmatic embodiment, or if it has all these parts but some (not including the brain) are misfunctioning, we will regard it as significantly similar to a paradigmatically animated body and will be willing, under some circumstances, to regard it as the body of a conscious person. Thus we have the cases of the multiple amputee and the blind and deaf paralytic. And whether or not it is medically possible for such a person to be restored or brought to a condition of paradigmatic embodiment, we have a notion of what it would be like for this to be done. It is perhaps because the case of the detached brain can be thought of as a limiting case of amputation – the amputation of everything except the brain – that many philosophers are prepared to allow that such a brain could be the brain of a still existing and still conscious person; and it goes with this that we have at least a crude idea of what it would be like for such a person to be restored to a state of paradigmatic embodiment. And here I should reiterate a point made earlier: it is because of the causal role played by the brain in cases of paradigmatic embodiment – roughly, its role in mediating connections between sensory stimuli and behavioral responses – that we are prepared to think of it as the physiological core of a person.

But now what are we to make of the idea that a person might exist in a *totally* disembodied state? We have some notion of what it would be for an amputee, a paralytic, or even the owner of a detached brain to be restored to a state of paradigmatic embodiment; but do we have any comparable idea of what it would be for a totally disembodied

person to be so restored? It is clear that the paradigmatic reembodiment of a human brain would require one sort of body, that of a
chimpanzee brain would require a different sort of body, that of a
robot brain made of transistors and the like would require a still
different sort of body, while that of a Martian brain (supposing there
to be intelligent life on Mars) would very likely require a sort of body
radically different from any of these. Crudely speaking, the structure
and causal powers of the body in each case would have to be such as to
"mesh" with the structure and causal powers of the brain, in such a
way as to bring about the causal connections between volitions and
bodily movements, and between sensory stimulation and sense-
experiences, that are constitutive of volitional and sensory embodiment. But what sort of body would be required for the paradigmatic
reembodiment of a completely disembodied mind? If someone says
that no particular sort of body is required, and that such a mind would
be capable of animating any body that could be the body of a subject
of mental states – human bodies, Martian bodies, robot bodies of
various constructions, and so on – this seems tantamount to the
admission that he has no notion of what it would be for such a mind to
be reembodied. Suppose, then, that it is said that a mind requires for its
embodiment a particular sort of body, and that an embodied mind is
related to its body, including especially its brain (presumably the point
of contact between mind and body on any plausible dualistic theory),
in a way analogous to that in which the brain is related to the rest of
the body. This requires that the mind be thought of as having a
structure, or at any rate a set of causal powers, which must "mesh" in
a certain way with the structure and causal powers of a physical body
if it is to be paradigmatically embodied in that body. I shall try to show
in what follows that conceiving the mind in this way (as it must be
conceived, I think, if the dualistic theory is to be at all intelligible) is
incompatible with conceiving it as something whose states *are* mental
states (which a Cartesian mind is supposed to be); on the former
conception a "mind" turns out to be a sort of ghostly brain, and
mental states will be related to it in whatever way a physicalist ought
to think of mental states as related to brain states (not all of which are
mental states, even on the "identity theory"). I assume that there is no
good reason to think that there are "minds" on this conception of
them (the ghostly brain conception). And the possibility (if it is one) of
there being such entities, and of their existing in "disembodied form,"
turns out to be of no more philosophical interest, from the point of
view of our current investigation, than the possibility of an ordinary

human brain existing in "disembodied form," that is, being detached from its body and kept alive *in vitro*.

I shall assume in the ensuing discussion that it makes good sense to suppose that creatures whose physical-chemical makeup is very different from ours might be capable of having the same mental states as we have, and that we could be justified in ascribing these states to such creatures on the basis of their behavior despite the differences between their physiology and ours. There are neither empirical nor conceptual reasons for thinking that if a creature having certain mental states has a certain physical-chemical makeup, then any creature having those mental states must have that physical-chemical makeup. In the debate over the mind–body "identity theory" this point has been urged, by philosophers like Fodor and Putnam, as showing that mental states (or at any rate mental properties) cannot be straightforwardly identified with physical states.[8] As the point is sometimes put, since the same mental state can be physically "realized" in a variety of ways (just as, to use a favorite analogy, the "abstract" machine states of a Turing machine will be realized in different ways in different sorts of "hardware"), a mental state cannot be identical with any of the physical states that realize it on particular occasions or in particular sorts of creatures. While this point seems to refute some versions of the identity theory, there are other versions that are immune to it; and as I hope to show, it is considerably more damaging to dualism than to physicalism.[9]

If a mind requires for its embodiment a certain sort of body (one whose structure "meshes" with its own in the right way), then equally a body should require for its "animation" a certain sort of mind (again, one whose structure "meshes" with its own in the right way). And if there are different sorts of bodies all of which are equally capable of being the bodies of persons having certain mental states, and if a body is the body of a person in virtue of being animated by a mind whose structure meshes with its own in the right way, then there

[8] See J. A. Fodor, "Explanations in Psychology," in M. Black (ed.), *Philosophy in America* (Ithaca, N.Y., 1965); H. Putnam, "The Mental Life of Some Machines" and "The Nature of Mental States," in *Mind, Language and Reality* (Cambridge, 1975).

[9] One version that seems immune to it is that of Donald Davidson in "Mental Events," in L. Foster and J. W. Swanson (eds.), *Experience and Theory* (Amherst, Mass., 1970). Another is that of David Lewis in "An Argument for the Identity Theory," in D. M. Rosenthal (ed.), *Materialism and the Mind–Body Problem* (Englewood Cliffs, N.J., 1971). See also Lewis's comments on Putnam's views in his review of *Art, Mind, and Religion*, in *The Journal of Philosophy*, (1969), 23–25.

will be different sorts of minds, all of which are equally capable of being the minds of persons having certain mental states. On the dualist view, states of minds play a crucial role in mediating the connections between sensory input and behavioral output in cases of paradigmatic embodiment. But presumably the states of minds needed to mediate in this way between input and output will be different in the case of radically different sorts of bodies. It is implausible to suppose, for example, that the very same sort of mental happening produces the movements constitutive of arm waving even when the inner physiological antecedents of the movements are entirely different in character; for since this mental happening would have to produce the arm movements by producing certain of the inner physiological antecedents, it would have to be the case that its immediate physical effects are radically different in .different cases, and yet that these effects are always events that lead, given the structure of the body as a whole, to the same gross bodily movements. In the absence of design, this seems unlikely. It seems far more likely that if two minds animate very different sorts of bodies, then what is in one of them a volition to perform a certain sort of action will be different (because of a difference in causal powers) from what in the other is a volition to perform that sort of action. And if volitions differ from one sort of mind to another, it would seem that other mental states – those that cause volitions, those that cause those that cause volitions, and so on – will differ as well. For example, if desires and beliefs cause volitions, then if a certain sort of volition (e.g., trying to wave one's arm) is something different in different sorts of minds, it will have to be the case that the desires and beliefs capable of causing that sort of volition (e.g., the desire to attract someone's attention, and the belief that waving will achieve this) also differ in nature depending on the nature of the mind in which they occur.

But what can it mean to say that the *same* mental state is something different (has a different nature) in different sorts of minds? I think that this makes no sense if we take minds to be entities whose states just are mental states, in the way bodies (or "material objects") are entities whose states just are physical states. It makes *prima facie* sense to say, as some physicalists would, that states of different *brains* can be the same *qua* mental states and different *qua* physical states (perhaps this will mean that the states are different physical "realizations" of the same "functional state," this being the mental state; or perhaps it will mean that the states are different disjuncts of a disjunctive state that is identical with the mental state; or perhaps it will mean just that it is a lawlike truth that the mental state is realized if any of the physical states is realized). But if states of different *minds* are the same *qua* mental states, *qua* what can they be different? They cannot be different *qua* physical states, for minds (on the dualist conception of them) do not have physical states.

Let us introduce the terms "immaterial substance" and the "immaterial state"; an immaterial substance will be a substance not possessing any physical properties, and an immaterial state will be a state that can belong only to immaterial substances, that is, cannot belong to anything having physical states. Now we might say that on the conception of minds under consideration (a conception on which minds are immaterial substances), states of different minds (or perhaps even of the same mind on different occasions) can be the same *qua* mental states and different *qua* immaterial states. But this involves abandoning an assumption that I think is commonly made in discussions of the philosophy of mind, namely that *if* there are immaterial states, then mental states just are immaterial states and immaterial states just are mental states (in such a way that being the same mental state necessarily goes with being the same immaterial state, and vice versa). And surely this assumption ought to be abandoned. It is hardly plausible to hold that it is analytic that all mental states are immaterial states (if it were analytic, opponents of dualism would hold a self-contradictory position unless they deny the existence of mental states), and it is hard to see why it should be thought to be analytic that all immaterial states are mental states.[10] And if the hypothesis that there are immaterial substances were introduced and adopted as an empirical hypothesis, one needed to explain human behavior, then questions would arise about the relationship between immaterial states and mental states that are

[10] In "Incorrigibility as the Mark of the Mental" (*The Journal of Philosophy*, 67 (1970), 399–424), Richard Rorty says that " 'immaterial' gets its sense from its connection with 'mental' " (p. 402). The trouble with this is that "immaterial" contrasts with "physical" (or "material") in a way that "mental" doesn't. It may well be, as Rorty goes on to say, that "The notions of 'ghostly stuff' and 'immaterial substance' would never have become current if Descartes had not been able to use *cogitationes* as an illustration of what he intended" (*ibid.*). But Rorty surely cannot think that what he regards as the essential "mark" of the mental, namely incorrigibility, makes mental states immaterial in the sense of being states of a substance having no physical properties. "Mental" does not contrast with "physical" in a way that suffices to get this sense of "immaterial" going. It may be that this sense of "immaterial" is no sense at all, because the notion of a substance having no physical properties is not coherent (and only seems coherent because of muddles about mental states). All I am saying is that there is no reason to think it analytic, or true, that *if* the latter notion is coherent then immaterial states are mental (or, conversely, that mental states are immaterial).

precisely analogous to the currently discussed questions about the relationship between brain states and mental states. Perhaps mental states could be held to be "functional states" that are "realized in" immaterial states. Perhaps they could be held to be disjunctions of immaterial states, or disjunctions of immaterial states and physical states. Conceivably particular mental events could be held to be identical with particular immaterial events in a way analogous to that in which Donald Davidson holds particular mental events to be identical with particular neurophysiological events, that is, in a way that does not require the existence of generic identities between kinds of mental events and kinds of immaterial events.[11] But if, as I have argued, the causal role played by mental states in the production of behavior would have to be played by different immaterial states in the case of different sorts of "minds" (i.e., minds that "mesh" with different sorts of bodies), then it is as much out of the question that anger, for example, should just be, in all possible circumstances, a certain immaterial state as that such a mental state should just be, in all possible circumstances, a certain neurophysiological state of the brain.[12]

But now for a qualification. I suggested earlier that the volition to wave one's arm would have different causal powers, and so would be "something different," in minds animating radically different sorts of bodies, because its immediate physical effects (on the brain, or whatever) would have to be different. More generally, I have suggested that if there were immaterial substances, different sorts of bodies would be animated by different sorts of immaterial substances. But this would not necessarily be the case, and I think that we can make sense of the notion of a mind (immaterial substance) that is capable of animating a variety of different sorts of bodies (assuming

[11] See Davidson, "Mental Events."

[12] I put the matter in this way so as to allow for a view parallel to David Lewis's version of the psychophysical identity theory (see Lewis, Review of *Art, Mind, and Religion*). As I understand him, Lewis would deny that the attribute of being angry is identical with any physical attribute, but would claim that "anger" nevertheless always names some physical state or other – perhaps a different physical state depending on the species of the creature (e.g., whether man or mollusk), and perhaps even a different physical state depending on the identity of the individual (e.g., whether Lewis or Putnam). Analogously, a dualist might deny (as I think my argument requires) that the attribute of being angry is identical with any immaterial attribute, but hold that "anger" always names some immaterial state or other, though perhaps a different one depending on the species or identity of the individual to which anger is ascribed. (But I think he would do better to take the view sketched in footnote 15.)

that we can make sense of the notion of an immaterial substance to begin with).

One way of making sense of this is to suppose, in effect, that the mind has a part – call it the "adaptor" – which mediates the causal connections between the remainder of it and the body it animates, and does so in a different way depending on the nature of the body. When the mind comes into "contact" with a body (what "contact" can mean here is of course totally unclear, since immaterial substances have traditionally been conceived as not having spatial location in their own right), the adaptor "scans" the body in order to determine of what sort it is, and then, depending on the outcome of this scanning, goes into an appropriate "mediating state"; and when the adaptor is in a mediating state appropriate to the body with which it is in "contact," the sensory input from the body is translated into a form suitable for the production of appropriate sense-impressions in the mind, and the volitional output from the mind is translated into a form suitable for the production of appropriate movements in the body, the total effect being that the mind is paradigmatically embodied in the body (unless the body is defective in some way). If minds were like this, it might seem, there would be no need to distinguish mental states from immaterial states, since the same mental state would always be "realized in" the same immaterial state, no matter what sort of body the mind is embodied in.

If we can make sense of the notion of an immaterial substance at all, I think we can make sense of the notion of an immaterial substance of the sort just described, that is, one having an "adaptor" as a part. But if anything this makes matters worse for the view that mental states just are immaterial states. To begin with, if there can be adaptor-equipped minds (immaterial substances) which are capable of animating any of a variety of sorts of physical bodies, there would seem to be no reason why there cannot *also* be simpler minds (immaterial substances) not having adaptors, each of these being capable of animating only one sort of body. Also, there would seem to be no reason why there should not be more than one sort of adaptor-equipped mind. Suppose A-type minds are capable of animating only Alpha-type bodies, while B-type minds are capable of animating only Beta-type bodies. If we can imagine an A-type mind augmented by an adaptor that enables it to animate bodies of other sorts, including Beta-type bodies, we can equally imagine a B-type mind augmented by an adaptor (one of a different sort than is required for A-type minds) which enables it to animate bodies of other sorts, including Alpha-type bodies. This introduces a new possibility, namely that two bodies of the same sort might be animated by minds of different sorts, the persons having the same mental states and the same physical states but their minds having different immaterial states. Thus, for example, one of the bodies might be animated by an adaptor-equipped A-type mind while the other is animated by an adaptor-equipped B-type mind, the total structure of each mind (including its adaptor) being such that when in "contact" with a body of that sort they both mediate in the same way between sensory input and behavioral output.

But there is another, and perhaps simpler, way of making sense of the notion of a mind that is capable of animating (paradigmatically) more than one sort of body. Since the immediate causal effects of any event or state depend on what other events or states occur or exist at the same time, why shouldn't the very same mental (or immaterial) state or event act differently on different sorts of bodies, its immediate physical effect depending on the antecedent physical state of the body affected?[13] Supposing that Alpha-type bodies, Beta-type bodies, Gamma-type bodies, and so forth are different sorts of bodies, all of which are capable of being bodies of persons having the same repertoire of mental states, it might be that the causal powers of a particular immaterial state I could be expressed in a set of conditionals stating how I affects these various sorts of bodies when a mind in which it occurs is in "contact" with them; thus we might have "If I occurs in a mind which is in 'contact' with an Alpha-type body, it produces physical state P_1 in that body," "If I occurs in a mind which is in 'contact' with a Beta-type body, it produces physical state P_2 in that body," and so on. And it might be, compatibly with this, that the effect of I on overt behavior is (*ceteris paribus*) the same in these various sorts of bodies, despite the fact that it produces this effect sometimes by producing inner physical state P_1, sometimes by producing state P_2, and so on. If in all cases the contribution of I to the causation of overt behavior is the same (despite the differences in the way in which it makes this contribution), and is that which is appropriate to a particular mental state (in other words, if I is, in D. M. Armstrong's terminology, "apt for bringing about" behavior manifesting a certain mental state,[14] no matter what sort of body is involved), let us say that

[13] Here I am indebted to Professor J. V. Canfield, who pointed out to me that I was mistaken in maintaining, in an earlier version of this essay, that this would violate the principle "Same cause, same effect."

[14] See David M. Armstrong, *A Materialist Theory of the Mind* (London, 1968), who suggests that "The concept of a mental state is primarily the concept of *a state of the person apt for bringing about a certain sort of behavior.*"

I "universally realizes" that mental state; and if the immaterial states of an immaterial substance universally realize a complete repertoire of mental states, let us say that it is a "universal mind."

I do not wish to deny the possibility of there being universal minds and immaterial states that universally realize mental states. But it seems at least equally possible that there should be immaterial states whose causal powers are more limited, each of these states being such that only in the case of one sort of body would the state contribute to the causation of overt behavior in the way appropriate to a particular mental state; these would be states that are "apt for bringing about" behavior manifesting a certain mental state only when the mind in which they occur is in "contact" with a body of a particular sort. So instead of, or in addition to, state *I*, which universally realizes (let us suppose) the state of trying to wave one's arm, we might have state I_a, which has the same effect as *I* on Alpha bodies (i.e., produces arm waving by producing physiological state P_1) but has no effect, or no relevant effect, on bodies of other sorts; state I_b, which has the same effect as *I* on Beta-type bodies (i.e., produces arm waving by producing physiological state P_2) but has no relevant effect on bodies of other sorts; and so on. Thus we seem to have the possibility of the same mental state (the volition to wave one's arm) being "something different" in different minds, that is, of immaterial states (I, I_a, I_b, etc.) being the same *qua* mental states and different *qua* immaterial states. And this is all that my argument requires, since it is enough to preclude a straightforward identification of mental states and immaterial states.

My argument has rested, of course, on the claim that if it is possible for there to be "immaterial substances" at all then it is possible that there should be different sorts of immaterial substances (as different from each other as human bodies are from the robot and Martian bodies of science fiction), which are capable of "animating" different sorts of bodies (or even, if augmented with "adaptors," the same sorts of bodies) in such a way as to yield the same potential for behavior. An opponent might deny this claim. But I do not see on what grounds he could deny it.

I shall not consider here the question of whether the notion of an immaterial state (and that of an immaterial substance) is a coherent one, and for the purposes of this discussion I am assuming (or pretending) that it is – I am assuming (or pretending) that the notion of a "physical state" can be given an intuitively satisfactory analysis which leaves it logically possible that there should be entities that are capable of interacting causally with entities having physical states but do not themselves have physical states. I shall not consider whether such entities could be assigned spatial location and, if not, how they might be individuated. One of the main points I have been concerned to make is that if there are such entities, their states have no more claim to *be* mental states than brain states do. Once this point is seen, it should be clear that there is no *conceptual* reason for supposing that the existence of mental states involves the existence of immaterial substances and immaterial states, and it should be clear, in particular, that the conceptual falsity of particular forms of the mind–body identity theory provides no such reason. Any reasons for adopting the hypothesis that there are immaterial substances would have to be empirical. I assume that if there is any empirical evidence for the existence of such substances (perhaps in phenomena reported by spiritualists and parapsychologists), it is not overwhelming. But even if there are such substances, and even if they do sometimes exist in "disembodied form" (i.e., without being related to bodies in such a way as to be capable of interacting causally with them in the ways constitutive of paradigmatic embodiment), this turns out, I think, to be compatible with my contention that paradigmatic embodiment is paradigmatic of the very existence of persons. The causal role played by such immaterial substances in the determination of behavior would be, at best, that which nowadays is generally ascribed to the brain; they would be, at best, ghostly brains. And the (perhaps) logically possible case of the disembodied immaterial substance seems in essential respects like the logically possible case of the detached brain kept alive *in vitro*; in both cases, I think, it is only the causal role that the states of the brain or quasi-brain would play if it were paradigmatically embodied which would justify regarding them as realizing, or in some sense being, mental states.[15]

I began this essay by pointing out that if we can establish both (1) that it is a necessary truth that if a person is embodied then certain of

[15] It is worth noting that the view that our mental states are realized in the states of immaterial substances, which serve as "ghostly brains" (this being, according to me, the only version of dualism that has a chance of being coherent), is perfectly compatible with the Strawsonian conception of persons as entities which are, irreducibly, subjects of both mental and physical states (as opposed to being subjects of mental states alone, or composites of subjects of mental states ("minds" or "souls") and subjects of physical states ("bodies")). The acceptance of this view would no more require one to identify the person with the immaterial substance whose states realize his mental states than the acceptance of the usual views about the causal role of the brain would require one to identify the person with his brain (and we cannot make the latter identification unless we are willing to say that no person ever weighs

his mental states will typically manifest themselves in certain ways in the behavior of his body, and (2) that it is a necessary truth that the existence of persons requires their embodiment, we will have established (3) that it is a necessary truth that certain of the mental states of persons typically manifest themselves in certain ways in bodily behavior. But only as a very rough approximation could one describe my strategy in this essay as that of arguing for a version of (3) by arguing for versions of (1) and (2). I summed up the first part of the essay by saying that what I have called "paradigmatic embodiment" is genuinely paradigmatic of the embodiment of persons, and hence that it is a conceptual truth that if a person is embodied then his volitions, or at least those volitions that are of types relative to which he believes himself to be embodied, normally issue in movements of his body that are "appropriate" to them. This, call it (1'), seems to qualify well enough as a version of (1). In the remainder of the essay I defended the view, call it (2'), that paradigmatic embodiment is paradigmatic of the very existence, and not just the embodiment, of persons. But (2'), while in the spirit of (2), is not really a version of it, and there is no version of (3) that follows from (1') and (2') in the way (3) follows from (1) and (2). Still, if the claim that paradigmatic embodiment is paradigmatic of the embodiment of persons warrants a conceptual claim about the normal or typical effects of volitions in cases of *embodied* persons, the claim that paradigmatic embodiment is paradigmatic of the very existence of persons would seem to warrant a corresponding claim about the normal or typical effects of volitions in the case of persons *simpliciter*. And the latter claim, that it is conceptually true that the volitions of a person (or at least those relative to which the person believes himself to be embodied) normally

more than a few pounds, that persons are grey in color and roughly hemispherical in shape, and so on). Although mental states will be realized in states of immaterial substances, on this view, they should not be thought of as being states of immaterial substances; instead, they will be states of persons, which, since they have physical states as well as mental states, are not immaterial substances (and do not have immaterial states). It is true that if it is possible for an immaterial substance to exist in disembodied form, it is possible for a person to exist without having physical properties. But even then the mental states of the person will not be immaterial states, since they will still be states that are capable of belonging to something having physical states. However, if this sort of disembodiment is possible, then it cannot be true, as was tentatively suggested in footnote 1, that whatever has physical properties is essentially something having physical properties – although it will be true (by definition) that whatever has immaterial properties is essentially something that lacks physical properties.

give rise to bodily movements appropriate to them, would seem to qualify as a version of (3).

Early in my discussion I put on one side, as being "psycho-psycho" rather than psychophysical, such connections as that between wanting to do something and trying to do it, that between fearing something and wanting to avoid it, and so on. But I have not really been able to keep such connections out of my discussion; for in order to get the result that a paradigmatically embodied person will have generally correct beliefs about the extent of his volitional embodiment, I had to stipulate that paradigmatic embodiment involves a significant degree of rationality and learning capacity, and this is to say that it involves the existence of psycho-psycho connections as well as psychophysical ones. To complete my examination of the logical status (i.e., the contingency or otherwise) of psychophysical connections I would have to consider the status of these psycho-psycho connections. Indeed, I think that it has often been connections of the latter sort (e.g., between wanting X, believing that doing Y is the most efficient way of getting X, and trying to do Y) that philosophers have had in mind in asserting that there are "conceptual connections" between mental states and behavior. I believe that in a consideration of the logical status of these psycho-psycho connections the notion of rationality can play much the same role that the notion of embodiment has played in my discussion here. Roughly, we can argue that it is necessarily or conceptually true that *if* a person is rational then certain lawlike connections will hold among his mental states (or, better, that such connections hold to the extent that the person is rational), and can then proceed to consider to what extent, if any, the very existence of the mental states requires rationality and hence the existence of these connections. While I cannot undertake this investigation here, my hunch is that its outcome would be, if combined with the conclusions of the present essay, a version of the "causal theory of mind" in which the various sorts of mental states are characterized as having, essentially, such causal powers as tend to yield lawlike connections constitutive of rationality and paradigmatic embodiment.[16]

I should remark, in conclusion, that while I have attempted to defend a version of the view that there are "conceptual connections"

---

[16] The causal theory of mind has been championed in recent years by a number of writers. See especially Armstrong, *A Materialist Theory of the Mind*; David Lewis, "An Argument for the Identity Theory" and "Psychophysical and Theoretical Identifications," *Australasian Journal of Philosophy*, 50 (1972), 249–257; and Alvin Goldman, *A Theory of Human Action* (Englewood Cliffs, N.J., 1970).

between mental states and behavior, nothing that I have said supports, or is intended to support, the view that there are necessary truths that directly license inferences from behavioral premises to mentalistic conclusions, for example, necessary truths of the form "If a body is moving in such and such ways, then (normally, or *ceteris paribus*) it is the body of someone having thus and such mental states." It is difficult enough to come up with a proposition of this form that is true, and it is quite impossible, I now think, to come up with one that is necessarily, or conceptually, true. If there is to be truth in the view that there are behavioral "criteria" for mental states, it must not be interpreted as implying that there are necessary truths of this sort.[17]

Postscript (1983)

The argument of this essay can be strengthened, I believe, by applying to it recent insights about reference, and in particular the point that Hilary Putnam has expressed by saying "Meaning ain't in the head."[18] Recently, in *Reason, Truth and History*, Putnam has applied the point to the skeptical hypothesis that we are brains in vats, arguing that the hypothesis is incoherent on the grounds that a brain in a vat could not have the thought that it is a brain in a vat.[19] Given the role of causal relations in the determination of reference, a brain in a vat could not, according to Putnam, mean by "I am a brain in a vat" what we mean by it; what "vat" means in its idiolect would perhaps be a state of the computer which is responsible for the brain's input, or perhaps a construction out of sense data. And what goes for the reference of words goes also for the reference of images and other psychic items.

For reasons I cannot go into here, I do not believe that Putnam's argument will support conclusions as strong as those he draws – in particular, I do not believe that it will support his anti-realism. But the main point he makes seems to me correct; a brain in a vat could not, even if its internal physical states were identical with (say) mine over a

[17] I tended to interpret it in this way in *Self-Knowledge and Self-Identity* (Ithaca, N.Y., 1963), but I did not there distinguish adequately between this view and the view that there are necessary truths of the form "If someone knows such and such about the behavior of a body, he is (*ceteris paribus*) entitled to take this as evidence that it is the body of a person having such and such mental states." It is possible that the latter view can be upheld even though the former cannot; but I would no longer put any stock in it.

[18] See especially Putnam's "The Meaning of Meaning," in *Mind, Language and Reality*. [19] Cambridge, 1981.

period of time, have mental states whose contents were the same as those of the states of a normally embodied person. The contents of propositional attitudes are determined in part by the same consider- ations that determine the reference of the words in which those attitudes are expressed, and so they are determined in part by states of affairs "outside the head" – or better, by states of affairs that link what is inside the head with what is outside it.

It would seem, moreover, that what bestows extramental content on mental states must always involve what I have called "para- digmatic embodiment," or something closely analogous to it. For both volitional and sensory embodiment are crucially involved in the causal transactions that determine reference. (Perhaps the brain in a vat attached to a computer which produces an input which duplicates that produced by a terrestial environment will not literally be paradigmatically embodied; but if there is a feedback relationship whereby the output from the brain into the computer influences the input from the computer into the brain, and does so in a way analogous to that in which a person's voluntary actions influence his sensory input, then the brain will be in a situation functionally equivalent to paradigmatic embodiment.) No doubt a person's mental states can have content even when the person is not currently paradigmatically embodied (or even quasi-paradigmatically em- bodied, in the manner of Putnam's brain-in-a-vat-attached-to-a- computer). But in such a case, e.g., the case of the deaf and blind paralytic, the content ascribed will be that appropriate to whatever sort of paradigmatic embodiment we regard as normal for that creature, i.e., that which the creature's internal states would have if it were paradigmatically embodied in that way. (Perhaps the "ap- propriate" sort will be the sort the creature has most recently had; if our brain in a vat has just been detached from its computer, perhaps we will be inclined to assign to its internal states the contents they would have if it were hooked up to the computer, rather than the contents they would have if it were paradigmatically embodied in a body of the sort from which it was originally taken.) In the essay I claimed that paradigmatic embodiment is paradigmatic of the very existence of persons (or, better, of persons *qua* subjects of certain sorts of mental states), and not just of their embodiment. This is surely so if (1) it is paradigmatic of the existence of certain sorts of mental states that they have content, i.e., are in some sense representations of states of affairs in the world, and (2) the paradigm (conceptually central) cases of states having content are states of paradigmatically embodied creatures.

7

Immortality and dualism

I

Someone who believes in immortality is not thereby committed, logically, to believing in dualism and in the possibility of disembodied existence. Nevertheless, any antidualist who believes in immortality is committed to believing things which most antidualists would find even less plausible than dualism. Observe that if at some future time I die and then undergo bodily resurrection, or if I arrange to have myself deep-frozen and then thawed a few millennia later,[1] or if I have my brain transferred to a younger and healthier body, or if I have my brainstates transferred to a younger and healthier brain, or if I undergo rejuvenation at the hands of the microsurgeons, then no matter how much my bodily existence will have been extended beyond threescore years and ten, I will still have an eternity ahead of me. None of the imagined life-prolonging (or life-restoring) episodes would, by itself, bring one immortality, as opposed to mere increased longevity. If someone believes that he is (will be?) immortal, but rejects dualism and the possibility of disembodied existence, he is committed to believing either (a) that beginning now or later he will live forever embodied in a body of the sort he currently has, one subject to all of the ills flesh is heir to, or (b) that at some future time his body will be transformed into, or replaced by, one that is imperishable and indestructible (by natural means), in which he will then be embodied forever, or (c) that he will undergo and survive an unending series of life-prolonging episodes (resurrections, brain transplants, rejuvenations, etc.). Even if none of these beliefs can be faulted on logical or conceptual grounds, most people would agree that there are overwhelming empirical grounds for rejecting all of them.

For anyone who wants to believe in personal immortality, dualism seems to offer obvious advantages over antidualism. A dualist can believe in immortality without clashing head-on with science and with

---

[1] See Robert C. W. Ettinger, *The Prospect of Immortality* (New York, 1966).

the fund of experience which has made "All men are mortal" a truism. While we have abundant empirical evidence of the perishability and impermanence of material substances, especially organic ones, we have none at all of the perishability and impermanence of immaterial substances. To be sure, we also have no empirical evidence of the *im*perishability and permanence of immaterial substances. But to many philosophers it has seemed that we are guaranteed the latter on a priori grounds. An undoubted attraction of the idea that persons are immaterial substances is the idea that such substances, being simple and without parts (a supposed consequence of their lacking spatial extension), will be incapable of going out of existence through dissolution of parts, and so will be "incorruptible" by natural means. Nowadays, of course, such ideas do not have the following they once had. There are few who subscribe to the sort of "rational psychology" attacked by Kant in the Paralogisms. But the effects of such ideas linger on, and the view persists that belief in dualism is appreciably more compatible with belief in immortality than is belief in materialism. One of my objects in this essay is to undermine this view.

II

Recent philosophers who reject dualism and deny the possibility of disembodied existence of persons tend to fall into one of two groups. Those in one group seek to show that the falsity of dualism can be demonstrated on conceptual grounds.[2] Those in the other group maintain that dualism is an intelligible and logically coherent doctrine, but that we have overwhelming empirical grounds for rejecting it as false.[3] On the first view there is no possible world in which dualism is true. On the second view dualism is true in some possible worlds, but not in the actual world.

I think that there is an element of truth in each of these views; roughly, they are true of different versions of dualism. There is a version of dualism, and one that implies that disembodied existence of persons is possible, to which there is, as far as I can see, no decisive logical or conceptual objection. This it seems reasonable to regard as a doctrine to be accepted or rejected (I opt for the latter) on empirical

[2] I have not been able to find an unequivocal and unqualified statement of this view in the literature; but it is implicit in my own book *Self-Knowledge and Self-Identity* (Ithaca, N.Y., 1963), and in the writings of other philosophers who have attacked dualism on conceptual (or logical) rather than empirical grounds.
[3] See David M. Armstrong, *A Materialist Theory of the Mind* (London, 1968), p. 19.

grounds. Once it is clearly distinguished from other versions, this version turns out not to be of much help to believers in immortality, and it is not, I think, the doctrine that such believers have ordinarily held. There is another version of dualism which at least some believers in immortality have held, and which seems in harmony with the doctrine of immortality. I believe that this second version is conceptually incoherent, but I shall content myself here with arguing that there is, and could be, no reason to believe it true.

Presumably any dualist who believes that it is possible for him to exist in disembodied form believes that there is an immaterial substance such that (a) what mental states he has depend on what states the immaterial substance has, (b) all causal connections involving mental states between his sensory "input" and his behavioral "output" are mediated by states of this immaterial substance, and (c) it is possible for him to exist, as a subject of mental states, without having a body, as long as the immaterial substance exists and has the appropriate states. Let us say that anyone of whom all of this is true has a minimally dualistic nature. I shall use the term "Minimal Dualism" for the doctrine that all persons have minimally dualistic natures – but it is worth noting that there is no evident incoherence involved in holding that some persons have minimally dualistic natures while others are purely material creatures.

Notice that Minimal Dualism does not say either (a) that the immaterial substance associated with a person *is* the person, or (b) that the states of the immaterial substance *are* the mental states of the person. Neither does it deny that (a) and (b) are true. So two versions of Minimal Dualism can be distinguished. Both of these hold that the person is something distinct from (nonidentical with) his body, and that physical states (height, weight, etc.) belong to a person only derivatively – so, for example, a person has a certain weight in virtue of having (rather than being) a body having that weight. And both hold that the mental states of a person belong to him nonderivatively – that a person's being angry, for example, is not a matter of his being related in a certain way to something (nonidentical to himself) that is angry. But one version affirms what the other denies, that a person is identical with an immaterial substance, the states of which are the mental states of the person. I shall call the version that says that persons are immaterial substances Cartesian Dualism, and shall call the other Non-Cartesian Dualism. But these are only suggestive names, and I do not claim that Descartes consistently adhered to the doctrine I call Cartesian Dualism.

It is worth noting that what Minimal Dualism says about

immaterial substances is the same as what many contemporary philosophers are prepared to say about *brains.* Many philosophers would hold that for each person there exists a brain such that (a) what mental states the person has depends on what states the brain has, (b) all causal connections involving mental states between the person's sensory input and behavioral output are mediated by states of the brain, and (c) it is possible for the person to exist, as a subject of mental states, as long as the brain exists and has the appropriate states. The only part of this that would ordinarily be regarded as at all controversial is (c), which is affirmed by those who think that a person could survive the destruction of his body if his brain were detached and kept alive *in vitro.* Now this view about brains does not seem to imply that persons *are* brains (and so weigh only a few pounds, are greyish in color, and so on), and that the mental states of persons just *are* states of their brains. And no more does Minimal Dualism seem to imply Cartesian Dualism. It seems compatible with Minimal Dualism that an immaterial substance should be related to a person in much the way we ordinarily think of a person's brain as related to him – that it should be, in effect, a ghostly brain.[4] And this is what I shall take Non-Cartesian Dualism to hold.

It should come as no surprise that the version of dualism I regard as conceptually coherent (although empirically very implausible) is Non-Cartesian Dualism, while that which I believe to be conceptually incoherent is Cartesian Dualism.

III

Before I can go on I must explain some terminology and state some assumptions.

A substance, as I shall use the term, is a "continuant" in W. E. Johnson's sense – something that can persist through time, and can have different properties at different times. A material substance I take to be a substance whose nonderivative and nonrelational properties are necessarily limited to (a) physical properties and (b) properties it has in virtue of what physical properties it has (in the way a machine can have a certain computational capacity in virtue of having a particular physical structure, even though things having very different physical structures, and perhaps even immaterial things, could have the same computational capacity).[5] And I take it that physical

---

[4] See "Embodiment and Behavior" (Essay 6 of this volume).

[5] I owe this example to Richard Boyd.

properties can belong, nonderivatively, only to material substances. Beyond this I shall not attempt to define the terms "material" and "physical." I shall simply assume, for the sake of this discussion, that the correct definitions of these terms (if there are such), or the ways in which their references are fixed, are not such as to make it self-contradictory to suppose that there might be properties and states that are not physical and substances that are not material.

It is misleading to treat the terms "material substance" and "immaterial substance" on a par. The relationship between them should be thought of as analogous, not to that between "iron" and "copper," but to that between "iron" and "nonferrous metal." If there can be immaterial substances at all, presumably there can be different kinds of immaterial substances, these being as different from one another as they are from material substances. For each possible kind of immaterial substances there will be a kind of properties which are essential to those substances in the way physical properties are essential to material substances. Just as physical properties can belong (nonderivatively) only to material substances, so immaterial properties of one of these kinds will be capable of belonging (nonderivatively) only to immaterial substances of the corresponding kind; and, conversely, the nonderivative and nonrelational properties of immaterial substances of a given kind will be necessarily limited to (a) immaterial properties of the corresponding kind and (b) properties they have in virtue of what immaterial properties of that kind they have.

A term that purports to refer to a kind of immaterial substances, and to be on a par with "material substance," is "spiritual substance." Spiritual substances are what Cartesian Dualists believe persons to be. They are (or would be if they existed) substances whose nonderivative and nonrelational properties are necessarily mental properties (if you like, modes of consciousness); and anyone who holds that there can be such substances is committed to holding that mental properties can belong (nonderivatively) *only* to such substances.

It might be supposed that "immaterial substance" could be defined as meaning simply "substance that is not a material substance." A reason for not so defining it (one that would not, however, impress a Cartesian Dualist) is that this would make Non-Cartesian Dualism logically incoherent. Persons are certainly substances in the broad sense I have defined; they are "continuants." Now Non-Cartesian Dualism denies that persons are material substances, and so would be committed, by the proposed definition of "immaterial substance," to holding that they are immaterial substances. But I have characterized

Non-Cartesian Dualism as the version of Minimal Dualism which denies that a person *is* the immaterial substance on which his mental states depend; and if a person is not that immaterial substance, what immaterial substance could he be? No answer seems forthcoming.

But there is another reason, and one that even a Cartesian Dualist should appreciate, for rejecting the proposed definition. On any version of dualism which allows for the possibility of causal interaction between material and immaterial substances (and only such versions are under consideration here) there can exist systems which consist of one or more immaterial substances interacting causally with one or more material substances. Such systems (I will call them "partly physical systems") will be continuants, and so substances in the broad sense. And such systems will have properties – dispositional properties at least – which they possess in virtue of what properties their material and immaterial components have, and of how these components are related to one another; something's having such a property will be a "partly physical" state of it. Clearly such a system will not be a material substance. Yet it will not do to characterize such systems as immaterial substances; for obviously a system which has material as well as immaterial components cannot be immaterial in the same sense in which its immaterial components are immaterial.

Immaterial substances, if there are any, will be substances whose nonrelational and nonderivative properties are neither physical nor partly physical. What we have just seen is that if we admit the possibility of there being immaterial substances as well as material substances, we must admit the possibility of there also being substances, or at any rate continuants, which are themselves neither material substances nor immaterial substances but whose existence in some way consists in the existence of material and immaterial substances. We cannot, I think, rule out a priori the possibility that persons, or even minds, will turn out to be such entities.[6]

[6] Even on the assumption that there are no immaterial substances, and that the existence of everything in some way consists in the existence of material substances, there may be a sense in which persons are neither material nor immaterial substances. For even on materialist assumptions, it is natural to hold that stones, trees, and automobiles are material substances in a sense in which corporations, nations, and political parties are not. If such a narrow sense of "material substance" can be defined (and I shall not attempt to define it here), it may be that even a materialist should deny that persons are material substances in the narrow sense – for one thing, the identity conditions for persons seem to differ importantly from those for paradigmatic "material objects," but not in ways that call materialism into question.

IV

I shall follow tradition by assuming that immaterial substances lack spatial properties, and so are not spatially extended, and that they do not have spatial location in their own right. Some philosophers have held that the nonspatiality of immaterial substances makes the very idea of an immaterial substance incoherent. Their argument has been that there could be no satisfactory way of individuating such entities; since immaterial substances are supposed to be particulars, rather than abstract entities, they could not be individuated by their nonrelational properties (for it ought to be possible for two particulars to share all of their nonrelational properties), and since they are supposed to be nonspatial they could not be individuated by spatial relations. Likewise, it has been objected that there is no way in which the notion of identity through time could be applied to entities to which the notion of spatiotemporal continuity is inapplicable.

Those who make such objections usually assume, as do most philosophers who write about dualism, that immaterial substances would be spiritual substances. It does seem logically possible that two numerically different persons should be exactly similar with respect to their mental or psychological attributes. And it may seem to follow that the notion of a spiritual substance, a substance having only mental (psychological) properties and states, is not a coherent notion.

Even if this constituted a valid objection against Cartesian Dualism, which takes persons to be spiritual substances, it would not refute Non-Cartesian Dualism, which is not committed to the existence of spiritual substances. And in fact it does not seem to me a convincing objection to Cartesian Dualism.

Both Cartesian Dualism and Non-Cartesian Dualism are versions of what I have called Minimal Dualism. And Minimal Dualism is committed to the claim that immaterial substances are such that they can interact causally with material substances; for it is essential to Minimal Dualism that the states of immaterial substances mediate the causal connections between the sensory input and the behavioral output of the bodies of living persons.[7] Now immaterial substances

---

[7] So I am not discussing Occasionalism, and other versions of dualism that deny interaction between material and immaterial substances. I believe, but have not the space to argue here, that interactionism is the only coherent form of dualism.

are usually thought to lack spatial position, and spatial relations, as well as spatial extension. And this makes it difficult to understand how there can be causal connections of the required sorts between immaterial substances (and their states) and material substances (and their states). There can be no spatial relationship, such as spatial contiguity, which relates the immaterial substance which is my mind, soul, or ghostly brain to *my* body and not to any other, and which relates my body to *my* mind (soul, ghostly brain) and not to any other immaterial substance. Why, then, do the states of my mind affect only the states of my body, and why is it only my mind that is directly affected by sensory stimulation of my body? Since I am supposing that Minimal Dualism is coherent, I must suppose that this difficulty can be overcome. And to suppose this we must suppose, I think, that there could be nonspatial relationships between immaterial substances ("minds") and material substances ("bodies") which play a role in determining what causal relationships can hold between these substances which is analogous to the role which spatial relationships play in determining what causal relationships can hold between material substances. Let us speak of these as "quasi-spatial relationships." Now there seems no reason why a Non-Cartesian Dualist cannot hold that immaterial substances are, or can be, related to material substances by such relationships; there seems to be no conflict between this claim and the essentially negative characterization of immaterial substances given by Non-Cartesian Dualism. If it is incompatible with the notice of a spiritual substance that such a substance should stand in quasi-spatial relationships to material substances, then Cartesian Dualism cannot make intelligible the possibility of interaction between mind and body, and can be rejected on that account. But it is not clear that this is incompatible with the notion of a spiritual substance. What we know from the notion of a spiritual substance, beyond the fact that spiritual substances are immaterial, is that the *non*relational properties of spiritual substances are mental properties. Offhand, this implies nothing about what relations such substances can enter into, except (perhaps) that they cannot enter into spatial relationships. But, and here is the point, if it is intelligible to suppose that immaterial substances can be related to material substances by such quasi-spatial relationships, there seems no reason why we should not suppose that they stand in quasi-spatial relationships to one another. And then their quasi-spatial relationships could play the role in their individuation, and in their identity through time, which spatial relationships play in the case of material substances. It seems that this could be held by Cartesian Dualists as well as by Non-Cartesian Dualists.[8]

V

Immaterial substances have traditionally been supposed to be "simple," in the sense of being indivisible and without separable parts, and this supposition has figured prominently in a priori arguments for immortality. One basis for this view has been the view that *persons* are simple and indivisible, this being based on considerations which we can lump together under the heading "the unity of consciousness." Given the premise that persons are simple and indivisible, that properly speaking nothing can be a *part* of a person, plus the premise that persons must be either material substances or immaterial substances, plus the obvious fact that material substances are *not* simple and indivisible, we can derive both the conclusion that persons are immaterial substances and the conclusion that at least some immaterial substances (namely those that are persons) are simple and indivisible. In order to reject this argument I do not need to dispute the

[8] Despite what I have said here, something must be conceded to the objection that there is no satisfactory principle of individuation for immaterial substances. In the sense in which we have a conception of material substance, which includes, as central to it, a partial specification of the identity conditions for material objects, we do not have a conception of immaterial substances, or of any particular kind of immaterial substances. The definition I have given of "spiritual substance" does not specify such a conception, for it says nothing positive about what relationships would hold between spiritual substances (to say that some of these relationships would be "quasi-spatial" is not to say what they would be). So it is in a rather thin sense that it is "conceivable" that there should be immaterial substances. It is not that we have a determinate conception of some kind of immaterial substances, and can conceive of there being things that satisfy this conception. It is rather that we can conceive of having (or acquiring) such a determinate notion, and of believing, intelligibly and consistently, that there are things that satisfy it. However, in the remainder of this essay I shall write as if we do have a determinate conception of immaterial substance; this can be thought of as a concession to my opponents.

One other common objection to dualism should be mentioned here. It is sometimes urged that there are intimate conceptual, or logical, connections between mental states and their behavioral manifestations or expressions, and that because of these connections it is logically incoherent to suppose that a person might exist in disembodied form. In order to assess this objection we must consider in what sense, if any, mental states and behavior are "conceptually connected." I cannot discuss this complex issue here; but I have argued elsewhere that what seems to me the most defensible version of the "conceptual connection thesis" is compatible with the view that disembodied existence is possible – see my "Embodiment and Behavior" (Essay 6).

claim that persons are (in some sense) simple and indivisible. For I have already rejected the second premise of the argument, namely that persons must either be material substances or immaterial substances. A Non-Cartesian Dualist, who denies that persons *are* immaterial substances, cannot conclude from the (alleged) simplicity of persons that immaterial substances are simple, and cannot cite the simplicity of persons as proof that there are immaterial substances.

It may be objected that even if persons are not identical with either material or immaterial substances, their existence must in some sense consist in the existence of substances of one, or both, of these kinds. With this I agree. And it might further be held that if something is simple and indivisible, its existence cannot consist in the existence of substances that are not themselves simple and indivisible. But this further claim seems to me unwarranted. I can imagine someone arguing that the United States Supreme Court, for example, is in some important sense without parts and indivisible, and that the relationship of the individual justices to the court is not that of part to whole (since, arguably, the court would continue to exist even if all of the justices were simultaneously to die or resign and since, presumably, the question, "How much does the Supreme Court weigh?" is one we should reject rather than answer by summing the weights of the individual justices). But nothing that could plausibly be meant by this would persuade a materialist that he must choose between denying the existence of the Supreme Court and abandoning his materialist view that the things that exist in the world are either material substances or things whose existence consists in the existence of material substances and their relationships to one another.

There is, however, a traditional reason for thinking that immaterial substances would have to be simple and indivisible which does not rest on the claim that persons are simple and indivisible. For it is taken for granted (as I do here) that an immaterial substance cannot be spatially extended, and from this it is concluded that immaterial substances, if there be such, are necessarily indivisible and without parts. No doubt this consideration and those leading directly to the conclusion that persons are simple have tended to reinforce each other – if someone has been persuaded on independent grounds that (a) persons are simple and (b) immaterial substances are simple, it will not be surprising if he concludes that immaterial substances are just the right sorts of things for persons to be.

But this second reason for thinking immaterial substances to be simple is undermined by the points made in section IV. We saw there that in order to make intelligible the possibility of causal interaction between immaterial substances and material bodies (as is required by both forms of Minimal Dualism) we must suppose that there are "quasi-spatial" relationships which immaterial substances can stand in which constrain what causal relationships they can stand in to material substances, and do so in a way analogous to that in which spatial relationships constrain what causal relationships can hold between different material substances. Moreover, we saw that in order to answer the "individuation" objection to dualism we must suppose that there are "quasi-spatial" relationships that hold between different immaterial substances. But given all this, it is surely intelligible (if talk about immaterial substances is intelligible at all) to suppose that immaterial substances can interact causally with one another, as well as with material substances, the causal connections between them being constrained by quasi-spatial relationships holding between them. And if there could be causal interaction between different immaterial substances, surely there could exist, in virtue of the holding of causal connections, *systems* of immaterial substances which constitute causal units in much the way a (physical) machine is a causal unit in virtue of the causal connections that hold between its parts. And such systems would have parts, or at any rate components, some of these being subsystems and some (perhaps) being "atomic" immaterial substances which are simple and without parts. Presumably such systems could have a quasi-spatial unity which goes with their causal unity in much the way that the spatial unity of material bodies goes with their causal unity.

Someone might allow that there could be such systems of immaterial substances, but deny that such systems would themselves be immaterial substances. If this denial stems from a stipulation that a substance, of whatever sort, must be simple and without parts, we can point out that this stipulation rules out talk of material substances (or at any rate excludes human bodies, and other macroscopic material things, from being substances). But there is no need for us to quibble here about the word "substance"; if need be, we can abandon it in favor of "thing," "entity," or "continuant." The point is that if there can be immaterial substances at all, of the sort required by Minimal Dualism, there seems no reason why there should not be immaterial entities that have parts. More specifically, if Non-Cartesian Dualism is coherent, there seems no reason why the "ghostly brain" of a person should not be a composite immaterial thing, a system of immaterial things which are so related as to constitute a causal unit, rather than an "atomic" immaterial substance. Certainly the view that we have immaterial brains that are such systems is no less intelligible than the view that we have immaterial brains that are immaterial atoms.

Finally, and this is, of course, the point of all this, if it is possible for immaterial substances (or things) to have parts or components, then there seems no reason to suppose that immaterial substances are not subject to destruction through the dissolution of their parts. Clearly we have no empirical evidence of the indestructibility of immaterial substances. Let us suspend, for a moment, our skepticism about purported cases of communication with the dead, "out-of-body experiences," and other spiritualistic phenomena. Even if such cases were evidence that there are immaterial substances, it is clear that they would provide no evidence that these substances are simple and indivisible, or that they are for any other reason indestructible. Likewise, if we discovered evidence that the structure of the human brain and nervous system is insufficiently complex to account for all aspects of human behavior, then while this might be evidence that there exist immaterial substances which function as the "ghostly brains" of persons, or which are the immaterial components of partly physical systems which function as "partly ghostly brains," it clearly would not be evidence that these immaterial substances are simple and indestructible.

It is plain that support for Non-Cartesian Dualism, if we had it, would not as such be support for the doctrine of immortality. Moreover, it seems (and I shall argue later) that whatever empirical evidence we can imagine having for the truth of Minimal Dualism would be compatible with Non-Cartesian Dualism – assuming, of course, that Non-Cartesian Dualism is a coherent position. If so, dualism can be used to buttress the plausibility of the doctrine of immortality only if it can be shown on a priori grounds that Non-Cartesian Dualism is not coherent and that Cartesian Dualism is – in other words, that Cartesian Dualism is the only coherent form of dualism. It will turn out that in order to maintain this one must maintain that it can be established a priori not merely that Cartesian Dualism is the only coherent form of dualism, but that it is the only coherent philosophy of mind. In other words, one must maintain that it can be established a priori that persons are spiritual substances and that mental states are immaterial states of such substances. As will become clear in the following sections, I think that there are no sound a priori reasons for believing this to be true, and that there are strong a priori reasons for believing it to be false.

VI

Let us consider what the status of mental states would be if Non-Cartesian Dualism were true. The brief answer, I think, is that their status would be much the same as it would be (or is) if materialism were (or is) true – where by "materialism" is meant the view that whatever exists (apart from "abstract entities" such as numbers) is either a material substance or something whose existence consists in the existence of material substances, their states, and their relations to one another.

Materialists sometimes assert that mental states are neurophysiological states of the brain. Now on one understanding of this, it implies something which many materialists would want to deny (and which, I think, any materialist *should* want to deny). Suppose that pain is said to be the firing of C-fibers. This might mean that the mental property, or attribute, *being in pain* is identical with the neurophysiological attribute *has its C-fibers firing*. Now this ought to imply, not merely that in all actual cases whatever has the mental attribute has the neurophysiological one, and vice versa, but also that this holds in all possible cases as well – for it is a principle of modal logic that if *a* is identical with *b*, *a* is *necessarily* identical with *b*.[9] And if every mental attribute were thus identical with some physical feature of human brains, it would follow (a) that disembodied existence of subjects of mental states is not even a possibility, and (b) that other physical creatures (e.g., the inhabitants of remote planets) cannot be subjects of mental states unless they have brains containing C-fibers. But many materialists would reject (a), and most would reject (b). There is, however, another way of taking the claim that mental states are neurophysiological states of the brain. To say that pain is the firing of C-fibers might mean that in the case of human beings (but not, necessarily, in the case of all possible creatures) being in pain "consists in," and "is nothing over and above," the firing of C-fibers. Or as it might be put, in human beings the attribute of being in pain is "realized in" the firing of C-fibers – which is compatible with its being realized in other ways in other creatures. It is even possible to hold that in the case of human beings a given mental state sometimes has one physical "realization" and sometimes another. Of course, it needs to be explained what this relationship of "being realized in," or

⁹ See Saul Kripke, "Identity and Necessity," in Milton K. Munitz (ed.), *Identity and Individuation* (New York, 1971), pp. 135–164.

"existing in virtue of," amounts to. I think that this can best be understood if we adopt a causal, or functional, analysis of mental concepts. Roughly, to say that in a certain person at a certain time the attribute of being in pain is realized in the firing of C-fibers is to say that in that person at that time the firing of C-fibers plays the causal role which is definitive of pain.[10]

Now a Non-Cartesian Dualist will not hold that mental attributes are identical to immaterial attributes of immaterial substances. Just as it seems possible that there should be creatures which, given their behavior, we would want to count as having mental states despite the fact that the physical makeup of their brains or "control systems" is very different from ours, so it seems possible (assuming the coherence of Minimal Dualism) that there should be creatures to which we would be willing to assign the same mental states despite the fact that they have "ghostly brains" having very different immaterial states. What the Non-Cartesian Dualist will hold is that the mental states of a person are realized in, that they exist in virtue of, immaterial states of an immaterial substance that functions as the person's "ghostly brain," and that it is possible (in principle, anyhow) for the same mental attribute to be realized in different immaterial states on different occasions or in different persons. Indeed, just as a materialist can hold that there *could* be creatures (though in fact there aren't) whose mental states are realized in immaterial states, so a Non-Cartesian Dualist could hold that there could be creatures (though in fact there aren't) whose mental states are realized in physical states. And somebody could hold, although I doubt if anyone ever has, that the mental states of some creatures are realized in physical states of brains, while those of other creatures are realized in immaterial states of "ghostly brains."

While the Non-Cartesian Dualist holds that mental states are "realized in" states of immaterial substances, he does not hold that they are themselves states of immaterial substances. They are states of persons; and just as a sensible materialist does not hold that persons *are* their brains, a Non-Cartesian Dualist does not hold that persons *are* the immaterial substances which function as their "ghostly brains." A person, according to Non-Cartesian Dualism, is an entity which normally exists, and has the properties it has, in virtue of the

[10] See Armstrong, *A Materialist Theory of the Mind*, and David Lewis, "An Argument for the Identity Theory," in D. M. Rosenthal (ed.), *Materialism and the Mind–Body Problem* (Englewood Cliffs, N.J., 1971), and "Psychophysical and Theoretical Identifications," in *Australasian Journal of Philosophy*, 50 (1972), 249–257.

existence of a "mind" and a "body" which are related in a certain way and have certain properties, but which can exist in virtue of the existence of the mind (immaterial substance) alone. Perhaps the Non-Cartesian Dualist can say, harking back to the discussion in section III, that a normal, i.e., embodied, person is a "partly physical system," but one whose identity conditions permit it to survive the loss of its physical components. But if he says this he must avoid saying that in becoming disembodied a person would become an immaterial substance; for immaterial substances are essentially immaterial, and nothing can become one or cease to be one. Likewise, a materialist who thinks that mental states are "realized" in physical states of the brain will not think (or should not think) that mental states are themselves states of the brain; for he will know that they are states of a person, and that a person is not identical with his brain (for one thing, the size, shape, weight, etc. of a person are not normally the size, shape, weight, etc. of his brain).[11]

VII

Now let us turn our attention to Cartesian Dualism. The Cartesian Dualist holds that mental attributes *are*, in the sense of being identical with rather than in the sense of being realized in, immaterial states of spiritual substances. This means that he must hold, not merely that neither materialism nor Non-Cartesian Dualism *is* true, but that neither of these positions *could* be, or *could have been*, true. If being in pain (say) were merely realized in some immaterial attribute (rather than being identical with it), this would not rule out the possibility of its also being realized (in other creatures, or in other possible worlds) in some physical attribute of a material substance. But if being in pain is *identical with* an immaterial attribute, it is plainly impossible that it should be realized in a physical attribute of a material substance. Likewise, if it is identical with an immaterial attribute (an attribute which can belong only to immaterial substances), it cannot belong to something which is *not* an immaterial substance (e.g., a person as conceived by Non-Cartesian Dualism), and so cannot do so in virtue

[11] It may be thought that if a person's brain is kept alive *in vitro*, and is all that physically remains of him, then (on materialist assumptions) he will be identical with it – and, likewise, that if all that is left of a person is a ghostly brain, he will be identical with it. But this cannot be so if, as I believe, it is impossible for entities X and Y to be numerically different at one time and numerically identical at another (or if, what would seem to come to the same thing, identical entities must have identical histories).

of some immaterial substance (someone's ghostly brain) having some *other* immaterial attribute (one that is not mental).

This is not yet to say that the Cartesian Dualist is committed to holding that it can be established a priori that both Non-Cartesian Dualism and materialism are false or incoherent. For while he is committed to holding that neither of these positions could possibly be true (that neither is true in any possible world), this would be compatible with his holding that the truth of his own position, and the falsity of these others, is necessary a posteriori (in Kripke's sense) rather than necessary a priori.[12] Just as an identity like "Hesperus is Phosphorus" is established empirically, despite the fact that if true it is necessarily so in the sense that it could not have been false (is false in no possible world), so it might be held that identities between immaterial attributes and mental attributes are (like all identities) necessary in this sense, but are known to hold a posteriori.

But this view has no plausibility at all. For suppose, first of all, that we wished to establish empirically an identity statement of the form "Mental state M is immaterial state I." Clearly we would need, to begin with, to have some way of identifying or picking out state I which guarantees that it is an immaterial state but which leaves it an open question, to be settled empirically, whether it is identical with M. In fact, of course, we lack any such way (or any way at all) of picking out immaterial states. But even if we had such a way of picking out immaterial states, what could we discover empirically that would show that a mental state M is identical with an immaterial state I, as opposed to being merely correlated with it, or being realized in it? We could rule out *mere* correlation if we could establish that effects (e.g., behavioral ones) which we confidently attribute to M are in fact due to I. But this would no more establish that M is identical to I than the discovery that pain behavior is produced by the firing of C-fibers would establish that the attribute *is in pain* is identical (and so identical in all possible worlds) to the physical attribute *has its C-fibers firing*. At best such a discovery would establish that, in the creatures investigated, state M is realized in state I; and this in no way rules out the possibility that there should be creatures in which it is realized in some other state, either immaterial or physical (i.e., that there should be creatures in which behavioral and other effects which would correctly be regarded as manifestations of M are due to some state

[12] See Kripke's "Identity and Necessity," already cited; see also his "Naming and Necessity," in D. Davidson and G. Harman (eds.), *Semantics of Natural Language* (Dordrecht, Netherlands, 1972).

other than *I*). Yet if this would not establish that *M* and *I* are identical, it seems to me that no empirical discovery would establish this.

Of course, someone might maintain that we could establish empirically that mental states are immaterial states without establishing identities of the form "Mental state *M* is immaterial state *I*" (just as many materialists would hold that we can establish that mental states are (realized in) physical states without establishing any statements of the form "Mental state *M* is (realized in) physical state *P*"). But essentially the same difficulty arises about this. For in the absence of an a priori argument against the possibility of Non-Cartesian Dualism being true, it seems that any conceivable evidence that might be thought to show that mental states *are* immaterial states would be compatible with the claim that they are merely realized in them, and that the same mental state could (in principle) be realized in more than one way. This is true, for example, of the (perhaps) imaginable discovery that we need to posit the existence of immaterial substances in order to explain the behavior that is attributed to mental states.

VIII

Let us turn, then, to the question of whether the Cartesian Dualist has any hope of establishing his position a priori.

The a priori arguments for dualism that I know of simply assume, and make no attempt to show, that Cartesian Dualism is the only viable form of dualism. I do not myself think that any of these arguments are sound. But what is relevant to our present concerns is that even if some of them were sound, and did establish Minimal Dualism, they would not establish Cartesian Dualism. For example, one typical argument goes (fallaciously, I believe) from the (alleged) fact that I can conceive of myself existing in disembodied form to the claim that it is possible for me to exist in disembodied form, where this is taken as a statement of *de re* modality to the effect that I am something that can exist in disembodied form,[13] from which in turn it is concluded (validly) that I am not a material substance. But even if

---

[13] The fallacy in this, I think, involves a confusion of a certain sort of epistemic possibility with metaphysical possibility. In the sense in which it is true that I can conceive of myself existing in disembodied form, this comes to the fact that it is compatible with what I know about my essential nature (supposing that I do not know that I am an essentially material being) that I should exist in disembodied form. From this it does not follow that my essential nature is in fact such as to permit me to exist in disembodied form. (See my "On an Argument for Dualism," Essay 13 of this volume.)

this conclusion were established, we could not legitimately go from it to the conclusion that I am a spiritual substance (or, more generally, that persons are spiritual substances), for nothing in the argument excludes the possibility that I am (that persons are) as Non-Cartesian Dualism represents persons as being. Or consider the arguments that purport to show that mental states are not physical states. If the conclusion means simply that mental attributes are not identical with physical attributes (and that it is therefore possible for them to be realized nonphysically), then even a materialist can accept it. If it means that mental attributes cannot be realized in physical states (that the having of a mental attribute cannot be "nothing over and above" the having of certain physical attributes), then I do not think it can be established a priori. But even if it could be, this would not establish Cartesian Dualism, for it would be compatible with the truth of Non-Cartesian Dualism. Still another argument is from the alleged "simplicity" of persons; we have already seen that this fails to establish Cartesian Dualism.

Moreover, I think we can see that there *could* be no sound a priori argument for Cartesian Dualism. For suppose (*per impossibile*) I had such an argument, and knew a priori that all mental states are identical with immaterial states of spiritual substances. And suppose that, having this knowledge, I am faced with what looks like someone who is, with great ingenuity and resourcefulness, repairing a complicated machine; that is, I am faced with what, as things are, I would take without question to be a person having certain mental states. On our supposition, I could not be entitled to regard what is before me as a person having these mental states unless I were entitled to believe that the body before me is animated by a spiritual substance. Someone might argue that since I would be entitled to believe that there is a conscious person before me, and since, *ex hypothesi*, I would know that all mental states are identical with immaterial states, I would ipso facto be entitled to believe that the body before me is animated by a spiritual substance having the appropriate immaterial states. But here it seems more appropriate to argue backward, and to say that since one *cannot* be justified on empirical grounds in believing that something is animated by a spiritual substance, and since, ex hypothesi, I would know that all mental states are immaterial states of spiritual substances, I could not be entitled to believe that what was before me was (or was the embodiment of) a person having those (or any) mental states.

To elaborate this, suppose that I am confronted with *two* creatures, one from Venus and one from Mars, both of which are exhibiting behavior which one would ordinarily take to show the existence of certain mental states. And suppose, what seems compatible with this, that the physical makeups of these two creatures are entirely different (their evolutionary histories having been different), and that I know this. There are two possibilities here; either the causes of the observed behavior are entirely physical, or they are at least partly immaterial. If I had good reason to believe the former, and was guaranteed on a priori grounds that mental states are immaterial states, I certainly could not be entitled to take the observed behavior as evidence of the existence of mental states. So let us suppose that I have good reason to believe that the causes of the behavior are at least partly immaterial. Now, given that the physical makeups of these creatures are entirely different, it seems reasonable to suppose that they would have to be acted on by different sorts of immaterial states or events in order to yield the same output of behavior (roughly, that there would have to be immaterial differences to compensate for the physical differences).[14] Moreover, if we can investigate immaterial substances empirically at all, it ought to make sense to suppose that we have investigated the immaterial substances that animate our Martian and Venusian and discovered that they have very different immaterial states. So let us suppose that I have discovered this. I would therefore know, given our supposition that I am guaranteed a priori that mental states are immaterial states of spiritual substances, that at least one of the creatures was not the subject of the mental states which seem to be manifested in the behavior of both. And this would be true *no matter what* the behavior was, and no matter how extensive it was. Moreover, given what I argued in section VII, nothing I could establish empirically would show *which* creature, if either, is a subject of those (or any) mental states – that is, there is nothing that would show which body, if either, is animated by a *spiritual* substance. More generally, on the supposition that we are guaranteed a priori that mental states are immaterial states of spiritual substances, the behavioral evidence we would ordinarily take as establishing that a creature is a subject of certain mental states does not establish this, and there is no empirical data which in conjunction with this evidence would establish it. In other words, on this supposition mental states are unknowable. And this seems to me a *reductio ad absurdum* of the supposition.

It seems, then, that we could have neither good empirical grounds nor good a priori grounds for believing Cartesian Dualism to be true. It does not follow from this, perhaps, that Cartesian Dualism could

[14] See my "Embodiment and Behavior" (Essay 6) for an elaboration of this.

not be true – that it is logically or conceptually incoherent. We could establish this stronger conclusion if we could establish that either materialism or Non-Cartesian Dualism *could* be true. For as we have seen, if it is so much as logically possible that either of these positions is true, Cartesian Dualism cannot be true. And if the falsity of Cartesian Dualism follows from a true statement of logical possibility, then it is not even logically possible that Cartesian Dualism should be true. We could establish the logical possibility of materialism or Non-Cartesian Dualism being true if we could establish a causal or functional account of what mental states are – for such an account would allow for the possibility of mental states being realized in a variety of physical states or a variety of immaterial states. I believe myself that only such an account makes sense of our ability to have knowledge of mental states (our own as well as those of others). But I have not the space to argue this here. If, however, I have succeeded in showing that there is and could be no good reason for believing in Cartesian Dualism, then, given what I argued earlier, I have shown that there is and could be no good reason for believing in a form of dualism that would make belief in immortality significantly more plausible than it is on antidualist assumptions.

8

Phenomenal similarity

I

I shall begin by quoting from some recent philosophical discussions of sensation. In his book *Myself and Others* Don Locke says that "My elders and betters taught me what 'pain' meant even though they did not and could not know how my sensations felt because they did not and could not feel them."[1] This is possible, according to Locke, because

A sensation's being a pain sensation is not a matter of how it feels, but a matter of its being of the sort caused by bodily damage and leading to pain behavior. Similarly a sensation's being a sensation of cold is not a matter of how it feels, but a matter of its being a sensation of the sort caused by frost and snow and leading to shivering, etc. And similarly for other sensations.[2]

Alan Donagan expresses much the same view in his paper "Wittgenstein on Sensation," and attributes it to Wittgenstein. On this view,

you and I correctly say that we have the same sensation, say toothache, if we both have something frightful that we would naturally express by holding and rubbing our jaws, by certain kinds of grimace, and the like. Whether the internal character of what is expressed in these ways is the same for you as for me is irrelevant to the meaning of the word "toothache."[3]

This view does not deny that there is and must be an inner "accompaniment" to pain behavior, having some "internal character" or other, if there is to be pain.

What is irrelevant [says Donagan] is not the existence of the object, but what it happens to be. You and I could not have a common word for pain unless our natural pain behavior was accompanied by something frightful; but whether the accompaniment is the same for both of us, or even whether it changes or not (provided we do not notice it) is irrelevant.[4]

I assume that this view will strike nearly everyone, even including those who are persuaded that there is something to it, as *prima facie*

---

[1] Oxford, 1968, p. 98.   [2] *Ibid.*, p. 101.
[3] In G. Pitcher (ed.) *Wittgenstein: The Philosophical Investigations* (Garden City, N.Y. 1966), p. 348.   [4] *Ibid.*, pp. 346–347.

paradoxical and counterintuitive. It seems to imply that it is possible that a sensation that feels exactly like my most recent pain might be, in someone else or me at another time, a tickle rather than a pain, and that a sensation having the "internal character" of my most recent tickle might be a pain rather than a tickle. This conflicts with the intuition which Saul Kripke recently expressed by saying that pain "is not picked out by one of its accidental properties; rather it is picked out by the property of being pain itself, by its immediate phenomenological quality. Thus pain . . . is not only rigidly designated by 'pain' but the reference of the designator is determined by an essential property of the referent."[5] I would suppose that what Kripke calls the "immediate phenomenological quality" of pain is what Donagan calls its "internal character" and what Locke refers to by speaking of "how it feels." Thus Kripke affirms, what Locke and Donagan deny, that what constitutes something's being a pain is its having a certain "internal character" or "phenomenological quality." If there is a common-sense view on this matter, it is surely much closer to Kripke's than to Locke's and Donagan's.

I suspect that the view of Locke and Donagan is the result of the pressure of two *prima facie* conflicting ideas. One of these is the idea that the concept of a particular sort of mental state centrally involves, and perhaps can be defined in terms of, the concepts of certain of its typical behavioral effects or manifestations, and in some cases, the concepts of its bodily causes. This is an idea shared, in one version or another, by philosophical behaviorists, Wittgensteinians, and proponents of "causal" or "functional" accounts of mental states, including some proponents of Central State Materialism. In *prima facie* conflict with this is the idea – or I should say the fact – that each of us is directly aware of phenomenal similarities and differences between his own mental states, especially his sensory states, in a way that does not involve knowing about corresponding similarities and differences in the causes and causal powers of these states, and in a way that seemingly leaves it a contingent matter whether states that are given as similar have correspondingly similar causes and tendencies to influence behavior and whether states that are given as different have correspondingly different causes and tendencies to influence behavior. These phenomenal similarities and differences are thought to exist in virtue of the intrinsic features of the mental states in question, their "internal" or "phenomenal" character. Thus the connection between these intrinsic features of mental states, on the

---

[5] "Naming and Necessity", in D. Davidson and G. Harman (eds.), *Semantics of Natural Language* (Dordrecht, Netherlands, 1972), p. 340.

one hand, and bodily states of affairs, on the other, seems purely contingent. And if one combines this view with the view that our concepts of mental states centrally involve the concepts of the bodily causes and/or behavioral effects or manifestations of these states, e.g., the view of David Armstrong that a particular mental state can be defined as a "state apt for bringing about" certain behavior, one gets the view, held by Locke and Donagan, that while sensations and the like have phenomenal features, which we can be immediately aware of in introspection, these features are logically irrelevant to their belonging to the kinds marked out by our mental concepts, e.g., the concept of pain.

The notorious problem of the "inverted spectrum" is relevant here. It is often suggested that it might be, for all that can be shown by any possible behavior (including linguistic behavior), that blue things standardly look to one person the way yellow things standardly look to another, and likewise for other pairs of colors. Now when this alleged possibility is used to raise epistemological problems, the relevant phenomenal similarities and differences are envisaged as holding interpersonally, e.g., between my experiences and yours, and so not being open to anyone's introspection. But I think that what primarily gives rise to the idea that such similarities and differences are possible interpersonally is the fact that we can imagine them occurring intrapersonally, where they would be immediately accessible to introspection or introspection *cum* memory. For example, it seems imaginable that my spectrum might become inverted relative to what it had been in the past, so that after a certain time blue things look to me the way yellow things looked to me before that time, and so on. Not only can I imagine this happening to me; I can also imagine behavior (verbal and otherwise) that would be evidence that it had happened to someone else. But presumably someone to whom this happened would eventually adjust to the change, and accommodate his usage of color terms to that of other persons; once this accommodation has taken place he will say not only that the sky *is* blue but that it *looks* blue, despite the fact that it looks to him the way yellow things looked to him before the change. And here something like the Locke-Donagan description seems appropriate; if someone underwent spectrum inversion, and accommodated to the change, it seems that we would say that at different times in his life experiences "of the same sort," e.g., experiences of blue, were phenomenally different, and sensations "of different sorts," e.g., an experience of yellow and one of blue, were phenomenally similar. And if inter-personal spectrum inversion is possible, this will amount to there being interpersonal differences between experiences of "the same sort" and interpersonal similarities between experiences of "different sorts," even if the persons having the experiences are behaving in identical ways in identical environments.

When we move from the case of visual experience to that of sensations like pain, the notion of "qualia inversion" becomes much more problematical. It is far from clear that we can make sense of the notion of someone having a sensation phenomenally just like pain which he does not find unpleasant or distressing, and which he responds to in the way other people respond to tickling sensations. Because this raises rather special problems. I shall say no more about pains and tickles and the like in this essay. I hope that what I have to say about phenomenal similarity can eventually be extended to cover the case of these so-called "intransitive" sensations. But my immediate purpose is to throw light on the application of the notion of similarity to perceptual experiences – for example, to similarities between the way various things look to us, or, in Chisholm's terminology, between various ways of being "appeared-to."

II

So much by way of introduction. I now want to consider the notion of similarity, first in general, and then as it applies to experiences. I shall approach this notion *via* a topic that may initially seem to have little if anything to do with it.

In his book *Fact, Fiction and Forecast*, Nelson Goodman posed what he called "the new riddle of induction." He introduced a predicate, "grue," which is defined as applying "to all things examined before t just in case they are green but to other things just in case they are blue," where t is some particular time, say noon, Eastern Daylight Time, on 4 July 2010. Goodman's definition has been interpreted in different ways by different commentators and critics. But for our present purposes it does not matter which interpretation we adopt. On any of them it will be true that all emeralds examined before t were green when examined before t if and only if all emeralds examined before t were grue when examined before t, and on any of them it will be true that an emerald examined for the first time after t will be grue when first examined just in case it will be blue when first examined. And this is enough to generate Goodman's puzzle. Supposing that the time is before t, the fact that all emeralds so far examined have been green seems clearly to provide good inductive support for the generalization that all emeralds are green and thus for the conclusion that emeralds examined for the first time after *t* will be green. But using the same principles of inductive inference, the fact that all emeralds so far examined have been grue seems to provide equally strong inductive support for the generalization that all emeralds are grue, and thus for the conclusion that emeralds examined for the first time after *t* will be grue, from which it follows that they will be blue. Yet in a sense the fact that all examined emeralds have been grue seems to be the same as the fact that all examined emeralds have been green, given that the time is before *t*. Clearly we cannot allow that incompatible conclusions can legitimately be inferred from the same evidence; so the problem is to explain why one of these inductive extrapolations (presumably that involving "green") is legitimate and the other not.

There is another problem that is raised by predicates like "grue," although not only by such predicates. If A and B are both grue, they have something in common, namely being grue. But intuitively this doesn't guarantee that A and B are in any significant way similar; for it may be, compatibly with this, that A is green and B is blue, and that they differ in size, shape, composition, etc. Evidently it is not true of just any predicate that the things to which it applies are alike, or similar, in virtue of the facts that make it true that the predicate applies to both. Indeed, it is obvious on slight reflection that given any two things, no matter how dissimilar they are (intuitively speaking), we can define any number of predicates that are true of both. Since sharing of predicates does not, in itself, give us similarity, what does give it to us? Another way of raising the same question is to ask what makes some classes, and not others, "natural kinds."

But now let us return to Goodman's "new riddle of induction." I shall not discuss here the solution Goodman offers to this "riddle," nor shall I discuss any other proposed solutions to it.[6] My present interest is not in the riddle as such but in a connection which Goodman implicitly establishes in posing it.

We of course believe that certain inductions involving the predicate "green" are acceptable while parallel inductions involving the predicate "grue" are not. In Goodman's terminology we can express this belief by saying that certain hypotheses involving "green" are "projectible" while corresponding hypotheses involving "grue" are not. Following the precedent set by other writers, including Quine, I shall depart from Goodman's usage by sometimes applying the terms "projectible" and "unprojectible" to predicates as well as to hypo-

---

[6] See Essay 4 for my views on this.

theses containing predicates; thus I will say that the predicate "green" is projectible and that the predicate "grue" is unprojectible. Projectible predicates are those that are, in Goodman's words, "well behaved" in inductive inference; roughly speaking, they are such that generalizations involving them that have been observed to be true in examined cases can reasonably be believed to hold in unexamined cases as well. Where a predicate is projectible, I shall allow myself to speak of the corresponding *property* as projectible as well; so, for example, I will say that the property green is projectible. Needless to say, this is not Goodman's usage.

Now as Goodman points out, the distinction between the projectible and the unprojectible is closely connected with that between "lawlike" and "accidental" generalizations. Lawlike generalizations, those that "sustain" counterfactuals, are confirmed by positive instances, and this will not in general be true of generalizations of the form "All A are B" unless either the predicates "A" and "B" are projectible or the generalization is equivalent to one of that form in which the "A" and "B" are projectible.

But the connection that especially interests me is that between the notions of projectibility and lawlikeness, on the one hand, and that of likeness or similarity, on the other. Goodman remarks that "the entrenchment of classes is some measure of their genuineness as kinds; roughly speaking, two things are the more akin according as there is a more specific and better entrenched predicate that applies to both."[7] Here Goodman is assuming the truth of his theory about projectibility, in which the notion of projectibility is defined in terms of the notion of "entrenchment"; to oversimplify, a predicate is entrenched, and so presumptively projectible according to Goodman, to the extent that it, or other predicates having the same extension, have been projected in the past. But it seems clear that Goodman is asserting here a connection, what I would call a conceptual connection, between a predicate's being projectible and its extension's being a "natural" or "genuine" kind. The same connection is more explicitly asserted by Quine, who remarks that "a projectible predicate is one that is true of all and only things of a kind."[8] And Quine goes on to link the notion of a kind with that of similarity or resemblance: "The notion of a kind and the notion of similarity or resemblance seem to be variants or adaptations of a single notion."[9] Although talk of properties is not congenial to Goodman and Quine, given their extensionalism, it

---

[7] N. Goodman, *Fact, Fiction and Forecast*, 2nd edn (New York, 1965), p. 121.
[8] W. V. O. Quine, "Natural Kinds," in *Ontological Relativity and Other Essays* (New York, 1969), p. 116.　　　　　　　　　　[9] *Ibid.*, p. 117.

would also seem that our intuitive notion of a genuine property is closely linked with the notion of projectibility; we are reluctant to say that things that are grue thereby share a genuine property, and this is of a piece with our unwillingness to say that the extension of "grue" is a natural kind, or that things that are grue thereby resemble one another – and all of this is connected with our belief that "grue" is not a projectible predicate.

Neither Goodman nor Quine thinks that the notion of similarity provides any help in explaining or applying the notion of inductive projectibility, but in both writers there is, as we have seen, the suggestion that the notion of projectibility is of some use in explaining the notion of similarity. And in a recent essay entitled "Seven Strictures on Similarity" Goodman expresses the suspicion that "rather than similarity providing any guidelines for inductive practice, inductive practice may provide the basis of some canons of similarity."[10] On the rather slender basis of the passages I have quoted, I shall use the term "Goodman–Quine account of similarity" to refer to the view that the notion of similarity is to be explicated, in part, in terms of the notion of inductive projectibility. This name should not be taken too seriously; for in fact, Goodman and Quine hold the notion of similarity in such low regard that they probably would not want to dignify it by offering their remarks as an "account" of it. Quine speaks of the "dubious scientific standing" of this notion, and remarks that "it is a mark of maturity in a branch of science that the notion of similarity or kind finally dissolves, so far as it is relevant to that branch of science." Goodman uses even harsher terms; in "Seven Strictures on Similarity" he says that similarity is "a pretender, an imposter, a quack."[11] Still, Goodman and Quine seem to concede that there is *some* basis to the intuitive distinction between genuine similarity and the mere sharing of predicates, and their remarks suggest the view that this distinction coincides, at least roughly, with the distinction between projectible predicates and unprojectible ones.[12]

[10] In L. Foster and J. W. Swanson (eds.), *Experience and Theory* (Amherst, Mass., 1970), p. 24.   [11] *Ibid.*, p. 19.

[12] My agreement with the Goodman–Quine account is not as complete as the body of this essay may suggest. What is wrong with this account is not what it says but what it leaves out. It makes no mention of the notion of causality; yet it is *via* this notion, I think, that the notion of inductive projectibility is linked with the notions of natural kinds, genuine similarity, and genuine properties. (For a causal account of properties, see "Causality and Properties" (Essay 10); for an application of this to the problem of induction, see my "Properties, Causation, and Projectibility," in L. Jonathan Cohen and Mary Hesse (eds.), *Applications of Inductive Logic* (Oxford, 1980).)

III

Now there is, I think, a very natural resistance to the idea that the notion of projectibility must enter into a satisfactory explication of such notions as that of a natural kind, that of a genuine property, and especially that of similarity or resemblance. Similarity and dissimilarity seem to be paradigm cases of relationships that can be directly "given" in experience, that is, relationships we can directly observe to hold. The notion of projectibility, connected as it is with the notion of lawlikeness, seems a close cousin of the notion of causality. And due in part to the influence of Hume there is a tendency to think that no fact involving concepts in this family can be directly experienced.

I think myself that this Humean view is the source of a good deal of philosophical mischief. And while Goodman and Quine write as if Hume were their ally on the topic of induction, the implications of their views about similarity and natural kinds seem to me fundamentally at odds with Humean assumptions. For Hume never questioned our ability to perceive genuine similarities or resemblances, yet, notoriously, he regarded the projectibility of these similarities, and of the properties in virtue of which they hold, as an open question which no sort of argument or evidence can close. Certainly Hume could not have raised the problem of induction in the way he does if he had thought that in being aware of similarities one is, ipso facto, aware of the sharing of projectible properties; for to hold the latter is to hold that in being aware of similarities one is already well on one's way toward knowing what inductions are legitimate.[13]

Still, the Humean view does have considerable initial plausibility, and if we are to defend what I am calling (with tongue in cheek) the Goodman–Quine account of similarity – the view that the notion of similarity is to be explained, in part, in terms of the notion of inductive projectibility – we must somehow explain away the seeming incompatibility between this account and the fact that similarities and dissimilarities are prominent among the immediate deliverances of experience. This amounts to the task of showing how the Goodman–Quine account applies to similarity with respect to "sensible qualities," and, ultimately, how it applies to similarity of

---

[13] According to the causal theory of properties suggested in Essay 9, genuine similarities consist in the sharing of properties that have the same potential for contributing to the causal powers of the things that have them; and it is certainly at odds with the Humean view to suppose that in being aware of similarities one is ipso facto aware of such a causal fact.

sensory experiences themselves. Thus we come back to the central topic of this essay, the notion of "phenomenal similarity."

The first part of the solution to this problem seems to be provided by the notion of what Quine has called an "innate quality space" and more recently "an innate standard of similarity, or innate spacing of qualities." Quine remarks that

A response to a red circle, if it is rewarded, will be elicited again by a pink ellipse more readily than by a blue triangle; the red circle resembles the pink ellipse more than the blue triangle. Without some such prior spacing of qualities, we could never acquire a habit; all stimuli would be equally alike and equally different. These spacings of qualities, on the part of men and other animals, can be explored and mapped in the laboratory by experiments in conditioning and extinction. Needed as they are for all learning, these distinctive spacings cannot themselves all be learned; some must be innate.[14]

While this point is most clearly illustrated by the case of language learning, in particular the learning of the color vocabulary, Quine stresses that an innate sense or standard of similarity is something we share with animals who lack the capacity for language; it is, as he says, "part of our animal birth-right."[15]

All such learning, according to Quine, involves induction; and the inductions we make depend on the similarities we see, and thus on our innate standard of similarity. The one part of the traditional problem of induction which Quine recognizes as a sensible question is the following:

why does our innate subjective spacing of qualities accord so well with the functionally relevant groupings in nature as to make our inductions tend to come out right? Why should our subjective spacing of qualities have a special purchase on nature and a lien on the future?[16]

For the answer to this Quine refers us to Darwin, and makes the pithy remark that "Creatures inveterately wrong in their inductions have a pathetic but praiseworthy tendency to die before reproducing their kind."[17]

But now, just what does it mean to say that a creature has an innate spacing of qualities that accords with "the functionally relevant groupings in nature?" Quine would presumably answer this in behavioral terms, referring to how the creature responds, or is capable of responding, to conditioning. And for his purposes such an answer may be entirely satisfactory; I should make clear that in what follows I do not take myself to be raising difficulties for Quine's account. But for those of us who are not averse to using mentalistic terminology, it is

[14] "Natural Kinds," p. 123. [15] *Ibid.* [16] *Ibid.*, p. 126. [17] *Ibid.*

natural to say that what it is for there to be such an "innate spacing" is for the relationships of similarity and difference holding between the person's perceptual experiences to reflect, or correspond to, relationships of similarity and difference holding between the things experienced. Or, translating this into a somewhat less philosophical jargon, there is such an innate spacing if likenesses and differences in the way things look, feel, and sound to the person correspond to similarities and differences between the things themselves. In accordance with the "Goodman–Quine account" of similarity we will suppose that the similarities between the things themselves, the similarities "in nature," involve the sharing of projectible properties, and that their existence requires that generalizations involving these properties be lawlike. And the fact that we have "immediate" or "direct" perception of these similarities, and the related fact that our inductions based on our experience of things in nature tend to come out right, is to be explained in terms of a sort of preestablished harmony, with natural selection playing the role of Leibniz' God. (Of course, it is not supposed, as it is by Leibniz, that the experiences are causally unrelated to the things they are of; on the contrary, the existence of the "preestablished harmony" consists in our being causally related to nature in such a way that, *ceteris paribus*, similarities and differences in our experience reflect significant similarities and differences in nature.)

But what of our immediate awareness of the similarities between the perceptual experiences themselves? It is not, indeed, part of the view I have sketched that we must be aware of these similarities in order to be aware of objective similarities in nature; the view is that perceptual awareness of similarities in nature involves *having* similar experiences, not that it involves *being aware of* similar experiences or of similarities between experiences. Still, by a mere shift of attention one can be aware of similarities between experiences; and as already noted, the awareness of such similarities seems a paradigm of "direct" or "immediate" awareness of similarity. But if we try to explain our awareness of these similarities in the way the account sketched above explains our awareness of similarities in nature (e.g., color similarities), we run into insuperable difficulties.

To begin with, there is the threat of an infinite regress; it seems offhand that we will have to posit experiences of experiences, experiences of experiences of experiences, and so on *ad infinitum*, and that along with this infinite hierarchy of experiences we will have to posit an infinite hierarchy of preestablished harmonies, each consisting in the existence of a general correspondence between the similarity and difference relationships holding between experiences at a certain level and similarity and difference relationships holding between items, namely the experiences at the next level down, of which these experiences are experiences. Clearly this will not do.

There is, indeed, a way of avoiding this infinite regress. Let us suppose that there are "levels" of experiences, the experiences at the first level being experiences of objects in the world, those at the second level being experiences of experiences at the first level, and so on. We can avoid the infinite regress if we are willing to hold that for some level of experiences n we are able to be aware of similarities and differences between experiences at levels below n but are not able to be aware of similarities and differences between experiences at level n itself – for then n could be the top level, and the regress would stop there. But even then there would be serious, and, I think, insuperable, difficulties. If one is aware of similarities between experiences by having similar experiences of those experiences, it would have to be possible for there to be a failure of correspondence here, and for one to misperceive the relationships between one's experiences (at any level) in a way analogous to that in which one can misperceive the color relationships between material objects. Just as it can look to one exactly as if two apples are similar in color without their being similar in color, it would have to be possible for it to appear to one exactly as if two color experiences are similar without their being similar – it would have to be possible for it to appear to one exactly as if one were seeming to see two things similar in color without its being the case that one does seem to see two things similar in color. And the latter seems to me clearly not to be possible. I am not claiming that beliefs about one's present visual experiences, about how things presently appear to one or about how one is "appeared to," are "incorrigible." I am merely saying that the ways of being mistaken about one's present experiences, about how things look or sound or feel to one, do not include anything analogous to hallucination or sensory illusion.

Yet it seems clear that we are immediately and noninferentially aware of similarities between perceptual experiences. And we now see that if we take *these* similarities as our "objective" facts, we cannot explain our awareness of them by reference to an innate "spacing" which is subjective relative to them and is, for evolutionary reasons, in accordance with them.

IV

This may lead to the thought that similarity of experience is an exception to what was said earlier, following Goodman and Quine, about the connections between the notions of similarity, projectibility and lawlikeness. And this is likely to go with the thought that it is similarity between experiences that is "intrinsic" similarity *par excellence*. Our first candidate for this status is likely to be color similarity between objects. For the fact that we can directly observe color similarities and dissimilarities in the physical world may at first incline us to think that these are simple and unanalyzable relationships, and that the holding of these relationships is logically independent of considerations of projectibility – since we do not have to *establish* that colors are projectible in order to be aware of these relationships. But on reflection *this* appears as an illusion, fostered by the innateness of our sense of color similarity, that is, by the fact that we are so constituted, presumably as the result of evolution, that in seeing things we have experiences that stand in relationships of similarity and difference that are isomorphic with relationships of color similarity and difference holding between the things seen. Yet it is tempting to suppose that the illusion arises from our projecting onto the color similarity relationships between things the simplicity and unanalyzability of the similarity and difference relationships holding between our perceptual experiences themselves – this would be a manifestation of the propensity of the mind, noted by Hume, to "spread itself on external objects, and to conjoin with them any internal impressions, which they occasion."[18] The apparent simplicity and unanalyzability of the similarity and difference relationships holding between the experiences themselves cannot in the same way be explained away as an illusion, and it is thus natural to conclude that it is genuine and not merely apparent. And if similarity as a relationship between experiences is unanalyzable, it cannot be analyzed in terms of the notion of projectibility. It should be noted that this way of thinking manifests a not uncommon association of epistemological immediacy and metaphysical simplicity.

But if we reject the Goodman–Quine account of similarity, and reject projectibility as a criterion of similarity and genuineness of kinds or properties, we are left with a problem which this rejection renders insoluble. Let us say that a property is "grue-like" relative to another property if it is related to it as the "property" of being grue is related to the property of being green. Given any set of properties or features of experiences, we can define properties that are grue-like relative to them, and relative to which they in turn are grue-like. And

[18] David Hume, *A Treatise of Human Nature*, ed. by L. A. Selby-Bigge (Oxford, 1888), p. 167.

for any such set of properties we can define a relationship of similarity (or quasi-similarity) that holds between experiences to the extent that they share properties in that set. What is it that determines which of these various properties of experiences are intrinsic, that is, are such that experiences that share them are intrinsically similar, and what is it that determines which of these various relationships of similarity or quasi-similarity is genuine or intrinsic similarity? This question seems to require an answer – and if it can be answered it would seem that the relationship of experience-similarity cannot after all be unanalyzable.

At this point one may be tempted to resort to the idea that the notion of similarity of experience is an undefinable notion which one can come to understand only by being acquainted with cases in which it is instanced. This goes with the idea that this notion and also the notions of particular features that are intrinsic to experiences, could be introduced, and perhaps could *only* be introduced, by "private ostensive definition." But I think that it is precisely when we try to divorce the notion of similarity and the notion of an intrinsic feature or kind from the notions of projectibility and lawlikeness that it becomes incoherent to suppose that either these notions or the notions of particular intrinsic features or kinds could be defined ostensively. Indeed, it is precisely on the assumption that such a divorce is legitimate that intrinsic features of experience acquire the status of the beetle in Wittgenstein's box; they become irrelevant, not merely to what we can know about the minds of others, but also to what we can know about our own minds.

It should be noted to begin with that there is a special difficulty about the idea that the notion of *similarity* might be introduced by a private ostensive definition. For giving an ostensive definition of a concept seems to involve having the thought that the concept applies to the case at hand *and* to cases relevantly *similar* to it, and thus seems to require that the definer already has the notion of similarity. But let us bypass this difficulty for the moment, and consider whether concepts of particular intrinsic features of experiences can be defined ostensively on the assumption that intrinsicness does not logically involve projectibility. I should make it clear that the idea I am attacking is not the idea – which I am sure no one holds – that the intrinsic features of experiences are not projectible; it is the idea that it is at most a contingent fact that the intrinsic features of experience are projectible, and that their intrinsicness has nothing logically to do with their projectibility.

If it is logically an open question whether the intrinsic features of experiences are projectible, it is logically possible that they should not be, and it is logically possible that a given intrinsic feature should not be projectible while one that is grue-like relative to it is projectible. But suppose that I apply a predicate "P" to a given experience, intending thereby to define it as the name of one of the features of that experience, and that subsequently I apply "P" to a number of other experiences. If I do not as yet know whether the intrinsic features of experiences are projectible, can I suppose that I have succeeded in introducing "P" as the name of an intrinsic feature of experiences and that I have correctly applied it to a number of different experiences? I can perhaps suppose that it is possible that I have applied "P" only to experiences having a certain intrinsic feature – but I must allow that if I have done this then either that intrinsic feature is projectible or, if it is not, then it is to some extent an accident or coincidence that I have applied "P" only to experiences that have that feature, in which case it is not *that* feature that I have named (if I have named any). If I think that I have named some feature "P," I must presumably think that my defining procedure or ceremony, whatever it is, is capable of establishing a connection between an experience of mine having that feature and my thinking that it is right, that is, in accordance with my definition, to apply that term to it. This involves thinking that there are lawlike connections between the instantiation of that feature and other facts. In particular, it involves thinking that something like the following is a lawlike truth: if someone has defined "P" in the way I defined it, then, *ceteris paribus*, if he has any opinion at all about whether "P" applies to an experience of his, he will think that it applies if and only if the experience has the feature in question. Moreover, in order to think that it is possible to establish that a present experience shares a given feature with the past experience by reference to which I defined the predicate "P," I must suppose that the feature is one whose past instantiation can be known on the basis of memory or on the basis of inductive inference. But memory provides knowledge of past experiences only on the assumption that there are lawlike connections between certain of those features and the character of subsequent memory impressions – this is the point that the notion of memory is a causal notion. And of course it is only lawlike generalizations that can be directly supported by inductive evidence and used to license inductive inferences concerning the past. All of this indicates that the only features of experiences that I could hope to name by a private ostensive definition are projectible features, that is, those that can enter into the most basic sorts of lawlike connections. Non-projectible predicates can of course be introduced, either by disjunctive definitions like Goodman's definition of "grue" or, in some cases, by exhaustive specifications, by enumeration, of their extensions. But it would seem that the only general features which words can come to name by ostensive procedures are projectible ones. So if I have succeeded in introducing "P" as the name of some feature of experiences, the feature will be a projectible one. And if I am ignorant as to whether projectible features are intrinsic, I cannot suppose that I have named an intrinsic feature.

Nor can there be any question of my naming a feature ostensively and then finding out empirically that it is intrinsic. To begin with, in order for there to be anything for me to find out I must have some notion of what it is for a feature to be intrinsic, or, what comes to the same thing, what it is for experiences to be intrinsically similar – and of course we are assuming that I am barred from taking projectibility as a criterion of intrinsicness. If the notion of intrinsic similarity is simple and unanalyzable, the only way in which I could introduce it is by a private ostensive definition. But what I have said about ostensive definition in general applies to the special case of the definition of the relational predicate "is intrinsically similar to." If I take myself to have successfully introduced this predicate by ostensive definition, I must take *it* to be projectible – that is, I must take it as being like the projectible relational predicate "is similar in color to" and not like the nonprojectible relational predicate we would have if we defined the expression "is similar in schmolor to" as being true of pairs of things that share properties that are grue-like relative to colors (properties like Goodman's *grue* and *bleen*).[19] But in that case I cannot regard it as an open question, and as a matter for empirical investigation, whether intrinsic features – that is, features the sharing of which contributes to intrinsic similarity – are inductively projectible.

It should be remembered that what led to the attempt to divorce the notion of intrinsicness from the notion of projectibility was the fact that we have immediate awareness of what we are inclined to regard as intrinsic similarities between experiences, together with the fact that this awareness cannot be explained in the way we can explain our immediate awareness of color similarities between material objects. But this fact, when properly understood, can be seen to be incompatible with the idea to which it naturally gives rise, namely the idea that the notion of experience similarity is "simple and unanalyzable."

[19] See J. S. Ullian, "More on 'Grue' and Grue," *The Philosophical Review*, 70 (1961), 386–389. See also my "On Projecting the Unprojectible" (Essay 4).

It will be agreed to be a fact that if someone believes two of his present experiences to be phenomenally similar then, *ceteris paribus*, they will be phenomenally similar. More briefly, though perhaps misleadingly, if experiences seem phenomenally similar, then, *ceteris paribus*, they are phenomenally similar. If this were not a fact, we could not be said to have the ability to be immediately aware of similarities between experiences. But we must ask whether this fact is contingent or conceptually necessary. If it is conceptually necessary, there is a conceptual connection between experiences being similar and their seeming similar to the person who has them, and thus an internal connection between experience similarity and awareness of experience similarity – and if this is so, the notion of experience similarity cannot be a simple and unanalyzable concept. So anyone who holds that this notion *is* simple and unanalyzable will have to hold that there is only a contingent connection between experiences being similar and their seeming similar to the person who has them, as well as holding that there is only a contingent connection between intrinsic similarity of experiences and projectibility. But if someone holds *this*, he is necessarily precluded from having any reason for holding that experiences that seem similar actually are similar, or for holding any other generalization of this sort. He could not hold that he had established such a generalization inductively, for this would require that he already know something which on his own assumptions he could have no way of knowing, namely that the intrinsic features of experiences are projectible and (hence) are such that generalizations involving them are lawlike and supportable by inductive evidence. Nor, for reasons already given, would memory afford him any help. But his situation is worse than this. For his assumptions about the notion of experience similarity (call them Humean assumptions) are such as to preclude the possibility of his *having* a notion satisfying those assumptions. He holds that this notion is not analyzable or definable in terms of other concepts. Nor, on his assumptions, can it be defined ostensively – for we have just seen that it is only on the assumption that the relationship of intrinsic similarity of experience is projectible, and hence that intrinsic features of experiences are projectible, that the notion of this relationship can be introduced by private ostensive definition. So if this notion is assumed to be simple and unanalyzable, and to be such that it is logically an open question whether the relationship of experience similarity is projectible, then there is no way at all in which this notion could be introduced.

Nor – to close a final escape route – would it help to maintain that the notion of experience similarity is innate. If someone claims to have a certain notion, acquired or innate, he must surely suppose that he can know that he is applying that same notion on different occasions. And the Humean assumptions about the notion of intrinsic experience similarity preclude the possibility of anyone's knowing that he has applied this notion on two or more occasions, since, for reasons already given, neither memory nor induction could support such a knowledge claim about an indefinable concept of a relationship that cannot be assumed to be projectible. On these assumptions one cannot claim even to know that certain experiences *seem* similar, let alone that they *are* similar – since in order to know that experiences seem similar one would have to have a notion, that of experience similarity, which on these assumptions no one could have.

The upshot of all this seems to be that projectibility is as much involved in the intrinsic, phenomenal, similarity of experiences as it is in similarities in the physical world, despite the fact that our awareness of the former has a kind of immediacy that the latter never has, and despite the fact that our awareness of the former cannot be given an explanation that parallels Quine's explanation of our awareness of the latter. But we have yet to give an account of experience similarity that makes this intelligible.[20]

V

When I mentioned the inverted spectrum problem at the beginning of this essay I remarked that I can not only imagine undergoing spectrum inversion myself but can also imagine behavior that would be evidence that someone else had undergone spectrum inversion. The behavior would include the person's verbal reports, but it would also include what might be called his recognitional and discriminatory behavior; for example, if the person keeps his paper clips in a blue box on his desk and his stamps in an identically shaped yellow box, and if we see him, newly addressed envelope in hand, reaching for the blue box, this will be some evidence that blue things look to him the way yellow things did previously.[21] Those who use the possibility of inverted spectrum to support the claim that sense-experiences have phenomenal qualities that are logically independent of their typical causes and effects (and hence cannot be adequately accounted for by causal or

[20] The argument in this section was suggested by some of Wittgenstein's remarks on "private language," but I would not wish to offer it as an interpretation of his "private language argument."

[21] For a fuller discussion of how intrasubjective spectrum inversion might show itself in behavior, see Essays 9 and 14.

functional analyses of mental states) cannot afford to deny that we have this sort of access to the intrinsic, phenomenal similarity of experiences in the intrapersonal case – to do so would be to undercut the only basis there is for thinking that spectrum inversion is possible. But reflection on what is involved in our having this access to the relationship of phenomenal similarity suggests that this relationship itself can be given a causal or functional characterization.

In order to bring this out, I want to consider a fanciful hypothesis, which was suggested to me by Wittgenstein's remark that one should get rid of the idea of a private object by assuming that the object constantly changes, but that one does not notice the change because one's memory always deceives one. According to the hypothesis, the way things look to us with respect to color is constantly changing. At the end of every minute, say, one's spectrum inverts, and a minute later it inverts back again. But this is compensated for by a systematic memory falsification. At any given time one misremembers how things looked during the minute immediately preceding the most recent change, and in every alternate minute before that, in such a way that if a thing has retained the same color throughout a long interval, with the result that the way it has looked to us has been constantly changing, it seems to us, because of the memory falsification, that the way it has looked has been the same throughout.

The question of course is not whether this hypothesis is true or probable but whether it is so much as coherent. And first reactions to this question are likely to be conflicting. One may be inclined to say that it is logically absurd to suppose that someone who can recognize and distinguish things by their colors, and can be counted on to make correct color assignments and correct judgments of color similarity and difference on the basis of what he sees and remembers, is regularly mistaken in such a radical way about the character of his color experience. On the other hand, it seems at first blush that there could be evidence that the hypothesis is actually true of some sub-species of human beings. For example, we might find that people in the sub-species alternate between physiological states S_1 and S_2 at one-minute intervals, and we might have discovered that in our own case changes in these states are correlated with changes in the way things look with respect to color, and we might also find in these people some periodic change in neural patterns (or whatever) which in our own case we know to be correlated with memory contents. Evidently, then, the question of the coherence of the hypothesis is not one to be settled out of hand.

Since likenesses and differences in the ways things appear to us are supposed to hold in virtue of the intrinsic natures of the experiences we have in being appeared-to in various ways, presumably experiences have intrinsic features corresponding to the observable features of objects, its being in virtue of these features of one's experiences that an object appears to have the features it does. Experiences will not themselves be colored, for we are not thinking of them as sense-data; but we will suppose that there must be some subset of features of experiences which stand to one another in relationships of resemblance, complementarity, and so forth, analogous to those relating determinate shades of color, that is, forming a "quality space" isomorphic with the quality space of colors. Suppose, then, that there is such a set of features which is such that there is a constant and systematic change with respect to which of these features a person's experience has when he sees something of a certain color under standard viewing conditions. Let us speak of one color as the *inverse* of another if its position in the inverted spectrum corresponds to the position of the other in the ordinary spectrum, and let us assume that there is a corresponding inverse relationship which holds between the features of experiences on which depend the ways things look with respect to color. Our fanciful hypothesis will now take the form of the supposition that at any given time the seeing of things of different colors goes with the presence of correspondingly different intrinsic features in one's visual experience, but that if at a given time seeing something of a particular color involves one's experience having a given intrinsic feature, a minute later it involves one's experience having the inverse of that feature.

Supposing there to be a set of features of experiences that alternate in this way, let us call these A-features. What A-features my experience has when I am seeing something blue varies from minute to minute. But using the notion of an A-feature we can introduce the notion of another set of features, which we can call B-features. Letting "φ" be a variable ranging over A-features, we will say that a person S's visual experiences at times t_1 and t_2 have the same B-features if and only if there is a φ such that *either* (1) t_1 and t_2 are within one-minute intervals which both began either an even number or an odd number of minutes before or after a certain time T (say noon today), and S's experience had φ at both t_1 and t_2, or (2) t_1 and t_2 are within one-minute intervals one of which began an even number of minutes before or after T and the other of which began an odd number of minutes before or after T, and S's experience at t_1 had φ and his experience at t_2 had the inverse of φ. A-features and B-features are thus so related, by definition, that the B-features of someone's visual experiences over a period of time remain the same just in case the A-features are replaced by their inverses at one-minute intervals, and vice versa.

But now let us consider again the idea that it might be true of some sub-species of human beings, or perhaps even of us, that the way things look to members of that species with respect to color is constantly changing, and that this is compensated for, and goes unnoticed because of, a systematic memory falsification. We have supposed, or rather stipulated, that there is a constant and systematic change with respect to what A-features a person's experience has when he sees things of certain colors, and we can allow that this amounts to there being a sense in which the way things of certain colors look to us is constantly changing. But given that this is so, what possible reason could there be for saying that it is in *this* sense that we use "appear" and related expressions in our memory statements? Let us mark with the subscript "A" the sense of "appears" and related expressions in which sameness in the way things appear, and sameness of ways of being appeared-to, goes with sameness with respect to A-features, and let us mark with the subscript "B" another sense of these expressions in which sameness of ways of being appeared-to goes with sameness with respect to B-features. Given our supposition (or stipulation) about A-features, and what it implies about B-features (given my definition), cases in which I *think* that I am appeared-to in the same way as on a past occasion are normally cases in which I am appeared-to$_B$ in the same way as on that past occasion. Moreover, it is precisely when I am in the same state of being appeared-to$_B$ on different occasions that I am able to recognize things by their similarities with respect to color, and it is precisely when things appear$_B$ different to me that I am able to distinguish them by their differences with respect to color. Given this, there seems every reason to say, and no reason not to say, that it is sameness and difference of states of being appeared-to$_B$, not sameness and difference of states of being appeared-to$_A$, that correspond to "intrinsic" phenomenal likeness and difference of experiences. And this makes it seem totally perverse to suggest that my memories of how things of various colors appeared to me in the past are memories of how they appeared$_A$, and thus false as often as true, rather than memories of how they appeared$_B$, and so mostly true; the perversity is comparable with that of taking an ordinary person to mean by "green" what Goodman means by "grue," and judging his inductive inferences accordingly. We can tie this up with the discussion in the preceding section by saying that if someone introduced by "private ostensive definition" a name for one of the "intrinsic features" of his visual experiences, there could be no reason for saying that he had introduced it as the name of an A-feature.

Given a sense of "appear" in which it is true that the way things of certain colors appear is constantly changing, or is different in one part of the visual field than in another, we can introduce, by means of the sort of definition employed above, a sense in which this is not true; and given a sense in which it is not true, we can introduce any number of senses in which it is true. So it is really a truism that there are possible senses in which it is true and possible senses in which it is not. The important question is what determines which of these possible senses is the actual sense, the sense in which we employ the words "appear" and "look" when we say that in fact the way blue things standardly appear remains the same and that only if there occurred phenomena of a very special sort – a certain sort of temporary breakdown in recognitional and discriminatory capacities, together with appropriate verbal reports – would it be reasonable to say that there had been a change in the way blue things standardly look to someone? And my suggestion is that what singles out one of these possible senses as the actual one is its being such that it is likenesses and differences in the way things appear to someone in that sense that explains his recognitional and discriminatory abilities.

One way of putting this view is to say that the notion of similarity of experience must be understood in terms of the more fundamental notion of experience *of* similarity, and, likewise, that the notion of dissimilarity of experience must be understood in terms of the notion of experience of dissimilarity. Thus we might say, as a first approximation, that experiences are similar if they jointly yield awareness of similarity, or, better, that they are similar if they would yield awareness of similarity if they were "co-conscious," that is, conscious to a person at the same time, where an experience counts as conscious to a person when he correctly remembers it as well as when he is actually having it. This account would of course be circular if the only similarities of which awareness is yielded were similarities between the experiences themselves – we would then be saying that what it means to say that experiences are similar is that they yield or tend to yield awareness of the similarity of those very experiences. The account will not be circular, however, if the similarity referred to in the *analysans* is, or includes, similarity of something other than experiences. So it is a possible view, and I think basically a correct one, that what it means to say that experiences are phenomenally similar is that they stand in a relation which is such that if two experiences are related by that relation, and are co-conscious, their joint occurrence yields, or tends to yield, awareness of similarities holding between material things, namely similarities with respect to their perceptible or observable qualities, the latter application of the notion of similarity, namely to material things, being explicable in terms of the Goodman–Quine account as involving projectibility and lawlikeness.

Phrases like "experience of similarity" must here be understood intentionally. For there to be similarity of experience, and so experience of similarity, there need not be an objective similarity in the world that is veridically perceived; it is enough if it looks as if, or sounds as if, or feels as if there were such an objective similarity, or that it would look, sound or feel this way if the experiences were co-conscious. On this view the connection between similarity of experience and projectibility and lawlikeness is rather complex. On the one hand it can be seen as an intentional connection; similar experiences are, when co-conscious, jointly *of* objective similarities which may or may not actually exist in the world but whose actual existence would involve the sharing of projectible properties. But in virtue of this connection, similarities between experiences, and the features in virtue of which they hold, are themselves projectible. Indeed, something stronger than projectibility is involved here. To say that features and relationships are projectible is not to say that they actually are connected in a lawlike way with other features; generalizations involving such features and relationships are lawlike in the sense that they would be confirmed by positive instances, but this is not to say that any such generalization is actually confirmed to any extent, or that any such generalization is actually true. But given the proposed account of similarity of experience, it appears that there must actually be lawlike connections between experience similarity and other states of affairs. Specifically, there must be a lawlike connection between a person's having phenomenally similar experiences and his believing that there exist, and that he is perceiving, objective similarities in the world, and likewise, there must be a lawlike connection between a person's having phenomenally different experiences and his believing, or tending to believe, that there exist, and that he is perceiving, objective differences in the world. This does not mean that, for example, whenever similar experiences are co-conscious there results a belief in objective similarity; rather, we can say that co-conscious experiences that are phenomenally similar *tend* to bring about such beliefs, and do so in the absence of "countervailing" factors.[22]

VI

But where does this leave our awareness of similarity and difference of experience? How does defining phenomenal similarity and difference of experience in terms of their causal role in awareness of objective similarities and differences explain our awareness of phenomenal similarities and differences themselves? To this question I have no fully satisfactory answer, and certainly none that I can give briefly. What I wish to contend is, to speak both vaguely and metaphorically, that our ability to be aware of experience similarities is implicit in, and is a sort of shadow or reflection of, our ability to be perceptually aware of objective similarities in nature. A crucial point here is that while there are ways in which a man or animal may fail to be aware of experiences he has, none of these is analogous to blindness. If, as I suppose, we are disposed to deny that dogs are aware of their experiences, this is not because we think that dogs lack an inner sense that we possess, but because we think that they lack concepts that such awareness would require. It makes no sense, I think, to suppose that there might be a creature of human intelligence who has these concepts, and who has

---

[22] When I read this paper in Mexico City, Mr. Gareth Evans pointed out in the discussion that there is an apparent circularity in this account. Since any two objects will be similar in some respect or other, and since any reflective person knows and believes this, we can hardly characterize the belief to which similar experiences give rise as simply the belief that the perceived objects are similar in some respect or other. But (so the objection runs) any characterization of the belief which is more specific is bound to bring in reference to perception, and, ultimately, to similarity of perceptual experiences. Thus we might characterize the belief as the belief that two objects are similar with respect to their perceptible properties. But what is a perceptible property, if not one whose instantiations tend to give rise to similar experiences in perceivers? Or one could perhaps characterize the belief as the belief that there is a similarity between the objects which accounts for the relation between the experiences of them – and what is the relevant relation between the experiences, if not their similarity? (This formulation of the objection is mine, and may distort what Evans had in mind.) I agree that the characterization of the belief is bound to bring in, eventually, reference to perception and perceptual experiences – indeed, this is closely connected with the essential "reflexivity" of perceptual awareness which I briefly discuss in section VI. But it is not clear to me that it will have to bring in reference to phenomenal similarity of experiences. Suppose we characterize the belief as the belief that there is a similarity between the objects which accounts for the relation between the experiences

perceptual experiences by means of which he perceives objective states of affairs, but who differs from us in lacking the ability to be aware of these experiences and of relations of similarity and difference between them. But this, I think, is to be explained in terms of what is involved in perceptual awareness of objective states of affairs. The propositional content of a perceptual awareness always involves a token reflexive element and, implicitly, a reference to the perceiver and his experiences. How this content should be articulated depends on the conceptual sophistication of the creature doing the perceiving. At a relatively primitive level the content might be expressed in some such words as "Tree here now." But for a creature who has the concept of himself, and the concept of seeing, a more adequate expression would be "I see a tree in front of me." This might be put by saying that in perceiving something to be the case one is (given human intelligence and conceptual ability) at least potentially aware that one perceives it to be the case. Here again no analogue to blindness is possible. It is not by an inner sense, which I might have lacked without lacking the ability to see, that I am aware that I see. It would scarcely be intelligible for someone to say "I know that there is a tree in front of me, but I have no idea whether I see a tree in front of me." But if seeing involves having visual experiences, then the ability to be aware that one sees, which is (I have claimed) involved in the ability to see, involves the ability to be aware of one's visual experiences. And I would hope to be able to show that the ability to be aware, in the

of them. While this relation will be, or include, their phenomenal similarity, it is not clear why this fact must be mentioned in the analysis. Again, while it may be necessarily true that instantiations of perceptible properties tend to give rise to similar experiences in appropriately located observers, it does not obviously follow that we cannot explain the notion of a perceptible property without explicitly invoking the notion of phenomenal similarity of experience.

But I would not be surprised if it could be shown that the circularity is unavoidable. For I think it is true in general that philosophical "analyses" of central concepts (causality, substance, property, etc.) are bound to be circular in this way, and that such circularity is not necessarily a defect. I cannot say in general what distinguishes "vicious" from "virtuous" circularity; but I think that I can sometimes tell the difference in particular cases. (There is an obvious difference between my account and the blatantly circular account which says that experiences are similar if they tend to give rise to the belief that they are similar. In both cases (let us suppose) the notion being analysed is invoked in the *analysans*. But in my account various other concepts are invoked as well, whereas in the other the only other concept that is invoked is the concept of belief – and there is something peculiarly unacceptable about any account that purports to explicate the notion of P's being the case in terms of the notion of someone's believing P to be the case.)

required sense, of perceptual experiences involves the ability to be aware of phenomenal similarities and differences between these experiences. But that, and the elaboration of the account crudely sketched in these last few pages, is a matter for another paper.

9

Functionalism and qualia

I

In their paper "What Psychological States are Not" N. J. Block and J. A. Fodor raise a number of objections to the 'functional state identity theory' (FSIT), which says that "for any organism that satisfies psychological predicates at all, there exists a unique best *description* such that each psychological state of the organism is identical with one of its machine states relative to that description."[1] FSIT is a version of 'functionalism,' which they characterize as the more general doctrine that "the type-identity conditions for psychological states refer only to their relations to inputs, outputs, and one another."[2] Most of the objections Block and Fodor raise they take to be objections only to FSIT, and not to functionalism more broadly construed. I shall not be concerned with these objections here. But they raise one objection which, they say, "might be taken to show that psychological states cannot be functionally defined *at all* and that they cannot be put into correspondence with *any* properties definable over abstract automata."[3] Briefly put, the objection is that the way of 'type-identifying' psychological states proposed by FSIT, and by functionalism generally, "fails to accommodate a feature of at least some such states that is critical for determining their type: namely their 'qualitative' character."[4]

Block and Fodor devote only a couple of pages to this objection, and raise it in a fairly tentative way; so it is quite likely that the length of my discussion of it here is disproportionate to the importance they put on it. But they have given a concise and vivid formulation to an objection which is felt, and voiced in conversation, more often than it is expressed in print, and which seems to me to raise fundamental issues. Other philosophers have raised much the same objection by saying that functionalism (or behaviorism, or materialism, or 'causal' theories of the mind – the objection has been made against all of these)

---

[1] N. J. Block and J. A. Fodor, "What Psychological States are Not," *The Philosophical Review*, 81 (1972), p. 165.   [2] *Ibid.*, p. 173.
[3] *Ibid.*, pp. 173–174.   [4] *Ibid.*, p. 172.

cannot account for the 'raw feel' component of mental states, or for their 'internal,' or 'phenomenological,' character. My primary concern here is not with whether this objection is fatal to FSIT; if I understand that theory correctly, it is sufficiently refuted by the other objections Block and Fodor raise against it. But as they characterize functionalism 'in the broad sense,' it is, while vague, a view which many philosophers, myself included, find attractive; and it seems to me worth considering whether it can be defended against this objection.

I shall follow Block and Fodor in speaking of mental states (or rather, of some mental states) as having 'qualitative character(s)' or 'qualitative content.' I hope that it will emerge in the ensuing discussion that this does not commit me to anything which a clear headed opponent of 'private objects,' or of 'private language,' should find objectionable.

II

Block and Fodor develop their objection in two stages. The first of these they call the 'inverted qualia argument,' and the second can be called the 'absent qualia argument.'

Because they are unpersuaded by the familiar 'verificationist' arguments against the conceptual coherence of the 'inverted spectrum hypothesis,' Block and Fodor are inclined to think that cases of 'inverted qualia' may be possible. They take it that there would be qualia inversion (presumably an extreme case of it) if it were true that "every person does, in fact, have slightly different qualia (or, better still, grossly different qualia) when in whatever machine table state is alleged to be identical to pain."[5] The possibility of this is incompatible with functionalism on the plausible assumption that "nothing would be a token of the type 'pain state' unless it felt like a pain, . . . even if it were connected to all of the other psychological states of the organism in whatever ways pains are."[6]

[5] *Ibid.*, p. 173.
[6] *Ibid.*, p. 172. It is worth noting that this assumption, or one very much like it, plays a crucial role in Saul Kripke's recent arguments against the psychophysical identity theory; Kripke expresses it by saying that pain "is not picked out by one of its accidental properties; rather it is picked out by the property of being pain itself, by its immediate phenomenological quality. Thus pain . . . is not rigidly designated by 'pain' but the reference of the designator is determined by an essential property of the referent"; "Naming and Necessity," in D. Davidson and G. Harman (eds.), *Semantics of Natural Language* (Dordrecht, Netherlands, 1972), p. 340.

Block and Fodor do not regard the possibility of qualia inversion as constituting by itself a decisive objection to functionalism, for they think that it may be open to the functionalist to deny the *prima facie* plausible assumption that pains must be qualitatively similar (and, presumably, the related assumption that anything qualitatively identical to a pain is itself a pain).[7] If qualia inversion actually occurred in the case of pain (i.e., if a state functionally identical to a pain differed from it in qualitative character), then, they say, "it might be reasonable to say that the character of an organism's qualia is irrelevant to whether it is in pain or (equivalently) that pains feel quite different to different organisms."[8] Such a view is not in fact unheard of. According to Don Locke, "A sensation's being a pain sensation is not a matter of how it feels, but a matter of its being of the sort caused by bodily damage and leading to pain behavior."[9] And Alan Donagan has attributed to Wittgenstein the view that

you and I correctly say that we have the same sensation, say toothache, if we both have something frightful that we would naturally express by holding and rubbing our jaws, by certain kinds of grimace, and the like. Whether the internal character of what is expressed in these ways is the same for you as for me is irrelevant to the meaning of the word 'toothache.'[10]

But while Block and Fodor do not dismiss this response to the inverted qualia argument as obviously mistaken, they see it as possibly opening the door to an argument much more damaging to functional-

---

[7] Block and Fodor mention another way, besides that mentioned in the text, in which a functionalist might try to meet the inverted qualia argument; he might maintain that "though inverted qualia, *if they occurred*, would provide counter-examples to his theory, as a matter of nomological fact it is impossible that functionally identical psychological states should be qualitatively distinct" (p. 172). The thought here must be that the mere logical, or conceptual, possibility of qualia inversion is not incompatible with functionalism. It would seem, however, that if the actual occurrence of inverted qualia would provide counterexamples to functionalism (as the envisioned reply concedes), then the mere logical possibility of inverted qualia is incompatible with functionalism; pain cannot be *identical* with a given functional state if there is a possible world, even a logically but not nomologically possible world, in which the functional state exists without pain existing, or vice versa. (On the general claim about identity here being invoked, namely that if *a* and *b* are identical they must be identical in any logically possible world in which either exists, see Kripke's "Naming and Necessity," already cited, and his "Identity and Necessity," in Milton K. Munitz (ed.), *Identity and Individuation* (New York, 1971).
[8] Block and Fodor, "What Psychological States are Not," p. 173.
[9] Don Locke, *Myself and Others* (Oxford, 1968), p. 101.
[10] Alan Donagan, "Wittgenstein on Sensation," in G. Pitcher (ed.), *Wittgenstein: The Philosophical Investigations* (Garden City, N.Y., 1966).

ism, namely the *absent* qualia argument. Their thought may be that once it is admitted that a given functional state can exist without having a given 'qualitative content,' it will be difficult to deny the possibility that it might exist without having any qualitative content (or character) at all. At any rate, they go on to say that

For all that we know, it may be nomologically possible for two psychological states to be functionally identical (that is, to be identically connected with inputs, outputs, and successor states), even if only one of the states has a qualitative content. In this case, FSIT would require us to say that an organism might be in pain even though it is feeling *nothing at all*, and this consequence seems totally unacceptable.[11]

And if cases of 'absent qualia' are possible, i.e., if a state can be functionally identical to a state having a qualitative character without itself having a qualitative content, then not only FSIT, but also functionalism in the broad sense, would seem to be untenable.

III

If mental states can be alike or different in 'qualitative character,' we should be able to speak of a class of states, call them 'qualitative states,' whose 'type-identity conditions' could be specified in terms of the notion of qualitative (or 'phenomenological') similarity. For each determinate qualitative character a state can have, there is (i.e., we can define) a determinate qualitative state which a person has just in case he has a state having precisely that qualitative character. For example, there is a qualitative state someone has just in case he has a sensation that feels the way my most recent headache felt. Now, qualitative states will themselves be 'mental' or 'psychological' states. And this calls into question the suggestion by Block and Fodor that a functionalist could deal with the 'inverted qualia argument' by maintaining that "the character of an organism's qualia is irrelevant to whether it is in pain." If mental states include qualitative states, what such a functionalist says about pain could not be said about mental states generally, since it would be self-contradictory to say that the character of an organism's qualia is irrelevant to what qualitative states it has. And of course, if qualitative states themselves could be functionally defined, then the possibility of qualia inversion would pose no difficulty for functionalism, and the functionalist would have no need to make the counterintuitive denial that the character of an

[11] Block and Fodor, "What Psychological States are Not," p. 173.

organism's qualia is relevant to whether it is in pain. But if, as Block and Fodor apparently assume, qualitative states cannot be functionally defined, then there is one class of mental states, namely the qualitative states themselves, that cannot be functionally defined.

This raises questions which I shall return to in later sections, namely (a) in what sense are qualitative states not functionally definable (or, in what sense are they not functionally definable if qualia inversion is possible), and (b) is their being functionally undefinable (in whatever sense they are) seriously damaging to functionalism? As we shall see in the remainder of the present section, this question is also raised by a consideration of the alleged possibility of 'absent qualia.'

We can establish the impossibility of cases of 'absent qualia' if we can show that if a state is functionally identical to a state having qualitative content then it must itself have qualitative content. One might try to do this by construing the notion of functional identity in such a way that qualitative states are included among the 'other psychological states' by relation to which, along with input and output, the 'type-identity' of a given psychological state is to be defined. Thus one might argue that if a given psychological state has a certain qualitative character, this involves its standing in some determinate relationship to some particular qualitative state (namely the qualitative state a person is in just in case he is in a state having that qualitative character), and that any state functionally identical to it must stand in the same relationship to that qualitative state, and so must have the same qualitative character.[12] But this argument is not very convincing. One objection to it is that since qualitative states cannot themselves be functionally defined (assuming the possibility of *inverted* qualia), it is illegitimate to include them among the psychological states by reference to which other psychological states are functionally defined, or in terms of which 'functional identity' is defined. I shall return to this objection later, since it is also a *prima*

---

[12] Just what is the relationship that a state must have to a qualitative state in order to have the qualitative character corresponding to that state? It cannot be, in the cases that concern us, the relationship of identity (that would permit only qualitative states to have qualitative character, and would not permit us to speak of the qualitative character of states whose 'type-identity' conditions are given in functional terms). And presumably it must be something stronger than the relationship 'is accompanied by,' or 'is coinstantiated with.' The best I can do is to say that a particular token of a state *S* had the qualitative character corresponding to qualitative state *Q* if on the occasion in question the tokening (instantiation) of *S* essentially involved the tokening (instantiation) of *Q*. Possibly, but I am not sure of this, we could strengthen this, and make it less vague, by saying that on such occasions the token of *S* *is* a token of *Q*.

facie objection against the more plausible argument I shall present next. Another objection is that the relationship which a state has to a qualitative state, in having the 'qualitative character' corresponding to that qualitative state, is not anything like a causal relationship and so is not the sort of relationship in terms of which a psychological state can be functionally defined. But the argument I shall present next is not open to this objection, and does seem to me to show that on any plausible construal of the notion of functional identity a state cannot be functionally identical to a state having qualitative character without itself having qualitative character.

One important way in which pains are related to other psychological states is that they give rise, under appropriate circumstances, to introspective awareness of themselves as having certain qualitative characters, i.e., as feeling certain ways. I shall assume that the meaning of this can be partially unpacked by saying that being in pain typically gives rise, given appropriate circumstances, to what I shall call a 'qualitative belief,' i.e., a belief to the effect that one feels a certain way (or, more abstractly, that one is in a state having a certain qualitative character, or, in still other terms, that one has a certain qualitative state). Any state functionally identical to a pain state will share with the pain state not only (1) its tendency to influence overt behavior in certain ways, and (2) its tendency to produce in the person the belief that there is something organically wrong with him (e.g., that he has been cut or burnt), but also (3) its tendency to produce qualitative beliefs in the person, i.e., to make him think that he has a pain having a certain qualitative character (one that he dislikes). According to the 'absent qualia argument,' such a state may nevertheless lack qualitative character, and so fail to be a pain. Let us consider whether this is plausible.

Supposing such cases of 'absent qualia' are possible, how might we detect such a case if it occurred? And with what right does each of us reject the suggestion that perhaps his own case is such a case, and that he himself is devoid of states having qualitative character? Indeed, with what right do we reject the suggestion that perhaps no one ever has any feelings (or other states having qualitative character) at all? It is, of course, a familiar idea that behavior provides inconclusive evidence as to what qualitative character, if any, a man's mental states have. But what usually underlies this is the idea that the man himself has a more 'direct' access to this qualitative character than behavior can possibly provide, namely introspection. And introspection, whatever else it is, is the link between a man's mental states and his beliefs about (or his knowledge or awareness of) those states. So one way of putting our question is to ask whether anything could be evidence (for anyone) that someone was not in pain, given that it follows from the states he is in, plus the psychological laws that are true of him (the laws which describe the relationships of his states to one another and to input and output), that the totality of possible behavioral evidence *plus* the totality of possible introspective evidence points unambiguously to the conclusion that he is in pain? I do not see how anything could be. To be sure, we can imagine (perhaps) that 'cerebroscopes' reveal that the person is not in some neurophysiological state that we ourselves are always in when we are (so we think) in pain. But this simply raises the question, on what basis can we say that *we* have genuine pain (i.e., a state having a qualitative character as well as playing the appropriate functional role in its relationships to input, output, and other psychological states)? Here it seems that if the behavioral and introspective evidence are not enough, nothing could be enough. But if they are enough in the case of us, they are enough in the case of our hypothetical man. In any event, if we are given that a man's state is functionally identical with a state that in us is pain, it is hard to see how a physiological difference between him and us could be any evidence at all that his states lack qualitative character; for if anything can be evidence for us about his psychological state, the evidence that his state is functionally equivalent to ours is ipso facto evidence that any physiological difference between us and him is irrelevant to whether, although not to how, the state of pain is realized in him.

To hold that it is logically possible (or, worse, nomologically possible) that a state lacking qualitative character should be functionally identical to a state having qualitative character is to make qualitative character irrelevant both to what we can take ourselves to know in knowing about the mental states of others and also to what we can take ourselves to know in knowing about our own mental states. There could (on this view) be no possible physical effects of any state from which we could argue by an 'inference to the best explanation' that it has qualitative character; for if there were, we could give at least a partial functional characterization of the having of qualitative character by saying that it tends to give rise, in such and such circumstances, to those physical effects, and could not allow that a state lacking qualitative character could be functionally identical to a state having it. And for reasons already given, if cases of 'absent qualia' were possible, qualitative character would be necessarily inaccessible to introspection. If qualitative character were something that is irrelevant in this way to all knowledge of minds, self-knowledge as well as knowledge of others, it would not be at all 'unacceptable,' but would instead be just good sense, to deny that pains must have qualitative character. But of course it is absurd to suppose that ordinary people are talking about something that is in principle unknowable by anyone when they talk about how they feel, or about how things look, smell, sound, etc. to them. (Indeed, just as a causal theory of knowledge would imply that states or features that are independent of the causal powers of the things they characterize would be in principle unknowable, so a causal theory of reference would imply that such states and features are in principle unnamable and inaccessible to reference.) And if, to return to sanity, we take qualitative character to be something that can be known in the ways we take human feelings to be knowable (at a minimum, if it can be known introspectively), then it is not possible, not even logically possible, for a state that lacks qualitative character to be functionally identical to a state that has it.

This is not a 'verificationist' argument. It does not assume any general connection between meaningfulness and verifiability (or knowability). What it does assume is that if there is to be any reason for supposing (as the 'absent qualia argument' does) that it is essential to pain and other mental states that they have 'qualitative character,' then we must take 'qualitative character' to refer to something which is knowable in at least some of the ways in which we take pains (our own and those of others) to be knowable. It also assumes that if there could be a feature of some mental state that was entirely independent of the causal powers of the state (i.e., was such that its presence or absence would make no difference to the state's tendencies to bring about other states, and so forth), and so was irrelevant to its 'functional identity,' then such a feature would be totally unknowable (if you like, this assumes a causal theory of knowledge).

Against this argument, as against an earlier one, it may be objected that the other psychological states by relation to which (along with inputs and outputs) a given psychological state is functionally defined must not include any states that cannot themselves be functionally defined. For, it may be said, the states I have called 'qualitative beliefs' can no more be functionally defined than can qualitative states themselves. The most important relationship of these states to other states would appear to be their relationship to the qualitative states that characteristically give rise to them, yet (so the argument goes) the latter cannot be functionally defined and so cannot legitimately be referred to in functional definitions of the former. Moreover (remembering that the possibility of cases of *inverted* qualia is not here being questioned), it seems plausible to suppose that if two people differed in the qualitative character of their pains, but in such a way that the difference would not be revealed in any possible behavior, then they would also differ in their qualitative beliefs, and this latter difference too would be such that its existence could not be revealed in any possible behavior. And if this is possible, there seems as much reason to deny that qualitative beliefs are capable of functional definition as there is to deny that qualitative states are capable of functional definition.

This objection does not touch one important point implicit in my argument, namely that we cannot deny, without being committed to an intolerable skepticism about the pains of others, that someone's saying that he feels a sharp pain is good evidence that he has some qualitative state or other, and is so because someone's saying this is, normally, an *effect* of his having a state having qualitative character – and this by itself strongly suggests that if a mental state of one person has qualitative character, and if an otherwise similar state of another person lacks qualitative character, then the states differ in the ways they tend to influence behavior ('output') and hence differ function-ally. Still, the possibility of 'inverted qualia' does seem to imply that qualitative states, and hence qualitative beliefs, cannot be functionally defined. To see whether this is compatible with functionalism, and whether it undercuts the argument given above, we need to consider in what sense it is true that qualitative states (and qualitative beliefs) are not functionally definable, and what limits there are on the ways in which reference to mental states that are not functionally definable can enter into functional definitions of other mental states.

In order to consider these questions I wish to change examples, and shift our consideration from the case of pain to that of visual experience. There are two reasons why such a shift is desirable. First, the possibility of 'spectrum inversion' (one person's experience of colors differing systematically, in its qualitative or phenomenological character, from another person's experience of the same colors) seems to me far less problematical than the possibility of 'qualia inversion' in the case of pain (pain feeling radically different to different persons). Second, and related to this, it is much easier to distinguish seeing blue (for example) from its qualitative character than it is to distinguish pain from its qualitative character, and accordingly much easier to consider how reference to qualitative states might enter into a functional account of seeing colors than it is to consider how reference to such states might enter into a functional account of pain.

IV

If I see something, it looks somehow to me, and the way it looks resembles and differs from, in varying degrees and various respects, the ways other things look to me or have looked to me on other occasions. It is because similarities and differences between these 'ways of being appeared to' correlate in systematic ways with similarities and differences between seen objects that we are able to see these objects and the properties of them in virtue of which the similarities and differences obtain.[13] Being appeared-to in a certain way, e.g., things looking to one the way things now look to me as I stare out my window, I take to be a qualitative state. So seeing essentially involves the occurrence of qualitative states. Moreover, reference to these qualitative states enters into what looks very much like a functional account of seeing. For it would seem that what it means to say that someone sees something to be blue is something like the following:

S sees something to be blue if and only if (1) S has a repertoire of qualitative states which includes a set of states K which are associated with the colors of objects in such a way that (a) visual stimulation by an object of a certain color under 'standard conditions' produces in the person the associated qualitative state, and (b) the degrees of 'qualitative' or 'phenomenological' similarity between the states in K correspond to the degrees of similarity between the associated colors, and (2) person S (a) is at present in the qualitative state associated with the color blue (b) is so as the result of visual stimulation by something blue and (c) believes, because of (a) and (b) that there is something blue before him.[14]

I must now qualify the assertion that 'being appeared-to' in a certain way is a qualitative state. If asked to describe how he is appeared-to, or, more naturally, how things look to him, a man might say, among other things, that a certain object looks blue to him, or that it looks to him as if he were seeing something blue, or (if he is a philosopher who speaks the 'language of appearing') that he is

[13] The 'being appeared-to' terminology I take from Roderick Chisholm; see his " 'Appear,' 'Take,' and 'Evident,' " in R. J. Swartz (ed.), *Perceiving, Sensing and Knowing* (Garden City, N.Y., 1965), especially p. 480, footnote 6. One is 'appeared-to' both in cases of veridical perception and in cases of illusion and hallucination, and can be appeared-to in the same ways in all of these sorts of cases. The technical locution 'appeared-blue-to' is used in the text as an abbreviation for the locution 'sees or seems to see something blue' (on a 'nonepistemic' understanding of that locution).

[14] As an analysis this will not quite do. I can see something to be blue even though it looks green (i.e., even if my visual qualitative state is that associated with green), if I have been 'tipped off' that in these circumstances blue things look green.

'appeared-blue-to.' And it is natural to make it a condition of someone's being appeared-blue-to that he be in the qualitative state that is, in him at that time, associated with visual stimulation by blue things; that is, it is natural to give an analysis of 'S is appeared-blue-to' which is the same as the above analysis of 'S sees something to be blue' except that clauses (b) and (c) of condition (2) are deleted. But if we do this, then being appeared-blue-to will not itself be a qualitative state. Or at any rate, this will be so if spectrum inversion is possible. We might sum up the situation by saying that being appeared-blue-to is, on the proposed analysis, a functional state whose functional characterization requires it always to have some qualitative character (or other) but does not require it to have the same qualitative character in different persons (assuming the possibility of intersubjective spectrum inversion) or in the same person at different times (assuming the possibility of intrasubjective spectrum inversion). But this raises again the question of whether qualitative states are themselves functionally definable and, if they are not, whether they can legitimately be referred to in functional characterizations of other mental states.

The expression 'appeared-blue-to' could, I think, have a use in which it would stand for a qualitative state. I could 'fix the reference' of this expression by stipulating that it refers to (or, since it is a predicate rather than a singular term, that it predicates or ascribes) that qualitative state which is at the present time (April 1974) associated in me with the seeing of blue things.[15] Understanding the expression in this way, if I underwent spectrum inversion tomorrow it would cease to be the case that I am normally appeared-blue-to when I see blue things, and might become the case that I am normally appeared-yellow-to on such occasions.[16] (By contrast, in the 'func-

[15] I take the notion of 'reference fixing' and the notion of a 'rigid designator' employed below, from Saul Kripke; see his "Naming and Necessity," pp. 269–275 and *passim*. The use of a definite description 'the x such that Fx' to 'fix the reference' of a term T contrasts with defining T as equivalent in meaning to, i.e., as an abbreviation of, the definite description; in the former case, but not in the latter, the statement 'if T exists, then T is the x such that Fx' will be contingently rather than necessarily true. An expression is a rigid designator if it designates the same object in all possible worlds (or in all possible worlds in which it designates anything). According to Kripke, ordinary names are rigid designators, while many definite descriptions are not. When a definite description is used to introduce a name (and hence a rigid designator), it is used to 'fix its reference' rather than to 'define' it or give its 'meaning.'

[16] My distinction between the 'functional' sense of 'appeared-blue-to' and a (possible) sense in which it rigidly designates (or, better, rigidly predicates) a qualitative state is similar to Chisholm's distinction between the 'comparative' and 'noncomparative' senses of expressions like 'looks blue.' See his *Perceiving: A Philosophical Study* (Ithaca, N.Y., 1957), ch. 4.

tional' sense of 'appeared-blue-to' sketched above, it could be true before and after intrasubjective spectrum inversion that I am normally appeared-blue-to when I see blue things, although of course being appeared-blue-to would have the qualitative character at the later time which another visual state, say, being appeared-yellow-to, had at the earlier time.) I do not think that there would be much utility in having expressions that were, in this way, 'rigid designators' (or 'rigid predicators') of visual qualia. On the other hand, I see no reason in principle why we could not have them. But if we did have them, they could not be functionally defined. Such terms would have to be introduced by Kripkean 'reference fixing' or (what is a special case of this) ostensive definition. To be sure, there is the theoretical possibility of giving a verbal definition of one of these expressions by making use of other expressions of the same sort; just as I might define 'blue' by means of a description of the form 'the color that is not yellow, or red, or green . . . etc.,' so I might define 'being appeared-blue-to' as equivalent to a description of the form 'the color qualia which is neither being appeared-yellow-to, nor being appeared-red-to, nor being appeared-green-to, . . . etc.' But this is of very little interest, since it is obviously impossible that names (or predicates) for all visual qualia should be defined in this way without circularity. So, assuming that talk of defining functional states is equivalent to talk of defining names or 'rigid designators' for qualitative states, there seems to be a good sense in which qualitative states cannot be functionally defined.

But what seems to force us to this conclusion is the seeming possibility of spectrum inversion. I think that what (if anything) forces us to admit the possibility of spectrum inversion is the seeming conceivability and detectability of *intra*subjective spectrum inversion. And if we reflect on the latter, we will see, I believe, that while we cannot functionally define particular qualitative states, there is a sense in which we can functionally define the *class* of qualitative states – we can functionally define the identity conditions for members of this class, for we can functionally define the relationships of qualitative (phenomenological) similarity and difference. This is what I shall argue in the following section.

V

Taken one way, the claim that spectrum inversion is possible implies a claim that may, for all I know, be empirically false, namely that there is a way of mapping determinate shades of color onto determinate shades of color which is such that (1) every determinate shade (including 'muddy' and unsaturated colors as well as the pure spectral colors) is mapped onto some determinate shade, (2) at least some of the shades are mapped onto shades other than themselves, (3) the mapping preserves, for any normally sighted person, all of the 'distance' and 'betweenness' relationships between the colors (so that if shades *a, b* and *c* are mapped onto shades *d, e* and *f*, respectively, then a normally sighted person will make the same judgments of comparative similarity about *a* in relation to *b* and *c* as about *d* in relation to *e* and *f*), and (4) the mapping preserves all of our intuitions, except those that are empirically conditioned by knowledge of the mixing properties of pigments and the like, about which shades are 'pure' colors and which have other colors 'in' them (so that, for example, if shades *a* and *b* are mapped onto shades of orange and red, respectively, we will be inclined to say that *a* is less pure than *b* and perhaps that it has *b* in it). But even if our color experience is not in fact such that a mapping of this sort is possible, it seems to me conceivable that it might have been – and that is what matters for our present philosophical purposes.[17] For example, I think we know well enough what it would be like to see the world nonchromatically, i.e., in black, white, and the various shades of grey – for we frequently do see it in this way in photographs, moving pictures, and television. And there is an obvious mapping of the nonchromatic shades onto each other which satisfies the conditions for inversion. In the discussion that follows I shall assume, for convenience, that such a mapping is possible for the full range of colors – but I do not think that anything essential turns on whether this assumption is correct.

Supposing that there is such a mapping (and, a further assumption of convenience, that there is only one), let us call the shade onto which each shade is mapped the 'inverse' of that shade. We will have *inter*subjective spectrum inversion if the way each shade of color looks to one person is the way its inverse looks to another person, or, in other words, if for each shade of color the qualitative state associated in one person with the seeing of that shade is associated in another

---

[17] In a book which came to my attention after this essay was written (*Form and Content*, Oxford, 1973), Bernard Harrison presents empirical evidence against the possibility of what I am calling spectrum inversion. He also tries to show on a priori grounds – and here I find him much less convincing – that "the linguistic and conceptual machinery which governs colour naming works in such a way that any difference in the perceived content of the colour presentations seen by different speakers must show itself in differences in the way in which they apply colour names, or in the privileges of occurrence in sentential contexts which colour names display in their discourse" (p. 133).

person with the seeing of the inverse of that shade. And we will have *intra*subjective spectrum inversion if there is a change in the way the various shades of color look to someone, each coming to look the way its inverse previously looked.

What strikes us most about spectrum inversion is that if it can occur *inter*subjectively there would appear to be no way of telling whether the color experience of two persons is the same or whether their color spectra are inverted relative to each other. The systematic difference between experiences in which intersubjective spectrum inversion would consist would of course not be open to anyone's introspection. And there would appear to be no way in which these differences could manifest themselves in behavior – the hypothesis that your spectrum is inverted relative to mine and the hypothesis that our color experience is the same seem to give rise to the same predictions about our behavior. Here, of course, we have in mind the hypothetical case in which the various colors have always looked one way to one person and a different way to another person. And the situation seems very different when we consider the case of *intra*subjective spectrum inversion. In the first place, it seems that such a change would reveal itself to the introspection, or introspection *cum* memory, of the person in whom it occurred. But if this is so, other persons could learn of it through that person's reports. Moreover, and this is less often noticed, there is non-verbal behavior, as well as verbal behavior, that could indicate such a change. If an animal has been trained to respond in specific ways to objects of certain colors, and then begins, spontaneously, to respond in those ways to things of the inverse colors, and if it shows surprise that its responses are no longer rewarded in the accustomed ways, this will surely be some evidence that it has undergone spectrum inversion. In the case of a person we could have a combination of this sort of evidence and the evidence of the person's testimony.[18]

If we did not think that we could have these kinds of evidence of intrasubjective spectrum inversion, I think we would have no reason at all for thinking that spectrum inversion of any sort, intrasubjective or intersubjective, is even logically possible. To claim that spectrum inversion is possible but that it is undetectable even in the intrasubjective case would be to sever the connection we suppose to hold between qualitative states and introspective awareness of them (between them and the qualitative beliefs to which they give rise), and also their connections to perceptual beliefs about the world and, *via* these

---

[18] See Essay 15, section II; the example used there was originally presented in a footnote to this essay.

beliefs, to behavior. No doubt one could so *define* the term 'qualitative state' as to make it inessential to qualitative states that they have these sorts of connections. But then it would not be in virtue of similarities and differences between 'qualitative states' (in that defined sense) that things look similar and different to people, and the hypothesis that people differ radically in what 'qualitative states' they have when they see things of various colors would be of no philosophical interest, and would not be the 'inverted spectrum hypothesis' as usually under-stood. Indeed, the supposition that intrasubjective spectrum inversion could occur, but would be undetectable, is incoherent in much the same way as the 'absent qualia hypothesis,' i.e., the supposition that states 'functionally identical' to states having qualitative content might themselves lack qualitative content. Neither supposition makes sense unless the crucial notions in them are implicitly defined, or redefined, so as to make the supposition empty or uninteresting.

But what, then, are we supposing about qualitative states, and about the relationships of qualitative or phenomenological similarity and difference between these states, in supposing that intrapersonal spectrum inversion *would* be detectable? In what follows I shall speak of token qualitative states as 'experiences,' and will say that experiences are 'co-conscious' if they are conscious to a person at the same time, where an experience counts as conscious to a person when he correctly remembers it as well as when he is actually having it. One thing we are supposing, if we take intrasubjective spectrum inversion to be detectable in the ways I have indicated, is that when experiences are co-conscious the similarities between them tend to give rise to belief in the existence of objective similarities in the physical world, namely similarities between objects in whose perception the ex-periences occurred, and differences between them tend to give rise to belief in the existence of objective differences in the world. And these beliefs, in turn, give rise (in combination with the person's wants and other mental states) to overt behavior which is appropriate to them. This explains how there can be non-verbal behavior that is evidence of spectrum inversion; the behavior will be the manifestation of mistaken beliefs about things which result from the fact that in cases of intrasubjective spectrum inversion, things of the same color will produce qualitatively different experiences after the inversion than they did before, while things of each color will produce, after the inversion, experiences qualitatively like those produced by things of a different color before the inversion.

But even if, for some reason, a victim of spectrum inversion were not led to have and act on mistaken beliefs about objective similarities and dissimilarities in this way, we could still have evidence that his spectrum had inverted – for he could tell us that it had. And in supposing that *he* can know of the spectrum inversion in such a case, and so be in a position to inform us of it, we are supposing something further about the relationships of qualitative similarity and difference, namely that when they hold between co-conscious experiences, this tends to give rise to introspective awareness of the holding of these very relationships, i.e., it tends to give rise to correct "qualitative beliefs" to the effect that these relationships hold.

Philosophers who talk of mental states as having behavioral 'criteria' have sometimes said that the criterion of experiences being similar is their subject's sincerely reporting, or being disposed to report, that they are.[19] If we recast this view in functionalist terms, it comes out as the view that what constitutes experiences being qualitatively similar is, in part anyhow, that they give rise, or tend to give rise, to their subject's having a qualitative belief to the effect that such a similarity holds, and, in virtue of this belief, a disposition to make verbal reports to this effect. But as a functional *definition* of qualitative similarity this would of course be circular. If we are trying to explain what it means for experiences to be similar, we cannot take as already understood, and as available for use in our explanation, the notion of believing experiences to be similar.

But no such circularity would be involved in functionally defining the notions of qualitative similarity and difference in terms of the first sort of relationship I mentioned, namely between, on the one hand, a person's experiences being qualitatively similar or different in certain ways, and, on the other, his believing in the existence of certain sorts of objective similarities or differences in the world, and, ultimately, his behaving in certain ways. I believe that a case can be made, although I shall not attempt to make it here, for saying that the tendency of sensory experiences to give rise to introspective awareness of themselves, and of their similarities and differences, is, for creatures having the conceptual capacities of humans, an inevitable by-product of their tendency to give rise to perceptual awareness of objects in the world, and of similarities and differences between these objects. And my suggestion is that what makes a relationship between experiences the relationship of qualitative (phenomenological) similarity is precisely its playing a certain 'functional' role in the perceptual awareness of objective similarities, namely its tending to produce perceptual

---

[19] See, for example, Carl Ginet, "How Words Mean Kinds of Sensations," *The Philosophical Review*, 77 (1968), p. 9.

beliefs to the effect that such similarities hold. Likewise, what makes a relationship between experiences the relationship of qualitative difference is its playing a corresponding role in the perceptual awareness of objective differences.[20]

This suggestion is, of course, vague and sketchy. But all that I have to maintain here is that the claim that we can give a functional account of qualitative similarity and difference along these lines is no less plausible than the claim that such mental states as belief and desire can be functionally defined. For my aim is not the ambitious one of showing that functionalism provides a fully satisfactory philosophy of mind; it is the much more modest one of showing that the fact that some mental states have 'qualitative character' need not pose any special difficulties for a functionalist. And an important step toward showing the latter is to show that the notions of qualitative similarity and difference are as plausible candidates for functional definition as other mental notions. I conceded earlier that there is a sense in which particular qualitative states cannot be functionally defined. But it will be remembered that what distinguishes qualitative states from other sorts of mental states is that their 'type-identity conditions' are to be given in terms of the notion of qualitative similarity. At the beginning of our discussion, specifying identity conditions in such terms seemed to contrast sharply with specifying them in functional terms. But this contrast becomes blurred if, as I have suggested, the notion of qualitative similarity can itself be defined in functional terms. And if the latter is so, and hence the identity conditions for qualitative states can be specified in functional terms, it seems not inappropriate to say, as I did earlier, that while particular qualitative states cannot be functionally defined, the *class* of qualitative states can be functionally defined.

VI

Now let us return to the question of whether it is legitimate to make reference to qualitative states in giving functional definitions of other sorts of mental states.

On one construal of it, functionalism in the philosophy of mind is the doctrine that mental, or psychological, terms are, in principle, eliminable in a certain way. If, to simplify matters, we take our mental vocabulary to consist of names for mental states and relationships (rather than predicates ascribing such states and relationships), the

[20] Further arguments for this view are presented in Essay 8.

claim will be that these names can be treated as synonymous with definite descriptions, each such description being formulable, in principle, without the use of any of the mental vocabulary. Mental states will indeed be quantified over, and in some cases identifyingly referred to, in these definite descriptions; but when they are, they will be characterized and identified, not in explicitly mentalistic terms, but in terms of their causal and other 'topic neutral' relations to one another and to physical inputs and outputs.[21]

Now what I have already said implies that names of qualitative states (if we had them) could not be defined as equivalent to such definite descriptions – on the assumption, of course, that 'qualia inversion' is possible. If the causal role played by a given qualitative state (in conjunction with other mental states) in mediating connections between input and output could be played by another qualitative state, and if that qualitative state could play a different role, then it is not essential to the state that it plays that causal role and it cannot be part of the meaning, or sense, of a term that rigidly designates it that the state so designated is *the* state that plays such a causal role. Moreover, since such a term could not be eliminated in this way in favor of a definite description, it could not occur within the definite description which functionally defines the name of some other mental state – assuming that the aim of such functionalist definitions is to eliminate mental terminology in favor of physical and topic neutral terminology.

But there is nothing in this to imply that qualitative states cannot be among the states quantified over in the definite descriptions that define other sorts of mental states. And it seems that it would be quantification over such states, rather than reference to particular states of this kind, that would be needed in the defining of other mental states. If spectrum inversion is possible, we do not want to make the occurrence of any particular qualitative state a necessary condition of seeing (or seeming to see) something blue, but we do want to require that at any given time in the history of a person there is some qualitative state or other that is (at that time) standardly involved in his seeing (or seeming to see) blue things. The specification of the roles of the qualitative states in the seeing of blue things will no doubt invoke the notions of qualitative similarity and difference; but this causes no difficulties for a functionalist if, as I have suggested, these notions can themselves be functionally defined.

There would appear, however, to be some mental states (other than

[21] See David Lewis, "Psychophysical and Theoretical Identifications," *Australasian Journal of Philosophy*, 50 (1972), 249–257. See also Essay 12.

qualitative states) that cannot be functionally defined in the strong sense here under consideration, namely in such a way that there is no essential (uneliminable) use of mental terminology in the *definiens*. For consider the states I have called 'qualitative beliefs,' i.e., beliefs about qualitative states and in particular beliefs to the effect that one is (oneself) in a particular qualitative state. Qualitative beliefs can be divided into two groups, those in whose propositional content there is reference to particular qualitative states, and those in whose propositional content there is quantification over qualitative states but no reference to particular qualitative states. So far as I can see, qualitative beliefs of the second sort provide no special difficulties for the functionalist; if other sorts of beliefs can be functionally defined, so can these. But qualitative beliefs of the first sort do seem to resist functional definition. Consider the belief I would express if I said 'I am in the state of being appeared-blue-to,' using the phrase 'state of being appeared-blue-to' to rigidly designate a particular qualitative state. If we tried to characterize this state of believing functionally, i.e., in terms of its relationships to other mental states and to input and output, it would seem that we would have to make references in our characterization to the qualitative state the belief is about – we would have to say that the state of believing that one is appeared-blue-to is typically the result of the state of being appeared-blue-to. If so, it is impossible to define such states (qualitative beliefs of the first sort) without making essential use of mental terms.

But this constitutes no obstacle to our functionally defining other sorts of mental states. For while we may want to include in our functional characterizations of some kinds of mental states that they give rise to qualitative beliefs of the first sort (i.e., those in whose propositional content there is reference to particular qualitative states), this need not involve our making identifying reference to beliefs of this sort in our functional characterizations; all that this need involve is quantifying over such beliefs. Thus, for example, we can build it into our functional characterization of pain that being in pain typically results in some qualitative belief to the effect that one has some specific qualitative state, without saying of any specific qualitative state that being in pain tends to give rise to a belief about it. And if quantifying over qualitative states is permissible in giving functional definitions, I see no reason why quantifying over functional beliefs should not be permissible as well.

Now let us return briefly to my argument in section III against the possibility of cases of 'absent qualia.' In that argument I pointed out that it is characteristic of pains to give rise to introspective awareness of themselves as having particular qualitative characters, and so to give rise to 'qualitative beliefs,' and I used this to argue that any state functionally identical to a state having qualitative character (e.g., a pain) must itself have qualitative character. The objection was raised to this argument that since qualitative beliefs, like qualitative states, cannot be functionally defined, they cannot legitimately enter into a functional account of the 'type-identity conditions' for other mental states. We can now answer this objection. No doubt pains give rise to qualitative beliefs of the sort that (so I am allowing) cannot be functionally defined, i.e., beliefs to the effect that one is having some specific qualitative state. But they also give rise to beliefs to the effect that one is in pain – and if (as the 'absent qualia argument' apparently assumes) pain is necessarily a state having qualitative character, then the belief that one is in pain presumably involves (at least in the case of a reflective person) the belief that one is in a state having some qualitative character or other. And while the latter belief is a qualitative belief, its propositional content quantifies over qualitative states rather than involving reference to particular qualitative states. No reason has been given why qualitative beliefs of this sort should not be regarded as functionally definable. And if they are functionally definable, there is no reason why the tendency of other states to give rise to such beliefs should not be part of what constitutes the functional identity of those other states. And this is all the argument of section III requires.

VII

Over the last few decades, much of the controversy in the philosophy of mind has involved a battle between two seemingly conflicting sets of intuitions. On the one hand there is the intuition that mental states are somehow logically, or conceptually, connected with physical states of affairs, in particular the behaviors that are taken to manifest them. This intuition has found expression in a succession of different philosophical positions – logical behaviorism, the 'criteriological' views inspired by Wittgenstein, and, most recently, functional or causal analyses of mental states (these usually being combined with some form of materialism or physicalism).[22] On the other hand there is the intuition that connections between mental states and behavior are,

[22] Some advocates of causal or functional theories of the mind would object to being put in this company. But others have clearly seen their accounts as incorporating what is correct in, or as explaining the intuitions which make plausible, behavioristic and criteriological views. See, for example, Lewis, "Psychophysical and Theoretical Identifications," p. 257, David Armstrong, *A Materialist Theory of the Mind* (London, 1968), p. 92, and Alvin Goldman, *A Theory of Human Action* (Englewood Cliffs, N.J., 1970), p. 112.

at bottom, contingent; that under the most 'intrinsic' descriptions of mental states, it is a contingent fact that they are related as they are to behavior and to other sorts of physical states. And a common expression of this view has been the claim that spectrum inversion and other sorts of 'qualia inversion' are logically possible; for to say that these are logically possible is apparently to say that what intrinsic, internal character these mental states have, their 'qualitative content,' is logically irrelevant to their being related as they are to their bodily causes and behavioral manifestations. I have conceded that there is a substantial element of truth in this view. For I have allowed that spectrum inversion is a possibility, and have allowed that this implies that at least some qualitative states (and qualitative beliefs) cannot be functionally defined. But I believe that there is a substantial element of truth in the other view as well. I think that where the other view – the view that mental states are 'logically' or 'conceptually' connected with behavior – has its greatest plausibility is in its application to such states as desire and belief, and I think that these states do not have 'qualitative character' in the sense that here concerns us, although they may sometimes be accompanied by qualitative states. But as I have tried to show, even qualitative states can be accommodated within the framework of a functional, or causal, analysis of mental states. While it may be of the essence of qualitative states that they are 'ineffable' in the sense that one cannot say in general terms, or at any rate in general terms that do not include names of qualitative states, what it is for a person to be in a particular qualitative state, this does not prevent us from giving a functional account of what it is for a state to be a qualitative state, and of what the identity conditions for qualitative states are. Thus it may be possible to reconcile these firmly entrenched, and seemingly conflicting, intuitions about the contingency or otherwise of relations between mental states and the physical world.

There are a number of issues that would have to be investigated before it could be claimed that this attempted reconciliation is successful. The account of qualitative similarity and difference that I have suggested was tailored to the case of perceptual experiences, and it needs to be considered whether it can be plausibly applied to sensations like pains. What its application to the case of pain may require is the acceptance of the view of pains as somatic sense impressions, i.e., impressions (which need not be veridical) of bodily injuries and the like.[23] Also, this account of qualitative similarity and

---

[23] Such a view has in fact been advanced by D. M. Armstrong and by George Pitcher. See Armstrong, *A Materialist Theory of the Mind*, pp. 313ff. and Pitcher's "Pain Perception," *The Philosophical Review*, 79 (1970), 368–393.

difference is tailored to the case in which the experiences being compared are experiences of one and the same person, and it needs to be considered whether it gives sense, and the right sort of sense, to intersubjective comparisons of experiences. This would involve, among other things, a consideration of whether it is possible for experiences of different persons to be 'co-conscious' in the sense defined earlier; and I think this reduces to the question of whether it is possible for there to be 'fusion' between persons of the sort envisaged in some recent discussions of personal identity, i.e., a merging of two persons into a single person (or single subject of consciousness) who then remembers, and is able to compare, the experiences the persons had prior to the fusion. (It is worth noting that if fusion is possible, then it is not after all the case that no possible behavior would reveal whether the color experience of two persons was the same or whether their color spectra were inverted relative to each other; for were the persons to fuse, the behavior of the resulting person could presumably settle this question.) But these are all complex issues, and I shall not attempt to discuss them here.

10
Causality and properties

I

It is events, rather than objects or properties, that are usually taken by philosophers to be the terms of the causal relationship. But an event typically consists of a change in the properties or relationships of one or more objects, the latter being what Jaegwon Kim has called the "constituent objects" of the event.[1] And when one event causes another, this will be in part because of the properties possessed by their constituent objects. Suppose, for example, that a man takes a pill and, as a result, breaks out into a rash. Here the cause and effect are, respectively, the taking of the pill and the breaking out into a rash. Why did the first event cause the second? Well, the pill was penicillin, and the man was allergic to penicillin. No doubt one could want to know more – for example, about the biochemistry of allergies in general and this one in particular. But there is a good sense in which what has been said already explains why the one event caused the other. Here the pill and the man are the constituent objects of the cause event, and the man is the constituent object of the effect event. Following Kim we can also speak of events as having "constituent properties" and "constituent times." In this case the constituent property of the cause event is the relation expressed by the verb 'takes,' while the constituent property of the effect event is expressed by the predicate 'breaks out into a rash.' The constituent times of the events are their times of occurrence. Specifying the constituent objects and properties of the cause and effect will tell us what these events consisted in, and together with a specification of their constituent times will serve to identify them; but it will not, typically, explain why the one brought about the other. We explain this by mentioning certain properties of their constituent objects. Given that the pill was penicillin, and that the man was allergic to penicillin, the taking of the pill by the man was certain, or at any rate very likely, to result in an

[1] See Jaegwon Kim, "Causation, Nomic Subsumption, and the Concept of Event," *The Journal of Philosophy*, 70 (1973), 27–36. I should mention that it was reflection on this excellent paper that first led me to the views developed in the present one.

allergic response like a rash. To take another example, suppose a branch is blown against a window and breaks it. Here the constituent objects include the branch and the window, and the causal relationship holds because of, among other things, the massiveness of the one and the fragility of the other.

It would appear from this that any account of causality as a relation between events should involve, in a central way, reference to the properties of the constituent objects of the events. But this should not encourage us to suppose that the notion of causality is to be analyzed away, in Humean fashion, in terms of some relationship between properties – for example, in terms of regularities in their instantiation. For as I shall try to show, the relevant notion of a property is itself to be explained in terms of the notion of causality in a way that has some strikingly non-Humean consequences.

II

Philosophers sometimes use the term 'property' in such a way that for every predicate F true of a thing there is a property of the thing which is designated by the corresponding expression of the form 'being F.' If 'property' is used in this broad way, every object will have innumerable properties that are unlikely to be mentioned in any causal explanation involving an event of which the object is a constituent. For example, my typewriter has the property of being over one hundred miles from the current heavyweight boxing champion of the world. It is not easy to think of a way in which its having this property could help to explain why an event involving it has a certain effect, and it seems artificial, at best, to speak of my typewriter's acquisition of this property as one of the causal effects of the movements of the heavyweight champion.

It is natural, however, to feel that such properties are not 'real' or 'genuine' properties. Our intuitions as to what are, and what are not, genuine properties are closely related to our intuitions as to what are, and what are not, genuine changes. A property is genuine if and only if its acquisition or loss by a thing constitutes a genuine change in that thing. One criterion for a thing's having changed is what Peter Geach calls the "Cambridge criterion." He formulates this as follows: "The thing called 'x' has changed if we have '$F(x)$ at time t' true and '$F(x)$ at time t^1' false, for some interpretations of 'F,' 't,' and 't^1.'"[2] But as

---

[2] Peter Geach, *God and the Soul* (London, 1969), p. 71. See also Jaegwon Kim, "Non-Causal Relations," *Nous*, 8 (1974), 41–52, and "Events as Property Exemplifications," in M. Brand and D. Walton (eds.), *Action Theory* (Dordrecht, Netherlands, 1976), pp. 159–177.

Geach points out, this gives the result that Socrates undergoes a change when he comes to be shorter than Theaetetus in virtue of the latter's growth, and even that he undergoes a change every time a fresh schoolboy comes to admire him. Such 'changes,' those that intuitively are not genuine changes, Geach calls "mere 'Cambridge' changes." For Geach, real changes are Cambridge changes, since they satisfy the Cambridge criterion, but some Cambridge changes, namely those that are *mere* Cambridge changes, fail to be real changes. Since it is mere Cambridge changes, rather than Cambridge changes in general, that are to be contrasted with real or genuine changes, I shall introduce the hyphenated expression 'mere-Cambridge' to characterize these. And I shall apply the terms 'Cambridge' and 'mere-Cambridge' to properties as well as to changes. Mere-Cambridge properties will include such properties as being 'grue' (in Nelson Goodman's sense), historical properties like being over twenty years old and having been slept in by George Washington, relational properties like being fifty miles south of a burning barn,[3] and such properties as being such that Jimmy Carter is President of the United States.

It is worth mentioning that in addition to distinguishing between real and mere-Cambridge properties and changes, we must also distinguish between real and mere-Cambridge resemblance or similarity, and between real and mere-Cambridge differences. Cambridge similarities hold in virtue of the sharing of Cambridge properties. And mere-Cambridge similarities hold in virtue of the sharing of mere-Cambridge properties: there is such a similarity between all grue things; there is one between all things fifty miles south of a burning barn; there is one between all beds slept in by George Washington; and there is one between all things such that Jimmy Carter is President of the United States. It will be recalled that the notion of similarity, or resemblance, plays a prominent role in Hume's account of causality. His first definition of *cause* in the *Treatise* is "an object precedent and contiguous to another, and where all the objects resembling the former are plac'd in a like relation of priority and contiguity to those objects, that resemble the latter."[4] Hume clearly regarded the notion of resemblance as quite unproblematical and in no need of elucidation.[5] Yet it is plain that he needs a narrower notion of resemblance

---

[3] I take this example from Kim, "Causation, Nomic Subsumption, and the Concept of Event."

[4] David Hume, *A Treatise of Human Nature*, ed. by L. A. Selby-Bigge (Oxford, 1888), p. 170 (bk. I, pt. III, sect. XIV).

[5] "When any objects *resemble* each other, the resemblance will at first strike the eye, or rather the mind, and seldom requires a second examination" (*ibid.*, p. 70 (bk. I, pt. III, sect. I)).

than that of Cambridge resemblance if his definition of causality is to have the desired content. Cambridge resemblances are too easily come by; any two objects share infinitely many Cambridge properties, and so 'resemble' one another in infinitely many ways. There are also infinitely many Cambridge differences between any two objects. What Hume needs is a notion of resemblance and difference which is such that some things resemble a given thing more than others do, and such that some things may resemble a thing exactly (without being numerically identical to it) while others resemble it hardly at all. Only 'real' or 'genuine' resemblance will serve his purposes. If it turns out, as I think it does, that in order to give a satisfactory account of the distinction between real and mere-Cambridge properties, changes, similarities, and differences we must make use of the notion of causality, the Humean project of defining causality in terms of regularity or 'constant conjunction,' notions that plainly involve the notion of resemblance, is seriously undermined.

I have no wish to legislate concerning the correct use of the terms 'property,' 'change,' 'similar,' and so forth. It would be rash to claim that the accepted use of the term 'property' is such that what I have classified as mere-Cambridge properties are not properties. But I do think that we have *a* notion of what it is to be a property which is such that this is so – in other words, which is such that not every phrase of the form 'being so and so' stands for a property which something has just in case the corresponding predicate of the form 'is so and so' is true of it, and is such that sometimes a predicate is true of a thing, not because (or only because) of any properties *it* has, but because something else, perhaps something related to it in certain ways, has certain properties. It is this narrow conception of what it is to be a property, and the correlative notions of change and similarity, that I am concerned to elucidate in this essay. (I should mention that I am concerned here only with the sorts of properties with respect to which change is possible; my account is not intended to apply to such properties of numbers as being even and being prime.)

III

John Locke held that "*Powers make a great part of our complex* Ideas *of substances.*"[6] And there is one passage in which Locke seems to suggest that all qualities of substances are powers; he says, in

---

[6] John Locke, *Essay Concerning Human Understanding*, ed. by Peter H. Nidditch (Oxford, 1975), p. 300 (bk. II, ch. 23, sect. VIII).

explanation of his usage of the term 'quality,' that "the Power to produce any *Idea* in our mind, I call *quality* of the Subject wherein that power is."[7] This suggests a theory of properties, namely that properties are causal powers, which is akin to the theory I shall be defending. As it happens, this is not Locke's view. If one ascribed it to him on the basis of the passage just quoted, one would have to ascribe to him the view that all qualities are what he called 'secondary qualities' – powers to produce certain mental effects ('ideas') in us. But Locke recognized the existence of powers that are not secondary qualities, namely powers (for example, the power in the sun to melt wax) to produce effects in material objects. These have been called 'tertiary qualities.' And he distinguished both of these sorts of powers from the 'primary qualities' on which they 'depend.' Nevertheless, the view which Locke's words unintentionally suggest is worth considering.

What would seem to be the same view is sometimes put by saying that all properties are dispositional properties. But as thus formulated, this view seems plainly mistaken. Surely we make a distinction between dispositional and nondispositional properties, and can mention paradigms of both sorts. Moreover, it seems plain that what dispositional properties something has, what powers it has, depends on what nondispositional properties it has – just as Locke thought that the powers of things depend on their primary qualities and those of their parts.

In fact, I believe, there are two different distinctions to be made here, and these are often conflated. One is not a distinction between kinds of *properties* at all, but rather a distinction between kinds of *predicates*. Sometimes it belongs to the meaning, or sense, of a predicate that if it is true of a thing then under certain circumstances the thing will undergo certain changes or will produce certain changes in other things. This is true of what are standardly counted as dispositional predicates, for example, 'flexible,' 'soluble,' 'malleable,' 'magnetized,' and 'poisonous.' Plainly not all predicates are of this sort. Whether color predicates are is a matter of controversy. But whatever we say about this, it seems plain that predicates like 'square,' 'round' and 'made of copper' are not dispositional in this sense. There are causal powers associated with being made of copper – for example, being an electrical conductor. But presumably this association is not incorporated into the meaning of the term 'copper.'

The first distinction, then, is between different sorts of predicates,

---

[7] *Essay*, p. 134 (bk. II, ch. 8, sect. VIII).

and I think that the term 'dispositional' is best employed as a predicate of predicates, not of properties. A different distinction is between powers, in a sense I am about to explain, and the properties in virtue of which things have the powers they have.[8] For something to have a power, in this sense, is for it to be such that its presence in circumstances of a particular sort will have certain effects.[9] One can think of such a power as a function from circumstances to effects. Thus if something is poisonous its presence in someone's body will produce death or illness; in virtue of this, being poisonous is a power. Here it is possible for things to have the same power in virtue of having very different properties. Suppose that one poisonous substance kills by affecting the heart, while another kills by directly affecting the nervous system and brain. They produce these different effects in virtue of having very different chemical compositions. They will of course differ in their powers as well as in their properties, for one will have the power to produce certain physiological effects in the nervous system, while the other will have the power to produce quite different physiological effects in the heart. But there is one power they will share, in virtue of having these different powers, namely that of producing death if ingested by a human being. Properties here play the role, *vis-à-vis* powers, that primary qualities play in Locke; it is in virtue of a thing's properties that the thing has the powers (Locke's secondary and tertiary qualities) that it has.

There is a rough correspondence between this distinction between powers and properties and the earlier distinction between dispositional and nondispositional predicates. By and large, dispositional predicates ascribe powers while nondispositional monadic predicates ascribe properties that are not powers in the same sense.

IV

On the view of properties I want to propose, while properties are typically not powers of the sort ascribed by dispositional predicates,

---

[8] What does "in virtue of" mean here? For the moment we can say that a thing has a power in virtue of having certain properties if it is a lawlike truth that whatever has those properties has that power. On the theory I shall be defending it turns out that this is a matter of the possession of the properties entailing the possession of the power (that is, its being true in all possible worlds that whatever has the properties has the power).

[9] In speaking of "circumstances" I have in mind the relations of the object to other objects; instead of speaking of "presence in circumstances of a particular sort" I could instead speak of 'possession of particular relational properties.' Being in such and such circumstances is a mere-Cambridge property of an object, not a genuine (intrinsic) property of it.

they are related to such powers in much the way that such powers are related to the causal effects which they are powers to produce. Just as powers can be thought of as functions from circumstances to causal effects, so the properties on which powers depend can be thought of as functions from properties to powers (or, better, as functions from sets of properties to sets of powers). One might even say that properties are second-order powers; they are powers to produce first-order powers (powers to produce certain sorts of events) if combined with certain other properties. But the formulation I shall mainly employ is this: what makes a property the property it is, what determines its identity, is its potential for contributing to the causal powers of the things that have it. This means, among other things, that if under all possible circumstances properties X and Y make the same contribution to the causal powers of the things that have them, X and Y are the same property.

To illustrate this, let us take as our example of a property the property of being 'knife-shaped' – I shall take this to be a highly determinate property which belongs to a certain knife in my kitchen and to anything else of exactly the same shape. Now if all that I know about a thing is that it has this property, I know nothing about what will result from its presence in any circumstances. What has the property of being knife-shaped could be a knife, made of steel, but it could instead be a piece of balsa wood, a piece of butter, or even an oddly shaped cloud of some invisible gas. There is no power which necessarily belongs to all and only the things having this property. But if this property is combined with the property of being knife-sized and the property of being made of steel, the object having these properties will necessarily have a number of powers. It will have the power of cutting butter, cheese and wood, if applied to these substances with suitable pressure, and also the power of producing various sorts of sense-impressions in human beings under appropriate observational conditions, and also the power of leaving an impression of a certain shape if applied to soft wax and then withdrawn, and so on. The combination of the property of being knife-shaped with the property of being made of glass will result in a somewhat different set of powers, which will overlap with the set which results from its combination with the property of being made of steel. Likewise with its combination with the property of being made of wood, the property of being made of butter, and so on.

Let us say that an object has power P conditionally upon the possession of the properties in set Q if it has some property r such that having the properties in Q together with r is causally sufficient for having P, while having the properties in Q is not by itself causally sufficient for having P. Thus, for example, a knife-shaped object has the power of cutting wood conditionally upon being knife-sized and made of steel; for it is true of knife-shaped things, but not of things in general, that if they are knife-sized and made of steel they will have the power to cut wood. When a thing has a power conditionally upon the possession of certain properties, let us say that this amounts to its having a *conditional power*. Our knife-shaped object has the conditional power of being able to cut wood if knife-sized and made of steel. The identity condition for conditional powers is as follows: if A is the conditional power of having power P conditionally upon having the properties in set Q, and B is the conditional power of having P' conditionally upon having the properties in set Q', then A is identical to B just in case P is identical to P' and Q is identical to Q'. Having introduced this notion of a conditional power, we can express my view by saying that properties are clusters of conditional powers. (I shall count powers *simpliciter* as a special case of conditional powers.) I have said that the identity of a property is determined by its causal potentialities, the contributions it is capable of making to the causal powers of things that have it. And the causal potentialities that are essential to a property correspond to the conditional powers that make up the cluster with which the property can be identified; for a property to have a causal potentiality is for it to be such that whatever has it has a certain conditional power.

This account is intended to capture what is correct in the view that properties just are powers, or that all properties are dispositional, while acknowledging the truth of a standard objection to that view, namely that a thing's powers or dispositions are distinct from, because 'grounded in,' its intrinsic properties.[10]

Before I give my reasons for holding this view, I should mention one *prima facie* objection to it. Presumably the property of being triangular and the property of being trilateral do not differ in the contributions they make to the causal powers of the things that have them, yet it is natural to say that these, although necessarily coextensive, are different properties. It seems to me, however, that

---

[10] After this was written I found that Peter Achinstein has advanced a causal account of property identity which, despite a different approach, is in some ways similar to the account proposed here. See his "The Identity of Properties," *American Philosophical Quarterly*, 11 (1974), 257–276. There are also similarities, along with important differences, between my views and those presented by D. H. Mellor in "In Defense of Dispositions," *The Philosophical Review*, 83 (1974), 157–181, and those presented by R. Harre and E. H. Madden in *Causal Powers: A Theory of Natural Necessity* (Oxford, 1975).

what we have good reason for regarding as distinct are not these properties, as such, but rather the concepts of triangularity and trilaterality, and the meanings of the expressions 'triangular' and 'trilateral.' If we abandon, as I think we should, the idea that properties are the meanings of predicate expressions, and if we are careful to distinguish concepts from what they are concepts of, I see no insuperable obstacle to regarding the properties themselves as identical.

V

My reasons for holding this theory of properties are, broadly speaking, epistemological. Only if some causal theory of properties is true, I believe, can it be explained how properties are capable of engaging our knowledge, and our language, in the way they do.

We know and recognize properties by their effects, or, more precisely, by the effects of the events which are the activations of the causal powers which things have in virtue of having the properties. This happens in a variety of ways. Observing something is being causally influenced by it in certain ways. If the causal potentialities involved in the possession of a property are such that there is a fairly direct causal connection between the possession of it by an object and the sensory states of an observer related to that object in certain ways, e.g., looking at it in good light, we say that the property itself is observable. If the relationship is less direct, e.g., if the property can affect the sensory states of the observer only by affecting the properties of something else which the observer observes, a scientific instrument, say, we speak of inferring that the thing has the property from what we take to be the effects of its possession. In other cases we conclude that something has a property because we know that it has other properties which we know from other cases to be correlated with the one in question. But the latter way of knowing about the properties of things is parasitic on the earlier ways; for unless the instantiation of the property had, under some circumstances, effects from which its existence could be concluded, we could never discover laws or correlations that would enable us to infer its existence from things other than its effects.

Suppose that the identity of properties consisted of something logically independent of their causal potentialities. Then it ought to be possible for there to be properties that have no potential whatever for contributing to causal powers, i.e., are such that under no conceivable circumstances will their possession by a thing make any difference to the way the presence of that thing affects other things or to the way other things affect it. Further, it ought to be possible that there be two or more different properties that make, under all possible circumstances, exactly the same contribution to the causal powers of the things that have them. Further, it ought to be possible that the potential of a property for contributing to the production of causal powers might change over time, so that, for example, the potential possessed by property *A* at one time is the same as that possessed by property *B* at a later time, and that possessed by property *B* at the earlier time is the same as that possessed by property *A* at the latter time. Thus a thing might undergo radical change with respect to its properties without undergoing any change in its causal powers, and a thing might undergo radical change in its causal powers without undergoing any change in the properties that underlie these powers.

The supposition that these possibilities are genuine implies, not merely (what might seem harmless) that various things might be the case without its being in any way possible for us to know that they are, but also that it is impossible for us to know various things which we take ourselves to know. If there can be properties that have no potential for contributing to the causal powers of the things that have them, then nothing could be good evidence that the overall resemblance between two things is greater than the overall resemblance between two other things; for even if *A* and *B* have closely resembling effects on our senses and our instruments while *C* and *D* do not, it might be (for all we know) that *C* and *D* share vastly more properties of the causally impotent kind than do *A* and *B*. Worse, if two properties can have exactly the same potential for contributing to causal powers, then it is impossible for us even to know (or have any reason for believing) that two things resemble one another by sharing a single property. Moreover, if the properties and causal potentialities of a thing can vary independently of one another, then it is impossible for us to know (or have any good reason for believing) that something has retained a property over time, or that something has undergone a change with respect to the properties that underlie its causal powers. On these suppositions, there would be no way in which a particular property could be picked out so as to have a name attached to it; and even if, *per impossibile*, a name did get attached to a property, it would be impossible for anyone to have any justification for applying the name on particular occasions.

It may be doubted whether the view under attack has these disastrous epistemological consequences. Surely, it may be said, one can hold that it is a contingent matter that particular properties have the causal potentialities they have, and nevertheless hold, compatibly with this, that there are good theoretical reasons for thinking that as a matter of fact different properties differ in their causal potentialities, and that any given property retains the same potentialities over time. For while it is logically possible that the latter should not be so, according to the contingency view, the simplest hypothesis is that it is so; and it is reasonable to accept the simplest hypothesis compatible with the data.

Whatever may be true in general of appeals to theoretical simplicity, this one seems to me extremely questionable. For here we are not really dealing with an explanatory hypothesis at all. If the identity of properties is made independent of their causal potentialities, then in what sense do we explain sameness or difference of causal potentialities by positing sameness or difference of properties? There are of course cases in which we explain a constancy in something by positing certain underlying constancies in its properties. It is genuinely explanatory to say that something retained the same causal power over time because certain of its properties remained the same. And this provides, *ceteris paribus*, a simpler, or at any rate more plausible, explanation of the constancy than one that says that the thing first had one set of under- lying properties and then a different set, and that both sets were sufficient to give it that particular power. For example, if the water supply was poisonous all day long, it is more plausible to suppose that this was due to the presence in it of one poisonous substance all day rather than due to its containing cyanide from morning till noon and strychnine from noon till night. But in such cases we presuppose that the underlying property constancies carry with them constancies in causal potentialities, and it is only on this presupposition that positing the underlying constancies provides the simplest explanation of the constancy to be explained. Plainly this presupposition cannot be operative if what the 'inference to the best explanation' purports to explain is, precisely, that sameness of property goes with sameness of causal potentialities. It is not as if a property had the causal potentialities in question as a result of having yet *other* causal potentialities, the constancy of the latter explaining the constancy of the former. This disassociation of property identity from identity of causal potentiality is really an invitation to eliminate reference to properties from our explanatory hypotheses altogether; if it were correct then we could, to use Wittgenstein's metaphor, 'divide through' by the properties and leave the explanatory power of what we say about things untouched.

It might be objected that even if my arguments establish that the causal potentialities of a genuine property cannot change over time, they do not establish that these causal potentialities are essential to that property, in the sense of belonging to it in all possible worlds. The immutability of properties with respect to their causal potentialities, it might be said, is simply a consequence of the immutability of laws – of the fact that it makes no sense to speak of a genuine law holding at one time and not at another. And from the fact that the laws governing a property cannot change over time it does not follow, it may be said, that the property cannot be governed by different laws in different possible worlds.

Let me observe first of all that in conceding that the immutability of the causal potentialities of genuine properties is a consequence of the immutability of laws, the objection concedes a large part of what I want to maintain. It is not true in general of mere-Cambridge properties that their causal potentialities cannot change over time; for example, this is not true of *grueness* on the Barker–Achinstein definition of *grue*, where something is grue just in case it is green and the time is before T (say A.D. 2010) or it is blue and the time is T or afterwards.[11] That genuine properties are marked off from mere-Cambridge properties by their relation to causal laws (and that it is nonsense to speak of a world in which it is the mere-Cambridge properties rather than the genuine ones that are law-governed in a way that makes their causal potentialities immutable) is a central part of my view.

There is, moreover, a *prima facie* case for saying that the immutability of the causal potentialities of a property does imply their essentiality; or in other words, that if they cannot vary across time, they also cannot vary across possible worlds. Most of us do suppose that *particulars* can (or do) have different properties in different possible worlds. We suppose, for example, that in some possible worlds I am a plumber rather than a philosopher, and that in some possible worlds my house is painted yellow rather than white. But it goes with this that particulars can change their properties over time. It is possible that I, the very person who is writing this essay, might have been a plumber, because there is a possible history in which I start with the properties (in this case relational as well as intrinsic) which I had at some time in my actual history, and undergo a series of changes which

---

[11] See S. F. Barker and P. Achinstein, "On the New Riddle of Induction," *The Philosophical Review*, 69 (1960), 511–522. The definition given there is not equivalent to that originally given by Goodman, in *Fact, Fiction and Forecast*, 3rd edn. (Indianapolis, 1975), p. 74, and it is the latter which is employed elsewhere in the present essay.

result in my eventually being a plumber. If I and the world were never such that it was then possible for me to *become* a plumber, it would not be true that I might have been a plumber, or (in other words) that there is a possible world in which I am one. There is, in short, a close linkage between identity across time and identity across possible worlds; the ways in which a given thing can be different in different possible worlds depend on the ways in which such a thing can be different at different times in the actual world. But now let us move from the case of particulars to that of properties. There is no such thing as tracing a property through a series of changes in its causal potentialities – not if it is a genuine property, i.e., one of the sort that figures in causal laws. And so there is no such thing as a possible history in which a property starts with the set of causal potentialities it has in the actual world and ends with a different set. To say the least, this calls into question the intelligibility of the suggestion that the very properties we designate with words like 'green,' 'square,' 'hard,' and so on, might have had different causal potentialities than they in fact have.

However, this last argument is not conclusive. My earlier arguments, if sound, establish that there is an intimate connection between the identity of a property and its causal potentialities. But it has not yet been decisively established that *all* of the causal potentialities of a property are essential to it. The disastrous epistemological consequences of the contingency view would be avoided if for each property we could identify a proper subset of its causal potentialities that are essential to it and constitutive of it, and this would permit some of a property's causal potentialities, those outside the essential cluster, to belong to it contingently, and so not belong to it in some other possible worlds. There would, in this case, be an important difference between the trans-world identity of properties and that of particulars – and it is a difference which there is in my own view as well. If, as I believe, the assertion that a certain particular might have had different properties than it does in the actual world (that in some other possible world it does have those properties) implies that there is a possible history 'branching off' from the history of the actual world in which it acquires those properties, this is because there is, putting aside historical properties and 'identity properties' (like being identical to Jimmy Carter), no subset of the properties of such a thing which constitutes an individual essence of it, i.e., is such that, in any possible world, having the properties in that subset is necessary *and sufficient* for being that particular thing. To put this otherwise, the reason why the possible history in which the thing has different properties must be a branching-off from the history of the actual world is that the individual essence of a particular thing must include historical properties. Now I am not in a position to object to the suggestion that properties differ from particulars in having individual essences which do not include historical properties and which are sufficient for their identification across possible worlds; for I hold that the totality of a property's causal potentialities constitutes such an individual essence. So a possible alternative to my view is one which holds that for each property there is a proper subset of its causal potentialities that constitutes its individual essence. Such a view has its attractions, and is compatible with much of what I say in this essay; in particular, it is compatible with the claim that within any possible world properties are identical just in case they have the same causal potentialities. But I shall argue in section IX that this view is unworkable, and that there is no acceptable alternative to the view that all of the causal potentialities of a property are essential to it.

VI

As was intended, my account of properties does not apply to what I have called mere-Cambridge properties. When my table acquired the property of being such that Gerald Ford is President of the United States, which it did at the time Nixon resigned from the presidency, this presumably had no effect on its causal powers. Beds that were slept in by George Washington may command a higher price than those that lack this historical property, but presumably this is a result, not of any causal potentialities in the beds themselves, but of the historical beliefs and interests of those who buy and sell them. And grueness, as defined by Goodman, is not associated in the way greenness and blueness are with causal potentialities. (In this sense, which differs from that invoked in section V, something is grue at a time just in case it is green at that time and is first examined before T, say, A.D. 2010, or is blue at that time and is not first examined before T.) It can happen that the only difference between something that is grue and something that is not is that one of them has and the other lacks the historical property of being (or having been) first examined before the time T mentioned in Goodman's definition of *grue*; and presumably this does not in itself make for any difference in causal potentialities. It can also happen that two things share the property of being grue in virtue of having properties that have different potentialities – that is, in virtue of one of them being green (and examined before T) and the other being blue (and not so examined).

There is an epistemological way of distinguishing genuine and mere-Cambridge properties that is *prima facie* plausible. If I wish to determine whether an emerald is green at *t*, the thing to do, if I can manage it, is to examine the emerald at *t*. But examination of a table will not tell me it is such that Gerald Ford is President of the United States, or whether it is fifty miles south of a burning barn. And if I am ignorant of the date, or if *t* is after *T* (the date in Goodman's definition), examination of an emerald will not tell me whether it is grue. Likewise, while scrutiny of a bed may reveal a plaque claiming that it was slept in by George Washington, it will not tell me whether this claim is true. Roughly, if a question about whether a thing has a property at a place and time concerns a genuine nonrelational property, the question is most directly settled by observations and tests in the vicinity of that place and time, while if it concerns a mere-Cambridge property it may be most directly settled by observations and tests remote from that place and time, and observations and tests made at that place and time will either be irrelevant (as in the case of the property of being such that Jimmy Carter is President) or insufficient to settle the question (as in the case of grue).

It would be difficult to make this into a precise and adequate criterion of genuineness of property, and I do not know whether this could be done. But I think that to the extent that it is adequate, its adequacy is explained by my account of properties in terms of causal powers. Properties reveal their presence in actualizations of their causal potentialities, a special case of this being the perception of a property. And the most immediate and revealing effects of an object's having a property at a particular place and time are effects that occur in the immediate vicinity of that place and time. To be sure, we cannot rule out on purely philosophical grounds the possibility of action at a spatial and/or temporal distance. And the more prevalent such action is, the less adequate the proposed epistemological criterion will be. But there do seem to be conceptual limitations on the extent to which causal action can be at a spatial or temporal distance. It is doubtful, to say the least, whether there could be something whose causal powers are *all* such that whenever any of them is activated the effects of its activation are spatially remote from the location of the thing at that time, or occur at times remote from the time of activation.

Causation and causal powers are as much involved in the verification of ascriptions of mere-Cambridge properties as in the verification of ascriptions of genuine ones. But in the case of mere-Cambridge properties some of the operative causal powers will either belong to something other than the object to which the property is ascribed, or will belong to that object at a time other than that at which it has that property. Thus if I verify that a man has the property of being fifty miles south of a burning barn, it will be primarily the causal powers of the barn, and of the intervening stretch of land (which, we will suppose, I measure), rather than the causal powers of the man, that will be responsible for my verifying observations.

VII

It will not have escaped notice that the account of properties and property identity I have offered makes free use of the notion of a property and the notion of property identity. It says, in brief, that properties are identical, whether in the same possible world or in different ones, just in case their coinstantiation with the same properties gives rise to the same powers. This is, if anything, even more circular than it looks. For it crucially involves the notion of sameness of powers, and this will have to be explained in terms of sameness of circumstances and sameness of effects, the notions of which both involve the notion of sameness of property. And of course there was essential use of the notion of a property in my explanation of the notion of a conditional power.

It is worth observing that there is a distinction between kinds of powers that corresponds to the distinction, mentioned earlier, between genuine and mere-Cambridge properties.[12] Robert Boyle's famous example of the key can be used to illustrate this.[13] A particular key on my key chain has the power of opening locks of a certain design. It also has the power of opening my front door. It could lose the former power only by undergoing what we would regard as real change, for example, a change in its shape. But it could lose the latter without undergoing such a change; it could so do in virtue of the lock on my door being replaced by one of a different design. Let us say that the former is an intrinsic power and the latter a mere-Cambridge power. It is clear that in my account of properties the word 'power' must refer only to intrinsic powers. For if it refers to mere-Cambridge powers as well, then what seems clearly to be a mere-Cambridge property of my key, namely being such that my door has a lock of a certain design, will make a determinate contribution to its having the powers it has, and so will count as a genuine property of it. But it

---

[12] This was called to my attention by Nicholas Sturgeon.
[13] See Boyle, "The Origins and Forms of Qualities," in *The Works of the Honourable Robert Boyle* (5 vols., London, 1744), vol. II, pp. 461 ff.

seems unlikely that we could explain the distinction between intrinsic and mere-Cambridge powers without making use of the notion of a genuine change and that of a genuine property. And so again my account of the notion of a property in terms of the notion of a power can be seen to be circular.

How much do these circularities matter? Since they are, I think, unavoidable, they preclude a reductive analysis of the notion of a property in terms of the notion of causality. But they by no means render my account empty. The claim that the causal potentialities of a property are essential to it, and that properties having the same causal potentialities are identical, is certainly not made vacuous by the fact that the explanation of the notion of a causal potentiality, or a conditional power, must invoke the notion of a property. As I see it, the notion of a property and the notion of a causal power belong to a system of internally related concepts, no one of which can be explicated without the use of the others. Other members of the system are the concept of an event, the concept of similarity, and the concept of a persisting substance. It can be worthwhile, as a philosophical exercise, to see how far we can go in an attempt to reduce one of these concepts to others – for both the extent of our success and the nature of our failures can be revealing about the nature of the connections between the concepts. But ultimately such attempts must fail. The goal of philosophical analysis, in dealing with such concepts, should not be reductive analysis but rather the charting of internal relationships. And it is perfectly possible for a 'circular' analysis to illuminate a network of internal relationships and have philosophically interesting consequences.

VIII

According to the theory of properties I am proposing, all of the causal potentialities possessed by a property at any time in the actual world are essential to it and so belong to it at all times and in all possible worlds. This has a very strong consequence, namely that causal necessity is just a species of logical necessity. If the introduction into certain circumstances of a thing having certain properties causally necessitates the occurrence of certain effects, then it is impossible, logically impossible, that such an introduction could fail to have such an effect, and so logically necessary that it has it. To the extent that causal laws can be viewed as propositions describing the causal potentialities of properties, it is impossible that the same properties should be governed by different causal laws in different possible worlds, for such propositions will be necessarily true when true at all.

It is not part of this theory, however, that causal laws are analytic or knowable a priori. I suppose that is analytic that flexible things bend under suitable pressure, that poisonous things cause injury to those for whom they are poisonous, and so on. But I do not think that it is analytic that copper is an electrical conductor, or that knife-shaped things, if knife-sized and made of steel, are capable of cutting butter. Nor does it follow from the claim that such truths are necessary that they are analytic. Kripke has made a compelling case for the view that there are propositions that are necessary a posteriori, that is, true in all possible worlds but such that they can only be known empirically.[14] And such, according to my theory, is the status of most propositions describing the causal potentialities of properties. The theory can allow that our knowledge of these potentialities is empirical, and that it is bound to be only partial. But in order to show how, in the theory, such empirical knowledge is possible, I must now bring out an additional way in which the notion of causality is involved in the notion of a property.

One of the formulations of my theory says that every property is a cluster of conditional powers. But the converse does not seem to me to hold; not every cluster of conditional powers is a property. If something is both knife-shaped and made of wax, then it will have, among others, the following conditional powers: the power of being able to cut wood conditionally upon being knife-sized and made of steel (this it has in virtue of being knife-shaped), and the power of being malleable conditionally upon being at a temperature of 100°F (this it has in virtue of being made of wax). Intuitively, these are not common components of any single property. By contrast, the various conditional powers a thing has in virtue of being knife-shaped – for example, the power of being able to cut wood conditionally upon being knife-sized and made of steel, the power of being able to cut butter conditionally upon being knife-sized and made of wood, the power of having a certain visual appearance conditionally upon being green, the power of having a certain other visual appearance conditionally upon being red, and so on – are all constituents of a single property, namely the property of being knife-shaped. The difference, I think, is that in the one case the set of conditional powers has, while in the other it lacks, a certain kind of causal unity. I shall now try to spell out the nature of this unity.

[14] See Saul Kripke, "Naming and Necessity," in D. Davidson and G. Harman (eds.), *Semantics of Natural Language* (Dordrecht, Netherlands, 1972), pp. 253–355.

Some subsets of the conditional powers which make up a genuine property will be such that it is a consequence of causal laws that whatever has any member of the subset necessarily has all of its members. Thus, for example, something has the power of leaving a six-inch-long knife-shaped impression in soft wax conditionally upon being six inches long if and only if it has the power of leaving an eight-inch-long knife-shaped impression in soft wax conditionally upon being eight inches long. Now some conditional powers will belong to more than one property cluster; thus, for example, there are many different shape properties that give something the power of being able to cut wood conditionally upon being made of steel. But where a conditional power can be shared by different properties in this way, it will belong to a particular property cluster only if there is another member of that cluster which is such that it is a consequence of causal laws that whatever has that other member has the conditional power in question. And at the core of each cluster there will be one or more conditional powers which are such that as a consequence of causal laws whatever has any of them has all of the conditional powers in the cluster. For example, if something has, conditionally upon being made of steel, the power of leaving a knife-shaped impression in soft wax, then it cannot fail to be knife-shaped, and so cannot fail to have all of the other conditional powers involved in being knife-shaped. I suggest, then, that conditional powers X and Y belong to the same property if and only if it is a consequence of causal laws that either (1) whatever has either of them has the other, or (2) there is some third conditional power such that whatever has it has both X and Y.

Returning now to the conditional power of being able to cut wood conditionally upon being made of steel and the conditional power of being malleable conditionally upon being at a temperature of $100°F$, it seems to me that these do not qualify under the proposed criterion as belonging to a common property. It is obviously not true that whatever has one of them must have the other. And it does not appear that there is any third conditional power which is such that whatever has it must have the two conditional powers in question.

If I am right in thinking that the conditional powers constituting a property must be causally unified in the way indicated, it is not difficult to see how knowledge of the causal potentialities of properties can develop empirically. The behavior of objects, that is, the displays of their powers, will reveal that they have certain conditional powers. Once it is discovered that certain conditional powers are connected in a lawlike way, we can use these to "fix the reference" of a property term to the cluster containing those conditional powers and whatever other conditional powers are related to them in the appropriate lawlike relationships.[15] And we can then set about to determine empirically what the other conditional powers in the cluster are.

IX

As I observed earlier, my theory appears to have the consequence that causal laws are logically necessary, and that causal necessity is just a species of logical necessity. While to some this may be an attractive consequence, to many it will seem counterintuitive. It does seem to most of us that we can conceive of possible worlds which resemble the actual world in the kinds of properties that are instantiated in them, but differ from it in the causal laws that obtain. My theory must maintain either that we cannot really conceive of this or that conceivability is not proof of logical possibility.

Anyone who finds both of these alternatives unacceptable, but is persuaded by the arguments in section v that the identity of properties is determined by their causal potentialities, will look for ways of reconciling that conclusion with the view that there can be worlds in which some of the causal laws are different from, and incompatible with, those that obtain in the actual world. I want now to consider two ways in which one might attempt to achieve such a reconciliation. First, it might be held that while propositions describing the causal potentialities of properties are necessarily true if true at all, there are other lawlike propositions, namely those asserting lawlike connections between conditional powers, which are contingent and so true in some possible worlds and false in others. According to this view, when we seem to be conceiving of worlds in which the same properties are governed by different laws, what we are really conceiving of are worlds in which the same conditional powers stand to one another in different lawlike connections than they do in the actual world, and so are differently clustered into properties. Second, it might be held that my condition for the identity of properties across possible worlds is too strict. The theory I have advanced might be called the 'total cluster theory'; it identifies a property with a cluster containing all of the conditional powers which anything has in virtue of having that property, and maintains that in any possible world anything that has that property must have all of the members of that cluster. One might attempt to replace this with a 'core cluster theory,' which identifies the

[15] For the notion of 'reference fixing,' see Kripke, *ibid.*, pp. 269–275.

property with some proper subset of the conditional powers something has in virtue of having that property. On this theory, it is only
some of the causal potentialities possessed by a property in the actual
world, namely those constituted by the conditional powers in its core
cluster, that are essential to it – so it is possible for the same property to
have somewhat different causal potentialities in different possible
worlds, because of different laws relating the conditional powers in its
core cluster with other conditional powers.

I do not believe, however, that either of these attempted reconcili-
ations is successful. The first involves the suggestion that it is at least
sometimes a contingent matter whether two conditional powers
belong to the same property, and hence that there could be a world in
which some of the same conditional powers are instantiated as in this
world, but in which, owing to the holding of different laws, these are
differently clustered into properties. The difficulty with this is that the
specification of a conditional power always involves, in two different
ways, reference to properties that are instantiated in our world and
which, *ex hypothesi*, would not be instantiated in the alternative
world in question. It involves reference to the properties on which the
power is conditional, and also to the properties in the instantiation of
which the exercise of the power would result. For example, one of the
conditional powers in the property of being knife-shaped is the power,
conditionally upon being made of steel, of leaving a knife-shaped
impression if pressed into soft wax and then withdrawn. This
conditional power, although not by itself identical to the property of
being knife-shaped, could not be exercised without that property
being instantiated. Neither could it be exercised without the property
of being made of steel being instantiated. And a conditional power
could not be instantiated in a world in which the causal laws would
not allow an exercise of it. So in general, a conditional power could
not be instantiated in a world in which the causal laws did not permit
the instantiation of the properties whose instantiation would be
involved in its instantiation or in its exercise.

Nothing I have said precludes the possibility of there being worlds
in which the causal laws are different from those that prevail in this
world. But it seems to follow from my account of property identity
that if the laws are different then the properties will have to be different
as well. And it does not appear that we have the resources for
describing a world in which the properties that can be instantiated
differ from what I shall call the 'actual world properties,' that is, those
that can be instantiated in the actual world. We have just seen that we
cannot do this by imagining the conditional powers that exist in this

world to be governed by different laws, and so to be differently grouped into properties.

It might seem that we can at least imagine a world in which *some* of the properties that can be instantiated are actual world properties while others are not. But a specification of the causal potentialities of one property will involve mention of other properties, a specification of the causal potentialities of those other properties will involve mention of still other properties, and so on. If there could be a world in which some but not all of the actual world properties can be instantiated, this could only be because those properties were causally insulated, as it were, from the rest – that is, were such that their causal potentialities could be fully specified without reference to the rest and vice versa. It seems unlikely that any proper subset of the actual world properties is causally insulated in this way – and any that are insulated from all properties we know about are thereby insulated from our knowledge and our language. But could there be a world in which the properties that can be instantiated include all of the actual world properties plus some others? This would be possible only if the two sets of properties, the actual world properties and the properties that cannot be instantiated in the actual world, were causally insulated from one another. And because of this, it would be impossible for us to say anything about the properties that cannot be instantiated in the actual world; for what we can describe is limited to what can be specified in terms of properties that can be so instantiated. What we could describe of such a world would have to be compatible with the laws that specify the causal potentialities of the actual world properties and, what we have found to be inseparable from these, the laws describing the lawlike connections between the conditional powers that constitute these properties.

Now let us consider the second attempt to reconcile the claim that the identity of a property is determined by its causal potentialities with the apparent conceivability of worlds in which the causal laws that obtain are different from, and incompatible with, those that obtain in the actual world. This involves the proposal that we adopt a 'core cluster theory' in place of the 'total cluster theory,' and make the identity of a property depend on a proper subset, rather than on the totality, of the causal potentialities it has in the actual world. Like the first attempted reconciliation, this involves the idea that at least some of the lawlike connections between conditional powers hold only contingently; it is this that is supposed to make it possible for the composition of the total cluster associated with a property to differ from one possible world to another, owing to different conditional powers being causally linked with the conditional powers in the property's essential core cluster. But it would seem that the lawlike connections between those conditional powers included in the essential core cluster will have to hold of logical necessity, i.e., in all possible worlds. For if they held only contingently, then in some possible worlds they would not hold. In such a world, the individual conditional powers which in the actual world constitute the essential core of the property could be instantiated, but the property itself could not be instantiated. Even if these conditional powers could be instantiated together in such a world, their coinstantiation would not count as the instantiation of a property, and so of that property, since the requisite causal unity would be lacking. But I have already argued, in discussing the first attempted reconciliation, that it is not possible that there should be a world in which conditional powers that are instantiated in the actual world can be instantiated while actual world properties cannot be instantiated.

But if, as I have just argued, the lawlike connections between conditional powers within the essential core cluster will have to hold of logical necessity, then we are faced with a problem. Some lawlike connections between conditional powers will hold contingently (according to the core cluster theory), while others will hold as a matter of logical necessity. How are we to tell which are which? It does not appear that we can distinguish these lawlike connections epistemologically, i.e., by the way in which they are known. For if, as I am assuming, there are truths that are necessary a posteriori, the fact that a connection is discovered empirically is no guarantee that it does not hold necessarily. Nor can it be said that we identify the necessary connections by the fact that they hold between conditional powers belonging to some property's essential core cluster; for this presupposes that we have some way of identifying essential core clusters, and how are we to do this if we do not already know which connections between conditional powers are necessary and which are contingent?

It might be suggested that what constitutes a set of conditional powers as constituting an essential core cluster is just its being a lawlike truth that whatever has any of its members has all of them, and that it is by discovering such lawlike truths that we identify essential core clusters. Given that the lawlike connections between members of essential core clusters hold of logical necessity, this would amount to the claim that if two conditional powers are so related that the possession of either of them is both causally necessary and causally sufficient for the possession of the other, then the lawlike connection between them holds as a matter of logical necessity, while if the possession of one is causally sufficient but not causally necessary for the possession of the other then the lawlike connection may be contingent. I have no knockdown argument against this view, but it seems to me implausible. If it is possible for it to be a contingent fact that the possession of one conditional power is causally sufficient for the possession of another, then it seems to me that it ought to be possible for it to be a contingent fact that the possession of one conditional power is both causally necessary and causally sufficient for the possession of another; that is, it ought to be possible for it to be contingently true of two conditional powers that the possession of either of them is causally sufficient for the possession of the other. So if we deny that the latter is a possibility, we should also deny that the former is.

It may be suggested that it is our linguistic conventions that make certain causal potentialities essential to a property, and so determine the makeup of a property's essential core cluster. But this cannot be so. It may in some cases belong to the conventionally determined sense of a property word that the property it designates has certain causal potentialities; while I think there is no need for property words to have such Fregean senses, and think that such words often function much as Kripke thinks natural kind terms do, I have no wish to deny that a property word can have a conventionally determined sense. But there is only so much that linguistic conventions can do; and one thing they cannot do is to dictate to reality, creating lawlike connections and *de re* necessities. Having discovered that certain conditional powers necessarily go together, and so are appropriately related for being part of an essential core cluster, we can lay down the convention that a certain word applies, in any possible world, to those and only those things having those conditional powers. But this leaves open the question of how we know that the conditional powers in question are appropriately related – that they must go together in any world in which either can be instantiated. And here appeal to convention cannot help us.

It begins to appear that if we hold that some lawlike connections are contingent, there is no way in which we could discover which of the lawlike connections between conditional powers are logically necessary and which are logically contingent, and so no way in which we could identify the essential core clusters of properties. This means that when we conceive, or seem to be conceiving, of a possible world in which the actual world properties are governed by somewhat different laws, there is no way in which we can discover whether we are conceiving of a genuine possibility. All that any of our empirical investigations can tell us is what lawlike connections obtain in the actual world; and without some way of telling which of these connections are contingent and which necessary, this gives us no information about what can be the case in other possible worlds. This makes all talk about what logically might be and might have been completely idle, except where questions of logical possibility can be settled a priori. If the core cluster theory makes the modal status of causal connections, their being necessary or contingent, epistemologically indeterminate in this way, it does not really save the intuitions which lead us to resist the total cluster theory, according to which all such connections are necessary. Unless we are prepared to abandon altogether the idea that there is a 'fact of the matter' as to whether there are logically possible circumstances in which a given property would make a certain contribution to the causal powers of its subject, I think we must accept the total cluster theory and its initially startling consequence that all of the causal potentialities of a property are essential to it.

X

If, as my theory implies, there are no situations that are logically but not causally possible, how is it that we are apparently able to conceive or imagine such situations? Saul Kripke has suggested one answer to a very similar question.[16] He holds that it is a necessary truth that heat is molecular motion, but recognizes that it seems as if we can imagine heat turning out to be something other than this. According to Kripke, this appearance of conceivability is something to be explained away, and he explains it away by claiming that the seeming conceivability of heat turning out not to be molecular motion consists in the actual conceivability of something else, namely of sensations of a certain sort, those that we in fact get from heat, turning out to be caused by something other than molecular motion. The latter really is conceivable, he holds, and for understandable reasons we mistake its conceivability for the conceivability of something that is in fact not conceivable.

But if conceivability is taken to imply possibility, this account commits one to the possibility that the sensations we get from heat might standardly be caused by something other than molecular motion (and so something other than heat); more than that, it commits

[16] *Ibid.*, pp. 331–342.

one to the possibility that this might be so and that these sensations might be related to other sensations and sense-experiences in all the ways they are (or have been to date) in the actual world. And since the property of having such sensations is one that is actualized in this world, this would commit one, in my view, to the claim that it is compatible with the laws of nature that prevail in the actual world that these sensations should be so caused and so related to other experiences. Now this claim may be true – if 'may be' is used epistemically. But it is hard to see how we are entitled to be confident that it is. For might there not be laws, unknown to us, that make it impossible that the standard cause of these sensations should be anything other than it is, given the way they are related to the rest of our experience? If the seeming conceivability of heat turning out to be something other than molecular motion does not prove the actual possibility of this, why should the seeming conceivability of certain sensations being caused by something other than molecular motion prove the actual, and so causal, possibility of that? And if seeming conceivability no more proves possibility in the latter case than in the former, there seems little point in distinguishing between conceivability and seeming conceivability; we may as well allow that it is conceivable (and not just seemingly conceivable) that heat should turn out to be molecular motion, and then acknowledge that conceivability is not conclusive proof of possibility. We could use the term 'conceivable' in such a way that it is conceivable that P just in case not-P is not provable a priori. Or we could use it in such a way that it is conceivable that P just in case it is epistemically possible that it is possible that P should be the case – that is, just in case P's being possible is compatible, for all we know, with what we know. These uses of 'conceivable' are not equivalent, but on both of them it is possible to conceive of what is not possible.

XI

Although many of the implications of the account I have advanced are radically at odds with Humean views about causality, it does enable us to salvage one of the central tenets of the Humean view, namely the claim that singular causal statements are 'implicitly general.' As I see it, the generality of causal propositions stems from the generality of properties, that is, from the fact that properties are universals, together with the fact which I began this essay by pointing out, namely that causal relations hold between particular events in virtue of the properties possessed by the constituent objects of those events, and the fact, which I have tried to establish in the essay, that the identity of a property is completely determined by its potential for contributing to the causal powers of the things that have it. If I assert that one event caused another, I imply that the constituent objects of the cause event had properties which always contribute in certain ways to the causal powers of the things that have them, and that the particular episode of causation at hand was an actualization of some of these potentialities. I may of course not know what the relevant properties of the cause event were; and if I do know this, I may know little about their causal potentialities. This is closely related to the now familiar point that in claiming to know the truth of a singular causal statement one is not committed to knowing the laws in virtue of which it holds.[17] Moreover, a singular causal statement does not commit one to the claim that the instantiation of the relevant properties in relevant similar circumstances always produces the effect that it did in the case at hand; for the laws governing these properties may be statistical, the powers to which the properties contribute may, accordingly, be statistical tendencies or propensities, and the causation may be nonnecessitating. Also, the claim that singular causal statements are implicitly general does not, as here interpreted, imply anything about how such statements are known – in particular, it does not imply the Humean view that causal relationships can only be discovered *via* the discovery of regularities or 'constant conjunctions.' But where the present theory differs most radically from theories in the Humean tradition is in what it claims about the modality of the general propositions, the laws, that explain the truth of singular causal propositions; for whereas on the Humean view the truth of these propositions is contingent, on my view it is logically necessary. I thus find myself, in what I once would have regarded as reactionary company, defending the very sort of 'necessary connection' account of causality which Hume is widely applauded for having refuted.

Postscript

(The following was appended to the original publication of this essay as a "Note Added in Proof.")
Richard Boyd has offered the following as a counter example to the account of properties proposed in this essay. Imagine a world in which the basic physical elements include substances *A, B, C,* and *D.* Suppose

---

[17] See, for example, Donald Davidson, "Causal Relations," *The Journal of Philosophy,* 64 (1967), 691–703.

that X is a compound of A and B, and Y is a compound of C and D. We can suppose that it follows from the laws of nature governing the elements that these two compounds, although composed of different elements, behave exactly alike under all possible circumstances – so that the property of being made of X and the property of being made of Y share all of their causal potentialities. (This means, among other things, that it follows from the laws that once a portion of X or Y is formed, it cannot be decomposed into its constituent elements.) It would follow from my account of properties that being made of X and being made of Y are the same property. And this seems counterintuitive. If, as appears, X and Y would be different substances, the property of being composed of the one should be different from the property of being composed of the other.

I think that this example does show that my account needs to be revised. I propose the following as a revised account which is still clearly a causal account of properties: for properties F and G to be identical, it is necessary *both* that F and G have the same causal potentialities *and* (this is the new requirement) that whatever set of circumstances is sufficient to cause the instantiation of F is sufficient to cause the instantiation of G, and vice versa. This amounts to saying that properties are individuated by their possible causes as well as by their possible effects. No doubt Boyd's example shows that other things I say in the essay need to be amended.

II

Identity, properties, and causality

I

I want to discuss in this essay a view about identity that goes back at least to Hume, namely that identity through time, or at any rate what we count as identity through time, consists at least in part in the holding of causal relations of certain kinds between momentary entities – events, or momentary thing-stages (phases, slices) – existing or occurring at different times. The idea is that what links these entities into the history of a single persisting object, or at least what makes us regard them as belonging to the history of a single object, is their being causally related in certain ways. The causal relation is, of course, not itself held to be the relation of identity. Rather, it is, in the terminology of John Perry, the "unity relation" for objects of the sort in question; that is, it is the relation such that its holding between numerically different entities constitutes their being stages of, or somehow belonging to (the history of), a single object of a certain kind.[1] Reichenbach seems to have been giving expression to such a view when he wrote that "A physical thing is . . . a series of events; any two events belonging to this series are called genidentical," and that "We apply the relation of genidentity only to events connected by a causal chain."[2] As Reichenbach uses the term, "genidentity" seems to be another word for Perry's unity relationship. An earlier expression of such a view occurs in W. E. Johnson's *Logic*: "The unity which I ascribe to the continuant is a causal unity of connection between its temporally or spatially separated manifestations; an observed or assumed causal formula, under which the character of these manifes-

  [1] See John Perry, "The Problem of Personal Identity," in his anthology *Personal Identity* (Berkeley and Los Angeles, 1975), pp. 3–30.
  [2] Hans Reichenbach, *The Direction of Time* (Berkeley and Los Angeles, 1956), p. 38. See also section XXVI of that book, "The Genidentity of Quantum Particles," and Reichenbach's earlier book, *The Philosophy of Space and Time* (New York, 1958), pp. 270–271.

tations may be subsumed, is the sole ground for regarding them as manifestations of one and the same continuant."[3]

I shall discuss this idea in connection with another idea with which it may seem to be naturally linked. Crudely put, the second idea is that what we regard as persisting objects are logical fictions, or at any rate logical constructions, whose supposed identity is reducible to the holding of relations of various sorts between nonidentical entities. The identity through time of these entities is thought of as being either wholly fictitious (which was Hume's view) or at least something somehow imposed on reality by human thought, human language, or human conventions. On such a view, one could in principle describe the world completely, or as completely as it can be described, without asserting any "cross-temporal identities" (as I shall call propositions asserting that something existing at one time is identical to something existing at a different time).

This formulation is, as I say, crudely put; it tars with the same brush a number of different views. To see what a range of views I mean to lump together for my purposes here, consider the variety of views compatible with the claim that a material object is "nothing over and above" a set, series, or mereological sum of temporary thing-stages. There are, of course, many sets, series, or sums of temporary thing-stages that we do not ordinarily think of as persisting objects – for example, the set or sum consisting of the stages of my knife on the even-numbered days of the month and the stages of my cat on the odd-numbered days. Now there are two *prima facie* very different views that agree in holding that the ontological status of what we ordinarily think of as persisting objects, that is, as "continuants," is on a par with that of such entities. On the one hand, there is the view that the identity of continuants is fictitious just because it is on a par with the identity of such spatiotemporally scattered objects. On the other hand, there is the view that the ontological status of such scattered objects, in being on a par with that of ordinary continuants, is much more robust than would ordinarily be supposed. What these views have in common is the idea that it is not a difference in ontological status, but only pragmatic considerations of various kinds, that accounts for the favored treatment which ordinary continuants receive in our language and "conceptual scheme" – for example, the fact that we have names for some of them, have common nouns and other sortal predicates that can be used to classify them, and so on.

[3] W. E. Johnson, *Logic, Part III: The Logical Foundations of Science* (New York, 1964), p. 99.

What the identity conditions are for a given kind of object will be a matter of linguistic convention, and only pragmatic considerations will limit what conventions are adopted, that is, what sorts of sets, series, or sums of thing-stages will be singled out for recognition in our language. On the one view, continuants are in a sense the creation of our conventions, and so are fictions. On the other view, what the conventions do is select rather than create; the various entities are all there, most of them scattered objects which we can afford to ignore, and our conventions provide rules for picking certain of them out. Both views can, I think, be described as conventionalist and reductionist views of the identity of material objects. On either view, what is asserted by a statement of cross-temporal identity can be expressed by a statement that does not invoke the notion of identity through time at all, and talks merely of momentary things and their interrelations.

I think it is natural to assume that anyone who proposes a causal analysis of cross-temporal identity, and says that the identity of material objects and persons over time consists in the holding of certain sorts of causal relations between momentary thing-stages, will be putting forward a conventionalist and reductionist view of this sort. And it has been common for philosophers who reject such views to reject any suggestion that the cross-temporal identity of genuine continuants can be said to consist in the holding of any relations other than the relation of identity itself. Thus Bishop Butler and Thomas Reid held that genuine identity is indefinable. And whenever, as in the case of organisms and artifacts, it seems plausible to say that identity over time does "consist in" the holding of certain relationships (spatiotemporal continuity, causal relationships, etc.) holding between entities existing or occurring at different times, they took this as showing that what we have in these cases is not identity in the "strict and philosophical sense" at all, but is, rather, what Butler called identity in a "loose and popular sense" and what Reid contrasted with "perfect identity" by calling it "something which, for conveniency of speech, we call identity."[4] This point of view is vigorously represented in our own time by Roderick Chisholm. Like Butler and Reid, Chisholm regards persisting tables and ships, and presumably trees and dogs as well, as "*entia successiva*," logical constructions out of more short-lived entities, and contrasts them with the "*entia per se*" to which alone identity through time in the "strict and philosophical

---

[4] See Joseph Butler, "Of Personal Identity," First Dissertation to the *Analogy of Religion* (reprinted in Perry (ed.), *Personal Identity*) and Thomas Reid, *Essays on the Intellectual Powers of Man* (Cambridge, Mass., and London, 1969), p. 344.

sense" can be ascribed.[5] And he thinks, again like Butler and Reid, that the identity of persons, unlike the identity of tables and the like, is identity in the strict and philosophical sense – in other words, that persons are *entia per se*. One source of this view which I shall not discuss here is the allegiance of these philosophers to the doctrine Chisholm calls "mereological essentialism," which says that whatever parts a thing has are essential to it and so must belong to it throughout its history. But I suspect that where this view does not rest on confusion, it rests on the idea that only arbitrary or pragmatically based conventions could account for the fact that certain changes in the composition of a thing and not others are counted as compatible with its continued existence, and on the idea that the truth conditions for assertions of identity in the strict and philosophical sense cannot be determined by such conventions.

Despite my disagreement with much of what Butler, Reid, and Chisholm say about identity, including their mereological essentialism, I am sympathetic with their rejection of reductivism and conventionalism about the identity of continuants over time. I believe that there is a difference between the ontological status of what we ordinarily regard as continuants, on the one hand, and that of sets, series, or sums of thing-stages, on the other, which makes it appropriate to regard the former and not the latter as genuine continuants having an identity, or unity, across time which is something over and above the unity which any two arbitrarily selected things partake of in virtue of their joint membership in indefinitely many different sets of mereological sums – and that this is a unity, moreover, that is not conferred by linguistic conventions, or by the pragmatic considerations that lead us to cut up the world in the way we do. But, and this will be my main point in this essay, I think that this is not only compatible with the view that identity through time "consists in" causal relations of a certain kind, but is actually implied by a causal account which I think is plausible on other grounds. The causal account I shall give, in fact, combines causal accounts of two different things – the nature of identity through time and the nature of the properties things have at the different times in their existence.

II

I shall begin with considerations that seem to me to show that it is a requirement for the cross-temporal identity of ordinary sorts of continuants that successive stages or phases in their histories stand in

---

[5] See Roderick Chisholm, *Person and Object* (La Salle, Illinois, 1976), ch. 3, "Identity Through Time."

appropriate causal relationships, and that there is a good sense in which the holding of these relationships may be said to be constitutive of the identity. One route to this conclusion is through a consideration of memory theories of personal identity. Beginning with Locke, many philosophers have held that, as Hume put it, in the case of persons "memory not only discovers the identity, but also contributes to its production,"[6] and various examples have been produced that seem to support the claim that facts about memory are at least partially constitutive of personal identity.[7] But recent discussion has convincingly shown that the concept of memory is itself a causal concept – that a present belief or impression counts as a memory of a past action or experience only if it stands to it in an appropriate causal relationship.[8] If you put the memory theory of personal identity together with the causal theory of memory, and then generalize the result in a suitable way, what you get is a causal theory of the identity through time of continuants.

A second route to our conclusion is through a consideration of the role of similarity as evidence of identity. Similarity is not always good evidence of identity, so we need to ask under what circumstances it is good evidence. And while it is obvious that resemblance with respect to a certain property will be poor evidence of identity if the possession of that property is known to be common among things of the sort in question, it is not so often noticed that resemblance with respect to a property can be no evidence, or poor evidence, of identity even if the having of that property is rare. Suppose that the chairs in a certain building are all of the same shape and size, but rarely of the same color. Suppose further that once a year, on 1 January, all of the chairs in the building are repainted, and that the color a given chair is painted is chosen at random, so that only by coincidence will a chair have the same color before and after the repainting. And suppose I know all of this. If in December I am asked whether a given chair is the one I saw in February of the same year, the fact that it has the same color as that chair had then will be very good evidence for an affirmative answer. But if in December I am asked whether a given chair is the same as one

[6] David Hume, *A Treatise of Human Nature*, ed. by L. A. Selby-Bigge (Oxford, 1888), p. 261.

[7] See, for example, Anthony Quinton, "The Soul," *The Journal of Philosophy*, 59 (1962), 393–409, and my *Self-Knowledge and Self-Identity* (Ithaca, N.Y., 1963), especially pp. 23–25. A classic statement of a memory theory of personal identity is H. P. Grice, "Personal Identity," *Mind*, 50 (1941), 330–350.

[8] See C. B. Martin and M. Deutscher, "Remembering," *The Philosophical Review*, 75 (1966), 161–196. See also David Wiggins, *Identity and Spatiotemporal Continuity* (Oxford, 1967) and my "Persons and Their Pasts" (Essay 2 of this volume).

I saw the previous December, the fact that it has the same color as that chair will be no evidence at all of identity. What this brings out is the following principle: if the way object B is at one time resembles the way object A was at an earlier time, it is reasonable to conclude from this that A is identical to B *only if* it is reasonable in the circumstances to conclude that B is the way it is at the later time *because*, among other things, A was the way it was at the earlier time. If we take the resemblance as evidence of identity, we are committed to thinking that if A had possessed different properties at the earlier time, B would have had correspondingly different properties at the later time – other things being equal, of course. This condition is satisfied in the first case involving the chairs. If the chair I saw in February was canary yellow, and the one I see now is canary yellow, then it is reasonable for me to conclude that this one is canary yellow because that one was, and that if that one had not been canary yellow, this one would not be canary yellow now; and in being entitled to believe this I am entitled to believe that they are one and the same chair. But in the second case, the condition is not satisfied. Supposing the chair I see now is sky blue, and the one I saw last December was sky blue, I am not entitled to suppose that this chair is sky blue because that one was then, or that if that one had not been sky blue then, this one would not be now. And just for this reason, I am not entitled to take the similarity as evidence of identity. It is worth observing that a similar principle governs our entitlement to take a correspondence between seeming memories and preceding actions or experiences as evidence of personal identity; if person S manifests at time t_2 an ostensible memory of doing an action of sort X at time t_1, and such an action was in fact done at time t_1 by person S', we are entitled to conclude on this basis that S is identical to S' only if it is reasonable in the circumstances to conclude that S has the seeming memory he does at t_2 because of what S' did at t_1, and that if S' had acted differently at t_1, S would have different memories at t_2.

What this strongly suggests is that those series of thing-stages that are histories of persisting things, genuine continuants, are distinguished from series that are not, that is, series made up of stages from histories of different things, by the fact that what properties are instantiated in later stages of a genuine history is a function of, among other things, what properties were instantiated in earlier stages of it. In the simplest case, where the thing has had minimal interaction with other things and has minimal internal complexity, the causal connections linking the stages will be what I shall call "property preserving" ones, and will result in similarity between successive stages. Such similarity is often used as evidence of identity; but as I have just argued, it is evidence of identity only insofar as it is evidence of counterfactual dependence, which in turn I take to indicate a causal relationship. And when things change, their new properties are normally a function of their old; how something is affected by interaction with other things will depend on what properties it had prior to the onset of the interaction, and in processes such as biological growth later stages are causally generated out of earlier ones in a way that yields a fixed pattern of change. If I squeeze a lump of clay, the shape of the resulting piece will depend on the shape and composition of the original piece as well as on how much force was applied and where. The mighty oak will have different properties than the sapling from which it grew; but the properties of the sapling provide a basis for predicting what the properties of the mature tree will be.

Returning briefly to personal identity, I think we can now see the relation of this to memory in a better light. That someone existing at a later time has the interests, values, and personality traits of someone existing at an earlier time can be just as good evidence of his identity with that person as the fact that he has seeming memories that correspond to things that person did at the earlier time. But mere cross-temporal similarity, whether it be physical or psychological, seems ill-suited for being constitutive of cross-temporal identity. It is probably because of this that philosophers who believe that personal identity consists in mental or psychological facts have concentrated their attention on facts involving memory – the other relevant mental facts have been seen as reducing to cross-temporal similarities or chains of such similarities (as when there is gradual change over time). But we have seen that cross-temporal similarity is evidence of cross-temporal identity only insofar as it is evidence of a causal dependence of later stages on earlier ones, and that memory involves a similar sort of causal dependence. Seen in this light, the fact that someone's personality traits, etc., stand in appropriate relations of causal dependence to those of someone in the past has as good a claim to be constitutive of a fact of personal identity as does the fact that his mental states include memories (or, to avoid a possible circularity, "quasi-memories"[9]) of that person's past actions or experiences. Remembering is best seen as just a special, albeit very important, case of the retention of acquired mental states, which in turn is a special case of the sort of causal dependence that is central to the unity relation for continuants in general.

---

[9] For this notion, see my "Persons and Their Pasts" (Essay 2).

III

The suggestion most frequently made about the cross-temporal identity of material things is that this consists in spatiotemporal continuity – that what links different table-stages into the history of a single table is their belonging to a spatiotemporally continuous series of table-stages. But it is not difficult to show that the spatiotemporal continuity account is inadequate and has to be replaced or supplemented by an account in terms of causality. I shall begin with some fanciful examples.

Suppose, contrary to fact, that the following remarkable machines are possible. The first is a table canceller; if you have set its controls so as to pick out a certain location, then pushing a button on the machine will cause any table at that location to vanish into thin air. The second is a table producer; if you have set its controls so as to pick out a certain location, then pushing a button on the machine will cause a table to materialize out of thin air at that location, and the properties of that table will depend on the setting of the machine and on nothing else. I shall suppose that we have tried out both of these machines separately on many occasions and that they have always performed as described. We have rid the world of many hideous tables and created many handsome new ones. But now we set the controls of the machines so that the location picked out on both is that of my dining room table, and we push both buttons simultaneously. Assuming that the controls of the table producer are set to produce tables of the shape, size, and color of my present dining room table, it will look as if nothing has happened. There will be a spatiotemporally continuous series of table-stages, and it will appear to the casual observer as if the same table has persisted throughout. But knowing the powers of the machines, we know that this is not so. If *t* is the time at which the buttons were pushed, then the nature of the table-stages that occurred after *t* is due to the pushing of the button on the table producer at *t*, and not at all due to the properties of the table that was there before *t*; given that the button was pushed, we would have had such a table there after *t* even if there had been no table, or a very different table, there before. It seems plain that in this case one table has been replaced by another.

If you prefer a theological example, imagine an absent-minded deity who decides to arrange some miracles. He decrees that at a certain time a certain object – let it be a stone tablet – will disappear into thin air. Then, having forgotten all about this decree, and all about the existence of that stone tablet, he issues another decree, this one to the effect that at that time there will come into existence at a certain place a stone tablet of a certain description – and by coincidence the place and description are precisely those of the existing tablet at the time of its decreed annihilation. The time comes and the decreed events both occur. But the multitudes are unimpressed, for what they observe is simple a spatiotemporally continuous series of tablet-stages which they reasonably, although mistakenly, take to be the continued existence of a single tablet. What our deity has inadvertently done is to replace one tablet with another just like it, and in such a way as to preserve spatiotemporal continuity.[10]

Both of these stories are unlikely, to put it mildly; but they do not seem to me to be incoherent. And the claim that they are coherent fits with a causal theory, but not with the view that the identity of material things consists in spatiotemporal continuity. I do not know whether material persistence requires spatiotemporal continuity; but I suspect that if it does, this is because the relevant sorts of causality require it.

IV

Another objection to spatiotemporal continuity and continuity of properties accounts of cross-temporal identity has been made, independently, by Saul Kripke[11] and D. M. Armstrong.[12] This is based on the close connection there is between the notion of persistence, or cross-temporal identity, and the notion of motion. Among the properties that can be ascribed to a thing at a time are what might be called states of motion – for example, moving relative to some other thing at a certain velocity, accelerating at a certain rate, rotating with a certain angular velocity, and so on. But it seems obvious that it is impossible to give a noncircular analysis of cross-temporal identity in terms of relations between momentary thing-stages if we include states of motion among the properties that characterize or define our

---

[10] In a paper entitled "Identity Through Time," which I saw in manuscript after this section was written, David Armstrong uses a very similar example to make essentially the same point. Armstrong's paper is in Peter van Inwagen (ed.), *Time and Cause. Essays Presented to Richard Taylor* (Dordrecht, Netherlands, 1980).

[11] In lectures on "Time and Identity" given at Cornell in the spring of 1978. In response to these lectures, I have added the present section and section VIII to this essay, and made minor changes elsewhere; but I cannot pretend to have done justice to Kripke's extremely rich, provocative, and illuminating treatment of the topic of identity through time.

[12] In "Identity Through Time."

momentary thing-stages. At any rate, this is so on the usual understanding of the notion of motion; for on that understanding, the notion of motion must be explained in terms of the notion of cross-temporal identity – something that existed only for (or at) a durationless instant could not move, and could not have an instantaneous velocity. Now on a continuity analysis of cross-temporal identity, the truth values of all cross-temporal identity propositions that hold in a world should follow from a description of the history of that world as a series of what Kripke calls "holographic states" (think of a three-dimensional moving picture, each "frame" of which is a hologram), each of which is given by a maximal description of the world as it was at a particular temporal instant, where the description is not such as to imply the existence at any other moment of time of any of the things referred to or quantified over in it. Thus while such a state could include the fact that a red cube of a certain size is at a certain distance from a blue sphere of a certain size, it could not include the fact that these objects are moving toward each other, or the fact that the sphere was rotating at a certain rate; states of motion, since they imply facts of cross-temporal identity, cannot be included in holographic states. But Kripke points out that if the world described includes a perfectly uniform disk made of homogeneous material, the description of the series of holographic states will be the same whether the disk is stationary or rotating, and will be the same no matter at what rate it is rotating. So there will be identity questions, for example, whether the portion of the disk occupying a certain portion of space at one time (for simplicity we shall assume an absolute Newtonian space-time) is the same as one occupying that portion of space at another time, which will not be answerable on the basis of a spatiotemporal continuity or continuity of properties criterion of cross-temporal identity. Armstrong's example is the same, except that the homogeneous object is a sphere rather than a disk.[13]

Despite the similarity of their examples, Kripke and Armstrong have different purposes. Kripke's argument is part of a general attack

---

[13] It might be suggested that the momentary states of a rotating disk or sphere will differ from those of a stationary one with respect to the forces that exist at each moment of time; the parts of the rotating object will be subjected to centrifugal forces, which must be balanced by centripetal ones. If reference to forces can be included in descriptions of "holographic states," then indeed the series of holographic states will be different depending on whether the object is rotating. But the notion of force is closely tied to the notion of acceleration, and so with the notion of motion. It would seem arbitrary, at best, to allow reference to forces in descriptions of holographic states while refusing to allow reference to instantaneous velocities and accelerations.

on the idea that there are constitutive "criteria" for the identity through time of material objects, one version of which is the view that such identity consists in the holding of certain relations (specifiable without the use of the notion of cross-temporal identity) between momentary thing-stages. But Armstrong is a supporter of the latter view, which he calls the "Relational View," and introduces the example of the sphere in order to show that a causal version of the Relational View avoids the difficulty this example poses for other versions of the view. If the sphere is stationary, he says, then the phases of the eastern portion from t_1 to t_2 will bear to each other that special causal relationship which must hold between different phases of the same thing; in particular, the existence of the earlier phases will be "nomically required" in a distinctive way for the existence of the later phases. The causal relations will be different if the sphere is rotating.

Armstrong's suggestion would seem to be supported by the fact that different counterfactuals will be true of the successive phases of the rotating sphere than will be true of the successive phases of the stationary sphere. Suppose that between t_1 and t_2 the sphere rotates 180°. Then it will be true (assuming that the sphere is made of scratch-retentive material) that if at t_1 the eastern portion of the sphere had had a scratch of a certain shape on it, and the sphere had been otherwised unscratched, then at t_2 the western portion of the sphere would have had such a scratch on it, and the sphere would have been otherwise unscratched. Whereas if the sphere had been stationary between t_1 and t_2, a different counterfactual would hold, namely that if at t_1 the sole scratch on the sphere had been on the eastern portion, then at t_2 it would also be the case that the sole scratch on the sphere is on the eastern portion. It would seem that this difference in what counterfactuals are true in the two cases must be due to a difference in the causal relationships that hold between the different "sphere-phases" in the two cases, and that if we incorporate such causal relationships into our unity relationship, we avoid the difficulty raised by the Kripke–Armstrong examples.

It is natural to object that it seems very unlikely that we can specify the relevant causal relationships without invoking the notion of motion and with it the notion of cross-temporal identity, or of a persisting thing, which we are trying to analyze.[14] Let E_1 be the eastern portion of our sphere at t_1, E_2 the eastern portion of our sphere at t_2, and W_2 the western portion of our sphere at t_2. In the case where the sphere

---

[14] Something like this objection was made to me in conversation by Saul Kripke; but my formulation of it may not capture all that he had in mind.

is stationary, the state of E_2 at t_2 is counterfactually dependent on the state of E_1 at t_1, and it seems reasonable to assume that this counterfactual dependence is grounded in causal relationships. Here, of course, E_1 and E_2 are identical. Likewise, in the case in which the sphere is rotating, and rotates 180° between t_1 and t_2 the state of W_2 at t_2 is counterfactually dependent on the state of E_1 at t_1, and again it seems reasonable to assume that this relation is grounded in a causal relationship. Here E_1 and W_2 are identical. But the causally relevant state of E_1 at t_1 cannot consist simply in its having a certain shape, size, and composition, for such properties are ones that E_1 has in both cases (that is, both when the sphere is stationary and when it is rotating) and so cannot account for the difference between the counterfactuals that hold in the one case and those that hold in the other. It would seem that the causally relevant state of E_1 at t_1 will crucially involve in the one case the fact that E_1 was stationary and in the other the fact that E_1 had a certain angular velocity. If the causally relevant properties include states of motion, then it seems that the attempt to analyze cross-temporal identity in terms of causality will be circular.

What we would have to do in order to answer this objection is to give an analysis of the notion of motion, and of such notions as the velocity of a thing at an instant, which does not invoke or presuppose the notion of cross-temporal identity. If the analysis is in terms of the notion of causality, then so much the better. Let us see how an attempt at such an analysis might go.

I shall assume that we have available to us the notion of a spatiotemporally continuous series of thing-stages. The case of the rotating sphere shows that not every such series is the history of a persisting thing; there will be infinitely many continuous series of hemisphere stages that are not histories of single persisting hemispheres – for example, the series of eastern hemisphere-stages in the case in which the sphere is rotating around its north-south axis. It should be possible to define the notion of the spatial length of the segment of such a series that occurs during a given temporal interval.[15] (Roughly, this will be the distance something would have traveled during that interval if the members of that series had been stages of its history – but, of course, we cannot use this as a definition if our object is to define the notion of a persisting object.) We can also speak of the temporal length of such a segment, which will be just the length of the

---

[15] This notion, and the notion of (linear) velocity defined in terms of it, should, of course, be defined so as to make the values of the lengths and velocities relative to frames of reference; but for present purposes this complication can be ignored.

interval. Using these notions, and the notion of a limit, we can define the notion of the "velocity" of such a series at an instant; if S is the class of segments of the series that occur during intervals containing instant i, then the "velocity" of the series at i will be the limit of the ratio of spatial length to temporal length of the segments in S as their temporal length approaches zero. In a similar way we can define other "states of motion" for spatiotemporally continuous series – for example, "rate of acceleration," "angular velocity," and so on. To illustrate the notion of the "velocity" of a series which is not necessarily the velocity of any persisting object, consider a case in which a light source is revolving around a sphere, illuminating one-half of it at any given moment. If the sphere is stationary, or rotating on an axis other than that on which the light source is revolving, the series of illuminated hemisphere-stages will not be the history of any particular part of the sphere. Nevertheless, it will have an "angular velocity" which depends on the angular velocity of the revolving light source.[16]

Let us now consider the subclass of spatiotemporally continuous series of stages which are such that for each stage S of the series, and for each segment of the series that includes S, that segment includes an earlier stage that stands to S in the appropriate sort of causal relationship. I shall speak of such a series as "causally connected." A thing-stage will include a certain state of motion for example, a certain velocity, just in case the stage belongs to a causally connected continuous series of thing-stages, for short a CCCS, having the corresponding "state of motion," for example, a "velocity" of a certain value, at the time in question. In the case of the series of illuminated hemisphere-stages, the "velocities" are not velocities, because the series is not causally connected. This way of defining states of motion does not in any direct way invoke the notion of a persisting thing. (It remains to be considered whether it does so surreptitiously in its reliance on the notion of an "appropriate" sort of

[16] It is worth noticing that there will be series of thing-stages that lack velocities at certain times because the distance-time ratios of the segments of the series around those times do not converge on limiting values. For example, suppose we have a sphere that is rotating at a certain uniform rate around its north-south axis. Let S_1 be the series of hemisphere-stages that is the history of the hemisphere that at time t is the eastern side of the sphere. Let S_2 be the series of eastern hemisphere stages of the sphere. At any time, S_1 has an "angular velocity" equal to the angular velocity of the sphere and S_2 has an "angular velocity" of zero. Now let S_3 be the series that includes the members of S_1 up to and including time t, and the members of S_2 at all times subsequent to t. S_3 will be a spatiotemporally continuous series. But at time t, the "angular velocity" of S_3 is undefined (at other times it has the "angular velocity" either of S_1 or S_2).

causal relation. I return to this in section VIII.) And there is no obvious reason why states of motion, as thus defined, should not have the required sort of causal efficacy.

V

It is obvious that not just any relation of causal dependence between successive thing-stages is sufficient to make the stages belong to the history of a single persisting object; otherwise forgeries of paintings would be identical to the originals from which they are copied, with all the absurdities that entails. I shall not attempt here the probably impossible task of giving a general and nontrivial characterization of a kind of causal dependence, the holding of which between successive thing-stages is always necessary and sufficient for their belonging to the same continuant. Instead, I shall content myself with a supervenience claim. Consider a world that is just like the actual world with respect to what properties are instantiated at each space-time point, and also just like the actual world with respect to what causal relations hold between these different property instantiations. I claim that if in the actual world a set of property instantiations all belong to the history of a single persisting object, then their counterparts in that other possible world likewise belong to the history of a single persisting object. More generally, if in any possible world a set S of property instantiations makes up the history of a single persisting thing, then in any world that is qualitatively identical to that world, in the sense that the same properties are instantiated at the same space-time points, and also identical to it with respect to the sorts of causal connections that hold between the various property instantiations, the set of property instantiations in that world which is the counterpart of S will likewise make up the history of a single persisting thing. This gives expression to the idea that the persistence through time of continuants is *nothing over and above* the holding of certain causal and spatiotemporal relations between different property instantiations – and since momentary thing-stages can be thought of as sets of simultaneous property instantiations that are related in certain ways, this can also be put by saying that the persistence through time of continuants is nothing over and above the holding of certain causal and spatiotemporal relations between momentary thing-stages.

The view I have just expressed must surely sound like extreme reductivism about identity through time – that is, it must sound just like the view I said at the outset I was going to oppose. But I think that it can be understood in such a way that it is not. In order to show this I must first put forward a view about the nature of properties.

VI

There is a broad sense of the word "property" in which there is a property corresponding to any grammatical predicate. Properties in the broad sense will include relational properties, like being fifty miles south of a burning barn (to use Jaegwon Kim's example), and historical properties, like being two hundred years old and having been slept in by George Washington, as well as such ordinary properties as being spherical, weighing fifty pounds, and being blue. They will also include what only a philosopher would think to count as properties, for example, being such that Jimmy Carter is President of the United States (a property that belongs to absolutely everything right now), and being grue in Goodman's sense.

Now I think that it will be agreed that usually we use the word "property" in a narrower sense than this. Suppose that someone claims that two pennies are exactly alike, that is, share all of their properties. We would doubtless think that this claim is unlikely to be true – surely when we get down to the microscopic and sub-microscopic levels, there will be some difference in their size and shape (in the number and arrangement of the particles of which they are composed). But we would not count it against the truth of this claim that the two pennies have had different histories and stand in different relations to other things – that is, that their historical and relational properties are different. Again, when my pencil loses the property of being fifty miles south of a burning barn (because the fire is extinguished, say), or when it loses the property of being such that Gerald Ford is President of the United States (because Jimmy Carter is inaugurated), we do not suppose that it thereby undergoes any genuine change. In other words, we seem to have a narrow sense of "property," which is correlative with our usual sense of "change," which excludes, as not genuine properties, relational and historical properties and the like. In the narrow sense, being spherical will be a property, but being such that Carter is President will not be. How are we to elucidate this sense? We could, of course, say that something is a property in the narrow sense if and only if its acquisition or loss constitutes a genuine change. But then we would be faced with the job of elucidating the required sense of "change," and distinguishing it from the broad sense in which everything in the universe underwent a change when Carter was inaugurated, or in which Socrates underwent a change when he became shorter than Theaetetus, in virtue of the latter's growth. We shall be going in a circle if we explain the latter by saying that a genuine change is one that involves the acquisition or loss of a genuine property. In the end, I am afraid, we shall have to settle for a circular account anyhow; but it is possible to make the circle a bit bigger than this.

My suggestion is that in order to elucidate these distinctions we must bring in the concept of causality. Consider a bed slept in by George Washington, and another bed, made by the same craftsman from the same design and the same stock of wood, that lacks this historical property. Our narrow sense of "property" should be such that it is possible for these beds to share all of their properties. Now it is plain that the beds could be so much alike that it would be impossible to *observe* any difference between them. But, of course, even if observation could detect no difference between them, one would allow that there was a genuine difference if they registered a different effect on some instrument. Suppose, however, that all of their causal powers and potentialities, all of their dispositions to influence other things or be influenced by other things, were exactly the same. Then, I suggest, they would share all of their properties in the narrow sense, all of their "intrinsic" properties. Likewise, when I say that the loss by my pencil of the property of being fifty miles south of a burning barn, or the property of being such that Gerald Ford is President, is not a real change, the cash value of this is that the acquisition or loss of these so-called properties does not in itself make any difference to the causal powers of a thing. This suggests a view about what intrinsic properties, properties in the narrow sense, are. According to this view, what constitutes the identity of such a property, what makes it the particular property it is, is its potential for contributing to the causal powers of the things that have it. Each of the potentialities that makes up a property can be specified by saying that in combination with such and such other properties that property gives rise to a certain causal power. Thus, for example, the property of having the shape of an ordinary kitchen knife – for short, the property of being knife-shaped – is partially specified by saying that if anything has this property together with the property of being made of steel, it thereby has the power of being able to cut wood if applied to it with suitable pressure. If we could indicate all of the ways in which the having of this property could contribute to the causal powers of things, we would have said all there is to say about the intrinsic nature of this property. Such, at any rate, is my suggestion.

This view recommends itself on epistemological grounds. If, *per impossibile*, there were properties whose possession made no difference whatever to the causal powers of the things that have them, there would be no way at all in which we could know of their existence, or have any reason whatever to believe in it. It is likewise true, I think, that if the identity of properties consisted in something other than and independent of their potential for contributing to the causal powers of the things that have them, then we would have no way of knowing things which in fact we are clearly capable of knowing; we would have no way of knowing whether two things possessed the same property, whether the properties possessed by something had changed, and so on. For it is only on the assumption that sameness of property goes with sameness of causal potentialities that our observations and instruments indicate what we take them to indicate.

I hasten to point out that this account of properties is circular. It tells us, in brief, that properties (intrinsic properties) are identical just in case it is true in all possible circumstances that their coinstantiation with the same properties gives rise to the same powers. This makes use of the notion of sameness of property, which is the very notion being elucidated. It also makes use of the notion of sameness of causal power, the elucidation of which would doubtless require the use of the notion of sameness of property. Despite this, the account has substantive content – it links the concept of an intrinsic property with that of causality in a way that is not customarily done, and it has some surprising consequences which I cannot go into here. And as will emerge later in this essay, if this account is right, then my earlier account of identity through time in terms of causality appears to be circular in much the same way.[17]

VII

I want now to apply this theory of properties to the problem of identity. Earlier I put the causal theory of cross-temporal identity by saying that the identity of persisting things consists in the holding of a certain sort of causal relation between momentary thing-stages, this causal relation being the "unity relation" for continuants. But we can

---

[17] The account of properties sketched in this section is developed and defended at greater length in my "Causality and Properties" (Essay 10).

achieve greater generality if we take the terms of the unity relation to be momentary property instantiations rather than momentary thing-stages. This enables us to ask, not merely how property instantiations occurring at different times must be related in order to have the same subject, but also how simultaneous property instantiations must be related in order to have the same subject – where the "subject" of a property instantiation is the thing in which the property is instantiated. In fact, we might as well take a momentary thing-stage to be just a set of simultaneous property instantiations that is closed under the unity relation, that is, a set that contains all and only the simultaneous property instantiations that stand in the unity relation to any of its members. We can then divide the problem of identity into two parts. There is the problem of specifying the relationship that unites simultaneous property instantiations into thing-stages (for short, the relationship of "synchronic unity"), and there is the problem of specifying the relationship that unites different thing-stages (and their constituent property instantiations) into histories of persisting things (this will be the relationship of "diachronic unity").

The first of these problems (if it can be called a problem) is seldom discussed.[18] And it has seldom been given the sort of reductivist and conventionalist answer that is so often given to the second question. But it is worth showing that such an answer could not be correct; this will prepare the ground for an argument against reductivist and conventionalist answers to the question about cross-temporal identity, that is, about the diachronic unity of property instantiations and thing-stages. What I shall argue is that such reductivist views are ruled out by the account of properties sketched earlier.

Consider the property of being knife-shaped and the property of being made of steel. Each of these properties, according to my account, has an essential nature which consists in its potential for contributing to the causal powers of the things that have it. The essential nature of the property of being knife-shaped includes the feature of being such as to give rise to the power of cutting wood if

[18] Except in connection with the problem of personal identity, where philosophers sometimes ask what makes simultaneous experience "co-personal," i.e., what makes them belong to the same "consciousness," or to the same "total temporary state." See Bertrand Russell, "On the Nature of Acquaintance," *Logic and Knowledge: Essays, 1901–1950*, ed. by R. C. Marsh (London, 1956); C. D. Broad, *Mind and Its Place in Nature* (London, 1925), ch. 13, "The Unity of the Mind"; Grice, "Personal Identity"; and my *Self-Knowledge and Self-Identity*, ch. 3. Where I speak in the text of "synchronic" and "diachronic" unity, Broad speaks of "transverse" and "longitudinal" unity.

combined with, that is, coinstantiated with, the property of being made of steel; and the essential nature of the property of being made of steel includes the feature of being such as to give rise to the power of cutting wood if combined with the property of being knife-shaped. In other words, it belongs to the essential natures of these two properties that if they are coinstantiated, that is, instantiated in the same subject at the same time, this gives rise to a certain causal power. This rules out a reductivist account of the synchronic unity of property instantiations. For if one cannot say what a property is without saying what happens when it is coinstantiated with other properties, that is, what happens when instantiations of it *stand in the unity relation to* instantiations of other properties, then it cannot be the case that the synchronic unity of property instantiations is an optional logical construction out of property instantiations and some relationship between them (that relationship being specifiable without the use of the notion of synchronic unity). Moreover, it is clear that on my account the nature of properties imposes severe constraints on what the synchronic unity relationship can be. Nothing could be the unity relation between simultaneous instantiations of the property of being made of steel and the property of being knife-shaped unless its holding between these instantiations guaranteed that they jointly give rise to the appropriate power, namely the power to cut wood if subjected to suitable pressure. Similar constraints will be imposed by the essential natures of any set of properties that can be instantiated together. These constraints leave little scope, if any, for conventional decision in determining the unity conditions for simultaneous property instantiations.

To illustrate this with an example of a different kind, suppose that the following mental properties are instantiated at the same time: a desire expressible by "I want to survive," a belief expressible by "To survive, I must do A," and a belief expressible by "I can do A." If these are all states of a single person, then, *ceteris paribus*, they had better give rise to an attempt to do A. There are circumstances in which this could serve as a criterion of mental unity; if in the case of a split-brain patient we have reason to ascribe certain desires to the possessor of the right brain hemisphere, and certain beliefs to the possessor of the left brain hemisphere, then whether it is correct to say that these are states of one and the same person, or of one and the same "mind," may depend on whether they jointly give rise to the effects, behavioral and otherwise, that ought to result from the coinstantiation of these mental properties. If, as seems conceivable, a set of mental property instantiations associated with a single human body could fail to pass this test for synchronic unity, then the essential nature of mental properties rules out any such relation as *occurring in the same body as* as the unity relation for simultaneous instantiations of mental properties.

Now let us return to the problem of identity through time – or, what comes to the same thing, the problem of specifying the unity relation for nonsimultaneous property instantiations and thing-stages. The essence of a property, I have argued, consists in its potential for contributing to the causal powers of the things that have it. A power, in turn, is specified by saying what will happen if the thing that has it is placed in various circumstances, or interacts in certain ways with other things. And usually this will involve saying what will happen if the thing remains in those circumstances over some interval of time, or is involved in an interaction lasting some period of time. For example, if a thing is malleable, then if subjected to sufficient force it will gradually undergo a change in shape, and will retain its new shape once the deforming force is removed; while if a thing is elastic, it will change shape when subjected to certain forces, but will resume its former shape when the forces are removed. Since a specification of the essential nature of a property will involve a specification of the powers to which it has the potential for contributing, and since a specification of the powers will say what happens to their subject *over time* given certain conditions, the essential nature of a property incorporates the persistence conditions, that is, the cross-temporal identity conditions, of the things to which it can belong. The attribution of a particular property will not have a determinate truth value unless the identity conditions for things having that property are already fixed; for the attribution of a property to a thing will imply propositions about what will happen to *that thing* under certain circumstances, and these propositions will have determinate truth value only if it is already settled under what circumstances a future happening is to count as an episode in the history of *that thing*. But if this is so, the unity conditions for nonsimultaneous property instantiations can be no more a matter for conventional decision than the unity conditions for simultaneous property instantiations.

One thing this brings out is that the laws that specify the contribution of particular properties to causal powers, and so (on my account) describe the essential nature of these properties, cannot be separated from the laws that say what happens over time to something having certain properties, including those that specify the conditions under which a property is retained or lost. In order to be able to specify the effects on a thing of various sorts of external influences, we need to be able to specify, as our baseline, the sort of history the thing would have if not subjected to those influences. And just as it is built into the nature of particular properties that a thing having those properties will undergo a certain change if subjected to a certain influence, so it is typically built into the nature of a property that in the absence of external influences (or of a change in external influences) a thing having that property will continue to have it. One might put this by saying that property instantiations have an inherent tendency to perpetuate themselves – although this would have to be qualified to allow for phenomena like biological growth and radioactive decay. The causality that works within a thing, and in general (although not invariably) works to preserve its properties, is what W. E. Johnson called "immanent causality" and contrasted with the "transuent causality" by which one thing influences another.[19] While the nature of properties consists, or so I maintain, in their potential for contributing to both sorts of causality, it is the connection with immanent causality that is of special interest here. For it follows from this that any series of thing-stages that constitutes the history of a persisting thing must be "causally connected" in a sense akin to that of section IV, not because talk of persistence is reducible to talk of causally connected series, but because of the very nature of the properties that are instantiated in these stages.

Let us say that a series of thing-stages is "immanently connected" if its later stages develop from its earlier ones in accordance with the laws of immanent causality that are, as it were, built into the nature of the properties instantiated in the states of the series (and in the stages of other series with which it interacts). What immediately follows from my account of properties is that it is a necessary condition of a series of thing-stages being the history of a persisting thing that it be immanently connected. The supervenience claim of section V can now be put by saying that this necessary condition is also sufficient – that if a series of thing-stages is such that each stage influences subsequent stages in precisely the ways it would have to, given the properties involved, if the series were the history of a single persisting thing, then the series will, in fact, be the history of a single persisting thing. This is not, as far as I can see, a consequence of my account of properties. But it is compatible with it and seems to me to be true. If something more than this is required for cross-temporal identity, for a series of thing-stages to be the history of a single persisting thing, then it is not clear

[19] See ch. 6, "The Continuant," in his *Logic*.

what this "something more" could be, or how we could know whether it was present in particular cases.

VIII

It will be recalled that in section IV the notion of a causally connected continuous series of thing-stages, or for short a *CCCS*, was introduced in order to provide a way of defining the notion of motion that did not employ the notion of a persisting thing. Such a definition was suggested as a way of defending causal analyses of cross-temporal identity against a charge of circularity; more specifically, the charge was that only if such analyses are so construed as to be circular can they handle the Kripke–Armstrong examples. The apparent circularity stemmed from the fact that the different momentary states of continuants will not be causally connected in the ways claimed by the causal theory unless they are construed as including states of motion, and the fact (or apparent fact) that the notion of motion has to be explained in terms of the notion of cross-temporal identity. If the notion of a *CCCS* can be explained without the use of the notion of cross-temporal identity, then the possibility of defining states of motion in terms of the "states of motion" of *CCCS*s would show that this circularity is only apparent.

But the definition of a *CCCS* invoked the notion of an "appropriate" causal connection between thing-stages, and this notion obviously cries out for clarification. We now have *a* way of clarifying it; we can say that the causal connection between thing-stages is appropriate just in case they belong to a series of thing-stages that is immanently connected. But as I have explained the notion of being immanently connected, this will reintroduce the circularity we were out to avoid; the notion of being immanently connected was explained in terms of the notion of immanent causality, which in turn was explained in terms of the notion of persistence, or cross-temporal identity.

Is there any hope of defining the notion of immanent causality, or the required notion of an "appropriate" causal connection between thing-stages, without the use of the notion of persistence? I do not think so. To do this we would have to be able to characterize the causal potentialities of properties without making use of the notion of persistence. We might be able to do this if we *already* had available a notion of a *CCCS* which was not explained in terms of the notion of persistence. If we had this, then instead of specifying the causal potentialities of a property by saying what will happen over time under various conditions to something having that property, we might try to specify them by saying what sorts of CCCSs would occur under various conditions when that property is instantiated. But it is precisely in order to define the notion of CCCS that we are trying to define the notion of an "appropriate" causal connection. So it now appears that in order to give a noncircular analysis of this notion, we would already have to have one; which is to say that it is not possible to give one.

The objection considered in section IV suggested that states of motion will be the Achilles' heel of any attempt to give a reductive analysis of cross-temporal identity in terms of relations between thing-stages. But these cause a problem only because of the difficulty, or impossibility, of giving a noncircular account of the notion of an "appropriate" causal connection, or of the notion of immanent causality. And this stems from the fact that what counts as an appropriate causal relation in a particular case depends on the nature of the particular properties involved in that case, and the fact that it seems impossible to characterize the relevant class of causal potentialities of properties, those relating to "immanent causality," without making use of the notion of persistence and cross-temporal identity.

IX

Now let us compare the status of those series of thing-stages (or property instantiations) that are histories of ordinary continuants (material objects or persons) with those – I shall call them "gerry-mandered series" – that are made up of stages (or property instantiations) taken from the histories of different ordinary continuants, for example, the series consisting of the stages of my knife on the even-numbered days of the month and the stages of my cat on the odd-numbered days. We can agree that these series are ontologically on a par *qua* series; likewise the mereological sums of the members of the series are ontologically on a par *qua* mereological sums. One series or mereological sum is just as real as any other. Some philosophers would conclude from this that ordinary constituents are ontologically on a par with entities whose existence is not ordinarily acknowledged – entities that correspond to, or simply are, the gerrymandered series (or mereological sums of the members thereof). This seems to me clearly wrong. First of all, from the fact that the histories of continuants are, *qua* series or sums of thing-stages, on a par with the gerrymandered series, it does not follow that the continuants themselves are on a par with the gerrymandered series; for continuants are not identical with the series or sums of stages that are their histories. And if it is said that ordinary continuants are ontologically on a par with entities of which the gerrymandered series are histories, I would reply that there simply are no such entities for them to be ontologically on a par with. At any rate, it follows from the account of properties I have given, and seems to me intuitively correct, that there is no entity corresponding to a gerrymandered series that relates to it in the way ordinary continuants relate to the series of thing-stages that are their histories.

An ordinary continuant has certain properties at a given time if and only if its history contains a stage occurring at that time which includes instantiations of those properties. So if a gerrymandered series is likewise the history of a persisting entity, then at any moment of time that entity should have, should be the subject of, whatever properties are instantiated in a member of the series occurring at that time.[20] So any entity whose history includes the stage of my knife's history that occurred at noon today has to have been knife-shaped and made of steel at noon today. But if what I have said about the essential nature of properties is right, any entity that has those properties must have the causal powers that my knife had at noon today. I have pointed out, moreover, that something's having such powers involves various conditionals being true of it, these saying what will happen to it over time under various conditions. But for any gerrymandered series, the existence of an entity having at each moment of time the properties instantiated in the series at that moment would falsify the conditionals that would have to be true of an entity having those properties. For example, if there were an entity having as its history the series consisting of the stages of my knife occurring on the even-numbered days of the month and the stages of my cat occurring on the odd-numbered days, then what happened to that entity at midnight on any given day (except on the thirty-first of the month) would violate the laws that spell out the essential natures of the properties that entity

---

[20] Anyone who thinks that stages of ordinary continuants are also stages of entities having gerrymandered series as their histories will want to put some restriction on what sort of property instantiations are to be taken as constituting these promiscuous thing-stages. Obviously such historical properties as "is something that a year earlier was in Paris" and "is something that will explode three minutes hence" will have to be excluded. And insofar as sortal concepts, like *table*, are thought of as encompassing criteria of cross-temporal identity for the entities that satisfy them, instantiations of sortal properties will have to be excluded as well. But as I argue in the text, these exclusions are not enough to protect this view from incoherence. To exclude instantiations of all properties whose natures constrain the identity conditions of the things that have them would be to exclude all property instantiations, or at least all instantiations of "intrinsic" properties.

would have to have, and would falsify the conditionals that would have to be true of it. So there could not be such an entity. Here, then, is the (or at any rate, a) difference in ontological status between those series of thing-stages that are histories of ordinary continuants, on the one hand, and gerrymandered series, on the other; the former are, while the latter are not, histories of entities that are subjects of the properties instantiated in the stages.

It may still seem to some that for any series of thing-stages, including gerrymandered series, we can introduce the notion of an object having that series as its history, and can do so in such a way as to guarantee that the object exists if the series does. If a household has exactly one table in the kitchen and exactly one in the living room, let us say that there exists a "klable" having as its history the series of stages consisting of the stages of the kitchen table from midnight to noon and those of the living room table from noon to midnight (call this the "klable series," and call table-stages that belong to such series "klable-stages"). We shall stipulate, as one of the rules defining the meaning of "klable," that at any given time the klable in a household has those properties that are instantiated in the klable-stage occurring at that time in that household. Given that there are households of the appropriate sort, it might seem that our rules guarantee (or would if we spelled them out fully enough) that there are entities that share the properties of tables at particular moments but have klable series as their histories. But this is an illusion. Such rules for the use of "klable" could not give it the status of a sortal predicate, and could not give to such expressions as "my klable" the status of being singular terms; at best they could assign to these expressions certain roles in a code for talking about tables. They might guarantee that sentences like "My klable is made of oak now, but was made of maple an hour ago" are sometimes true. But the truth of such a sentence will no more imply that something was first made of maple and then of oak than the truth of "The average man has 2.3 children" implies that there is someone who has 2.3 children. What superficially appear to be the grammatical subjects of these sentences are not genuine terms, and are not accessible to existential quantification. If our rules, together with the facts, assign the truth-value "true" to the sentence "Klables exist," then in this use of the word "exist" it will be part of the code for talking about tables and will not have its ordinary meaning.

Of course, instead of introducing "klable" as part of a code (that is, by a set of rules assigning truth conditions to certain sentences or quasi-sentences containing it) we might introduce it by the following explicit definition: "x is a klable = df. x is an entity of a kind such that, necessarily, entities of that kind are paired one–one with households having exactly one kitchen table and exactly one living room table, and each such entity shares from midnight till noon the properties of its associated kitchen table and from noon to midnight the properties of its associated living room table." Now "klable" will be, syntactically at least, a genuine sortal term. But it will be false, and I think necessarily false, that there are any klables. Only if we confuse such an explicit definition with a set of rules assigning a word like "klable" a role in a code will it seem that entities with bizarre identity conditions can be defined into existence (or that they are there all along, awaiting linguistic recognition).

If indeed the term "table" had the same status as "klable" (on the code construal of it), then it would be appropriate to say that tables are logical fictions – or, to put this more appropriately in the formal mode, that the term "table" does not refer, despite the fact that it occurs as a quasi-noun in sentences that mimic existential and subject-predicate sentences and are so defined as to be true. But there is no reason whatever to suppose that this is true; to put this in the material mode (where it cannot really be said), there is no reason whatever to suppose that tables are ontologically on a par with klables.

X

I shall end by commenting briefly on the implications of what I have been saying for the topic of personal identity. People often do philosophy of mind in a way that implies that the nature of personal identity and the nature of mental states are pretty much unrelated topics. If the thesis of this essay is right, this is a mistake. The most important properties of persons are mental or psychological ones. And an understanding of what particular mental or psychological properties are will intimately involve an understanding of both the unity conditions for simultaneous instantiations of such properties and the unity conditions for nonsimultaneous properties of them – in other words, it will intimately involve an understanding of the identity conditions for the subjects of such properties.

Interestingly enough, this is just what functionalist accounts of mental states imply. On such accounts, one says what it is for a person to have a certain mental state, for example, a certain belief, by saying how the possession of that mental state combines with the possession of various combinations of other mental states (in particular, desires and other beliefs) to influence the person's behavior and his subsequent mental states. But to speak of the possession of a mental state "combining" with the possession of others is to invoke the unity relation between simultaneous mental states, while to speak of the influence of a mental state on subsequent mental states of the same person is to invoke the unity relation between nonsimultaneous mental states.

This is not to claim, however, that the notion of personal identity is logically or conceptually prior to that of particular sorts of mental states. Such claims of conceptual priority are to be avoided. To claim the conceptual priority of the notion of personal identity *vis-à-vis* other mental notions would be to move in the direction of the sort of account of identity favored by Butler, Reid, and Chisholm, according to which personal identity (and "strict" identity generally) is "indefinable" and propositions of personal identity have no nontrivial truth conditions. To claim the conceptual priority of notions of momentary mental states or property instantiations, or of momentary "person-stages," *vis-à-vis* the notion of personal identity would be to move in the direction of a fictionalist, or at any rate reductivist, account of personal identity. Both views seem to me mistaken. On the view I would urge, the notion of personal identity and the notions of particular mental states are internally related, but neither can be said to be conceptually prior to the other. If we want philosophical illumination here, we have no choice but to move in a circle. In elucidating particular mental concepts, we shall have to help ourselves to the notion of personal identity, while in elucidating the concept of personal identity, we shall have to help ourselves to various mental concepts. And so it is in general with the concept of persisting substance or continuant, the concept of an intrinsic property, and the concept of causality; any elucidation of any of these concepts will have to make use of at least one of the others, and none of them can be eliminated in favor of the others.

12

Some varieties of functionalism

I

I take as my point of departure a procedure for formulating functional definitions which is due to David Lewis.[1] To appreciate the virtues of this procedure one should recall the circularities that have plagued attempts to give behavioral definitions of mental states. Someone who believes that it is raining may be disposed to take an umbrella when he goes out – but only if he wants to keep dry. And someone who wants to keep dry may be disposed to take an umbrella – but only if he believes that it is raining. It appears that to give a behavioral definition of either of these mental states (the belief, or the want), one would have to mention the other; so there appears to be no way of formulating a noncircular dispositional definition of both, or a purely behavioral definition of either. Lewis has shown that the functionalist, unlike the logical behaviorist, can avoid such circularities by making use of the notion of a Ramsey-sentence. One starts off with a theory which incorporates propositions stating all of the causal facts about mental states – about their relations to inputs, outputs, and one another – in terms of which one proposes to define them. One then constructs the Ramsey-sentence of this theory, which says that there is a set of states satisfying the open sentence which results from the replacement of the psychological terms in the original theory by variables (or, on Lewis's version of the procedure, one constructs the "modified Ramsey-sentence," which says that there is a unique such n-tuple of states). From the Ramsey-sentence (or modified Ramsey-sentence) one can then extract noncircular definitions of each of the mental terms that figured in the original theory. I shall refer to this as the "Ramsey–Lewis technique." As a first approximation, let us use a

[1] See Lewis's "Psychophysical and Theoretical Identifications," *Australasian Journal of Philosophy*, 50 (1972), 291–315. See also Ned Block's "Troubles with Functionalism," in C. Wade Savage (ed.), *Perception and Cognition, Issues in the Foundations of Psychology, Minnesota Studies in the Philosophy of Science* (Minneapolis, 1978), vol. IX, and Block's introduction to his anthology *Readings in the Philosophy of Psychology* (Cambridge, Mass., 1980), vol. I.

version of this procedure recently described by Ned Block.[2] Let T be our psychological theory, so written that all of its psychological terms are predicates. The Ramsey-sentence of T can be written as

$$\exists F_1 \ldots \exists F_n \, T(F_1 \ldots F_n)$$

If 'F_1' is the variable that replaced 'believes that it is raining' in the formulation of the Ramsey-sentence, and 'F_2' is the variable that replaced 'wants to keep dry,' then the following biconditionals will hold:

(1) $\times$ believes that it is raining $\leftrightarrow \exists F_1 \ldots \exists F_n[T(F_1 \ldots F_n) \, \& \, \times$ has $F_1]$ and

(2) $\times$ wants to keep dry $\leftrightarrow \exists F_1 \ldots \exists F_n[T(F_1 \ldots F_n) \, \& \, \times$ has $F_2]$.

The functional definition of believing that it is raining will identify this property with the property expressed by the predicate on the right side of the biconditional in (1), and the functional definition of wanting to keep dry will identify this property with that expressed by the predicate on the right-hand side of the biconditional in (2).[3] These predicates quantify over mental properties, or states, but do not mention any specific ones (the Ramsey-sentence having been purged of mental predicates); so no circularity is involved in defining the belief in terms of (1) and the desire in terms of (2).

I am going to assume that for every satisfiable predicate of the form of the right-hand side of (1) and (2) (for short, for every satisfiable functional predicate) there is a property "expressed" by the predicate, i.e., a property something has just in case it satisfies the predicate. (I shall not, in this essay, attempt to make any distinction between properties and states (state types); in some contexts I find 'property' more natural, while in others I prefer 'state' – but nothing of substance will turn on the difference.) Should we say that every property expressible by such a predicate is a functional property? To avoid trivializing the notion of a functional property we will have to make some restrictions. Suppose that our "theory" is "Someone is in pain just in case he has a sensation that hurts." From this we can construct a "functional predicate," namely '$\exists F[\forall y(y$ is $F \leftrightarrow y$ has a sensation that hurts) $\& \, \times$ is $F]$,' which is necessarily coextensive with '$\times$ is in pain.'

[2] Ned Block, "Are Absent Qualia Impossible?", *The Philosophical Review*, 89 (1980), p. 257, footnote 1.

[3] Of course, no functionalist would maintain that each different belief and each different want must be defined separately; in the case of belief, for example, the functionalist will want a definition of 'S believes that P' which holds for all values of 'P.'

Supposing that we allow that the property expressed by this predicate is none other than the property of being in pain, we still will not want to count *this* as showing that the property of being in pain is a functional property. This suggests the following restriction: in order to express a functional property, such a predicate must not contain any predicate which is necessarily coextensive with the functional predicate itself (nor, to cover our bets, may it contain predicates from which such a predicate can be constructed truth-functionally). Henceforth I will restrict the term 'functional predicate' to predicates that satisfy this condition.

It may seem obvious that we want a much stronger restriction, namely that the functional predicate must contain no mental predicates whatever. But while this is a reasonable restriction to make when our concern is with the functional definition of mental states or properties, it is not one we want to make in characterizing the general notion of a functional property. Consider the property, possessed by certain drugs, of being an anti-depressant. Presumably this ought to count as a functional property, whether or not it is possible to eliminate mental predicates (such as 'depressed,' 'in good spirits,' etc.) from the *definiens* of its functional definition.

But now let us focus our attention again on the functional definition of mental states. Sometimes it is said that pain, for example, is functionally definable if it is definable "in terms of its causal relations to inputs, outputs, and other mental states."[4] But suppose that pain were definable in terms of its causal relations to inputs, outputs, and certain beliefs and desires, but that those beliefs and desires were not definable in any such way. In that case being in pain would be a functional property, in a sense, but what functionalists have meant in claiming that it is a functional property would not be true. What they have meant is that it is expressible by a functional predicate which contains no mental predicates whatever, and not merely that it is expressible by one that contains no predicate which is necessarily coextensive with 'is in pain'; and if the other mental properties by relation to which it is defined include beliefs and desires, this requires that those properties likewise be expressible by such functional predicates. Let us say that a mental state is functionally definable in the weak sense just in case it is definable in terms of its causal relations to inputs, outputs, and other mental states, regardless of whether those other mental states are so definable. And let us say that a state (mental or otherwise) is functionally definable in the strong sense just in case it

---

[4] See, for example, Block, "Are Absent Qualia Impossible?", p. 257.

is expressible by a functional predicate that contains no mental predicates (or mental terminology) whatever. States that are functionally definable in the strong sense I will call 'SS-functional states'; and it is functional states in this sense which functionalism takes mental states to be.

II

Now let us consider the relationship between functional properties, or states, and what are sometimes called their "realizations." Let '$\exists F_1 \ldots \exists F_n [T(\ldots F_j \ldots) \ \& \ x \ \text{has} \ F_j]$' be a functional predicate which contains no mental terminology, i.e., one that expresses an SS-functional property. Let us pretend, in fact, that the functional property expressed by this is identical to the property of being in pain, and that 'F_j' is the variable that replaced the predicate 'is in pain' in forming the Ramsey-sentence of the psychological theory from which this predicate was derived. And now suppose that we find a person A, and a set of physical predicates 'P_1' . . . 'P_n,' such that if we replace 'F_1' . . . 'F_n' in our functional predicate with 'P_1' . . . 'P_n,' respectively, and remove the initial quantifiers (since there are no longer any variables for them to bind), the resulting physical predicate is true of A. There are now two different physical properties which might naturally be said to "realize" in A the property of being in pain. First, there is that named by 'P_j' – perhaps this might be something like 'has C-fibers firing.' Second, there is the property expressed by the physical predicate '$T(\ldots P_j \ldots) \ \& \ x \ \text{has} \ P_j)$.'

Before we go on we must correct an inadequacy in our current formulation. Presumably "$T(\ldots P_j \ldots)$" will be a general proposition about how states $P_1 \ldots P_n$ relate causally to one another and to inputs and outputs, in whatever creatures these states occur. It will have the same form as the psychological theory from which our Ramsey-sentence was derived; to expose a little more of its form, let us rewrite it as "$\forall x[T(\ldots P_j x \ldots)]$," where the variable 'x' takes persons as values. But must this general proposition be true, i.e., must these states behave as it says wherever and whenever they occur, in order for it to be true that in the case of person A the having of P_j realizes the property of being in pain? Suppose as before, that 'P_j' abbreviates 'has C-fibers firing,' and suppose that there are creatures whose brains are wired differently than A's, so that in them C-fiber firings do not have the characteristic causes and effects of pain. In that case "$\forall x[T(\ldots P_j x \ldots)]$" will be false. But on the assumption that being in pain is a functional property derived from theory T, this should have no bearing on whether A has pain in virtue of having C-fibers firing (i.e., having P_j); all that should be required for the latter is that A's brain should be wired in such a way that *in him* C-fiber firings have the required sorts of causes and effects. What we want as a first conjunct of our physical predicate is not the proposition '$\forall x[T(\ldots P_j x \ldots)],$' but rather a predicate – '$T(\ldots P_j x \ldots),$' or 'Tx' for short – which results from the removal from that proposition of the universal quantifier binding the variable 'x'; this predicate will be true of a person just in case the person is as all subjects of P_j would have to be in order for "$\forall x[T(\ldots P_j x \ldots)]$" to be true, but it can be true of a person without that general proposition being true. For the same reason, our functional predicate should be rewritten as '$\exists F_1 \ldots \exists F_n [T(\ldots F_j x \ldots) \& F_j x]$' or (for short) '$\exists F_1 \ldots F_n (Tx \& F_j x),$' and the physical predicate which results from replacing 'F_1' $\ldots$ 'F_n' with 'P_1' $\ldots$ 'P_n' will read '$T(\ldots P_j x \ldots) \& P_j x$' or (for short) '$Tx \& P_j x.$'

Now let us return to the notion of physical realization. As I said earlier, there are two different physical properties that might be said to be the realization in A of the property of being in pain. There is P_j, i.e., having C-fibers firing. Whether A is in pain depends on whether he has P_j, and clearly his having P_j is in some sense constitutive of his being in pain, as opposed to being a cause of it. But this is true only because A has the property expressed by 'Tx'; this can be thought of as a determinate form of the property: *being physically constituted in such a way that P_j plays the causal role definitive of pain.* So the physical property of A which is unconditionally sufficient for being in pain is not P_j by itself, but rather the conjunctive property expressed by '$Tx \& P_j x.$' I will say that the latter property is a *total realization* of being in pain, and that P_j is a *core realization.*

A common functionalist claim is that the same mental state can be physically realized in a variety of different ways. This can be put by saying that there can be indefinitely many different physical properties which are total realizations of the same functional property. So while having a given total realization of a functional property is sufficient for having that property, it is not necessary for it – that same functional property could be instantiated in virtue of the instantiation of some quite different total realization of it. Some writers have said that it is also true that the same physical state can realize different functional properties at different times, or in different circumstances, or in different creatures.[5] This is true if 'realize' means 'be a core realization

---

[5] See, for example, Ned Block and Jerry Fodor, "What Psychological States are Not," *The Philosophical Review,* 81 (1972), 159–181, p. 163.

of,' but it is false if it means 'be a total realization of.' Supposing that in us C-fiber firing is a core realization of pain, there might be creatures, with brains wired differently from ours, in which C-fiber firing is a core realization of some altogether different mental state – say the desire to fly to the moon. But in no such creature could a physical property which in us is a total realization of the property of being in pain be a realization of any other mental property, or fail to be a realization of that one.

I shall have more to say about the distinction between core realizations and total realizations in the next section. First, however, I should say something about the relationship between functionalism (as understood here) and materialism. Some early formulations of functionalism suggested that it is incompatible with materialism.[6] The fact that functional states are "multiply realizable" implies that a functional state cannot be identical to any particular physical realization of it; and on the assumption that materialism requires such identities, this implies that materialism is false if functionalism is true. But it should be apparent by now that if functionalism is true, *and* if all of the total realizations of functional states that actually occur are physical states, then materialism is true on any reasonable interpretation of what it says. (It is perhaps worth observing that if materialism really did require the identities which functionalism holds to be unavailable, it would be refuted by the existence of such horological properties of clocks and watches as those expressed by 'keeps accurate time,' 'is five minutes slow,' and 'registers five o'clock'; for these, like mental properties as conceived by the functionalist, are multiply realizable and not identifiable with any of their physical realizations.)

A natural suggestion is that a functional property can be identified with the property which is the disjunction (perhaps infinite) of all of its total realizations. Now it *may* be that all possible total realizations of mental properties (or of functional properties generally) are physical properties, and in that case each functional property will be identical to a physical property – assuming that it is permissible to speak of infinite disjunctions. But it cannot be excluded a priori that it is possible that functional states should have realizations that are wholly or partially nonphysical (perhaps involving, as Putnam once imagined, the operation of "bundles of ectoplasm"). And if that is a possibility, then the disjunctive property with which such a functional

---

[6] See especially Hilary Putnam, "The Mental Life of Some Machines," in *Mind, Language and Reality* (Cambridge, 1975).

state is identifiable will have some nonphysical disjuncts, and so cannot be said to be a physical property. But even if this is so, if it is nevertheless true that only the physical disjuncts of such properties are ever instantiated in the actual world – or, in other words, if all actual realizations of functional properties are physical – then materialism will be true. If one interprets materialism as requiring that all properties be identical to physical properties, and if one also allows for uninstantiated properties and holds that the disjunction of any two properties is a property, one is in effect taking materialism to hold, not only that there are no nonphysical entities, but that it is logically impossible that there should be any. And that, surely, is a much stronger claim than the materialist is committed to simply in virtue of being a materialist.

III

While the functionalist approach I favor employs a procedure for formulating functional definitions which is due to David Lewis (the "Ramsey–Lewis technique"), the view I end up with is importantly different from Lewis's. To bring out the differences and (I hope) illuminate the virtues of my account, I shall briefly discuss Lewis's recent paper "Mad Pain and Martian Pain."[7]

Lewis wants an account of pain that allows for the possibility of a certain sort of "madman" – a man whose pain differs radically from ours in its causes and effects. The madman's pain has none of the typical causes and effects of normal human pain; instead, it is caused by "moderate exercise on an empty stomach," it "turns his mind to mathematics, facilitating concentration on that but distracting him from anything else," it causes him to "cross his legs and snap his fingers," and so on.[8] The madman is not in the least motivated to prevent pain or to get rid of it. Lewis also wants his account to allow certain imaginary Martians to have pain, precisely because they have states that have the typical causes and effects of pain, despite the fact that the physical realization of pains in the Martians is totally different from that in us. In the case of a Martian, what plays the causal role played in us by C-fiber firing is "the inflation of many smallish cavities in his feet."[9] According to Lewis, the case of the madman shows that pain is only contingently connected with its causal role, while the case

---

[7] In N. Block (ed.), *Readings in the Philosophy of Psychology*, vol. 1. Hereafter I shall refer to this as 'MP&MP.'

[8] MP&MP, p. 216.   [9] *Ibid.*

of the Martian shows that it is only contingently connected with its physical realization.

Lewis remarks that "[a] simple identity theory straightforwardly solves the problem of mad pain," but it "goes just as straightforwardly wrong about Martian pain."[10] We are to suppose, then, that the madman's pain has the same physical realization as ours – that it is realized in some physical state, let it be C-fiber firing, with which a "simple" identity theory might want to identify pain. Such a simple identity theory is wrong because it cannot account for the pain of the Martians, who lack C-fibers altogether. On the other hand, according to Lewis, "[a] simple behaviorism or functionalism goes the other way: right about the Martian, wrong about the madman."[11] We are to conclude from this that the madman does not have any state that satisfies the (best possible) functional characterization of pain.

What we need, according to Lewis, is a mixed theory. Briefly, his account is as follows. The concept of pain "is the concept of a state that occupies a certain causal role, a state with certain typical causes and effects."[12] Whatever does occupy that causal role is pain. If "the state of having neurons hooked up in a certain way and firing in a certain pattern"[13] is the state apt for causing and being caused in relevant ways, then that neural state is pain. But it is only contingent that that state is pain. "Pain might not have been pain."[14] Lewis says that the concept of pain is "a *non-rigid* concept," and that 'pain' is a non-rigid designator.[15] Not only can 'pain' designate different things in different possible worlds; it can designate different things in different "populations" in the actual world. What is pain for a given population is what occupies the relevant causal role for that population. Since (we will suppose) what occupies the causal role in our population is C-fiber firing, and since (we will stipulate) Lewis's madman is a member of our population, the madman is in pain when his C-fibers are firing – for when his C-fibers are firing he has the state which, in the relevant population, has the typical causes and effects definitive of pain, even though in him (an atypical member of this population) this state does not have these causes and effects. The Martians, however, are a different population. In that population what occupies the causal role definitive of pain is the inflation of tiny cavities in the feet, so in that population it is that state, and not C-fiber firing, which is designated by 'pain.' (We are not talking, of course, about what the *Martian* word 'pain' (if there is one) designates; we are talking about what Martian states fall within the extension of *our*

[10] *Ibid.*, p. 217.   [11] *Ibid.*   [12] *Ibid.*, p. 218.   [13] *Ibid.*   [14] *Ibid.*   [15] *Ibid.*

word 'pain.') Lewis's account does give the result he wants: it allows both his Martian and his madman to have pain. But we have to consider the cost.

Lewis does not say much about what constitutes a "population." He does say that "an appropriate population should be a natural kind – a species, perhaps."[16] But species can accommodate freaks – otherwise Lewis's madman could not be a member of our species. One wonders what Lewis would say of a Martian freak (progeny of Martian parents) who is physically indistinguishable from one of us, or a human freak (progeny of human parents) who is indistinguishable from a Martian. (Perhaps the Martians are so different from us, physiologically, that such freaks are biologically impossible – but if so we can pose the difficulty by imagining some Venusians who are not quite so different.) If Lewis holds that the Martian freak lacks pain, because it lacks the state which among Martians plays the causal role definitive of pain, he will hold a view which it ought to be difficult for a materialist to stomach – that a creature could fail to be in pain despite being physically indistinguishable from a creature which is in pain. This puts the property of being in pain in the company of such manifestly non-intrinsic properties as that of being a Baptist inhabitant of a state whose Governor is a Methodist, and offhand this seems to be just the sort of property it is not. On the other hand, if Lewis assigns the Martian freak to our population because of his physical similarity to us, it becomes unclear on what basis his madman is assigned to our population; would the madman not belong to our population, and not be in pain, if somewhere else (on Venus, say) there were a race of creatures physically just like him, among whom some physical state utterly different from C-fiber firing plays the causal role of pain, and C-fiber firing does not?

But even if these difficulties can somehow be met, it seems to me that the attractiveness of Lewis's position is considerably diminished once we apply to it the distinction, made in section II, between "core realizations" and "total realizations" of a functional state or property. Lewis's madman is supposed to have a state which in typical members of our population, but not in him, plays the causal role of pain, and it is natural to express this by saying that the madman has a state which in our population "realizes" pain, or is the (or a) "realization" of pain. But this, we now see, is ambiguous; it can mean that the madman has a state which is, in our population, the (or a) core realization of pain, or it can mean that he has a state which in our population is the (or a)

---

[16] *Ibid.*, p. 220.

total realization of pain. If the latter were meant, there would certainly be no objection to saying that the madman has pain – although there would be a question as to how Lewis can consistently characterize the madman as someone who "is not in a state that occupies the causal role of pain for him" (I will return to this shortly). But if this is how the example is to be understood, then the admission that the madman has pain poses no threat to a "simple" functionalism, and provides no grounds for the claim that we must go to a "mixed theory" of the sort Lewis proposes. It also provides no grounds for Lewis's belief that 'pain' is a non-rigid designator. Lewis expresses the latter belief by saying that "pain might not have been pain," and presumably would say that the state that "is" pain in the Martian (and us) might not have been pain. But if 'is' means 'is the total realization of,' this will surely not be true – or at any rate, one would suppose that Lewis's functionalist intuitions would lead him to deny it. On the other hand, this will be true if 'is' means 'is the core realization of'; in creatures who are "hooked up" differently than us, so that in them the standard causes and effects of C-fiber firing are utterly different than they are in us, C-fiber firing would not be a core realization of pain, even though it is so in us. And I think that the most natural reading of Lewis's example is that according to which the madman has a state which in us is a core realization of pain, but does not have the total realization of which that state is the core – and does not have any other total realization of pain. This goes with his characterization of the madman as someone who is "hooked up wrong." But now the question is, why should we allow that the madman has (or could have) pain? It would be sheer confusion to say that he must have pain because he has a state which is a realization of pain; this would involve an equivocation on the notion of realization. And Lewis would have to agree that the inductive argument "C-fiber firing is invariably accompanied by pain in us; the madman has C-fiber firing; therefore (probably) the madman has pain" is worthless, given that we know that the madman is hooked up differently than we are. (If that argument were cogent, we could use an analogous inductive argument, based on the fact that in us pain is always accompanied by C-fiber firing, to show that the Martians do not have pain!) Of course, given Lewis's theory we would have a basis for assigning pain to the madman; for the madman belongs to our population, and he has the state which in our population is the (core) realization of pain – or, as Lewis puts it, he is in the state which occupies the causal role of pain for most members of that population (notice that 'occupies the causal role of' shares the ambiguity of 'realizes'). What I am suggesting is that once we are clear that the madman is not supposed to have any total realization of pain, the assignment of pain to him has no plausibility independently of Lewis's theory, and so cannot be used to support it.

Near the beginning of his paper Lewis remarks of his madman case that "my opinion that this is a possible case seems pretty firm. If I want a credible theory of mind, I need a theory that does not deny the possibility of mad pain."[17] Now I think that Lewis's initial description of the case can be read in such a way as to make reasonable Lewis's conviction that the case is possible. But I think that this reading, unlike the interpretation which Lewis subsequently puts on the case, is compatible with the madman's having a total realization of pain (as functionally defined, *à la* Lewis, in terms of a "common-sense" psychological theory) – and on such a reading, as we have seen, the claim that mad pain is possible does not support Lewis's view that 'pain' is a non-rigid designator, that pain is population-relative, and that we need a "mixed theory." Since Lewis doesn't say which of the typical causes and effects of pain are to be taken as defining, the fact that the madman's pain – or rather, the state of him which supposedly realizes pain – does not have certain of the typical causes and effects of pain, and has other causes and effects which are not typical, does not by itself imply that it does not have those that are defining. Perhaps the proper conclusion from the possibility of mad pain is that the defining causal role of pain is other than its total causal role, and other than what one might initially suppose it to be. Moreover, there is an ambiguity in the notion of "playing a causal role." To say that a state plays the causal role of pain may mean that it actually has causes and effects of certain kinds, or it may mean that it is "apt" for causing and being caused in certain ways. And the truth of the latter is compatible with the falsity of the former. There are various ways in which a creature could have a state which is apt for causing and being caused in certain ways without that state's having, when instantiated in that creature, the relevant causes and effects. To mention just one, it may be that the generalizations that comprise "common-sense psychology" are studded with 'probably's and 'normally's, and that instead of saying that pain has such and such causes and effects, they say that it "tends" to be caused by certain sorts of events, and "tends" to cause, in conjunction with certain other states, certain effects. If one holds this, one will also hold that it is possible for there to be, as a sort of statistical fluke, a creature who has states whose nature it is to tend to have such and such causes, but in whom these states seldom if ever do have such causes and effects. But if this is how we think of the

[17] *Ibid.*, p. 216.

madman, we will be thinking of him as having a physical makeup such that certain conditions (the typical causes of pain) are likely to cause his C-fibers to fire, and such that his C-fibers firing is likely to have certain behavioral effects (the typical behavioral effects of pain). But we will also be supposing that in his case the likely does not happen – he is a statistical fluke, analogous to the fair coin which comes up heads a thousand times in a row. Of course, this is not compatible with Lewis's subsequent characterization of the madman as someone who is "hooked up" differently than the rest of us, presumably in such a way that C-fiber firing does not even have the tendency to cause the typical effects of pain, or to be caused by its typical causes. My point is simply that Lewis's initial characterization of mad pain is such that the admission of its possibility does not imply that there can be pain in the absence of total realizations of pain (as functionally defined), and so does not support the claim that a "simple" functionalism must give way to a "mixed theory."

IV

Ned Block has distinguished two main varieties of functionalism, analytical functionalism, or what Block calls 'Functionalism' (with a capital 'F'), and 'Psychofunctionalism.'[18] These two versions of functionalism do not differ in the sorts of ontological claims they make. Both assert that mental states are identical to SS-functional states (i.e., states expressible by functional predicates containing no mental vocabulary). Nor, I assume, need there be any difference in the modal status they assign to these claims; both can agree with Kripke that identity propositions are metaphysically necessary (assuming that the terms involved are rigid designators). But whereas analytical functionalism views the enterprise of formulating functional definitions as an a priori one, one of conceptual analysis, Psychofunctionalism views it as an empirical enterprise. While both can use the Ramsey–Lewis technique for constructing functional definitions, they will seek different sorts of theories as the bases for constructing their definitions. The analytical functionalist seeks to extract his definition from a "theory" consisting of analytic or conceptual truths about the relations of mental states to inputs, outputs, and other mental states. For the Psychofunctionalist, on the other hand, the definitions are to be extracted from the best theory provided by empirical psychology.

It may be that we should distinguish three rather than two versions

[18] See Block, "Troubles with Functionalism."

of functionalism. David Lewis is often classified as an analytical functionalist. But Lewis characterizes the theory from which the functional definitions are to be derived as consisting of "common-sense platitudes" about the mental – and while he suggests that at least some of these have the flavor of analyticity about them, it is by no means clear that he wants to include only those platitudes that could be claimed to be analytic. At any rate, there is a possible view which says that mental states are identical to functional states which are definable, by the Ramsey–Lewis technique, in terms of a common-sense psychological theory (sometimes referred to as "folk psychology"), as opposed to a scientific one, but which does not claim that the propositions in that common-sense theory have the status of analytic or conceptual truths. But this seems to me an unpromising view. Assuming that our "common-sense platitudes" are synthetic, if one of them should be contradicted by scientific findings we presumably would not want to include it in the theory to which the Ramsey–Lewis technique is applied; we do not want to define our mental terms in terms of a *false* theory. And if our functional "definitions" are not meant to capture the meaning, or sense, of the mental terms, why should the information included in them be limited to facts that are common knowledge? We might say that the analytical functionalist looks for functional characterizations that give the "nominal essence" of mental states, while the Psychofunctionalist looks for functional characterizations that give the "real essence" of such states; what is unclear is what sort of essence the "common-sense functionalist" would be looking for. At any rate, in what follows I shall ignore "common-sense functionalism," and shall concentrate my attention on analytical functionalism and Psychofunctionalism.

There is, however, a version of functionalism which someone could hold without holding either analytical functionalism or Psycho-functionalism – although it could be held together with one or the other of these, or even with both. One might label this view 'minimal functionalism.' But that name isn't really appropriate, since it is a view which some proponents of analytical functionalism and Psycho-functionalism will want to reject. My procedure in the remainder of this essay will be as follows. I shall first characterize this sort of functionalism, and make some observations about it. I shall then consider the relative merits of analytical functionalism and Psycho-functionalism, first on the assumption that this other sort of functionalism is true, and then on the assumption that this other sort of functionalism is false.

V

Properties have two main sorts of (what I shall call) causal features. One sort are causal potentialities; a property has a causal potentiality in virtue of being such that its instantiation in a thing contributes, when combined with the instantiation of certain other properties, to the possession by that thing of a certain causal power. For example, one of the causal potentialities of the property of having a sharp edge consists in the fact that if coinstantiated with the property of being made of steel, this property bestows on its possessor the power of being able to cut wood and various other substances. The second sort of causal feature has to do with the ways in which the instantiation of a property can be caused; a property's having a causal feature of this sort amounts to its being such that its instantiation in a thing will be caused by the instantiation of such and such other properties in things standing in such and such relations to the thing. Every property has many, perhaps in some cases uncountably many, causal features of each of these kinds.

If we could specify all of the causal features of a property in a set of propositions of finite length, then using that set of propositions as our "theory" we could use the Ramsey–Lewis technique to construct a functional predicate which is true of a thing, in all worlds having the same causal laws as the actual world, just in case it has that property. The functional property expressed by that predicate could be called the "functional correlate" (or the "actual world functional correlate") of that property. There is, however, no guarantee that such a finite specification of the causal features of a property is possible. Nevertheless, there is a natural extension of the notion of a functional property which will enable us to speak of each property as having associated with it a functional property which is its functional correlate. It is obviously true of finite sets of causal features that if all of the members of the set can belong to the same property, there is a functional property which something has just in case it has a property having all of the causal features in the set. I propose that we extend the notion of a functional property by stipulating that this is true of infinite and uncountable sets of causal features as well; the functional property corresponding to such a set will be the property of having a property having all of the causal features in the set. This allows there to be functional properties that are not expressible in functional predicates. And if we may speak of the totality of the causal features of any property (and I see no reason why we should not be able to) then we may say that corresponding to any property P there is a functional property, its functional correlate, which something has just in case it has a property having the totality of the causal features possessed by P.

Mental properties, just like others, have infinitely, perhaps uncountably, many causal features. Some of these are ones that no analytic functionalist or Psychofunctionalist would want to mention in his functional definition of the property. For example, if pain can be realized (as earlier) in a certain physiological state $T \& P_j$, and if the coinstantiation of that physiological state with another physiological state P^* results in a rise in body temperature, then one of the causal features of pain is that its coinstantiation with T and P^* results in a rise of body temperature. This causal feature belongs essentially to the functional property which is the functional correlate of the property of being in pain, but it is presumably without conceptual or psychological significance.

What the causal features of a property are depend on what causal laws hold. If the same properties can be governed by different causal laws in different possible worlds, then there will be worlds in which something has a property without having its functional correlate, and perhaps vice versa. In that case properties cannot in general be identified with their functional correlates. However, a number of philosophers have recently offered causal accounts of property identity.[19] On all of these accounts, it is necessary and sufficient for the identity of properties A and B in the actual world that A and B share all of the same causal features. This amounts to the requirement that properties in the actual world are identical just in case they have the same functional correlate. I have argued elsewhere that a similar condition holds for the "transworld" identification of properties: property P in world w is the same as property P′ in world w′ just in case P has in w just the causal features that P′ has in w′.[20] Or, in other words, P in w is the same as P′ in w′ just in case the functional correlate of P in w is the same as the functional correlate of P′ in w′. I shall refer to this as the causal theory of properties – for short, CTP.

If CTP is true, then every property will be identical to its functional correlate, and every property will be a functional property. And if this is true of properties in general, it will be true of mental properties in particular. However, to say that every mental property is a functional property is not yet to say what functionalism asserts, namely that

---

[19] See Peter Achinstein, "The Identity of Properties," *American Philosophical Quarterly*, 11 (1974), 257–276, and David Armstrong, *A Theory of Universals, Universals and Scientific Realism* (Cambridge, 1978), vol. II. See also my "Causality and Properties" (Essay 10 of this volume).

[20] See my "Causality and Properties."

every mental property is an SS-functional property. Earlier I characterized SS-functional properties as those that are functionally definable in the strong sense, i.e., are expressible by functional predicates containing no mental terminology. Now that I have broadened the notion of a functional property, a corresponding broadening of the notion of an SS-functional property is called for. Let us say that a causal feature of a property is an SS-causal feature if there is an SS-functional property which something has just in case it has a property having that feature – or, in other words, if it can be specified without the use of mental terminology. If all of the members of a set (even of an uncountable set) of causal features are SS-causal features, then the functional property something has just in case it has a property having all of the causal features in that set is an SS-functional property. The "minimal" functionalism mentioned earlier is the view that (a) every mental property is identical to its functional correlate, and (b) the functional correlate of every mental property is an SS-functional property. Since to hold this is to hold that CTP holds for mental properties, I shall refer to it as CTP-functionalism. But while it is obvious that (a) follows from CTP, it is not at all obvious that (b) does; and therefore it is not obvious that CTP-functionalism is a consequence of CTP. I believe that it is a consequence, but I shall not attempt to demonstrate this here. I shall, however, make some remarks about the relationship between the two, which will bring out what must be shown if this is to be demonstrated.

It is clear, I think, that CTP-functionalism does follow from the conjunction of CTP and the version of materialism which says that every property is a physical property, where this is understood as implying that every property has a physical description. On the latter assumption, all of the causal features of mental properties can be specified in physical and "topic neutral" terms, and this means that all are SS-causal features, and thus that the functional correlate of a mental property is an SS-functional property; so if (as CTP says) every property is identical to its functional correlate, every mental property is an SS-functional property.

If we understand materialism as the weaker thesis that all actual realizations of mental states (but not necessarily all possible realizations) are physical, then it is easy to see that from materialism and CTP it follows that for each mental state there is an SS-functional state which is (as a matter of metaphysical necessity) sufficient for its existence, and is such that in the actual world having the mental state is "nothing over and above" the having of that SS-functional state. Let us here understand 'realization' in such a way that if a property P can be construed as the disjunction of properties Q and R, then Q and R are both realizations of P. On the version of materialism now under consideration, while there may be possible worlds in which mental states are realized nonphysically, this does not happen in the actual world. This means that every mental property is construable as a disjunction of properties, and that each of these disjunctions contains as a disjunct a physical property (itself, no doubt, a disjunction of properties) such that (a) its instantiation is sufficient for the instantiation of that mental property, and (b) in the actual world it is by having that physical property that something has the mental property. By the argument of the preceding paragraph, if CTP is true, then all of the physical disjuncts of mental properties are SS-functional properties.

To establish the stronger claim that CTP-functionalism follows from CTP even on the assumption that nonphysical realizations of mental states are possible and sometimes occur, and even on the antimaterialist view that *only* nonphysical realizations of mental states are possible, we would have to show the logical impossibility of the following sort of situation. Suppose that $a_1 \ldots a_n$ and $b_1 \ldots b_n$ are two sets of irreducibly nonphysical properties, and that the a's can be paired with the b's in such a way that for any such pair $\{a_j, b_j\}$, the members of the pair differ in some of their causal features but share all of the same SS-causal features. If a_j has the causal feature of being caused to exist in x by x's having a_j and physical state P, then b_j will have not this but the counterpart feature of being caused to exist in x by x's having b_j and physical state P; and in virtue of this, both will share an SS-causal feature expressible by a predicate of the form 'α is such that $\exists$ F[. . . F . . . & ($\forall$x) (x's having F and P causes x to have α)].' And if a_j has the causal feature that in conjunction with a_k it causes physical state of affairs P*, then b_j will have not this but the counterpart feature that in conjunction with b_k it causes P*; and in virtue of this, both will share an SS-causal feature expressible by a predicate of the form 'α is such that $\exists$ F[. . . F . . . & ($\forall$x) (x's having α and F causes P*)].' Let us call such a pair of properties 'functional counterparts.' Let us suppose further that there are two individuals A and B which are exactly alike in all respects (and so in all of their physical properties), except that A's repertoire of possible properties includes the a's and not the b's, while B's repertoire includes the b's but not the a's, and A has a given a-property a_j just in case B has its functional counterpart b_j. Let us speak of individuals related as A and B are as 'functional twins.' Finally, let us suppose that $a_1 \ldots a_n$ are mental states and that $b_1 \ldots b_n$ are not. Thus B, although indistinguishable in its behavior and physical makeup from A, would altogether lack the mental states that A has.

The situation just described is compatible with CTP; since functional counterparts would differ in their causal features, although not in their SS-causal features, they would satisfy CTP's requirement that different properties differ in their causal features. But the situation is of course not compatible with CTP-functionalism. So if the situation is possible, CTP-functionalism does not follow from CTP. To me it seems obvious that this situation is not possible. But I know of no way of arguing for this that does not involve invoking epistemological principles that are at best no less controversial than the claim they would be used to establish. For example, it would be easy enough to show that a mindless creature who was a functional twin of a minded one would be absolutely indistinguishable, by any logically possible observation or test, from the minded one. It is tempting (at least to me) to argue that it follows from this that on the assumption that functional twins are possible we are reduced to total skepticism about the possibility of knowledge of other minds, and that this amounts to a *reductio ad absurdum* of the assumption. But such an argument requires some such principle as the following: if state of affairs S is in principle indistinguishable from state of affairs S', which is incompatible with it, and if it is logically possible that state of affairs S' should obtain, then it is impossible to know that state of affairs S obtains. And there are plenty of contemporary epistemologists who would deny that principle.[21] So while I think that CTP-functionalism should seem plausible to anyone to whom CTP seems plausible, I do not claim to be able to establish conclusively that the latter entails the former.

VI

Let us suppose for the moment that CTP and CTP-functionalism are true. I have said that CTP-functionalism is compatible with either analytic functionalism or Psychofunctionalism. But supposing that we accept the former, what reason could we have for accepting either of the latter?

What distinguishes the CTP-functionalist who accepts analytic functionalism from one who rejects it is not their ontological views, but their views about the semantics of mental terms. Both hold that

[21] See, for example, Alvin I. Goldman, "Discrimination and Perceptual Knowledge," *The Journal of Philosophy*, 73 (1976), 771–791.

mental states are identical to functional states, and they need not differ as to what functional states a given mental state is identical to. But CTP-functionalism does not, as such, offer any account of how mental terms latch onto the particular functional states they designate. The analytic functionalist offers an explanation of this along the following lines. Each mental term has analytically associated with it its functional definition, which gives its meaning and specifies the "nominal essence" of the mental state it designates. Although the functional property or state picked out by this definition will have, according to CTP-functionalism, infinitely (perhaps uncountably) many causal features, only a tiny and finite subset of these will be mentioned in the analytic functional definition. What makes the others essential to the functional property is the fact that they are connected by nomological necessity (and so, according to CTP, by metaphysical necessity) with those that are mentioned.

An account along these lines is at least a possible explanation of how a property-term connects with its designatum. There are many terms in the language, such as 'poisonous' and 'mousetrap,' for which only such an account is plausible, and the analytic functionalist holds that the same is true of words like 'pain' and 'desire.'

If Psychofunctionalism offers an alternative account of the semantics of mental terms, presumably it will be one along the following lines. Mental terms refer in basically the same way as Kripke and Putnam have held that natural-kind terms like 'gold' and 'water' refer. Such terms apply to certain paradigms and to whatever other things share with those paradigms a scientifically discoverable "real essence." In the case of gold or water, we turn to the science of chemistry to determine what the real essence is. The Psychofunctionalist, as I am now construing him, holds that just as chemistry can tell us the real essence of gold or water, psychology (once it is developed further) can tell us the real essence of pain, anger, belief, desire, and thought. Whereas on analytical functionalism the infinitely many causal features of pain belong to the property designated by 'pain' in virtue of their nomological connections with the causal features which are mentioned in the analytic definition of 'pain,' according to Psycho-functionalism these features belong to that property in virtue of their nomological connections with a real essence, presently unknown but in principle discoverable by the science of psychology.

A CTP-functionalist who rejects analytical functionalism would not necessarily have to accept Psychofunctionalism. But if he did not, I think that his account of the semantics of mental terms would have to be similar to that just ascribed to the Psychofunctionalist. The difference would be that whereas the Psychofunctionalist sees mental terms as standing for natural kinds whose natures are to be discovered by psychology, this third sort of functionalism sees them as standing for natural kinds whose natures are the subject matter of some other science – most likely physiology. The materialist version of this view would be a version of the psychophysical identity theory, which says that mental properties (states) just are certain physiological properties (states). This is a version of what I have elsewhere called the 'parochial view' about the nature of mental states and the semantics of mental terms.[22] To distinguish it from Psychofunctionalism, which could also be called a parochial view (it makes having *our* "depth psychology" essential to having mental states), let us refer to it as 'physiological parochialism.'

One thing that analytic functionalism and Psychofunctionalism are agreed on is that there are conceivable creatures in whom mental states have very different physical realizations than they do in us – thus both could agree on the conceivability of David Lewis's Martians, whose pains are realized in the inflation of tiny cavities in the feet. Of course, it may turn out to be nomologically impossible given the physical laws that obtain in the actual world (and so metaphysically impossible, if CTP is true), that any functional property with which either sort of functionalist would hold that pain is identifiable could be realized in such a way. What both of these sorts of functionalism are agreed upon, however, is that the mere fact that a creature's physical states are radically different from ours does not in itself preclude them from being realizations of mental states. So both the analytical functionalist and the Psychofunctionalist are persuaded by reflection on (*prima facie*) possible cases that no simple form of the psycho-physical identity theory can be true, and that physiological parochialism is false. In Ned Block's terminology, both hold that physiological parochialism is "chauvinistic" – that there are possible circumstances in which it would require us to deny mental states to creatures that have them.

The argument which leads both analytical functionalists and Psychofunctionalists to reject physiological parochialism as chauvinistic might be called the 'argument from science fiction' – it is an argument from our "semantic intuitions" about, i.e., what it seems natural to say about, certain conceivable situations. I want now to suggest that if the argument from science fiction provides a good reason for rejecting physiological parochialism, it provides an equally

[22] See Essay 14.

good reason for favoring analytical functionalism over Psychofunctionalism.

Presumably the psychological theory which the Psychofunctionalist envisages as giving us the real essence of mental states will not consist exclusively or primarily of common-sense platitudes; presumably it will go into some detail about the nature of the underlying psychological processes and mechanisms involved in perception, memory, information processing, and the like. But what reason is there for thinking that these underlying processes and mechanisms must be the same in all creatures having mental states? In other words, what reason is there for thinking that all creatures having mental states must have the same "depth psychology"? As far as I can see, there is no reason for thinking that this is so, and there is good reason for thinking that it is not. As I have said, the analytical functionalist and the Psychofunctionalist agree that the physical differences between Lewis's Martians and us do not in themselves preclude their having the same sorts of mental states we have – or rather, that they preclude this only if they preclude the Martians having the right sorts of functional states. But now suppose that we are investigating the Martians' "psychology" (I put the word 'psychology' in scare quotes, so as not to beg the question as to whether the functional states we assign to them in order to explain their behavior, and which we find to be realized in their physiology, are genuine mental states or not). And let us suppose that not only do the Martians have states which satisfy the best functional definitions of mental states that any analytic functionalist has been able to come up with, but also that if we take their states to be the mental states which satisfy these functional definitions in us then all of the facts that empirical psychology will discover prior to (say) 1985 are true of them – except, of course, those having to do with their relations to neurophysiological states. In other words, if we purge scientific psychology as it will exist in 1985 of whatever mistaken claims it will contain, and also of whatever neurophysiology it will contain, then the remaining theory will do equally well as a theory about human mental states and as a theory about Martian "mental states." For convenience, let us suppose that we make this discovery in 1985. From that time on there are two groups of psychologists at work, one studying us and the other studying the Martians. And let us suppose that for each theoretical issue that is put to experimental test, the issue is decided one way by the experiments on us, and in a different and incompatible way by the experiments on the Martians. Ultimately the psychologists decide that while it requires highly sophisticated experiments to detect the difference, the underlying mechanisms and processes operating in the Martians are radically different from those operating in us – for short, their depth psychology is radically different from ours. To repeat, the difference does not have to do primarily with the radical difference there is (by hypothesis) between the Martian physiology and ours. Indeed, we can suppose that subsequently we find creatures who are superficially very much like us physiologically but who have the Martian "depth psychology," and still other creatures who are superficially very much like the Martians in their physiology but who have the human (Earthling) depth psychology. What we are imagining is that the best possible scientific psychological theory true of human mental states is not true of the Martians – although there is true of them a theory which, relative to our psychological knowledge in 1985, could (epistemically) be the best psychological theory true of us.

The Psychofunctionalist (as I understand his position) has to say that in the case just imagined the Martians don't have such mental states as pain, desire, belief, etc. Here I can only appeal to intuition. It seems to me that this view is obviously wrong – that it is ruled out by the understanding we all tacitly have of our mental vocabulary. Psychofunctionalism is exposed by this thought experiment as being, like physiological parochialism, a "chauvinist" view about the mental.[23]

It may be helpful to compare this bit of science fiction with a comparable story about gold. Let us suppose that at some time, it will have to be considerably earlier than 1985, we find (on Mars, say), samples of a metallic substance which passes all of the layman's and jeweler's tests for being gold, and obeys all of the laws which the chemistry of the time has established to be true of gold. Subsequently we find that the microstructure of this substance is entirely different from that of our paradigms of gold, and that it is a compound rather than an element. I share the intuition of Kripke and Putnam that this substance is not gold. Of course, if we had become habituated to calling it 'gold,' that usage might stick; but in that case the word 'gold' would have become ambiguous – the stuff in question would not fall within the extension of our present word 'gold' although it would fall within the extension of one of the senses that word would have in the imagined situation. But I, for one, have no inclination to say that words like 'belief,' 'desire,' and 'pain' would be used ambiguously if

[23] Cf. Ned Block, "Troubles with Functionalism," pp. 310–314, especially his remarks on "cross-world psychology."

applied to us and to my imaginary Martians. It is perfectly consistent to accept the Kripke–Putnam account of the semantics of natural kind terms like 'gold' and 'water' while rejecting such an account for mental terms. The notion of a natural kind is not the most luminous of notions; but I do not think we should be bothered if we are required to say that pains, like poisons and mousetraps, are not a natural kind, and lack a scientifically determinable essence.

I should mention that there is an understanding of Psychofunctionalism on which it is compatible with analytical functionalism – on the assumption that CTP-functionalism is true. If Psychofunctionalism incorporates a Kripke–Putnam account of the semantics of mental terms, then it is incompatible with analytical functionalism. But if it holds merely that there is a scientifically discoverable essence of mental states, and that there is in principle available a psychological theory from which functional definitions of mental states could be derived by the Ramsey–Lewis technique, then it is perfectly compatible with analytical functionalism. The analytical functionalist might put the matter as follows: while it is not in any way analytically or conceptually necessary, it may for all we know be nomologically necessary, that in order to satisfy the analytic functional definitions of the various mental states, the states in question must be governed by certain psychological laws which require that they stem from, or involve, certain specific sorts of underlying psychological processes and mechanisms. In other words, it may be that Lewis's Martians (or rather my recent version of them, whose underlying depth psychology is radically different from ours) are a nomological impossibility. If, as a matter of nomological fact, there is only one possible depth psychology which is compatible with the common-sense psychology from which our analytic definitions are derived, then functional definitions extracted from that psychology may be said to express the real, scientifically determinable, essence of mental states. To be sure, the functional predicates extracted from that theory will not be equivalent in meaning to those extracted from the common-sense theory. The predicate that expresses the scientific definition of pain will be very different, and presumably much more complex, than that which expresses the analytic definition. But, assuming CTP-functionalism, this does not prevent these from expressing the same functional property. What we will have are different ways of picking out the same functional property; it will be picked out by two different finite subsets of the infinite set of causal features that "define" the property, and both subsets will determine the same total set because it is in each case a matter of nomological necessity – and so, according to CTP, metaphysical necessity – that whatever has that subset of features has that total set.

It is worth observing that if physiological parochialism is divorced from the Kripke–Putnam account of the semantics of mental terms, and is merely the view that mental states are identical to the functional counterparts of certain physiological states (roughly, those which in us are total realizations of the best possible analytic functional definitions of those states), then on the assumption that CTP is true, physiological parochialism is compatible with analytical functionalism and Psychofunctionalism. For it is compatible with the latter views that in fact the only nomologically possible realizations of the functional states with which they identify mental states are the physiological states which realize them in us. Given CTP, the only nomologically possible realizations will also be the only metaphysically possible realizations. And it would seem that a functional state can be identified with the disjunction of its metaphysically possible realizations.

VII

Now let us consider how things stand if CTP and CTP-functionalism are rejected. To reject CTP is to allow that the causal features of properties can vary from one possible world to another, and thus that a property cannot be identified with its functional equivalent. In other words, it is to hold that the same properties can be governed by different causal laws in different possible worlds. To reject CTP-functionalism is to hold (assuming that one does not believe in the possibility of "functional twins," *à la* section v) that this is true of mental properties and states in particular.

First of all, if CTP-functionalism is false, it seems very unlikely that analytic functionalism and Psychofunctionalism can *both* be true. Suppose that analytical functionalism is true, and suppose further, as we did at the end of section vi, that in the actual world the causal laws are such that it is nomologically impossible for a creature's states to satisfy the "correct" analytic functional definitions without conforming to a certain depth psychology. In the actual world, then, mental states have a certain scientifically determinable essence. As we have seen, if CTP-functionalism were true then in these circumstances both analytical functionalism and Psychofunctionalism would be true – both the best analytic definition of a functional state and the best scientific definition of it would pick out the same functional state, namely the functional counterpart of that state. But if CTP and CTP-functionalism are false, and mental properties have different causal features in different possible worlds, then of course it will not follow from the fact that the best analytic definition and the best scientific one are nomologically equivalent in the actual world that they are nomologically equivalent in all possible worlds, and so it will not follow that they are metaphysically equivalent.

But another point of importance merges here. If CTP is false, then from the supposition that in the actual world it is nomologically necessary that whatever creatures have mental states (of the sorts we have) must have the same depth psychology, it does not follow that this is true in all possible worlds. Assuming, then, that there is a depth psychology which all "minded" creatures in the actual world share, if we use the Ramsey–Lewis technique to define functional states or properties in terms of this theory, then while each of these will be coextensive with some mental property in the actual world (and in all worlds nomologically like it), we cannot infer from this, if CTP is false in the case of mental properties, that this coextensiveness holds in all metaphysically possible worlds – as it must do if the mental properties are to be identified with the functional ones. If analytical functionalism is true, but CTP is not, then there seems no reason in principle why there should not be worlds in which the depth psychologies underlying mental states are very different from the one we are supposing there to be in the actual world, and also worlds in which there is no *one* depth psychology, but rather different ones for different species of minded creatures (as I suggested earlier may well be the case in the actual world). And it is hard to see why this shouldn't be a possibility quite apart from whether analytical functionalism is true. Psychofunctionalism is often advanced as an empirical thesis. But it is hard enough to see how it could be discovered empirically that it is nomologically impossible for there to be more than one depth psychology in the actual world. And if we assume the falsity of CTP, it is even harder – I think it is quite impossible – to see how it could be discovered empirically that the one nomologically possible depth psychology in the actual world is also the only nomologically possible depth psychology in all possible worlds in which there are mental states.

One possible out for the Psychofunctionalist who rejects CTP is to hold that while there are possible worlds in which the causal laws, and so the causal features of properties, are different from what they are in the actual world, these are worlds in which mental properties do not exist (or, at any rate, cannot be instantiated). This would enable him to identify mental properties with their functional correlates, and so would amount to holding CTP-functionalism while rejecting CTP as a general view about properties. Assuming (as I do in this section) that CTP does not hold in general, it is hard to see what reason there could be for thinking that it holds in the special case of mental properties. Certainly there seems to be little prospect of its being an empirical discovery (say of psychology) that this is so; it is not easy to see how empirical data could support the conclusion that certain properties can only be instantiated in worlds nomologically equivalent to this one.

In the absence of some a priori reason why we should hold CTP-functionalism without holding CTP, the prospect of Psychofunctionalism being true seems even dimmer on the supposition that CTP is false than on the supposition that it is true. On the other hand, analytic functionalism can live equally well with CTP and with its denial. If CTP is false, then there may be logically or metaphysically possible realizations of the best analytic functional definitions which are not nomologically possible, given the laws that hold in the actual world. In that case, the functional properties picked out by the analytic functional definitions will not be metaphysically coextensive with, and so cannot be identical to, the actual-world functional correlates of the corresponding mental properties. But it is no part of the thesis of analytic functionalism that such an identity holds; analytical functionalism is compatible with CTP-functionalism, as we have already noted, but it does not imply it.

VIII

I have not, in this essay, offered any reason for thinking that any version of functionalism is true. My primary aim has been to clarify some of the different versions (no doubt there are more than I have distinguished) and the relations between them. But I think that it emerges from this clarification that some versions have less prospect of being established than others. Reflection on the nature of properties, or on the notion of a property, may give us reason to accept CTP-functionalism, and reflection on our mental concepts may give us reason to accept analytical functionalism. But there is no prospect of Psychofunctionalism being established by unaided philosophical analysis. And even if philosophical analysis is supplemented by empirical research in psychology, the prospects of Psychofunctionalism being established seem nonexistent unless CTP-functionalism can be established, and dim even if it can be.

13

On an argument for dualism

I

It is a striking fact about contemporary philosophy of mind that, while scarcely anyone thinks that it is a live possibility that a mind–body dualism anything like Descartes's is true, considerable effort continues to be spent on the construction, consideration, analysis, and refutation of arguments in favor of such dualistic positions. While much of this activity takes the form of Descartes scholarship, the amount of it cannot be explained as simply a manifestation of a widespread historical interest in Descartes's philosophy; on the contrary, it seems plausible to suppose that the interest in Descartes's philosophy is due in part to the continued fascination of philosophers with the dualistic outlook of which Descartes is the classical proponent. Nor can it be supposed that the interest in dualism among philosophers is to be explained by the prevalence of dualistic convictions among non-philosophers. While there are pockets of dualistic belief in the general populace, and even among neurophysiologists, such belief seems out of tune with the intellectual temper of the times. In popular writings on scientific topics relating to the nature of man it tends to be simply taken for granted that dualism is no longer credible; and it seems a safe bet that most readers of such writings have little inclination to question this assumption. It seems unlikely, to say the least, that this intellectual climate is the result of the antidualistic efforts of such philosophers as Wittgenstein, Ryle, and Strawson. As Richard Rorty remarks in a recent paper, "The reason Cartesian dualism is so unpopular nowadays is not because of any applications of the powerful methods of modern analytic philosophy, but simply because we keep reading in *Life* and *The Scientific American* about cerebral localization, the production of any desired emotion, thought, or sense impression by the insertion of electrodes, and the like."[1] Nor is it only *recent* developments in the biological sciences (or exaggerated popular accounts of them) that have led to the unpopularity of

[1] Richard Rorty, "Functionalism, Machines, and Incorrigibility," *The Journal of Philosophy*, 69 (1972), pp. 218–219.

Cartesian dualism; as a theory about man as a natural phenomenon, dualism has been increasingly incredible since the time of Darwin.

It is worth asking, in the light of this, why it is that the attitude of philosophers towards dualism is not more like that of chemists towards phlogiston theory – i.e., why dualism is not regarded as a discredited theory whose current interest can only be historical. But while I hope that this essay will throw some light on this question, this is not its primary purpose. On the whole the essay will be an exemplification and illustration, rather than an analysis, of this *prima facie* perverse philosophical preoccupation with mind–body dualism.

I wish to consider an argument in favor of dualism which is the subject of a recent paper by Norman Malcolm.[2] Malcolm reports that the argument was brought to his attention by an unpublished paper by Robert Jaeger, and I shall refer to it as the "Jaeger–Malcolm argument." It should not of course be assumed that either Malcolm or Jaeger actually subscribes to the argument; their interest in it is basically of the same sort as mine, the nature of which will soon be apparent. Malcolm's own analysis and evaluation are subtle and complex, and any brief summary would be bound to distort them. It is different enough from my own that a consideration of it would take me away from the issues I want to consider, so I shall not attempt to discuss it here.

I also shall not consider the historical question of whether Malcolm is correct in attributing the argument to Descartes. While the attribution strikes me as plausible, it does not matter for my purposes whether it is correct. Whether or not the Jaeger–Malcolm argument is Cartesian, it is certainly "Cartesian." This is really an auto-biographical remark; what I mean is that the argument strikes a responsive chord in me which is akin to that struck by certain passages in Descartes's writings. While I am as certain as I am of anything that mind–body dualism has to be false, I am nevertheless aware of a suppressed inclination in myself to believe that it is true. There is, as it were, a tiny dualist faction in my soul which has not been completely quieted by the much larger materialist faction. And the Jaeger–Malcolm argument appeals to the dualist faction in me in much the way the dualistic passages in Descartes do. While such philosophical inclinations are bound to be multiply overdetermined, it strikes me as possible, or even likely, that my produalist inclinations

[2] Norman Malcolm, "Descartes' Proof That He Is Essentially a Non-Material Thing," in *Thought and Knowledge, Essays by Norman Malcolm* (Ithaca, N.Y., 1977), pp. 58–84.

are partly to be explained by the initial plausibility, the initial semblance of soundness, of this argument. This of course involves supposing that a person's beliefs and inclinations to believe can be influenced by arguments which he has never explicitly formulated. But I am sure that this is true. An important part of philosophical activity consists in making explicit, so that they can be subjected to analysis and criticism, lines of reasoning which have previously been only implicit in our thinking. In any case, I am sure that I am not alone among contemporary antidualist philosophers in having some produalist inclinations. Many of us have within us a little dualist which we would like to exorcise; and the way in which we hope to do this is by bringing to light the sources of our produalist inclinations, so that these can be exposed as involving confusions, misconceptions, fallacious reasoning, and the like. As I have indicated, it would be unrealistic to hope that one might discover some *single* argument or line of reasoning which is the sole source of one's produalist inclinations and is such that once one has seen it refuted the inclinations will wither away. It is more likely that these inclinations have a plurality of causes, some of which, perhaps, have little to do with reason and argument. Nevertheless, the Jaeger–Malcolm argument strikes me as a likely candidate for being *one* of the sources of produalist inclinations, including my own, and to warrant our attention for that reason.

It is worth remarking, before we proceed to an examination of the argument, that the Jaegar–Malcolm argument resembles other arguments in favor of dualism which have commanded the attention of philosophers in being, at least *prima facie*, of an a priori character. It has, in fact, been quite common in recent philosophy to treat the issue of whether dualism is true as one to be settled by a priori reasoning. To be sure, dualism is occasionally argued for on empirical grounds. Spiritualistic phenomena might, if taken to be genuine, be regarded as supporting dualism. And occasionally a neurophysiologist attempts to argue that the mechanisms in the brain are not up to the task of doing all that the mind does, and that a nonphysical mind must therefore be postulated.[3] But it is not such considerations that motivate the little dualist in me, and I suspect that the same holds for most other philosophers interested in dualism. Insofar as we are tempted to believe in dualism, we are so tempted on the basis of considerations

---

[3] See, for example, Wilder Penfield, *The Mystery of the Mind* (Princeton, 1975), and John Eccles's essay in Karl R. Popper and John C. Eccles, *The Self and Its Brain: An Argument for Interactionism* (Berlin, 1977).

that are a priori rather than empirical. Nor is it only *pro*dualist arguments that tend to have an a priori character. The a priori reasonings of antidualist philosophers have often been directed at showing on a priori, or "conceptual," grounds that dualism is false – or senseless, or conceptually incoherent – and not merely that the a priori arguments offered in its favor are fallacious or confused. This is rather striking in the light of the fact, mentioned earlier, that the antidualism which characterizes the present-day intellectual climate seems to be due mainly to such scientific developments as Darwinian evolutionary theory, the discovery of the physical basis of heredity, the vast increase in knowledge of the workings of the brain, and advances in the field of artificial intelligence and computer simulation of human intellectual functions. Surely philosophers have been influenced by these developments at least as much as anyone else. But it seems odd that someone should be strongly inclined to reject a view on empirical grounds (e.g., because of discoveries in biology) while also being inclined to accept that same view on a priori grounds. And it seems even odder that someone who rejects a view on empirical grounds should feel that it ought to be possible to give an a priori disproof of that view. This gives rise to a doubt as to whether the dualism which philosophers talk about can really be the same as the dualism which philosophers and educated laymen alike find unbelievable because of developments in empirical science. And perhaps this helps to explain the preoccupation with dualism that I mentioned at the beginning of this essay. The produalist inclinations that some philosophers find in themselves are not merely an intellectual itch which those philosophers would like to be rid of; the existence of these inclinations, and the fact that they go with an inclination to regard the truth or falsity of dualism as something to be settled by a priori reasoning, e.g., by "conceptual analysis," are signs that we don't really have a very clear idea of what we are denying when we deny that dualism is true. But if our idea of this is unclear, so is our idea of what we are affirming when we assert that materialism, or physicalism, is true; for as far as intelligibility is concerned, these doctrines take in one another's washing.

II

I turn now to a consideration of the Jaeger–Malcolm argument. It is formulated by Malcolm as follows:

(1) *I think I am breathing* entails *I exist*
(2) *I think I am breathing* does not entail *I have a body*

Therefore
(3) *I exist* does not entail *I have a body.*

The first thing to be said about this argument is that it is logically valid; it is impossible that its premises should be true without its conclusion being true. It is an instance of the formally valid argument form:

p entails q
p does not entail r
Therefore, q does not entail r.

So any successful challenge to the argument will have to be a challenge to one of its premises.

But before we begin to consider such challenges, we should notice that on the face of it the argument falls short, even if sound, of establishing the Cartesian conclusion that one's mind, or self, is something distinct from any body – that it is a spiritual, incorporeal substance lacking all physical characteristics. Proposition (3), the stated conclusion of the argument, is logically equivalent to the proposition "It is logically possible for me to exist without having a body." This does not of course entail that I *do* exist without a body, and Descartes would not suppose that it does; it was of course no part of his purpose to deny that he *had* a body. But given that I have a body, why shouldn't it be the case that right now, while I have it, I possess its corporeal characteristics, even if, as (3) says, it is possible that I should exist without having such a body, and so without having any physical characteristics? In other words, one might suppose that just as the claim that I could exist without having a body is compatible with my actually having one, so the claim that I could exist without having physical characteristics is compatible with my actually having such characteristics. But if the latter is so, then if we take dualism to imply that I, as the subject of my mental states, am something nonphysical or noncorporeal, something not having any physical characteristics, then the conclusion of the Jaeger–Malcolm argument does not imply dualism.

But there are strong *prima facie* objections to such an attempt to reconcile acceptance of (3) with the rejection of dualism. If right now, while I have a body, I necessarily have the physical characteristics which that body has, it would seem that I ought to be identical to that body. But how could it be true both that I am identical to that body and that it is possible for me to exist without it existing? It can be replied that I needn't be identical to my body in order to have its physical characteristics. Perhaps my relationship to my body is like that of a ship to the particular collection of wooden planks that constitute it at a given time, or of a statue to the portion of bronze that constitutes it. Since the ship can survive the replacement of some of the planks, or even all of them if the replacement is gradual enough, it is not identical to the collection of planks; but its shape, size, etc. at a given time is precisely that of the collection of planks that constitute it at that time. In an analogous way, it might be suggested, I might share my body's corporeal characteristics and yet not be identical to it. I think that this suggestion is correct. But this analogy does not help us make sense of the claim that I might at one time have all of the physical characteristics of a certain body and at a later time have no physical characteristics at all – for if we substitute "collection of planks" for "body," this is plainly not something our ship can do.

There is, indeed, one way in which we can make sense of this claim – but it is one that is of no help to someone who is out to reconcile (3) with the rejection of dualism. Descartes himself can perfectly well allow that there is a sense in which I am the subject of whatever corporeal characteristics my body has, even though he thinks I can exist without having any body at all. Descartes can agree that if my body weighs 170 pounds, I weigh 170 pounds. But his view must be that I have these characteristics in a derivative way. They do not belong to myself, that which I call "I," in the direct way in which my mental characteristics belong to it. What they directly belong to is the body with which I am "intimately united," and what directly belongs to me is the relational property of being united to a body which has such characteristics. A Cartesian can hold that we sometimes use predicates like "weighs 170 pounds" to ascribe such relational properties; and when such a predication is true, the subject may be said to have the nonrelational property in question – in this case, weighing 170 pounds – "derivatively." To have a property derivatively is to have the relational property of being related in a certain way – roughly, the way Descartes thinks souls are related to their bodies when they are embodied – to some other entity which directly (and so nonderivatively) has the property.[4] Descartes's dualist doctrine is that he, what he calls "I," is something that does not directly, or *non*derivatively, have any corporeal characteristics. And while it is *prima facie* intelligible that something should at one time have

---

[4] I would not want to say that the ship possesses only derivatively the properties that belong to the collection or aggregation of planks that constitute it at a particular time; the relation of the ship to the collection of planks is obviously of a very different sort from the relation Descartes believes to hold between a person and his body.

physical characteristics derivatively and then subsequently cease to have any – at any rate, we have a picture, of the soul being released from the body, which goes with this – it is much harder to understand the suggestion that something could at one time have physical characteristics in a *non*derivative way and then cease to have any.

It is clear enough, in any case, what we have to add to our argument in order to get the explicitly dualistic conclusion which Descartes could express by saying "I am something incorporeal – something having no corporeal, or physical, characteristics." What we have to add is what I shall call the "essentialist premise." This says that whatever has corporeal characteristics nonderivatively is essentially, or necessarily, something that has corporeal characteristics. In other words, if something has, nonderivatively, any corporeal characteristics, then it is not possible for it to exist without having some corporeal characteristics or other. This is, it should be observed, a principle which Descartes was committed to in any case, and certainly would have had no hesitation about using. Spatial extension being, on his view, the essential attribute of material substance, and all corporeal characteristics being modes of extension, the only changes a subject of corporeal characteristics is capable of undergoing are those that involve the replacement of one mode of extension with another; it is logically possible for something spherical to change into something cubical, but it would be logically impossible for something spherical to change into something having no shape whatever and no corporeal characteristics whatever. And it is not only Cartesians who find this principle compelling. Bernard Williams, a staunch antidualist, argues from the claim that "the understanding of what a given sort of thing is closely involves an understanding of under what determinables a thing of that sort exemplifies determinates" to the conclusion that "the possibility of disembodiment would show, not just that a person was a sort of thing that *did not necessarily* exemplify physical determinables, but that it was a sort of thing that *necessarily did not* exemplify such determinables."[5] In that case, he says, "even embodied persons would not have physical attributes, but would be nonphysical things associated with a body, i.e., a Cartesian account would apply." It certainly follows from this that if the dualist can establish (3) he is home clear.

Doubts can be raised about the essentialist premise, and I shall return to these later on. But it is, *prima facie*, a very plausible principle, and for now I shall assume that it is true.

[5] Bernard Williams, "Are Persons Bodies?" in *Problems of the Self* (Cambridge, 1973), p. 71.

In order to integrate the essentialist premise into the Jaeger–Malcolm argument, I shall take the liberty of substituting slightly different propositions for (2) and (3). The argument now goes as follows:[6]

    (1)   *I think I am breathing* entails *I exist.* (Premise)

    (2′) *I think I am breathing* does not entail *I have corporeal characteristics.* (Premise)

    (3′) *I exist* does not entail *I have corporeal characteristics.* (From (1) and (2′))

    (4)   Whatever has corporeal characteristics nonderivatively is essentially something having corporeal characteristics. (Premise)

    (5)   I do not have corporeal characteristics nonderivatively. (From (3′) and (4))

(3′) follows from (1) and (2′) for the same reason that our original (3) followed from (1) and (2); the form of the argument up to that point is the same. (4) is our essentialist premise. That (4) and (3′) together entail (5) can be seen as follows. According to (3′), it is logically possible that I should exist without having corporeal characteristics. This means that I am not essentially something having corporeal characteristics. But if I am not essentially something having corporeal characteristics, then according to (4) I am not something having corporeal characteristics nonderivatively. And that is our conclusion.

I have resolved to leave premise (4) unchallenged for the time being. Premise (1) is a special case of Descartes's "Cogito," and would be regarded as incontestable by most philosophers, antidualists as well as dualists. If we had to drag our feet at (1) in order to resist dualism, then at the very least the dualist would have won a very considerable moral victory. This leaves (2′) as the premise to attack.

Before we consider how (2′) might be attacked, we should notice that it seems on the face of it to be a very weak, even innocuous, claim. It merely asserts that it is not a *logical* consequence of my having a certain thought that I have corporeal characteristics. Putting it another way, it merely asserts that it is *logically* possible that I should have a certain thought without having any physical characteristics. Offhand one would have thought it unlikely that we could find

    [6] I use the term "corporeal" in formulating the argument to give it an appropriate seventeenth-century flavor. When it suits my purposes I sometimes use "physical" or "material" instead.

incontestable, or at least highly plausible, premises which in conjunction with this seemingly very weak claim would entail a metaphysical doctrine as extreme as mind–body dualism. This is one of the things that makes the argument interesting.

But the central role played by (2′) in our argument is interesting for another reason. (2′) can be seen as an expression of the doctrine that mental states are "only contingently" connected with physical states of affairs, in particular bodily behavior. Among some recent philosophers, especially those influenced by the later philosophy of Wittgenstein, this doctrine is closely associated with Cartesian dualism. Wittgenstein remarks that "an 'inner process' stands in need of outer criteria," and his remarks about the status of behavior as criteria for the existence of mental states have been seen as an attack on Cartesianism and – what some have thought inseparable from this – as asserting a closer than contingent connection between mental states and behavior. A remark of Wittgenstein, noted by Malcolm, which seems directly in conflict with (2′) is the following: "Only of a living human being and what resembles (behaves like) a living human being can one say: it has sensations; it sees; is blind; hears; is deaf; is conscious or unconscious."[7] On the other hand, there are other philosophers, equally opposed to dualism, who think it a mistake to link the rejection of dualism with the acceptance of what I shall call the "conceptual connection thesis," namely the view that it in some way belongs to the concepts of the various mental states that any subject of these states must have a body in which, under appropriate conditions, the states can have certain appropriate behavioral manifestations. These philosophers (e.g., those proponents of the psychophysical identity theory who hold that the psychophysical identities are contingent) think that the falsity of dualism is a contingent matter, something that has been (or is in the process of being) discovered empirically, e.g., by the scientific developments mentioned earlier. And they see the conceptual connection thesis as a thinly disguised version of behaviorism, a doctrine they assume to have been discredited.

Now it might seem that a consideration of the Jaeger–Malcolm argument, and in particular the realization that (2′) is apparently the premise to reject if one is to reject the argument, supports the former of these views – that which links the rejection of dualism with the

---

[7] Ludwig Wittgenstein, *Philosophical Investigations*, ed. by G. E. M. Anscombe and R. Rhees, trans. by G. E. M. Anscombe (Oxford, 1953), para. 281.

acceptance of the conceptual connection thesis. To reject (2′) one must assert that there *is* an entailment from the self-ascription of thoughts to the claim that one has some corporeal characteristics. It can easily appear that the only plausible account of how there could be such an entailment would be along the lines of a behaviorist or criteriological account of mental concepts, one that entails the conceptual connection thesis. This would also seem to vindicate those who have seen the issue of whether dualism is true as an a priori issue. For whether (2′) is true depends on whether one proposition *entails* another; and it is natural to assume – or at any rate traditional to assume – that whether one proposition entails another is something to be established a priori. The Jaeger–Malcolm argument appears to be an a priori argument in favour of dualism. And if we can refute that argument by showing the falsity of (2′), then, it seems, we will have an a priori argument *against* dualism. If this is so, then the recent developments in biological science are far less central to the case against dualism than most people, or at any rate most nonphilosophers, tend to assume.

But as we shall see, it is in fact not necessary to claim that dualism can be refuted on a priori or conceptual grounds in order to refute the Jaeger–Malcolm argument. There is a refutation of it which is perfectly compatible with its being an empirical matter whether dualism is true. That this refutation can be given does not imply that it is not *also* possible to refute dualism on a priori grounds. But it is useful to see that it is possible to refute the argument without giving an a priori argument for the necessary falsity or conceptual incoherence of dualism – and in particular that it is possible to do so without invoking some version of the conceptual connection thesis. If we think that we can reject dualism only by rejecting (2′), and that we can reject (2′) only by accepting the conceptual connection thesis, then we may feel that we have to accept the conceptual connection thesis as the price of rejecting dualism. And then we will be under pressure to believe something false. For while I think that there is an important truth lying behind the conceptual connection thesis, I think that this truth is not such as to imply the falsity of dualism; so anyone who accepts the conceptual connection thesis in order to avoid accepting dualism will not only be accepting it for the wrong reason but will be accepting a mistaken version of it. Once we have seen that our argument for dualism can be refuted without the use of the conceptual connection thesis, the latter doctrine can be considered on its own merits, without our being under pressure to accept too strong a version of it.

Now let us proceed to an examination of (2'). (2') says that the proposition "I think that I am breathing" (call this "A") does not entail the proposition "I have corporeal characteristics" (call this "B"). Propositions A and B are both subject–predicate propositions, and both have the same subject – the grammatical subject being in both cases the word "I." Now when the question arises whether one such proposition entails another, what is usually in question is whether there is between them what I will call a "predicate entailment." There is a predicate entailment between two such propositions just in case they have the same subject and it is a necessary truth that whatever satisfies the predicate of the one also satisfies the predicate of the other. In other words, there is such an entailment from the proposition "a is F" to the proposition "a is G" just in case the proposition "Whatever is F is G" is a necessary truth. Thus there is a predicate entailment from "Jones is a bachelor" to "Jones is unmarried," since it is a necessary truth that whoever is a bachelor is unmarried, and there is a predicate entailment from "This figure is trilateral" to "This figure is triangular," since it is a necessary truth that whatever is trilateral is triangular.

If the universal necessary truth which backs up a particular entailment is analytically true, let us say that the predicate entailment is an analytic entailment. The entailment from "Jones is a bachelor" to "Jones is unmarried" is an analytic predicate entailment, if anything is. Many philosophers have thought that all predicate entailments are analytic. An even more common assumption has been that all such entailments are knowable a priori. Thus, consider the entailment from "This book is red" to "This book is not green," which holds in virtue of the necessary truth "Nothing is both red and green." Some philosophers have held that the latter proposition is synthetic rather than analytic; but even these philosophers have generally held that this proposition, or our knowledge of it, is a priori; it has in fact been offered as a non-Kantian example which supports the Kantian doctrine that there are synthetic a priori truths. If someone thinks that in order to refute the Jaeger–Malcolm argument one must be able to give an a priori disproof of dualism, this will be because he assumes that the entailment at issue in (2') would have to be a predicate entailment, and one that is analytic or at least a priori. And I think it is just this assumption that underlies the plausibility of (2'), i.e., the denial that there is an entailment from proposition A to proposition B. It is very plausible, indeed I think it is true, that there is no analytic predicate entailment from A to B; and the view that there is a predicate entailment which is a priori without being analytic does not seem more promising than the view that there is an analytic predicate entailment.

Recently the assumption that all predicate entailments are a priori has been called into question by Saul Kripke's contention that there are necessary truths about natural kinds that are a posteriori, i.e., empirical, rather than a priori. For example, according to Kripke the proposition "Gold is the element having the atomic number 79" is necessarily true, if true at all, even though it is not a priori; so assuming that it is true, the entailment from "My ring is made of gold" to "My ring is made of the element having atomic number 79" is a predicate entailment that is not a priori. So it would be possible for someone who agrees that there is no a priori entailment from A to B to reject (2′) on the grounds that there may be a predicate entailment from A to B that is not a priori.

But while this is a possible way of challenging the Jaeger–Malcolm argument, it is not the one I shall pursue. What I shall argue is that there may be an entailment from A to B which is not only not an a priori entailment but is not a predicate entailment at all, and that to assume without argument that there is not such an entailment amounts to begging the question in favor of dualism. Or at any rate, this is so on the assumption that premise (4) of the argument is true. That there are entailments between propositions like A and B that are not predicate entailments is another of the consequences of Kripke's work. But as we shall see, this claim is in fact something Descartes himself is committed to. Indeed, it is a consequence of one of the premises of the very Cartesian argument we are considering; it is implied by premise (4), the "essentialist premise."

Let us suppose that Kripke is right in thinking that it is necessarily true, if true at all, that Margaret Truman was born of Harry and Bess Truman. Or, more exactly, it is necessarily true that if Margaret exists (or ever existed) she was born of those parents. This follows from the plausible claim that in any possible world in which Margaret exists she was born of those parents; that however much a possible history of Margaret differs from her actual history, it cannot differ from it in starting with a birth from different parents. If this is so, the proposition "Margaret Truman sings" entails the proposition "Margaret Truman was born of Harry and Bess Truman" – assuming, of course, that the name "Margaret Truman" is used to refer to the right Margaret Truman. This is plainly not a predicate entailment; it is not necessarily true, or true at all, that whatever sings was born of Harry and Bess Truman. Yet it seems to be an entailment. Let us call such entailments "subject entailments." Where P and Q are subject–predicate propositions having the same subject, there is a subject entailment from P to Q if P entails the existence of its subject and Q ascribes to that subject some essential property.[8]

It is not necessary to maintain that there actually are any essential properties, and that there are any subject entailments that are not predicate entailments, in order to refute the Jaeger–Malcolm argument. For we can argue ad hominem by pointing out that any proponent of that argument is committed to there being such entailments. According to premise (4), anything having corporeal characteristics necessarily has corporeal characteristics. So consider the propositions expressed by "This is ten years old" and "This has corporeal characteristics," where the word "this" refers to something, let it be my watch, which has some corporeal characteristics. If (4) is true, the first proposition will entail the second; for according to (4) the thing in question must have corporeal properties in order to exist, and since it must exist in order to be ten years old, it follows that it must have corporeal characteristics in every world in which it is ten years old. And one proposition entails another just in case it is logically impossible for the one to be true without the other being true; or in other words, just in case the second is true in every possible world in which the first is true.

Many philosophers have found Descartes's First and Second Meditations a convincing proof that there can be no entailment from propositions like A to proposition B; for if one can coherently doubt the existence of a material world, and so of one's own body, while being unable to doubt one's own existence as a thinking being, it is natural to conclude that there can be no entailment from propositions like A (self-ascriptions of thoughts) to proposition B. A related argument for (2′) is from the supposed imaginability of oneself, or someone, lacking corporeal characteristics. I think that this comes to much the same thing as arguing to the logical possibility of "I think but have no corporeal characteristics (or will at some time have no

---

[8] It might be better to speak of subject entailments and predicate entailments as holding between *statements*, where the identity of a statement depends on the sentence used to express it as well as on its propositional content. I would then want to stipulate that statements count as "having the same subject" only if they both have the same grammatical subject (contain the same singular referring expression) and the grammatical subject has the same referent in both. The statements I would express by saying "Hesperus is a planet" and "Phosphorus has physical characteristics" would not have the same subject in this sense, and there would be neither a subject entailment nor a predicate entailment between them.

corporeal characteristics)" from its epistemic possibility. But the most such arguments show is that there is no a priori predicate entailment from A to B, and we have now seen that establishing this is far from enough to establish (2'). To have a case for (2') we must have a case for thinking, not merely that there is no a priori predicate entailment from A to B, but also that there is no a posteriori subject entailment between them. But how could it be argued that there is no subject entailment here? Given that one accepts premise (4) of the argument, one could do so only by arguing that one does not possess, nonderivatively, any corporeal characteristics. But that is precisely the conclusion of our argument. So it appears that in order to establish the crucial premise of the argument one would have to establish its conclusion. The argument therefore appears to be question-begging.

In order to reject the Jaeger–Malcolm argument one need not claim to know that premise (2') is false; one need only claim that no good reason has yet been given for thinking that it is true – and in particular, that the fact (if it is one) that there is no predicate entailment from A to B is no reason for thinking this. Also, if one does in fact claim that (2') is false of oneself, one is not thereby committed to denying that there are creatures for which it is true. Whether there is a subject entailment between propositions expressed by sentences A and B will depend entirely on the essential nature of the creature referred to by the word "I" in these sentences; and it is at least *prima facie* conceivable that there should be creatures for which the entailment holds and others for which it does not. Perhaps dualism is true of the Martians but not of us. Or vice versa. There is a tendency to suppose that if the entailment holds for anyone it holds for everyone, and that if it fails for anyone it fails for everyone. If one thinks this, and also thinks that it is logically possible that there should be a creature which has thoughts but no body (perhaps because one thinks one can imagine becoming such a creature, or can imagine discovering that someone else has), one will think that the entailment fails for everyone and will thereby be committed to holding that dualism is true of all creatures having minds. If one makes the same assumption, but is convinced that dualism is false, one will think that one has to deny the logical possibility of there being creatures that have thoughts without having bodies. But what leads to this assumption is the uncritical acceptance of the assumption that all entailments are predicate entailments. Once it is seen that this assumption is unfounded, or at any rate not available to anyone who accepts premise (4), it can be seen that the entailment at issue in (2') could hold for some creatures and not for others. And then it can be seen that it is at least *prima facie* consistent to hold that one is oneself an essentially corporeal being whose existence depends on its having corporeal characteristics, while holding that there may be other thinking beings which are capable of disembodied existence. It goes with this that whether a particular person is, nonderivatively, a subject of corporeal characteristics is a matter for empirical investigation, and not something to be discovered by a priori philosophical reflection.

III

It is possible that one source of the view that it is entirely an a priori matter whether dualism is true is the idea, which I have just argued to be mistaken, that in order to avoid dualism one must hold the view that for every mental state there is a predicate entailment from the having of that state to the having of some corporeal characteristics, together with the view that all predicate entailments must be a priori. But I am sure that this is not the only source. For I believe that there is an important version of dualism of which this view is true – a version such that the issue of whether it is true should be regarded as an a priori one. What partly accounts for the ambiguous status of dualism mentioned at the beginning of this essay, the fact that it is sometimes treated as an a priori thesis and sometimes as an empirical one, is that philosophers have not clearly distinguished the a priori version from a version which is, at least *prima facie*, empirical. What I say about these two versions of dualism here will be in part a summary of what I have said in more detail elsewhere; my excuse for going over this again is in part its bearing on the general theme of this essay, in part the fact that I must do so in order to fulfill my promise to reexamine premise (4) of my version of the Jaeger–Malcolm argument.[9]

Let me begin by characterizing a position I will call "Minimal Dualism." According to this, for each person having mental states there is an incorporeal substance such that (a) what mental states the person has depends on what states the incorporeal substance has, (b) all causal connections involving mental states between the person's sensory input and behavioral output are mediated by states of this immaterial substance, and (c) it is possible for the person to exist, as a subject of mental states without having a body, as long as the incorporeal substance exists and has the appropriate states. Now on one version of this view, the version I will call "Cartesian Dualism,"

[9] See my "Embodiment and Behavior" and "Immortality and Dualism" (Essays 6 and 7 of this volume).

the subject of mental states (i.e., the person) *just is* the incorporeal substance, and the states of the incorporeal substance *just are* the person's mental states. But notice that this is not implied by Minimal Dualism. It is compatible with Minimal Dualism, as I have characterized it, that the relation of the incorporeal substance and its states to the person and his mental states should be analogous to the relationship which a materialist thinks there is between a person's brain and its physiological states, on the one hand, and the person and his mental states, on the other. Most materialists would not want to say that a person *is* his brain; and whether or not the materialist says that the person's mental states are states of his brain, he will not say that all of the states of the person's brain are mental states. What our materialist will say is that the person's mental states are in some sense constituted by, or realized in, states of his brain. And on the version of Minimal Dualism which I will call "Non-Cartesian Dualism," the mental states of a person are constituted by, or realized in, the states of an incorporeal substance which can be thought of as a kind of ghostly brain. The situation in which a person exists in disembodied form, with the incorporeal substance separated from his body, will be analogous to the situation, envisaged as possible by some materialists, in which the person exists as a brain in a vat.[10]

It will perhaps come as no surprise that the version of Minimal Dualism which seems to me an a priori thesis, and which I believe to be a priori false, is Cartesian Dualism, while the version which seems to me to be *prima facie* an empirical thesis, and empirically false, is Non-Cartesian Dualism. In the scope of the present essay I can do no more than sketch my reasons for thinking this.

Let me begin by trying to imagine a set of empirical observations which is as favorable to dualism as possible, and asking what sort of dualism, if any, these observations would support. I suppose that the observed phenomena should include lots of "spiritualistic" phenomena, apparent communications with the dead and the like, for which no physical explanations could be found. They should also include observations that indicate that neither the brain nor any other part of

[10] The possibility of the position I have called "Non-Cartesian Dualism" was recognized by Hilary Putnam in "The Nature of Mental States" and "The Mental Life of Some Machines," when he pointed out that "the functional state hypothesis is not incompatible with dualism," and that a soul, or a system consisting of a body and a soul, could perfectly well be a Turing Machine or Probabalistic Automaton of the sort the "functional state hypothesis" holds minds to be. See Putnam, *Mind, Language and Reality, Philosophical Papers* (Cambridge, 1975), vol. II, pp. 412 and 436.

the body has the degree of complexity and the sort of organization it would have to have if its states were the sole causal basis of the enormously complex behavioral repertoires a person has in virtue of having the various mental states. It would also help if the observations were such as to give comfort to opponents of evolutionary theory, and supported the view that the gulf between the intellectual capacities of man and those of other animals is every bit as large as Descartes believed it to be.

Now if such a set of observations established dualism, what they would directly establish is the truth of what I have called Minimal Dualism – the view that we must postulate something over and above material things and physical processes in order to explain the observed phenomena we attribute to the mental states of human beings. Assuming that Non-Cartesian Dualism is a coherent version of dualism, then in establishing Minimal Dualism these observations would not establish Cartesian Dualism. And it seems plain that there are no additional empirical observations that would tip the balance in favor of Cartesian Dualism over Non-Cartesian Dualism. Of course, so far the situation is symmetrical; if Cartesian Dualism is a coherent form of dualism, then in establishing Minimal Dualism these observations would not establish Non-Cartesian Dualism. But on further examination the symmetry breaks down.

Let us ask how Non-Cartesian Dualism could fail to be coherent. It would of course be incoherent if the very notion of an incorporeal substance turned out to be incoherent, or if it turned out that it is incoherent to suppose that material and incorporeal substances could interact causally. But in that case Cartesian Dualism would be incoherent as well, since *all* versions of Minimal Dualism would be incoherent. Let us suppose that this is not the case. Assuming, then, that the notion of an incorporeal substance is in order, and that causal interaction between material and immaterial substances is not a logical impossibility, it would seem that Non-Cartesian Dualism could fail to be coherent only if it were incoherent to suppose that mental states are related to states of incorporeal substances in the way materialists think that mental states are related to physical states of the brain. But since the notion of an incorporeal substance is a negative notion, i.e., is the notion of a substance that is *not* physical or material, such an incoherence could not be due to some special feature of this notion which precludes the possibility of mental states being realized in, or constituted by, states of incorporeal substances. Assuming, as we are, that there are coherent forms of dualism, it cannot belong to the concept of mental states that the only sorts of states they can be

realized in, or constituted by, are physical states of material substances. So if, despite this, Non-Cartesian Dualism is not coherent, this
can only be because it is not coherent to suppose that there are any
states whatever that realize or constitute mental states in the way that
materialists believe physical states of the brain realize or constitute
them. But this is to say that Non-Cartesian Dualism will fail to be
coherent only if noneliminative materialism fails to be coherent –
where by "noneliminative materialism" I mean the version of
materialism which holds that there are mental states but that these are
"nothing over and above" physical states. (Henceforth I shall take
"noneliminative" as understood when I speak of materialism.) So
anyone who thinks that it is an empirical issue whether materialism or
dualism is true must think that Non-Cartesian Dualism is a coherent
doctrine. There is no such argument to show that such a person must
think that Cartesian Dualism is a coherent doctrine; and as I shall now
indicate, I think there are reasons to hold that such a person ought to
think that Cartesian Dualism is *not* a coherent doctrine.

A proponent of Non-Cartesian Dualism could hold that Non-
Cartesian Dualism is true in the actual world but that there are other
possible worlds in which materialism is true. For while he holds that in
fact mental states are realized in, or constituted by, certain nonphysical states of incorporeal substances, it is compatible with this
that these states could be realized physically – just as it is compatible
with the view that certain mental states are in fact realized in certain
physical states that they could be realized in different ones. Indeed, just
as a materialist can hold that the same mental states can have one sort
of physical realization among human Earthlings and another sort of
physical realization among the denizens of some remote planet, so
someone who holds that Non-Cartesian Dualism is true of himself and
the rest of his kind might nevertheless allow that elsewhere in the
universe there may be creatures psychologically like him whose
mental states are realized physically, and are purely physical beings. A
Cartesian Dualist, however, must hold that there is no possible world
in which materialism is true, or in which there are purely physical
beings which have mental states. According to him, each mental
property just is a certain nonphysical property, and it is logically
impossible that any such property should belong to a purely physical
thing. If we could assume the traditional view that questions of logical
possibility are always a priori, this would be enough to show that a
proponent of Cartesian Dualism cannot regard the question of
whether dualism or materialism is true as an empirical one. For such a
dualist would have to think that the truth of materialism is logically

impossible, and therefore not something it makes sense to investigate empirically. However, Kripke has complicated our lives by showing that propositions whose truth or falsity is logically necessary can have the epistemological status of being a posteriori. So we need to carry the argument a bit further. In the present essay I can only indicate the direction in which the continuation of the argument would have to go.

Let me begin by formulating a doctrine, which I shall call "conceptual functionalism," which has recently been advanced by a number of philosophers.[11] This says, roughly, that the concept of a mind is the concept of a system of states that stand in certain relations, in particular causal relations, to one another and to behavior. What constitutes a particular state as being a particular mental state is its playing the role in such a system which is definitive of that mental state. For example, what constitutes a state as being a certain belief is the way in which it combines with certain desires, and with other beliefs, in the production and control of behavior directed at the satisfaction of those desires; perhaps, as a first approximation, it is the belief in a certain proposition because its contribution to behavior is such that it tends to maximize the satisfaction of the person's desires (whatever they might be) in circumstances in which that proposition is true.[12] As long as a state plays the appropriate role, it doesn't matter what it is like otherwise; thus it is that the same mental state can be "realized" in a variety of different ways. It is essential to this position, as I am characterizing it, that it is a conceptual truth that mental states are functional states, and that it is at least to some extent a conceptual matter what the functional definitions of particular sorts of mental

[11] Versions of this view can be found in David Armstrong, *A Materialist Theory of the Mind* (London, 1968); in David Lewis, "An Argument for the Identity Theory," in D. M. Rosenthal, (ed.), *Materialism and the Mind–Body Problem* (Englewood Cliffs, N.J., 1971), and "Psychophysical and Theoretical Identifications," *Australasian Journal of Philosophy*, 50 (1972); and in my own "Functionalism and Qualia" and "Some Varieties of Functionalism" (Essays 9 and 12 of this volume). A similar view can be found in Paul Grice, "Method in Philosophical Psychology (From the Banal to the Bizarre)," *Proceedings and Addresses of the American Philosophical Association*, 48 (1974–75), 23–53. Other advocates of a functionalist approach to the philosophy of mind would deny the status of "conceptual truth" to both the functionalist position itself (the view that mental states are functional states) and to the functional definitions of particular states, and would instead assign to these the status of empirical hypotheses. See, for example, Hilary Putnam, "The Nature of Mental States." For an account of the different sorts of functionalism, and a criticism of functionalist theories, see Ned Block, "Troubles With Functionalism," in *Readings in the Philosophy of Psychology* (Cambridge, Mass., 1980), vol. I.

[12] See Paul Grice, "Method in Philosophical Psychology (From the Banal to the Bizarre)."

states (beliefs, desires, pains, etc.) are. I also take it that conceptual functionalism and Cartesian Dualism are logically (and conceptually) incompatible. According to Cartesian Dualism, mental terms rigidly designate certain nonphysical properties and states, and all that belongs to their sense is that the properties and states thus designated are nonphysical. So if conceptual functionalism can be established by conceptual analysis, then Cartesian Dualism is not only false but conceptually false. This is what I believe to be the case. But in the present essay I have given no argument whatever in favor of conceptual functionalism. I have merely offered it as something which it is plausible to think can be established by conceptual analysis, and so a priori, and which rules out an interesting form of dualism.

It is worth observing that if conceptual functionalism is true, it can fairly claim to capture the germ of truth in the idea, mentioned earlier in connection with the Jaeger–Malcolm argument, that dualism is false, and conceptually false, *because* it denies the conceptual connections between mind and body. Conceptual functionalism is a cousin of what I earlier called the conceptual connection thesis; like the latter it makes the relations of mental states to bodily behavior partly definitive of them. It is not strong enough to warrant the claim that there is an analytic entailment between propositions A and B in premise (2′) of the Jaeger–Malcolm argument, and so it is not strong enough to rule out all forms of dualism. In particular it does not rule out Non-Cartesian Dualism – for the latter can be seen as simply the view that the way in which mental states are in fact realized is in the incorporeal states of incorporeal substances. It is, however, strong enough to rule out Cartesian Dualism.

But now let us return to Non-Cartesian Dualism. If this is a coherent form of dualism, and perhaps (as I think) the only coherent form of dualism, it becomes necessary to reconsider premise (4) of the Jaeger–Malcolm argument (or, rather, of my reconstruction of that argument). According to Non-Cartesian Dualism, an embodied person is a system which is partly material and partly immaterial, the two parts interacting causally. The immaterial part is supposed to play the causal and functional role which materialists think is played by the brain. But if there could be such systems, why couldn't there also be systems in which what plays this causal and functional role is itself a system which is partly material and partly immaterial? In other words, if there can be persons animated by ghostly brains, why can't there be systems animated by partly ghostly brains? And if there could be such systems, why couldn't they undergo changes consisting in the replacement of material components with functionally equivalent immaterial ones, or vice versa?[13] But if this is possible, then it would seem as if it should be possible for someone to start off as a completely physical being and to end up, as the result of a series of such replacements, having a completely immaterial substance playing the role of the brain. And if the continued existence and functioning of this ghostly brain could be sufficient for the existence of the person even if it were separated from his body (again, this may be compared with the case in which a brain is kept alive *in vitro*), then it would be true of something which at one time was a purely physical being, and had physical characteristics in a nonderivative way, that it could exist without having any physical properties at all. And if this is true then premise (4) of my reconstruction of the Jaeger–Malcolm argument is false. If so, then one cannot say, as I did earlier, that premise (2') of the argument begs the question. For if (4) is false, the assertion of (2') is not after all tantamount to the denial that one has corporeal characteristics in a nonderivative way. But this will be cold comfort for the proponent of the Jaeger–Malcolm argument, for he can now be impaled on the horns of a dilemma. We can point out that on the assumption that (4) is true premise (2') begs the question, while on the assumption that (4) is false the argument is simply unsound.

It may be objected that if so-called immaterial substances could be functionally equivalent to material substances in the way just imagined, and if they could interact causally with them in ways analogous to those in which parts of the brain interact with one another and the rest of the body, then there could be no good reason for calling them "immaterial" or "nonphysical." I suspect that if this objection is pressed consistently it will deny the possibility of any sort of causal interaction between the material and the immaterial, or between the physical and the nonphysical. The idea will be that whatever can interact causally with physical systems must itself be physical. In the end, I think, this will amount to a denial that the notion of an immaterial substance, a substance whose properties are nonphysical, is a coherent one. To argue this is to mount an a priori attack on dualism which is very different from the sorts of attack I have considered so far. This objection raises the difficult question of how, precisely, the terms "physical" and "material" are to be understood in formulations of the mind–body problem, and whether there is any acceptable understanding of them which makes dualism a coherent answer to the problem. I cannot pursue this question in any

[13] Richard Boyd envisages a similar possibility in "Materialism Without Reductionism: What Physicalism Does Not Entail," in Block (ed.), *Readings in the Philosophy of Psychology*, vol. i.

detail here, and will conclude with just a couple of brief remarks on it. First of all, the view that it follows from the correct analysis of the meaning of the term "physical" that whatever can interact causally with a physical system must itself be physical, and that any substance that interacts causally with human bodies is ipso facto a material substance having physical properties, is difficult to reconcile with the fact, mentioned earlier, that we can imagine a history of empirical observations which would seem to establish, or at least support, some version of dualism. If such observations actually occurred, a material-ist who tried to use such an analysis to convince dualists that their views had not been vindicated would be accused, with some justice, of semantic hanky panky, to say nothing of being a sore loser. On the other hand, we certainly would not want to limit the application of the term "physical" to phenomena that are reducible to phenomena *currently* recognized by physics, and I think that we have some tendency to so use that term that any entity or phenomenon which we have to posit in order to explain physical phenomena will itself count as physical. Perhaps there is some indeterminacy in our notion of the physical, and there is simply no fact of the matter as to whether certain imaginable happenings should count as the discovery of nonphysical, or immaterial, substances, or whether, on the other hand, they should count as the discovery of physical entities of a novel kind. If so, we have a further explanation, beyond those already given in this essay, of why the issue of dualism seems to be constantly shifting its status, presenting itself sometimes as an a priori issue and sometimes as an empirical one.

14
Absent qualia are impossible – a reply to Block

I

In his recent paper "Are Absent Qualia Impossible?" (hereafter AAQI),[1] Ned Block attempts to rebut an argument I gave for an affirmative answer to his title question in my paper, "Functionalism and Qualia" (hereafter F&Q).[2] The issues raised by this controversy go far beyond the question of whether a particular argument of mine is successful. The question of what account we are to give of "qualia" (of the "qualitative"/"phenomenal"/"subjective"/"raw feel" aspects of the mental), or of what can and cannot sensibly be said about them, is one of the most central issues in the philosophy of mind. Block's formulation of this question focuses it on the issue of "functionalism." To hold that absent qualia are possible – that a state lacking qualitative character can be functionally equivalent to a "qualitative state" like pain (one that necessarily has qualitative character) – is to hold that functionalism fails as a general philosophy of mind. Block is certainly not alone in regarding qualia as the Achilles' heel of functionalism; a well-known expression of the same view is Thomas Nagel's claim that the "subjective character" of experience, "what it is like" to have it, is "not captured by any of the familiar, recently devised, reductive analyses of the mental, for all of them are logically compatible with its absence."[3]

Block's paper has helped me to see deficiencies in my argument in F&Q against the possibility of absent qualia. Certainly the argument was less clear than it should have been. Since I remain convinced of the truth of its conclusion and believe that it is supported by the sorts of considerations I adduced, and since I agree with Block's criticisms of

---

[1] *The Philosophical Review*, 89 (1980), 257–274.

[2] Essay 9 of this volume. My paper was a reply to a paper by Ned Block and Jerry Fodor, "What Psychological States are Not" (*The Philosophical Review*, 81 (1972), 159–181), which raised the "inverted qualia" and "absent qualia" objections to functionalism (see pp. 172–174).

[3] Thomas Nagel, "What is it Like to be a Bat?", in *Mortal Questions* (Cambridge, 1979).

the two interpretations of the argument which he considers, I am naturally unwilling to accept his interpretations as correct. But his interpretations are *prima facie* plausible ones, and reflecting on them has helped me to get clearer both about the issues and about my own past intentions. The issues matter a great deal more than the past intentions, and my purpose in the present essay is not primarily to defend the argument as it was formulated in F&Q: instead, it is, first, to clarify the issues and, second, to defend what I now take to be the intended conclusion of that argument.

II

I have characterized a case of absent qualia as a case in which a state lacking qualitative character is "functionally equivalent" to a state, like pain, that necessarily has a qualitative character. To get clear about what this means we must consider the notion of "functional equivalence" and the closely related notion of a functional definition. I begin with the latter.

Block says that "[f]unctionalism is the doctrine that pain (for example) is identical to a certain functional state, a state definable in terms of its causal relations to inputs, outputs, and other mental states."[4] Suppose, however, that pain were definable in terms of its causal relations to inputs, outputs, and certain other mental states, but that some of those other mental states (beliefs, say) were not so definable. Would pain count as functionally definable, if this were so? From the passage just quoted from Block one would judge that it would be, but from the footnote in which Block offers a more precise characterization one would judge the opposite; according to the footnote, the *definiens* of a functional definition of pain would contain no mental terminology, and this means that the "other mental states" by relation to which pain is defined would themselves have to be functionally definable.[5] It will be useful to allow both answers. Let us

---

[4] AAQI, p. 257.

[5] Block's more precise characterization is given in his footnote 1, p. 257 of AAQI. It is a variant of one proposed by David Lewis in "Psychophysical and Theoretical Identifications" (*Australasian Journal of Philosophy*, 50 (1972), 249–257). On this characterization, functional definitions of mental predicates are extracted from the Ramsey sentence of a psychological theory (on Lewis's view, one consisting of common-sense "platitudes" about relations of mental states to one another and to inputs and outputs); in forming the Ramsey sentence all of the mental predicates in the theory are replaced by variables, so that none occur in the *definiens* of a functional definition. I shall refer to this as the "Ramsey–Lewis technique."

say that a mental state is functionally definable in the *weak sense* if it is definable in terms of its causal relations to inputs, outputs, and other mental states, regardless of whether those other mental states are functionally definable. And let us say that a mental state is functionally definable in the *strong sense* if it is functionally definable in the sense of Block's footnote, that is, in such a way that no mental terminology occurs in the *definiens*. In a definition of the latter sort, the *definiens* will quantify over what are in fact mental states, or rather over what are in fact mental states *if* the definition is correct, but it will not contain expressions designating particular mental states. Functionalism, as a general theory of mind, should be understood as the thesis that all mental states are functionally definable in the strong sense. But the weak sense is nevertheless important; as we shall see, the claim that absent qualia are possible has different senses corresponding to these different senses of "functionally definable."

To say that state *A* is "functionally equivalent" to state *B* is presumably to say that there is a functional definition of some sort that *A* and *B* both satisfy. But what sort? To say merely that there is some functional definition or other that both satisfy is much too weak, for that could not fail to be the case. On the other hand, where *B* is a mental state it will not do to say that *A* is functionally equivalent to *B* just in case *A* satisfies a *correct* functional definition of the mental state *B* is; for the proponent of the possibility of absent qualia denies that there is a correct functional definition of pain, but still wants to say that a state can be functionally equivalent to pain while lacking qualitative character. I shall say that a state is functionally equivalent to a given mental state just in case it satisfies a "maximally good" functional definition of that mental state (if the equivalence is between state types) or of the most determinate mental state type of which it is a token (if the equivalence is between state tokens). It remains to explain what I mean by a "maximally good" functional definition.

Suppose that I have offered a functional definition of a certain mental state, and suppose that you then offer me what, on reflection, I agree is a counterexample to my definition. Obviously this need not persuade me that the state in question is not functionally definable, and that functionalism is false. I may in fact gratefully accept your counterexample as showing me a way in which my definition can be improved; I will then try to come up with an emended version of the definition to which your example is not a counterexample. Presumably this is just the way in which a functional definition gets refined. We think up possible cases, compare what seems intuitively the right thing to say about them with what our current definition dictates that we should say, and emend the definition if it doesn't give us the right answers – unless, of course, we find some reason for thinking that our initial intuitions were wrong. Let us call this the method of refinement by successive approximations. What I mean by a maximally good functional definition of a mental state is one that has been refined by this method to the point where it is not improvable by further consideration of thought experiments (or real experiments); D is such a definition of mental state M if it is not possible to formulate an alternative functional definition D' of M such that there are logically possible cases that are counterexamples to D but not to D', and none that are counterexamples to D' and not to D.

We can now say that to hold that absent qualia are possible is to hold that there can be states that satisfy maximally good functional definitions of qualitative states like pain, but lack qualitative character and so in fact are not such states. This is of course to claim that in the case of qualitative states, maximally good functional definitions are not good enough, and thus that such states are not functionally definable. But now let us recall our distinction between the weak and the strong senses of "functionally definable." There are two distinct theses that could be expressed by saying that qualitative states are not functionally definable, and that absent qualia are possible. I shall call these Absent Qualia Thesis One (AQT-1), and Absent Qualia Thesis Two (AQT-2).

AQT-1 holds that qualitative states are not functionally definable in even the weak sense. A weak functional definition of pain would define it as a state standing in various causal relations to (among other things) other mental states; so to have a state that satisfies a maximally good functional definition of this sort a creature would have to have, or at least be capable of having, some genuine mental states, namely those mentioned in the *definiens* of the weak functional definition of pain (these might include, for example, believing that one is in pain, wanting to be rid of pain, and so on). If a state (token) satisfies a maximally good functional definition (in either the weak or the strong sense) of mental state M, for example, pain, but in fact is not a genuine (token of) M, let us say that it is an "ersatz M," for example, an "ersatz pain."[6] According to AQT-1, it is possible for there to be a creature, an "imitation man,"[7] whose nonqualitative mental states, such as beliefs, are all genuine (not ersatz), but those pains and other qualitative states are ersatz, in the sense that they satisfy maximally

---

[6] The term "ersatz pain" is due to Larry Davis – see AAQI, p. 259.

[7] I take the term "imitation man" from Keith Campbell; see his *Body and Mind* (Garden City, N.Y., 1970), chs. 5 and 6.

good weak functional definitions of those states but lack qualitative character and so are not genuine tokens of them.[8]

AQT-2 holds that qualitative states are not functionally definable in the strong sense. This means that it is possible for there to be a creature that has states that satisfy maximally good *strong* functional definitions of qualitative states like pain, but in fact lacks such qualitative states because all of its states lack qualitative character. This would of course be true if there could be an imitation man of the sort AQT-1 holds to be possible (so AQT-1 entails AQT-2). But AQT-2 is not committed to this possibility; even if such an imitation man is impossible (that is, even if qualitative states are functionally definable in the weak sense), AQT-2 would still be true if there could be what we might call a super-imitation man, namely a creature having states satisfying maximally good strong functional definitions of the various mental states, but such that all of these states, the putative non-qualitative mental states as well as the putative qualitative ones, are ersatz rather than genuine.

It is clear that AQT-1 implies AQT-2, but the converse is not true. The possibility of there being an imitation man and the possibility of there being a super-imitation man are independent; neither implies the other, and the denial of neither implies the denial of the other.[9] But

[8] Given the way I defined "weak sense" above, the requirement that the proponent of AQT-1 deny that qualitative states are functionally definable in the weak sense is perhaps a bit too strict; it is sufficient that he deny that they are functionally definable in a slightly stronger sense, which I shall call the "pretty-weak sense." A pretty-weak functional definition of a mental state is one that defines it in terms of its causal relations to inputs, outputs, and *nonqualitative* mental states – where "nonqualitative" is understood as excluding not only qualitative states proper, such as pain, but also a certain kind of what in F&Q I called "qualitative beliefs," namely introspective beliefs to the effect that one has a state having a certain specific qualitative character (not excluded are introspective beliefs to the effect that one has a state having some qualitative character or other that satisfies some causal or functional condition – see F&Q, pp. 203–4 of this volume). AQT-1 is best taken as saying that any maximally good pretty-weak functional definition of any qualitative state can be satisfied by a state that lacks qualitative character, or at least that this is true of some such functional definitions. Hereafter, "weak sense" in the text may be read as having the meaning here assigned to "pretty-weak sense." This makes a difference only if it should turn out (what seems to me unlikely) that maximally good weak (in the original sense) functional definitions of qualitative states always define them (in part) in terms of their relations to other qualitative states, or to beliefs that assign specific qualia, and so do not qualify as pretty-weak functional definitions. Someone who held that such definitions might be correct (and so incapable of being satisfied by states lacking qualitative character) could consistently accept AQT-1, as I am interpreting it.

[9] As I use these terms, a super-imitation man is not an imitation man – to be an imitation man a creature must have genuine nonqualitative states as well as ersatz qualitative states.

whereas AQT-1 implies the possibility of there being an imitation man, what AQT-2 implies is that it is possible either that there should be an imitation man or that there should be a super-imitation man or (perhaps) that some situation intermediate between these should obtain. Since AQT-1 is a stronger thesis than AQT-2, the denial of AQT-2 is a stronger thesis than AQT-1. Indeed, the denial of AQT-2 is virtually tantamount to the affirmation of the correctness of functionalism as a general philosophy of mind; for given the connections that hold between qualitative mental states and other mental states, and would have to be mentioned in any plausible functional definition of these states, the denial of AQT-2 implies that all or most mental states are functionally definable in the strong sense. The denial of AQT-1, on the other hand, is compatible with the falsity of functionalism; it is compatible with its being the case that some mental states (nonqualitative ones) are not functionally definable in even the weak sense, and it is compatible with no mental states being functionally definable in the strong sense (that is, it is compatible with the possibility of there being a super-imitation man).

In F&Q I claimed to show, by a rather brief argument, that absent qualia are impossible. That argument (which is the target of Block's AAQI) was a preliminary to the main part of the essay, in which I attempted to show that functionalism is compatible with "qualia inversion" (for example, "spectrum inversion" – red things looking to me the way green things look to you, and so on), and that the notion of qualitative similarity, and of qualia (thought of as features of mental states), can be functionally defined in a way that allows for this possibility. In the main part of the essay I construed my task as that of rebutting what Block calls "qualia centred objections" to functionalism, and explicitly disavowed any intention of establishing the general adequacy of functionalism; to quote from myself, "my aim is not the ambitious one of showing that functionalism provides a fully satisfactory philosophy of mind; it is the much more modest one of showing that the fact that some mental states have 'qualitative character' need not pose any special difficulties for a functionalist."[10] But if my preliminary argument had shown the impossibility of absent qualia in the sense affirmed by the denial of AQT-2, then it would have shown the main part of what I disavowed any intention of showing – it would have shown that qualitative states are functionally definable in the strong sense, which would require (at least) that most other mental states are also functionally definable in the strong sense. When I wrote

[10] F&Q, p. 201 of this volume.

F&Q I had not seen (clearly) the necessity of distinguishing between the weak and strong senses, and thus of distinguishing AQT-1 and AQT-2. But once the distinction is made, it is clear both from the nature of my preliminary argument and from my statements of intent that the argument should be seen as aimed at refuting AQT-1, and not at refuting AQT-2. If AQT-1 is false, then while it may still be the case that functionalism is false, it is hard to see how it can be false *because* there is something special about qualitative states that makes them not functionally definable. For anyone who holds AQT-2, but denies AQT-1, it will be difficult to maintain that qualia are the Achilles' heel of functionalism. And what F&Q, taken as a whole, was intended to show is that functionalism has nothing to fear from qualia.

It is clear enough that Block wants to defend AQT-2. It is not so clear whether he believes, or is interested in defending, AQT-1. The putative case of absent qualia he describes in AAQI, his example of the "homunculus-headed system," is a putative case of a super-imitation man rather than of an imitation man – it is supposed to lack mental states generally, and not just qualitative states. So at best it supports AQT-2 but not AQT-1. If Block is interested only in defending AQT-2, then while he is defending a thesis I reject, he is not defending one that I have argued against.

III

Let us take pain as our example of a qualitative state, that is, of a mental state that necessarily has qualitative character. And let us understand the phrase "causal features" in such a way that the causal features of a state (type) will include facts about how the state is capable of being caused as well as facts about what sorts of effects it is capable of causing, by itself or in combination with other factors. Presumably it is the causal features of a state that enable us to have knowledge of it, and nothing we can know of the state can be independent of these. My argument in F&Q against the possibility of absent qualia was directed against the idea that there could be a state that has all of the functionally relevant causal features of pain, including its causal relations to other mental states, but altogether lacks qualitative character. This would be the case of an imitation man having ersatz pain – a case of absent qualia in the sense of AQT-1. Since one of the causal features of pain is that it is accessible to introspection – that is, that it gives rise under certain circumstances to a belief in its occurrence on the part of its possessor – it would have to be true of ersatz pain that it gives rise to the same introspective beliefs on the part of its possessor, as well as the same behavior, as pain does. The gist of my argument against the possibility of absent qualia was that the supposition that ersatz pain is possible gives rise to insuperable epistemological difficulties. There is, of course, the problem of how we could know that our friends and neighbors are not imitation men. But there is also, on this supposition, a problem about how we can know that we ourselves are not imitation men. For one thing, it appears that my grounds for thinking that my own pains are real and not ersatz can be no better than the grounds that an imitation man would have for thinking the same about his ersatz pains.

Block's first formulation of my argument (the only one I shall explicitly address) is as follows: "if absent qualia are possible, then the presence or absence of the qualitative character of pain would make no difference to its causal consequences; and so, according to a causal theory of knowledge, we could have no knowledge of the qualitative character of pain; but given that we *do* have knowledge of the qualitative character of pain . . . , absent qualia are not possible."[11] His objection to this argument is to its first premise, which he rejects on the grounds that "[t]he causal role of genuine pain may be crucially *dependent on its qualitative character*, even if the homunculus-head's pains are ersatz," that is, even if in some possible creature the same causal role is played by states lacking qualitative character.[12]

I would accept this formulation of my argument only if the first premise is emended to read as follows (call the emended premise EP): "If absent qualia are possible, then the presence or absence of the qualitative character of pain would make no difference to its causal consequences *that would make it possible for anyone to distinguish cases of genuine pain from cases of ersatz pain*" (the emendation consists in the addition of the italicized clause). And this emendation circumvents Block's objection. To refute EP it is not enough to point out, as Block does, that the friends of absent qualia (to use his phrase) are not committed to the view that the qualitative character of pain is epiphenomenal.[13] Nor is it enough to point out, as Block points out in criticizing a slightly different reconstruction of my argument, that the fact that ersatz pain would have the same "functional causal role" as pain (that is, would share with it the functionally relevant causal features of pain – whatever features a state must have in order to

---

[11] AAQI, p. 259.

[12] AAQI, p. 262.

[13] A friend of absent qualia who does embrace the view that qualia are epiphenomenal is Keith Campbell; see his *Body and Mind*, ch. 6.

satisfy a best possible functional definition of pain) does not imply that it has the same "total causal role" as pain (that is, shares all of its causal features, including those not required by the best possible functional definition of pain). We can agree that any case of ersatz pain would differ in its total causal role (that is, in some causal feature or other) from any case of pain. What is at issue is whether the differences could be such as to make it possible to distinguish such cases, not merely in the sense of ascertaining that they are in some way different from each other (after all, there can be differences between different cases of genuine pain), but in the sense of being able to tell that one is a case of genuine pain and the other a case of ersatz pain. In F&Q there was the germ of an argument (hardly more than that) for a negative answer to the question just posed, and that amounts to an argument for EP. In what follows I shall present, in this order, that argument, an objection to it (not quite the same as Block's but related to it), and an attempt to remedy its shortcomings.

The "functional causal role" of pain will be the causal role assigned to pain by a maximally good functional definition.[14] This will be different from its total causal role, that is, the totality of its causal features (otherwise it would not be possible, as functionalists insist it is, for pain to be physically realized in different ways – each possible realization will correspond to a total causal role, and the functional causal role will be what all these have in common). But it would seem offhand that this is a difference that it would be impossible to exploit in order to distinguish pain from ersatz pain, or vice versa. What we need, in order to do the latter, is a difference in causal roles between two states that will tell us that one is genuine pain and the other ersatz pain, and, moreover, will tell us which is which. But where can this difference lie? It cannot lie in the functional causal role, since by hypothesis this is possessed in common by genuine pain and ersatz pain. But suppose that there is some feature F possessed by state S and lacked by state S^*, such that S's possession of it shows that S is genuine pain and S^*'s lack of it shows that S^* is ersatz. The possession of F must lie outside the functional role of pain (and so must any other feature of which F is a reliable indicator and which is possessed by S and lacked by S^*). But it seems plausible to argue that this cannot be. Perhaps the best functional definition of pain so far devised places F (and its correlates) outside the functional role of pain. But this would

---

[14] This will cause trouble if there can be two or more "maximally good" functional definitions of a mental state which are not equivalent. I do not believe that this is possible, but have no proof that it is not.

merely show, it would seem, that our best current definition is not a maximally good one, and that we can improve on it by redrawing the line between functionally relevant and functionally irrelevant causal features, so that *F*, or some feature of which it is a reliable indicator, becomes functionally relevant. So once we have a maximally good functional definition, there will be no such feature *F* that can be used to distinguish pain from ersatz pain. And from this EP does seem to follow.

If correct, this line of argument would show that it is impossible to show by counterexamples that a given mental state is not functionally definable, and that the most any counterexample can do is to contribute to the process of "refinement by successive approximations" by showing that a particular functional definition is not maximally good and so should be emended or replaced. If the argument works at all, it applies to functional definability in the strong sense as well as functional definability in the weak sense, and so shows that it is not possible to conceive of a case in which we would be entitled to assert the existence of absent qualia, either in the sense of AQT-1 or in the sense of AQT-2. It would dispose of Block's "homunculus-head" counterexamples to functionalism, and of all others of the same sort. It seems too good to be true that such a conclusion could be established so easily. And in fact the argument is defective. The objection I shall raise to it is related to one Block raises, but I shall put it in my own way.[15]

It is widely held nowadays, under the influence of Kripke and Putnam, that it is not possible to give what I shall call "Lockean

---

[15] Block's objections are stated on pp. 267–270 of AAQI. A theme that runs through much of what he says is that definitional refinement of the sort I have described might require the incorporation into a definition of "physiological information" that would be out of place in an analytic functional definition. To the extent that I can understand this, it comes to the objection I raise in the text in the following pages. But Block also suggests that certain sorts of definitional refinement that do not depart from functionalism in *this* way might nevertheless render the definition no longer a functional definition; specifically, he thinks that this is true of those that involve adding to a functional condition "whatever negative conditions can be motivated by a priori thought experiments" (p. 268). Suppose that we have a definition that says that a creature is in pain just in case it satisfies functional description *D*, and that we modify it (to avoid a counterexample) by adding the condition that a creature that satisfies *D* counts as being in pain only if it is *not* the case that its satisfaction of *D* results in a certain way from the operation in it of a "homunculus" satisfying a certain functional description. Block apparently thinks that the new definition would not be a functional definition because it would not define pain solely in terms of its "causal role." But not to count such a negative causal condition as a partial specification of the causal role of a state seems to me arbitrary, and so does the requirement that a

definitions" of natural kind terms like "gold," that is, definitions that assert analytic equivalences of the form "x is gold if and only if x has features $F_1 \ldots F_n$." Now, if the line of argument given above were correct, an analogous line of argument would show that it is not possible to show by counterexample that natural kind terms cannot be given Lockean definitions; the most that any counterexample could show, so the argument would run, is that a particular Lockean definition is not a "maximally good Lockean definition," and needs to be emended or replaced. I think that Kripke has shown that this argument is mistaken. Even if something satisfies a maximally good Lockean definition of "gold," we can establish that it is not gold by establishing that it lacks some property (say, a certain atomic structure) that scientific investigation of our "paradigm" samples of gold has shown to be essential to gold. Indeed, it is not necessary that the scientific investigation should actually have taken place; if we can so much as imagine discovering that our paradigm examples of gold have a certain underlying feature F, and if it is clear to us on reflection that we would take such a discovery as showing that gold is essentially F, then we see right away that no Lockean definition of "gold" can be correct, since we see that the satisfaction of any such definition would be compatible with the absence of what scientific investigation might show to be essential to gold. And supposing that an essential underlying feature has been discovered by scientific investigation, it will not be open to us to incorporate a reference to it into an "improved" Lockean definition of "gold"; for Lockean definitions are supposed to be analytic and a priori, and to capture the ordinary, prescientific meaning of natural kind terms.[16]

---

functional definition define a state solely in terms of a causal role, in this narrow sense of "causal role"; no such restriction is motivated by the intuitions that lead to functionalism. Since the issue now threatens to become verbal, I will simply say that I count as a functional definition any "topic-neutral" definition constructed by what I earlier called the "Ramsey–Lewis technique," and that this lets in definitions containing negative conditions of the sort in question. (See footnote 5. See also my "Some Varieties of Functionalism" (Essay 12 of this volume).)

[16] Two caveats. First, while my term "Lockean definition" is meant to evoke memories of Locke's "nominal essences," I do not want to claim that the conception of definition it expresses is precisely that of the historical Locke. Second, it is not essential for my purposes to claim that Kripke is right about terms like "gold." The point is that he has described a way in which some kinds of terms *could* work (whether or not any in fact do work this way), and one such that if a term did work this way, a maximally good Lockean definition of it could be shown to be mistaken. And this is enough to make it incumbent on me to consider the possibility that mental terms work in such a way.

Obviously, it would be possible to hold a view about mental terms that is analogous to the Kripke–Putnam view about natural kind terms. One version of this view, the only one I shall discuss here, is an antifunctionalist version of materialism that holds that mental terms have their references fixed, *à la* Kripke, to what are in fact (although the users of the terms need not know this) certain physiological states.[17] We can suppose that these states are the physical realizations *in us* of maximally good functional definitions of the mental states. Or, if we want to be more liberal, we can suppose that the reference is fixed to those physical states of us and to whatever other physical states resemble them in certain ways, where the resemblance required is something other than purely functional resemblance (that is, satisfying the same maximally good functional definitions). Now if such a view were true, and if reflection on our intuitions about possible cases would reveal that it was true, then it would be possible for us to discover that a creature lacked mental states despite having states that are "functionally equivalent" to mental states, that is, despite having states that satisfy maximally good functional definitions of mental states. We could discover this by, first, discovering how our own mental states are physically realized and, second, discovering that the physical states of the other creature that realize the same functional states in it do not resemble in the required way the realizations of those states in us. That we might discover this (and so, with sufficient imagination, could imagine discovering it) would not show that our functional definitions of the mental states were not maximally good. For if we were to try to emend our definitions so that the creature's states no longer satisfy them, we might find that there is no way of doing so without incorporating into them physiological requirements that have no place in functional definitions that are supposed to be analytic and a priori – this would be like incorporating reference to atomic structure into a Lockean definition of "gold." And of course, if a maximally good functional definition could be overthrown by the actual discovery of such a case, it could equally well be overthrown by the imagined discovery of one. Even if I know nothing of my own neurophysiology, I can imagine finding that my mental states are realized physically in one way and that functionally equivalent states in another creature are realized physically in some quite different way

---

[17] One could easily enough concoct a dualist version of the view, according to which the states to which the reference of the mental terms is fixed are nonphysical ones; but what I say about the physicalist version of the view applies equally to the dualist version. (See, in this connection, my "Embodiment and Behavior" and "Immortality and Dualism" (Essays 6 and 7 of this volume).)

– and if the imagined differences were such that its actual discovery would show that the other creature lacked mental states, then the mere fact that I can imagine discovering it would show that the maximally good functional definition was in fact incorrect. (It might of course be extensionally correct; what would be shown by the thought experiment is that it fails as an analytic functional definition.) So while it is true by definition that a maximally good functional definition is not improvable by consideration of further thought experiments, there is a possible view according to which such functional definitions are one and all refutable by thought experiments. But the point most relevant to our present concerns is that on such a view it would be possible for cases of absent qualia to exist, and possible for them to be detected and distinguished from cases of "present qualia." So far as I can see, it is *only* on such a view that such cases could be detected.

I shall call this view the "parochial view" of mental states. It is parochial in the sense that it makes *our* mental states of each sort (pains, beliefs, fears, etc.) paradigmatic of mental states of that sort, and makes it a requirement of a state's being of a sort that it have to our mental states of that sort a resemblance that no analytic functional definition could capture. As I see it, the chief shortcoming of my argument in F&Q against the possibility of absent qualia is that it did not take account of this view.

The parochial view could be held about mental states generally, or it could be held only about qualitative states. Let us call these, respectively, the unrestricted and the restricted versions of the parochial view. Now if someone thinks that it is precisely on the matter of qualia that functionalism founders, and that it might be acceptable if it were not for the fact that mental states necessarily have qualitative character, then he would seem to be subscribing to the restricted rather than the unrestricted version. Moreover, it is the proponent of the restricted version who is committed to AQT-1. So it is the restricted version we must consider.

Here it will help to consider some imaginary Martians. The Martians I want to consider have a psychology isomorphic with ours (at least with our "commonsense psychology"), and have states functionally equivalent, in the sense explained above, to our mental states – that is, they have states satisfying maximally good functional definitions of the various mental states we have. But their biochemistry and neurophysiology are radically different from ours. And let us stipulate that their physical differences from us are such that according to the restricted version of the parochial view they lack qualitative states. According to the restricted version of the parochial view, the beliefs, desires, etc., of these Martians are genuine but their "pains," and in general their qualia-involving states, are ersatz.

According to the restricted version of the parochial view, we should be able to discover that the Martian pains, etc., are ersatz. We would discover this by discovering what the physical realizations of our mental states are, what the physical realizations of theirs are, and that these differ in a certain way. This is supposed to be an advantage of the parochial view – it enables it to avoid the epistemological difficulties with which I have tried to embarrass the friends of absent qualia. But notice that if we can discover that the Martian pains, etc., are ersatz, then it ought to be possible for the Martians to discover this, too. The physiological discoveries that would reveal it to us should also reveal it to them – and of course there is no reason in principle why they should not make the same physiological discoveries as we make. But is this – that they lack qualia and that their pains are ersatz – what *they* should conclude from discovering that they differ physically from us in some recondite way? Why on Earth (or why on Mars) should they conclude *that*?

For the moment let us suppose, with the proponent of the restricted version of the parochial view, that in *our* language words like "pain" have their references fixed to a class of states that we have and the Martians don't, and that the same is true of philosophers' terms like "qualia." And let us suppose that the Martians speak a language that sounds for all the world like English. If you don't want to suppose that by an incredible coincidence they independently developed a language like ours, you can suppose that they picked up English from us some time ago and made it their own language. But I want it understood that the Martians we are dealing with have been speaking this language all of their lives. Now, is it plausible to suppose that the words "pain" and "qualia" in *their* language refer to states that only *we* have (or features which only our states have), and that the Martians are systematically mistaken when they claim to have what they call "pains" and "qualia"? It seems to me that this is not in the slightest plausible and, moreover, that it would be ruled out by any of the best current accounts of reference.[18] In the Martian language, surely, these terms will refer to states of the Martians, with which they will be causally connected in ways that make for reference. And if our

[18] I have in mind causal or "historical" accounts of reference, along the lines of those advanced by Kripke, Donnellan, and Putnam, and also the more recent account in terms of "epistemic access," advanced by Richard Boyd in "Metaphor and Theory Change," in Andrew Ortony (ed.), *Metaphor and Thought* (Cambridge, 1979).

philosophers are entitled to say that Martian pains lack qualia, and that their pains are ersatz, plainly the Martian philosophers will be entitled to use the same words (with their Martian senses and references, of course) to say the same about us. If ours are right in saying that there is "nothing it is like to be a Martian," theirs will be right in saying there is "nothing it is like to be an Earthling." It will, of course, be true in this case that we will have *something* they don't have, and that they will have *something* we don't have – for it is true by hypothesis that their physiological states are very different from ours. But I hope that it is beginning to be clear that it would be preposterous to say that what we have and they lack are qualitative states, and that what they have and we lack are states denoted in Martian–English by the phrase "qualitative state." Imagine trying to explain to a Martian the Earthling use of "what it is like" so as to be able to tell him that there is nothing it is like to be him!

The costs of denying qualitative states to the Martians are fairly obvious, given that (as the restricted version of the parochial view allows) they have a common-sense psychology isomorphic with ours and share our nonqualitative mental states. Plainly they must be allowed to see and hear. And while it seems obvious that seeing and hearing involve qualitative states, this cannot be said if "qualitative" is given the parochial interpretation that precludes its application to the Martians. Again, we will not want to deny that the Martians enjoy basking in the sun, having their backs scratched, and the like. But if we give "qualitative" the parochial interpretation we will not be able to say that basking in the sun produces in them feelings having a pleasant qualitative character – although that is what they seem to say about themselves. If we insist on the parochial interpretation of "qualia," "qualitative state," and the like, these expressions will simply fail to express the philosophically interesting concepts they were introduced to express. I think it is obvious that if we mingled with the Martians, did business with them, struck up friendships with them, talked philosophy with them, and so on, we would use "pain" and the rest as if they applied univocally to them and us, and would have no inclination to give these words a parochial interpretation. A proponent of the parochial view would have to say that in doing so we would be changing the meanings and references of these words. I suppose that it is not possible to *prove* that this view is wrong; but it seems to me utterly implausible.[19]

[19] In claiming that these Martians would have qualia, I am not claiming that they would have the same qualia as we do – that their pains would feel just like ours, that colors would look to them the way they look to us, and so on. On the contrary, given

My reason for considering the parochial view (restricted version) was to buttress my argument in favor of EP – the claim that if absent qualia were possible, then the presence or absence of the qualitative character of pain would not make any difference to its causal consequences that would make it possible for anyone to distinguish cases of genuine pain from cases of ersatz pain. If the parochial view can be ruled out, I can maintain my claim that anything that seems to show the existence of absent qualia, in the sense of AQT-1, will merely show instead that our current functional definitions of pain, qualia, etc., are not maximally good, and need to be refined. From EP, generalized to apply to qualitative states generally, my initial argument would conclude that AQT-1 has the unacceptable consequence that qualitative states are unknowable, and would conclude from that the falsity of AQT-1. I think that there are philosophers who would dispute the inference from EP to the claim that AQT-1 implies the unknowability of qualitative states.[20] But while I am inclined myself to think that the inference is valid, it is unnecessary for me to insist on this. For we can bypass EP, and use the argument against the parochial view to argue directly that AQT-1 is false. If AQT-1 is true, then there is a possible world in which there are imitation people as well as genuine ones. In such a world, both the genuine people and the imitation people would have beliefs about qualitative states, and thus would have concepts of such states; and both would use words like "pain" that refer to such states. How can it be supposed that in the case of the imitation people these concepts and words might have a reference that makes their introspective beliefs about themselves systematically false? If we ask what "pain" refers to in the case of the imitation people, the answer ought to be what it was in the case of the

that their physical makeup is radically different from ours, and thus that the physical properties that realize their qualia are bound to be ones that couldn't characterize our mental states (and vice versa), I think that their qualia would have to be very different from ours. See Essay 15. But it is important not to confuse having qualia with having *our* qualia; such a confusion may be one source of the "absent qualia objection" to functionalism.

[20] Someone might argue, invoking an account of knowledge along the lines of Alvin Goldman's (see his "Discrimination and Perceptual Knowledge," *The Journal of Philosophy*, 73 (1976), 771–791), that if *in fact* there are no cases of absent qualia, then our current ways of acquiring beliefs about mental states constitute a "reliable mechanism" for the acquisition of true belief, and that the mere logical possibility of ersatz pain does not make my (or your) having ersatz pain a "relevant alternative" to my (or your) having genuine pain, and so does not make it a requirement of my knowing that I (or you) have pain that I be able to distinguish cases of genuine pain from cases of ersatz pain.

Martians; it ought to refer to a state of them, to which it is causally connected in ways that make for reference. (If it were not so connected, they would not be functionally equivalent to the real people, as they are supposed to be.) Indeed, we can repeat my argument against the parochial view, with "imitation people" in place of "Martians," and with "genuine people" in place of "Earthlings" (or "us"). The conclusion will be that each of these groups uses "pain" to refer to a state that they themselves have, but that both groups means the same by words like "pain" (and words like "qualia" if they are philosophical enough to have them), from which it follows that the pains of the (supposedly) imitation people are genuine rather than ersatz, and that the people are not imitation. AQT-1 is thus reduced to absurdity.

The line of argument I have just used cannot, of course, be used against a philosopher who holds the unrestricted version of the parochial view. Such a philosopher won't concede that my Martians have any mental states at all, and so won't concede that they speak a language. So we cannot work on him by getting him to reflect on what "pain" and "qualia" would refer to in the Martian language. Although the unrestricted version of the parochial view seems to me just as implausible as the restricted version, I shall not attempt to refute it here. The case against unrestricted parochialism would be nothing other than the case for functionalism as a general philosophy of mind. Only if the claim that absent qualia are possible is taken in the sense of AQT-2 does refuting it require refutation of unrestricted parochialism. And my target here is only the absent qualia thesis asserted by AQT-1. If that thesis can be refuted then, to say the least, the burden of proof is shifted to those who claim that qualia present a special difficulty to functionalism.

IV

In the final section of this paper Block takes up my reply in F&Q to the "inverted qualia objection" to functionalism. This objection is based on the premise, with which I agree, that cases of "qualia inversion," for example, spectrum inversion, are logically possible. In such a case, states that are functionally equivalent (for example, states satisfying maximally good functional definitions of "seeing red") would be qualitatively different, and states that are functionally different ("seeing red" in Jones and "seeing green" in Smith) would be qualitatively the same; the possibility of this shows that individual qualia cannot be functionally defined, and can easily seem to show that functionalism is false. Very briefly, my reply to this objection was as follows. The best support for the claim that qualia inversion is possible is that there are imaginable circumstances in which *intra-subjective* qualia inversion would be shown to have occurred. But a consideration of how this would be shown suggests that the relationships of qualitative similarity and qualitative difference between experiences are themselves functionally definable in terms of the effects that the intrasubjective holding of these relations has on beliefs and other mental states. In terms of these relationships, in turn, one could give a functional account of the identity conditions for qualia, and of what it is to be a quale. And this, I argued, is all the functionalist needs. In order for qualitative states like pain to be functionally definable, what is necessary is that we should be able to quantify over qualia in our functional definitions, and be able to formulate, in functional terms, requirements to the effect that certain states have qualitative character, that certain states differ in qualitative character, and so on. For this it is not necessary that individual qualia be functionally definable; all that is required is that the notion of a quale, and the similarity and identity conditions for qualia, be functionally definable.

Block does not take issue with the details of this reply. But he makes the point (which is obviously correct) that a definition of qualitative similarity of the sort I suggest could be correct only if absent qualia were impossible (this would be true of any functional definition of this relationship), and concludes that my reply to the inverted qualia objection fails if absent qualia are possible. Now I, of course, do not think that absent qualia are possible. But Block is just mistaken in thinking that my reply to the inverted qualia objection fails if they are. For a reply to an objection to be successful, it is not necessary that the position it defends be correct, and still less is it necessary that it be shown to be correct by the reply; all that is necessary is that the reply show that the position is not shown to be mistaken by the objection in question. And my reply did show that functionalism is not shown to be false by the fact that qualia inversion is possible. Block may think that my reply rests on the premise that a certain functional definition of qualitative similarity is correct, and thus rests on a false premise if absent qualia are possible. But this is a mistake; what my reply needs as a premise is not the claim that such a functional definition is correct, but only the claim that, for all the objector has shown or given any reason for believing, such a definition may well be correct. And this premise is true even if (what I deny) there is some *other* objection that shows that absent qualia are possible and thus that no such definition can be correct.

15
The inverted spectrum

As best I can determine, the idea of spectrum inversion made its first appearance in the philosophical literature when John Locke, in the *Essay*, entertained the possibility that *"the same Object should produce in several Men's Minds different Ideas at the same time; e.g. the Idea, that a Violet produces in one Man's Mind by his Eyes, were the same that a Marigold produced in another Man's, and vice versa."*[1] It was obviously part of Locke's supposition that the color experiences of the two people differ in such a way that the difference could not manifest itself in their behavior and their use of color words, and we will take this as an essential feature of full-fledged intersubjective spectrum inversion. This "inverted spectrum hypothesis" was revived in the early years of this century, and in the heyday of logical positivism it was a favorite target for application of the verificationist theory of meaning; there are classic formulations and discussions of it in the writings of C. I. Lewis, Moritz Schlick, Hans Reichenbach, John Wisdom, Max Black, and J. J. C. Smart,[2] and it lurks beneath the surface, and sometimes at it, in many of Wittgenstein's discussions of "private experience."

I

Wittgenstein seems to have been the first to give this idea a new twist by envisioning the possibility of *intra*subjective spectrum inversion:

Consider this case: someone says "I can't understand it, I see everything red blue today and vice versa." We answer "it must look queer!" He says it does and, e.g., goes on to say how cold the glowing coal looks and how warm the clear (blue) sky. I think we should under these or similar circumstances be

---

[1] *Essay Concerning Human Understanding*, ed. by Peter H. Nidditch (Oxford, 1975), p. 389 (bk. II, ch. 32, sect. XV).

[2] See Lewis, *Mind and the World Order* (New York, 1929), p. 75; Schlick, "Positivism and Realism," in A. J. Ayer (ed.), *Logical Positivism* (New York, 1959), pp. 92–95; Reichenbach, *Experience and Prediction* (Chicago, 1938), pp. 248–258; Wisdom, *Other Minds* (New York, 1952), pp. 10–11; Black, *Language and Philosophy* (Ithaca, N.Y., 1949), pp. 3ff; Smart, *Philosophy and Scientific Realism* (New York, 1963), pp. 66–69.

inclined to say that he saw red what we saw blue. And again we should say that we know that he means by the words 'blue' and 'red' what we do as he has always used them as we do.[3]

What is imagined here is that there should be a systematic difference between the character of someone's color experience at a certain time and the character of that *same* person's color experience at another time. If Wittgenstein was indeed the first to describe such a case, there is a mild irony in this. For there is a natural line of argument, which we will come to shortly, from the possibility of *intra*subjective inversion to the conclusion that it makes sense to suppose, and may for all we know be true, that *inter*subjective spectrum inversion actually exists – that among normally sighted people, i.e., those who are not color blind, there are radical differences in the way things look with respect to color. And Wittgenstein is associated, probably more than any other philosopher, with the view that this supposition makes no sense. In the midst of the attack on the notions of "private language" and "private objects" in the *Philosophical Investigations*[4] there occurs the following passage:

> The essential thing about private experience is really not that each person possesses his own exemplar, but that nobody knows whether other people also have *this* or something else. The assumption would thus be possible – though unverifiable – that one section of mankind has one sensation of red and another section another. (p. 95)

I think it is pretty clear from the tenor of the surrounding passages that Wittgenstein thinks that this "assumption" is in fact senseless or conceptually incoherent and takes it to be a *reductio ad absurdum* of the notion of "private experience" he is attacking that it implies that this "assumption" might be true.

I said that there is a natural line of argument from what Wittgenstein seems to admit – the logical possibility of intrasubjective spectrum inversion – to what he apparently denies the meaningfulness of asserting – namely, the possibility that intersubjective spectrum inversion actually exists. One reason why the claim that intrasubjective inversion is logically possible makes a natural starting point for such an argument is that it seems immune from verificationist objections; as Wittgenstein's example shows, it is easy to imagine phenomena we would take as verifying that such a change in color

---

[3] "Notes for Lectures on 'Private Experience' and 'Sense Data,'" ed. by Rush Rhees, *The Philosophical Review*, 77 (1968), p. 284.
[4] Trans. by G. E. M. Anscombe, 3rd edn (New York, 1958).

experience had occurred. One can imagine this happening in oneself, one can imagine another person reporting that it had happened to him, and one can imagine nonverbal behavior that would be evidence of such a change. But – and here comes the promised argument – it seems, offhand, that if intrasubjective spectrum inversion is possible, intersubjective inversion must also be possible. For suppose that someone, call him Fred, undergoes intrasubjective inversion at time t.[5] Assuming that others did not also undergo inversion at t, it would seem that either before t or afterward (or both) Fred's color experience must have been radically different from that of others. But if we allow that there can be intersubjective inversion in cases in which there is intrasubjective inversion, it seems that we must allow that there could be intersubjective inversion without intrasubjective inversion; if the color experience of a person can differ from that of others at some point during his career, it should be possible for such a difference to exist throughout a person's career. But if this is a possibility, then it does seem perfectly coherent to suppose, and perfectly compatible with all the behavioral evidence we have about the experiences of others, that, in Wittgenstein's words, "one section of mankind has one sensation of red and another section another."[6]

Suppose one allows the premise of this argument: that intrasubjective inversion is possible; how, if at all, can one resist its conclusion? How is one to reject the inference from the possibility of intrasubjective spectrum inversion to the possibility of intersubjective spectrum inversion? One way is to maintain that the relevant notion of similarity and difference, what I shall call *qualitative* similarity and difference, is well defined only for the intrasubjective case. This allows one to deny the possibility of intersubjective inversion, but does so at the cost of forbidding one from saying that one's color experiences are qualitatively similar to those of others. On this view (see section IV), experiences belonging to different persons can be neither qualitatively similar nor qualitatively different.

It does not appear, however, that Wittgenstein could have taken this way out. In the passage in which he seems to allow the possibility of intrasubjective inversion he seems to allow that the case he describes would also be a case of intersubjective inversion; he says that "we should under these or similar circumstances be inclined to say that we saw red what he saw blue." Why then is Wittgenstein not committed

[5] For Fred's first appearance in the discussion of this problem see D. M. Taylor, "The Incommunicability of Content," *Mind*, 75 (1966), 527–541.

[6] See Taylor, *ibid.*, where this point is made.

to the very thing he seems to deny? He was not unaware of the problem, for in a later passage he wrote:

We said that there were cases in which we should say that the person sees green what I see red. Now the question suggests itself: if this can be so at all, why should it not always be the case? It seems, if once we have admitted that it can happen under peculiar circumstances, that it may always happen. . . . This is a very serious situation. ("Notes for Lectures," p. 316)

A full discussion of how Wittgenstein thought he could solve or avoid this problem would take me too far afield – and the answer is none too clear. Briefly, however, I think that it is only in a qualified sense that he allowed that intrasubjective inversion is possible, and only in a similarly qualified sense that he allowed that in a case of intrasubjective inversion we would also have intersubjective inversion. I think he thought that such a case would have to be one in which the person who has undergone inversion describes things as looking "queer," and says, for example, that the clear sky looks warm and that the glowing coal looks cold. Now, if the difference between someone's color experience and ours went with a tendency on his part to describe his experience in such ways, then of course it would not be a difference that could not manifest itself in behavior (since verbal behavior is behavior), and so would fail to amount to a case of "full blown" intersubjective spectrum inversion.

But it would seem offhand that Wittgenstein was mistaken if he thought that any case in which we could know that someone's experiences of colors at one time were radically different from his experiences of the same colors at another time would have to be one in which at one or the other of the times the person describes his experiences as "queer." Suppose that it was thirty years ago that Fred underwent his spectrum inversion. We have monitored him closely since then, and at no time has he reported a "reinversion," or given any behavioral indication of one. He has, however, gradually become accustomed to the new look of things and to describing the colors of things in the same words others use; for some time now it has come natural to him to say that the sky is blue and daffodils yellow, and, moreover, that the sky *looks* blue and daffodils *look* yellow. Each day during the last thirty years we have asked him how things looked compared with how he remembered their looking the day before, and each day (after the first) he has confidently reported that things look the same with respect to color as they did the day before – although in the early years of this period he also reported that their looking this way was seeming less strange with the passage of time, that he was again finding it natural to describe glowing coals as looking warm rather than cold, and so on. In such a case I think we could have good reason to think that Fred's color experience now is systematically different from what it was before the inversion, even though he does not now, and did not then, describe his experience as "queer."[7] But if this case is possible, then it seems that full-fledged intersubjective spectrum inversion should also be possible.

II

I have so far talked as if we would have a case of spectrum inversion if blue things looked to you the way yellow things look to me, and vice versa. But a little reflection shows that this is not enough. If you and I differed *only* in this way and if all other colors looked the same to us, it is obvious that the difference would manifest itself in behavior, both verbal and nonverbal. One of us would find yellow things more similar to orange things, and less similar to violet things, than blue things are, while the other would find just the opposite. What is required for full-fledged intersubjective inversion is that the color "quality spaces" of the two people should have the same structure, which requires (among other things) that under the same lighting conditions they make the same judgments of relative color similarity ("*A* is more similar to *B* than to *C*") about the same visually presented objects. If this condition is satisfied, then any difference in how the two people see colors will ramify through all the colors; all, or virtually all, will have to look different to the one person than they do to the other. Pretending, for the moment, that we have only the pure, "saturated," colors to deal with, we might have such a systematic difference if to each of our two persons each color looked the way its complementary color looked to the other.

---

[7] Though I think we could have good reason to believe this, I do not claim that the behavioral evidence I have described entails it. As Gilbert Harman and David Lewis have pointed out to me, what I have described of Fred's behavior is compatible with there having been over the thirty years a change in Fred's color experience so gradual that the change from one day to the next would not be noticeable (as Lewis put it, a rotation of the color circle so slow that it took it thirty years to go 180 degrees), the net effect of which was to undo the initial inversion. But we could have reason to discount this possibility if we had evidence that over the thirty years there had not occurred in Fred any physiological change such that, if it occurred suddenly rather than gradually, it would produce noticeable behavioral manifestations of intrasubjective inversion. Further possible behavioral evidence of inversion is described in section II, and the relevance of physiological considerations to questions about inversion is discussed in section V.

The same applies, *mutatis mutandis*, to the case of intrasubjective inversion. And this puts us in a position to answer an objection that is sometimes raised against putative cases of intrasubjective spectrum inversion. Suppose Fred claims to have just undergone spectrum inversion. How do we know, it is asked, that what has changed in Fred is his color experience, and not his understanding of color words or his memory of how things looked to him in the past – that he is not the victim of some peculiar sort of aphasia or memory illusion? The suggestion behind such questions is often that the questions are unanswerable and that this undermines the claim that we could know that intrasubjective inversion had occurred. To parry such objections, let me complicate our case slightly. Let us suppose that the relationships between the different colors can be represented by associating each determinate shade of color with a point on the circumference of a circle, the distances between the points along the circumference corresponding to the perceived differences between the shades, and the point corresponding to any shade being opposite the point corresponding to its complementary. Let us label the points on the circle as they are on the face of a clock, with the numerals 1 through 12. I will suppose, indeed, that we have a circle, call it a "color circle," on which the points on the circumference actually have the colors they represent. And now let us imagine our case as follows. At time t_1 Fred was perfectly normal in his use of color words, his discriminatory abilities, and the like. But at time t_2 he tells us that a remarkable change has occurred. Although most things look to him the way they used to, a sizable minority look different. He describes the change by saying that, if he looks at a color circle, it looks the way it would have looked at t_1 if the shades between 12 and 2 had been interchanged with their complementaries (those between 6 and 8), the rest of the circle remaining unchanged. According to this, the structure of Fred's visual color space at t_2 is different from its structure at t_1. And, because of this, we can suppose that Fred's testimony is supported by his nonverbal discriminatory and recognitional behavior – the ease with which he discriminates certain shades that formerly were difficult for him to discriminate (and are so for the rest of us) and the difficulty with which he discriminates other shades that seem to us (and previously seemed to him) very different. At t_3 Fred tells us that another such change has occurred, adding itself to the first one; this time it is the shades between 2 and 4 that have changed places with their complementaries (those between 8 and 10). Again we can suppose there is behavioral evidence to substantiate his claim. Finally, at t_4 he tells us that still another such change has occurred; this time it is the shades between 4 and 6 which have changed places with their complementaries (those between 10 and 12). Again there is behavioral evidence to substantiate his claim. But at t_4, unlike t_2 and t_3, Fred's judgments of color similarity and difference will coincide with ours and those he made at t_1; at t_4 the structure of Fred's color space is the same as it was at t_1. Yet Fred reports that his color experience is systematically different from what it was at t_1; each color looks the way its complementary looked then. And this claim seems to be supported by the behavioral evidence that supported his claims that there were changes in his color experience between t_1 and t_2, between t_2 and t_3, and between t_3 and t_4; for these partial inversions add up to a total spectrum inversion. It does not appear that any sort of aphasia or memory failure could account for the phenomena imagined here.[8]

Returning to the case of intersubjective spectrum inversion, I suspect that the main reason why many philosophers are hostile to the claim that such spectrum inversion is possible is that they suspect that admitting that claim will put one on a slippery slope which will eventually land one in skepticism about other minds. If I cannot know from the behavior of others that their color experiences are like my own, neither can I know that when they are cut or burned they have experiences phenomenally or qualitatively like my pains; and if I cannot know even that much, it is natural to suppose, then I cannot know anything about their minds. A common counterargument, which argues from the falsity of skepticism to the impossibility of spectrum inversion, goes as follows. According to our ordinary standards of evidence, if two individuals Jones and Smith make the

[8] It might be objected that it is compatible with the behavior I have imagined on the part of Fred that between t_1 and t_2 he underwent a series of experience *cum* memory changes that resulted in his color experience at t_4 being the same as his color experience at t_1, despite his seeming to remember it as being different. I do not deny this, but do not think it follows that in the case as described we would not be justified in thinking that Fred at t_4 was spectrum-inverted relative to Fred at t_1. In general, a memory change having a certain behavioral effect seems far less likely than an experience change having the same effect (where either could produce the effect); on any plausible assumption about how perception and memory are realized physically, a change that alters the way specific kinds of stimuli are linked with specific color qualia (as happens when someone puts on tinted spectacles) seems far more likely than one that systematically modifies all a person's memories of how things looked with respect to color prior to a certain time, leaving these memories otherwise unchanged. And, quite apart from this, in the absence of overriding physiological evidence (and I do not deny that there could be such), the hypothesis that someone has undergone an experience change that would produce a certain behavioral effect is obviously to be preferred, on grounds of simplicity, to the hypothesis that the person has undergone an experience change *and* a memory change which jointly would have the same effect.

same color discriminations, agree in their judgments of color similarity and difference, and apply color words in the same way, this is sufficient evidence that they mean the same by their color words. And if in addition they have learned to use 'looks,' 'appears,' etc. in the same ways in the same objective circumstances – for example, both say of what they know to be a white wall illuminated by red light that it "looks" red – this is sufficient evidence that they mean the same by expressions like 'looks red.' But if Jones says, truthfully, that an object looks red to him, and Smith says the same of the object, and if they mean the same by the expression 'looks red,' this surely shows that with respect to color the object looks pretty much the same to them and that their experiences of it are similar. Yet, according to the view that intersubjective spectrum inversion is possible, this information about Jones's and Smith's use of color words, discriminatory abilities, and so forth would leave it an entirely open question whether red things look alike to them. So we must choose between rejecting our ordinary standards of evidence concerning such matters and rejecting the view that intersubjective spectrum inversion is possible. But we cannot abandon our ordinary standards of evidence here without accepting an absurd general skepticism about other minds. So, the argument concludes, we must reject the claim that spectrum inversion is possible.

I will not deny that if it is possible to have some knowledge of other minds, it must be possible to know whether others mean the same as we do by their color words. Nor will I deny that if we can know what someone means by expressions like 'red' and 'looks red,' we can also know that something looks to him the way it looks to us. What I dispute in the argument just given is the claim that this conclusion, *in the sense in which it is true*, contradicts the claim that spectrum inversion is possible. What emerges here is that expressions like 'looks the same' are potentially ambiguous. And this can be seen from further reflection on Fred and his intrasubjective spectrum inversion.

We have supposed that Fred eventually accommodates to the change in his color experience, and says that an object looks yellow in just those objective circumstances in which others would say this – even though the way something looks to him when he says it looks yellow is the way things formerly looked to him when he said they looked blue. But this accommodation will cause him some difficulty in the use of such expressions as 'looks the same' and 'looks similar in color to.' Others will assume that from the premises "X looked yellow to Fred at time t_1," and "Y looked yellow to Fred at time t_2," we can infer the conclusion "The way X looked to Fred at t_1, with respect to color, is the way Y looked to Fred at t_2, with respect to color." But if t_1 is a time before Fred's spectrum inversion and t_2 is a time after he has accommodated to it, then that conclusion will be false on one interpretation of it, although true on another, if the premises are true. Fred needs, and we need, a distinction between different senses of the expression 'looks the same,' and of related expressions. If Fred's house looked yellow to him at both t_1 and t_2, then with respect to color his house "looked the same" to him at those two times in the sense that his experiences of it on those two occasions were *of* the same objective color, or had the same color as their "intentional object." Call this the *intentional* sense of 'look the same.' But in another sense his house did not "look the same" to him at the two times; call this the *qualitative* sense of that expression. That Fred has undergone spectrum inversion requires that things look different to him than they did before in the qualitative sense, but not (once he has accommodated to the change) that they look different to him in the intentional sense.

Applying this distinction to the case of Jones and Smith in the anti-inversion argument, we can say that it is only in the intentional sense of 'looks the same' that the information about Jones and Smith – their use of color words, their abilities to distinguish and recognize colors, and so forth – establishes that red things look the same to them. What this information does not establish, by itself, is that red things look the same to them in the qualitative sense – that their visual experiences of redness are qualitatively as well as intentionally similar. So long as our ordinary standards of evidence are taken as standards for establishing intentional similarity of experiences, the adherence to these standards is perfectly compatible with allowing the possibility of spectrum inversion. And, I think, it is only if the standards are taken in this way that it is plausible to maintain that abandoning them would lead to general skepticism about other minds.

It may appear that I have conceded part of the claim that allowing the possibility of spectrum inversion leads to skepticism, namely, that it leads to skepticism about our ability to have knowledge of the qualitative character of the experiences of other persons. But I have not conceded that; on the contrary, whether this is so will be one of the main issues under consideration in the rest of this essay. What I have conceded is that it follows from the possibility of spectrum inversion, and is indeed true, that the *behavioral* evidence that establishes intentional similarities and differences between experiences of different persons is not by itself sufficient to establish qualitative similarities and differences between such experiences. And it was such behavioral evidence I had in mind in speaking of our "ordinary standards of evidence." It remains to be considered whether other sorts of evidence, e.g., evidence of physiological similarities or differences of some kind, might enable us to make intersubjective comparisons of the qualitative character of experiences.

III

The last objection to the possibility of spectrum inversion which I shall discuss (and there are many I shall have to ignore) is empirical. A brief consideration of it will help me bring into focus some of the problems raised by the possibility of spectrum inversion.

If spectrum inversion is to be possible, there must be a mapping which maps every determinate shade onto some determinate shade and at least some onto shades other than themselves, which preserves, for any normally sighted person, all the "distance" and "between-ness" relationships between the shades, and which maps primary colors onto primary colors. Now as long as we restrict ourselves to the pure saturated colors, various such mappings seem to be possible; one is the mapping of shades onto their complementaries, and others can be got by rotating the "color circle" in different ways. It has been questioned whether even these mappings satisfy the condition that primaries be mapped onto primaries.[9] But it seems even more questionable that we can get a mapping that satisfies these conditions once all the unsaturated colors (beige, olive, rust, etc.) and non-chromatic colors (black, white, and the various shades of grey) are taken into account. Obviously the simple color circle is inadequate for the representation of the relationships of these to one another and to the "pure" colors.

The question of whether our color experience does have a structure that allows for such a mapping – whether it is "invertible" – is an empirical question about our psychological makeup. And it is one I intend to by-pass. Even if our color experience is not invertible, it seems obviously possible that there should be creatures, otherwise very much like ourselves, whose color experience does have a structure that allows for such a mapping – creatures whose color experience *is* invertible. And the mere possibility of such creatures is sufficient to raise the philosophical problems the possibility of spectrum inversion has been seen as posing.

Let me be more explicit about what these problems are. One problem, call it the *metaphysical* problem, is about the nature of

---

[9] See Bernard Harrison, "On Describing Colors," *Inquiry*, 10 (1967), 38–52.

"qualia" – the qualitative or phenomenal features of sense-experience, in virtue of having which they resemble and differ from each other, qualitatively, in the ways they do. If spectrum inversion is so much as a logical possibility – whether or not it is a possibility *for us*, as we are currently constituted – then it is clear that no behavioristic account of qualia will do. For what the possibility of interpersonal spectrum inversion comes to is that two people might be behaviorally indistinguishable, might share all the same behavioral dispositions, even though their color experiences were radically different in qualitative character – and this means that there might be a psychological difference between people who would have to be psychologically identical if behaviorism were true. This is perhaps not such a great problem, since there are plenty of independent reasons for regarding behaviorism as false. But it also appears that the possibility of intersubjective spectrum inversion is incompatible with what many regard as the most respectable descendant of behaviorism, namely functionalism, where this is understood as the view that mental states are definable in terms of their causal relations to sensory inputs, behavioral outputs, and other mental states. Now if spectrum inversion is a logical possibility, then the quale currently involved in my perception of blue things cannot be defined by the functional role it plays in the likes of me, since in someone whose spectrum was inverted related to mine a different quale (perhaps the quale involved in my perception of yellow things) would play that functional role, and this quale would play a different role. This is a version of what has been called the "inverted-qualia objection" to functionalism – spectrum inversion being a special case of "qualia inversion."[10]

The other main problem posed by the possibility of spectrum inversion is what I shall call the *epistemological* problem – the problem of how we can know about the qualitative states of other persons. Now if it turns out that our color experience is not invertible, there is one epistemological problem we do not face: we do not have to worry about the possibility that the color experience of others is inverted relative to our own. But once it is clear that qualia are not behavioristically or functionally definable, other possibilities have to be contemplated. For example, it seems compatible with two creatures having color quality spaces with the same structure that none of the color experiences of either creature should bear any qualitative similarity to any of the color experiences of the other – e.g., the

[10] See Ned Block and Jerry Fodor, "What Psychological States are Not," *The Philosophical Review*, 81 (1972), 159–181, pp. 172–174.

sensations of red of the one are not only not like the sensations of red of the other, but also are not like the other's sensations of green or his sensations of any other color. So we must consider what grounds, if any, we have for thinking that we do not differ from our friends and neighbors in this radical way. And the fact, if it is a fact, that our color experience is not invertible, i.e., that its structure does not yield mappings of the sort described above, is no reason whatever for thinking this.

I conclude that there is no fundamental epistemological or metaphysical problem here which is solvable on the assumption that our experience is not invertible but not solvable on the assumption that it is. So it will do no harm – and will make exposition easier – to assume from now on that it is.

IV

I now want to take up the view, mentioned earlier, that the relationships of qualitative similarity and difference are well defined only for the intrasubjective case. This view solves the epistemological problem about the qualia of others, not by offering an account of how we know which color experiences of others are qualitatively similar to our own, but by denying that there is anything of this sort for us to know.

A view something like this is suggested by remarks of Frege in his essay "The Thought." Frege discusses the case in which he and a color-blind companion are looking at a strawberry field, and he declares to be "unanswerable, indeed really nonsensical," the question "does my companion see the green leaf as red, or does he see the red berry as green, or does he see both as one colour with which I am not acquainted at all?"[11] He goes on to say that "when the word 'red' does not state a property of things but is supposed to characterize sense-impressions belonging to my consciousness, it is only applicable within the sphere of my consciousness." Putting this in my terminology, Frege is saying that insofar as he uses 'red' as applying to experiences qualitatively similar to certain experiences of his, it will be applicable only to experiences of his. This is not a solipsist claim that assigns a special status to his sense experiences; it merely asserts that the relationship of qualitative similarity can hold only intrasubjectively. A similar view was held by Moritz Schlick in "Positivism and

[11] Gottlob Frege, "The Thought: A Logical Inquiry," *Mind*, 65 (1956), 289–311, p. 299.

Realism," on explicitly verificationist grounds: "The proposition that two experiences of different subjects not only occupy the same place in the order of a system but are, in addition, qualitatively similar has no meaning for us. Note well, it is not false, but meaningless: we have no idea what it means" (93).[12]

This view, call it the *Frege–Schlick view*, does not fly as violently in the face of common sense as it may initially seem to do. It does not imply that we are talking nonsense, or that our remarks are without truth value, when in ordinary circumstances we speak of different persons having similar or dissimilar experiences, or when we say that something looks the same, or different, to two different people. For it is open to us to construe such remarks as about the *intentional* similarity or difference of experiences, rather than as about the *qualitative* similarities and differences; and the view in question does not of course deny that the relationships of intentional similarity and difference are well defined for the intersubjective case.

One attraction of the Frege–Schlick view is that it solves, or dissolves, the epistemological problem about our knowledge of the qualitative states of others. But this view also suggests an answer to the "inverted-qualia objection" to behaviorism and functionalism, and thus a solution to the metaphysical problem. Part of the

[12] A more recent expression of this view (minus the verificationism) is that of Thomas Nagel: "A type of relation can hold between elements in the experience of a single person that cannot hold between elements in the experience of distinct persons: looking similar in color, for example. Insofar as our concept of similarity of experience in the case of a single person is dependent on his experience of similarity, the concept is not applicable between persons" ("Brain Bisection and the Unity of Consciousness," in *Mortal Questions* (Cambridge, 1979), footnote 10, pp. 160–161). Nagel informs me that he is now doubtful about this view. I suggested such a view myself in my "Critical Notice: *Myself and Others* by Don Locke," *Philosophical Quarterly*, 19 (1969), 272–279, pp. 276–278.

As I am interpreting this view, it regards qualitative similarity as well defined for diachronic intrasubjective comparisons as well as for synchronic ones. But another version of the view is possible. Reichenbach held that "if we call the impression of two persons incomparable, we are obliged to call the impressions of one person at different times incomparable as well" (*Experience and Prediction* p. 252), and this could lead (although I do not find that it did in Reichenbach – he uses his claim to attack the very notion of a quale) to the view that qualitative similarity and difference are well defined only for synchronic intrasubjective comparisons. On such a view intrasubjective inversion is no more possible than intersubjective inversion. I shall not consider this view, partly because it seems to me to have little intrinsic plausibility (especially the sharp epistemological distinction it has to make between synchronic and diachronic intrasubjective comparisons), and partly because I am investigating what options are open to someone who allows the possibility of intrasubjective inversion.

motivation for holding that qualitative similarity is well defined only for the intrasubjective case is that it is only in the intrasubjective case that we can have direct behavioral evidence of the holding of this relationship. It is this, after all, which makes *intra*subjective spectrum inversion, but not *inter*subjective inversion, behaviorally detectable. Now if intrasubjective qualitative similarity is the only sort of qualitative similarity there is (as the Frege–Schlick view holds), and if it is behaviorally detectable, then for all that has been shown it is behaviorally *definable* as well. But a much more promising view that is suggested by the same considerations is that this relationship is *functionally* definable, i.e., definable in terms of how the holding of the relationship between experiences is causally related to sensory inputs, behavioral outputs, and other mental states. It would be central to the functional account that when this relationship holds between different visual experiences of a person it tends to produce in that person the belief that there are objective similarities in the things he is seeing – to put it roughly, similarity of color qualia tends to produce belief in similarity of seen colors. And, via their effects on the person's beliefs, the qualitative similarities between his experiences would affect his behavior, in particular his recognitional and dis-criminatory behavior. But in addition, the holding of this relationship between different experiences of a person will produce in that person the belief that the experiences themselves are similar and, via this belief, will affect his verbal behavior – thus it is that Fred's saying that marigolds look today the way violets looked yesterday is taken as evidence that he has undergone inversion. Similar remarks apply to the relationships of qualitative identity (a special case of qualitative similarity) and qualitative difference. It is obvious that it is only when these relationships hold intrasubjectively that the holding of them can play such causal roles. But if, as the Frege–Schlick view holds, the relationships *can* hold only intrasubjectively, then there seems to be no reason why they should not be functionally definable in terms of such causal roles. Given this, there seems no reason why we should not be able to define in functional terms what it is for a state to have a qualitative character – a state will have a qualitative character if it is qualitatively similar to or different from some other state or states, and we are supposing that we already have a functional account of qualitative similarity and difference. And this clears the way for making states like pain functionally definable; at any rate, the fact that pain necessarily has a qualitative character, one that is unpleasant and distracting, is no bar to its being functionally defined. If individual qualia are not functionally definable, then of course no individual quale can be mentioned in the functional definition of pain; but if the similarity and identity conditions of qualia are functionally definable, it will still be possible to quantify over qualia in such a definition, and that is all that seems to be required. If such an account can be made to work, functionalism has nothing to fear from qualia.[13]

It is natural to suppose that a functional account of qualia of the sort just sketched requires the Frege–Schlick view. And it may seem unpromising for just this reason. For the Frege–Schlick view clashes with strongly felt intuitions. Most of us, I suspect, cannot help feeling that a visual experience of mine can be like a visual experience of yours in exactly the way it can be like another visual experience of mine, even though this intersubjective similarity differs from intrasubjective similarity in not being directly experienceable or rememberable by anyone. Call this the *common-sense view*.[14] I shall now try to show that, although the common-sense view is of course incompatible with the Frege–Schlick view, nevertheless, the functional account of qualia, which is suggested by the Frege–Schlick view and may seem to imply it, is in fact not only perfectly compatible with the common-sense view but can be used to defend it.

V

Let us begin by seeing why the functional account of qualitative similarity does not imply the Frege–Schlick view. The word 'qualia,' it will be remembered, is intended to refer to those features of sensory states in virtue of which they stand to one another in relationships of

[13] See my "Functionalism and Qualia" (Essay 9).

[14] It is worth observing that if, as has often been supposed in recent discussions of personal identity (e.g., Derek Parfit's "Personal Identity," *The Philosophical Review*, 80 (1971), 3–27), "fusion" of persons is a logical possibility, then the Frege–Schlick view must be false. For if persons A and B fuse to form C, and C's subsequent mental life is psychologically continuous with the past lives of A and B (and so, among other things, contains memories of them), then, since the pre-fusion experiences of A and B must be qualitatively comparable with the post-fusion experiences of C (must stand to them in determinate relationships of qualitative similarity and difference), they must be qualitatively comparable to each other. But suppose that A and B *could* fuse at time t, but do not in fact do so. It would seem that, since A's and B's experiences prior to t will be qualitatively comparable in the case in which fusion subsequently occurs, they must also be qualitatively comparable in the case in which it doesn't occur; it can scarcely be the case that whether experiences occurring before t are qualitatively comparable depends on what happened at t or afterwards. It thus appears that, if creatures are "fusible," their experiences are qualitatively comparable. But this supports the common-sense view only if human beings are fusible – and that seems rather questionable.

qualitative similarity and difference. States will be qualitatively similar in virtue of having identical or similar qualia – so our functional account of qualitative similarity must say what it is for qualia to be qualitatively similar. The first point to be emphasized is that qualia are properties and, therefore, universals. Suppose, then, that Q_1 and Q_2 are two different qualia. What the functional analysis of qualitative similarity tells us is that Q_1 and Q_2 are similar to a certain degree if it is the case that when Q_1 and Q_2 characterize two different experiences belonging to one and the same person, this tends to have certain effects on that person's beliefs and behavior. There is nothing in this to say that Q_1 and Q_2 can characterize only experiences belonging to one and the same person. And, if they characterize experiences belonging to different persons, those experiences will be similar to the appropriate degree, even though this pair of instantiations of Q_1 and Q_2 will not have, or tend to have, the effects definitive of qualitative similarity; the similarity will hold in virtue of the fact that Q_1 and Q_2 are such that, if they *were* to be instantiated in experiences of the same person, this *would* tend to have these effects.

But these remarks presuppose that one and the same quale can be instantiated in the experiences of different persons, and it may be objected that no sense can be made of this, given the sort of functional account of qualitative similarity and identity I have suggested. The answer to this is, in brief, that qualia can be shared by experiences of different persons in virtue of their being "realized" in other properties, presumably physical properties, that can be shared by experiences of different persons. Here we must remember that although there is a sense in which qualia are not functionally definable (if qualia inversion is a possibility), there is also a sense in which they are – their similarity and identity conditions, I have claimed, are functionally definable. Now functional states and properties can be said to have physical "realizations." A physical state or property *realizes* a functional state or property in a particular creature if in the workings of that creature it plays the "causal role" definitive of that functional state or property, i.e., if it interacts causally in the required ways with inputs, outputs, and other internal states of the creature. Given the sense in which they are functionally definable, qualia too can be said to have physical realizations, which in principle we could discover by physiological investigations. The physical properties that realize qualia will be properties that can be instantiated in different people. This makes it possible for the same qualia to be instantiated in different people and, thus, for experiences of different people to be qualitatively similar and different in all the varying degrees. Moreover, it makes it possible that such similarities and differences should be discovered.

I am not saying that it is automatically true that, for any two creatures who have experiences having qualitative character, the color experiences of each will stand to those of the other in determinate relationships of qualitative similarity and difference – or, to abbreviate this, that the color experiences of the two creatures will be "qualitatively comparable." The color experiences of two different creatures will be qualitatively comparable only if those creatures are capable of having states having the same qualia, and on my account this in turn will be true only if, for at least one color quale, both creatures are capable of having states that share at least some of the physical properties that are realizations of that quale. Suppose, to invoke a favorite functionalist fantasy, that we come across a race of Martians who are behaviorally indistinguishable from us and have a "psychology" isomorphic with ours, but whose internal physical makeup – their neurophysiology and biochemistry – is utterly different from ours. These Martians are to be creatures who share our mental states, at least on a functionalist view, but in whom the physical realizations of these states are as different as they could possibly be from their realizations in us. On my functional account of qualia, these Martians would have states having qualia – there would be something it would be like for them to have these states. But their experiences would not share any of the qualia our experiences have; for I am assuming that none of the properties that realize qualia in us could be instantiated in them. When it comes to comparing Martian experiences and ours, something like the Frege–Schlick view holds: their experiences and ours are not qualitatively comparable. But I do not say, with Schlick, that it is meaningless to assert that our experiences are qualitatively similar to those of the Martians; on my view, that our experiences are not qualitatively comparable with theirs would be something to be discovered empirically, by discovering the physiological differences between them and us.

Now let me fill this account out a bit. Let $Q\text{-}BY$ be the quale currently involved in my perception of the color blue, and let $Q\text{-}YB$ be the quale currently involved in my perception of the color yellow. And let us make the simplifying assumption that only one sort of spectrum inversion is possible for humans and that this involves $Q\text{-}BY$ playing the causal role in the visual perception of one person, or at one time, which $Q\text{-}YB$ plays in another person, or at another time, and vice versa. As I have already said, it is not possible (if spectrum inversion is possible) to give a purely functional characterization of either $Q\text{-}BY$ or $Q\text{-}YB$. But if the notion of a quale can be functionally defined (i.e., if its similarity and identity conditions can be), then the following will be a functional description: 'pair of qualia such that, at any given time, one member of that pair characterizes perceptions of blue while the other characterizes perceptions of yellow.' And, given our simplifying assumption, this description will pick out a unique pair of qualia for each creature having a color quality space with the same structure as our own, although the unique pair may be different in different creatures (e.g., it will be different in a Martian than in one of us). And we can ask how the satisfaction of this description is physically realized in the case of a particular creature at a particular time. In principle we can go hunting in the physiology of a creature for a pair of physical properties which play the functional role of qualia, which are involved only in the perception of blue and yellow, and which are such that, as long as one of them characterizes perceptions of blue the other can characterize only perceptions of yellow, and vice versa (given that the structure of the total color experience is normal). If the creature is me, one member of any such pair will be a realization of Q-BY and the other will be a realization of Q-YB. There may in fact be a number of different realizations of each of these qualia. To be realizations of the same quale, different properties must be qualitatively identical in the following sense: the experience someone has in virtue of being in a state having the one has the same color quale as the experience he has in virtue of being in a state having the other. These qualia can, in fact, be identified with the disjunctions of the properties in their respective realization classes. What realizes in me the above functional description of a "blue-yellow invertible pair" is the pair of disjunctive properties consisting of the disjunction of the realizations of Q-BY and the disjunction of the realizations of Q-YB.

Having discovered that in a certain creature a certain pair of disjunctive properties realize this description, we could of course discover which of the properties is, at a given time, involved in a creature's perception of blue and which is involved in the creature's perception of yellow. If in another creature we find that the same members of this pair of properties are involved in the perception of the same colors, we know that blue and yellow look qualitatively the same to these two creatures. If we find the reverse, we know that we have a case of spectrum inversion. But for blue to look to me as it does to you, it is not essential that we be in physically similar states. Q-BY, I have said, can be identified with a disjunction of different properties, and it may be that my experience has Q-BY in virtue of having one of these properties while yours has Q-BY in virtue of having a different one. But unless you and I are enough alike physically that there is some physical realization of Q-BY that *can* be instantiated in both of us, it is impossible for us both to have experiences having Q-BY. What I am supposing about my Martians is that the sets of possible physical realizations in them of their qualia do not overlap at all with the sets of possible realizations in us of our qualia – and from this it follows that none of our qualitative states are qualitatively similar, to any degree at all, to any of theirs.

But now let us confront a problem. Let us suppose that in me having visual experiences is realized in X-fiber firings, and that my visual experiences' having a certain color quale, say Q-BY, is realized in the X-fiber firings occurring in a certain pattern. And so it is with you too. In the Martians, let us suppose, the having of visual experiences is realized in having Z-fibers firing, and particular qualia are realized in certain properties of the patterns of Z-fiber firings. Let X_1 be a realization in me of the quale Q-BY, and let Z_1 and Z_2 be realizations in the Martians of a pair of qualia that constitute a blue-yellow invertible pair. Now there are various physical properties that can be instantiated in both us and the Martians, and among these are the disjunctive properties X_1-or-Z_1 and X_1-or-Z_2. Why shouldn't one of these be a physical realization of the quale Q-BY? Of course, it is not possible that *both* should be, since in the Martians Z_1 and Z_2 realize different and incompatible qualia. And I am supposing that the physical differences between the Martians and us are such that there would be no reason for picking one of these rather than the other as a realization of Q-BY. But what is it that disqualifies these disjunctive properties as realizations of qualia? The answer cannot be just that they are disjunctive. For any property that can be shared by things that are different in any way can be construed as disjunctive. You and I will be physically different in a variety of ways; at the very least, our DNA will be different. So the property X_1, which we share, can be construed as the following disjunctive property: (having X_1 and being the experience of someone having my DNA) or (having X_1 and being the experience of someone having a DNA different from mine). But this suggests yet another problem. How could we know, and what could make it true, that what realizes Q-BY in me is X_1 and not a more specific property (a disjunct of X_1) which cannot be instantiated in you – perhaps one that can be instantiated only in creatures having my DNA?

The problem raised is one about the individuation of qualia realizations.[15] What is it that makes it appropriate to say that X_1, but not the disjunctive property X_1-or-Z_1 and also not the more

---

[15] I am grateful to John Bennett and Richard Boyd for making me aware of this problem and of the inadequacy of earlier attempts of mine to solve it.

determinate property of having X_1 and being an experience of someone having my DNA, is a particular physical realization of a quale? I think the answer is given by the following rule. Property P realizes a quale if (1) it is a consequence of functional definitions and causal laws that, whenever different states of the same person share P, they are qualitatively identical in some respect (e.g., with respect to color qualia); (2) P is not equivalent to conjunctive property P_1-and-P_2 such that (i) P_1 satisfies condition (1) and P_2 doesn't, and (ii) P satisfies condition (1) because, and only because, P_1 does; and (3) if P is equivalent to a disjunctive property Pa-or-Pb such that Pa and Pb both satisfy conditions (1) and (2), then it must be that Pa and Pb satisfy (1) and (2) because P satisfies them, and not that P satisfies them because Pa and Pb satisfy them.[16] Let me illustrate this with an example.

Suppose the property X_1, which can be instantiated in both you and me, satisfies condition (1); more specifically, it is a consequence of functional definitions, including the functional definition of qualitative identity, that whenever different states of the same person share X_1 they realize experiences identical with respect to color qualia. Suppose, further, that X_1 satisfies condition (2) as well. This means,

---

[16] In an earlier version of this essay clause (ii) of condition (2) did not contain the word 'only,' and condition (3) did not refer to condition (2). That version of the rule was open to the following counterexample (due to Mr. Mark Johnston). Suppose that the brain contains a "backup system" in which qualia are realized quite differently than in the primary system. In the primary system a particular quale is realized by property Pa, and in the backup system it is realized by Pb. If at a particular point t in a person's life the backup system takes over from the primary system, then the person's pre-t experiences characterized by Pa will be color-qualia-identical to the person's post-t experiences characterized by Pb. It would seem offhand that the disjunctive property Pa-or-Pb should count as a realization of this quale. But though this disjunctive property can be presumed to satisfy conditions (1) and (2), it will fail condition (3) (as originally formulated); for it will satisfy (1) because Pa and Pb do, whereas, if it is to satisfy (3), it would have to be because it satisfies (1) and (2) that Pa and Pb do.

Actually, the objection as just stated does not work even against the original formulation, for the disjunctive property Pa-or-Pb will not in fact be a realization of the quale (although a closely related property will be). If before t an experience realized in the primary system has property Pa and after t an experience realized in the backup system has property Pb, this will not amount to those experiences being color-qualia-identical unless the backup system and the primary system are connected in an appropriate way (e.g., so that they will contribute jointly to the person's recognizing after t things he had seen before t). Let C be a property an experience has in virtue of belonging to a brain in which such a primary system and such a backup system are appropriately connected. What will satisfy (1) in such a case is not Pa-or-Pb but rather $(Pa$-or-$Pb)$-and-C. But the original formulation of the rule is nevertheless in trouble. On a natural interpretation of (2), $(Pa$-or-$Pb)$-and-C fails to satisfy condition (2); for

among other things, that my having the particular DNA I do have plays no essential role in the physiological explanation of the behavior that manifests the existence of my qualitative states and the qualitative similarities and differences between them. This might be because what matters, for purposes of such explanation, is the organization of the brain at the neuronal level, so that, so long as the neurons are such as to interrelate causally in certain ways, differences in their microstructure are irrelevant. On this supposition, of course, the conjunctive property of having X_1 and being an experience of someone with my DNA is ruled out, as a realization of a quale, by condition (2).[17] Both X_1 and the Martian property Z_1, we can suppose, satisfy conditions (1) and (2). But the disjunction of X_1 and Z_1, although it satisfies conditions (1) and (2), is ruled out by condition (3) – clearly this disjunction satisfies (1) because its disjuncts do, and not vice versa. We can coherently suppose, however, that X_1 itself satisfies (3) (and, if we like, that Z_1 does also). Though it is not coherent to suppose that X_1 is

its first conjunct satisfies (1) but its second conjunct doesn't, and it is at least plausible to say that the property as a whole satisfies (1) because the first conjunct does. Moreover, $(Pa\text{-or-}Pb)\text{-and-}C$ is equivalent to the disjunctive property $(Pa\text{-and-}C)\text{-or-}(Pb\text{-and-}C)$, and this might be said to fail condition (3) on the grounds that it satisfies condition (1) because its disjuncts do.

The amended version of the rule in the text avoids these difficulties. The inclusion of 'and only because' in (2) enables $(Pa\text{-or-}Pb)\text{-and-}C$ to satisfy (2). For it is not the case that the latter satisfies (1) only because its first conjunct does; sometimes (when the similarity is between experiences realized in different subsystems) the second conjunct, i.e., C, plays an essential role. And $(Pa\text{-or-}Pb)\text{-and-}C$ (or, equivalently, $(Pa\text{-and-}C)\text{-or-}(Pb\text{-and-}C)$) does not fail the amended version of (3), since it is not the case that it satisfies condition (2) because its disjuncts do, rather than vice versa. For $Pa\text{-and-}C$ and $Pb\text{-and-}C$ satisfy condition (2) because of the essential role played by C, a common conjunct of both of them, in making Pa experiences realized in the primary system color-qualia-identical to Pb experiences realized in the backup system. And this seems to me tantamount to saying that they satisfy (2) because $(Pa\text{-or-}Pb)\text{-and-}C$ satisfies it, and not vice versa.

[17] It is worth noting that, if condition (2) did not include clause (ii), X_1 would be ruled out as a quale realization as well, contrary to what we want. For let Z_1 be (as before) a property of Martian states which satisfies condition (1), and let Q be any property of states which is independent of X_1 and Z_1 and is such that possession of Q in the absence of X_1 or Z_1 is not enough to satisfy (1). Then X_1 is equivalent to the complex conjunctive property $(X_1\text{-or-}Z_1)\text{-and-}[X_1\text{-or-}(Q\text{-and-not-}Z_1)]$. (Here I am indebted to John Bennett.) But whereas the first conjunct of this, $X_1\text{-or-}Z_1$, satisfies condition (1), it surely cannot be said that it is *because* this conjunct of X_1 satisfies (1) that X_1 satisfies it; on the contrary this conjunct satisfies (1) because both X_1 and Z_1 satisfy it. Whereas it plainly is true that the conjunctive property expressed by 'has X_1 and is an experience of someone with my DNA' satisfies (1) because X_1 satisfies it, given what we are assuming about the case. Thus the latter property, but not X_1, is ruled out by condition (2).

not equivalent to a disjunctive property, it is coherent to suppose that it is not equivalent to any disjunctive property that does not violate condition (3). And if this supposition is true, then Xɪ will be a qualia realization of the sort we are looking for.

Conditions (2) and (3) both make use of the notion of something's being the case *because* something else is the case, where this is not simply a matter of the latter thing's being a logically or nomologically sufficient condition of the former. I have no analysis of this notion to offer; but it seems to me that it is clearly a notion we do have, and one that has application. The word 'because' of course signals that something is being said to be explanatory of something. And, on my account, what singles out certain properties as realizations of qualia is the fact that they are suited, and have the right degree of specificity, to play a certain explanatory role. Some properties will be ruled out as too specific because they are analyzable into conjunctions having conjuncts irrelevant to the explanatory role. Others will be ruled out as not specific enough, in that they are analyzable into disjunctions of properties, each of which plays the relevant causal role by itself. But if I am not mistaken, those which satisfy conditions (1)-(3) are just those which are capable of playing the causal role and have just the right degree of specificity.

VI

What I have just been saying was addressed to what I earlier called the "metaphysical problem." Where does all of this leave us with respect to the epistemological problem? On the account I have suggested, there is no reason in principle why we should not be able to discover whether the color experiences of different human beings are qualitatively comparable and, if they are, whether they are qualitatively similar in similar circumstances or, on the other hand, are spectrum-inverted relative to each other. We could discover this by finding how qualia are realized in the brain and by determining whether the relevant physiological similarities hold between the brains of different human beings.[18] But, given that such physiological investigations are

---

[18] It may be thought that, if Martian color experiences are not qualitatively comparable with our own, there is one thing that is in principle unknowable – we cannot know "what it is like" to have experiences possessing the Martian color qualia (cf. Thomas Nagel, "What is it Like to be a Bat?", in his *Mortal Questions*). There is a sense in which this is true, but it does not imply that there would be facts about Martian experiences which would be unknowable by us. If, as I have suggested, qualia can be identified with disjunctive physical properties (the disjunctions of their possible

still far in the future, what are we to say about our present epistemological situation? Do I have good reason right now to think that my experiences of violets and marigolds are similar to those of others, or even that my color experiences and those of others are qualitatively comparable?

If we do have good grounds for such beliefs, I think it will be an essential part of these grounds that the creatures whose experiences are being compared are members of a single species and, therefore, can be presumed to share a genetic endowment. By and large, different members of our own species have color-quality spaces having the same structure – i.e., they make the same color discriminations, see the same similarity relationships between objects, and so forth. Even in the exceptional case of color-blind people, the breakdown of this structural uniformity is very limited. The existence of this uniformity can scarcely be a coincidence, and it calls out for an explanation in terms of our shared genetic endowment. The situation would be altogether different if the structural similarity in question were that between human color-quality spaces and those of my hypothetical Martians, supposing them to exist. The existence of such an interspecies similarity could very well be a coincidence; and in any case, it could not be explained by a shared genetic endowment, since, *ex hypothesi*, the Martian evolutionary history would be entirely independent of our own. The similarity between different Martians could be explained in terms of their genetic endowment, and the similarity between different humans could be explained in terms of ours; but the similarity between humans and Martians would have to be explained in some quite different way, if at all.

What would seem the simplest explanation of the uniform structure of human color-quality spaces is that, as part of our shared genetic endowment, we are all "wired" in such a way that the same

realizations), there is no reason in principle why we should not be able to pick out the Martian qualia, assign names to them, and know which of them characterize the experiences of a Martian on a given occasion. Granted, this would not be to know what it is like to have experiences characterized by these various qualia. But what would it be to know this? I suggest that to know what it is like to have an experience having a certain quale is (a) to have such experiences in one's own repertoire of possible experiences, and' (b) to be able to recognize such experiences as such "introspectively," i.e., simply by having them. Where we fail to satisfy condition (b) but not condition (a), there is no reason to suppose that our failure to "know what it is like" is irremediable. And our failure to satisfy (a) in the case of Martian color experience, which presumably would be irremediable, would not as such preclude us from knowing any facts; it would merely preclude us from knowing certain facts in a certain way (namely that way which involves the satisfaction of (b)).

environmental stimuli give rise to the same color qualia in our visual experiences. This, of course, would guarantee both that color experiences of different human beings are qualitatively comparable and that, under similar conditions, they have qualitatively similar color experiences – i.e., that there is no intersubjective spectrum inversion among human beings. But if we suppose that our experiences are not qualitatively comparable or that some of us are spectrum-inverted relative to others, then, in order to explain this uniformity of structure, we must suppose there is something in our genetic endowment that compensates for the differences there are in our qualia, so as to make the differences cancel out so far as their effects on behavior are concerned. This is not impossible, but presumably it would call for more complex neural mechanisms than the first arrangement; and from an evolutionary standpoint it seems unlikely that we would have the more complex rather than the less complex arrangement. Obviously no such considerations could be used to support the claim that our experiences are qualitatively comparable with, or similar to, those of my Martians. And this is as it should be; if we know that Martian evolutionary history is completely independent of our own, then even before we discover the physiological differences between them and us, it will not be reasonable to think that our color experiences and theirs are qualitatively similar, or even qualitatively comparable.

It seems to me that if we are indeed entitled to think that, as John Locke put it, "the sensible *Ideas*, produced by any object in different Men's Minds, are most commonly very near and undiscernibly alike,"[19] our entitlement will rest on an empirical argument along the lines of that just sketched. I shall not attempt to elaborate the argument or to rebut the various objections that might be made to it; for part of the point I want to make is that the argument is at best fairly weak. It gives its conclusion – that our experiences are qualitatively comparable with those of others and that spectrum inversion does not occur – the status of a hypothesis which, although perhaps reasonable on the basis of current evidence, could easily be overthrown by future discoveries about how mental states are realized in the brain. We do not, if this is so, know with certainty at the present time that this conclusion is true. If one finds this counterintuitive, one should remember a point I made earlier: given the distinction between qualitative similarity and intentional similarity, our everyday claims about the experiences of others need not be taken as implying

[19] *Essay*, bk. II, ch. 32, sect. XV.

anything specific about the qualitative character of those experiences, and thus the certainty we would like to ascribe to some of our everyday claims need not be undermined by the admission that we lack certain knowledge of the qualitative character of the experiences of others.

A more expeditious, if not wholly satisfying, treatment of the epistemological problem is that of John Locke:

> I am nevertheless very apt to think, that the sensible *Ideas*, produced by an Object in different Men's Minds, are most commonly very near and undiscernibly alike. For which Opinion, I think, there might be many Reasons offered; but that being besides my present Business, I shall not trouble my reader with them, but only mind him, that the contrary Supposition, if it could be proved, is of little use, either for the Improvement of our Knowledge, or Conveniency of Life: and so we need not trouble ourselves to examine it.[20]

Locke was not always so anxious not to "trouble his reader," and one could wish that he had not been so here.

Postscript (1983)

In the original publication of this essay the following "Note Added in Proof" was appended to it:

> Saul Kripke has called my attention to a mistake in what I say in section v about the realization of qualia. Suppose that in person A quale Q_1 has the properties P_1 and P_2 as its only possible realizations, that in person B the quale Q_2 has properties P_2 and P_3 as its only possible realizations, and that in person C the quale Q_3 has properties P_3 and P_4 as its only possible realizations. Suppose further that there is no possible creature in which P_1 and P_4 can both be instantiated. According to what I say in section v, the last supposition implies that P_1 and P_4 are not "qualitatively identical," and thus that Q_1 and Q_3 are not the same quale. Yet plainly Q_1 and Q_3 would have to be the same quale, by the transitivity of identity. Let R be the relationship that holds between two qualia realizations when (a) they can be instantiated in the same creature (i.e., it is possible for there to be a creature in which both are instantiated), and (b) they are such that when they are so instantiated the experiences that have them are qualitatively identical in some respect. Then the relation "being realizations of the same quale" should be equated not with R but with its ancestral R^*; and what I must stipulate about my imaginary Martians is not only that they do not share any qualia realizations with us, or have any that stand in R to any of ours, but also that they do not have any qualia realizations that stand in R^* to any of ours. I believe,

[20] *Ibid.*

however, that an elaboration of the considerations adduced in footnote 16 will show that it is to a very limited extent, if at all, that qualia realizations can be related by R^* without being related by R.

It turns out, I think, that the specific difficulty raised here is fairly easily met (and without the problematic rejection of R in favor of R^* as the qualitative identity relation). But the reflection on the considerations adduced in footnote 16, which the note encouraged, had the unexpected result of bringing to light a much more serious difficulty with the view presented in section v, one that suggests that the Frege–Schlick view may be right after all.

First let me address the difficulty raised in the note. It is implicit in the account of qualitative similarity given in the essay that the relation of qualitative similarity between qualia, and also the relation of qualitative identity between different quale realizations (the relation that holds between two quale realizations just in case they are realizations of one and the same quale) can hold only between qualia, or quale realizations, that can be instantiated together in experiences of one and the same person – for short, qualia or quale realizations that are capable of cosubjective instantiation. For the basic idea of the account is that these relations are defined in the first instance in terms of what the consequences are when they hold intrasubjectively. The account says that two qualia stand in a certain relation of qualitative similarity if they are such that if they were to be instantiated in experiences of a single subject, this would have certain effects on the beliefs and behavior of that subject; and it is surely implicit in this that the similarity relationships are well defined only for cases in which the antecedent of that subjective conditional is satisfiable. Similarly, qualitative identity between qualia realizations can be thought of, as a first approximation, as a kind of indistinguishability or functional interchangeability; and only quale realizations that are capable of cosubjective instantiation can be indistinguishable in the sense that the behavioral and introspective effects of their cosubjective instantiation is the same as that of an otherwise identical pattern of property instantiations in which all instantiations of one of the realizations are replaced by instantiations of the other. Of course, indistinguishability is not transitive, so in order to make the relation of qualitative identity an equivalence relation we must complicate the account slightly. We can say that two quale realizations are qualitatively identical if and only if (1) they are indistinguishable in the sense indicated, and (2) any realization indistinguishable from either of them is indistinguishable from the other. This makes the example in the note impossible. If $P1$

and $P4$ (likewise, $P1$ and $P3$, and $P2$ and $P4$) are not capable of cosubjective instantiation, then $P2$ and $P3$ (likewise $P1$ and $P2$, and $P3$ and $P4$) are not qualitatively identical, even if they are indistinguishable. (Kripke's objection was, however, cogent against the somewhat confused version of section V I had presented to him in conversation; he had not seen the essay.)

But now let us consider a variation on the example described in footnote 16. Suppose that S_1 is a brainlike system in which quale realization Pa can be instantiated, and S_2 is a brainlike system in which quale realization Pb can be instantiated. If S_1 and S_2 are joined in a certain way – call it "way C" – into a larger system S_3, then each of these systems serves as a "backup system" to the other in the sense indicated in footnote 16, and Pa and Pb are qualitatively identical, or at least indistinguishable, and so realize a common quale, or at least realize very similar qualia. For the moment assume that they realize a single quale. As I explain in footnote 16, strictly speaking it is not Pa and Pb *simpliciter* that realize this single quale, but rather the properties Pa-and-C and Pb-and-C, where C is the relational property a quale has just in case it occurs in a system in which subsystems like S_1 and S_2 are joined in way C. In the terminology of Essay 12, Pa and Pb will be "core realizations" of the single quale, and Pa-and-C and Pb-and-C will be "total realizations" of it.

Now if it is because of the particular way S_1 and S_2 are joined in S_3, i.e. the fact that they are joined in way C, that Pa and Pb are core realizations of a single quale (or of very similar qualia), then it would seem that it should be possible for S_1 and S_2 to be joined in a different way, call it C^*, such that when they are so joined Pa and Pb (or the total quale realizations of which they are the "cores") are not qualitatively identical, and instead are qualitatively different to a considerable degree – let it be that they (or the qualia they realize) differ as the character of seeing red differs from the character of seeing green. Of course, the total realizations here are Pa-and-C^* and Pb-and-C^*; so the total realizations that differ in this case are not the ones that are qualitatively identical in the other. There is no difficulty about Pa and Pb being core realizations of the same quale in one sort of system and core realizations of different qualia in another sort of system. So far, then, there is no problem.

The problem begins to emerge when we notice that Pa and Pb can themselves be total quale realizations, namely when they are instantiated in the unjoined systems S_1 and S_2, respectively. Suppose that at t_1, when the systems have not yet been joined, a Pa experiences (i.e., an experience having Pa) occurs in S_1. At t_2, after the systems have been joined in way C, another Pa experience occurs in S_1. The latter experience also has the property Pa-and-C (since all experiences in the larger system have C). It will hardly do to say that the experience at t_2 instantiates two different qualia, one realized in Pa and the other realized in Pa-and-C. And we can plausibly suppose (and stipulate as part of the example) that the effects of these successive qualia instantiations are precisely what, on our functional account, the effects of successive instantiations of one and the same qualia should be. It would seem that we must say that just one quale was realized by Pa and Pa-and-C at t_2, and that this is the same quale that was realized by Pa at t_1.

Similar considerations will apparently show that Pb is qualitatively identical to Pb-and-C. But our example is supposed to be one in which Pa-and-C and Pb-and-C are qualitatively identical. Since qualitative identity is a transitive relation, it follows that Pa and Pb are qualitatively identical. But surely something has gone wrong. For the considerations that show that Pa is qualitatively identical to Pa-and-C will also show that Pa is qualitatively identical to Pa-and-C^*, and that Pb is qualitatively identical to Pb-and-C^*. But since Pa-and-C^* and Pb-and-C^* differ significantly in their qualitative character, we can infer from this that Pa and Pb differ qualitatively in exactly the same way. And now we have a contradiction on our hands; for our earlier conclusion was that Pa and Pb were qualitatively identical.

We might attempt to avoid the contradiction by trying to avoid the conclusion that Pa is qualitatively identical to Pa-and-C (likewise with Pb and Pb-and-C, and so on). First, we might insist that when system S_1 exists by itself (unjoined with S_2), what serves as a total realization is not Pa by itself, but something of the form Pa-and-X, where X is some property which is incompatible with C and C^* (it could be just the property of not occurring in a composite system of the sort S_3 is). Now Pa will be only a core realization, and not a proper term for our qualitative identity relationship. But we still need to block the argument that would seem to show that Pa-and-X is qualitatively identical to Pb-and-X (in virtue of their being qualitatively identical to, respectively, Pa-and-C and Pb-and-C, which in turn are qualitatively identical), since a parallel argument would show that these are qualitatively very different (in virtue of their being qualitatively identical to, respectively, Pa-and-C^* and Pb-and-C^*, which are qualitatively very different). We could block this by strengthening the requirement that qualitatively identical quale realizations must be capable of cosubjective instantiation into the requirement that such realizations must be capable of *simultaneous* cosubjective instantiation. For Pa-and-X and Pa-and-C (and other such pairs) are not capable of simultaneous instantiation in experiences of a single subject. But notice that this will achieve the desired result only if we also strengthen the conditions for qualitative similarity, so that qualia can count as qualitatively similar only if they are capable of simultaneous cosubjective instantiation. For if we allow that Pa-and-X is qualitatively very similar to (even though not qualitatively identical to) both Pa-and-C and Pa-and-C^*, that Pb-and-X is qualitatively identical to both Pb-and-C and Pb-and-C^*, and that Pa-and-C and Pb-and-C are qualitatively identical while Pa-and-C^* and Pb-and-C^* are qualitatively very different, then we still have a contradiction on our hands.

Alternatively, we might try to avoid the contradiction by denying that Pa-and-C and Pb-and-C could be qualitatively identical in the case envisaged. But this will be ineffective unless we also deny that these properties, or the qualia they realize, would be even qualitatively very similar. For if we allow that they would be qualitatively very similar, and allow that Pa-and-C^* and Pb-and-C^* would be qualitatively very different, and allow the other qualitative relationships that generated our original contradiction, then we still have a contradiction. We will be able to infer both that Pa-and-X and Pb-and-X are qualitatively very similar (being qualitatively identical to, respectively, Pa-and-C and Pb-and-C, which are very similar) and that they are qualitatively very different (being qualitatively identical to, respectively, Pa-and-C^* and Pb-and-C^*, which are qualitatively very different); and both conclusions cannot be true, given that there is here only one relevant dimension of similarity-and-difference.

But is either of these ways of avoiding the contradiction compatible with the view of qualia sketched in section v? It will be useful to resolve that view into two components. First, there is the functional account of qualitative similarity (and difference, etc.) sketched in section IV (and in Essays 8 and 9) – that according to which qualitative similarity is defined in the first instance for the intrasubjective case, and is defined in terms of its effects on the subject's beliefs and behavior. Second, there is what I shall call the standard conception of qualia. This says that qualia are intrinsic properties of experiences (they are not "mere-Cambridge" properties in the sense of Essay 11), that they are the primary relata of the relationships of qualitative similarity and difference, and that the similarity and difference relations of a quale to other qualia are internal to it. On this conception, experiences are qualitatively similar or different in virtue of what qualia they have, i.e., in virtue of similarities and differences between their qualia, and each quale essentially and eternally stands to other qualia in whatever relations of qualitative similarity or difference it has to them – so it makes no sense to speak of the same pair of qualia being qualitatively similar under one set of circumstances and qualitatively different under another.

Now consider the consequences of adopting one or the other of the suggested ways of avoiding our contradiction. If we adopt the first, and say that Pa-and-X and Pa-and-C cannot be qualitatively identical or even qualitatively very similar (because they are not qualitatively comparable, being incapable of simultaneous cosubjective instantiation), then we must either give up the view that qualia (or quale realizations) are the primary relata of the relations of qualitative identity, similarity and difference, or else we must deny that the experience at t_1 and the experience at t_2 are qualitatively similar in virtue of their successive instantiation of Pa-and-X and Pa-and-C, respectively. But the former denial involves abandoning the standard conception of qualia, and the latter denial is sharply at odds with the functionalist account of qualitative similarity, given that the case is one in which the experiences would count as qualitatively very similar on the functionalist account. And the same is true if we attempt to avoid the contradiction by denying that Pa-and-C and Pb-and-C are qualitatively identical or (at least) qualitatively very similar – for the case is one in which experiences having these quale realizations would count as at least qualitatively very similar on the functionalist account. So unless we can find some grounds on which we can deny the possibility of the sort of situation envisaged (one in which there are two different ways of combining brainlike systems into larger brainlike systems, such that on a functionalist account the similarity and difference relations between experiences realized in the different subsystems depend on which mode of connection is in effect) we must apparently choose between rejecting the functionalist account of qualitative similarity and rejecting the standard conception of qualia.

I would prefer not to have to make this choice; but if I am forced to make it, I reject the standard conception of qualia. And to hold the functionalist view of qualitative similarity without the standard conception of qualia is tantamount to holding the Frege–Schlick view. If one adopts this view one must say either that there are no such things as qualia or that the similarity and difference relations between qualia are not internal to them, and that qualia are not the primary relata of the relations of qualitative similarity and difference. And if one says either of these things one will deprive oneself of the way, sketched at the beginning of section v, of giving the functionally defined relations of qualitative similarity and difference an inter-subjective application. It will be impossible to say that my experience can resemble yours in virtue of having qualia that resemble those yours have (where the resemblance between qualia consists in their being such that their cosubjective instantiation would have certain effects on beliefs and behavior). Obviously this cannot be said if there are no such things as qualia; and it also cannot be said if the same qualia can stand in different relations of qualitative similarity and difference in different circumstances. On such a view there seems to be no alternative to holding that qualitative identity (and similarity, etc.) is well defined only for the intrasubjective case, just as the Frege–Schlick view holds.

16

On what there are

Philosophers, and I suspect only philosophers, know about grue – the property (if that is what it is) that something has just in case it is green and examined before 2010 AD or blue and not so examined. Nelson Goodman introduced the predicate "grue" in order to raise an important problem about induction. But my concern here is not with the philosophy of induction; I am interested in grue only as an example of a fishy property. There are lots of other examples. Properties that are arbitrary disjunctions of ordinary properties, like *being red or weighing thirty pounds*, will strike most people as fishy. So also will such properties as *being 50 miles south of a burning barn* and *having once been touched by the drummer of a rock band*. So also will properties like *being such that Reagan is President*, a property that now belongs to absolutely everything but once (believe it or not) did not, and ones like *being such that 2 + 2 = 4*, a property that always has belonged and always will belong to absolutely everything.

In addition to fishy properties, there are fishy things. I have elsewhere written about klables – if you have both a kitchen table and a living room table, the midnight till noon stages of the one and the noon till midnight stages of the other are together the stages of a klable, a table-like object which shifts back and forth twice a day between your kitchen and your living room.[1] Eli Hirsch has written about incars and outcars, and about contacti-persons.[2] As your car leaves your garage an incar slowly goes out of being as an outcar comes into being; the process is reversed when your car reenters your garage. The histories of contacti-persons are traced like those of ordinary persons, with one important difference – when two human bodies come into contact, each comes to be the body of the contacti-person who previously had the other one, and a corresponding reversal occurs when two human bodies cease to be in contact.

Peter Geach has characterized the sort of change that Socrates

[1] See Essay 11.
[2] See his book *The Concept of Identity* (New York, 1980).

undergoes when he becomes shorter than Theaetetus, owing to the latter's growth, as a mere "Cambridge" change – possibly in honor of the Cambridge philosopher McTaggart.[3] Following his lead, others have used the term "Cambridge property" for grue and the like; and I suppose one could speak of klables, incars, contacti-persons and the like as "Cambridge things." But I will stick with "fishy."

On the face of it, the status of the fishy properties and things mentioned is not the same as that of such putative properties as being bewitched and such putative things as goblins and ghosts. It is, most of us think, just false that anything is bewitched, and just false that there are goblins and ghosts. But given Goodman's definition of "grue," there are as many grue things in this room as green things, and given Hirsch's rules for the use of "contacti-person," there are always exactly as many contacti-persons as there are persons.

I have been inclined to say, and still am inclined to say, that while "grue" and "is such that Reagan is President" are well-defined predicates, they do not stand for genuine properties. Likewise, I have been inclined to say, and still am inclined to say, that there are no such entities as klables, incars, and contacti-persons. One can choose to speak in such a way that the sentence "There is a klable in my house which this morning was made of maple and now is made of walnut" expresses a truth; but if one does, I have maintained, the word "klable" is simply functioning as part of a code for talking about ordinary tables, and not as a name for a peculiar sort of object, one capable of instantaneous change of place and instantaneous change of composition.

Going with this rejection of fishy properties and fishy objects has been a view about the identity conditions for genuine properties and objects, namely that these intimately involve the concept of causality. Genuine properties, I have maintained, are individuated by the ways they contribute to the causal powers of the things that have them, and also by the ways their own instantiation can be caused.[4] And the identity over time of genuine objects essentially involves there being relations of causal or counterfactual dependence of their later stages on their earlier ones, a special case of which is the persistence of traits – something having a trait because it previously had it.[5]

But much of what I want to say about the role of causal considerations in the identity conditions for properties and things is compatible

---

[3] See his *God and the Soul* (London, 1969).
[4] See Essay 10.
[5] See Essay 11.

with a more permissive view about fishy properties and things, and
this view, too, I have sometimes found attractive. According to this
more permissive view, there really are such properties as grueness – it
is just that there are good reasons for not being interested in them,
outside of philosophy. Similarly, there really are klables, incars, and
all the rest; but for all ordinary and scientific purposes, these can
safely be ignored in favor of the sorts of entities that figure in our
ordinary and scientific talk about the world. An expression of the
permissive view about objects is Quine's statement that "Any arbitrary congeries of particle-stages, however spatiotemporally gerrymandered or disperse, can count as a physical object."[6] An expression
of the permissive view about properties is David Lewis's view that a
property "is just the set of all its instances – all of them, this- and
other-worldly alike," and that "the properties are just as numerous as
the sets themselves, because for any set whatever there is the property
of belonging to that set."[7] It is, of course, compatible with the
permissive view that what marks off, from all the rest, the properties
and objects we are interested in outside of philosophy, those that are
recognized in ordinary and scientific language, is the role causal
considerations play in their identity conditions.

A way of trying to shed light on these matters is to begin by trying
to characterize in some way all of the possible ways of cutting the
world up into (putative) things and properties, and then inquiring
into what accounts for our finding some of them natural and some
fishy. One need not at the outset decide whether fishiness implies
unreality; one needn't decide between the view that there are no such
things as grueness, klables, and incars, and the more permissive view
that their fishiness is just some sort of unsuitability for recognition in
our ordinary thought and talk about the world, and that they do
indeed exist.

One way of indicating alternative ways of cutting up the world is
to begin with our ordinary ontology and then use the resources of set
theory, mereology, and plain old-fashioned definition to construct
novel sorts of entities out of the familiar ones. Thus, we go from
green, blue, and our temporal framework to grue. And we go from
tables to table stages to sets or mereological sums of table stages, and
this (one may think) gets us klables. Those who think of tables as
four-dimensional entities of which table stages are momentary parts
will find this unproblematic. My own resistance to klables stems in

[6] Quine, *The Roots of Reference* (La Salle, Ill., 1973), p. 54.
[7] *The Plurality of Worlds* (Oxford, 1986), p. 50 and p. 60.

part from my resistance to temporal parts. Assuming that the notion of a momentary table stage can be satisfactorily introduced, and I don't doubt that it can be, I have no objection to allowing series or sums of these – including those series or sums composed of morning stages of a kitchen table and afternoon stages of a living room table from the same household. But I don't think that a table can be identified with a series or sum of table stages, for the reason that the very same table could have existed without that very series of table stages occurring. And so I don't think that the existence of a series or sum of table stages automatically gives us a table-like entity. Roughly, I think that it does so only if the right sort of causal continuity runs through the entire series – which is not so in the case of the putative klable history. But an important point that emerges here is that entities that are merely sets, series, or sums of familiar entities (or of stages thereof) will not in general have the same sorts of modal properties as the familiar entities. Various things could have been true of a given table that are not in fact true of it – it can have quite different careers in different possible worlds.[8] Indeed, the modal properties of familiar entities are closely tied up with their causal properties. It is above all the truth of counterfactuals that obliges us to allow that the careers of such things might have been different from what they are; and the counterfactuals true of a thing are grounded in its actual causal properties. (This is one basis of the "essentiality of origins" principle; to the extent that the alternative careers of a thing are those described in the consequents of conditionals whose antecedents describe activations of its causal powers, those alternative careers will be branchings off of its actual career.) At any rate, if we want klable-like entities to have different careers in different possible worlds, we cannot simply equate them with sets or sums of momentary thing stages.

No doubt any way of sketching alternative ontologies will have to be based to some extent on our actual one. But it is desirable to minimize the extent to which this is true, while maximizing the number of putative entities that our sketch gives us. The way I shall propose takes as its point of departure a standard way of characterizing properties in terms of possible worlds; a property is "represented" by a function from possible worlds to extensions of things in those worlds. If we take every such function to represent a property, we will be

---

[8] Here I employ the simplest way of translating modal talk into possible worlds talk; I do not think that it would make a substantial difference to what I say if instead I employed a counterpart theory *à la* David Lewis.

adopting a very permissive view about propertyhood – grueness, being such that Reagan is President, and even stranger things will be properties. This will be so even if the things in the extensions are limited to familiar sorts of objects. But we can use a similar device to broaden our class of (putative) objects, thereby broadening still further our class of (putative) properties. We want our objects to include ones that have modal properties of the sort ordinary continuants have, ones that give them different careers in different possible worlds. We might represent the career of an object in a possible world by a collection of spacetime points – the points occupied by the object during its career (in that world). And so we might represent the object by a function from possible worlds to collections of spacetime points. If we take there to be an object represented by every such function, then while we will perhaps have left out some of the objects dreamt of in some philosophies, we will certainly have more objects than are dreamt of in most.[9]

One additional complication is needed. If properties are represented by functions from possible worlds to extensions, then the objects in these extensions will have these properties *simpliciter*, i.e., timelessly – these won't be the sort of properties something can have at one time and not at another. And this means that they won't include familiar properties like color, shape, and size. Presumably, we can get around this by representing the properties by somewhat more complex functions – functions from possible worlds to sets of ordered pairs, each pair consisting of an object and a time, or, since the relativity of simultaneity makes times dubious entities, functions from possible worlds to ordered pairs consisting of objects and temporal cross-sections of their spacetime paths.[10] For the sake of simplicity, however, I shall pretend that the simpler functions will do.

Supposing that any two functions of either of these sorts (from

[9] Among the putatively possible entities not allowed for by this scheme are Cartesian minds. Since these are not supposed to have spatial location in their own right, and are supposed to be capable of a disembodied existence in which they have no spatial location at all, their possible careers apparently cannot be represented by sets of spacetime points. I have suggested elsewhere that the individuation of such entities might require that they stand in "quasi-spatial" relationships that play a role in their individuation analogous to that played by spatial relations in the individuation of material things (see Essay 7). Perhaps their careers can only be presented in worlds (supposing there to be such) in which the spatial framework in which material things exist is supplemented by a quasi-spatial one. Or perhaps they are not possible at all.

[10] For this last suggestion I am indebted to Phil Gasper. David Lewis finds such constructions "misguided," and prefers an account according to which things have or lack properties *simpliciter*, and so according to which "it is by having temporal parts which are thirsty that a person is thirsty at various times" (*The Plurality of Worlds*, p. 53).

possible worlds to collections of spacetime points, and from possible worlds to extensions within worlds) have different objects or properties corresponding to them, it is obvious that the vast majority of these objects and properties are ones that it would be in principle impossible for us to refer to or have any knowledge of. We could not pick them out by specifying the corresponding functions. The collections of spacetime points which are the values of these functions would be in many cases nondenumerably numerous random selections from all the spacetime points there are, and so could not be specified by simple enumeration, or by any other means available to us. And most of these entities would not stand to us in any of the causal relations that make for the most basic sorts of epistemic access (e.g., sense-perception), would not stand in causal or explanatory relations to entities that do in turn stand in such causal relations to us, and would not be finitely definable or describable in terms of properties to which we have such access. It is obvious enough why such putative entities do not get recognition in our language. They hardly get as far as seeming fishy to us, since we cannot consider particular ones of them in the way we can consider grueness and klables.

Others of the putative entities will be like grueness or klables. These, supposing them to exist, are not inaccessible to our reference and knowledge. But our access to them seems clearly indirect compared with our access to more familiar entities. We learn about grueness by learning about greenness and blueness and the time, and we learn about klables by learning about familiar sorts of tables. This is partly a matter of how we interact causally with the rest of the world. Our "quality space" is suited to the perception of colors and not the perception of schmolors (like grueness), and I have argued elsewhere that it is not really conceivable that it should have been otherwise.[11] It is also arguable that our ability to perceive objects is tied up with an ability to track objects over time, and that this requires that the objects of which we get our basic perceptual knowledge be ones whose identity conditions are suited to our perceptual capacities. Here we might speculate that if we were different in certain ways the objects and properties to which we have our most direct epistemic access might be different: e.g., if we underwent instantaneous changes in position at periodic intervals, we might look more kindly on klable-like entities – and if our own instantaneous shifts lined up with theirs we might even regard ourselves as having the ability to track them perceptually.[12]

---

[11] See Essay 4.
[12] We would, of course, be wrong to do so if there are really no such things as klables.

There are other cases in which we not only can conceive of alternative ways of classifying and individuating things, but can conceive of creatures otherwise very similar to ourselves for whom these modes of classification and individuation are basic, rather than being defined in terms of ours (as we define "grue" in terms of "green," "blue," and a date). Supposing that Kripke and Putnam are right about how *we* apply natural kind terms like "water" and "gold," it seems conceivable that there should be people pretty much like us who have terms with more or less the same extensions as these in normal circumstances, but whose response to Twin Earth cases shows that they regard the extensions of their terms as determined by Lockean nominal essences, i.e., phenomenal properties, rather than by Kripke–Putnam real essences, i.e., explanatory properties in the underlying substrate. The basis of such a difference might be cultural. But one can also imagine it residing in part in innate psychological makeup. Wittgenstein has stressed the extent to which meaning and linguistic practice are based in "general facts of nature" about language users; that our words mean what they do is based in part in the fact that having been introduced to them in certain ways, perhaps by ostensive teaching, we just do go on in certain ways rather than others in applying them. It might be that for a people to have a language whose semantics was consistently Lockean rather than Kripkean, they would have to differ from us in how they spontaneously go on in response to linguistic training, and so would have to differ from us in their nature.

But however it may be with such differences, there will also be differences in practices of classifying and individuating whose basis is entirely cultural – and these will include differences that are actual and not just imagined. For example, there are the differences in the ways things are divided up by the color vocabularies of different languages.[13] And there are all those words for snow in Eskimo.

Returning to our plethora of putative properties and things, those that we do not recognize in our ordinary dealings with the world range from, at one extreme, those that it is absolutely impossible for us, or any other finite minds, to refer to or have knowledge of, to, at the other extreme, those that we do not recognize because of conven-

What we *would* be able to track would be objects (were there such) whose instantaneous shifts lined up with ours and were such that their post-shift states are causally and counterfactually dependent on their pre-shift states – it is in part the lack of such causal and counterfactual dependence in the case of klables that makes them dubious entities.

[13] But see B. Berlin and P. Kay *Basic Color Terms* (Berkeley and Los Angeles, 1969), which indicates that these differences are not as great as is commonly assumed.

tions that happen to be in force in our linguistic community, conventions that might easily have been different. And what determines the position of these entities along this continuum is the extent to which they are governed by causal laws in ways that permit them to stand to us, or to other minds, in the sorts of causal connections involved in knowledge and reference. To be within semantic and epistemic reach, the properties will have to have the sorts of causal features that make for inductive projectibility, and some of them will have to have causal features that make them suitable objects of perception. The epistemic and semantic accessibility of objects will depend on their identity through time being constituted in a way that permits of their reidentification, and this requires that such changes of property and position as they undergo be governed by lawlike principles that the knowing minds in question are capable of grasping. It is to be noted here that the identity through time of a knowing mind must itself be governed by lawlike principles – those that govern the accumulation of information in memory, and its utilization in reasoning, for example. And an entity that is knowable by (or referable to by) a knowing mind must be such that its career over time has a causal structure that can mesh, as it were, with that of a knowing mind, in such a way as to make it an object of knowledge and reference by that mind. It is natural to speculate that there may be entities that would be within the semantic and epistemic reach of minds of a different sort than ours, if only there were such, but are not within reach of ours. And of those that are within reach of ours, our access to some is, as we have noted, more direct and more natural (given *our* nature) than our access to others. The further we get from these, as we move along the spectrum, the stranger, or fishier, the entities will seem.

If we think of the matter in this way, the involvement of causal considerations in the identity conditions of the properties and objects we recognize may seem not a deep metaphysical fact about the nature of properties and objects as such, but rather a consequence of what it is for a property to be within the semantic and epistemic reach of a knowing mind. It is rooted in the causal nature of knowledge and reference, and the causal nature of mind itself. This may seem to give support to the "permissive" view about properties and things I sketched at the beginning. The following picture may be suggested. There really are objects corresponding to all of the functions from possible worlds to collections of spacetime points, and properties corresponding to all of the functions from possible worlds to extensions. The identity conditions for most of these are quite independent of causal considerations. But the causal conditions for knowledge and reference filter these out, so that the only properties and objects that get through to us are those whose identity conditions are governed by causal considerations – only these attract our notice, and get recognition in our language. Of course, this is a slight exaggeration, since we can define predicates like "grue," and we can introduce notions like that of a klable. But in a way the exceptions prove the rule; these notions could not be introduced ostensively, and their introduction is necessarily parasitic on the prior possession of concepts of entities that are causally well behaved.

I should mention some considerations that seem to support the permissive view. It is plausible, to begin with, that there are identity propositions about familiar sorts of objects that are indeterminate in truth value. And it is plausible that the source of this indeterminacy is indeterminacy of reference: e.g., if the proposition that is indeterminate is "The building Jones is in is the building Smith is in," the source of this is the vagueness of the term "building," which leaves it indeterminate whether the referent of "the building Jones is in" is a structure that excludes Smith or a larger structure that includes him. But if there is to be this sort of indeterminacy of reference, then there must *be* in the world all of the entities that are the potential referents. In this case there must be both an entity which is a candidate for being the referent of "the building Jones is in" that contains both Jones and Smith and one that contains only Jones. And if there is indeterminacy of identity in Thomas Hobbes's Ship of Theseus case, then in that case there must be two different ship-like continuants – one that retains the same planks throughout its career, though existing for a while as a scattered object, and one that survives the one-by-one replacement of all of its planks – that are competing candidates for being the referent of the expression "the ship" as it figures in the story. Much the same point can be made by pointing out that it seems at least to some extent a matter of convention how we cut up the world into properties and things. Since the adoption of conventions can hardly be thought to *create* the entities to which it gives recognition, it would seem that the role of convention can only be that of selecting from a set of preexisting entities certain ones to give linguistic recognition to. And if we think that there are still other ways of cutting up the world that are not available to us, because of the way we are built, but which would be available to possible creatures whose sensory and cognitive constitutions are different from our own, then it seems that we must allow that there are the entities such creatures would or might recognize – we must allow this as the cost of rejecting the idealist view that what exists is mind dependent.

But if we expand our ontology to include all the entities we need in order to explain indeterminacy of identity in terms of indeterminacy of reference, and all those we need to give scope for conventional decision and to allow for the possibility of minds who see the world differently than we do, it may seem that we have opened the floodgates and that we cannot stop short of adopting the permissive view.

An attraction of the permissive view that I will mention in passing is that it provides a quick way of dismissing the view, represented in one form by David Hume and in another by Bishop Butler and Thomas Reid, that some or all of the identities we claim to hold in everyday life are "fictitious," or identities only in a "loose and popular sense," and that identity in the "strict and philosophical sense" is either not to be found or is found only in indivisible souls and indivisible atoms. On the permissive view, identity in the strict and philosophical sense could not be more plentiful; for any two spacetime point s and s' there will be infinitely many thing-kinds K, each such that a thing of kind K at s is identical to a thing of kind K at s'. (One might question, of course, whether one has to go to such extremes of profligacy to avoid the stinginess about identity one finds in Butler, Hume, and Reid.)

One objection I used to raise against the permissive view now seems to me answerable. Let's take the case of klables, and let us suppose that while klables have different identity conditions than tables, the properties of a klable at a time are always the properties possessed by a table at that time – those of a kitchen table if it is the morning, those of a living room table if it is after noon. This means that a klable will have, among other things, a certain mass. Let us suppose our klable is on wheels in the middle of a smooth kitchen floor, and that a half second before noon I give it a hefty push in a direction in which there are no obstructing objects until you get to the wall. Something with that mass and those circumstances ought, subjected to such a force, to glide along the kitchen floor till it hits the wall. And that is what the *table* does. But this is not what the *klable* is supposed to do, given the identity conditions for klables that I stipulated; it is supposed to move instantaneously to the living room at noon, acquiring instantaneously the properties of the living room table (which happens to be at rest throughout this interval). The klable, if there is such a thing, seems to violate all sorts of physical laws governing things having the properties it has. And that seems a good reason for denying that there is such a thing.

I can think of two ways this objection might be countered. The first, which I do not find very congenial, is to hold that it is a mistake to think that these causal laws hold of all entities, of whatever sort, that have the properties in question. They hold for table-like entities, but not for klable-like entities. More generally, they hold only for entities that are intuitively genuine, but not for ones that are intuitively fishy. A different response to the objection, and the one I favor when I am feeling friendly to the permissive view, is to deny that klables have the very same properties tables do. A klable will perhaps have a property that is a counterpart of a certain mass, but it won't have that mass. After all, on the permissive scheme I am considering, which gives us a property for every function from possible worlds to extensions, there will be properties aplenty. While there will be extensions that include both tables and klables, there will also be ones that include tables but not klables, and others that include klables but not tables, and this makes it possible to hold that our familiar table properties, and more generally the properties invoked in the laws of physics, are ones represented by functions to extensions that do not include klables. There will then be no danger of klables violating the laws of physics. A similar maneuver will keep contacti-persons from violating the laws of psychology.

But let us consider further the question of how the notion of causality is connected to the notions of propertyhood and objecthood. I have suggested that to be within semantic and epistemic reach of knowing minds, objects and properties must be governed by lawlike principles of certain kinds. And, as I have noted, it may seem that this is all the involvement of causality in the identity conditions for properties and objects amounts to. This might suggest a modified Humean view of what causality is, somewhat along the lines of Donald Davidson's in "Causal Relations."[14] Let us say that there are properties corresponding to all the functions from possible worlds to extensions, and let us speak of these as "thin" properties. Among the thin properties there are some that conform, in all possible worlds (or in all nearby ones), to certain sorts of laws. These, it might seem, are the "genuine" properties my causal theory of properties attempted to characterize. And it might be suggested that for one event to cause another is just for the two events to involve properties belonging to this subset in such a way that the event sequence is subsumable under laws that hold in all possible worlds in which these properties are instantiated, and which sustain the appropriate counterfactuals. Roughly, causality will consist in constant conjunctions of thin prop-

[14] *The Journal of Philosophy*, 64 (1967), reprinted in Davidson's *Essays on Actions and Events* (Oxford, 1980).

erty instantiations that hold in all possible worlds (or all possible worlds in some privileged subclass).

As might be expected, this does not work, if its aim is to effect a distinction between genuine and nongenuine properties. Thin properties are so plentiful that for every thin property there will be bound to be other thin properties with which it is connected in a quasi-lawlike way.[15] Nor will it help to restrict genuineness to those properties governed by laws that resemble in some way the laws governing the familiar properties. For as we shall now see, as long as the required resemblance does not require that the properties actually stand in lawlike connections with the familiar properties, the amended proposal will still give us, unless we are extremely permissive, altogether too many "genuine" properties and objects and altogether too many causal connections.

Consider the collection of spacetime points that constitute my spacetime path in the actual world, and the collections that constitute it in every other possible world in which I exist. And now consider, for each of these collections of spacetime points, another collection that has the same spatiotemporal "shape" as it, but is shifted slightly in spatiotemporal position – e.g., it begins five minutes earlier (relative to some reference frame). These will be values of a function from possible worlds to collections of spacetime points, and on the permissive ontological view I am playing with this function determines an object which in each possible world has the corresponding collection of spacetime points as its spacetime path. Call this object a "shadow" of me. Obviously, I will have nondenumerably many shadows, corresponding to the nondenumerably many ways of mapping the spacetime points in my spacetime path onto other spacetime points. And every other ordinary object in the world will have nondenumerably many such shadows. For any given shadow of me gotten by a certain way of mapping, consider the family of shadows which includes the shadow of every other ordinary thing determined by that way of mapping. And now consider the properties determined by the functions from possible worlds to extensions, where the extensions are made up of shadows belonging to this family. These will be thin properties that stand in lawlike connections to one another that exactly mirror the lawlike connections of the genuine properties of the genuine things of which these shadows are the shadows. According to the suggestion made earlier, these shadow properties will themselves

---

[15] That this is true of all thin properties, and not merely of the "shadow" properties discussed later, escaped my notice till it was pointed out to me by Carl Ginet.

be genuine properties and will stand in causal relations. My shadow will have a set of shadow properties that stand in causal relations to one another and to things in its shadow environment that are exactly isomorphic to the relations my properties stand in to one another and to things in my environment. On a causal theory of mind, my shadow has a mind and has exactly the same sorts of mental states as I do – except that the intentional objects of its representational states are shadows of the intentional objects of mine. And, of course, I have nondenumerably many such shadows, each belonging to a family of shadows to which it is related just as I am related to the genuine objects in the world. We have no need of Putnam's Twin Earth; each of us has nondenumerably many "doppelgängers" right here!

But these shadow-like entities are not limited to shadows of actual entities. Take any work of fiction you like – say the Sherlock Holmes stories; fill it out so as to be consistent and to be a "complete novel" – i.e., to contain every sentence or its negation – and in such a way that it assigns its fictional events to actual places and times. Then write as many other complete novels as it takes to describe the alternative possible careers of all of the things mentioned in the first complete novel. Then assign these arbitrarily to possible worlds, and consider the set of functions from possible worlds to sets of spacetime points each of whose members takes as its value for each possible world the spacetime path one of these fictional entities would have if the associated novel were a true description of the world. On our permissive view about what there is, there *is* an object corresponding to each of these functions. And, of course, we can now go on to define a set of functions that give us appropriate properties for these objects. Now things are *really* getting crowded. Right in this room there will be shadowlike counterparts of Sherlock Holmes, David Copperfield, Huck Finn, and all the rest. Indeed, since "complete novels" amount to complete descriptions of possible worlds, each possible world will contain shadows of everything that exists in every other possible world – in fact, it will contain as many different shadows of each thing as there are possible worlds in which that thing exists.[16]

Initially I assumed that this would offend everyone's sense of reality. Even David Lewis, who thinks that all possible things are equally real, doesn't think that they all exist *right here*. But somewhat to my

---

[16] This will not be so if the spacetimes of different possible worlds differ in size and structure (see Lewis, *The Plurality of Worlds*). What will be true is that every possible world will contain shadows of everything that exists in any possible world whose spacetime matches its own in size and structure.

surprise I have sometimes met with the following response. "Why should these shadow things bother you. They don't get in our way, or compete with us for space, food and other resources. Once we see that the family of ordinary properties and things and the various families of shadow properties and things can interpenetrate each other without resistance, and are causally insulated from each other, why not live and let live? Why not allow that all are equally real, but allow also that we are within our rights in ignoring them for all ordinary and scientific purposes, as indeed the shadow people are within their rights in ignoring us?"

Call this the "extreme permissive view." It may seem that the proponent of the extreme permissive view is committed to denying things that any sensible person would assert. For example, any sensible person would assert that no one has ever done all of the things that Sherlock Holmes is described as doing in the Arthur Conan Doyle stories, yet it would seem from what I said earlier that the extreme permissive view is committed to there being, in this very room, nondenumerably many people who have done those things. But the proponent of the extreme permissive view has a ready reply to this. Following the lead of David Lewis, he can say that in our ordinary and scientific existence claims we often implicitly restrict the range of our variables so that it does not include all of the things there are. To use Lewis's example, this happens when I say all the beer is in the fridge.[17] The claim of the proponent of the extreme permissive view would be that ordinarily we restrict the range of our variables so that it includes only "ordinary" properties and things, and does not include the various shadows of these. Given such a restriction, the claim that no one has ever done all the things Sherlock Holmes is described as doing is presumably true. But it is compatible with this that the claim is false if we enlarge the range of the variables to include absolutely everything. So the proponent of the extreme permissive view will have no trouble reconciling what he says with commonsense platitudes, or with what is said in history books and scientific texts.

A common response to Goodman's "grue" and "bleen" is to say that these are really disjunctive predicates, because definable in terms of "green" and "blue" and a date, and for that reason do not stand for genuine properties, or at any rate projectible ones. The standard Goodmanian response to this is to say that "green" and "blue" are equally definable in terms of "grue" and "bleen" and a date, and that the situation is therefore symmetrical. I have elsewhere given reasons for holding that the standard Goodmanian response is not satisfactory, but I do not want to go into that now.[18] I want rather to point out that there is a parallel set of responses to the issue about the status of the shadow entities vis à vis the ordinary ones. Parallel to the claim that "grue" is disjunctive because defined in terms of "green" and "blue," etc., will be the claim that the shadow entities have at best a derivative status because they can only be characterized by reference to the ordinary ones. For one thing, the characterization relies on the idea of a plurality of different possible worlds, and (it will be said) it is differences in the way ordinary things and instantiations of ordinary properties are distributed in the different worlds that make them different. Parallel to the Goodmanian response will be the claim that it is only from our point of view that the ordinary properties have a privileged status. From the point of view of the shadow people, supposing them to exist, we and our "ordinary" properties will be among the derivative ones, for it is in terms of properties and things belonging to *their* family of properties and things that they will give what will seem to them the basic descriptions of the different possible worlds.

Despite the availability of these replies, it still seems to me outrageous to maintain that, quantifying over absolutely everything, there are in the actual world nondenumerably many doppelgängers of all the ordinary objects plus nondenumerably many instantiations of every individual concept, and that *sub specie aeternitatis* the entities we recognize in our ordinary and scientific dealings with the world do not have a special status. So what other views are available?

One might hold that the shadow entities do exist, but that they have some deficiency which warrants stigmatizing them as in some sense nongenuine. If this view is to have any advantage over the extreme permissive view, it ought at least to deny that the shadows of persons are themselves persons possessed of psychological, or mental, properties. What suggested earlier that these shadows would be persons possessed of mental properties was the idea that they would have properties that are causally isomorphic with the mental properties of persons. We could justify denying that they are persons possessed of mental properties by holding that the deficiency of shadow entities generally is one having to do with causality. I will call this the moderate permissive view; this allows that there are the shadow objects and properties, but holds that despite the lawlike

---

[18] See Essay 4.

uniformities holding among the instantiations of their properties, they are totally devoid of causal efficacy.

It is a consequence of this view that there cannot be a reductive analysis of causality in terms of lawlike uniformities, or in terms of counterfactuals. To see more fully what this involves, suppose (contrary to fact) that it were possible to write out a complete theory about what I am calling "ordinary" properties and objects, where these include all of the properties and things that will be recognized "in the limit" by ideal science. The ideal theory tells us not only what uniformities hold in the actual world but also which ones hold in all possible worlds or (if that is too much) in all possible worlds similar enough to ours to count as nomologically possible. Suppose now that we form the Ramsey sentence of this theory, in such a way that the only constants remaining in the sentence, aside from logical ones, are terms for spatiotemporal properties and relations. Taking the variables in this sentence to range over "thin" properties and things, it will be made true by the ordinary properties and things, but it will also be made true by the shadow properties and things belonging to each of nondenumerably many shadow families. If, indeed, the properties and things belonging to those shadow families are devoid of causal efficacy, what is asserted by the Ramsey sentence of the theory cannot imply anything about causality. But presumably what is asserted by the sentence would include everything, in the way of relations between properties, that might be thought to be constitutive of causality by any reductive account. It follows that on the moderate permissive view no reductive account of causality can be correct.

If lawlike and counterfactual connections are not sufficient for causality, what more is needed? I think that it is not possible to say what more is needed without referring to the particular properties that are intuitively the "genuine ones," i.e., what I have been referring to as the ordinary ones. *These* properties having certain lawlike connections with each other is sufficient for there being certain causal facts; but this is because these are the properties they are, and not because it is true generally of thin properties that their having lawlike or counterfactual connections is sufficient for the existence of causal facts. The suggestion is that just as it is, or so I have argued elsewhere, essential to the ordinary properties that they have certain causal powers, it is essential to causality that it governs *these* properties. The connection between causality and these properties is an internal one. Hilary Putnam has suggested that our natural kind concepts are in a way indexical; to be gold is to have the underlying structure that explains the phenomenal features of *these* things, or of the things *around here* that have these phenomenal features.[19] Perhaps the notion of causality is indexical in a similar way – causality is what underlies the lawlike connections that hold between *these* properties, and any other properties that stand in lawlike connections with them. On this view the introduction or explanation of the notion of causality must involve an ostensive component, a reference to certain paradigms.

On the moderate permissive view, then, the shadow objects and properties exist, but lack something that the ordinary objects and properties have, something the lack of which makes the term "shadow" appropriate for them. What they lack is causal efficacy. And the notion of causality is indexical in the way just suggested.

This suggests a way of formulating the restrictive view. The restrictive view agrees with the modestly permissive view in holding the notion of causality to be indexical, but extends this attribution of indexicality to the notion of an individual substance, or continuant, and to the notion of a property of an individual substance. We ourselves, and the things we have certain kinds of epistemic access to, will be the paradigms of individual substances, and the properties of ourselves and the things to which we have epistemic access will be paradigms of genuine properties. Other putative substances and properties will be real just in case they are related in certain ways to these paradigms.

On one way of construing this view it is very little different from the moderate permissive view. This will be so if the view is construed as saying that there do exist entities corresponding to all of the functions from possible worlds to collections of spacetime points, and from possible worlds to extensions within worlds, but that only some of these entities, namely those endowed with causal efficacy, count as individual substances or properties of individual substances. If one allows that the shadows exist, and that ordinary things and properties are entities otherwise like them which are blessed with causal efficacy, then there seems hardly more than a verbal difference between saying, on the one hand, that the lack of causal efficacy on the part of the shadows makes them very anemic substances and properties, and saying, on the other hand, that it disqualifies them from counting as substances and properties at all. It seems better to construe the restrictive view as denying the very

---

[19] See his "The Meaning of 'Meaning,'" in his *Mind, Language and Reality: Philosophical Papers*, vol. II (Cambridge, 1975).

existence of the shadow objects. But I do not think that the proponent of the restrictive view need be taken to deny that there are set-theoretical entities corresponding to the various functions from possible worlds to collections of spacetime points or sets thereof. For example, there is no need for him to deny qua proponent of the restrictive view that corresponding to a function from possible worlds to extensions there is the set of all the actual or possible entities belonging to any of these extensions, and that corresponding to a function from possible worlds to collections of spacetime points there is a set of collections of spacetime points. What he will deny is that genuine substances and properties are just a subset of these set-theoretical entities, namely those that are somehow endowed with causal efficacy. There is, he will maintain, a categorical difference between genuine substances and properties and set-theoretical entities of these sorts – and most of these set-theoretical entities, and their corresponding functions, have no substances or properties corresponding to them.

To be defensible, the restrictive view must be somewhat more permissive than some philosophers would like. It must allow enough unrecognized entities to give scope for conventional decisions about how to cut up the world, and enough to explain indeterminacy of truth value of identity statements in terms of vagueness and indeterminacy of reference. It must also allow for the entities that would be recognized by possible creatures having quality spaces, and natural ways of "going on," different from our own. But here I have in mind creatures we can actually imagine discovering and learning about – not the shadow persons. To the latter, and all the shadow entities, the restrictive view denies existence.

Unlike the modestly permissive view, the restrictive view can allow that statements of lawlike or counterfactual connections between property instantiations can entail statements of causality, for unlike that account it does not admit that there are causally inefficacious shadow properties which stand in lawlike and counterfactual relations to one another. But unlike the extreme permissive view, it is barred from holding that such entailments hold because causality is reductively analyzable in terms of regularities and counterfactuals. If it employs the notion of causality in an essential way in its characterization of what constitutes a genuine property, it cannot claim that causal claims simply reduce to regularity or counterfactual claims.

Before we consider the question of how we are to decide between these views, it will be instructive to consider what they have in common. Let us return to the extreme permissive view. This admits all of the putative shadow entities as genuine, and accords them the same metaphysical status as ordinary individual substances and properties thereof. But it allows that for ordinary purposes we exclude them from the range of our variables of quantification – adding, even-handedly, that for ordinary purposes the shadow people exclude us from the range of *their* variables of quantification. But what determines which things are admitted to the range of these variables? If we speak, as I have done, of the shadow entities as falling into "families," and if we speak of ordinary things and properties as forming one family, then we might begin our answer by saying that for any speaker or thinker the range of the variables is either all of the things belonging to the same family with it or some contextually determined subclass of those things. But this, of course, raised the question: What determines whether properties and things belong to the same family? A special case of this is the question of what determines whether properties and things are "ordinary" properties and things, i.e., belong to the same family with us.

This, clearly, is a question that needs answering on all three of the views I have sketched. On the extreme permissive view we need an answer to it for the reason already indicated, namely in order to say what things are admitted to the range of variables of quantification. On the moderate permissive view we need to answer it in order to say which the things are that have genuine causal efficacy. On the restrictive view we need to answer it in order to say what is required for the existence of genuine substances and properties. I think that all three views can answer it on pretty much the same lines, and that what these answers have in common is an important part of the truth in causal accounts of the identity conditions for properties and substances, and in causal accounts of mind, perception, reference, and knowledge. For the notion of causality plays an important role throughout.

This common answer is really implicit in what I said in the first part of this essay. The entities that are candidates for belonging to the range of our variables are, to begin with, we ourselves, the things in our environment to which we have our most direct epistemic access, and the properties of ourselves and those things to which we have direct epistemic access. Our direct epistemic access to these things (via perception, introspection, etc.) of course brings with it direct semantic access to them; they are the things we can refer to demonstratively, or by means of descriptions whose references are fixed demonstratively. These will be, for us, the paradigmatically genuine things. That we have direct epistemic and semantic access to these things of course involves there being a mesh between their causal nature and ours. Our "nature" here includes our "quality space" (*à la* Quine), whatever we bring to the world (*à la* Kant) in the way of innate conceptual structure, and our propensity to "go on" in certain ways (*à la* Wittgenstein) in applying language and concepts to the world. The properties and things these will lead us to recognize and quantify over will be ones that stand in certain sorts of causal and explanatory connections to the paradigmatically genuine ones.

On the extreme permissive view there will be sets of things and properties that are causally related to the shadow people in the same way that the ordinary things and properties are related to us, and it is these sorts of causal relations and features that group "thin" properties and things into families, one of which is the family of ordinary entities. On the moderate permissive view it is the presence of these causal relations and features that distinguishes the ordinary things and properties from the causally anemic shadows. On the restrictive view it is the presence of these causal relations and features that constitutes the very existence of substances and properties.[20]

---

[20] It is natural to suppose that there are possible worlds (call them alien worlds) in which there are instantiated properties (call them alien properties) that are not instantiated in the actual world and could not enter into causal relations with any of the actual world properties which the restrictive view counts as genuine. For example, it is natural for a materialist to think that while there are no Cartesian minds in this world, there are possible worlds in which such minds do exist, and that such worlds are alien in the above sense. What does the restrictive view say about such alleged possibilities? (I am grateful to Mark Richard for forcing me to consider this question.)

One might suppose that there are two sorts of alien worlds – those (fully alien worlds) in which only alien properties are instantiated, and those (partially alien worlds) in which are instantiated both some alien properties and some actual world properties. Clearly the restrictive theorist must deny that there are partially alien worlds; if in the actual world a putative property fails to be genuine because of a lack of causal relations to the paradigm genuine properties, the same should be true of any other possible world in which the paradigms (or properties that are genuine in virtue of their causal relations to the paradigms) are instantiated. And if the restrictive theorist allows the possibility of totally alien worlds, he will be left with no way of making a distinction in such worlds between genuine properties (and things) and mere "shadows" of these. I think he should deny that there are such worlds.

This does not mean that a restrictive theorist who is a materialist cannot allow that it is in some sense possible that there should be, or should have been, Cartesian minds. He might think that the nonphysical states of Cartesian minds are not, after all, alien properties; that while they are in fact not instantiated in the actual world, they could be, and that if they were their instantiations would stand in determinate sorts of causal relations to instantiations of the ordinary properties that are in fact instantiated. Alternatively, his claim that Cartesian minds are possible might express some sort of epistemic possibility, or (what may or may not come to the same thing) the claim that there is nothing *conceptually* amiss with the idea that there are Cartesian minds.

Which view is right? I have already expressed my preference for the restrictive view. But as I have already indicated, proponents of the other views can easily enough reconcile their claims with commonsense and scientific assertions about what does and does not exist, by maintaining that in these assertions the range of the variables of quantification is implicitly restricted. So if someone does not find the permissive view (extreme or moderate) absurd on the face of it, it is not easy to see how one could show her that it is. It may be thought that the permissive view offends against Occam's razor. But it does not offend against this principle qua scientific methodological principle; one would offend against that principle only if one postulated more ordinary entities, more entities belonging to *our* family, than are needed for explanatory purposes, and the proponent of the permissive view does not do that. Perhaps the principle offended against is just: Don't postulate entities you have no reason to postulate. But the proponent of the permissive view can offer us reasons for admitting the shadows into his ontology. He can cite, for what they are worth, the considerations in favor of the permissive view mentioned earlier. He can also say that if we have possibilia anyhow, it is metaphysical excess to suppose that in addition to sets of possibilia we have properties – and that gives us a reason for reducing properties to sets of possibilia, which gives us all of the shadow properties (and lots of others besides). And sets of spacetime points seem to give us the shadow objects. This seems to get us at least to the moderate permissive view; and if we add a reductionist account of causality it gets us to the extreme permissive view. I would prefer to run the argument backwards – to say that since it is absurd to claim that there are the shadow persons and things, the reductionist view of causality must be false; and that since the moderate permissive view is absurd as well, the reduction of properties to sets of possibilia is mistaken as well. But I do not know how to defend this preference for running the argument the one way rather than the other.[21]

I would be reluctant, in any case, to rest my opposition to the permissive view on an appeal to the principle that we should not postulate entities we have no reason to postulate. For I want to *deny* the existence of the shadow entities, and not merely to refrain from affirming their existence – and there is no acceptable principle that

[21] Christopher Hill has impressed on me that the relevant versions of Occam's razor are not limited to those just considered. My hunch is that any version of the principle that can be used to support the restrictive view will be as much in need of support as the restrictive view itself; but I cannot claim to have shown that here.

says that one is entitled to deny the existence of so-and-so's if one has no reason to affirm their existence. And, of course, we cannot say of the shadows, as we can say of ghosts and phlogiston, that if they did exist then there would be evidence of their existence which, in fact, there is not; our experience of the world is just as we should expect it to be if there were the shadow entities. The question whether they exist cannot be an empirical one which is decided negatively by the observed facts, nor an empirical one on which the evidence is not yet in.

It also does not seem acceptable to say that the shadows may or may not exist, and that there is no way of telling whether they do or not. If it were sensible to say that, it would be equally sensible to say that it may be that some of the families of shadow entities exist and others do not, and that there is no way of telling which do and which do not. And the latter does not seem sensible. The same goes for the "fishy" entities discussed earlier in this paper – putative properties such as grueness, and putative things such as klables, contacti-persons, and the like. If statements like "Klables exist" have truth conditions, these must somehow be bestowed on them by our semantic intentions. It does not seem credible that our semantic intentions may have bestowed truth conditions that make "Klables exist" true and "Contacti-persons exist" false, or vice versa, but in such a way that we have no way of telling that this is the case. And no more does it seem credible that our semantic intentions have bestowed truth conditions that make all such statements true, or all of them false, in such a way that we have no way of telling which is the case.

It appears that if the question whether these things exist has an answer, it ought to be decidable a priori what that answer is. I would like to have a decisive a priori proof of the restrictive view, but I do not have one. And, as I have thought about the matter, I have become increasingly skeptical as to whether the question is decidable a priori, and so whether it does have an answer. If it does not, I think, this can only be because of something like vagueness in our concepts, perhaps in concepts like that of a property, perhaps in the concept of existence itself. Fortunately, this vagueness, if such there is, does not threaten the determinacy of existence questions that arise outside of philosophy. When I began writing this essay I thought that I had to defend the restrictive view in order to defend claims, close to my heart, about the involvement of causality in the identity conditions for properties and substances. But as I have indicated, I think that the core of what I want to say about this is compatible with both the moderate and the extreme versions of the permissive view, and so with the view that it is indeterminate which of these views is correct. So my hankering for a knockdown proof of the restrictive view has abated. Still, I would be grateful if someone would give me one.[22]

[22] I am grateful to Carl Ginet, Phil Gasper, Christopher Hill, Jill Raitt, Mark Richard, and Robert Stalnaker, and to audiences at Cornell University, Williams College, Reed College, Yale University, and North Carolina State University, for comments on earlier versions of this essay.

17
Self and substance

I

Nowadays the question whether the self is a substance, and whether the identity over time of a person requires the identity of a substance, has a musty smell to it. We recognize it as a question that played a central role in the intriguing discussions of personal identity in Locke, Butler, Hume, and Reid; but it has not been the central question in contemporary discussions of personal identity, and in most such discussions it is simply not addressed.

Yet the question does have echoes in contemporary discussions. Contemporary "reductionists" about personal identity hark back to Locke and Hume, and contemporary antireductionists hark back to Butler and Reid. As I shall try to show, some of the intuitions of the antireductionists – e.g., their denial that the person who comes out at one end of a "teleportation" process can be the same as the person who went in at the other end – can be seen as expressions of the idea that in some good sense of "individual substance," a person must be an individual substance. And such a view seems at odds with the view of a reductionist like Derek Parfit, who says that while we can allow that a person is a "subject" of experiences, since this is "the way we talk," it is nevertheless true that facts about persons and their experiences admit of an impersonal description that reveals them to be nothing over and above facts about the relations of experiences to one another and to bodies.[1]

There is always a danger that framing a current philosophical issue in traditional metaphysical terms – here, in terms of the concepts of substance, inherence, etc. – will result in obfuscation rather than clarification. But that is a risk I shall take. I shall try to show that it is possible to combine some of the central intuitions that go with the claim that the self is a substance with some, although certainly not all, of the intuitions that go with reductionist views about personal

---

[1] See Parfit 1984, pp. 223, 225, 226, 251, 341.

identity. Among other things, I shall be developing the view, which I have presented elsewhere, that the psychological continuity view of personal identity, the contemporary heir to Locke's memory theory, can usefully be seen as complementary to – the "reverse side of the coin of" – a functionalist view about the nature of mental states. And I shall be arguing that there is a version of this view that is compatible with much of what Peter Unger argues on behalf of a "physical" view of personal identity in his *Identity, Consciousness and Value*, a work I place (somewhat hesitantly) in the Butler–Reid tradition.

Owing in large part to the work of Derek Parfit, the emphasis in recent literature on personal identity has shifted somewhat from the metaphysical issue of what constitutes such identity to questions about its importance – in particular, the question of whether it is identity "as such" that matters in "survival." My primary concern here will be with the metaphysical issue, not the issue of importance. But at the end I shall briefly discuss the relation between these.

II

As is well known, Locke denied that the identity of a person over an interval of time requires that it be one and the same substance that thinks "in" the person throughout that interval. As is also well known, Hume made the more radical denial that there is any substance at all involved in the existence of a person or self, unless our "perceptions" themselves count as substances.

Here Locke and Hume can be pitted against Joseph Butler and Thomas Reid, both of whom insisted that a self or person *is* a substance and that the identity over an interval of time of a self just *is* the identity over that interval of the substance the person is. Butler and Reid were dualists, and took it for granted that the substance involved in personal identity is an immaterial one. Locke and Hume were committed to denying that a self or person is an immaterial substance. But they were equally committed to denying that it is a material substance. Hume, of course, rejected the notion of substance altogether. And Locke says that those "who place Thought in a purely material, animal Constitution, void of an immaterial Substance" plainly "conceive personal Identity preserved in something else than Identity of Substance; as animal Identity is preserved in Identity of Life, and not of Substance" (Locke 1975, p. 337).

There is, as Butler and Reid both pointed out, a seeming contradiction involved in Locke's position. He defines "person" as meaning "a thinking intelligent Being, that has reason and reflection, and can consider it self as it self, the same thinking thing in different times and places" (p. 335). This seems to imply that a person is a subject of a thought, and thereby a thinking substance, yet Locke denies the evident consequence of this, that the identity of a person requires the identity of a thinking substance.

One might suggest, as I have done elsewhere[2], that Locke can be extricated from this apparent contradiction if we distinguish, as he (and Butler) did not, between two different senses of "substance". Call these the "subject of properties sense" (elsewhere I have called this the "Aristotelian sense") and the "parcel of stuff sense." What Locke's definition of "person" commits him to is that persons are substances in the subject of properties sense. This is compatible with the denial that a person is a substance in the parcel of stuff sense, and with the claim that one and the same person can at different times be constituted by different substances, in the latter sense.[3] Admittedly, this works better for the denial that a person is a material substance than for the denial that a person is an immaterial substance. Locke says that "those, who place thinking in an immaterial Substance only ... must show why personal Identity cannot be preserved in the change of immaterial Substance, or variety of particular immaterial Substance, as well as animal Identity is preserved in the change of material Substances ..." (p. 337). To suppose that "substance" here means "parcel of stuff" is to invoke the notion immaterial stuff – which sounds disturbingly like immaterial matter. Yet *something* like that seems to be going on in Locke, given the comparison he is making between change of immaterial substance and change of material substance.

Hume presumably could have agreed with the Lockean definition of person as "a thinking, intelligent Being ... etc." So why isn't he committed to persons being substances in the subject of properties sense? Here the obvious reply is that Hume thinks that a person's having a certain thought just consists in a certain bundle of perceptions having a perception of a certain sort as one of its members. So merely assenting to the truth of subject-predicate propositions about persons should not by itself commit one to persons being substances in the subject of properties sense. Following a suggestion of Paul

---

[2] See my 1984.
[3] A parcel of stuff can be thought of as a "quantity" of stuff in Helen Cartwright's sense (see her 1970) that at no time is a scattered object. It must be composed of the same stuff at every moment of its existence. This is what Locke seems to take a "body" to be in Essay, II. xxvii. 3.

Grice, in his classic 1941 paper on personal identity, let us say that a self is a substance in the subject of properties sense if and only if (1) statements of the form "S thinks, experiences, etc. such and such" are sometimes true, and (2) such statements are not analyzable in a certain way.[4] Bundle theorists *à la* Hume deny (2). The sort of analysis that would make (2) false would be one whose *analysans* does not refer to or quantify over persons or subjects of mental properties.

The view that statements about persons are analyzable in a way that relieves us of commitment to mental subjects as constituents of the world seems at least akin to the "reductionist" view, championed by Derek Parfit and others, that personal identity is analyzable in terms of "psychological continuity and connectedness." And some proponents of the latter view have said things that seem at least in the spirit of the Humean denial that selves are substances. Parfit says that "because we are not separately existing entities, we could fully describe our thoughts without claiming that they have thinkers" (Parfit 1984, p. 225). And he repeatedly says that it is "because of the way we talk" that it is true that persons are subjects. This strongly suggests that while condition (1) of the Gricean rendering of "Selves are substances" is satisfied, condition (2) is not.

III

Critics of reductionist views of personal identity are especially hostile to versions of reductionism that maintain that such imagined procedures as the teleportation of science fiction, and what I have called the "brain state transfer (BST) procedure," whereby the states of one brain are imposed on another without any transfer of matter, can be person-preserving.[5] To say that such a procedure is person-preserving means that a person A existing at time t_1 and a person B existing at a later time t_2 can be one and the same despite having different bodies and different brains, the identity holding in virtue of the mental states of A at t_1 and those of B at t_2 being linked by a chain of mental states exhibiting a certain sort of continuity and connectedness, which the procedure is sufficient to bring about.

The case against such versions of reductionism often rests on intuitions about what Parfit calls the "branch-line" case. In the branch-

---

[4] See Grice 1941. Grice expresses (2) by saying that the self is not a logical construction.

[5] See my 1984, sect. 10.

line case, two later persons stand in relations of psychological continuity and connectedness (psychological C&C) to one earlier person;
in the case of one of these the body and brain are the same as those
of the earlier person, and the chain of psychological C&C is carried
in the normal way by physical processes in that body and brain,
while in the case of the other the psychological C&C is due to an
episode of teleportation or BST transfer. There are widespread intuitions that favor the former of these – the one having normal physical continuity with the original person – as being the original person.
And these same intuitions are often seen as favoring the view that
even where there is only one later person whose states are psychologically C&C with the states of an earlier one, the holding of the
relationship of psychological C&C is not sufficient for identity.[6]

One might think of such intuitions as rejecting one sort of reductionism, one that says that personal identity consists in psychological C&C, for another, one that says that it consists in physical
continuity of a certain sort. But often those who are moved by such
intuitions think of themselves as opposing reductionism generally.
Such thinkers are in the tradition of Butler and Reid. And a natural
way to express their view is by saying that persons have to be individual substances of a certain kind, and that if the conditions of
personal identity were as the psychological C&C account claims – if
they allowed teleportation and the BST-procedure to be person-
preserving – persons could not be substances. In the branch-line case
there is, intuitively, "substantial unity" between one of the candidates and the original person, and not between the other candidate
and the original person.

What notion of substance is at work here? Proponents of the
psychological C&C view can assent to the truism that persons are
subjects of thought and experience; they think of themselves as giving
the transtemporal identity conditions for such subjects. Are they
committed to the denial that selves are substances in the Gricean
version of the subject of properties sense, because they hold judgments
of personal identity to be analyzable in a certain way? But while some
proponents of the psychological C&C view may be committed to the
view that judgments about persons have an analysis of the sort ruled

[6] One way in which psychological continuity theorists attempt to handle such cases is
by holding a "closest continuer view" which allows physical continuity to be the tie-
breaker in cases in which two or more later persons are competitors for being identical with
one earlier person, both being related to it to an equal degree by psychological C&C, but
holds personal identity to consist in psychological C&C in cases where there is no such
competition. See Nozick 1981, ch. 1.

out by condition (2) of the Gricean rendering of "Selves are substances," others are not. Presumably philosophers who hold that the truth conditions for judgments of personal identity can be framed in terms of the notion of *physical* continuity are not thereby committed to the denial that (2) is satisfied; so it is far from clear that those who hold that these truth conditions can be framed in terms of psychological C&C are committed to this denial, even if they think that these truth conditions allow teleportation and the like to be person-preserving.

Could the notion of substance here be the parcel of stuff notion? It is true that in some versions of the branch-line example the preferred candidate for being the continuation of the original person is one that is composed of the same matter of the original person. But this will not in general be true. Everyone agrees that in normal, paradigmatic cases of persistence of persons over time there is constant interchange of matter with the environment. So the view cannot be that it is a requirement of personal identity that a person always be composed of the same parcel of matter. It could of course be held that it is a requirement of personal identity that there be a certain sort of continuity of material composition – one that requires that over very brief intervals the material composition remains nearly the same. But this would not of course imply that a person *is* a substance in the parcel of matter sense.

So proponents of the psychological C&C view of personal identity are not committed to the denial that selves are substances in the logical subject sense. And while they are committed to the denial that selves are substances in the parcel of matter sense, that is a denial they share with their opponents. So in what sense is it the latter, rather than the former, who are the proponents of the substantiality of the self?

IV

There is a strand in the traditional conception of substance that until now I have not mentioned. Substances are ontologically *independent* in ways in which other entities are not. What metaphysicians call "modes" and "affections," and what all of us call states, are entities whose existence is logically parasitic, or as C. D. Broad put it "adjectival," on the entities of which they are modes, affections, or states; their existence just consists in certain things being modified, affected, or qualified in certain ways. Entities on which other entities are dependent in these ways, and which are not themselves dependent in such ways on other entities, are individual substances.[7]

The independence criterion of substantiality is closely related to the conception of individual substances as subjects of properties, if that is understood as including condition (2) of the Gricean rendering of that conception. Suppose that the only tenable notion of mental particulars, such as thoughts, sensations, etc., is one on which these are modes or affections of – on which their existence is adjectival on – minds or selves that "have" them. In that case minds or selves will be independent relative to such mental particulars, and on that account will qualify as substances. And by the same token, there will be no possibility of a reductive analysis of judgments ascribing thoughts or experiences to minds or selves into judgments solely about mental particulars and their relations to one another – and no possibility of a reduction of facts about minds or selves to facts about mental particulars. So minds and selves will count as substances by the Gricean criteria.

But I think that there is another way in which independence can function as a criterion of substantiality. As many have noted, it is a feature of the "continuants" that are paradigm individual substances that their persistence through time involves there being relations of causal and counterfactual dependence of their properties at later times on their properties at earlier times.[8] Other things equal, if this piece of wax had not had the shape it had an hour ago, it would not have the shape it has now; and it is, in part, *because* it had that shape then that it has its present shape now. This will be true if the shapes are the same. But it may also be true even if the shapes are different; the piece of wax has a certain shape now because it had a certain other shape an hour ago and has been sitting in the sun for the last hour. (Of course, if the wax is left in the sun too long, the contribution of its earlier shape to its later shape may become negligible.) The causation involved here is largely what W. E. Johnson called

---

[7] The idea is not that substances can exist without having any states or affections at all, but that the existence of a substance does not require the existence of any particular state or affection. By contrast, each state or affection depends for its existence on the particular substance of which it is a state or affection.

But suppose that it is essential to substance *S* that it have properties of kind *K*: e.g., it is essential to a person that it have certain psychological capacities. Then there will be, corresponding to such a substance, the state-like entity: *S*'s having properties of kind *K*. *S* will depend for its existence on the existence of that entity. The independence claim about substances must be qualified to allow for this sort of dependence, on what might be called higher-order states. (Here I am indebted to Harold Langsam.)

[8] See Essay 11.

"immanent" causation: causation that is internal to the thing's career, as contrasted with the "transeunt" causation involved in the action of one thing on another.[9] It is not always true that the resemblance between the later and earlier stages of a thing is due to immanent causation. If I take a watch to a jeweler to be repaired, its post-repair similarity to its pre-damage state is due in part to the intervention of the jeweler, which involves transeunt causation. But by and large, and especially in the case of those things (plants and animals) that are often taken as the paradigm individual substances, it is by immanent causation that things retain their properties over time and undergo those changes that are characteristic of the kinds of things they are. In organisms, we now know, this immanent causation takes place in accordance with genetic "instructions" encoded in DNA molecules. (At the molecular and submolecular levels much of the causation involved here will of course be transeunt; it is only relative to the career of the organism as a whole that it is to be classified as immanent.)

We might sum all this up by saying that individual substances are autonomous self-perpetuators. Or, better, *relatively* autonomous self-perpetuators. Some things – e.g., images on movie screens – appear to be autonomous self-perpetuators when they are not; and to these we deny the status of being individual substances. In the case of inanimate objects like rocks, this self-perpetuation is a pretty boring affair – simply a matter of retaining the same properties over time, in the absence of influence of other things. In the case of organisms, and minds, it is a much more dynamic affair. Here there are characteristic kinds of change which something must undergo, or be apt to undergo, if it is to be a thing of the sort in question. Some of these are triggered by impacts of the environment, and involve transeunt causation. But there will always be a large element of immanent causation. And it is largly immanent causation which is responsible for the thing's continuing to exist as a thing of a certain kind, one embodying certain principles of change and unchange.

The existence of things that are autonomous self-perpetuators is not, of course, totally independent of other things. Organisms are sustained by nutrition derived from their environments, and even nonorganic things depend for their continued existence on things and conditions that lie outside their boundaries. But things can be said to be independent to the extent that the causation involved in their continued existence is immanent causation. The extent to which this

---

[9] See Johnson, 1964.

is so varies from one sort of thing to another. At one extreme we have organisms, at the other we have images on movie screens. Among things between these extremes, self-regulating and self-repairing mechanisms have it to a greater extent than machines that need constant repair through human intervention. It seems plausible that it is to the extent that something is viewed as an autonomous self-perpetuator that we find it natural to regard it as an individual substance. It is a view that goes back to Aristotle that organisms have an edge over artifacts with respect to substantiality. It is also plausible to suppose that persons (or selves) have a high degree of this sort of independence – at least as high as that of organisms generally.[10] And my suggestion is that this is a source of the view that persons are substances in a way they could not be if their identity conditions allowed teleportation and the BST-procedure to be person-preserving.

Here it is instructive to consider a thought experiment of Peter Unger's.[11] Unger describes a scenario, or rather a series of scenarios, in which a brain is "superfrozen," all of its matter is rapidly replaced in a way that preserves structure, and the resulting brain is then "superthawed," the result being a person psychologically indistinguishable from the owner of the original brain prior to the super-freezing. In one scenario, the replacement of the brain matter takes place in four stages, each involving the replacement of one quarter of the brain with an exactly similar chunk of brain matter. In another, the replacement has as many stages as there are atoms in the brain, and each stage involves the replacement of one atom. In both cases the whole process takes only a tenth of a second. Unger thinks that in the first case the person does not survive the procedure, while in the second case the person does survive. I think this is a natural view to take about these cases. And I think we can see it as a special case of

---

[10] It should be noted, however, that the independence of persons, qua subjects of mental states, is compromised in one way in which that of other organisms is not. Assuming an "externalist" view about mental content, the content of a person's mental states is determined in part by her causal relations to things in her environment and, if Tyler Burge is right, by what linguistic practices exist in communities to which she belongs. To the extent that personal identity consists in a psychological continuity that involves the content of mental states, it requires a certain amount of constancy in the external factors that enter into the determination of such content. This is a further reason, beyond the dependence of persons, qua biological organisms, on an appropriate environment, for qualifying the term "autonomous self-perpetuator" with the team "relatively." The independence of persons is compromised still further if, as Robert Wilson maintains in a recent paper (Wilson 1994), much of the computation involved in a person's mental life is "wide" rather than "narrow," i.e., involves systems lying outside the person's boundary.

[11] See his 1990, pp. 123–125. I have slightly altered the details of his examples.

the intuition that a person should be an autonomous self-perpetuator whose characteristic continuity over time is carried by immanent causation.

Both of Unger's procedures are of course radically invasive,
involving a large dose of transeunt causation. But there is an
important difference. In the first case, where the replacement takes
place in four stages, it is essential to the success of the procedure
that the replacement parts have the right psychologically relevant
structure, namely that of the parts they replace. Miracles aside,
this would require that the state of the original brain be somehow
recorded, this providing a "blueprint" that can be used to
construct replacement parts having the right structure. This means
that if we regard the procedure as person-preserving, we will have
to say that the process whereby the psychological traits of the
person are "perpetuated" is not one of *self*-perpetuation, and not
one involving only immanent causation – it involves a large
measure of transeunt causation, namely that involved in the
recording and in the manufacture of duplicates on the basis of the
recording.[12] By contrast, in the second procedure the replacement
parts – the individual atoms – have no psychologically relevant
structure.[13] No recording of psychologically relevant states need
take place, and no construction of psychological duplicates need
be involved. Here there seems much less reason to deny that the
causation by which the psychological traits of the person are
perpetuated is immanent causation.

The cases of teleportation and the BST-procedure resemble the
first of Unger's replacement scenarios. In these it seems very natural
to say that the causation involved in the perpetuation of mental
states, and in bringing about psychological continuity over time, is
transeunt rather than immanent causation. And insofar as that is
true we cannot count these procedures as person-preserving without compromising the independence of persons, i.e., their status as
autonomous self-perpetuators. It is in that sense that the view that
such procedures can be person-preserving offends against the intuition that persons are individual substances.

---

[12] As Tamar Gendler pointed out to me, if brains naturally produced duplicates of their
quadrants, and then stored them like spare tires somewhere in the body, then replacing the
four quarters with *these* duplicates might seem more plausibly person-preserving.

[13] Of course, they have a structure that suits them to play various roles in the physical
realization of mental states. What I mean is that their structure encodes no information
about anyone's psychological makeup.

Of course, if we are willing to be flexible enough about what count as the boundaries of a person, we can say in all of these cases that the psychological trait perpetuation takes place by immanent causation. In Unger's replacement example, let the recording mechanism and the duplicate-making mechanisms count, temporarily, as part of the person. Do the same with the mechanisms involved in teleportation and the BST-procedure. But such gerrymandering is of course extremely unnatural. Moreover, it simply postpones the difficulty. For what explains how it is that a person at a certain time acquires these additional parts, and subsequently loses them? This – the person coming to be, and then ceasing to be, a certain sort of scattered object – can hardly be due to the operation of immanent causation! To say the least, the view of these procedures as person-preserving cannot be made to fit comfortably with the view of persons as beings that are essentially autonomous self-perpetuators.

One aspect of the view that substances are autonomous self-perpetuators finds expression in an extreme form in Leibniz's theory of monads, according to which the future states of an individual substance are "contained in" its current state, and flow from it in accordance with a "rule of development" that is internal to its nature. The picture of the later states of a thing "flowing from" its previous ones of course requires that its history be temporally continuous. And if the substance is thought of as being a material thing (as of course Leibniz's monads are not), it seems to require a spatiotemporally continuous history. This does not mean only that the chains of causality involved in the thing's history should be spatiotemporally continuous. That much would presumably be true of the chains of causality involved in teleportation. What it requires in addition is that the thing's history should occupy a spatiotemporally continuous series of spacetime locations, at each of which the thing exists with properties of the sort characteristic of that sort of thing, those properties "flowing" from the properties the thing has at earlier members of the series. And that will not be true in cases of teleportation and BST. On any such procedure, there will be short intervals in which there is nothing to the existence of the person but a series of radio signals, or a set of data stored in the memory of a computer. And of course it goes with this that, on the assumption that such procedures could be person-preserving, the causation involved in the perpetuation of the person's properties would in some cases have to be something other than immanent causation.

V

I have distinguished two parts of the claim that selves, or persons, must be such as to satisfy the "independence" criterion of substantiality. The first was that selves (persons, minds) are independent relative to mental particulars such as thoughts and sensations, the latter being "adjectival on" selves qua mental subjects. The second was that selves are (relatively) autonomous self-perpetuators. In this section I shall develop the first of these ideas further, relating it to certain general themes in the philosophy of mind, and in the next section I shall do the same with the second.[14]

That certain mental particulars are adjectival on mental subjects can be read off (almost) from the expressions that designate them. Assuming that "S" designates anything at all, what is designated by such a gerundial phrase as "S's feeling pain at t" or "S's seeing red at t" will be an entity that is adjectival on what "S" refers to. By itself, this cuts no metaphysical ice. Suppose for a moment that selves are what Hume said they are, bundles of perceptions, and that it is such bundles that personal pronouns and names of persons refer to. It will be true even on such a Humean account that "S's seeing red at t" designates an entity that is adjectival on what "S" refers to. What this entity will be, on a Humean account, is something like: *the inclusion of a perception of red in S (a certain bundle of perceptions)*. But while that entity is adjectival on S, its existence clearly involves the existence of mental particulars whose existence is not (on the Humean view) adjectival on S, or in any way logically dependent on it, namely the perceptions that make up the bundle. Perceiv*ings* are adjectival on perceivers, but perceptions, as Hume conceives them, are not.

So to support the claim that mental particulars are adjectival on mental subjects it is not enough to argue on grammatical grounds that certain mental particulars, those designated by gerundial phrases, are adjectival on subjects. For one thing, not all of the mental particulars we speak of in everyday life are so designated; it takes some rather ruthless regimentation to construe talk of pains, for example, in such a way that the only entities referred to or quantified over are mental subjects and states of mental subjects. For another, and this was the point of the preceding paragraph, it is compatible with a particular's being so designated that its existence involves the

---

[14] There are precursors of the discussions in these sections in, respectively, my 1985 and my 1984.

existence of mental particulars that do not have this adjectival status
– as is true on the Humean view.

In part, the case for the dependent status of mental particulars is
the case against the "act-object" conception of sensory states, and its
close relative, the sense-datum theory of perception. On such a view,
experiencing red and feeling pain (entities that are plainly adjectival)
are given the relational analysis their superficial grammar suggests:
being in such a state is held to consist in being related in a certain way
to (experiencing, or feeling) a mental particular of a certain kind (a
red image, or a pain). And the mental particular to which one is thus
related is not conceived of as being the sort of thing that could be
designated by a gerundial phrase, or by any other designator that
makes manifest that its existence is logically dependent on that of
anything else. As it happens, proponents of the act-object conception
and the sense-datum view have typically thought that these particulars *do* have a logically dependent status – that their *esse* is *percipi*. It
is one of the embarrassments of their view that they have no satisfactory account to give of this dependence – it is not the dependence
of affections or states on their subjects, and it is not clear what else it
can be. No doubt this is one source of bundle theories; having been
committed to such particulars by the act-object/sense-datum mode of
thinking, and being embarrassed by one's inability to explain their
dependence, one drops the dependence claim and attempts to regard
these mental particulars as the mental building blocks out of which
the mind is built. But there are well-known objections to the act-
object conception and the sense-datum theory, and I shall take it for
granted that this way of thinking is mistaken.

Even if one rejects the act-object conception and the sense-datum
theory, and resolutely resists the reification of mental images and the
like, one might think that a bundle theory is available to one. One
allows that sens*ings* and experienc*ings* are entities whose existence is
adjectival on mental subjects. But one thinks that a sensing or experiencing is just the inclusion of a sensation or experience in a bundle
of suitably interrelated mental particulars, and takes sensations and
experiences to be entities whose existence, unlike that of sense-data
and the like, is unproblematical.

It is of course controversial whether we can distinguish, in the
way this view must, between sensings and sensations, and between
experiencings and experiences. But I think that there is a case against
this view which does not depend at all on the claim that mental
particulars can be shown to have a dependent status because of the
gerund-like status of their designators (that claim being one that

some will see as claiming primacy of mental subjects on the basis of "the way we talk"). The more fundamental case rests on a consideration about the mental that has been put in a variety of different ways.

It is widely held, and not only by those who call themselves functionalists, that the identity of a mental state, e.g., its being a belief with a certain content, depends on what other states its subject has or is capable of having. Someone cannot have the belief that the cold war is over, or that the United States is in a state of political reaction, without believing and knowing a vast number of other things. The identity of beliefs is partly determined by their inferential connections – what beliefs they tend to give rise to when combined with other beliefs. And the identity of mental states generally is partly determined by the ways they combine with other states to influence behaviour (as when a set of beliefs and desires produce a piece of behaviour they jointly "rationalize") and to generate other mental states (as when new beliefs and desires arise from reasoning and deliberation). This remains true if we abstract from the status of these as "states," i.e., entities whose existence is adjectival, and speak of them simply as mental particulars. Insofar as these particulars have mental identities, as beliefs, desires, sensations, etc., of certain kinds, they are what they are in virtue of their membership in a system of states (or, if you like, particulars).

While in some cases having a certain mental state actually requires having others, as the belief that the cold war is over requires the belief that it occurred and the knowledge of what it was, this is not the most important point. The important point is that the existence of a mental state of a certain kind brings with it the truth of a vast number of conditional propositions about what other states would be apt to exist, or what behaviors would be apt to occur, were that state to be combined with – were it to be coinstantiated with – other states of certain kinds.

I think that the point can be clarified by reflecting on the notion of a "realization" of a mental state. Assuming physicalism and the supervenience of the mental on the physical, a mental state must be physically realized. Here I assume the functionalist view that the realization of a mental state is a physical state apt for playing a functional or causal role definitive of that mental state. So, it has been suggested, the firing of C-fibers may realize pain in human beings, because it is the neural state that has the characteristic causes and characteristic effects of pain. But, as I have insisted elsewhere, here it is essential to distinguish between the "core realization" and the "total realization" of a mental state.[15] C-fiber firing will not play the functional role of pain unless the brain as a whole is wired in such a way as to enable C-fiber firing to have those characteristic causes and effects. So C-fiber firing is at most the core realization of pain; the total realization will be C-fiber firing *plus* the brain's having that enabling wiring. In general, one can think of the total realization of a mental state as a realization of a sizable fragment of a psychology or psychological makeup, namely that part of it that serves as the categorical base – the truth-maker – for the conditional propositions that must be true of the core state if it is to be the core realization of that particular mental state. If we want to identify a token mental state with a physical state, and if we take it to belong to the essence of a token mental state that it is a state of a certain kind (a pain, or a hope or fear with a certain content), then we should identify it with the total realization rather than the core realization. If we are willing to give up the claim that the mental identity of a token mental state is essential to it, we can perhaps identify a token mental state with a core realization. But in either case, it will be essential to the existence of a mental state of a certain kind that the core realization of it be embedded in a total realization which includes a fragment of a psychological makeup.

It is obvious that there will be a good deal of overlap between the total realization of different mental states of the same individual. The realizations of both the belief that it is raining and the desire to keep dry will include the realization of the fragment of folk psychology which dictates that these states, in combination with others (e.g., certain beliefs about umbrellas), will lead to taking an umbrella if one goes outside. But to speak of what mental states will do when they are "combined" is just to speak of what they will do when they belong to the same subject – the same person, self, or mind. That notion, of what Bertrand Russell called the relation of co-personality and what we might call the psychological unity relation, will enter essentially into the characterization of any of the psychological makeup fragments that enter into the total realizations of mental states.

Now let us return to the status of mental particulars. Assuming physicalism, it is plausible to suppose that mental particulars are identical to physical particulars, these being token realizations of mental states and events. Insofar as they are token *states*, they already have an adjectival status. What in the first instance they are states of

---

[15] See Essay 11.

are brains and nervous systems, and their having this status doesn't automatically make them adjectival on persons or mental subjects. But if these token mental states are token total realizations, and if total realizations include fragments of psychological makeup whose charactization essentially involves the mental unity relation (the relation of *belonging to the same subject as*), then it seems that the existence of such a token state essentially involves its being the state of a subject having the psychological makeup in question.[16,17]

Here is it important to distinguish two components of reductionist views about the self. One is the claim that the unity relation between mental particulars – e.g., Russell's "co-personality" relation between experiences – can be characterized without explicit mention of any subject of which these particulars are affections, or on which their existence is adjectival. The other is the claim that the terms of the mental unity relation are entities that are not essentially affections of mental subjects – are entities that could, in principle, exist without

---

[16] Suppose that one believes in the possibility of person-preserving teleportation, or the like, and so denies that a person can be strictly identical to a particular brain or living human body. It might seem (as it does to Peter van Inwagen – see his 1997) that if one is also a materialist one is committed to the absurdity that when one has a mental state, that mental state is realized in two different things – the brain or living human body, and the person that is temporarily constituted by that brain or living human body. But that is a mistake. The most that is shared by the person and brain/body on this view is the core realization. If, as this view holds, the identity conditions for persons and brains/bodies are different, then it is only the former that are capable of instantiating total realizations of mental states – and it is only where there is a total realization of the state that the state is realized. That persons and their brains share core realizations but not total realizations seems to me very plausible – most of us do not think that a person is identical with his or her brain, and do not think that one's brain is one's mental twin. The view that persons and living human bodies, or persons and human beings, share core realizations but not total realizations is intuitively much less plausible, but certainly not incoherent.

[17] It might be held that the most that has been established here is that there is a conceptual dependence of the existence of mental particulars of given kinds on there being a mental subject, and that this does not establish, by itself, that there is any ontological dependence of the particulars that are of these kinds on a mental subject. If we identify the token mental states and events with token *core* realizations rather than with token *total* realizations, then we can say that their existence does not depend on there being any mental subjects, although their having the status of being token core realizations of particular sorts of mental states or events does depend on this. The cost of adopting this view is that it requires us to give up the plausible view that a mental particular that is in fact of a given mental kind is essentially of that kind. But some are already prepared to give this up on the basis of externalist considerations about mental content – what is in fact a token thought about water, so they say, is only contingently so, since that same token event might have occurred on Twin Earth and been about twater instead. Of course, even those who say this typically allow that a token thought is essentially a thought, even though it is only accidentally a thought about water; whereas to avoid the view that token thoughts are ontologically dependent on minds one must hold that token thoughts are only accidentally thoughts.

their existence constituting some mental subject's being in a certain mental state. The view I have sketched accepts the first claim but rejects the second. It accepts the first because it holds that the mental unity relation can be analyzed in functional terms, in a way that does not involve explicit reference to mental subjects. It rejects the second, because it holds that the terms of this relation are entities whose very existence involves, in the way indicated above, their being related, or being disposed to be related, to other such entities in certain ways, this in turn constituting their being states of a mental subject.

You cannot please everyone, and this view will not please advocates of an extreme version of the substance doctrine. It will not please those who think that the relation of subjects to affections is prior to the unity relation between affections, and that all that can be said about the latter is that it is the relation that holds between two affections when there is a single subject of which each of them is an affection. But I think that view is mistaken – and not just for the case of subjects and affections that are mental. Dents in fenders are a prime case of affections – entities whose existence is adjectival on other entities. But it is certainly not the case that nothing can be said about what it is for two dents to stand in the unity relation except that there is a single thing of which both are affections. Dents must be in surfaces, and to say what it is for there to be a surface on which there are two dents one must appeal to the unity relation whereby different bits of surface count as parts of the same surface. In general, as John Perry has brought out, the concept of a kind of objects essentially involves the unity relation whereby different events belong to the career of an object of that kind.[18]

VI

I turn now to the further development of the idea that individual substances are "relatively autonomous self-perpetuators," and its application to the case of personal identity. I want to show that this is compatible with, indeed finds natural expression in, a version of the psychological continuity view of personal identity. The version is closely connected to the functionalist conception of mental states; as I have put it elsewhere, it sees the psychological continuity that is

---

[18] See his 1975b. One example he uses is that of a baseball game; unless one knows how baseball events (pitches, hits, etc.) must be related in order to count as parts of the same game (as opposed, e.g., to being parts of different parts of a double-header), one doesn't have the concept of a baseball game.

constitutive of personal identity as the "playing out over time" of the functional natures of the various sorts of mental states.[19] Since psychological continuity views of personal identity are commonly seen as "reductionist" views, one might expect them to be more in a spirit of the bundle theory of the self than of the view that the self is a substance. But I will be suggesting that a psychological continuity account of the sort indicated is not only compatible with the view that the self is a substance, in the sense elucidated earlier, but gives that view its best chance of being true.

Consider someone who at a given time has a typical set of mental states. The states include not only conscious mental states, but also all of the beliefs, desires, preferences, intentions, hopes, anxieties, etc., that are present only in dispositional form. Suppose that a functionalist account of mental states is true. It is a commonplace that an important part of the functional role of a mental state is to give rise, in combination with other mental states, to yet other mental states. This happens when people reason and deliberate. But it also happens in ways that involve no exercise of agency. The "cognitive dynamics" and "cognitive kinematics" of mental states is such that over time they change in certain ways depending on what other mental states accompany them. An expectation of something as being in the remote future evolves into an expectation of something immediately forthcoming, given normal awareness of the passage of time. And one need not engage in any deliberate reasoning or deliberation for one's understanding of a situation to mature over time, and for separate items of knowledge or belief to merge into a unified conception. One important way in which mental states give rise to later mental states is by laying down memories of themselves. And of course certain sorts of mental states have natural upshots which in the normal course of events they ultimately give rise to, as intentions give rise to decisions and decisions give rise to the initiation of courses of action. So given our person who starts at a particular time with a certain set of mental states, we expect there to be a series of mental states which develops from that set of mental states and which exhibits a kind of continuity.

It is the grossest oversimplification to characterize this continuity, as is commonly done, by saying that later stages of the series will contain memories of the contents of earlier stages, that temporally proximate stages of the series will have significant similarities, and that there will be relations of causal and counterfactual dependence

[19] See my 1984.

of later stages of the series on earlier ones. All of that is true, but it vastly underdescribes what happens. A better description is that the later stages of the series are the consequences of the earlier stages in it playing the functional roles that are constitutive of their being the kinds of mental states they are.

That the mental histories of persons do in fact display this sort of continuity is not a controversial claim. But what the psychological continuity view says, in the version presented here, is that there being this sort of continuity in a series of mental states is constitutive of that series being the history of an individual person, or individual mental subject.

There is a threat of circularity here. Functional characterizations of mental states make free use of the notion of mental unity – of belonging to the same mental subject. What a functional definition tells us is that if a given state stands in this relation to other states of certain kinds (e.g., the belief that it is raining is accompanied by the desire to keep dry and certain beliefs about umbrellas), it will contribute to the production of another mental state (e.g., a decision to take an umbrella) which is related to it by this relation. Given this, it is *of course* the case that a series exhibiting the sort of functionally characterized continuity described above will be the mental career of an individual person or subject – for it follows from the description that successive stages of the series will be glued together by the mental unity relation. But that means that the account relies on the very notion, that of mental unity, which it purports to be defining.

The seeming circularity we confront here is akin to a seeming circularity that confronts functionalist accounts generally, and which is generally conceded to be avoidable. Functionalist accounts characterize particular kinds of mental states in terms of their relations to, among other things, other kinds of mental states. If all kinds of mental states are given such a characterization, the total set of characterizations will apparently display a kind of circularity – state A is characterized (in part) in terms of a relation to state B, which is characterized (in part) in terms of a relation of state C . . . which is characterized (in part) in terms of a relation to state A. The circle needn't even be very large; it belongs as much to the functional nature of a certain desire that in combination with a certain belief it gives rise to a certain action as it does to the functional nature of that belief that in combination with that desire it gives rise to that action. What all of this brings home is that functional definitions of mental states must be, in David Armstrong's words, "package deals"; and the Ramsey–Lewis technique for defining mental states is a way of giving such package-deal definitions which ensures that no vicious circularity is involved.[20] What we now see is that the "package" must include not only the individual mental states but also the mental unity relation. What we are talking about is a certain sort of relation between mental state instantiations, one such that token mental states related by that relation will tend to have certain joint consequences. This will be a multiply realizable functional relation, in just the way that the mental states are multiply realizable functional states. In a particular case it might be realized by the holding of certain neural connections between the neural states that realize particular mental states. But here we must remember the distinction drawn earlier between "core" and "total" realizations. What in the first instance the neural connections will connect are the neural states that are the core realizations of the mental states – e.g., of a particular belief and a particular desire. But these count as realizations of those mental states only because they are embedded in total realizations of them. And their being so embedded consists in the overall "wiring" of the brain being such that certain conditional propositions are true of states of these sorts. Part of what makes this true in a particular case might be that these two core states stand in a neural connection whereby they are apt to produce (in a relatively direct way) certain kinds of effects. But the holding of the neural connection will be only a core realization of the mental unity relation. The total realization will require this to be embedded in a realization of a fragment of a psychological makeup, one rich enough to make it true that the related states are indeed core realizations of mental states of the kinds in question, and that the consequence of their being so related is of the appropriate psychological kind.

Now the account I have suggested seems to make personal identity consist in the continuity of what Peter Unger has called "individual psychology." Unger denies that it does, holding that it consists instead in the continuity of what he calls "core psychology." Continuity with respect to core psychology, in turn, he holds to consist in a certain sort of physical continuity. And he represents his view as a physical, as opposed to psychological, view of personal identity, despite his holding that personal identity involves a kind of psychological continuity, namely continuity with respect to core psychology. Philosophers he regards as holding the psychological view he opposes include Derek Parfit, David Lewis, and myself.

Continuity with respect to core psychology, as Unger understands

----

[20] See Lewis 1972.

it, is continuity with respect to basic psychological capacities. These are traits something must have in order to count as a mental subject, of the human sort, at all. So they are not traits by which different people can be distinguished. He takes it that these are realized in states of brains and nervous systems. And I take it he would agree that human beings – embodied brains – are autonomous self-perpetuators with respect to such traits. It is the kinds of physical continuity that make them self-perpetuators with respect to these traits that he regards as constitutive of personal identity. That, I think, is what places him in the tradition of those who hold that the self is a substance.

The version of the psychological continuity theory I am presenting in this section agrees with Unger that continuity with respect to core psychology is necessary and sufficient for personal identity, and agrees that being an autonomous self-perpetuator with respect to core psychology is necessary and sufficient for personal identity. But it accepts this, not in opposition to the view that continuity with respect to individual psychology is necessary and sufficient for personal identity, but as a consequence of that view.

At this point I should warn the reader of a potentially confusing clash between Unger's terminology and my own. He speaks of "core" psychology, contrasting this with individual psychology, and I speak of "core" realizations, contrasting these with total realizations. So far there is no clash; the "cores" are just of different things. The clash comes when we see that on my view what constitutes the core psychology of an individual is made up of, not the core realizations of the person's mental states, but the *non*-core components of the total realizations of the person's mental states. I have said that the total realization of a mental state includes a fragment of a realization of a psychological makeup – something that provides the categorical base or truth-maker of the conditional propositions that must be true if particular physical states are to count as core realizations of certain mental states. Collectively, these realizations of fragments of psychological makeup, these non-core components of the total realizations of a person's mental states, constitute the realization of what Unger would call the person's core psychology.

If there is the sort of functionally characterized continuity I spoke of earlier, this must, assuming physicalism, be realized in continuity in the series of physical states that are the realizations of the mental states that make up the series that displays the psychological continuity. And these must of course be total realizations. But continuity with respect to the total realizations will require continuity with

respect to the fragments of realizations of psychological makeup that
are the non-core components of the total realizations. And continuity with respect to these will amount to continuity with respect to
core psychology, in Unger's sense.

Could there be continuity with respect to core psychology without
there being continuity with respect to individual psychology, i.e.,
without there being the functionally characterized sort of continuity
described earlier? And could there be the latter without the former?[21]
Not if continuity with respect to core psychology is as I have
described it. Continuity with respect to core psychology is an aspect
of continuity with respect to individual psychology, and is necessarily involved in it. There are cases in which individual psychology is
minimal, and virtually all there is to psychological continuity is continuity with respect to core psychology. Perhaps, as a limiting case,
there can be a creature that has core psychology and no individual
psychology at all; a creature born in a coma, who has never had
sensory experiences of any sort, has never had any beliefs, desires,
intentions, etc., and has never laid down any memories. What there
cannot be is a case in which, at a given time, a creature has both a
core psychology and an individual psychology, but tracing the core
psychology over time takes us to one later person while tracing the
individual psychology takes us to a different one. Tracing an individual psychology will include tracing a core psychology.

VII

I have been arguing that certain conservative intuitions about
personal identity, intuitions I have associated with the claim that the
self is a substance, are compatible with a version of "reductionism,"
i.e., with a psychological continuity view of personal identity. These

[21] In my 1992, I present an example, that of "Brainland," which at first sight seems to
be one in which a core psychology always stays with the same brain while an individual
psychology is regularly moving from one brain to another – and I there favor the view that
the career of a person follows an individual psychology. But the brains of Brainland are
programmed *not* to realize continuity with respect to individual psychology for more than
short intervals, and this means that they are programmed not to realize continuity with
respect to core psychology for more than short intervals. Those who oppose the liberal
version of the psychological continuity theory I favored in that paper, and favor instead the
conservative (self as substance) version presented here, should not say that the careers of
Brainland persons coincide with the careers of the brains there; they should say either that
there are no persons there or that the persons there are exist only for brief intervals. It is
partly because I find that view unattractive that I face the conflict described in the next
section.

conservative intuitions are ones that I respect, and which – some of the time – I share. But they are, in me, at war with other intuitions. When I consider certain situations involving teleportation and BST-procedures, I am strongly inclined to say that these procedures are, in those situations, person-preserving. And that is incompatible with the view I have been presenting here.

What we see here is the introduction into the debate of the issue of "what matters." One can, without outright inconsistency, combine a conservative view about the metaphysics of personal identity with a Parfitian view about what matters. Consider, for example, the case in which people submit to the BST-procedure every few years because, as they see it, this is the only way to survive in the face of radiation in their environment.[22] (Clones of their bodies are grown in radiation-proof vaults, and every few years the brain states of a person are transferred to one of his or her clones, by a procedure that destroys the original body.[23]) Here are some possible views about the case. (1) It is false that these people survive the BST-procedure, and they are mistaken in thinking that it gets them what they want in wanting to survive (even though for thousands of years these people have lived happily – none of them for more than a year or two – with this mistaken belief). (2) It is false

---

[22] See 1984, sect. 10.

[23] In his 1997, p. 307, Peter van Inwagen maintains that it is biological nonsense to suppose that cloning could result in a "blank brain" onto which a set of mental states could be imposed. No doubt he is right. Perhaps we should envisage instead something like Peter Unger's "informational taping" procedure, in which the molecular structure of a brain is recorded and a duplicate is constructed out of a stock of molecules. Judging from his remarks on teleportation, van Inwagen thinks that this would be physically impossible (given the time constraints). That could well be true. I think that the possibility that it is true can usefully be compared with the possibility that it is physically impossible for the functional organization that gives human beings their behavioral repertoire to be realized in an inanimate computer, or in aliens having a physical makeup radically different from that of ordinary human beings. Philosophers who suspect that the latter is so nevertheless take sides on the truth of the conditional "If (perhaps *per impossibile*) an electronic computer, or an alien with silicon based physiology, could pass the Super Turing Test (had a functional organization that made it behaviorally indistinguishable from a normal human being), it would have mental states of the sort we have." (For example, John Searle takes sides on this, because he denies the truth of the conditional.) To consider whether such conditionals are true is a useful way of probing our mental concepts. (Compare: it may be chemically impossible for there to be a substance other than the element with atomic number 79 that passes all of the layman's and jeweler's tests for being gold; certainly "fool's gold" (iron pyrites) doesn't pass them. That doesn't destroy the interest of the question of whether such a substance, were it to exist, would count as gold.) Similarly, philosophers who share van Inwagen's suspicion can take an interest in the truth or falsity of the conditional "If (perhaps *per impossibile*) there were psychological continuity via a BST-procedure, the procedure would be person-preserving." Van Inwagen himself takes sides on the issue; he gives reasons (bad reasons, as we shall see) for thinking the conditional false.

that these people survive the BST-procedure, but identity is not what matters in survival; so it is perfectly reasonable for these people to believe that the BST-procedure gets them what they want in wanting to survive. (3) The BST-procedure is person-preserving, and for that reason it gets these people what they want in wanting to survive. It is view (2) that combines a conservative view about the metaphysics of personal identity with a Parfitian view about what matters.

Position (1) I regard as unacceptable. Perhaps these people could be making a metaphysical mistake in thinking that the BST-procedure is person-preserving – they are if selves are substances in the sense I have sketched. But suppose they don't think that, or are agnostic about the matter, but nevertheless think that the BST-procedure is "as good as" survival; given that they are under no illusions about the sorts of psychological continuity the BST-procedure will provide, it is not intelligible that their belief that that procedure gives them "what matters" could be mistaken. The same holds even if they have the mistaken belief that the procedure is person-preserving, as long as their belief that the procedure gives them what matters is not grounded on that mistaken belief.

Insofar as I am drawn to the version of the psychological continuity view that respects the conservative intuitions about personal identity, I am drawn to position (2). But while I think that there are possible cases in which identity and the proper object of special concern come apart, e.g., cases of "fission," I think that there is nevertheless a close conceptual link between these. I think that it is a constraint on the concept of a person that the truth conditions for judgments of personal identity should, so far as possible, make it true that persons are identical with the future persons for whom they rationally have a special sort of concern.[24] This conceptual link makes (2) an unstable position; the two parts of it, although not strictly inconsistent, do not go comfortably together. If one starts with (2), but is more convinced of the conservative (self as substance) intuitions that make up its first part than of the Parfitian intuitions that make up its second part, one will be under pressure, because of the conceptual link, to revert to (1). If one starts with (2), and is more convinced of the Parfitian intuitions about what matters than of the conservative intuitions about the metaphysics of personal identity, one will be under pressure, again because of the conceptual link, to move to (3).

What I just said is right only on the assumption that the liberal

[24] See my 1969a.

version of the psychological continuity view, that on which the BST-procedure and the like could be person-preserving, is at least coherent. And this has been questioned. Peter van Inwagen says that "if one is a materialist and if one believes that persons really exist, then one must concede that every person is strictly identical with *some* material being." He goes on to say, "Someone who holds views like Shoemaker's [he has in mind a combination of materialism and the liberal version of the psychological continuity view] is therefore committed to the proposition that there could be two simultaneously existing material things such that one of them could become strictly identical with the other simply in virtue of a flow of information between them."[25] And this, he says, violates a well-established modal principle, which earlier in the paper he expresses by saying, "a thing and another thing cannot become a thing and itself."

This argument is mistaken, and it is instructive to see why. I fully agree that it is incoherent to hold that something could become strictly identical with another thing in virtue of a flow of information – or in any other way. But the combination of materialism and the liberal version of the psychological continuity view does not commit one to the possibility of this. What *does* commit one to the possibility of this is the combination of these views with the view that persons are substances in the sense I tried to elucidate earlier in this essay – in particular, the view that they are autonomous self-perpetuators. But of course the clear-headed advocate of the liberal version of the psychological continuity view will deny this. And she can consistently do this without abandoning materialism. The claim that a person is a "material thing" might mean simply that a person is a thing whose existence consists in various of the material/physical components of the world standing in certain relations and having certain properties. A materialist is of course committed to persons being material things in that sense; she is also committed to baseball teams, corporations, religious sects, and so on being material things in that sense, assuming she agrees (as it is not clear van Inwagen does) that such things exist. From something's being a material thing in that sense, nothing much follows about its transtemporal identity conditions. But "material thing" is more likely to mean something like: something that is a material thing in the first sense *and* is a substance in the sense I have discussed. And being a materialist who believes in the existence of persons does not, by itself, commit one to persons being material things in this second sense. I have acknowledged that

[25] 1997, p. 312.

the view that persons are substances – and so, given materialism, are material things in this second sense – is a view that has a strong intuitive appeal. It is a view to which I am strongly drawn. But this view is not, I think, underwritten by any more general principle or theory which has an independent claim on our acceptance – independent, I mean, of the prima facie intuitive plausibility of this particular view. And if it conflicts, as I think it does, with other views that also have strong intuitive appeal, I know of no higher court of appeal that can be counted on to decide matters in its favor.

So I think that there are conflicting tendencies in our thinking. There are tendencies that might be summed up in the slogan that the self is a substance; these are what this essay has mainly been about. And there are tendencies that emerge when we think about certain possible situations, e.g., ones in which the "survival" afforded by teleportation or the BST-procedure is the only survival available, and put ourselves in the place of those in those situations. Now, of course, given the way the world actually is, we don't need to count teleportational and BST-procedures as person-preserving in order to make it the case that personal identity is what matters. And it might be suggested that our concept of a person is made for the kinds of situations that actually exist – ones in which personal identity can matter in the right way *and* be the identity of an individual substance – and that we should not expect it to apply to imaginary situations radically different from these. But this seems too easy a way out of the difficulty. If the concept of a person does not apply to the imaginary community I have described, neither does the notion of being a subject of such mental states as belief, hope, fear, etc. And if that notion doesn't apply, neither do the notions of those mental states themselves. And that is too much to swallow. So there is a conflict here I do not know how to resolve.

18
Causal and metaphysical necessity

I

There was a time, within the memory of some of us, when it was widely accepted that there are just two kinds of necessity. There was logical necessity, which was generally construed as including the necessity of analytic truths. This was assumed to be something to which we have an a priori access. And there was causal necessity, to which our only access is empirical. Since the dominant views about causality then current were Humean in inspiration, there was some question as to how so-called causal necessity, the distinctive status of causal laws and their consequences, deserved the name of "necessity" at all. But that was what it was frequently called.

Since then the boat has been radically rocked, first by Quine and then by Kripke. The intended effects of their attacks on the traditional view were of course very different. Quine's attack on the analytic-synthetic distinction sought to contract, if not to empty, the class of truths that are called necessary. Kripke, on the other hand, argued that the class of truths deserving this label is much larger than had traditionally been supposed. And, in his most radical departure from the traditional view, he held that many of these truths have the epistemic status of being a posteriori. One important class of these truths included statements of identity, such as "Hesperus is Phosphorus" and "Water is H$_2$O." Another included statements about the essences of natural kinds, such as "Gold is an element" and "Tigers are mammals."

Such truths were characterized as being true in all possible worlds. That might suggest that they can be called logical truths. And that seems a radical departure from the traditional notion of logical truth. But so also, one might claim, was the earlier extension of the notion of logical truth to cover analytic truths such as "All bachelors are unmarried." If such truths are logical truths, they owe this status to the fact that their truth is guaranteed by certain paradigmatic logical truths – say that all unmarried men are unmarried – *together with* semantic facts, say that "bachelor" is synonymous with "unmarried male." What Kripke showed is that the class of semantic facts that can contribute to the bestowal of the status of necessary truth is much broader than the class of synonymies or analytic equivalences, supposing there are such; it includes such facts as that the term "gold" refers to a substance with a certain essential nature.

I favor the usage that restricts the term "logical truth" to what logicians would count as such, excluding both analytic truths like "Bachelors are unmarried" and Kripkean necessities like "Gold is an element." So I shall refer to the latter as metaphysical necessities, rather than as logical necessities. But this is not to say that metaphysical necessity is a weaker kind of necessity than logical necessity. A statement can be metaphysically necessary without being conceptually necessary, and without being logically necessary. This is true of "Gold is an element." But it is not plausible to put this by saying that there is a possible world in which gold is not an element, or by saying that the world might have been such that gold is not an element. We can compare this with the fact that "Bachelors are unmarried" is not, in the strict sense, a logical truth; we would not want to put this by saying that the world might have been such as to contain married bachelors.

So if Kripke is right, we have a set of truths, the metaphysically necessary ones, that are necessary in the strongest possible sense, and yet whose epistemological status is that of being a posteriori. Such truths are knowable, if at all, only empirically. And this epistemological status they of course share with statements of causal necessity. What, then, of the traditional view that causal necessity, if it deserves to be called necessity at all, is a weaker sort of necessity – that in possible worlds jargon, the causal laws hold in only a subclass of the metaphysically possible worlds? I think this view is widely held by philosophers who accept the Kripkean view that there are necessities a posteriori. But of course there is another possibility. Maybe the view that causal necessity is a weaker sort of necessity, or necessity only in a stretched meaning of the term, is a holdover from the pre-Kripkean view, which took it that genuine necessities, or at least those of the strongest sort, are knowable a priori because a priori reducible to truths of logic. Maybe, instead, causal necessity is just a special case of metaphysical necessity, and is necessity in the strongest sense of the term.[1]

---

[1] Kripke explicitly recognized this possibility in *Naming and Necessity* (1980): "Physical necessity, *might* turn out to be necessity in the highest degree. But that's a question which I don't wish to prejudge" (p. 99).

This is a view I defended in a paper published over fifteen years ago.[2] In that paper I put forward the view that properties are individuated by their causal features – by what contribution they make to the causal powers of the things that have them, and also by how their instantiation can be caused. Collectively, causal features of this sort constitute the essence of a property. So insofar as causal laws can be construed as describing the causal features of properties, they are necessary truths. One way to get the conclusion that laws are necessary is to combine my view of properties with the view of David Armstrong, Fred Dretske, and Michael Tooley, that laws are, or assert, relations between properties.

Views similar to mine have been defended by Chris Swoyer, and by Evan Fales.[3] But I think it is fair to say that it is definitely a minority view. The established view, even among those who have absorbed Kripke's lessons, is that causal laws are contingent, not just in the sense that their epistemic status is that of being a posteriori, but in the sense that there are genuinely possible situations in which they do not hold.

I shall not here repeat all of the arguments with which I supported the causal theory of properties and the necessitarian view about laws – although I will give a version of what I now take to be the central one. My main concern here is to clarify this view by exploring some of the sources of resistance to it.

II

The source of resistance that most immediately leaps to mind lies in the fact that we can easily imagine what it would be like to experience a world in which the laws are different. We can imagine conducting crucial experiments and having them come out differently than they do here. And as Hume reminded us, we can imagine bread failing to nourish, water failing to suffocate, and so on.

But, of course, in the sense in which we can imagine these things we can imagine analyzing gold and finding that it is not an element, analyzing water and finding that it is not H_2O, dissecting tigers and finding that they are reptiles, and so on. Most philosophers are now persuaded, by Kripke's arguments, that such imaginings are no real threat to the claim that it is necessary that gold is an element, that

---

[2] See Essay 10.
[3] See Swoyer 1982 and Fales 1993.

water is H$_2$O, and that tigers are mammals. Perhaps one wants to redescribe a bit what one actually succeeds in imagining; e.g., let it be analyzing what *looks like* gold, or what passes the layman's and jeweler's tests for being gold, and finding that it is not an element – or analzying what passes the ordinary observational tests for being water and finding that it is not H$_2$O. Then one can grant that what one actually does imagine is possible, but say that it is wrong to describe the possibility as that of gold not being an element or water not being H$_2$O. Some would prefer to stick to the original description of what is imagined, but deny that imaginability establishes possibility. In any event, the same resources are available for someone who wants to maintain, in the face of all that we can imagine or seem to imagine, that causal laws are metaphysically necessary. If one's preferred strategy for dealing with the Kripkean examples is to challenge the claim that imaginability is proof or evidence of possibility, one can employ the same strategy here. If one's preferred strategy is to allow that imaginability is at least evidence of possibility, but to claim that what we can really imagine in these cases is not what we initially take it to be, that strategy too is available here.[4] Let the law be that strychnine in a certain dosage is fatal to human beings. We can grant it to be imaginable that ingesting vast amounts of what passes certain tests for being strychnine should fail to be fatal to what passes certain tests for being a human being, but deny that this amounts to imagining a human being surviving the ingestion of that much strychnine.

But of course there was more to Kripke's argument than deploying such strategies to ward off challenges to his necessity claims that are based on imaginability or seeming imaginability. He had direct arguments for the necessity of identity propositions. He had a compelling case for the view that names and other singular terms are rigid designators. And, what is most pertinent here, he had a view of the semantics of natural kind terms that both implied that some statements expressed by the use of such terms are necessarily true and made it intelligible that such statements have the epistemological status of being a posteriori. It was part of that view that the semantic intentions underlying our use of natural kind terms are such that the underlying makeup of a natural kind, the properties responsible for the phenomenal features of the paradigm exemplars of the kind, is essential to it. So, for example, if the paradigm exemplars of gold are

---

[4] But if the position defended in this paper is correct, there are limitations on the applicability of this strategy – see note 11 below.

instances of an element having atomic number 79, it will be necessary that gold is such an element. This explains why something lacking that makeup can't be gold, whatever its phenomenal features. And it therefore explains why the imaginability of something having the phenomenal features characteristic of gold but lacking that physical makeup is no threat to the claim that it is necessary that gold has that makeup.

My claim will be that the causal theory of properties can provide a parallel explanation of why the imaginability or seeming imaginability of worlds in which the causal laws are different is no threat to the claim that the causal laws that hold have the status of being metaphysically necessary. Corresponding to Kripke's claim that our semantic intuitions are such that the underlying natures of natural kinds are essential to them will be the claim that the causal features of properties are essential to them. Just as we can refer to a natural kind, and identify instances of it, without knowing what its essential underlying nature is, so we can refer to a property, and pick out instances of it, without knowing what most of its causal features are. Our ability to pick out instances of a property perceptually, or with the use of instruments, will of course depend on exercises of the causal powers which the property contributes to bestowing. For example, it may involve the power to produce experiences having a certain phenomenal character. But having the power to produce such experiences will not in general be sufficient for having the property in question; so the imaginability of something having such a power but lacking any property having certain other causal features is compatible with those other causal features being essential to the property in question.

III

Before pursuing further the parallels between Kripke's claims and the claim that causal laws are metaphysically necessary, and before examining further the imaginability or seeming imaginability of the causal laws being other than they are, I must say more about what is, and what is not, asserted by the causal theory of properties I favor.

In expounding my theory in my paper "Causality and Properties" I made use of the notion of a "conditional power": something has a conditional power if it is such that it would have a certain power if it had such and such properties, where the possession of those properties is not itself sufficient to bestow that power: e.g., to use the example I used there, something that is knife-shaped has, among others, the conditional power of being able to cut butter if it is made of wood or steel. And I claimed there that properties can be identified with "clusters" of conditional powers, where the members of the cluster are causally unified in certain ways.

I now reject that formulation. One reason for rejecting it can be found in a postscript to that paper. I there consider a case offered by Richard Boyd, which purports to be a case in which two different properties bestow the same cluster of causal powers. We are to suppose that X is a compound of substances A and B and Y a compound of substances C and D, where A, B, C, and D are all different substances, and that it is a consequence of the laws of nature that X and Y behave exactly alike in all possible circumstances – so being made of X and being made of Y bestow exactly the same conditional powers. If, as seems plausible, X and Y are different substances, and therefore being made of X and being made of Y are different properties, we have a counterexample to the claim that properties are the clusters of conditional powers they bestow. This is not, however, a counterexample to the claim that it is essential to a property that it bestow a particular cluster of conditional powers. And if we include among the causal features of properties not only their "forward-looking" causal features, i.e., their being such as to contribute in certain ways to what their possessors cause, or what powers their possessors have, but also their "backward-looking" causal features, i.e., their being such that their instantiation can be caused in such and such ways, then Boyd's example is not a counterexample to the claim that properties are identical just in case they share all of the same causal features. In the example, the properties of being made of X and being made of Y share all of their forward-looking causal features, but not all of their backward-looking causal features.

Boyd's example raises another worry about the causal theory of properties, and I will return to it shortly. But even if his example could be shown to be impossible, and properties could be said to be necessarily coextensive with clusters of conditional powers, I would want to reject the formulation of the causal theory which says that a property *is* a cluster of conditional powers. That formulation has a reductionist flavor to it. And the reduction it seems to promise is a cheat. We must make use of the notion of a property in explaining the notion of a conditional power, so there is no question here of reducing properties to some more fundamental sort of entity.[5]

---

[5] I pointed this out in Essay 10, but did not see then that it clashes with the reductionist flavor of some of my formulations.

The formulation of the causal theory of properties I now favor is one that is in no way reductionist – and it is one that is compatible with the view that in Boyd's example being X and being Y are different properties. It says that the causal features of a property, both forward-looking and backward-looking, are essential to it. And it says that properties having the same causal features are identical.

You may well ask what exactly this theory is a theory *of*. Obviously it will not serve as a theory about the "abundant" properties recognized by David Lewis, where there is such a property corresponding to every set of possibilia, or every function from possible worlds to extensions. More plausibly, it is a theory about what Lewis calls "natural" properties, and what intuitively are "genuine", as opposed to "mere-Cambridge," properties. But for present purposes, we can take it as a theory about those properties that do contribute to determining the causal powers of things. Here I will be neutral as to whether there is a property common to all the things, future as well as past and present, that the predicate "grue" is true of. Even if there is, it is not this property that contributes to the causal powers of the things Goodman's predicate is true of. It is true that right now, something will produce a certain visual appearance only if it is grue – so you can make it produce that appearance by making it grue. But that is because right now being grue goes with being green, and something's being green contributes to its producing that appearance. Or, if you are doubtful about the causal role of color properties, consider the predicate "negapos," which is true of something just in case it has negative charge and the time is before T (some time in the future), or it has positive charge and the time is T or after. Right now, things attract things with positive charge and repel things with negative charge just in case they are negapos. But, so I say, the property of them that bestows this power is the property of having negative charge, not the property, supposing there is one, of being negapos. Perhaps grue and negapos have causal features; but they have them only derivatively, in virtue of their relations to green and negative charge, respectively.

So the claim of the causal theory of properties is that the properties that have causal features *non*derivatively have them essentially, and are individuated in terms of them.[6] I think this comes to much

---

[6] There is a case for saying that mental properties, and in general "higher-order" properties that are not themselves physical but which supervene on physical properties, have their causal features derivatively – that their causal efficacy derives from that of the physical properties in which they are realized. But there are ways and ways in which the causal features of a property can be "derivative"; it seems obvious that the causal efficacy of

the same thing as saying that the properties that enter into causal laws have their causal features essentially, and are individuated in terms of them. I should observe that there is nothing to prevent a proponent of this view from saying that ordinary properties are not themselves dispositions, but are instead the "categorical bases," the having of which bestows on things the dispositions they have. Some writers, such as David Armstrong, appear to think that one can think of properties as categorical only if one takes it to be contingent that properties bestow the dispositions they do. But I see no reason to think this. There is, to be sure, a kind of dispositional property that is only contingently bestowed by categorical properties. To use Robert Boyle's famous example, it is only contingent that the intrinsic categorical properties of a key bestow the *extrinsic* power of opening a certain door, since their doing so depends on the door's lock having a certain structure and composition. But it is compatible with this that the *intrinsic* powers of the key, e.g., its capacity of opening locks of a certain structure and composition, are necessarily bestowed by its categorical properties.

In my original defense of the causal theory of properties I put considerable weight on epistemological arguments aimed at showing that there cannot be properties that make no contribution to causal powers, that there cannot be two or more properties that share all of their causal features, and that properties cannot change their causal features over time. These arguments have often been charged with being "verificationist." I think that charge is confused.[7] But in any case, my present formulation of the view makes it possible to dispense with most of them. If there are properties that make no contribution to causal features, the account does not apply to them. Since laws are supposed to hold timelessly, or omnitemporally, we can be sure that the properties that figure in laws retain the same causal features over time.[8] Where there is still room for the deploy-

---

mental properties, and properties that figure in the "special sciences," is much more robust than the causal efficacy (if such it is) of the properties (if they are such) grue and negapos. The nature of the causal relevance and causal efficacy of higher-order properties raises large issues that I cannot go into here; but the causal theory of properties is meant to apply to at least some such properties.

[7] Those who make this charge, and they are legion, confuse verificationism (which involves commitment to a verificationist theory of meaning) with the use of a certain sort of epistemological argument, one that argues from the premise that we know facts of a certain sort (e.g., that two things share a property), together with the premise that we could not know them if such and such a view (e.g., that sameness of causal features is not sufficient for sameness of properties) were true, to the conclusion that that view is not true.

[8] I take the view stated here to be the standard view about laws. But it is sometimes

ment of an epistemological argument is in attacking the idea that there can be properties that share all of their causal features. And what epistemological considerations show, in the first instance, is that if there are sets of properties whose members are identical with respect to their causal features, we necessarily lack the resources for referring to particular members of these sets. Supposing there are such properties, it cannot be these that we intend to be referring to when we use singular property-referring terms – all we can plausibly be said to intend to refer to are equivalence classes of such properties. So if there are such properties, they don't fall within the extension of *our* term "property." Which seems to imply that if there are such properties, they aren't properties; which seems to imply that there are no such properties.

At any rate, what divides proponents of the causal theory of properties from most other philosophers is not what they think about the *intra*-world identity conditions for properties. What divides them is what they think about the *inter*-world identity conditions. The controversial claim of the theory is that the causal features of properties are essential to them – are features they have in all possible worlds. That is what implies that causal laws are metaphysically necessary, and that causal necessity is metaphysical necessity.

IV

Now let me return, as promised, to Richard Boyd's example, involving the properties *being made of X* and *being made of Y* which are identical with respect to their forward-looking causal features. The first thing to be said about it is that it is not at all clear that the case is metaphysically possible. It is not clear that it is nomologically possible, and what is in question here is whether metaphysical possibility

suggested that it is conceivable that the laws might change over time; e.g., that certain physical constants involved in them might gradually change their values. Faced with an opponent who claims that that is a real possibility, I would fall back on my epistemological arguments. But I would also suggest that it may be that some of what we call laws are lawlike generalizations that hold in virtue of (a) "strict" laws and (b) boundary conditions that are highly stable but can (compatibly with the strict laws) undergo gradual change. If so, then it is not these laws, but only the strict laws, that I hold to be necessary and internally related to the properties involved in them. The suggestion that all laws hold in virtue of stable but mutable boundary conditions seems to me incoherent. If the stability of the boundary conditions were just a cosmic accident, it could not confer lawlikeness on generalizations. And to hold that the stability is the result of laws, but that these laws themselves hold in virtue of stable but mutable boundary conditions, generates an unacceptable regress.

can outrun nomological possibility. The case is supposed to be one in which two substances, X and Y, have different compositions and yet are such that under no nomologically possible circumstances will they behave differently. This means that it is nomologically impossible for them to be decomposed into the different sets of elements of which they are composed. This is of course not true in ordinary cases in which different substances are phenomenally alike, e.g., in the case of the two sorts of jade, and it is at least questionable whether, given the physics and chemistry that actually obtain, it could be true of any pair of substances.

But let us waive this point, and assume that the example is possible. If it is, then there is a way in which the response I have already made to it, on behalf of the causal theory of properties, is inadequate. That response involves saying that the causal features in terms of which a property is individuated include its "backward-looking" as well as its "forward-looking" causal features. Now it is true that it is compatible with the example that properties are identical just in case they share the same total set of forward-looking and backward-looking causal features. But how is it that we know that the property of being made of X and the property of being made of Y do not satisfy this condition? Is it because you get the first by combining the elementary substances A and B, and you get the second by combining the elementary substances C and D? That can't be it – there can be more than one way in which the instantiation of a single property can be caused, so for all that we have said so far it might be that there is a single property which can be gotten either by combining A and B or by combining C and D. Clearly, the intuition that being made of X and being made of Y are different properties stems from the intuition that X and Y are different substances. And the intuition that they are different substances stems from the presumed fact that they have different compositions. The presumption that they have different compositions of course comes from the way samples of the substances come into existence – namely, the fact that samples of the one are compounded out of the elements A and B, while samples of the other are compounded out of elements C and D. And the background assumptions operating here are not principles about the individuation of properties; they are assumptions about chemistry.

One might wonder if these assumptions would continue to be reasonable if cases of the sort Boyd imagines actually occurred; if some substances couldn't be decomposed into elements, it might be reasonable to think when they are formed out of elements those elements "fuse" in a way that destroys their identity – so that what is formed by combining A and B would not differ in composition from what is formed by combining C and D. But let's waive this worry, along with the earlier worry about whether the case is metaphysically possible at all, and assume that our A and B and our C and D are the elementary substances that make up, respectively, the compound substances X and Y.

What we now have to allow is that where properties are of the sort in question here, what we might call compositional properties, then there is a principle of difference that applies to them that does not have to do in any direct way with causality. The property of being made of x is different from the property of being made of y if x and y are different substances, and x and y are different substances if they differ in composition. This enables us to distinguish properties that are alike in their forward-looking causal features and that can be shown to differ in their backward-looking causal features only by the use of this principle. So it is not true without qualification that properties are "individuated by" their causal features.

As I have said, this in no way counts against the claim that properties are identical just in case they share the same total sets of causal features – it merely implies that non-causal considerations can come into deciding whether properties do in fact share the same total sets of causal features. And none of this is any threat to the claim of the causal theory of properties that especially concerns us here, namely that causal laws are metaphysically necessary. Arguably this follows from a part of the causal theory of properties that is in no way challenged by Boyd's example, namely that the forward-looking causal features of properties are essential to them. This implies that the laws about the effects of instantiating the various properties are metaphysically necessary. Moreover, if you hold fixed across worlds what properties there are, it is obvious that in fixing the forward-looking causal features of properties across worlds you at the same time fix their backward-looking causal features – just as in fixing what telephone calls are made by each of the members of the total population of telephone users one fixes what telephone calls are received by members of that population. So, again assuming that what properties there are is held fixed across worlds, if the forward-looking causal features of properties are essential to them, then all of the causal laws without exception, those about how property instantiations can be caused as well as those about what they can cause, will be necessarily true.

V

But now I must address the question of why we should think that the causal features of properties are essential to them. I will approach this by considering first Kripke's case for the metaphysical necessity of statements about natural kinds. Since I am painting with a rather wide brush, I will here lump this together with Hilary Putnam's case for the same position, and draw on Putnam's examples as well as Kripke's.

Kripke asks us to consider a case in which, having discovered what we have discovered about the chemical makeup of gold, we discover, say on Mars, a substance that is phenomenally indistinguishable from gold, but which on chemical analysis turns out not to be an element at all, let alone one with atomic number 79. Elsewhere he asks us to consider creatures which look and act just like tigers but which biological analysis reveals to be reptiles, not mammals. And Putnam's Twin Earth contains a stuff which is just like water in its phenomenal properties, but which is XYZ rather than H_2O. We are expected to agree, and I do, that the Martian "gold" is not gold, that the reptilian "tigers" are not tigers, and that the Twin Earthian "water" is not water. And such examples seem to support the claims that the chemical makeup of gold and water, and the biological makeup of tigers, are essential to them.

But notice that what these examples have to do with in the first instance are the *intra*-world identity conditions for natural kinds. The world in which a goldlike substance on Mars turns out to be not an element is supposed to be one in which the actual samples of gold on earth are samples of an element with atomic number 79. And what Putnam imagines in imagining Twin Earth is not an alternative possible world but a remote planet in this world, or at any rate a world in which the watery stuff on Earth is H_2O. Now of course, it may well be nomologically impossible for there to be a compound that perfectly mimics the phenomenal properties of gold; what is called "fool's gold," namely iron pyrites, is very far from doing so. It may also be nomologically impossible for there to be reptiles that mimic the phenomenal properties of tigers, and non-H_2O that mimics the phenomenal properties of H_2O. I think that whether that is so is irrelevant to the philosophical point Kripke and Putnam are making. The question they address is whether, *supposing* that it is nomologically possible for there to be phenomenal duplicates of gold, tigers, and water that differ from paradigm samples of these things in their underlying nature, these duplicates would count as instances of the kinds gold, tiger, and water. That question they answer in the negative – and expect us to agree with them in answering in the negative, on the basis of our sense of how natural kind terms of this sort are applied.

No one, to my knowledge, has replied: "Yes, it's true that given that the actual samples of gold or water have a certain underlying constitution, all samples of gold or water in the actual world, or in worlds in which the laws are the same as here, must have the same underlying constitution. But what of worlds in which the laws of nature are different? May not the underlying constitution of these kinds be different there?" Such a reply would seem strange, and I think we can see why. We go on the reasonable assumption that whatever restrictions there are on the variation of a kind in the actual world also restrict its variation across worlds. If we take it that there are worlds in which the laws are different, this will be seen as restricting the instantiation of these natural kinds to a subclass of worlds, namely those that are nomologically possible – those in which the laws are the same as here. Only in these can we sensibly speak of the same phenomenal features being produced by the same underlying constitution. But I think that there is a natural generalization of this line of thought that undermines the idea that this class of worlds – the nomologically possible ones – is a proper subclass of all the possible worlds.

It seems to me a general feature of our thought about possibility that how we think that something could have differed from how it is in fact is closely related to how we think that the way something is at one time could differ from the way that same thing is at a different time. In possible worlds jargon, the ways one and the same thing of a given sort can differ across worlds correspond to the ways one and the same thing of that sort can differ at different times in the same world.[9] Could I have been a plumber or an accountant instead of a philosopher? The answer seems to be yes – and this goes with the fact that we acknowledge the possibility of a scenario in which someone who was exactly as I was at some point in my life undergoes a series

---

[9] This principle needs to be qualified, as Randy Clarke pointed out to me. The property of being the child of someone who has visited Paris is not one that one can have and then lose; but it is one that one can have in the actual world and not have in some other possible world. The principle is meant to apply only to non-historical properties; it says that where a non-historical property is not one that a given sort of thing can have and then lose, it is not one that a thing can have in the actual world and fail to have in some other possible world.

of changes resulting in his eventually being a plumber or an accountant. Could I have been a poached egg? *Pace* Lewis, the answer seems to be no – and this goes with the fact that our principles of transtemporal identity rule out the possibility of a scenario in which something starts off as a human being of a certain description and ends up as a poached egg.

When we move from particulars to kinds, the relevant intra-world variation includes variation across space as well as variation across time. So, for example, the underlying constitution of gold cannot be different on Mars than it is here, just as it cannot be different tomorrow than it is today. Assuming that the constraints on intra-world variation are also constraints on inter-world variation, this gives us the Kripkean view that the underlying constitution of gold is essential to it, and belongs to it in all possible worlds.

But now consider the case of properties. Different things can be true of a property at different places, and at different times: e.g., the frequency of its instantiation can be different, and it can be coinstantiated with different properties, insofar as this is compatible with the laws. But it cannot be governed by different laws at different places or at different times. Applying again the principle that constraints on intra-world variation are also constraints on inter-world variation, we get the conclusion that the same property cannot be governed by different laws in different worlds. Since I take it that the causal features of properties are features they have in virtue of the laws that govern their instantiation, this is equivalent to my claim that the causal features of properties are essential to them. And it implies that causal necessity is a special case of metaphysical necessity.

VI

I want now to return to the point that we seem offhand to be able to imagine the causal features of properties being different, and, what goes with this, the laws of nature being different. I have already pointed out that a proponent of the causal theory of properties can respond to this point in ways that parallel Kripke's responses to the claim that, for example, we can imagine heat being something other than motion of molecules. But more can be said about it.

One natural thought is that for each of a wide range of properties there is a perceptual "mode of presentation," and that when we take ourselves to be imagining something being true of certain of these properties what we are in the first instance imagining is that the thing in question is true of properties having that mode of presentation, and that that much, at least, is possible. If we could be sure that these modes of presentation necessarily always present the same properties, we could be sure that we are imagining what we seem to be imagining, and that it is indeed possible. What Kripke pointed out in his discussion of heat is that if we take as the mode of presentation certain sensations, there is no warrant for thinking that it is necessarily the case that these always present the same properties; in creatures with different sensory apparatus, the same sensations might be produced by something different than what produces them in us, namely motion of molecules, and in such a case the property they present would be something other than heat.

Pretending for the moment that perceptual modes of presentation are always sensations, there is one sort of property these are necessarily always modes of presentation of; sensations of sort S can always be taken to present the dispositional property of producing sensations of sort S under certain conditions. And it may be thought that we are at least in a position to establish via our imaginings the possibility that properties of this sort are governed by different laws than they are in the actual world. But this idea does not bear much examination. One can certainly imagine the regularities obtaining among one's sensations being very different than they in fact are. But obviously that is not to imagine any laws being different, for there are no laws that imply, by themselves, anything about what regularities obtain among sensations. Such laws as are relevant here will be ones about what sorts of sensations will be produced in a creature with certain sorts of sensory apparatus given certain sorts of stimulation from the environment. Imagining different patterns of instantiation among one's sensations will amount to imagining the breakdown of such laws only if the sensations can be taken as presenting the right sort of facts about one's own physical makeup and sensory apparatus, and about what sorts of stimuli are impacting on this physical makeup. And that is a very big "only if."

Now let me drop the fiction that sensations are the modes of presentation of perceptible properties. Indeed, I will drop talk of modes of presentation altogether. In its place I will adopt the following way of talking about the imaginings that are taken as establishing possibilities. What in the first instance one imagines, I will say, is a phenomenal situation. This phenomenal situation, in turn, is one whose existence is taken to indicate the existence of a state of affairs whose proper description is in "objective," non-phenomenal, terms. I use the notion of a "phenomenal situation" in a somewhat elastic way.[10] Sometimes it will involve the actual (as opposed to merely apparent) instantiation of what are naturally thought of as directly observable properties – colors, shapes, etc. Sometimes it seems appropriate to construe the phenomenal situation as something more subjective, namely its appearing to one, perhaps over a significant interval of time, that such and such properties are being instantiated. In any case, the argument for possibility will go in two steps. What is in the first instance shown to be possible, by the imagining, is the phenomenal situation. The possibility of this, in turn, is taken to show the possibility of the more objective situation whose existence the phenomenal situation indicates. Perhaps there will be more than two steps – e.g., from the possibility of things appearing a certain way to the possibility of things *being* a certain way, in terms of directly observable properties, and from that to the possibility of some nonphenomenal state of affairs obtaining.

It is not only in the fantasies of philosophers that this sort of thinking goes on. It also goes on in scientific thinking. Entertaining a certain hypothesis leads one to consider what might be evidence for it. We can think of the possible evidence as a possible phenomenal situation. Having thought of, imagined, such a possible phenomenal situation, we think that the hypothesis may well be true. And to test whether it is true we set up an experiment having that phenomenal situation as a possible outcome. Or perhaps instead we are doing history of science, and considering some hypothesis that is incompatible with what we now know to be the case. We consider whether there are ways in which certain experiments in the past might have come out – phenomenal situations they might have produced – that would have established the truth of that hypothesis. We may well find that there are. So we conclude that something we now know to be nomologically impossible was possible.

Now I think it is apparent on slight reflection that in these cases the possibility of the hypotheses is epistemic. When we are considering the possible outcomes of an experiment we are about to conduct, and considering the different hypotheses we would take these outcomes as establishing or supporting, the hypotheses are possible relative to our current state of knowledge. When we consider a past situation, and say that a certain hypothesis, now known to be nomologically impossible, was then possible, we mean that it was possible

---

[10] Obviously my notion of a phenomenal situation is very similar to, and derives from, Kripke's notion of an "epistemic situation" – I have introduced my own terminology so as to be able to use it in a rather elastic way without getting entangled in exegetical issues.

relative to the then current state of knowledge. And I think that often when we say that a state of affairs is imaginable and so possible, what we really mean is that the thing is possible relative to some unspecified state of knowledge; we are considering some phenomenal situation we take to be possible, and saying that given some possible body of background knowledge, or justified background belief, knowledge of that phenomenal situation would make it reasonable to believe in the existence of that state of affairs. And I think that epistemic possibility, relative either to our actual state of knowledge or to some hypothesized state of knowledge, is all we need to account for cases in which we say that something is or was possible, where this is compatible with the thing in question being nomologically impossible. What we do not need are metaphysically possible worlds which are not nomologically possible.

But what of the possibility of the phenomenal situations that figure in our imaginings? I think that there is a good case for saying that this is straightforward *nomological* possibility which we believe in on inductive grounds. We have abundant empirical evidence that when we can imagine some phenomenal situation, e.g., imagine things appearing certain ways, such a situation could actually exist – things really could appear that way to someone. In days of yore the evidence came from such things as the artistry of stage magicians and trompe l'oeil painters. Now this is supplemented by the productions of Hollywood special effects designers, holograms, "virtual reality" devices, and so forth. There is no need here, in the realm of phenomenal states of affairs, to suppose that metaphysical possibility outruns nomological possibility.

Of course, if it is on empirical grounds that we are entitled to think that the phenomenal situations we can imagine are nomologically possible, it should be imaginable that this should have turned out otherwise – that the empirical evidence should have supported the claim that some imaginable phenomenal states of affairs are nomologically impossible. And if that is so, it might be held, then it is imaginable, and so possible, that there should be phenomenal states of affairs that are possible, because imaginable, but not nomologically possible. And if it is possible that there should be possible states of affairs that are not nomologically possible, don't we after all need a notion of metaphysical possibility that outruns nomological possibility?

Let me observe first that there is a conception of imagination on which imagining a phenomenal state of affairs involves creating in one's mind an inner simulacrum of that state of affairs. To the extent that imagining is like this, imagining could be said to demonstrate the possibility of a phenomenal state of affairs by actualizing it. And in that case there is of course no question of the state of affairs not being nomologically possible.

But for most of us, most of the time, it is not like this. And I agree that it is imaginable, conceivable, that it should have turned out that what we can imagine in the way of phenomenal states of affairs outruns what is nomologically possible: e.g., experimental psychology might have discovered that there is a "speed limit" on certain sorts of phenomenal changes, which is such that these changes cannot occur as rapidly as we can imagine them occurring. But this, empirical psychology making such a discovery, is not itself a phenomenal state of affairs. And I say about its possibility what I said above about the possibility of scientific hypotheses that are not nomologically possible – there is no reason to think that this is anything other than epistemic possibility, relative to some envisaged body of background knowledge. So regarded, it gives no support to the idea that imaginability gives us access to metaphysical possibility that outruns nomological possibility. It may further be observed that were this epistemic possibility to be realized then the imaginability of phenomenal states of affairs would establish nothing more than their epistemic possibility.

There is another sort of possibility that imaginability might be said to give us access to, namely conceptual possibility. By and large, we come to believe situations to be conceptually possible by reflecting on their descriptions and seeing no contradiction or incoherence. But the more theoretical the concepts involved in such a description, the less confident we can be that there is not a contradiction or incoherence that escapes our notice. And, conversely, the more the description is couched in phenomenal terms, the more confident we can be that there is not such a contradiction or incoherence. And what imagining a situation often amounts to is considering a description of it in phenomenal terms, or largely in phenomenal terms. Where the description is entirely in phenomenal terms, we will be entitled to regard the situation as not only conceptually possible but nomologically possible, given what I said earlier. When the description is not in phenomenal terms, we may nevertheless be justified in taking it to express a conceptual possibility. But as is well known, what is conceptually possible, like what is epistemically possible, may fail to be metaphysically possible.[11]

---

[11] Some writers, taking their lead from Kripke's discussion of the seeming possibility of heat being other than molecular motion, have suggested that whenever we seem to be able

So there are three sorts of possibility we may reasonably come to believe in by reflecting on what we can imagine. There is the nomological possibility of phenomenal states of affairs. There is the epistemic possibility of nonphenomenal states of affairs. And there is the conceptual possibility of states of affairs of both kinds. But nowhere in all this, I submit, do we find any reason for supposing that there are states of affairs that are metaphysically possible but not nomologically possible.

VII

The causal theory of properties is so alien to what most philosophers believe that the burden of proof is commonly taken to fall on those who hold it. But I want to suggest, in conclusion, that once we accept with Kripke that there are metaphysically necessary truths whose epistemological status is that of being a posteriori, the burden of proof should be shifted to the other side. As is suggested by the way "necessity" is used in ordinary speech, and is defined in dictionaries, causal necessity is, pretheoretically, the very paradigm of necessity.[12]

to imagine something there is a metaphysically possible world that we are imagining, although it may be one we are misdescribing (as it is in Kripke's heat example). I do not disagree with this if it means that in those cases in which the imagining is in the first instance the imagining of what I have called a "phenomenal situation," the phenomenal situation, as opposed to the interpretation we put on it, is metaphysically possible. But some writers assume something stronger than this. They think that while we would be mistaken in taking Twin Earth imaginings to show that there can be water that is not H_2O, we are entitled to take them as showing that it is metaphysically possible for there to be a planet otherwise like Earth on which the "watery stuff" is not H_2O, where the watery stuff behaves, outside chemistry laboratories, just as water behaves here. If the view defended here is correct, this is a mistake. As noted earlier, it may well be that Putnam's XYZ, a substance that exactly mimics the behaviour of H_2O except in certain laboratory conditions, is a nomological impossibility. And if it is a nomological impossibility, then according to me it is a metaphysical impossibility.

This may have the effect of undermining Kripke's argument against the idea that pain might be identical with some physical state, such as C-fiber stimulation. Granted that there is some sense in which one can imagine pain without C-fiber stimulation, or C-fiber stimulation without pain, this provides no guarantee that either of these situations is nomologically possible – and so, on the present view, no guarantee that either is metaphysically possible. If what one imagines here in the first instance is a phenomenal situation, no doubt that will be possible. It might be, e.g., feeling pain while having experiences "as of" a negative autocerebroscope reading (saying that there is no C-fiber stimulation going on in one), or having experiences "as of" a positive autocerebroscope reading while feeling no pain. But the metaphysical possibility of these situations is no proof of the metaphysical possibility of the situations whose possibility Kripke is out to establish.

[12] The first non-circular definition of "necessity" given in the *American Heritage Dictionary* (3rd edn, p. 1207) is "Something dictated by invariable physical laws." Much

The main theoretical obstacle to according it that status has been the deeply rooted conviction that necessary truths should be knowable a priori. Once that obstacle has been removed, anyone who holds that causal necessity is not really necessity, or has only a second-class kind of necessity, owes us a reason for thinking this. I have not seen a reason that seems to me persuasive.[13]

the same is true in the *Shorter Oxford English Dictionary* (3rd edn, p. 1391), where definitions is terms of "determined" and "constraining power" are followed by the definition "Constraint or compulsion having its basis in the natural constitution of things; *esp.* such constraint conceived as a law prevailing throughout the material universe and within the sphere of human action."

[13] This paper was written for the Kripke Conference held in San Marino in May 1996. I am grateful for helpful comments from the participants of that conference, from audiences at the University of Iowa and Auburn University, and from members of John Heil's 1996 NEH Summer Seminar. I am also grateful to Eric Hiddleston for written comments on an earlier draft, and to Richard Boyd for discussion of these issues. It need hardly be said that I am greatly indebted to the work of Saul Kripke.

19

Realization and mental causation

The problem of mental causation is at the heart of the mind–body problem. And for physicalist or materialist views of mind, the key to solving the problem of mental causation is getting a satisfactory understanding of how the mental is realized in the physical. Recent discussions of physicalism have focused on the notion of supervenience; but I think that the focus should instead be on the notion of realization. Supervenience comes in a variety of forms – and the form we need to understand, in order to understand mental causation, is that in which the properties in the supervenience base can be said to realize the properties that supervene on them. Any physicalist theory, whether or not it is a functionalist theory, needs to maintain that the mental is realized in the physical, and so needs an account of realization. But my main focus will be on the realization of functional properties.

I

I take as my point of departure a recent paper by George Bealer that attempts to show that functionalist accounts of mind cannot give a satisfactory account of self-consciousness.[1] Although Bealer's primary target is functionalism, he takes his arguments to establish a version of property dualism. They are supposed to show that mental properties are "first-order properties," not the higher-order properties functionalists take them to be. And because Bealer thinks that there are decisive reasons for rejecting type physicalism, he thinks that the only way for mental properties to be first-order is for them to be nonphysical. His central claim is that functionalist views are incoherent, because they imply that when a person self-ascribes a property such as pain, the property self-ascribed is a first-order property, a physical "realizer" of the second-order functional property the

[1] Bealer 1997.

mental property pain is supposed to be, rather than that second-order property. The only way pain can be what is self-ascribed in such self-ascriptions is if pain is a first-order property, contrary to what Bealer takes functionalism to hold. And given the falsity of type physicalism, the only way for pain to be a first-order property is for it to be a nonphysical property. Property dualism follows.

Rather than expound Bealer's rather complex argument, I will present a simpler and cruder argument (not to be ascribed to him) that I hope conveys its flavor. This argument shares with Bealer's argument an assumption that I shall later question.

Bealer's central argument is directed against what he calls "Ramsified Functionalism," which defines mental states in terms of the Ramsey sentence of a folk-psychological theory in the way proposed by David Lewis.[2] On Bealer's interpretation (a standard one) the quantifiers prefacing the Ramsey sentence of the psychological theory range over first-order properties. So what the definition of a particular mental property or relation says is that an individual instantiates that property or relation just in case the individual instantiates some first-order property or relation that occupies a certain position in a complex network of causally interrelated first-order properties or relations. For short, it says that an individual instantiates the mental property just in case it instantiates some first-order property that plays a certain causal role, where playing the causal role is a matter of belonging to a family of properties that are such that their instantiations stand in certain causal relations to one another and to sensory inputs and behavioral outputs.

It is part of the causal role of pain that under certain conditions its instantiation results in an awareness on the subject's part that it has this property. As we might put it – and here begins my cruder version of the argument – it is part of its causal role that its instantiation results in its being self-ascribed. But if the instantiation of this property is a matter of some first-order realizer of it being instantiated, and if a realizer of it is a property that plays this causal role, then the instantiation of it should result in some first-order realizer property of it being self-ascribed – or, more precisely, in some first-order realizer property of it standing to the subject in a first-order relation that realizes the self-ascription relation. And this is the wrong result. Assuming that the property of being in pain is not identical with any first-order property, the self-ascription of pain cannot consist in, and should not involve, the self-ascription of any first-order property.

[2] See Lewis 1972.

There is an interesting parallel between this argument and the argument that functionalism makes mental properties epiphenomenal. Again, functionalism is taken to hold that mental properties are higher-order properties. Being in pain, for example, is the higher-order property something has just in case it has some first-order property or other that plays a certain causal or functional role. But then whatever causal work we might be inclined to attribute to the mental property will be done by one or another of its first-order realizer properties. The first-order properties will "preempt" whatever causal role the mental property might be supposed to have. So where Bealer's argument faults functionalism for coming to the wrong conclusion about what properties we introspectively self-ascribe, this argument faults functionalism for coming to the wrong conclusion about what causes the things mental events and properties are supposed to cause.

Perhaps the second argument needn't be taken as showing that functionalism is incoherent or false – perhaps it only shows that functionalism has the surprising consequence that mental properties are epiphenomenal. But there does seem to be a threat of incoherence here. For what is the causal role that the realizers of a mental property are supposed to play? It is (at least on some versions of functionalism) precisely the role that the mental property is taken to play in "folk psychology." And it is precisely that role that is supposed to define the mental property. It hardly seems coherent to say that a mental property is defined as the property that plays a certain causal role, and then say that what plays this causal role is not the mental property itself but rather one or another of the physical properties that realize it.

What we need if we want to avoid the conclusion of the second argument is a notion of realization on which realizer properties do not preempt the causal roles of the properties they realize. And I think that a notion that satisfies this need will also enable us to avoid the conclusion of Bealer's argument. Bealer considers the suggestion that we drop from the Ramsey definitions the requirement that the properties be first-order, so as to allow the mental properties themselves to be the properties that play the defining functional roles. He argues that this will have the consequence that the mental properties will themselves be first-order properties. And, as already mentioned, he thinks that because there are compelling reasons to reject type physicalism (the view that mental properties are identical with physical properties), the view that mental properties are first-order properties leads to property dualism. I shall argue that this whole line of thought rests on a mistaken conception of realization, and a distorted conception of the distinction between "first-order" and "higher-order" properties.

II

It seems tautological to say that if mental properties have defining causal roles, then it is the mental properties that play these roles. Of course, someone might think that it is only a first approximation to the truth that it is the mental property that plays the defining causal role. The truth behind the intuition that this is so is that there is a causal role "associated with" each mental property and in some sense defining it – but, the suggestion would be, it turns out on investigation that this causal role is played not by the mental property itself but by a physical property that realizes it. If what it means to say that a physical property realizes a given mental property is that it plays the causal role associated with that property, and if we cannot suppose without introducing an absurd sort of overdetermination that in each case of (supposed) mental causation the causal role is played twice, once by the mental property and once by whatever physical property realizes it on that occasion, such a view would seem to be forced on us. But such an error theory about our mental concepts is to be avoided if at all possible.

What we need is a different account of realization. The account I am about to suggest is partly due to Michael Watkins, and draws on a view about properties that I advanced some years ago.[3] While parts of the latter view are controversial, the part on which I will draw seems to me not to be so.[4]

Any property whose instantiation can be a cause or partial cause of something will be such that its instantiation bestows on its subject a set of what I call "conditional powers." A thing's having a power *simpliciter* is a matter of its being such that its being in certain circumstances, for example, its being related in certain ways to other things of certain sorts, causes (or contributes to causing) certain

---

[3] See Essays 10 and 18. I am indebted to Michael Watkins for pointing out to me that one can think of what I call the forward-looking causal features of a functional property as a proper subset of the causal features of the physical properties that realize it. Watkins develops his version of the view in his *Discovering Colors* (forthcoming). The same view is suggested, independently, by Lenny Clapp in his paper "Disjunctive Properties: Multiple Realization" (2001).

[4] I think, however, that we get a more satisfactory account of realization if we adopt all of my theory of properties rather than just this part. See notes 12 and 26.

effects. A thing has a *conditional* power if it is such that if it had certain properties it would have a certain power simpliciter, where those properties are not themselves sufficient to bestow that power simpliciter. So, for example, the property of being knife-shaped bestows on its possessor the conditional power of being able to cut wood if it is made of steel, and the conditional power of being able to cut butter if it is made of wood. Some properties confer powers simpliciter all by themselves; and we can think of powers simpliciter as a special case of conditional powers. But the more usual case is for the powers simpliciter of a thing to be determined jointly by a number of different properties of it – as the knife's cutting powers are determined jointly by its composition, shape, and size. Saying what conditional powers a property confers specifies what contribution its instantiation can make to the powers simpliciter of the object in which it is instantiated.

The controversial part of my account of properties consists in the claim that it is essential to a property that it confers the particular set of conditional powers it does in the actual world, so that these are conferred by it in any possible world in which it can be instantiated, and that properties that confer exactly the same sets of conditional powers, and also are alike with respect to the possible causes of their instantiation, are identical. But here I shall not assume this part of the account. I assume only that in the actual world the same property always confers the same conditional powers, and that no two properties confer exactly the same conditional powers.

Now sometimes the conditional powers bestowed by one property will be a proper subset of those bestowed by another. This will be true where the one property is a determinable of which the other is a determinate. The set of conditional powers bestowed by redness will be a proper subset of the conditional powers bestowed by scarlet, for example. The different determinates of redness will each confer its distinctive set of conditional powers – but these will have in common the set of conditional powers conferred by redness. Stephen Yablo has given us the example of the pigeon Sophie, who has been conditioned to peck at red things.[5] Being red, together with being of an appropriate size, confers the power of evoking a pecking response from a pigeon such as Sophie under certain conditions. And so does the property of being scarlet. The latter, of course, confers powers not conferred by redness. For example, it confers the power of evoking a pecking response in the likes of Sophie's sister Alice, who was conditioned to peck at scarlet

[5] Yablo 1992.

things but not at things of other shades of red. In such a case we could say that the determinate property realizes the determinable in virtue of the fact that the conditional powers bestowed by the latter are a proper subset of those bestowed by the former.

It is likewise true that the conditional powers conferred by a functional property will be a proper subset of the conditional powers bestowed by whatever physical property realizes it on a particular occasion. Suppose, then, that pain is a functional property, and that someone is in pain in virtue of instantiating a particular physical realization of pain, physical property P_1. What makes P_1 a realization of pain is that the conditional powers conferred by the instantiation of P_1 include the conditional powers conferred by the instantiation of the property of being in pain. Of course, the instantiation of P_1 bestows a number of conditional powers that are not among those associated with the property of being in pain – powers that are specific to it, and are not conferred by other properties that are realizers of pain. For example, it might bestow the power of producing a "P_1" reading on a cerebroscope attached to the subject's head.

In general, then, property X realizes property Y just in case the conditional powers bestowed by Y are a subset of the conditional powers bestowed by X (and X is not a conjunctive property having Y as a conjunct).[6] Where the realized property is multiply realizable, the conditional powers bestowed by it will be a proper subset of the sets bestowed by each of the realizer properties. The different realizer properties will differ from one another in the total sets of conditional powers they confer but will be alike in conferring the conditional powers conferred by the realized property.[7] Being such as to confer a certain conditional power can be said to be a "forward-looking causal feature" of a property. So we can also say that property X realizes property Y just in case the forward-looking causal features of Y are a subset (a proper subset in cases of multiple realization) of those of property X.[8]

---

[6] The need for the condition added in parentheses will be discussed in section VI.

[7] Here I oversimplify. When a concept is a cluster concept, the corresponding property (if we allow there is one) will be disjunctive, and instead of there being a single set of conditional powers corresponding to it there will be a number of overlapping sets.

[8] Because the only causal features of properties I shall be concerned with here are forward-looking ones, I shall sometimes omit the qualifier "forward-looking." But properties also have "backward-looking" causal features, which consist in their being such that their instantiation can be caused in certain ways. These have as much claim to be essential to the properties that have them as do the forward-looking causal features. But it cannot be said that the backward-looking causal features of a property are a subset of the back-

III

Before developing this account further, let us see how it deals with the problem of mental causation, and with the threat that the causal role we attribute to mental properties is preempted by their physical realizers. Suppose physical property P_1 is one of the realizers of the property of being in pain, and that in a particular case the causing of a piece of "pain behavior," say taking an aspirin, involved the exercise of some of the conditional powers conferred by P_1. But suppose further that these conditional powers were all ones belonging to the subset that the property of being in pain and the property P_1 both confer. Which of these property instantiations, that of being in pain or that of P_1, should we say was a cause or partial cause of the piece of behavior? It seems natural to say that it is the instantiation of the property of being in pain. Of course, the person was in pain *by* having P_1. But if we say that it was (in part) in virtue of the instantiation of P_1 that the causing occurred, we should add that it was in its capacity of being a realization of pain, that is, by conferring the conditional powers constitutively bestowed by the property of being in pain, that the instantiation of P_1 made its causal contribution. It is qua realization of pain that P_1 made its contribution to causing the behavior; for the conditional powers it conferred that are independent of those conferred by the property of being in pain were irrelevant to its making this contribution.

Some writers have suggested that when a determinable property is instantiated in virtue of a certain one of its determinates being instantiated, the instance (instancing, instantiation) of the determinable and that of its determinate are identical.[9] So, in a particular case, the instance of redness and that of scarlet are one and the same. Similarly, it is suggested that when a mental property is instantiated in virtue of the instantiation of a physical property that is a realization of it, the instance of the mental property and the instance of its realization are the same. This, of course, has the consequence that

ward-looking causal features of the properties that realize it. On the contrary, the backward-looking causal features of the realizer property seem to be a subset of those of the realized property. The possible causes of instantiations of scarlet are a subset of the possible causes of instantiations of red, and the possible causes of instantiations of P_1 (a realizer of pain) are a subset of the possible causes of instantiations of pain. But I see no need to bring the backward-looking causal features into the account of realization.

[9] See MacDonald and MacDonald 1995. See also Robb 1997, although what his account identifies are mental and physical "tropes," rather than instances of mental and physical properties.

the mental property instance causes whatever effects the physical realizer instance causes. It might seem that this provides a neat solution to the problem of how the mental can be causally efficacious in a physicalist world.

Even supposing the claim about the identity of instances to be correct, it is not clear that this would solve the problem of mental causation. As a solution to that problem it might be held to have the same drawback that a number of writers have charged against Davidson's anomalous monism, as a solution to the problem of mental causation. Anomalous monism claims that token mental events are identical with token physical events, and so cause whatever those physical events cause. But it does not follow from this that these events cause what they do in virtue of being mental events of the kinds they are; on the contrary, it rather seems that they don't, because (Davidson holds) they cause what they do in virtue of being subsumed under physical laws, and they are subsumed under physical laws in virtue of their physical properties, not their mental properties. A similar worry might be raised here. If what is in fact an instance of a mental property causes something (or contributes to causing something), but does so in virtue of being an instance of a physical property rather than in virtue of being an instance of that mental property, then the causal efficacy of the mental does not seem to have been adequately vindicated.

But in any case, it seems doubtful that we should identify the mental property instance with the instance of the physical property that realizes it – or that we should identify the instance of red and the instance of scarlet. If we think of the instantiation of a property as the conferring on something of the conditional powers associated with that property, then when properties confer different sets of conditional powers, the instantiation of one of them is not identical with the instantiation of the other.[10] But it does seem right to say that properties are causally efficacious in virtue of their instances being efficacious. And there is an intimate relation between an instance of a determinable and the instance of the determinate that realizes it on a particular occasion. Likewise, there is an intimate relation between an instance of a functional property and the instance of the property that realizes it on a particular occasion. While it seems wrong to say that a determinable property is part of each of its determinates, or that a functional property is part of each of its realizer properties, it

---

[10] Another reason for not identifying instantiations of determinates and instantiations of determinables with them is given in Yablo 1992, p. 259 fn. 32.

does not seem inappropriate to use the part–whole relation to characterize the relationship between the instances of these pairs of properties.[11] The instantiation of the determinate entails the instantiation of the determinable, and can quite naturally be said to *include* it. It seems natural to me to say that being scarlet is in part being red. Likewise, the instantiation of a realizer property entails, and might naturally be said to include as a part, the instantiation of the functional property realized.[12] The conditional powers conferred by the instance of the determinable or functional property are a proper subset, and in that sense a part, of the conditional powers conferred by the instance of the more determinate property that realizes it on a particular occasion.

Suppose then that we say that the instance of scarlet involved in Yablo's Sophie example has the instance of red as a part. Because the part–whole relation is not identity, we cannot argue that the instance of red caused whatever the instance of scarlet caused. But given that Sophie's pecking was a consequence of the instance of scarlet, we can ask whether what caused it was this instance as a whole or some

[11] At one time I thought that one could simply *identify* a property with a "cluster" of conditional powers having a certain kind of unity. If one could do that then, because the conditional powers associated with the property of being in pain are a proper subset of each of the sets of conditional powers associated with the properties that realize pain, one could say that the property of being in pain is literally a *part* of each of the realizer properties. In that case there is certainly no question of the realizer properties "preempting" the realized property with respect to causal efficacy – not if the realized property is a part of the realizing property, and is the part that includes the conditional powers involved in the episode of causation. For reasons I cannot go into here, I no longer want to identify a property with a cluster of conditional powers (see essay 18). While rejecting that identification bars me from construing realized properties as parts of their realizer properties, it does not bar me from construing instances of realized properties as parts of instances of realizer properties.

[12] Here it matters whether the causal features of a property belong to it essentially (as on the causal theory of properties I favor), or belong to it only contingently. If they belong to it essentially it will be straightforwardly true that the instantiation of the realizer property entails the instantiation of the realized property. If they belong to it contingently then what entails the instantiation of the realized property is not the instantiation of the realizer property by itself, but its instantiation *having the causal features it in fact has*, or, what comes to the same thing, *being governed by the causal laws that in fact hold*. If *realize* means something similar to *make real*, perhaps we should say that the realization includes the possession of those causal features, or the holding of those causal laws – so that where the causal essentialist view says that the realizer property is physical property P, the contingency view says that it is P *and such that* L, where "L" stands for the causal laws that actually obtain. Then it will be true on both views that the instantiation of the realizer property entails the instantiation of the realized property.

This seems required if we are to say that realizations of functional properties are determinates of them; for I think that it is part of the usual conception of the determinable–determinate relationship that the instantiation of a determinable is entailed by the instantiation of any of its determinates.

proper part of it. (Compare: Someone's dying might be said to be a consequence of the fusillade of shots from the firing squad, but because many of those shots may have missed it may be that what caused his death was not the fusillade as a whole but some part of it.) And here it seems appropriate to say that it was a part of it, namely the instance of red, that did the causing, because it was the conditional powers conferred by that part that were relevant to the effect (they are the ones that were conferred in other cases, when Sophie pecked at things of other shades of red). Similar circumstances exist in the case where the instances are instances of a functional property and of one of its physical realizations.

Stephen Yablo has suggested that where one event is a determinate of another, in the way Socrates' guzzling hemlock is a determinate of Socrates' drinking hemlock, the events do not compete for causal relevance to a particular effect or for causal sufficiency for that effect, but do compete for the status of being a cause of that effect.[13] And he suggests that the one that is the (or a) cause is the one that is, in a sense he spells out, "proportional" to the effect.[14] I think that Yablo's notion of proportionality can be applied here. Where the only causal features of property P_1 that play a role in producing an effect are ones that belong to property P_2, of which P_1 is a determinate or realizer property, there seems a good sense in which considerations of proportionality favor the instantiation of P_2 over the instantiation of P_1 as a cause of the effect.

IV

I will now explain more fully how this view of realization works. It is a commonplace that the behavior we attribute to mental states is typically the manifestation of a combination of mental states rather than any single state taken by itself.[15] Assuming that the manifestations of mental states are caused by them, we can illustrate this by saying that a given belief causes a piece of behavior in conjunction with certain of the subject's desires and certain of the subject's other beliefs. So the conditional powers conferred by the property *believes*

---

[13] Yablo 1992.

[14] Proportionality requires that effects be *contingent* on their causes, and that causes be *adequate* for their effects, *required* by them, and *enough* for them. See Yablo 1992 for details.

[15] This point, commonly attributed to Roderick Chisholm and Peter Geach, is the core of an important criticism of philosophical behaviorism.

that it is raining include, among countless others, one that can be roughly characterized as *being such that if one wants to keep dry and believes that umbrellas keep off rain, this will result in one's taking an umbrella if one goes out.* Suppose that on a particular occasion the belief that it is raining, call it Br, is realized in physical property P_1. I say that the conditional power just characterized is among those conferred by P_1. P_1 is such that in combination with certain other mental states, certain desires and other beliefs, it causes certain behaviors.

But of course, those other mental states will themselves be physically realized. Suppose that in the case just envisioned the relevant desires and other beliefs are realized in physical properties P_2, P_3, and P_4. P_1 will "combine" with the mental properties in question to produce the behavior by combining with the realizations of those properties, in other words, P_2, P_3, and P_4. So in the first instance the conditional power bestowed by P_1 is *being such that if one has P_2, P_3, and P_4, this results in one's taking an umbrella if one goes out.* But given that P_2, P_3, and P_4 are realizations of the mental states in question, being such as to confer this conditional power will amount to being such as to confer the conditional power that belongs to the belief-property that P_1 realizes. Being such as to confer a certain conditional power is a forward-looking causal feature of a property. Let's say that such a causal feature is a *mental causal feature* if the properties referred to in specifying the conditional power are mental properties, and that it is a *physical causal feature* if the properties referred to in specifying the conditional power are physical properties. We can now say that when mental property Br is realized by physical property P_1, the mental causal features of Br are realized in physical causal features of P_1. But I should emphasize that these mental causal features of Br are shared by P_1; they are realized in P_1 by its physical causal features.

Assuming that Br is multiply realizable, it will have possible realizations other than P_1. Each of these will share the mental causal features of P_1 and Br. But they will not necessarily share the physical causal features in which these are realized. A creature in which Br cannot be realized by P_1, because P_1 is not in its repertoire of possible properties, will most likely be such that P_2–P_4 are also not in its repertoire of possible properties. Its having the causal feature that interests us, that is, being such as to confer a certain mental conditional power, will not consist in its being such that in combination with P_2–P_4 it causes certain results. For it will not be capable of combining with those properties. Its mental causal features will be realized in some quite different physical features, including its being such that in combination with some quite different physical properties – call them Px, Py, and Pz – it causes certain behavior.

It should be clear that when mental properties $M1 \ldots Mn$ combine to produce certain effects, and these properties are physically realizable, it will not be the case that just any set of physical properties $P1 \ldots Pn$ that are, respectively, realizations of $M1 \ldots Mn$ will combine to produce those effects. This will be so only if $P1 \ldots Pn$ are jointly instantiable. The different physical properties that are realizers of mental properties will fall into a number of different "families" of properties, the members of each family being jointly instantiable. The forward-looking causal features of a realizer property will have to do with how instantiations of it can combine with other members of the same family to produce various effects. Presumably the physical realizations of mental states in Earthlings and the physical realizations of the same mental states in the Martians and supercomputers of philosophical fiction will typically not be jointly instantiable, and will not belong to a single family.[16]

---

[16] There is one challenge to this view of realization that requires a more extended treatment than it is possible to give here. Some mental states have "wide content," which makes the associated mental properties partly historical and relational. For example, the property of believing that there is water in the glass is a property one has partly in virtue of having a certain sort of history of interaction with a certain sort of environment (Earthlike rather than Twin Earthlike) – having this history is partly constitutive of having the property. Any realization of this property will itself have to be a property that is partly historical and relational. But in that case, how can the relation between realizer property and property realized be simply a matter of the conditional powers bestowed by the former being a superset of those bestowed by the latter? It is natural to suppose that the causally efficacious part of the instantiation of such a realizer property, what bestows the conditional powers, will be the contemporary intrinsic state of the subject's brain, and that the historical/relational part will be without causal efficacy. Yet given that the realized state essentially has wide content, and so is partly historical and relational, this causally efficacious part of the realizer property will not be sufficient for the instantiation of the realized property.

The first step toward answering this objection is to notice that it is possible for the possession of a power to require, constitutively, the having of properties that are partly historical and relational. For example, only someone with a certain sort of history, the details of which are spelled out in the U.S. Constitution, has the power to veto acts of Congress. Other examples involve the power of ministers to make couples husband and wife, the power of professors to pass and fail students, and the power many of us have to make purchases with credit cards. I think that if we get a satisfactory understanding of the sort of causation involved in these cases, we will be in a position to see how the powers bestowed by mental properties can be such that they can only be bestowed by properties that are partly historical and relational. Here I think Fred Dretske's distinction between "triggering causes" and "structuring causes" can be put to use (see Dretske 1993). But that is a topic for another paper.

V

Now let us return to Bealer's argument that functionalism leads to the wrong result about what a person is self-ascribing when self-ascribing pain. It will be recalled that his argument assumes that the properties quantified over in Ramsey–Lewis-style functional definitions are first-order properties, presumably physical ones, and that according to functionalism mental properties are second-order properties. The undesired result is that what a person self-ascribes is not pain but one of the first-order properties that realize it.

Bealer takes it to be a primary tenet of what he calls ontological functionalism that mental properties are "definable wholly in terms of the general pattern of interaction of ontologically prior 'realizations' " (p. 105). He clearly takes ontological functionalism to be committed to the notion of realization I have rejected, that which seems to make mental properties epiphenomenal.

On the alternative view of realization I have suggested, realized properties can be causally efficacious, and it can sometimes be the case that it is the instantiation of a realized property rather than an instantiation of a realizer of it that should be regarded as causing a certain effect. So on this view, there is every reason not to require that the properties quantified over in a Ramsey–Lewis-style functional definition be restricted to the first-order realizer properties. The properties quantified over turn out to include the mental properties. And then there is no route to Bealer's conclusion that Ramsified Functionalism leads to the absurd result that what should be self-ascriptions of pain are really self-ascriptions of physical realizers of pain.

Does that mean that we should reject Bealer's characterization according to which the properties quantified over are first-order properties? That depends on whether functional properties can count as first-order. Bealer tells us that first-order properties of individuals are "either primitive properties or properties of individuals definable in terms of primitive properties of individuals plus quantification over individuals" (pp. 70–1), but he does not tell us what it is for a property to be primitive, or how "definable in terms of" is to be understood. If the fact that functional properties are realized in properties other than themselves makes them nonprimitive and "definable in terms of" the realizer properties, then functionalism denies that mental properties are first-order. But if it is sufficient for a property's being first-order that its instantiation can be

Identity, cause, and mind

causally efficacious, then functional properties can count as first-order.[17]

I think that functionalists (including myself) who have championed the sort of Ramsified functional definitions Bealer discusses have gotten into trouble by trying to combine two tasks. They have tried to define (or to provide a recipe for defining) mental states in terms of their causal or functional roles. And they have tried to give an account of how mental properties are physically realized. These are combined by saying that to have a certain mental state, or instantiate a certain mental property, is to instantiate some realizer property or other that plays a certain causal role. If Bealer is right, this leads to the wrong result about what we self-ascribe in what should be self-ascriptions of mental properties such as being in pain. And it also leads to epiphenomenalist worries, because it lends support for the view that physical properties preempt the causal roles we want to ascribe to mental properties.[18]

So I suggest that functionalists should separate these two tasks. Their definitions of mental states should be of the sort Bealer envisages "ideological" functionalists as giving – mental properties should be characterized in terms of *their* causal relations to one another and to inputs and outputs. And then they should give a separate account of what it is for these properties to be realized. The latter account will be along the lines I have been suggesting. The realizer properties will be physical ones whose forward-looking causal features include those of the mental property as a proper subset.

Does this mean that, in Bealer's terms, I advocate abandoning "ontological functionalism" in favor of "ideological functionalism"? In advocating separating the two tasks just distinguished, I do favor a formulation of functionalism that does not incorporate one ontological claim that virtually all functionalists accept, namely the claim

---

[17] There is a sense in which any determinable property, and any multiply realizable property, is second-order. Each such property is associated with a class of properties, of which it is not a member, such that it is necessary and sufficient for something's having that property that it have some property or other in that class. (Of course, unless we put some restriction on what count as properties, any property whatever will be second-order in this sense. For let P be any property, and Q any other property. P is not a member of the class $[P\&Q, P\&-Q]$, yet it is necessary and sufficient for something's having P that it have some member or other of this class. So we will want to stipulate that the members of the class are not logical compounds involving our property.)

[18] One way to avoid these difficulties is to follow David Lewis in denying that terms such as *pain* are rigid designators, and holding that they always refer to one or another of the realizers of a functional property rather than to the functional property. See Lewis 1980. I dissent from Lewis's view in Essay 12, although I do not there consider this reason for holding it.

that mental properties are realized in properties with which they are not identical. But I do not see why the claim that mental properties are themselves defined by certain causal roles, and have certain causal features essentially, should not itself count as an ontological thesis, and should be said to have "only 'ideological' significance" (p. 90).[19]

VI

On the account I am suggesting, traditional examples of the determinable–determinate relation are instances of the relation between a property and a realizer of it; for example, being red can be said to be realized by being scarlet. And while this may depart from the traditional notion of the determinable–determinate relation, I shall sometimes speak of realizers as determinates of the properties they realize, and so shall construe the relation of mental properties to their physical realizers as an instance of the relation of determinables to their determinates.[20] In any case, it seems clear that properties fall into hierarchies, where the properties higher in a hierarchy are those

[19] There is one strand in Bealer's paper I have not discussed. He gives a "diagonal argument" to show that there is "a system of nonstandard properties that behave with respect to each other and the external environment in exactly the same way that the standard mental properties behave with respect to each other and the external environment" (p. 107). And he takes this to show that even ideological functionalism fails, unless it allows that the standard mental properties, which he thinks he has already shown to be first-order and nonphysical, are "natural" universals as well.

Now I have already argued that Bealer's argument fails to show that the mental properties are first-order in a way that precludes their having physical realizations, and so fails to show that they are nonphysical. And I take it that their "naturalness" is a consequence of the fact that their instantiation plays a role in the causing of what goes on in the world. I have no idea whether Bealer's argument succeeds in establishing that mental properties are necessarily coextensive with "deviant" properties such as his "thunking," the deviant relation that supposedly mimics the functional behavior of thinking, for I confess to being unable to take the argument in. But supposing there are such deviant properties, he could not hold that these are causally efficacious in the way mental properties are without holding that the behavioral effects of mental property instantiations are massively overdetermined. And because in any case he holds that thunking and its ilk are not natural, presumably he does not want to hold this. So functional definitions as I would want to formulate them, ones that require that the properties being defined have genuine causal efficacy, could not be satisfied by Bealer's deviant properties. Bealer points out (personal communication) that logically equivalent sentences are substitutable *salva veritate* within the scope of causal-necessity operators. So, if thinking and thunking are necessarily coextensive, and if the causal role of properties is specified only by the use of such operators, thunking will have a causal role that parallels that of thinking. This can be avoided either by using causal idioms of a different sort (e.g., "*x*'s being *F* causes . . .") in one's functional definitions, or by stipulating that the properties quantified over in the definitions are natural ones.

[20] Here I follow Yablo, in his 1992.

whose forward-looking causal features are included in the causal features of properties lower in the hierarchy.

One thing that could be meant by "first-order property" is a property that is, as I shall say, *self-realized* – in other words, is such that its instantiation does not consist in the instantiation of some other property of which its causal features are a proper subset. To understand *first-order property* in this way would be to restrict its application to properties that are ultimate determinates. There is, I think, no plausibility in the view that only such properties can be causally efficacious.

A self-realized property will be at the bottom of one of the hierarchies mentioned previously. It will realize properties above it in the hierarchy, which in turn will realize properties still higher in the hierarchy.

It might be supposed that if we start with the set of causal features of a self-realized property, there will be a property associated with every subset of this set, and each of these will have the self-realized property as a realizer. If this were so, then what is grounded in the self-realized property would not be a single hierarchy but a very complex treelike structure.

But it clearly will not do to say that given a property and its set of causal features, there is a property corresponding to every subset of that set. It also will not do to say that in every case in which the causal features of one property are a subset of the causal features of another, the second is a realizer of the first and is determinate relative to it.

Let me start with the last point. Assuming that there are conjunctive properties, it is clear that the causal features of such a property will have as subsets the sets of the causal features of its conjuncts. But plainly we do not want to say that each of the conjuncts of a conjunctive property is a determinable relative to it, and is realized by it. Assuming there is a conjunctive property corresponding to every pair of properties that can be instantiated together, and that every property belongs to such a pair, this would have the consequence that every property is a determinable relative to other properties. Clearly, if we are to define realization in terms of the subset relation, we need to impose some restriction that rules out conjunctive properties as realizers of their conjuncts.

Let's turn to the suggestion that there is a property corresponding to every subset of the causal features of a property. I have said that the causal features of the property of being red are a subset of the causal features of being scarlet. But consider those causal features of being scarlet that are *not* included in the set associated with being red. If there is a property corresponding to the subset consisting of these, then the property of being scarlet is the conjunction of the property of being red and some other property. Intuitively this is not so. And it is commonly said about the determinate–determinable relationship that a determinate cannot be regarded as the conjunction of the determinable and some other property.

What we saw previously is that what is commonly said about the determinate–determinable relationship should also be said about the relation between realizers and the properties they realize – realizers cannot be just conjunctive properties having the realized property as a conjunct. A realizer of the property of being in pain cannot be being in pain *and* being F, for some F. And that goes with the fact that not every subset of a property's causal features defines a property having just that set of causal features. To put it in another way, not every subset of the conditional powers conferred by a property is such that there is a property that confers just that subset.

What we need here is an account of the conditions under which a set of conditional powers is such that there is a property that confers just that set of conditional powers. Given such an account, we can say that property P realizes property Q just in case the conditional powers conferred by Q are a subset of the conditional powers conferred by P *and* there is no property R such that R confers just the conditional powers that are conferred by P and not by Q. This, of course, rules out conjunctive properties as realizers of their conjuncts.

In an earlier paper I addressed this issue, for a different reason, and suggested the following as a "unity relation" for properties: conditional powers X and Y are conferred by the same property if and only if it is a consequence of causal laws that either (1) whatever has either of them has the other, or (2) there is some third conditional power such that whatever has it has both X and Y.[21] In line with this, we could suggest there is a property that confers all and only the members of a set just in case every pair of members of the set satisfies this condition. This has the disadvantage that it rules out conjunctive properties. Obviously, if for any coinstantiable properties P and Q there is a property something has just in case it has both P and Q, then where P and Q are nomically independent (neither is such that its instantiation requires that the other be coinstantiated with it) there will be conditional powers C_1 and C_2, conferred by P and Q respectively and conferred by the conjunction of the two, that

---

[21] See Essay 10.

will not satisfy this condition. We might, however, give this as an account of what it is for there to be a basic, nonconjunctive, property that confers all and only the conditional powers in a set, and then allow for conjunctive properties by saying that there is a property that confers all and only members of a set just in case either (1) the set satisfies the condition just stated, or (2) the set can be partitioned into two or more sets, each of which satisfies that condition.

While I am inclined to think that satisfaction of the condition I have just formulated is a necessary condition for a set of conditional powers being such that there is a property corresponding to it, I am not sure that this is so. In any case, it is not sufficient. A further requirement is that the set be closed under nomic and metaphysical entailment – that for every conditional power contained in the set, the set contains every conditional power nomically or metaphysically entailed by that conditional power.[22] In what follows, I will assume only this necessary condition for a set of conditional powers having a property corresponding to it.

Let us return to the example of red and scarlet, and let us consider the set of conditional powers that are conferred by scarlet and not by red. These will include the power to elicit pecking in the likes of Alice (the pigeon conditioned to peck at scarlet things, but not at things of other shades of red), the power to produce an experience having a certain phenomenal character in human observers, and so forth. Although these are not conditional powers conferred by the property of being red, it would appear that they cannot be instantiated in something unless it is red and so has the conditional powers conferred by the property of being red. So the set in question fails to contain conditional powers that are nomically entailed by conditional powers in it; it is not closed under nomic and metaphysical entailment. That being so, there cannot be a property corresponding to that set of conditional powers.

I think the same will be so if we consider a physical realizer of a functional property and consider the conditional powers bestowed by it that are not bestowed by that functional property. The property of being a braking system is a multiply realizable functional property. Consider then a complex physical property the instantiation of which would give us a mechanical braking system of a certain design. This

---

[22] One conditional power nomically entails another just in case it is a consequence of causal laws that whatever has the first has the second; and one metaphysically entails another just in case it is a metaphysically necessary truth that whatever has the one has the other. On the causal theory of properties I favor, nomic entailment is a special case of metaphysical entailment – but I do not assume this here.

property confers whatever conditional powers are conferred by the functional property of being a braking system, but confers a number of others that are not conferred by other physical realizers of that functional property, for example, those that give us hydraulic braking systems, or electronic ones. So consider the conditional powers it confers that are not conferred by the functional property. I think it is clear that there is no property that confers these and only these conditional powers. If there were, the realizer property would be a conjunctive property having two nomically independent conjuncts, one of which is the functional property. And that is certainly not the case.

VII

On the account I am defending, functional properties are genuine properties whose instantiations confer conditional powers and play a role in the production of various effects. But a number of recent writers have questioned the genuineness of functional properties. Sometimes the challenge is based on the worry that the causal efficacy of functional properties is preempted by their realizations.[23] I have tried to show that that worry is baseless. A related worry, recently voiced by Jaegwon Kim, is that functional properties fail to be inductively projectible, and are for that reason unsuited for entering into causal laws.[24]

Kim compares pain, as construed by functionalists, with the property of being jade. Jade is a "disjunctive kind" rather than a natural kind. The two kinds of jade, jadeite and nephrite, are entirely different minerals that are alike only in their superficial properties (and in properties common to all minerals). And according to Kim, the property of being jade is not inductively projectible. This is supposedly shown by the fact that if our inductive sample consisted solely of pieces of jadeite, or solely of pieces of nephrite, the fact that all members of the sample are F would not give inductive support to the generalization that all pieces of jade are F. Kim suggests that if being in pain is a functional property, realizable in a variety of different physical properties, it fails to be projectible in the same way. For Kim this makes it questionable whether, assuming functionalism, there

---

[23] See Block 1990, and various papers by Jaegwon Kim in his 1993*b*, including his 1993*a*.
[24] See Kim 1993*a*.

really is a genuine property shared by the things the predicate "is in pain" is true of.

But compare the property of being jade with the property of being an acid, which I assume Kim would count as a genuine property, well suited to figuring in causal laws. Being an acid is a multiply realizable property. There are many different ways of being an acid – being sulfuric acid, being hydrochloric acid, being citric acid, and so forth. And just as we will go wrong in our inductions about jade if we rely on a sample consisting of only jadeite, so we will go wrong in our inductions about acids if we rely on a sample consisting of only sulfuric acid. For example, we may conclude, falsely, that all acids contain sulfur.[25]

There is a difference having to do with projectibility between the property of being jade and the property of being an acid, but it is not happily put by saying that the latter is projectible and the former is not. What is true is that if we do induction on a sample containing various kinds of acid, we stand a good chance of turning up generalizations true of acids generally. While if we do induction on a sample containing the various (two) kinds of jade, we are unlikely to turn up generalizations true of jade generally, except where these are generalizations true of minerals generally and so not specific to jade. If indeed we do find that the members of our sample share some property beyond those used to pick them out as jade, and not shared by minerals generally, we can take this as supporting the claim that that property is shared by pieces of jade generally. So the hypothesis that it is so shared is inductively projectible. But believing what we do about jade, we do not expect that to happen. (If it did happen, we might revise our beliefs about jade, and decide that it is a "natural kind" after all.)

But what underlies the difference between these two properties? Both properties confer sets of conditional powers, and both are multiply realizable. Why should they differ with respect to inductive projectibility?

The kind of induction we are here concerned with aims at discovering the causal features of a property, that is, discovering what conditional powers it confers. Obviously, if a property is picked out as the property having all and only a certain set of causal features, there is no room for this sort of induction concerning it – in picking it out we already know what this sort of induction seeks to discover. Assuming that properties are picked out by their causal features, it

<hr>

[25] A similar point is made by Louis Antony and Joe Levine in their 1997.

would seem that induction is possible only when a property is picked out by some proper subset of its causal features. We "fix the reference" of a property term by a description specifying such a subset, and then proceed to investigate empirically what further causal features the property referred to possesses. But as we have noted, the same set of causal features can belong to a number of different properties; so a description of the form "The property having thus and such causal features" will not in general be uniquely referring. And as we have also noted, a description of the form "The property having all and only thus and such causal features" will not pick out a property we can proceed to do induction on.

What will give us what we want is a description of the form "The most determinate property having thus and such causal features that is instantiated around here – or is instantiated in thus and such objects." This can pick out a unique property, and one that we can learn about by induction. If we think of the reference of terms such as *acid* as fixed by descriptions of this sort, we can understand how induction with respect to them is possible. Let's use the term *acidish* as a name for the property having all and only the causal features by reference to which the property of being an acid was initially picked out, and let's call those features acidish causal features. These features will include such powers as corrosiveness, and the disposition to turn blue litmus paper red. It may be that something could be acidish without being an acid. We cannot exclude a priori, or by simple induction, the possibility that being acidish relates to being an acid as being jade relates to being jadeite. And with respect to projectibility, the property of being acidish would be on a par with the property of being jade. But we can suppose that the reference of the term *acid* is fixed by the description "The most determinate property shared by thus and such things that has the acidish causal features." We can then set about to discover what other causal features the property so designated has – and can eventually discover the subatomic basis of acidity, namely that acids are proton donors. A functional definition of a property can be thought of as specifying a set of conditional powers and saying that anything having those conditional powers has that property; or as specifying a set of causal features and saying that anything having a property having those causal features has that property. It might be thought that this amounts to defining the property as the property having all and only certain causal features. But this isn't quite right. While a functional definition leaves open the possibility that the property defined is multiply realizable, it does not, taken by itself, exclude the possibility that there is just one nomologically possible way of realizing it, or the possibility that while there are a number of different ways of realizing it, all of the nomologically possible realizer properties share causal features in addition to those that define it. Should either of these possibilities be realized, it would seem that the functional property would have causal features over and above those that define it – it would have those that belong to its sole nomologically possible realizer, or those shared by all of its nomologically possible realizers.[26]

So there is room for an empirical discovery of a "hidden nature" of a functional property. But such a discovery is unlikely to be made by enumerative induction. It could not be an extrapolation from the fact that in examined cases the realizers of a functional property share some causal feature not included in the set of features that define the property – for such a fact would give scant support to the claim that it is nomically impossible for a property lacking that

---

[26] Here is a place where it may matter whether one accepts my view that it is true generally of properties, and not just of (what are generally regarded as) functional properties, that their causal features are essential to them, and that nomological necessity is a special case of metaphysical necessity. On this view, if it is nomologically necessary that a certain functional property be realized by a property having certain causal features, then this is metaphysically necessary. Given this, the case would seem very strong for saying that those causal features belong to the functional property. On the other hand, if one thinks that causal laws are contingent, and that while the causal features of functional properties are essential to them the causal features of other properties are not, then it may seem possible to hold that the causal features that belong to all of the nomologically possible realizers of a functional property do not belong to the functional property itself, on the grounds that in other possible worlds the functional property can be instantiated without being realized by a property with those features. Of course, if a proponent of this view holds that what are essential to functional properties are only their defining causal features, and does not insist that these are their only causal features, he can hold that functional properties possess, although only contingently, those causal features that belong to all of their nomologically possible realizer properties.

It occurs to me that one reason why some philosophers find functional properties suspect is that they assume that it is true of paradigmatic "natural" properties that they have their causal features contingently. From this vantage point, properties defined as having certain causal features essentially may seem to be a kind of artifact. On the view I recommend, that all properties have their causal features essentially, there will not be this difference in status between functional properties and other properties.

A related reason why functional properties may be found suspect is that on the usual view that "ordinary" properties, including all first-order properties, have their causal features contingently, it will be possible for things in different possible worlds to be exactly alike in their intrinsic first-order properties, and so (it would seem) to be duplicates, and yet differ in their functional properties. And then it may seem that functional properties fail to be intrinsic, despite the monadic character of the predicates that express them. On the view that properties have their causal features essentially there of course will not be this reason for regarding functional properties as nonintrinsic. (Of course, externalism about content provides a reason for regarding some mental properties as not intrinsic; but this is a consideration independent of functionalism.)

feature to realize the property. (At one time all computers contained tubes, but the inference from this to the conclusion that it is nomically necessary for computers to contain tubes would surely have been unwarranted.) What might ground such a discovery are theoretical considerations showing that, given the fundamental laws governing the physical entities out of which possessors of the functional property are built, only microphysical properties of a certain sort could realize the functional property.

But let us return to properties, such as being an acid, that are prime examples of projectible properties. I have suggested that it is characteristic of these that reference to them is fixed by reference to paradigm exemplars of them in a way that leaves open what many of their causal features are. Such a property might be picked out as the most determinate property having certain causal features that is commonly found in a certain class of things, a class whose specification might be in part indexical, and we might well find that such a property has additional causal features. But there is more to it than this. When a property is picked out in this way, we expect not only that the property will have causal features beyond those by which it is picked out, these being shared by its different realizer properties, but also that there is something in common to the various realizer properties that *explains* their shared causal features. The property of being an acid has many different realizations, differing from one another in many of their causal features. But in addition to sharing the "acidish" causal features, they share microphysical features, including those that make their possessors proton donors, that explain their acidish causal features. The causal features of the microstructural chemical property that realizes the property of being an acid on a particular occasion will include as a subset the causal features of that property. But that won't be the explanatory relationship. The explanatory relationship will be between, on the one hand, certain properties of, and certain relations between, protons and other subatomic particles and, on the other, the macroproperties of assemblages of these that have the conditional powers that go with acidity. The former will be the properties and relations that make something a proton donor and account for the fact that proton donors do the things acids do. Precisely what properties and relations of these sorts are involved will vary from acid to acid – but there will be a good deal in common to the explanatory stories in the case of different sorts of acid, and different realizers of the property of being an acid.

We can, of course, be wrong in expecting there to be this sort of commonality between different ways of realizing a property – but if we do turn out to be wrong, we will cease to regard the property as well suited for doing induction on.

In the case of functional properties we do not expect there to be this sort of commonality. As already indicated, the ways these are picked out make them unsuited for induction. And while it is possible that we might find theoretical reasons for supposing there is some commonality in the explanatory basis of different realizations of them, nothing in the way they are picked out gives us reason to expect this.

Where the defining functional role of a functional property is fairly thin, its explanatory potential will be limited. Being a functional property, it will (most likely) have no hidden nature that suits it for being invoked in explanations beyond the obvious ones, those that invoke the defining functional role. And when the defining role is thin, the obvious ones are likely to seem superficial – as in the explanation of someone's going to sleep in terms of the dormativity of the pill he took. This does not at all call into question the causal efficacy of such properties. Saying that taking the pill caused sleep because it was dormative can be true even though it fails as an explanation because it fails to give us causal information we did not already possess, or causal information of the sort we were after.

In any case, what is distinctive about mental properties, on a functionalist understanding of them, is that their defining functional roles (unlike that of dormativity) are extremely rich, and make possible illuminating explanations that are far from obvious. Arguably, there are no properties whose causal and explanatory roles are richer. They differ, in the ways I have indicated, from such properties as being an acid. The differences are what we should expect, given the differences in the ways the properties are picked out. But these differences provide no reason for denying that these properties have either explanatory or causal efficacy.

If mental properties are not functional properties, but are nevertheless multiply realizable, the way they are picked out must be more similar to the way the property of being an acid is picked out than was supposed previously. It will still be the case that each mental property will confer a set of conditional powers, which will amount to its playing a distinctive causal or functional role. And on a causal theory of properties this will be essential to it. But the way mental properties are picked out may carry the presupposition that there is the sort of commonality between the different realizers of a mental property that we expect there to be between the different realizers of a property such as being an acid, and do not expect there to be between the different realizers of a functional property. This is what I have called a "parochial" view of mental properties, and it allows for the possibility of "ersatz" mental states – states functionally similar to the mental states of various kinds that do not count as mental states of those (or any) kinds. To my way of thinking, the reality of the properties with which such a view would identify mental properties is no more robust than that of the functional properties with which functionalism identifies them. Both sorts of properties are "there," instantiated in creatures that are said to have mental states. It is a semantic question, which I do not here address, which sort our mental terms refer to, or our mental concepts pick out.

VIII

I have suggested that one property's realizing another is a matter of the forward-looking causal features of the first containing the forward-looking causal features of the second as a subset, with the proviso (discussed in section VI) that the realizing property not be a conjunctive property of which the realized property is a conjunct. Such a view makes it unmysterious that the causal efficacy of a multiply realized property is not preempted by that of its realizer properties, especially if combined with Stephen Yablo's point that causes should be proportionate to their effects. It has the added benefit that it disarms George Bealer's argument that functionalism leads to the wrong conclusion about what property a person is self-ascribing when, so we would think, she is self-ascribing pain.[27]

---

[27] A shorter version of this chapter was delivered in August 1998 at the 20th World Congress of Philosophy, and was published in volume 9 of the proceedings of that congress. I am grateful to George Bealer, Barry Loewer, Zoltan Szabo, Michael Watkins, and Steve Yablo for comments on an earlier version of the chapter.

References

Achinstein, Peter (1974). "The Identity of Properties."*American Philosophical Quarterly*, 2.

Antony, Louise, and Levine, Joseph (1997). "Reduction with Autonomy." *Philosophical Perspectives*, v, 11.

Aristotle (1941). *Physics. In the Basic Works of Aristotle*, trans. by R. P. Hardie and R. K. Gaye, ed. by Richard Mckeon. New York: Random House.

Armstrong, David (1968). *A Materialist Theory of Mind*. London: Routledge and Kegan Paul.

—— (1973). "Acting and Trying." *Philosophical Papers*. Reprinted in Armstrong, *The Nature of Mind*. Ithaca, N.Y.: Cornell University Press.

—— (1978). *A Theory of Universals, Universals and Scientific Realism*. Cambridge: Cambridge University Press.

—— (1980). "Identity Through Time." In Peter van Inwagen (ed.), *Time and Cause, Essays Presented to Richard Taylor*. Dordrecht, Netherlands: Reidel Publishing Co.

Aune, Bruce (1962). "Fatalism and Professor Taylor." *The Philosophical Review*, 71.

Ayer, A. J. (1956). *The Problem of Knowledge*. Harmondsworth: Penguin Books.

Barker, S.F., and Achinstein, P. (1960). "On the New Riddle of Induction." *The Philosophical Review*, 69.

Bealer, George (1997). "Self Consciousness." *The Philosophical Review*, 106, 1.

Bennett, Jonathan (1966). *Kant's Analytic*. Cambridge: Cambridge University Press.

Berlin, B., and Kay, P. (1969). *Basic Color Terms*. Berkeley and Los Angeles: California University Press.

Black, Max (1949). *Language and Philosophy*, Ithaca, N.Y.: Cornell University Press.

Block, Ned (1978). "Troubles with Functionalism." In C. Wade Savage (ed.), *Perception and Cognition, Issues in the Foundations of Psychology. Minnesota Studies in the Philosophy of Science*. Minneapolis: Minnesota University Press. Reprinted in Block 1980b.

—— (1980a). "Are Absent Qualia Impossible?" *The Philosophical Review*, 89.

—— (1980b). *Readings in the Philosophy of Psychology*, vol. I. Cambridge, Mass.: Harvard University Press.

—— (1980c). "Introduction" to Block 1980b.

—— (1990). "Can the Mind Change the World?" in G. Boolos (ed), *Meaning *and Method, Essays in Honor of Hilary Putnam.* Cambridge: Cambridge University Press.

—— and Fodor, J. A. (1972). "What Psychological States are Not." *The Philosophical Review*, 81. Reprinted in Block 1980*b*.

Boyd, Richard (1979). "Metaphor and Theory Change." In Andrew Ortony (ed.), *Metaphor and Thought.* Cambridge: Cambridge University Press.

—— (1980). "Materialism without Reductionism: What Physicalism Does not Entail." In Block 1980*b*.

Boyle, Robert (1744). "The Origins and Forms of Qualities." In *The Works of the Honourable Robert Boyle.* London.

Broad, C. D. (1938). *An Examination of McTaggart's Philosophy*, vol II. Cambridge: Cambridge University Press.

Butler, Joseph (1975). "Of Personal Identity." First Dissertation to the *Analogy of Religion.* Reprinted in Perry 1975*a*.

Campbell, Keith (1970). *Body and Mind.* Garden City, N.Y.: Anchor Books.

Cartwright, Helen, (1970). "Quantities." *The Philosophical Review*, 79.

Castañeda, Hector-Neri (1966). " 'He': A Study in the Logic of Self-Consciousness." *Ratio*, 8.

—— (1967). "Indicators and Quasi-Indicators." *American Philosophical Quarterly*, 4.

Chisholm, Roderick, (1963). *Perceiving, A Philosophical Study.* Ithaca, N.Y.: Cornell University Press.

—— (1965). " 'Appear,' 'Take,' and 'Evident' ". In R. J. Swartz (ed.), *Perceiving, Sensing and Knowing.* Garden City, N.Y.: Anchor Books.

—— (1969). "The Loose and Popular and the Strict and Philosophical Senses of Identity." In N. S. Care and R. H. Grimm (eds.), *Perception and Personal Identity.* Cleveland: Press of Case Western Reserve University.

—— (1976). *Person and Object.* La Salle, Ill.: Open Court.

Clapp, Leonard (2001). "Disjunctive Properties." *Journal of Philosophy*, 98.

Davidson, Donald (1966). "Emeroses by Other Names." *The Journal of Philosophy*, 63.

—— (1967). "Causal Relations." *The Journal of Philosophy*, 64.

—— (1970). "Mental Events." In L. Foster and J. W. Swandon (eds.), *Experience and Theory.* Amherst, Mass.: University of Massachusetts Press.

Donagan, Alan (1966). "Wittgenstein on Sensation." In George Pitcher (ed.), *Wittgenstein, The Philosophical Investigations.* Garden City, N.Y.: Anchor Books.

Dretske, Fred (1993). "Mental Events as Structuring Causes of Behavior." In J. Heil and A. Mele (eds.), *Mental Causation.* Oxford: Clarendon Press.

Ducasse, C. J. (1965). "Mind, Matter and Bodies." In J. R. Smythies (ed.), *Brain and Mind.* London: Routledge & Kegan Paul.

Ettinger, Robert C. W. (1966). *The Prospect of Immortality.* New York:

Fales, Evan (1993). "Are Causal Laws Contingent?" In J. Bacon, K. Campbell, and L. Reinhardt (eds.), *Ontology, Causality, and Mind.* Cambridge: Cambridge University Press.

References

Flew, A. G. N. (1961). *Hume's Philosophy of Belief.* New York: Humanities Press.

Fodor, J. A. (1965). "Explanations in Psychology." In Max Black (ed.), *Philosophy in America.* Ithaca, N.Y.: Cornell University Press.

Frege, Gottlob (1956). "The Thought, A Logical Inquiry." *Mind,* 65.

Geach, Peter (1969). *God and the Soul.* London: Routledge & Kegan Paul.

Ginet, Carl (1968). "How Words Mean Kinds of Sensations." *The Philosophical Review,* 77.

Goldman, Alvin (1970). *A Theory of Human Action.* Englewood Cliffs, N.J.: Prentice-Hall.

Goodman, Nelson (1965). *Fact, Fiction and Forecast,* 2nd edn. New York: Bobbs-Merrill.

—— (1966). "Comments." *The Journal of Philosophy,* 63.

—— (1967). "Two Replies." *The Journal of Philosophy,* 64.

—— (1970). "Seven Strictures on Similarity." In L. Foster and J. W. Swanson (eds.), *Experience and Theory.* Amherst, Mass.: University of Massachusetts Press.

Grice, H. P. (1941). "Personal Identity." *Mind,* 50. Reprinted in Perry 1975a.

—— (1961). "The Causal Theory of Perception." *Proceedings of the Aristotelian Society,* suppl. vol. 35.

—— (1975). "Method in Philosophical Psychology (From the Banal to the Bizarre)." *Proceedings and Addresses of the American Philosophical Association,* 48.

Harman, Gilbert (1965). "The Inference to the Best Explanation." *The Philosophical Review,* 74.

Harre, R., and Madden, E. H. (1975). *Causal Powers, A Theory of Natural Necessity.* Totowa, N.J.: Rowman & Littlefield.

Harrison, Bernard (1967). "On Describing Colors." *Inquiry,* 10.

—— (1973). *Form and Content.* Oxford: Basil Blackwell.

Hesse, Mary (1969). "Ramifications of 'Grue.'" *The British Journal of the Philosophy of Science,* 20.

Hirsch, Eli (1980). *The Concept of Identity.* New York: Oxford University Press.

Hume, David (1888). *A Treatise of Human Nature,* ed. by L. A. Selby-Bigge. Oxford: Oxford University Press.

Johnson, W. E. (1964). *Logic, Part III, The Logical Foundations of Science.* New York: Dover.

Kim, Jaegwon (1973). "Causation, Nomic Subsumption, and the Concept of Event." *The Journal of Philosophy,* 70.

—— (1974). "Non-Causal Relations." *Nous,* 8.

—— (1976). "Events as Property Exemplifications." In M. Brand and D. Walton (eds.), *Action Theory.* Dordrecht, Netherlands: Reidel.

—— (1993a). *Supervenience and Mind, Selected Essays.* Cambridge: Cambridge University Press.

—— (1993b). "Can Supervenience and 'Non-Strict Laws' Save Anomalous Monism." In J. Heil and A. Mele (eds.), *Mental Causation.* Oxford: Clarendon Press.

Kretzmann, Norman (1966). "Omniscience and Immutability." *The Journal of Philosophy*, 63.

Kripke, Saul (1971). "Identity and Necessity." In Milton K. Munitz (ed.), *Identity and Individuation*. New York: New York University Press.

—— (1972). "Naming and Necessity." In D. Davidson and G. Harman (eds.), *Semantics of Natural Language*. Dordrecht, Netherlands: Reidel.

Lewis, C. I. (1929). *Mind and the World Order*. New York: Dover.

Lewis, David (1966). "An Argument for the Identity Theory." *The Journal of Philosophy*, 63.

—— (1969). Review of W. H. Capitan and D. D. Merrill (eds.), *Art, Mind, and Religion*. In *The Journal of Philosophy*, 66. Reprinted in Block 1980a.

—— (1972). "Psychophysical and Theoretical Identifications." *Australasian Journal of Philosophy*, 50. Reprinted in Block 1980a.

—— (1980). "Mad Pain and Martian Pain." In Block 1980a.

—— (1983). "New Work for a Theory of Universals." *Australasian Journal of Philosophy*, 61.

—— (1986). *The Plurality of Worlds*. Oxford: Basil Blackwell.

Locke, Don (1968). *Myself and Others*. Oxford: Oxford University Press.

Locke, John (1975). *Essay Concerning Human Understanding*, ed. by Peter H. Nidditch. Oxford: Clarendon Press.

Macdonald, C. M., and MacDonald, G. (1995). "How to be Psychologically Relevant." In C. M. MacDonald and G. MacDonald (eds.), *Philosophy of Psychology*. Oxford: Blackwell.

McTaggart, J. M. E. (1927). *The Nature of Existence*. Cambridge: Cambridge University Press.

Malcolm, Norman (1963). "Three Forms of Memory." In Malcolm, *Knowledge and Certainty*. Ithaca, N.Y.: Cornell University Press.

—— (1977). "Descartes' Proof that He is Essentially a Non-Material Thing." In *Thought and Knowledge Essays by Norman Malcolm*. Ithaca, N.Y.: Cornell University Press.

Martin. C. B., and Deutscher, Max (1966). "Remembering." *The Philosophical Review*, 75.

Mellor, D. H. (1974). "In Defense of Dispositions." *The Philosophical Review*, 83.

Moore, G. E. (1959). "Wittgenstein's Lectures in 1930–33." In Moore, *Philosophical Papers*. London: Allen & Unwin.

Nagel, Thomas (1965). "Physicalism." *The Philosophical Review*, 74.

—— (1971). "Brain Bisection and the Unity of Consciousness." *Synthese*, 22. Reprinted in Perry 1975a.

—— (1974). "What is it Like to be Bat?" *The Philosophical Review*, 83.

Nerlich, G. C. (1959). "On Evidence for Identity." *Australasian Journal of Philosophy*, 37.

Nozick, Robert (1981). *Philosophical Explanations*. Cambridge, Mass.: Harvard University Press.

O'Shaugnessey, Brian (1973). "Trying (as the Mental 'Pineal Gland')." *The Journal of Philosophy*, 70.

Parfit, Derek (1971). "Personal Identity." *The Philosophical Review*, 80. Reprinted in Perry 1975*a*.
—— (1984). *Reasons and Causes*. Oxford: Oxford University Press.
Penfield, Wilder (1975). *The Mystery of the Mind*. Princeton, N.J.: Princeton University Press.
Perry, John (ed.) (1975*a*). *Personal Identity*. Berkeley and Los Angeles: California University Press.
—— (1975*b*). "The Problem of Personal Identity." In Perry 1975*a*.
Pitcher, George (1970). "Pain Perception." *The Philosophical Review*, 79.
Popper, Karl R., and Eccles, John C. (1977). *The Self and Its Brain: An Argument for Interactionism*. New York: Springer International.
Prior, A.N., (1957). "Opposite Number." *Review of Metaphysics*, 11.
—— (1965). "Time, Existence and Identity." *Proceedings of the Aristotelian Society* (1965–6).
Putnam, Hilary (1975*a*). *Mind, Language, and Reality*. Cambridge: Cambridge University Press.
—— (1975*b*). "The Meaning of Meaning." In Putnam 1975*a*.
—— (1975*c*). "The Mental Life of Some Machines." In Putnam 1975*a*.
—— (1975*d*). "The Nature of Mental States." In Putnam 1975*a*.
Quine, W. V. O. (1969). "Natural Kinds." In Quine, *Ontological Relativity and Other Essays*. New York: Columbia University Press.
—— (1973). *The Roots of Reference*. La Salle, Ill.: Open Court.
Quinton, A. M. (1972*a*). "Spaces and Times." *Philosophy*, 57.
—— (1972*b*). "The Soul." *The Journal of Philosophy*, 59.
Reichenbach, Hans (1938). *Experience and Prediction*. Chicago: University of Chicago Press.
—— (1956). *The Direction of Time*. Berkeley and Los Angeles: University of California Press.
—— (1958). *The Philosophy of Space and Time*. New York: Dover.
Reid, Thomas (1969). *Essays on the Intellectual Powers of Man*. Cambridge, Mass.: MIT Press.
Robb, David (1997). "The Properties of Mental Causation." *Philosophical Quarterly*, 47.
Rorty, Richard (1972). "Functionalism, Machines, and Incorrigibility." *The Journal of Philosophy*, 67.
Russell, Bertrand (1956). *Logic and Knowledge, Essays, 1901–1950*, ed. by Robert C. Marsh. London: George Allen & Unwin.
Schlick, Moritz (1959). "Positivism and Realism." In A. J. Ayer (ed.), *Logical Positivism*. New York: Free Press.
Shaffer, Jerome (1966). "Persons and Their Bodies." *The Philosophical Review*, 75.
Shoemaker, Sydney (1959). "Personal Identity and Memory." *The Journal of Philosophy*, 56. Reprinted in Perry 1975*a*.
—— (1963). *Self-Knowledge and Self-Identity*. Ithaca, N.Y.: Cornell University Press.

—— (1966). "On Knowing Who One Is." *Common Factor*, 4.

—— (1969a). "Comments." In N. S. Care and R. H. Grimm (eds.), *Perception and Personal Identity*. Cleveland: Press of Case Western Reserve University.

—— (1969b). "Critical Notice: *Myself and Others* by Don Locke.' *Philosophical Quarterly*, 19.

—— (1980). "Properties, Causation, and Projectibility." In L. J. Cohen and Mary Hesse (eds.), *Applications of Inductive Logic*. Oxford: Clarendon Press.

—— (1984). "Personal Identity: A Materialist's Account." In S. Shoemaker and R. Swinburne, *Personal Identity*. Oxford: Basil Blackwell.

—— (1985). Critical Notice of D. Parfit, *Reasons and Persons*. Mind, 44.

—— (1992). "Unger's Psychological Continuity Theory." *Philosophy and Phenomenological Research*, 52/1.

Slote, Michael (1970). *Reason and Scepticism*. London: George Allen & Unwin.

Small, Kenneth (1961). "Professor Goodman's Puzzle." *The Philosophical Review*, 70.

Smart, J. J. C. (1963). *Philosophy and Scientific Realism*. New York: Routledge & Kegan Paul.

Smythies, J. R. (ed.) (1965). *Mind and Brain*. London: Routledge & Kegan Paul.

Squires, Roger (1969). "Memory Unchained." *The Philosophical Review*, 78.

Strawson, Peter (1959). *Individuals*. London: Methuen.

Swoyer, C. (1982). "The Nature of Causal Laws." *Australasian Journal of Philosophy*, 60.

Taylor, D. M. (1966). "The Incommunicability of Content." *Mind*, 75.

Teller, Paul (1969). "Goodman's Theory of Projection." *The British Journal for the Philosophy of Science*, 20.

Thomson, Judith Jarvis (1966). "Grue." *The Journal of Philosophy*, 63.

Ullian, J. S. (1961). "More on 'Grue' and Grue." *The Philosophical Review*, 70.

Unger, Peter (1990). *Identity, Consciousness and Value*. New York: Oxford University Press.

van Inwagen, Peter (1997). "Materialism and the Psychological Continuity Account of Personal Identity." *Philosophical Perspectives, 11, Mind, Causation and World*.

Wiggins, David (1967). *Identity and Spatio-temporal Continuity*. Oxford: Basil Blackwell.

Williams, Bernard (1957). "Personal Identity and Individuation." *Proceedings of the Aristotelian Society*, 57 (1956–7). Reprinted in Williams 1973.

—— (1960). "Bodily Continuity and Personal Identity, A Reply." *Analysis*, 21. Reprinted in Williams 1973.

—— (1970). "Are Persons Bodies?" In Spiker (ed.), *The Philosophy of the Body*. Chicago: Quadrant Books. Reprinted in Williams 1973.

—— (1973). *Problems of the Self*. Cambridge: Cambridge University Press.

Wilson, Robert (1994). "Wide Computationalism." *Mind*, 103.

Wisdom, John (1952). *Other Minds*. New York: Basil Blackwell.

Wittgenstein, Ludwig (1953). *Philosophical Investigations*, ed. by G E. M. Anscombe and R. Rhees, trans. by G. E. M. Anscombe. Oxford: Basil Blackwell.

—— (1958). *The Blue and Brown Books*. Oxford: Basil Blackwell.

—— (1968). "Notes for Lectures on 'Private Experience' and 'Sense Data,' " ed. by Rush Rhees. *The Philosophical Review*, 77.

Yablo, Stephen (1992). "Mental Causation." *The Philosophical Review*, 101.

Zabludowski, Andrzej (1974). "Concerning a Fiction about How Facts are Forecast." *The Journal of Philosophy*, 71.

Index